AHMANSON · MURPHY
FINE ARTS IMPRINT

THE AHMANSON FOUNDATION
has endowed this imprint
to honor the memory of
FRANKLIN D. MURPHY
who for half a century
served arts and letters,
beauty and learning, in
equal measure by shaping
with a brilliant devotion
those institutions upon
which they rely.

THE PUBLISHER GRATEFULLY ACKNOWLEDGES THE GENEROUS SUPPORT OF THE ART ENDOWMENT FUND OF THE UNIVERSITY OF CALIFORNIA PRESS FOUNDATION, WHICH WAS ESTABLISHED BY A MAJOR GIFT FROM THE AHMANSON FOUNDATION.

PUBLICATION OF THIS BOOK HAS BEEN AIDED BY A GRANT FROM THE MILLARD MEISS PUBLICATION FUND OF THE COLLEGE ART ASSOCIATION.

MM

THEORIES OF THE NONOBJECT

# CONTENTS

# ACKNOWLEDGMENTS

This book has been in the making for many more years than I want to acknowledge. Its outline was delineated while I wrote my doctoral dissertation at the Graduate Center of the City University of New York under the effect of an intellectual excitement that was motivating but lacked a predictable framework—a symptom of the interdisciplinary and theoretical intoxication of the early 1990s. Plus, there I was in New York, fresh off the boat, as they say, with an acceptable command of the English language that however did not allow me to blink in class or write polished papers. By the time dissertation writing came about, the problem was not so much one of language but of concepts: how to think about a group of artists considered Latin American constructivists or under the rubric of Latin American geometric abstraction, while complicating those categories, as well as many others dear to my immediate discursive framework: modernity, medium specificity, environmental art, participation, performativity, center, periphery.

Those days at CUNY, almost the whole decade of the 1990s, to be precise, were filled with discoveries, surprises, encounters, and engagement with a field that was in constant transformation and whose rapid pace I can only equate to the intensity of New York at the turn of the twentieth century. I could not have navigated that intensity without some important people who populated my CUNY universe: Alessandra Gouldner, my dearest and first friend; John Angeline; Natasha Kurchanova; Fernando Azevedo; Marek Bartelik; Michele White; Noah Chasin, my first editor and still one of my favorite interlocutors; Rhea Anastas, whose peripheral but constant presence has always been an inspiration; and Janet Kraynak, who left CUNY soon after I arrived only to become, years later, a sympathetic friend whose intellectual rigor and work ethic I truly admire. Carol Armstrong's theoretical breadth and love for the materiality of the object were exemplary to my work; Jack Flam was a steady and comforting presence during my time at the Graduate Center and remains a supporter; and Anna Chave joined my dissertation committee to co-advise with Carol a dissertation that must have been a mystery to everyone, including me!

Beyond CUNY, at Columbia University, where I took and audited as many classes as the system allowed, I found nonstop intellectual stimulus through a network of colleagues whose effects on my professional development are every day visible: specially Margaret Sundell and T. J. Demos, who have been encouraging and enthusiastic about my work, and also Judith Rodenbeck and Stephanie Schwartz. I want to thank George Baker, Tom McDonough, and Branden Joseph for letting me test some of my ideas in *October* and the incredible journal *Grey Room*. At Columbia, thanks also to Benjamin H. D. Buchloh, whose rigorous approach to history and its aesthetic products has been a beacon of excellence to my generation. But no doubt my art history training and work is indebted to many more gestures of generosity and dialogues with friends and colleagues: Lisa Blackmore, Tom Cummins, Leah Dickerman, Alexander Dumbadze, Okwui Enwezor, João Fernandes, Jose Gabriel Fernández, Andrea Giunta, Robin Greeley, Suzanne Hudson, Miwon and Sowon Kwon, Pam Lee, James Meyer, Nicola Pezolet, Vicente Todolí, and Frazer Ward.

In 2004, after an instrumental postdoc at the David Rockefeller Center for Latin American Studies at Harvard, I joined the faculty of the Maryland Institute College of Art to teach modern and contemporary art in the Art History Department. I want to thank my incredibly supportive colleagues there, specially Joe Basile, Jenny Carson, Suzanne Garrigues, Jennie Hirsh, and Kerr Houston; our administrative assistant, Judith Lidie; our provost, Ray Allen; our vice provost for research and graduate studies, Gwynne Keathley; as well as our librarian, Chris Drolsum. Special thanks to Daniela Sandler, our missed architectural historian, for her help with some tricky translations from Portuguese to English. Throughout the years several of my students have embraced the material in this book with enthusiasm. I want to thank them for showing me how truly rewarding teaching can be.

When a sabbatical finally came, it was thanks to a generous grant from the American Philosophical Society that I was allowed to take the whole academic year. Then I confronted a radically different field, shaped and transformed by the serious and exciting work of younger colleagues who generously shared their work with me: Marita Garcia, Karin Kyburz, Aleca Le Blanc, Adele Nelson, and Irene Small. That wonderful year of dedicated research and writing was spent at the Fisher Fine Arts Library of the University of Pennsylvania: I want to thank Holly Pittman and Karen Beckman for extending my visiting lecturer privileges and the excellent and wonderful staff at the library whose work makes ours possible: Kirby Bell, Ed Deegan, Ken Graitzer, and Bob Lawley.

Beyond the United States, I owe much to colleagues and lifelong friends who generously shared information and facilitated research at a time when the Xerox machine ruled my life and who, to this day, remain crucial interlocutors: Guy Brett, Sylvia Cedeño, Katherine Chacón, Fernando Cocchiarale, Brenda Danilowitz, Fernanda Engler, Heloisa Espada, Henrique Faria, Jesús Fuenmayor, Hannía Gomez, Karen Kundig, Daniela Matera Lins, Gabriela Rangel, Tahia Rivero, Felipe Scovino, and Guilherme Wisnik. The Gego Foundation, in Caracas, and "O Mundo de Lygia Clark" and Projeto Hélio Oiticica, in Rio de Janeiro, were incredibly kind with time and materials. My deepest thanks go to Barbara Gunz, Josefina Manrique, Priscilla Abecasis, Claudia Garcés, Mariana Reyes, Esther Crespin, Alvaro Clark, Alessandra Clark, Sonia Meneses, Cesar Oiticica, Cesar Oiticica Filho, and Ariane Figueredo.

Once the manuscript was ready, the pre-production phase benefited from many more individuals. I want to thank my anonymous reader for her detailed reading of the text and invaluable recommendations, to Susan Best for her precise suggestions, and for a last-minute fulfilled request to read chapters 3 and 4 to Sérgio Martins and Michael Asbury, respectively. Their work too has been instrumental to mine. Thanks so much to Tom Fredrickson for helping me refine the text and for the enthusiasm and hard work of the UC Press team: my first editor, Kari Dahlgren, who embraced the project as soon as she received my proposal; her successor, Karen Levine; assistant editor Jack Young; project editor Rose Vekony; copy editor Lindsey Westbrook; and designer Lia Tjandra. The daunting task of collecting images and permissions for reproduction would have been impossible without Jess Bither's incredibly attentive, responsible, and detailed work. I want to thank those who relinquished reproduction fees and/or approved the reproduction of images: Ivan Cardoso, Ana Espinosa, Paolo Gasparini, Gyula Kosice, Carlos Raúl Lozza, Tomás Maldonado, Claudia Molenberg, Angela Thomas Schmid, Kenneth Snelson, Atelier Soto / Anne Soto, Cecilia de Torres, Moderna Museet in Stockholm, the Museo de Arte Latinoamericano de Buenos Aires, the Museum of Fine Arts Collection in Houston, the Fundación Archivo Fotográfico, the Fundación Archivo Fotografiá Urbana, the Fundación Villanueva, the Fundación Gego, and the Josef and Anni Albers Foundation. Thanks also to Mauro Herlitzka, Raúl Naon, and Alejandro Faggioni for helping me track down images and people in Buenos Aires.

Many thanks to the Colección Isabel and Agustín Coppel for helping me defray production costs, and to the Jewish Foundation for the Education of Women for giving me my first important grant while I was working on my dissertation. The David Rockefeller Center for Latin American Studies at Harvard, the American Philosophical Society in Philadelphia, and a Lucas grant from the Maryland Institute College of Art allowed further research and writing, and I am forever indebted to these grants and fellowships for the precious gift of time to read, think, and write—one of the greatest privileges in life.

Finally, I want to thank some dear friends not mentioned above who have been equally important to my life work: Molly Rath, Terry O'Hara, Clarissa Alcock Bronfman, Boyd Johnson, Nicholas Baume, and Allison Arieff. And last but certainly not least, thanks to my family for joining in the adventure and supporting it every step of the way, sometimes in doubt of concrete results: my mom, Morella de Amor; my dad, Carlos Amor; my sister, Maria Alejandra Amor; and the brother I never had but somehow got: Roberto Redondo. Every line written in this book I owe to the passion I share with my partner in life and thought, Carlos Basualdo, for the material presented here. He keeps my mind and imagination in a constant state of urgency. This book is dedicated to him and our two amazing kids: Lucas and Maya.

# INTRODUCTION
## Theories of the Nonobject

The imminence of the act, the abandonment of a process of transference to the object, the very dissolution of the concept of work and artist, all of that plunged me into a severe crisis that I had long been unconsciously searching for.

LYGIA CLARK, "TO CAPTURE A FRAGMENT OF SUSPENDED TIME"[1]

In 1962, the Brazilian artist Hélio Oiticica disparaged the term *geometric art* as "horrible and deplorable . . . [a] superficial formulation that . . . clearly indicates its formalistic meaning."[2] His aversion, expressed in the context of his reconceptualization of the term *constructive* and his reconsideration of constructivism, calls to mind the German-Venezuelan artist Gego's rejection of the word *sculpture* in favor of *bichos* ("bugs" in Spanish) to define her three-dimensional works. This, in turn, evokes the Brazilian artist Lygia Clark's own *Bichos* ("critters" in Portuguese), a series of metal sculptures initiated in 1960. In 1959, the Brazilian poet and critic Ferreira Gullar formulated the concept of the "nonobject" to address the demise of the frame and the base in the painting and sculpture of the neoconcrete artists he supported at the time. As Gullar repeatedly explained, the term *nonobject* was inspired by a work of Clark's that he later described as a "dismembered picture." He also called this work *troço*—a Portuguese slang term meaning an undefined thing, something, stuff.[3] It is unclear which specific work triggered these terms, but by October 1959, Clark appears to have embarked on a new series of works that Gullar identified in the press as evading the qualities of traditional mediums: not painting, not relief, not sculpture.[4]

These semantic negotiations speak to a crisis of mediums and representation that stimulated a series of aesthetic investigations by artists in Argentina, Brazil, and Venezuela—investigations that departed from the trajectories of Soviet constructivist and European geometric abstract art that influenced the cultural landscapes of those countries in the 1940s, 1950s, and 1960s. At that time and in those places, myriad international references—Kazimir Malevich's suprematism, Dutch De Stijl, Piet Mondrian's neoplasticism, Soviet constructivism, Bauhaus, Parisian concrete art, Swiss concrete art, and the work of such artists as Alexander Calder and Max Bill—shaped the efforts of South American artists to negotiate local cultural realities and construct an avant-garde practice based on the pure forms of geometry. In discussing these artists I use such terms as *constructivist, constructivism,* and *geometric abstraction* to refer to these various Russian, Soviet, and European influences, and I use the term *concrete art* to refer to the work and influence of Theo van Doesburg and Max Bill, especially when discussing the Argentine and Brazilian artists who developed carefully crafted responses to pre- and postwar concrete art. In turn, the chapters of this book address the dialogues that arose among specific artists and works from these foreign locales and the work of the South American artists considered in this study.

This book is not, however, a history of the constructivist trajectories that developed in Latin America during the postwar period—a subject about which much has been written in the last fifteen years, following the invaluable work done regionally by figures such as Aracy A. Amaral, Frederico Morais, Ronaldo Brito, Nelly Perazzo, and Marta Traba, and internationally by Guy Brett.[5] Instead, I take as my starting point Ferreira Gullar's concept of the nonobject and trace, through case studies, the disintegration of conventional approaches to painting and sculpture in work that was symptomatic of the uneven spaces and rhythms of modernity in the region. Specifically, I investigate the Asociación Arte Concreto Invención in Argentina (1944–46); the conceptual makeup of concrete art and the intellectual sources of the neoconcrete writings (1959–61) by Ferreira Gullar in Brazil (b. 1930); the neoconcrete and post-neoconcrete works and writings (1959–66) of the Brazilian artists Lygia Clark (1920–1988) and Hélio Oiticica (1937–1980); and the late-1960s work of the German-born Venezuelan artist Gego (Gertrud Louise Goldschmidt, 1912–1994). These artists and critics were invested in reinventing a constructivist tradition that was seen, in Paris and New York, as inadequate to the realities of the devastation wrought by World War II.[6] But what distinguishes the neoconcrete work of Lygia Clark, for example, from that of the Brazilian concrete artist Waldemar Cordeiro, or the work of Gego from that of the kinetic artist Jesús Rafael Soto, is its profound distrust of both art's reliance on the language of mathematics and objectivism and its steadfast faith in universalism. While Clark, Oiticica, and Gego employed a geometric vocabulary, they privileged the affective alliances of work, subject, and place. Additionally, the artistic agendas and artists addressed here developed an inquiry into the nature of the art object (e.g., the conventions of medium specificity) and leaped into environmental practices that abandoned the confinement of the object.

As its title suggests, this book pivots around the neoconcretist writings of the Brazilian poet Ferreira Gullar (chapters 2 and 3) and the artworks and writings of Lygia Clark (chapter 3) and Hélio Oiticica (chapter 4) between 1959 and 1966, but it also considers the interventions of the Asociación Arte Concreto Invención in Argentina in the 1940s (chapter 1) as an introduction to the crisis of mediums and representation that the nonobject embodied. My analysis of Gego's work in Venezuela in the 1960s (chapter 5) stands as a coda to this disruption of the conventions of the artwork posited by Gullar's concept. Therefore, I mobilize the notion of crisis in several directions:

1. to explore the transvaluation and transfigurations of the constructivist and concrete models that these artists drew from;
2. to underscore the historical, social, political, and cultural conditions that informed art production at the margins of a geopolitical configuration that privileged Europe and the United States; and
3. to foreground the aesthetic and theoretical operations that led to, or facilitated, an understanding of these artists' redefinition of pictorial and sculptural modernism, the space of art, and the role of the spectator.

This last point is related to what I call throughout a "crisis of representation," which was closely linked to a rejection of pictorial illusionism, but went beyond it to problematize representation as such. To the Argentine artist Alfredo Hlito, for example, aesthetics ignored the material and historical aspects of the art object, and speculation about beauty confused "the properties of the natural object with those of the aesthetic object."[7] This led the Argentine concretists to develop a materialist artistic practice that was attentive to the contingencies of real space and that destabilized the ontological—that is, intrinsic—definition of art. For Lygia Clark, a focus on the material constituents of painting led her to reject the frame and the traditional pictorial support. Writing in 1960 about the pictorial plane, she emphasized how it arbitrarily organizes space, delimiting it with notions of high and low, front and back. Consequently, she rejected subjective projection (the projection of the artist's ego onto the surface of the painting) and the transcendence of the surface and the ego that resulted from it—a dynamic she associated with the "old idea of continuing to express the world."[8]

Nowhere is this crisis of mediums and representation best articulated than in Gullar's seminal essay "Teoria do não-objeto" (Theory of the Nonobject), published in December 1959 (fig. 0.1).[9] This essay posited the nonobject as the inevitable culmination of the move away from realistic representation in modern painting, while it radically broke with the prevailing emphasis in concrete art on a modernist pictorial ontology that concerned the organization of a painting's constituent elements. Indeed, for van Doesburg and Bill, concrete painting is inherently self-referential. The 1930 concrete manifesto stated: "The picture must be entirely constructed from purely plastic elements, that is, planes and colors. A pictorial element has no other meaning than 'itself' and thus the picture has no other meaning than 'itself.'"[10]

In his essay, Gullar focused instead on the role of the frame. The frame mediated between fiction and reality, protected the picture and the fictional space that it contained, and facilitated its legibility in and distance from real space. But once the fictional space of representation had been rejected, as in the works of Mondrian and Malevich,

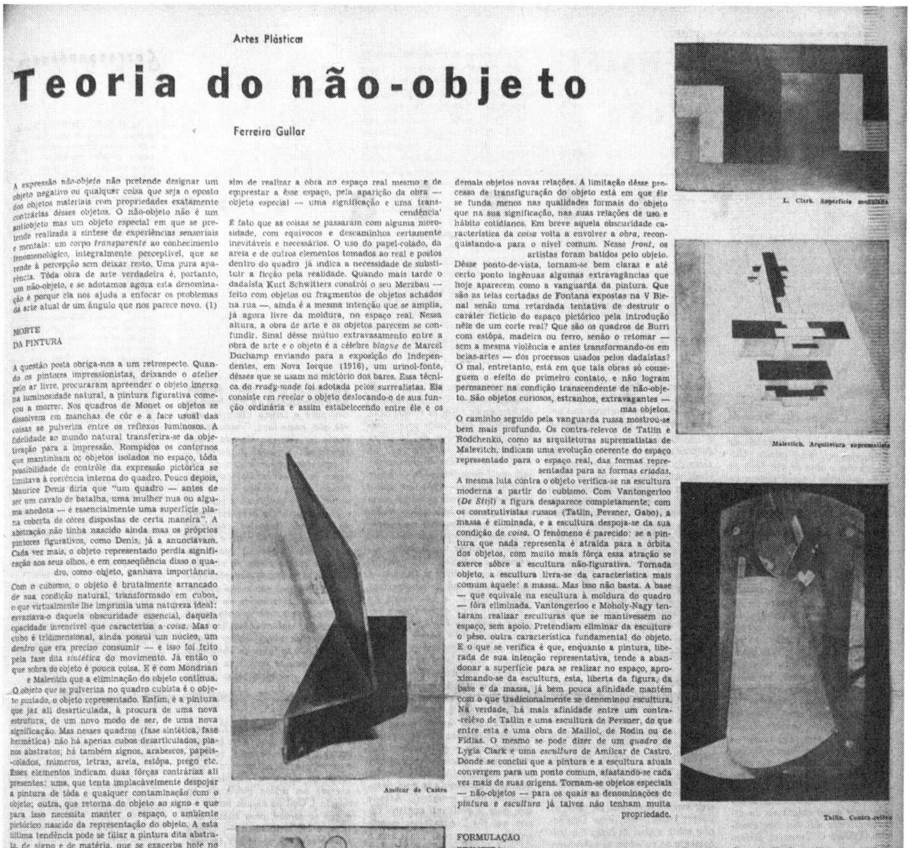

Artes Plásticas

# Teoria do não-objeto

Ferreira Gullar

A expressão *não-objeto* não pretende designar um objeto negativo ou qualquer coisa que seja o oposto dos objetos materiais com propriedades exatamente contrárias dêsses objetos. O não-objeto não é um antiobjeto mas um objeto especial em que se pretende realizada a síntese de experiências sensoriais e mentais: um corpo *transparente* ao conhecimento fenomenológico, integralmente perceptível, que se rende à percepção sem deixar resto. Uma pura aparência. Tôda obra de arte verdadeira é, portanto, um não-objeto, e se adotamos agora esta denominação é porque ela nos ajuda a enfocar os problemas da arte atual de um ângulo que nos parece novo. (1)

## MORTE DA PINTURA

A questão posta obriga-nos a um retrospecto. Quando os pintores impressionistas, deixando o *atelier* pelo ar livre, procuraram apreender o objeto imerso na luminosidade natural, a pintura figurativa começou a morrer. Nos quadros de Monet os objetos se dissolvem em manchas de côr e a face usual das coisas se pulveriza entre os reflexos luminosos. A fidelidade ao mundo natural transferira-se da objetivação para a impressão. Rompidos os contornos que mantinham os objetos isolados no espaço, tôda possibilidade de contrôle da expressão pictórica se limitava à coerência interna do quadro. Pouco depois, Maurice Denis diria que "um quadro — antes de ser um cavalo de batalha, uma mulher nua ou alguma anedota — é essencialmente uma superfície plana coberta de côres dispostas de certa maneira". A abstração não tinha nascido ainda mas os próprios pintores figurativos, como Denis, já a anunciavam. Cada vez mais, o objeto representado perdia significação aos seus olhos, e em conseqüência disso o quadro, como objeto, ganhava importância.

Com o cubismo, o objeto é brutalmente arrancado de sua condição natural, transformado em cubos, o que virtualmente lhe imprimia uma natureza ideal: esvaziava-o daquela obscuridade essencial, daquela opacidade invencível que caracteriza a *coisa*. Mas o cubo é tridimensional, ainda possui um núcleo, um *dentro* que era preciso consumir — e isso foi feito pela fase dita *sintética* do movimento. Já então o que sobra do objeto é pouca coisa. E é com Mondrian e Malevitch que a eliminação do objeto continua.

O objeto que se pulveriza no quadro cubista é o objeto pintado, o objeto representado. Enfim, é a pintura que jaz ali desarticulada, à procura de uma nova estrutura, de um novo modo de ser, de uma nova significação. Mas nesses quadros (fase sintética, fase hermética) não há apenas cubos desarticulados, planos abstratos; há também signos, arabescos, papéis-colados, números, letras, areia, estôpa, prego etc. Esses elementos indicam duas fôrças contrárias ali presentes: uma, que tenta implacàvelmente despojar a pintura de tôda e qualquer contaminação com o objeto; outra, que retorna do objeto ao signo e que para isso necessita manter o espaço, o ambiente pictórico nascido da representação do objeto. A esta última tendência pode se filiar a pintura dita abstrata, de signo e de matéria, que se exacerba hoje no tachismo.

Mondrian é quem percebe o sentido mais revolucionário do cubismo e lhe dá continuidade. Compreende que a nova pintura, proposta naqueles planos puros, requer uma atitude radical, um recomêço. Mondrian limpa a tela, retira dela todos os vestígios do objeto, não apenas a sua figura, mas também a côr, a matéria e o espaço que constituíam o universo da representação: sobra-lhe a tela em branco. Sôbre ela, o pintor não representará mais o objeto: ela é o espaço onde o mundo se harmonizará segundo os dois movimentos básicos da horizontal e da vertical. Com a eliminação do objeto representado, a tela — como presença material — torna-se o novo objeto da pintura. Ao pintor cabe organizá-la mas também dar-lhe uma transcendência que a subtraia à obscuridade do objeto material. A luta contra o objeto continua.

O problema que Mondrian se propôs não podia ser resolvido pela teoria. Se êle tentou destruir o plano com o uso das grandes linhas pretas que cortam a tela de uma borda a outra — indicando que ela confina com o espaço exterior —, ainda essas linhas se opõem a um fundo, e a contradição espaço-objeto reaparece. Inicia, então, a destruição dessas linhas e o resultado disso está nos seus dois últimos trabalhos: *Broadway Boogie-Woogie* e *Victory Boogie-Woogie*. Mas a contradição não se resolve de fato, e se Mondrian vivesse mais alguns anos talvez voltasse à tela em branco donde partira. Ou partisse dela para a construção no espaço, como o fêz Malevitch, ao cabo de experiência paralela.

## OBRA E OBJETO

A tela em branco, para o pintor tradicional, era o mero suporte material sôbre o qual êle esboçava a sugestão do espaço natural. Em seguida, êsse espaço sugerido, essa metáfora do mundo, era rodeada por uma moldura cuja função fundamental era inseri-lo no mundo. Essa moldura era o meio-têrmo entre a ficção e a realidade, ponte e amurada que, protegendo o quadro, o espaço fictício, ao mesmo fazia-o comunicar-se, sem choques, com o espaço exterior, real. Por isso, quando a pintura abandona radicalmente a representação — como no caso de Mondrian, Malevitch e seus seguidores — a moldura perde o sentido. Não se trata mais de erguer um espaço metafórico num cantinho bem protegido do mundo, e sim de realizar a obra no espaço real mesmo e de emprestar a êsse espaço, pela aparição da obra — objeto especial — uma significação e uma transcendência'

É fato que as coisas se passaram com alguma morosidade, com equívocos e descaminhos certamente inevitáveis e necessários. O uso do papel-colado, da areia e de outros elementos tomados ao real e postos dentro do quadro já indica a necessidade de substituir a ficção pela realidade. Quando mais tarde o dadaísta Kurt Schwitters constrói o seu Merzbau — feito com objetos ou fragmentos de objetos achados na rua —, ainda é a mesma intenção que se amplia, já agora livre da moldura, no espaço real. Nessa altura, a obra de arte e os objetos parecem se confundir. Sinal dêsse mútuo extravasamento entre a obra de arte e o objeto é a célebre *blague* de Marcel Duchamp enviando para a exposição do Independentes, em Nova Iorque (1916), um urinol-fonte, dêsses que se usam no mictório dos bares. Essa técnica do *ready-made* foi adotada pelos surrealistas. Ela consiste em *revelar* o objeto deslocando-o de sua função ordinária e assim estabelecendo entre êle e os demais objetos novas relações. A limitação dêsse processo de transfiguração do objeto está em que êle se funda menos nas qualidades formais do objeto que na sua significação, nas suas relações de uso e hábito cotidianos. Em breve aquela obscuridade característica da *coisa* volta a envolver a *obra*, reconquistando-a para o nível comum. Nesse *front*, os artistas foram batidos pelo objeto.

Dêsse ponto-de-vista, tornam-se bem claras e até certo ponto ingênuas algumas extravagâncias que hoje aparecem como a vanguarda da pintura. Que são as telas cortadas de Fontana expostas na V Bienal senão uma retardada tentativa de destruir o caráter fictício do espaço pictórico pela introdução nêle de um corte real? Que são os quadros de Burri com estôpa, madeira ou ferro, senão o retomar — sem a mesma violência e antes transformando-os em belas-artes — dos processos usados pelos dadaístas? O mal, entretanto, está em que tais obras só conseguem o efeito do primeiro contato, e não logram permanecer na condição transcendente de não-objeto. São objetos curiosos, estranhos, extravagantes — mas objetos.

O caminho seguido pela vanguarda russa mostrou-se bem mais profundo. Os contra-relevos de Tatlin e Rodchenko, como as arquiteturas suprematistas de Malevitch, indicam uma evolução coerente do espaço representado para o espaço real, das formas representadas para as formas *criadas*.

A mesma luta contra o objeto verifica-se na escultura moderna a partir do cubismo. Com Vantongerloo (*De Stijl*) a figura desaparece completamente; com os construtivistas russos (Tatlin, Pevsner, Gabo), a massa é eliminada, e a escultura despoja-se da sua condição de *coisa*. O fenômeno é parecido: se a pintura que nada representa é atraída para a órbita dos objetos, com muito mais fôrça essa atração se exerce sôbre a escultura não-figurativa. Tornada objeto, a escultura livra-se da característica mais comum àquele: a massa. Mas isso não basta. A base — que equivale na escultura à moldura do quadro — fôra eliminada. Vantongerloo e Moholy-Nagy tentaram realizar esculturas que se mantivessem no espaço, sem apoio. Pretendiam eliminar da escultura o pêso, outra característica fundamental do objeto. E o que se verifica é que, enquanto a pintura, liberada de sua intenção representativa, tende a abandonar a superfície para se realizar no espaço, aproximando-se da escultura, esta, liberta da figura, da base e da massa, já bem pouca afinidade mantém com o que tradicionalmente se denominou escultura. Na verdade, há mais afinidade entre um contra-relêvo de Tatlin e uma escultura de Pevsner, do que entre esta e uma obra de Maillol, de Rodin ou de Fídias. O mesmo se pode dizer de um *quadro* de Lygia Clark e uma *escultura* de Amílcar de Castro. Donde se conclui que a pintura e a escultura atuais convergem para um ponto comum, afastando-se cada vez mais de suas origens. Tornam-se objetos especiais — não-objetos — para os quais as denominações de *pintura* e *escultura* já talvez não tenham muita propriedade.

## FORMULAÇÃO PRIMEIRA

O problema da moldura e da base, na pintura e na escultura, respectivamente, nunca tinha sido examinado pelos críticos em suas implicações significativas, estéticas. Registrava-se o fenômeno, mas como um detalhe curioso que escapava à verdadeira problemática da obra de arte. O que não se percebia é que a própria obra colocava problemas novos e que ela procurava escapar, para sobreviver, ao círculo fechado da estética tradicional. Romper a moldura e eliminar a base não são, de fato, questões de natureza meramente técnica ou física: trata-se de um esfôrço do artista para libertar-se do quadro convencional da cultura, para reencontrar aquêle "deserto", de que nos fala Malevitch, onde a obra aparece pela primeira vez, livre de qualquer significação que não seja a de seu próprio aparecimento. Dissemos, no início dêste artigo, que tôda obra de arte verdadeira é um não-objeto. Melhor será dizer que tôda obra de arte *tende a ser* um não-objeto e que êsse nome só se aplica, com precisão, àquelas obras que se realizam fora dos limites convencionais da arte, que trazem essa necessidade de deslimite como a intenção fundamental de seu aparecimento.

Colocada a questão nestes têrmos, as experiências tachistas e informais, na pintura e na escultura, mostram-nos a sua face conservadora e reacionária. Os artistas dessa tendência continuam — embora desesperadamente — a se valer dos apoios convencionais daqueles gêneros artísticos. Nêles o processo é contrário: em lugar de romper a moldura para que a obra se verta no mundo, conservam a moldura, o quadro, o espaço convencional, e põem o mundo (os materiais brutos) lá dentro. Partem da suposição de que o que está dentro de uma moldura é um quadro, uma obra de arte. É certo que, com isso, também denunciam o fim dessa convenção, mas sem anunciar o caminho futuro.

Esse caminho pode estar na criação dêsses objetos especiais (não-objetos) que se realizam fora de tôda convenção artística e que reafirmam a arte como formulação primeira do mundo.

---

(1) A expressão não-objeto foi, por sugestão minha, adotada por Lygia Clark para designar os seus últimos trabalhos que são construções feitas diretamente no espaço. Mas o sentido de tal expressão não se restringe a ser o nome de trabalhos particulares, pois não-objetos são também as esculturas de Amílcar de Castro e Franz Weissmann, as últimas obras de Hélio Oiticica, Aloísio Carvão e Décio Vieira, bem como os livros-poemas dos poetas neoconcretos.

L. Clark. Superfície modulada

Malevitch. Arquitetura suprematista

Amílcar de Castro

Tatlin. Contra-relêvo

Marcel Duchamp. Ready-made, 1921

Mondrian. Pintura

suplemento dominical

JORNAL DO BRASIL sábado, 19 e domingo 20 de dezembro de 1959

FIGURE 0.1

Ferreira Gullar, "Teoria do não-objeto" (Theory of the Nonobject) in *Suplemento Dominical do Jornal do Brasil*, December 19–20, 1959.

the frame served no purpose. The rejection of the frame, however, was not without risks: Gullar invoked Kurt Schwitters's *Merzbau* (1923–36) as a symptom of the confusion between art and everyday objects prompted by the abandonment of the frame. And while Marcel Duchamp's readymades exemplified the total collapse of traditional mediums, Gullar found readymades limiting, since the transfiguration of the object and the new relations that it established with other objects do not depend on the object per se but on meaning as generated by everyday use; the readymades, he argued, remained ordinary objects and not artworks. Instead, Gullar looked to the Russian and Soviet avant-garde: to the counter-reliefs of Vladimir Tatlin (1914–15), the suprematist architectures of Malevich (1920s), and the spatial constructions of Alexander Rodchenko (ca. 1920)—works that signaled a move into real space and challenged the role of the frame in painting and the base in sculpture, and with them, the normative modalities of these mediums.[11] In the abstract structures of the Russians and the Soviets, the elimination of the base suggested a move away from the conventions of sculpture (mass, volume). At the same time, with the relaxation of artistic codes that the dismissal of the frame and the base signified, these works approached the status of ordinary objects and abandoned the space of representation. Gullar concluded that "contemporary painting and sculpture converge at a common point, increasingly distant from their origins. They become special objects—nonobjects—for which the denominations of *painting* and *sculpture* might not be appropriate."[12]

Thus, for this book I borrow Gullar's title to demarcate the distinctive crisis of mediums and representation that took place in Argentina, Brazil, and Venezuela through an engagement with the legacies of constructivism, concrete art, and geometric abstraction in general. However, without Gullar's follow-up essay, "Diálogo sobre o não-objeto" (Dialogue on the Nonobject), published a few months later, his initial short text would have been prophetic but incomplete, raising more questions than it answered. The longer "Diálogo," an imaginary interview between Gullar and an unidentified interlocutor, delves deeper into the philosophical and aesthetic roots of the nonobject.[13] It attempts to provide answers to what must have seemed to many readers of "Teoria do não-objeto" a riddle and a sarcastic affront.

Indeed, two cartoons made by the Brazilian illustrator Fortuna on one of the foldouts that served as the catalogue for the second exhibition of neoconcrete art in December 1960 (and later published in the *Suplemento Dominical do Jornal do Brasil*) depict onlookers at the exhibition pondering what the nonobject is, how it can be made, how one should interact with it, and how it relates to ordinary things and traditional sculpture (fig. 0.2). The cartoons poke fun at the existential tenor of the term *nonobject* and the confusing terminology proposed by Lygia Clark's *Bichos,* which blurred the boundaries, at least nominally, between artworks and critters just as the nonobject blurred the boundaries between artworks and objects.[14] Therein lies the kernel of the riddle: Gullar insisted that although the nonobject transcended the conventional categories of painting and sculpture, it was not an ordinary object. To substantiate his claims, he turned

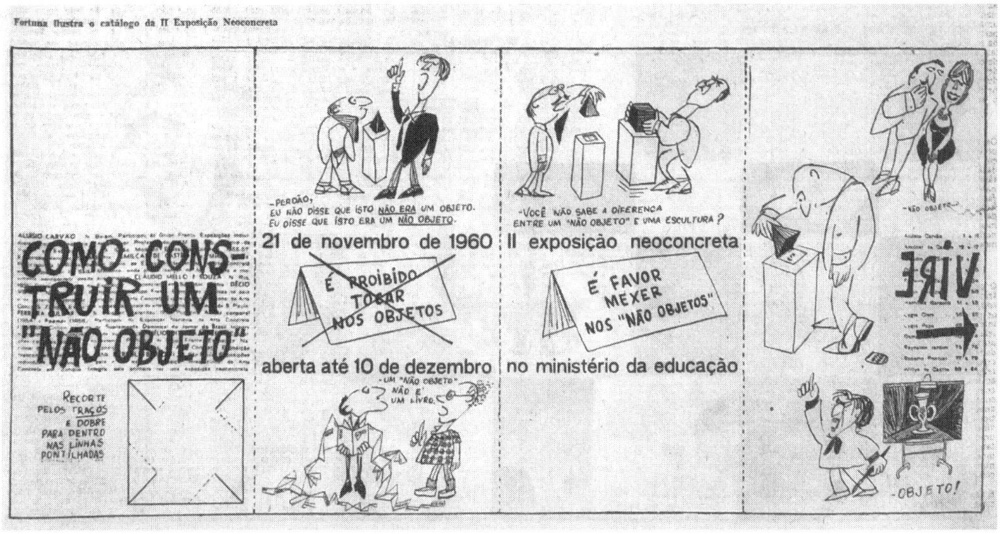


FIGURE 0.2

Fortuna, "Como Construir um 'Não Objeto'" (How to Construct a 'Nonobject'), a cut-and-fold cartoon in *Suplemento Dominical do Jornal do Brasil,* December 3–4, 1960.

to phenomenology, proposing that these "naked" objects—objects lacking the definitional markers of the base and the frame—aspired to produce modes of signification that rejected a priori meanings and resulted instead from the work's appearance in the spectator's field of vision, a return to the thing itself that implied a realization outside the conventions of art. This mode of signification, he argued, made the nonobject transparent to perception, with no need for mediation, no need for frame or base, no need for conceptual backing. Ordinary objects, by contrast, required language to be recognized, as they are exhausted, their meanings foreclosed, by their utility and linguistic designation. This is why, Gullar explained, "when we withdraw from the cultural order of the world, we see objects *without name*"—how such a thing is possible is not addressed by Gullar—"and we confront the opacity of things. . . . [T]he object becomes an absurd presence, opaque, with which perception clashes." However, what applies to these ordinary "objects-without-name" does not apply to neoconcrete works: "[T]he nonobject does not have that opacity . . . the nonobject is transparent to perception."[15] In other words, the nonobject—unique in our phenomenal world—is conducive to the suspension of knowledge and to the experience of astonishment because it is free from attachments to the worlds of language and use.

The nonobject announced the collapse of the modernist paradigm of aesthetic self-referentiality and universal signification that concrete art entailed—though it did not avoid contradictions in doing so. Caught between the realms of art and reality, the nonobject manifested a sort of identity crisis of the artwork. It signaled a radical recasting of the ontological project of definition that had characterized modernist painting and that Gullar associated with concrete art's emphasis on the self-referential nature of the artwork constituted by its plastic elements alone. The essence of painting posited by European concrete art—in which line, color, and pictorial space alluded to painting alone and not to the world of objects or the space of illusionism—was questioned by the various practices that concern us in this book. In the following chapters, I address how the self-sufficient nature of the pictorial and sculptural signifier was dismantled by the elimination of the frame and the base in the work of these artists—and by their engagement with real space, the body, and the vernacular.

## GEOMETRIC HISTORIES

As the recent literature has demonstrated, the development of geometric abstraction in Latin America was far from homogeneous. The tendency, though, has been to construct a chronological narrative that begins with the return of the Uruguayan artist Joaquín Torres-García to his native land after a forty-three-year exile in Europe and his efforts to communicate his knowledge of the avant-garde—as well as his own version of constructivism, called Universalismo Constructivo—through lectures, articles, and La Escuela del Sur (School of the South). As we will see in chapter 1, Torres-García was very influential in the Rio de la Plata region, but his impact on Brazilian and Venezuelan artists was limited. This artistic trajectory, springing from Uruguay and spreading to Argentina, Brazil, and Venezuela, has been rehearsed by several exhibitions over the last ten years. Their catalogues tend to follow a classic format: essays by experts in the different geographical areas covered by the exhibition, illustrations, a chronology, a bibliography, and usually a selection of translated documents from the period. The essays invariably revolve around the abovementioned countries and the various movements involved in the reconfiguration of European geometric abstraction: Universalismo Constructivo in Uruguay, the Asociación Arte Concreto Invención and Arte Madí in Argentina, concrete and neoconcrete art in Brazil, and kinetic art and geometric abstraction in Venezuela.[16]

Indeed, to understand the current institutional status of what is poorly defined as "Latin American geometric abstraction," it is important to acknowledge that the historiography of the field in the United States has been partly shaped by the exhibition and publication of private collections that fit Donald Preziosi's definition of what he has called "representational adequacy, wherein [the] exhibition is presumed to 'represent' more or less faithfully some set of extra-museological affairs; some 'real' history which, it is imagined, pre-exists its portrayal; its re-presentation, in exhibition space."[17] These collections tend to be organized around national or regional references, and the artworks in them are made to fit into a history of progress—a dynamic that can sometimes obscure larger political, economic, and cultural contexts and the contradictory projects that informed the various geometric abstract tendencies that concern us here.

The Colección Patricia Phelps de Cisneros (CPPC) in Caracas and the Adolpho

Leirner Collection in São Paulo stand out in this regard. The CPPC has been particularly active in the production of an extensive discursive apparatus around the works it collects.[18] Early exhibitions conceived by two curators at the CPPC, Ariel Jiménez and Luis Enrique Pérez-Oramas, initiated a critical dialogue around Venezuelan kinetic art (cinetismo) that remains among the most important contributions to the historiography of the field. Indeed, while the exhibition *Geometric Abstraction: Latin American Art from the Patricia Phelps de Cisneros Collection* (presented in 2001 at the Fogg Art Museum at Harvard University in Cambridge, Massachusetts) set up a template that subsequent shows would follow, it also unleashed a fascinating discussion around the meaning of kinetic art in Venezuela and its relationship to modernity in that country.

Pérez-Oramas's complex and compelling analysis of Venezuelan kinetic art sheds light on the contradictory projects that emerged from what is sometimes simplistically portrayed as an alliance between geometric abstraction and modernity in Argentina, Brazil, and Venezuela. The kinetic works by Jesús Rafael Soto and Carlos Cruz-Diez, legitimized by these artists' success in Paris in the 1950s and 1960s, enjoyed ample recognition and corporate and government support in Venezuela in the 1960s and especially the 1970s. They can be seen as aspiring to an ideal "absolute space," an unblemished territory of rhythmic combinations of color and lines in which the contradictions of modernity in Latin America would be erased. Instead, as we will see in the following chapters, the various projects of artists such as Tomás Maldonado and Alfredo Hlito in Argentina, Clark and Oiticica in Brazil, and Gego in Venezuela are defined by their engagement with the material specificities of site and their implicit awareness of the subaltern position their local contexts occupied within the geopolitical arena. The political and economic environments of Argentina in the 1940s and Brazil and Venezuela in the 1950s and 1960s were clearly different; however, the artists of these regions shared the experience of working at the margins of a canonical narrative of modernity that centered around Eurocentric visions of artistic value. Their artistic practices were shaped by the peripheral place of their nations during colonial and postcolonial times—a situation echoed by the material displacements and attention to real space, site specificity, and place that we detect in the various practices that occupy us here.

The critical corpus developed by Pérez-Oramas around the uncritical stance of Venezuelan kinetic art contrasts with the more optimistic vision of geometric abstraction in Latin America voiced by the most ambitious exhibition of the CPPC, *The Geometry of Hope* (2007), curated by its current director, the art historian Gabriel Pérez-Barreiro. He writes in his introduction to the exhibition's publication, "The title of this catalogue and exhibition brings together the two threads that epitomize abstract art from Latin America: on the one hand, geometry, precision, clarity, and reason; on the other, a utopian sense of hope."[19] He thus put forth the works of art included in the show as emblematic of a hopeful, optimistic, and playful utopia that echoed the urban aspirations and intellectual debates of the cities involved in this constructivist revival: Montevideo, Paris, São Paulo, Rio de Janeiro, and Caracas. "The exhibition and this catalogue," he writes, "should remind us that there was a time when Latin America was a beacon of hope and progress in a world devastated by war, genocide, and destruction."[20] It is once again Pérez-Oramas who deconstructs the exhibition's jovial premise and its unbroken arc of progress. In his catalogue essay, he refers to different phases of a "constructivist stage" in Caracas: one is associated with the architect Carlos Raúl Villanueva's Ciudad Universitaria (University City; plate 1), a prime example of a synthesis of the arts that gave ample visibility to local and international geometric abstraction and was built under the aegis of Colonel Marcos Pérez Jiménez's dictatorship (1952–58); the other, with kinetic art's proliferation during the democratic period (1959–76). "The same flippant critical outlook that fused Venezuela's different historical periods, dominant trends in the arts, and leading artists from 1948 to 1957 and from 1959 to 1976 turned the dictatorship into the golden age of modern optimism,"[21] writes Pérez-Oramas, highlighting the discord between modern aesthetics and regressive politics. Writing in 1973 about that second phase of kinetic celebration, the Argentine critic Marta Traba called attention to an alliance between "the society of power" in Caracas and the monumental works of kinetic artists as critical silence surrounded the antisculptural and residual aesthetics of Gego.[22]

The contradictions and tensions between the discourses of modernity and its locales has prompted other discordant voices to interrupt the univocal trajectory suggested by these exhibitions. As more collections, more institutions, and a new cadre of scholars emerge, new stories have begun to unfold. In his catalogue essay for the 2007 exhibition *The Sites of Latin American Abstraction,*[23] for example, the Venezuelan art historian and curator Juan Ledezma (despite following the exhibition template described above) warns of the differences between the constructivist project of Torres-García and the concrete work of the 1940s and 1950s in Argentina and Brazil. In the work of the Uruguayan, he writes, the grid organizes the pictorial surface as a template on which to inscribe highly codified pictograms that stand for a world of essences. Torres-García was concerned with delineating a project of regional identity that had little to do with the (not unproblematic) politicized universalism to which concrete art in Argentina aspired, or, at the other extreme, the provocative interactions between the vernacular and the somatic, the environmental and the body, that percolate through the work of Clark, Oiticica, and Gego. The works of these artists unsettled regional representation; motivated by a crisis of representation that interfered with the semantic transparency of the work of art, they explored the contingent materialism of place and subject. This inquiry led to spatial practices that abandoned the object and failed to coalesce around a discourse that identified geometric abstraction with rationalism and national progress. Not by chance, Gullar's nonobject eschewed disciplinary boundaries and implicitly complicated the spectatorial positions authorized by traditional museums. The challenges that many of the works addressed in this book present to museums (exemplary national and regional institutions) and exhibition spaces in general is a testament to their critical modalities.

In the early 1990s, however, a number of European museums initiated pioneering research on Clark and Oiticica, following the solid work developed in Brazil by the art historians and curators Celso Favaretto, Maria Alice Milliet, Ricardo Nascimento Fabbrini, and Paulo Herkenhoff, among others.[24] The retrospective catalogues published on Clark by the Tàpies Foundation in Barcelona and on Oiticica by Witte de With in Rotterdam still stand as fundamental references.[25] These publications offer overviews of the neoconcrete work of Clark and Oiticica and their transition into nonobject-based practices as well as the first selection of English translations of these artists' prolific writings.[26]

Encompassing, monographic exhibitions on Gego and Oiticica have been realized by the Museum of Fine Arts in Houston under the leadership and curatorial expertise of Mari Carmen Ramírez. Their titles, *Gego: Between Transparency and the Invisible* (2006) and *Hélio Oiticica: The Body of Color* (2007), attest to the formal methodology of the curatorial approach. For example, the framework through which the work of Gego is analyzed revolves around the theme of transparency and proposes her drawings as producers of illusion. For Ramírez, Gego's drawings and constructions oscillate between the illusion of lines "floating in layers of fine air" and "three-dimensional structures that read, in space, like two-dimensional linear drawings."[27] Her interpretations are apt, as Gego was indeed interested in transparency. But I would argue, as the more contextual and historical literature has suggested, that transparency is not the condition through which we can assess the most radical contributions of Gego to contemporary art.

In the following chapters I don't give priority to formal analysis—although an analysis of form is fundamental to understanding the alliance between theory and form that I propose, following not only the ambivalent suggestion of Gullar's title ("Theory of the Nonobject") but also these artists' inclinations to theorize and write. While Gullar and the neoconcrete artists were emphatic in their rejection of theory as a referential horizon—they objected specifically to concrete art's reliance on references imported from mathematics and science and its correspondence with systematic compositional methods (seriality, permutations, gestalt)—their attraction to philosophy, especially the phenomenology of the French philosopher Maurice Merleau-Ponty, was undeniable. Both Gullar and Oiticica were impressive and systematic readers; Clark was less so, but the discussions among these artists and critics clearly affected her writings of the period.[28] The indisputable enthusiasm for dialectical materialism and Marxism in the writings of the Argentines and the structural and thematic affinities of Gego's work with architectural and feminist theories of space has led me to dwell on the discursive dimension of their work.

If this book follows a chronology, my intention is to trace an alternative to the received narrative of Latin American geometric abstraction—one that posits these constructivist tendencies as the logical outcome of economic prosperity and modernist aspirations. I propose that this alternative is less harmonious than the standard history produced by more than a decade of exhibitions of geometric abstraction in Latin America suggests, and that the works and writings of the artists addressed here represent evidence of crisis more than accord with national projects of progress.[29] My account also aspires to disrupt canonical histories of postwar art that have overlooked the contributions of these artists to key debates in modern and contemporary art. Such accounts of modernism and modernity are usually structured around binaries, continuities, and wholes that leave no space for the "oblique"[30] tactics deployed by the artists who concern us here. However, as we shall see, these artists redirected the work of Tatlin, Malevich, Rodchenko, Mondrian, Bill, Calder, and Josef Albers, among others, and, in tandem with their European and American peers, they employed strategies that emphasized the wall, the exhibition space, the urban environment, spectatorship and subjectivity, and public address. These stratagems were executed under the aegis of constructivism and concrete art, but they were often manifested in crisis and displaced the tenets and forms associated with these artistic legacies—namely autonomy, rationalism, functionalism, objectivity, systematicness, technological optimism, and self-referentiality.

## CANONS AND NON-CANONS OF ART HISTORY

This book has its origins in a doctoral dissertation written in indeterminacy and uncertainty, to use terms that define strategies and operations that were favored by the artists, texts, and works that occupy me here. I arrived in New York from Venezuela in the early 1990s to study modern and contemporary art at a moment when all narratives of contemporary art descended from American minimalism.[31] In conceiving a dissertation topic, I felt an urgency to look at parallel moments in South America—to understand how artists there negotiated mediums, techniques, materials, space, and the viewer, and how these practices were the locus of much experimentation relevant to contemporary art. At the time that I was writing my dissertation, there were few comparative models to follow, and my grasp of the material and the proper discursive modalities that would make it legible was insufficient. So, despite the intellectual excitement that facilitated the formulation of my work then, it required further sedimentation, more research, and a sabbatical before it acquired its present shape. This shape is far from ideal, for the material that I deal with welcomes multiple readings and approaches—as the ever-growing literature on Oiticica's *Parangolés,* for example, demonstrates.[32] Additionally, much has been left out, much remains to be done.[33]

As I did many years ago in my doctoral dissertation, colleagues in Europe and Latin America continue to compare neoconcretism to minimalism, Gego to Eva Hesse, theatricality to opticality.[34] The ruptures that Gullar's "Teoria do não-objeto" signified in Brazil are in the Anglo-American context commonly, if not exclusively, identified with Donald Judd's "Specific Objects" from 1965.[35] Published in *Arts Yearbook* magazine as a piece of criticism, "Specific Objects" is a benchmark in contemporary art discourse that has come to define a concern with extra-artistic materials, anticompositionality, real space (the space of the viewer and the space of ordinary things), the readymade, and, most importantly, the limitations of the mediums of painting and sculpture (fig. 0.3). In

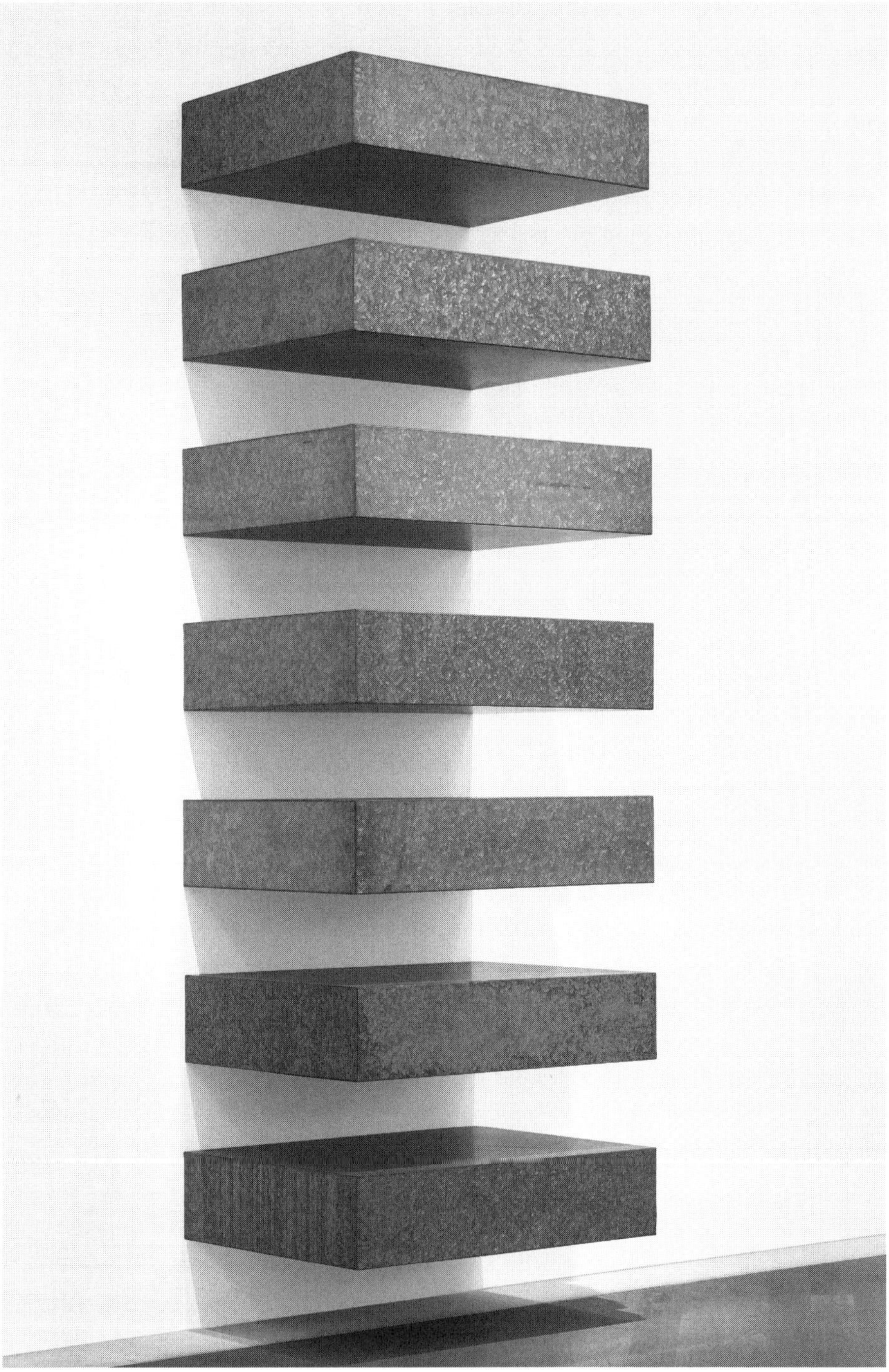

FIGURE 0.3
Donald Judd, *Untitled,* 1965, sheet metal, 9 × 39½ × 30 in. each unit.

the text, Judd posited wholeness as a prerequisite of a new category of work that he called "specific objects": "The thing as a whole. Its quality as a whole, is what is interesting. The main things are alone and are more intense, clear and powerful."[36]

A precedent for this kind of work existed in the Dada readymade, which the "Teoria do não-objeto" acknowledged as an alternative to traditional mediums but ultimately rejected due to its inescapable conventional meaning. By contrast, the readymade suited the literalist enterprise of Judd, who highlighted how Duchamp's readymades were seen "at once and not part by part"[37]—they were given objects. It was, however, in Frank Stella's shaped canvases that Judd recognized several important characteristics of the new three-dimensional work: the unifying correspondence between frame and internal structure, the objectlike quality of the works (a consequence of Stella's thick stretchers), and the use of seriality.[38] Seriality bypassed compositionality: "the order is not rationalistic and underlying but it is simply order, like that of continuity, one thing after another."[39] Stella's paintings embodied, then, two crucial traits that became associated with so-called minimalism: seriality and unity. Seriality provided a means to avoid the authorial mark or conceptualization of the artist and suggested the standardized economy of the machine. Lygia Clark would, however, define this mode of spatial organization as mechanical,[40] and Judd's call for objectivity, specificity, and explicitness would have appalled the Brazilians, focused as they were on the affective dimension of their geometric—but certainly not literalist—forms. In this sense, a "specific object" was the opposite of a "nonobject." The assertiveness of the first term is in clear opposition to the irresoluteness of the second, although both concepts responded to the exhaustion of the conventions of painting and sculpture: the move away from traditional mediums was posited by both Judd and Gullar as the litmus test of advanced art.

Also important in facilitating a comparison between the reductivist morphologies of minimalism and neoconcretism has been the phenomenological reading of minimalism, paramount in assessments of the movement for the past thirty years and advanced by Robert Morris in his "Notes on Sculpture, Part 2," published in *Artforum* in 1966.[41] In his essay, Morris identified phenomenology with a model of spectatorship contingent on the bodily movement of the viewer—a model that was radical in its privileging of the spectator's position and his or her relationship with the object in the gallery space.[42] This point is related to Morris's earlier advocacy—in "Notes on Sculpture, Part 1" (published in February 1966)—of "unitary form" or "gestalt," which, in accordance with then-current parlance, promoted wholeness as a desirable property of three-dimensional art. Here, shape emerged as the crucial quality of these new sculptures: "Their parts are bound together in such a way that they offer a maximum resistance to perceptual separation. In terms of solids, or forms applicable to sculpture, these gestalts are the simpler polyhedrons."[43] The "good form" advocated by Morris was meant to produce an instantaneous apprehension of the work on the viewer's part—an approach that, paradoxically, could become an obstacle to the phenomenological model of viewership upon which he would later insist. In discussing the nature of three-dimensional gestalts, the artist wrote:

> In the simpler regular polyhedrons such as cubes and pyramids, *one need not move around the object* [emphasis added] for the sense of the whole, the *Gestalt,* to occur. One sees and immediately "believes" that the pattern within one's mind corresponds to the existential fact of the object. Belief in this sense is both a kind of faith in spatial extension and a visualization of that extension. In other words, it is those aspects of apprehension that are not coexistent with the visual field but rather the result of the experience of the visual field.[44]

What Morris was articulating here—despite the fact that his own work contradicted this logic from within (e.g., his *Four Mirrored Cubes* of 1965)[45]—was an apprehension facilitated by the perceptual habit of looking at regular geometric shapes such as the cube. A cube is easy to visualize because the viewer's idea of the object matches his or her recurrent experience of the object.[46]

A few months later, in "Notes on Sculpture, Part 2," Morris mobilized the concept of gestalt in a different direction. The unitary form, divested of detail, relations, and spectatorial intimacy, called attention instead to the situation in which it was found. Morris wrote: "The better new work takes relationships out of the work and makes them a function of space, light, and the viewer's field of vision. The object is but one of the terms in the newer esthetic."[47] Here, the temporal suspension that gestalt intimated in "Notes on Sculpture, Part 1" was rejected in favor of a mode of interaction in which the unitary shape propels the viewer to focus on all of the exterior variables that relate to the object: light, space, physical viewpoint. This emphasis on positionality and situation, as well as the propensity of Morris's artwork to undo architectural space as a container (fig. 0.4), finds a parallel in the works produced by Oiticica and Gego in the 1960s.[48]

I offer this brief comparison of North and South American artistic practices to situate the strand of abstraction that occupies us here vis-à-vis the more familiar context of American art of the postwar period. I invoke the words of Judd and Morris to highlight different responses to common discursive horizons and legacies: European geometric abstraction and Russian and Soviet constructivism, the theories of form (Gestalt) that circulated among artists and designers, and the philosophical discourses (phenomenology) that influenced critics and artists at the time. Radically different institutional landscapes and politico-economic situations on the two sides of the continent produced different proposed paths forward for modern art, but there is no doubt that the South Americans were invested in parallel reflections on the limits and possibilities of modernism and its culture.

Indeed, as the Brazilian critic Mário Pedrosa (1900–1981, who was, as we will see in chapter 2, responsible for introducing gestalt theory in Brazil) observed in the late 1950s, his country was condemned to be modern—an allusion to what seemed an end-

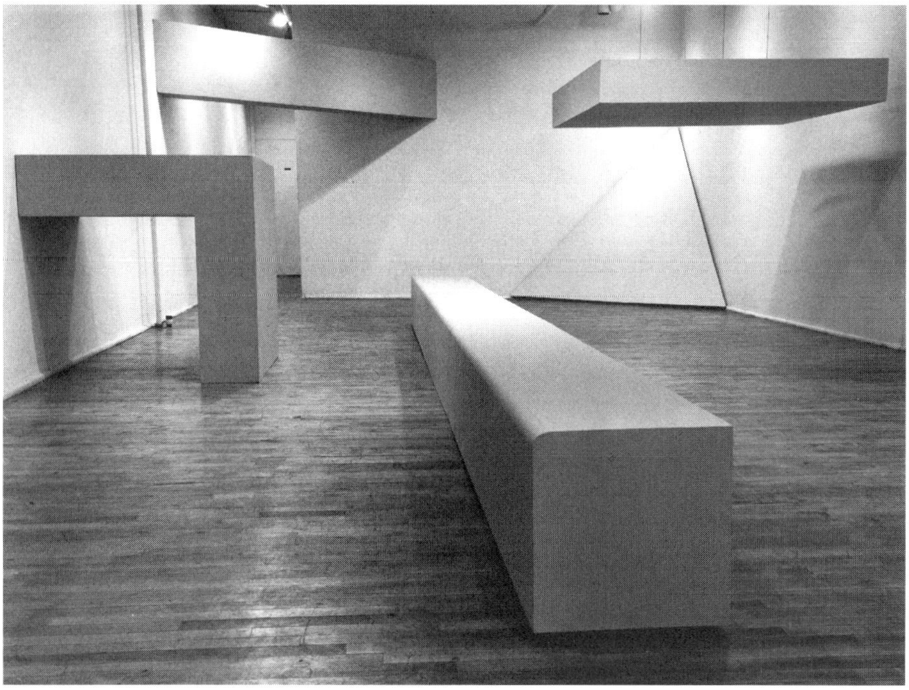

FIGURE 0.4
Robert Morris, installation at Green Gallery, New York, 1963–64.

less capacity to embrace the new and experimental, especially in the context of Brazilian architecture and the creation of the country's new capital, Brasília (fig. 0.5).[49] Yet Pedrosa also employed the term *postmodern* in reference to the art and cultural conditions of the mid-1960s, arguing that radical technological transformations and the rise of the mass media thrust the subject into a reality of information and consumption to which the subject's perceptual apparatus urgently needed to respond; as a result, art had to produce new images and forms of mediation. I summon the elasticity of Pedrosa's thinking to underline how, in his writings, *modern* did not define a period that opposed antiquity, but represented a constant search for what suited the progressive aspirations of his country. This operational use of the *modern* delineated a condition that rendered the definite meaning of the terms *modern, modernity,* and *postmodernity* fallacious and focused instead on the mutational processes and dynamics of cultural exchange unleashed by colonization and globalization. Following this logic, "normative" Western art, identified with an Anglo-European tradition, was not perceived by the Brazilian artists and critics who concern us here as some inviolable, immutable, hegemonic paradigm that was foreign to them. Rather, they considered these various modernist legacies as rich raw material that might be employed to shape Brazil's culture. At the same time,

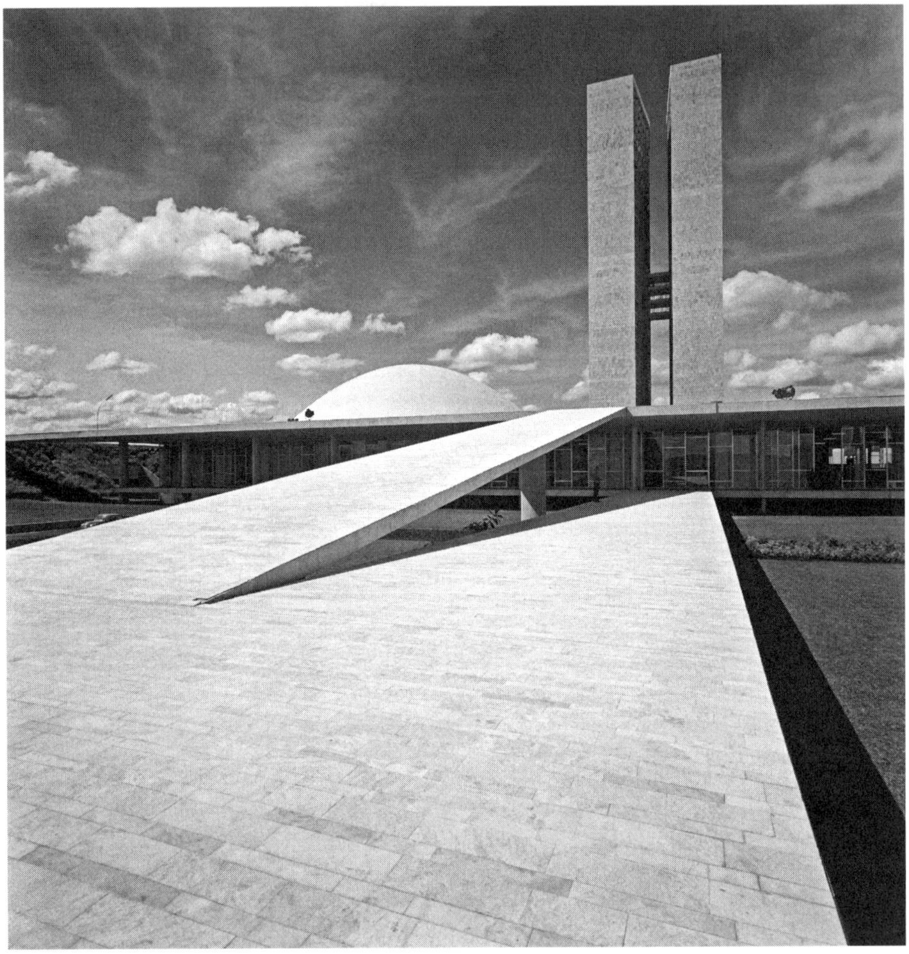

FIGURE 0.5
Marcel Gautherot (photographer), National Congress, Esplanade of Ministries, Brasília, ca. 1960.

this strategy allowed them to engage with the more materially powerful nations of the West through experimental agendas that nonetheless resisted the categorical proclivities of canonical modernism.

For Pedrosa, the colonial history of Brazil—a narrative defined by transplantation—facilitated the revolutionary desire to create something new in a territory that, lacking any trace of ancient civilization, provided modernism's ideal tabula rasa: a place of endless new beginnings.[50] It was thus in the history of colonial domination that Pedrosa paradoxically founded Brazil's ahistoricity and delivered a *modernus* without a *classicus* against which to stand. The Brazilian tabula rasa facilitated other paradoxes as well. First among these was the rise of modern architecture in the midst of dictatorship (1930–45). This dynamic was accelerated by the self-aggrandizing nature of the government and the favorable economic situation that followed in the 1950s and produced the artificiality of Brasília (1956–60). The city was planted more than six hundred miles away from the metropolitan hubs of Rio de Janeiro and São Paulo, and boasted the utopian plan of the architect Lúcio Costa, who believed in the self-sufficiency of the region yet remained keenly aware of the incongruity of the project. The discontinuity between these grand aspirations and the realities of the country resulted in a vision of modernism and modernity predicated on political vagaries, geographic dispersion, spatial contradictions, and discontinuous temporalities as well as on urbanism, architecture, and art as a societal model. This utopian élan called for the public reinstitution of the aesthetic dimension in Brazilian life and may help explain neoconcretism's preoccupation with the participation of the spectator and its relation to Pedrosa's chimerical vision of Brasília as an exemplary urban space and the ultimate collective work of art.

Indeed, a crucial reference for Pedrosa, Gullar, Clark, and Oiticica was Mondrian's aspiration for a synthesis of the arts that involved, but had to go beyond, an integration of the mediums of painting, sculpture, and architecture. In the Brazilian context, this interest ultimately led to the dissolution of the conventions of painting and sculpture in much experimental work of the 1960s and 1970s. The aesthetic investigations of neoconcretism were performed from within a unique modern preoccupation with space whose antecedents were Tatlin's *Counter-reliefs* (1914–15), Rodchenko's *Spatial Constructions* (ca. 1920), and Malevich's *Arkitektons* (early 1920s). Thus, the nonobjects Clark and Oiticica conceptualized and produced during the brief lifespan of the movement (approximately 1959–61) unleashed a phase of intense experimentation that advanced issues still being explored today in Brazil and abroad—for example, post-studio, post-medium, and situational and participatory aesthetics. In the chapters that follow, I trace the specific modernist lineage that these artists produced for themselves as a consequence of their localized thinking—an environmental art interwoven with the contradictions and antinomies of modernity on the periphery of international culture. Their work, fraught with productive material inconsistencies and symbolic "misreadings," critically reassessed the nature of the art object and the question of representation.

Let me now turn to the general plan of the book, which is based on a case-study approach. Chapter 1, "At Painting's Edge: *Arte Concreto Invención,* 1944–46," examines the genesis of concrete art in Buenos Aires with the publication of *Arturo* magazine in 1944 and its development in the works of the artists of the Asociación Arte Concreto Invención (AACI). This was a period of febrile experimentation, as evidenced by the key essay in *Arturo,* "El Marco: un problema de plástica actual" (The Frame: A Problem in Contemporary Art) by the Uruguayan-born, Argentina-based artist Rhod Rothfuss. This essay proposed an attack on orthogonal painting as the foundation of post-Renaissance illusionistic space through the strategy of the irregularly shaped cutout frame (*marco recortado*). The concrete art of Theo van Doesburg, which proclaimed the autonomy of painting via a self-referential manipulation of plastic elements—line, color, plane—

served as the point of departure for the investigations of the artists of the AACI. In their hands, however, plasticity became directly linked to a materialist aesthetic grounded in the Argentines' embrace of dialectical materialism and their membership in the Communist Party. In 1946 this ambition was summarized with the following words: "[T]he value and significance of the *invencionista* [from 'invention'] revolution lies . . . in having reframed the aesthetic and spiritual problem of humanity on a scientific basis, but without ignoring the specific problem of the economic liberation of the working class, and, rather, searching for a close coordination between the strictly political activities of the Marxists and the *invencionista* attempts to overcome the mental and aesthetic forms of the bourgeoisie."[51]

This revolution in form (and politics) manifested itself in the displacement of attention from the pictorial plane—painting as container and object of contemplation—to the edge of the canvas and beyond. The frame was understood as the structuring principle of what happened inside the painting, and the Argentines' experiments with the cutout frame led to an unprecedented analysis of the pictorial signifier. Specifically, the AACI's investigations yielded the so-called "coplanal"—a fragmented plane, broken down in sections and situated parallel to the wall—that shattered the pictorial support as the container of representation. This dismantling of the most entrenched conventions of painting, the frame and the pictorial support, was tantamount to a destruction of figure-ground relations—a necessary step in unmasking the fallacy of illusionism, or, in the words of the artist Tomás Maldonado, of painting as a "containing organism." The artists of the AACI aspired to a revolution in form that paralleled attempts at a Marxist revolution, but unlike their Russian and Soviet constructivist predecessors, their objects were not to be transitional forms ultimately leading to industrial production, but rather new modalities of painting to suit a future Communist society. New parameters of production, exhibition, and reception would oppose bourgeois painting and define the revolutionary instrument that painting was to become.

These experiments were a response to a crisis of representation in general and not just a crisis of pictorial representation, as the artist Alfredo Hlito observed in 1946.[52] In Argentina this crisis was signaled by the AACI's embrace of Marxism and dialectical materialism, and their coming of age during the politically tumultuous period that gave rise to Peronism in Argentina (1943–46). The reactionary, nationalistic, and militaristic tenor of Colonel Juan Domingo Perón's government foiled the aspirations of intellectuals, artists, and the traditional Left (Socialists and Communists), but it succeeded in luring the working class, whose interests—as recent political analyses have demonstrated—factored little in the Moscow-oriented agenda of the Argentine Communist Party. This rift between the Left and the proletarian masses made the working class vulnerable to Perón's tactics—among them reforms affecting industrial workers, who had become for the Argentine Communist Party little more than a figure of speech. The historian Carlos Altamirano, addressing a moment of soul-searching by local Communists after the disappointing but democratic election of Perón in February

1946, summarized the rift with a question about form that is relevant to our discussion of the marriage of abstraction and Communism that the artists of the AACI envisioned: "Against the prescriptions of Marxism-Leninism, hadn't (political) forms been valued more highly than (social) contents at the moment in 1945 when the terms of the dichotomy were being defined?"[53]

My inquiry in this chapter can be summarized with a riposte to Altamirano: How did the formal experiments proposed by the artists of the AACI articulate their political aspirations? And how was all this connected to the actual political circumstances in which their meticulous deconstruction of painting was situated? The first question has been addressed in the recent literature on these artists,[54] but the second query has, because of a perceived chasm between the Marxism of the AACI and the populism and authoritarianism of Perón's rule, gone unanswered. Consequently, chapter 1 considers how, between 1944 and 1946, artists associated with *Arturo* and later the AACI theorized and formalized this intertwining of aesthetics and dialectical materialism in an effort to cope with their cultural and political situation. How these issues were elaborated in the debates and works of this period is crucial to my articulation of a thematic of crisis and dispersal regarding the autonomous status of the pictorial and sculptural signifier, and to a fuller understanding of subsequent artistic responses to geometric abstraction on the South American continent.

Chapter 2, "The Concrete Idea on Its Way to the Nonobject, 1949–59," maps the intellectual genealogy that informs Gullar's propositions in the "Manifesto Neoconcreto" (1959, coauthored with the group of neoconcretists he was supporting at the time) and the "Teoria do não-objeto." The pre-neoconcrete lineage that I trace here is not the only one worth considering, but it unpacks material previously underdeveloped in accounts of the Brazilian transition from concrete to neoconcrete art. Excellent work has been done lately on the institutional developments that facilitated contemporary art in Brazil in the 1950s—namely, its museums and the São Paulo Bienal, inaugurated in 1951, where in that year the influential Swiss artist Max Bill won first prize in sculpture.[55] The Argentine art historian María Amalia García has written the most in-depth work to date on Bill's relationship to Argentina and Brazil. I, too, focus on his sway over the Brazilian context, but I specifically target his writings of the early 1950s to see how they compare to and contrast with those of Pedrosa and Gullar. My scope is limited, and my intention is to complement existing work done by García, upon whose archival thoroughness I've sometimes relied. Thus, I focus for example on the contested notion of gestalt—which, like the word *organic,* permeates contemporary discussions of what a work of art should or should not be. The word *gestalt* figures prominently in Bill's writings of the 1950s. As he uses it, it refers not to Gestalt theory or psychology, but (in keeping with its common German usage) connotes shape or form or "shape-form" as an attribute of things. It is obvious, however, that Bill was borrowing from Gestalt theory and psychology as developed in Germany in the 1920s to articulate his own concept of the term as a definitional aspect of his aesthetic program.

As has been amply observed elsewhere, the "Manifesto Neoconcreto" attacked, among other things, concrete art's a priori compositional strategies.[56] The geometric abstract works produced during the 1950s by Brazilian artists, especially those hailing from São Paulo, were characterized by painterly and graphic configurations that aspired to test the perceptual laws of Gestalt theory through heuristic arrangements of line, space, color, and shapes over the pictorial field. Pedrosa was exposed to Gestalt theory as a student at the University of Berlin between 1927 and 1929, and in 1949 he reviewed its principles in a thesis titled "Da natureza afetiva da forma na obra de arte" (On the Affective Nature of Form in the Work of Art). Chapter 2 compares Pedrosa's use of the term *gestalt* to Bill's and focuses on the Brazilian critic's privileging of the phenomenological source of Gestalt theory. Pedrosa introduced Gullar to the writings of the French philosopher Maurice Merleau-Ponty, and this facilitated a critique of concretism—specifically a rejection of its privileging of preestablished compositional methods to probe the objectivist parameters of geometry, seriality, and gestalt within painting. In his neoconcrete writings, Gullar instead advocated a phenomenological apprehension of the artwork that favored a "primal—total—experience of the real."[57]

Chapter 3, "From Work to Frame, In Between, and Beyond: The Topology of the Nonobject, 1959–66," follows closely the ideas introduced in the preceding chapter. It addresses the implications of Gullar's theoretical position as put forward in his neoconcrete writings "Manifesto Neoconcreto" (March 1959), "Teoria do não-objeto" (December 1959), and "Diálogo sobre o não-objeto" (March 1960). My focus on Gullar, Clark, and Oiticica as a triumvirate follows a common trajectory that views their dialogue and work as the foundation of neoconcretism. Here, however, I make no claims for neoconcretism as a movement or for the rest of its members; rather, I focus on the rapport between Clark's and Oiticica's work of the period (1959–61) and on Gullar's writings. I've opened up their conversation to include Pedrosa and Merleau-Ponty in their critique of not just pictorial representation but representation as such.[58] In their active engagement with real space and their consideration of the spectator (along with their copious writings and those of their supporters), Clark and Oiticica initiated a radical questioning of the status of the object and the subject of representation by rejecting contemplation and the art object itself as the product of the projection of artistic subjectivity. This endeavor led them to literalize the nonobject by abandoning painting and sculpture and developing participatory and environmental practices—thus my focus on these two artists and not on neoconcretism as a movement.

Projection, representation, and the plane as a repository of ideas and feelings were undermined through formal strategies based on the folding of wooden boards and metal plates in works produced by Clark and Oiticica between 1959 and 1961. Clark's *Bichos,* constructed of geometric plates of metal connected by hinges, are exemplary of this type of work: they opened up the support, dispersed the structures of geometry, and incorporated the surrounding space and the viewer. But the dynamics unleashed by these works—also staged in Oiticica's *Spatial Reliefs* (1960), *Nuclei* (1960–63), and

*Penetrables* (1961)—did not facilitate the unmediated relation between viewer and object (to which the "Manifesto Neoconcreto" pointed), and posited instead spatiotemporal ambivalences related to the topological logic of these works. Indeed, the manifesto sought to bracket all knowledge and theoretical understandings of the art object via a rejection of the techno-scientific and mathematical rhetoric of geometric abstraction. Against the (rational, scientific, or mathematical) "concept" and "idea" invoked in the serial form and illustrative inscriptions of much concrete art, Gullar insisted on "direct perception" as the means of grasping signification, paradoxically suggesting the circumstantial embeddedness of both the work and the spectator in a social, somatic, and psychological matrix that implicitly took into account the work's relationship to culture and historical time.[59]

This suspension of knowledge to which the "Manifesto Neoconcreto" aspired is clearly related to the disputed concept of the "phenomenological reduction" posited by the German philosopher Edmund Husserl. The reduction is an extreme method that aspires to avoid all abstract knowledge of the world, to strip all theory and scientific knowledge from the phenomenon so that it can appear in all its plenitude. The phenomenological reduction suspends factual conditions, as well as the forms of understanding them, so that the philosopher can reveal them anew. Partially following this call for a suspension of habit, the "Manifesto Neoconcreto" declared: "What we mean by the spatialization of the work is the fact that it is always making itself present, always recommencing the impulse that generated it and of which the work was the origin. And if this description also takes us back to the first experience—total—of the real, it's because neoconcrete art wants nothing less than to re-create this experience. Neoconcrete art founds a new, expressive space."[60]

The "total" transparency to which the "Manifesto Neoconcreto" aspired was idealistic and incompatible with Merleau-Ponty's more complicated account of perception and subjectivity. The unsustainability of this idealistic core became evident in the actual works of Clark and Oiticica—by the "situatedness," the "embeddedness," they demanded, by the "thisness" that Merleau-Ponty himself asked of phenomenology and that facilitated his most important axiom of "being in the world" (*être au monde*).[61]

Chapter 3, then, takes a close look at Gullar, Oiticica, and Clark's uses of phenomenology to facilitate their inquiry into the nature of the art object, their embrace of the body, and their alternative understanding of expression—one that rejected artistic subjectivity (conceived as interiority to be expressed) and was instead mediated by the temporal unfolding of the work and its consequent opening toward the other. This openness, enunciated by the "Manifesto Neoconcreto," was later abandoned by Gullar even as Clark and Oiticica advanced it. In 1961 the critic circled back to self-referentiality, arguing that if nonrepresentational work that was severed from the appearance of things can't coincide with those things, then it has to coincide with itself. This action of self-reflection (akin to the self-consciousness of the Cartesian cogito that Merleau-Ponty rejected) was resolved by Gullar in a most traditional concept of expression that signaled his rupture with the potentialities of the neoconcrete project: "[T]he work has to be the authentic manifestation of the interior reality of the artist. That reality will be more authentic when more individual, more individual when more interior, more interior when least contaminated by exterior reminiscences."[62]

Chapter 4, "Forms of Affect: Hélio Oiticica's *Parangolés,* 1964–65," explores Oiticica's relationship to the leftist positions of the early and mid-1960s, which were manifest in Gullar's engagement with the Centros Populares de Cultura (Centers for Popular Culture, or CPC), an organization devoted to the creation of a national culture based on popular roots, and the much less dogmatic so-called Festive Left. Though uninterested in the representational art that the CPC promoted, Oiticica was clearly influenced by the political and vernacular dimension that informed local culture at the time. His *Parangolés*[63] of 1964, conceived in the favela (shantytown) of Mangueira, were, in light of their connections to the urban and social fringes of the city, enmeshed in a politicized cultural agenda that valued collective participation while mobilizing the concept of affect that presided over the "Manifesto Neoconcreto." The *Parangolé capa* (Parangolé Cape, 1964), consisting of layers of plastic and cloth painted in bright colors, including protuberances and pockets, to be worn by the artist and others, is the focus of my discussion, which delineates the body-subject of phenomenology and affect that the cape proposed. I suggest that Oiticica's *Parangolé capa,* with its participatory structure of wearing and watching, conceived "embodied subjectivity" (the body-subject) as the intersection of multiple encounters between the self and the material world. Clearly informed by the syncretic dynamics of the favelas and the transformative logic of carnival, the *Parangolés* articulated, within the specific context of Mangueira, the interweaving of self and world proposed by Merleau-Ponty. What in 1959 had begun as a rejection of the ideationality, rationalism, and objectivism of geometric abstraction through an attempt to produce forms of affect related to the quasi-corpus of the work of art[64] in 1964 delivered the body in flux. In other words, the *Parangolé capa* can be seen as a modality on the quasi-corpus that the "Manifesto Neoconcreto" posited. Indeed, the cape fundamentally denied the normative and unified body, and mobilized an affective economy that stood against the authoritarian models of representation advocated by the CPC and later the Brazilian dictatorship, but also by normative society at large.

If chapter 1 is an introduction to the crisis of mediums and representation central to the book, then chapter 5, "Another Geometry: Gego's *Reticulárea,* 1969–77," can be read as a coda to the neoconcretist core of the book. The *Reticulárea,* made of metal meshes and nets connected and dispersed irregularly within the space of a room, addressed the Venezuelan artist's preoccupations with antiarchitectural space and antisculptural form—approaches that she developed in relation to her architectural training and teaching, and amid the urban disarray of Caracas in the 1960s. During this period, Gego proposed models of aesthetic production that defied the techno-scientific traits, optical effects, and dematerializing formulations that her colleagues Jesús Rafael Soto and Carlos Cruz-Diez favored in their kinetic art. Instead, she mobilized precarious materials and processes, used flexible configurations and radial structures, and made unpredictable connections between the constitutive elements of her works through modes of display and production that opposed the precision and sleekness favored by contemporary geometric abstract art in Venezuela. Gego's nets of the late 1960s, especially in their dialogue with the medium of drawing, embodied the demise of the sculptural signifier through her rejection of not only the base but also mass, volume, and the containment of the object.

Unlike the artists discussed above, Gego wrote little about her work, or about art in general.[65] She produced her most experimental work at the age of fifty-seven, and, while a beloved figure in her local context, she received limited critical attention and international exposure. I bring these aspects, and the fact that she was an émigré woman working at the periphery, to bear in my analysis of her work. To this end, I rely on the writings of several thinkers preoccupied with contesting the authority of architecture and monumentality through feminist philosophy. The philosopher Elizabeth Grosz proposes a theoretical analogy for the unique tectonics of Gego's work, linking feminist concerns about monstrosity (also present in Gego's antisculptural tendencies) with an architecture of excess. Others, such as the architect Greg Lynn, the feminist writer Rosi Braidotti, and the philosopher Luce Irigaray, complement the theoretical matrix that allows me to articulate crucial vectors in the *Reticulárea*—antiarchitectural, antimonumental, and antisculptural—as well as Gego's attention to site, morphological mutation, and connectivity.

The *Reticulárea,* too, is a nonobject: it challenges the universalism and rationalism of geometric abstraction and speaks to a crisis of mediums as the work oscillates between, without ever settling on, drawing and sculpture, sculpture and architecture. But unlike Gullar's nonobject, which he posited as the epitome of an evolution, Gego's "modernist sensibility" was openly at odds with the grand avant-gardist aspirations of the AACI and the Brazilians. The crisis constitutive of these earlier practices unfolded in aesthetic projects that developed corresponding theoretical templates; in Gego we encounter crisis as the foundation from which her mature work springs. Nowhere is this more visible than in her negotiations with the "organic," evident in the terms *bichos* (bugs), *chorros* (jets), and *breñales* (weeds) that she used to title or describe her works and their installations during the 1960s and 1970s. These semantic appropriations deny the functionalism of interdependent parts cohering into a whole that we associate with the organic, and instead privilege the residual and the fluid. Moreover, the weaving of nets became Gego's preferred technique from 1969 on. The handmade production of her meshes and screens, nets and bundles, contrasts with the retinal calculations of Venezuelan cinetismo. Much of this work aspired to the purity of total abstraction, to a universal space of sublimity where body becomes eye, the locus of a riveting experience that—as the scale of the projects that incorporated this art, and their budgets, grew—approached the mesmerizing effects of spectacle.

This tacit discord between the large-scale works of geometric abstract and kinetic

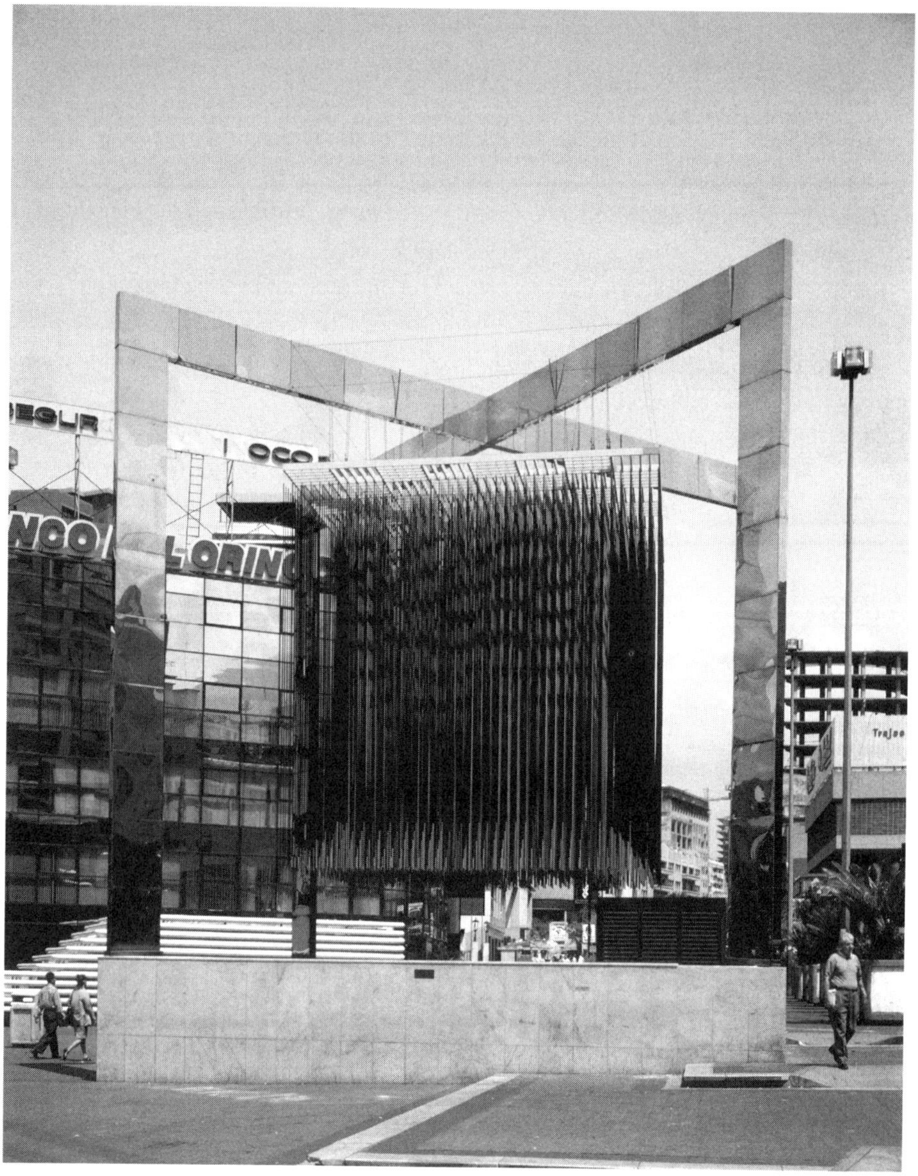

FIGURE 0.6

Jesús Rafael Soto, *Cubo virtual azul y negro* (Virtual Cube Blue and Black), 1982, aluminum and nylon, 400 × 6 × 400 in.

artists in Venezuela (fig. 0.6) and the lessons taught by Gego's *Reticulárea* is a productive point from which to consider the vicissitudes of modernity at the periphery. In Caracas this was manifested in the abysmal gap between infrastructural progress and urban poverty, and the political and artistic desire to obscure that disarray through a mirage of public art. But crisis is also evident in the culture of migration that Gego represents, the diasporic movement through which information circulates and translations and readjustments of ideas and purposes take place: from Paris to Buenos Aires, from Hamburg to Caracas, from Berlin to Rio de Janeiro, from Ulm to São Paulo, and so on. In this sense, the budding artistic and educational institutions of Buenos Aires, Rio de Janeiro, São Paulo, and Caracas through which the artists of the AACI, Pedrosa, Gullar, Clark, Oiticica, and Gego engaged with and contested European modernity were spaces to inhabit and reject—especially as the nonobject abandoned the normative modalities of painting and sculpture and thus the walls of gallery spaces and/or conventional forms of display. For these artists, the precarious, peripheral, and conflictive logic of their contexts unleashed a critical reassessment of artistic legacies, mediums, and practices. In the process, their works opened zones of communication and friction with the other, the vernacular, and the environment, and produced, against theory, modernity from within adversity.

# 1

# AT PAINTING'S EDGE

## *Arte Concreto Invención*, 1944–46

> The crisis of representational art does not constitute the crisis of art, only the crisis of representation.
>
> ALFREDO HLITO, "REPRESENTATION AND INVENTION," 1946[1]

"For us Marxists," wrote Tomás Maldonado in 1946, reality "is what action, practice, can verify."[2] This statement defined the stance of a group of Argentine avant-garde artists in the mid-1940s—one that deemed the illusionism of representational art a "mirage from which man always returned disappointed and weakened,"[3] and which posited the concrete materials of painting as the basis for a new aesthetic practice. This radical approach to painting was developed between 1944 and 1946 in Buenos Aires by artists associated with the magazine *Arturo* and, later, the Asociación Arte Concreto Invención (Association of Concrete Art Invention, or AACI). These artists were committed to defying the conventions of pictorial representation by employing strategies that challenged the orthogonal format of painting. Their experiments with the frame and the support of the pictorial plane resulted in a number of responses to the crisis of representation: canvases shaped by irregular cutout frames (*marcos recortados*) and mapped by grids based on the golden section; works consisting of painted wooden panels shaped in various forms; and "coplanals" (*coplanares*), in which a fragmented, multipart pictorial plane rests on a supporting wall (plate 2). These heterogeneous propositions owed much to the intermedial quality of relief, situated as they were between the two-dimensional space of painting and the three-dimensional space of sculpture. In other words, these wall-mounted works aimed at asserting their identity as paintings, but their formal configurations—whether as cutout frames, with their irregular perimeters, or as coplanals, with fragmented supports actively incorporating the wall into the composition—clearly questioned the conventional boundaries of traditional pictorial modes.

The events surrounding these developments—the 1944 publication of *Arturo* magazine (the seed of these investigations), the emergence of the AACI and Arte Madí in 1945–46, and the various international activities and exhibitions of concrete art[4] in the 1950s—have been well chronicled and the conceptual and theoretical underpinnings of these radical formal experiments have been thoroughly explored, particularly in the last decade.[5] This chapter, then, specifically addresses the AACI's embrace of European concrete art and the ways in which that movement's dedication to the plastic elements of art (plane, color, line) and to the precision of the creative process were reconfigured in Buenos Aires through an embrace of the writings of the young Karl Marx, ultimately leading to a dedicated dismantling of the conventions of painting. More particularly, it examines the relationship between the AACI's Communist alliances and its formal experiments, and how these related to the politics of the period, marked as it was by crisis at home and abroad.

## A REVOLUTION IN REALITY AND FORM

In his recent study of the Argentine avant-garde, Alejandro Crispiani focuses on how the term *dialectical materialism* was explicitly employed by the artists of the AACI. The implicit objective of these artists, writes Crispani, was to "reintegrate art objects into the reality of man."[6] He notes that these artists used the term *dialectical materialism* in tandem with a concept of humanism that surfaces in the early writings of Marx, reflecting the Argentines' proclivity to link Marx's work to the Communist Party that purported to speak on his behalf.[7] Indeed, the philosopher Étienne Balibar observes that this linking of dialectical materialism and humanism involves two sets of ideas that are, at times, actually quite different. *Dialectical materialism* should be understood as a term that attempts to bridge Marx's writings and Communist Party dogma. It was never used by Marx; rather, it was apparently coined in 1877 by Joseph Dietzgen, a worker who exchanged letters with the German philosopher. In 1931, Stalin decreed dialectical materialism the official philosophy of Marxism-Leninism, and in 1938 he delineated its tenets in "Dialectical and Historical Materialism." These so-called "laws of the dialectic" concerned the foundations of the science of history and its correspondence with the "proletarian worldview." They became cultural and intellectual dogma in Socialist countries and, writes Balibar, were imposed "with varying degrees of resistance on Western Communist parties."[8] Thus, the embrace of dialectical materialism by the artists of the AACI suggests that their absorption of Marxist doctrine was partly mediated by interactions with the Argentine Communist Party—indeed, several AACI artists became party members. Further, by grounding their formal experiments in dialectical materialism, the Argentine artists seemed to be attempting to think beyond theory and enter the field of realpolitik.[9]

None of this means, however, that the Argentine artists' field of action fell outside art: art remained their primary concern, and their espousal of a Marxist and Marxist-inspired vocabulary was explicitly linked to a rejection of representation in painting. In the early writings that inspired them, Marx did not dismiss artistic activity as superfluous. Rather, as the philosopher William Adams observes, he saw human beings as "distinguished by their creative powers, for creativity, in Marx's view, is what lies at the heart of productive practices. . . . [T]his is who and what we are, in other words, makers, creators, *homo fabricans*."[10] Yet the relationship between the political intent and the formal propositions of the Argentine avant-garde was an uneasy one, as key works and texts, particularly those created and written between 1944 and 1946, demonstrate.

What, then, was so compelling about Marxism and dialectical materialism for these Argentine artists who in 1944 found themselves shaking the cultural foundations of a rather conservative artistic milieu operating primarily between cubist/expressionistic figurative and realistic models of representation? Two events help frame the answer to that question: World War II and the Argentine military coup of June 4, 1943. The war in Europe produced a wave of immigration that shook up and reshaped the cultural, social, economic, and political dynamics of the country. Swift urban growth had transformed Buenos Aires, which by 1940 had 2.5 million inhabitants, making the city one of the largest in the world.[11] Within a few years it was clear that the country's existing political structure—a traditional, conservative, oligarchic-imperialist axis dominated by the all-encompassing power of the upper classes—was incompatible with its new social formations: a solid working class (composed of foreign immigrants and Argentines who had moved to the city from the country) increasingly aware of its role within the economic apparatus, a new industrial bourgeoisie, and a military class that became the conduit for a strong nationalist current. At a moment crying out for change, the Argentine Left found itself in disarray. Its workers' movement was ineffective, dominated by foreign interests and clotted by bureaucracy; its political parties were decaying; and it was hampered by what many perceived as an ideology of an abstract, European character more concerned with international conflict than with local realities. This was the background for the 1943 coup of June 4 (called a revolution by the military), led by the the nationalist and authoritarian Grupo Obra de Unificación (Unification Work Group), which catapulted Colonel Juan Domingo Perón to the center of Argentina's political life.[12] Perón initially served as secretary of labor but also acted as minister of war and vice president until he was removed from power by a coalition of parties, including Socialists and Communists, on October 10, 1945. A few days later, on October 17, he was reinstated as interim president by a massive mobilization of workers who had paralyzed the country with a general strike, and on February 24, 1946, he was elected president and remained in power until 1955. This political trajectory was identified by local (leftist) intellectuals as reactionary, nationalistic, and militaristic. Just seven years after the divisive experience of the Spanish Civil War,[13] Argentina's intellectuals saw the newly installed military regime echoing all too clearly the totalitarian, authoritarian, and Fascist developments of Europe in the 1930s. They were discouraged by how the military government thwarted progressive intellectuals and artists by suppressing the leftist press, previously established unions, political parties, and independent voices such as the university professors who had demanded the rupture of diplomatic relations with Germany during the war.[14]

In fact, Argentina maintained its neutrality in World War II until just a few months before the official end of hostilities, at which point it declared war on Germany and Japan.[15] By 1945 the victory of the Allied forces in Europe rendered Argentina's own incipient "fascist" experiment illegitimate—at least in the eyes of an opposition that included Communists and Socialists[16]—and prompted a local assembly to organize the Marcha de la Constitución y de la Libertad (Constitution and Liberty March) on September 19, 1945, in Buenos Aires to celebrate the end of the conflict and to tacitly protest against the local military regime. That same day, an item in *Orientación*—the "central organ of the Communist Party," as the journal was subtitled—announced that artists and writers of the concrete art movement—Edgar Bayley, Tomás Maldonado, Manuel Espinosa, Alfredo Hlito, Claudio Girola, and Aldo Prior—had become members of the Argentine Communist Party.

By the time of the march, the connection between a Marxist-inspired vocabulary and the aethetic strategies of artists pursuing the cutout frame was firmly established. In an April 1945 interview in *Contrapunto* magazine, Tomás Maldonado laid out the basics of his artistic agenda: a rejection of representation, and thus illusionism, through an art that focused on the tangible and the real and prioritized invention over reflection, presentation over representation. This art, he explained, would suit the new (victorious) "man," the "man" enganged in (postwar) reconstruction; it would be anonymous and practical; and it aspired to effectively participate in the life of all men.[17] Two months later in the same publication and in answer to the same questionnaire, Manuel Espinosa confirmed the association between concrete painting and leftist politics, insisting that modern art was an affirmation of man's mental and technical power. He illustrated his point with a painting that stands as an early statement of the cutout frame.[18] His *Pintura* (Painting, 1945; fig. 1.1) is one of two very similar works he made at this time in which overlapping, skewed rectangles create intersecting planes whose compartmentalized, angular surfaces echo the asymmetrical perimeter of the work. In both paintings the frame is replaced by a black grid that maps the entire pictorial surface: edge and internal grid unify the painting-object, making it impossible to distinguish figure from ground. The stained-glass-window effect of the fragmented colored surface animates the grid structure. While hues of yellow predominate in the work that survives today (plate 3),[19] some planes—in red, purple, green, and blue—jump from the canvas toward the viewer, thereby denying any allusion to imagery but retaining the illusion of receding and advancing space. In composing his paintings, Espinosa relied on the golden section to establish proportions among different segments of the pictorial surface, to create systematic rhythms, and to relinquish hierarchical organization. But this preplanned approach did not impede the optical push-pull effect—an illusionism that these young abstractionists would purge from subsequent

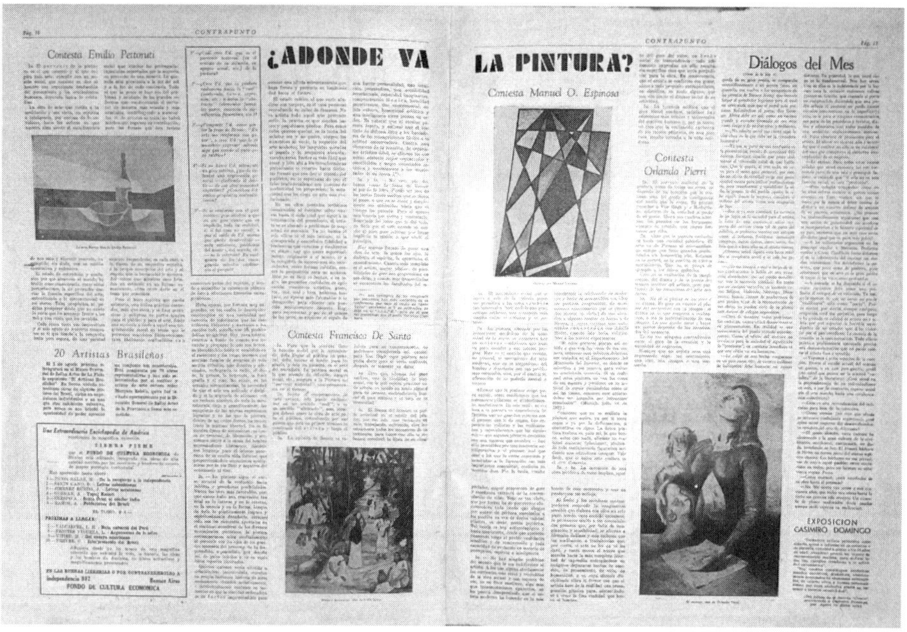

CONTRAPUNTO

Contesta Emilio Pettoruti

¿ADONDE VA LA PINTURA?

Contesta Manuel O. Espinosa

Diálogos del Mes

Contesta Orlando Pierri

20 Artistas Brasileños

Contesta Francisco De Santo

EXPOSICION CASIMIRO DOMINGO

FIGURE 1.1

Manuel Espinosa, *Pintura* (reproduced at top left of second page), in *Contrapunto,* no. 5, June 1945.

explorations by restricting the use of color and the proliferating compartmentalization of the picture plane.

After Perón's ascent to power, the cultural institutions of Buenos Aires became contested areas of ideological negotiation.[20] The Salón Nacional, for example, became a de facto state venue, ruled by decree and offering monetary prizes that encouraged subject matter on national themes that would appeal to a broad audience.[21] In opposition to this official venue, progressive artists formed their own salon in 1945: the Salón Independiente (which opened on September 19, 1945, the same day as the Marcha de la Constitución y de la Libertad). The artists associated with the Salón Independiente supported the Allied forces in World War II and democracy in Argentina, opposed the military government, and were united in "a concerted militancy of the brush."[22] A number of allegorical figurative paintings of the Salón Independiente alluded to the end of the war. The art historian Andrea Giunta, for one, interprets those works as an implicit affront to the military regime, which these artists associated with the vanquished Fascist forces in Europe. These war-themed paintings can also be seen as expressing empathy with the culture of the Old World—attempts to reestablish a connection that had been severed by the war. These negotiations with the culture and art of Europe were crucial for the artists associated with *Arturo* and later the AACI, in their search for original—that is, native—forms that would respond to their avowed European referents. These artists categorically rejected, however, the intrusion of figuration and realism into painting. This they associated with illusionism, contemplation, and idealism, concepts that Marx rejected in favor of action, change, social relations, and "worldliness."[23]

Despite these artists' overt commitment to certain Marxist concepts and the combative political rhetoric of their writings, there isn't any substantial discussion in their texts of 1944–46 of specific domestic political realities or the working masses that in October 17, 1945, put Perón in power and in whose name these artists spoke *in abstracto*. This omission can be explained in part by the fact that the ideological stance of the Argentine Communist Party at this time was highly compromised. The opinionated words of Jorge Abelardo Ramos shed light on the political landscape the Argentine avant-garde occupied circa 1944–47: "The decisive factor that forever transformed [Argentine Stalinism, and thus the Communist Party] into a small sect, well financed and sterile, was its alienation from the profound necessities of the Argentine people and the proletariat. Like any politics derived from variants of Soviet diplomacy, it rarely coincided with the national aspirations of our people."[24] More recently, the sociologist Juan Carlos Torre has singled out the Communist unions' rejection of economic concessions made by Perón as a key event. In retaliation, these unions were subjected to repression and defamation orchestrated by the regime, hastening the dissolution of ties between the Communist Party and the working class in Argentina. Whatever the exact temporality of this break, the record suggests that by 1945 Communism in Argentina was embraced primarily by "a coalition of middle-class and economic interests [that] mobilized against the vast popular movement composed of the same workers for whom, with so much loyalty, they had fought in the past."[25] This disidentification with the newly formed proletarian masses facilitated the emergence of new union leaders and made members of the working class with rural origins vulnerable to Perón's tactics. These included labor reforms, improved conditions for the growing population of industrial workers, and support for their nascent organizations, which crystallized with a wave of new labor unions in 1946.[26] The historian Carlos Altamirano, addressing a moment of soul searching by the Argentine Communist Party after the election of Perón, asks a crucial question: "Against the prescriptions of Marxism-Leninism, hadn't (political) forms been valued more highly than (social) contents at the moment in 1945 when the terms of the dichotomy were being defined?"[27] With these words, Altamirano echoes debates in art concerning (formal) abstraction and (representational) figuration that were characteristic of these years, especially within the French Communist Party. But most importantly, his words suggest a failure on the part of the Argentine Communist Party to address the loss of the proletariat to Peronism.

By proclaiming their association with the Communist Party, the artists of the AACI found themselves in a paradoxical position: they pursued an art of forms at a time when Communism and its aesthetics, especially the roles and values of abstract versus realistic figurative art, were being debated. As Maria Cristina Rossi and Alejandro Crispiani have noted, the terms of the abstraction/figuration debate were set in large part by French models to which Argentine intellectuals were highly receptive. This dynamic was related to the Francophile character of the cultural elites in Argentina, which were also attracted to the rapprochement between Communism and modern art that took place in France after World War II.[28] At the time, several factors suggested a common ground for Communism and modernism: the rejection of modernism by the Fascist regimes of Europe in the 1930s, the role of modern artists in the French Resistance, and the membership of certain artists in the Communist Party (Pablo Picasso being the most celebrated example). Tomás Maldonado made this case in 1946. Reviewing the Communist and antifascist credentials of the Parisian avant-garde—Fernand Léger, Tristan Tzara, Paul Éluard, and Picasso were among the figures he named—he declared, "In recent years, modern artists, so maligned, have demonstrated in the public square their love for the people."[29] And in defense of their identification with humanism—more commonly associated with representational, figurative art—he argued that "arte concreto-invención" was humanist because it was based on an "unlimited faith in the practical capacity of man."[30] "We are humanists," he wrote, "if humanism is revolutionary fervor, even in the field of culture and faith in the historical destiny of the proletariat."[31]

In the immediate postwar period, the French Communist Party was not only popular, due to its role in the Resistance, but the political organism around which a majority of intellectuals and artists coalesced. After 1947, however, the art historian Serge Guilbaut observes, "The Communist Party changed its previously more open . . . policy and, wanting to influence the restructuring of French culture, started promoting Social Realism against what in the 1930s they called bourgeois abstraction."[32] In light of these developments, it is not surprising that, in a 1947 article in *Orientación,* Maldonado would argue: "In truth, there is no official Communist aesthetic; there cannot be one. There is, however, a Communist ethics that the militant artist cannot ignore."[33] Nevertheless, he *did* have a specific aesthetic platform in mind for politically engaged Argentine artists: that of concrete art. By 1947, though, Maldonado and his circle had begun to abandon the radical strategies—the cutout frame and the coplanal—that had been conceived to bring about a revolution in form equivalent to a revolution in reality. At that time, the nature of that reality, like the art in question, was contested territory.

The previous year, also in the pages of *Orientación,* Edgar Bayley (Maldonado's older brother) published an apology for concrete art in more assertive terms. He wrote: "The era that is about to begin, an era of reconstruction and Socialism, demands an art in keeping with the material life of the society that is born and develops."[34] This statement was published just days before Perón's triumph in the presidential election and suggests that Bayley was blind to such a possibility. Perhaps he was channeling the hopes of the opposition, including Socialists and Communists—hopes that the election would shatter. In any case, not much seems to have changed for progressive Argentine artists with the triumph of Perón's "Labor Party." In the texts and works that followed, the artists who had embraced concrete art as a point of departure for their own investigations continued to pursue the lines of thought and formal experiments related to the cutout frame as well as those that would lead to the coplanal. Indeed, despite their desire for a transvaluation of the plasticity of European concrete art into concrete materiality and action, the AACI's focus remained aesthetic and theoretical. Bayley's ambivalent conclusion to his article attests to a tension between the self-referentiality of the concrete artwork and the communicative demands of propaganda, and to the uncertain place art occupied in Communist society. Despite the technical precision and efficient communication offered by the applied arts and propaganda, Bayley argued that concrete art was poised to make a "significant contribution to the liberation of man [by] asserting his dominance over the world . . . working against fiction through the inventive act and the techniques of propaganda and education, whose progress it promotes."[35] Here, Bayley links propaganda to political education, posters, and collective art, all of which opposed so-called "propaganda art," which confused communicative efficacy with diluted subjectivism and expressionism and was anathema to these artists. The task of concrete art, wrote Bayley, was the "invention of objective realities," a practice that supported politics by dislodging the fallacy of representational art (illusionism) that conspired "against the intelligibility and technical achievement of the poster."[36]

The political contradictions inherent in the works and texts of these artists are further illuminated by a revealing anti-Perón editorial from March 1945 by Américo Ghioldi in *La Vanguardia,* the Socialist newspaper he founded in Buenos Aires. Ghioldi argued that salary and labor concessions recently orchestrated by Perón were transitory and would be surpassed by advances in the process of production. What is "fundamental," he wrote, "is the consciousness of the working class, of its rights and its own strength."[37] And with a scorn that revealed the gap between the Argentine Left and the workers who supported Perón, Ghioldi referred to the latter as an easily bought mass ready to take advantage of perks, roasted meat, drinks, and "cotton handkerchiefs." Against this amorphous crowd—which, he argued, Perón called a "clientele"—Ghioldi posited an abstract notion of "the people" as the Socialists' real interlocutor. "We will go to [the people] with thoughts and ideals in search of affective and mental comprehension."[38] These words suggest that, to intellectuals, who found a natural correspondence between labor movements and democratic and progressive values, the task was mainly a pedagogical one: education would lead to the people's agency as world actors.[39]

The adoption of Marxist concepts by artists of the AACI can be seen as a compensatory discourse aimed at supplementing the absence of the traditional (representational) functions of painting and as part of an effort to transform painting into an epistemological tool that would dislodge illusionism and its contemplative mechanism of consumption. Materialism was probably the most relevant Marxist concept mobilized by the AACI. It facilitated a groundbreaking analysis of the pictorial signifier, threatening the identity of painting while simultaneously serving as the basis for an analysis of its constituent physical elements. This critical analysis and deconstruction of painting would trigger new modes of art production and perception and, arguably, lead to a revolutionary praxis based on action and thus to change.

Although art historians have identified resonances between the art of the Argentines and Russian and Soviet constructivism, the abstractionists associated with the AACI differed fundamentally from their Soviet counterparts.[40] The latter were firmly invested in the postrevolutionary social and political life of the USSR and, for a brief period, actively participated in the institutional cultural structure of the new political order.[41] For the most committed corps—the productivists, led by Alexander Rodchenko, Varvara Stepanova, and Aleksei Gan at Inkhuk (the Institute of Artistic Culture)—the development of a postrevolutionary project that implied the abandonment of art was far more important than the deconstruction of artistic mediums. Responding to urgent issues such as the role of art and the artist in a Communist society without class distinctions, the productivist agenda proposed experiments that would facilitate the transition of art into industrial production. In a program that delineated the foundations of what we today call design, these artists defined their task as "practical work on constructive structures according to received commissions . . . [and the] exploratory development of new technical possibilities of building."[42] This was not to be the Argentine way. Soviet and Argentine abstract artists faced radically different political realities, triggering unique relations to the realpolitik and producing discrete (if comparable) aesthetic projects. The art historian Paul Woods's statement that "the [Soviet] avant-garde actually aspired to an interventionist role"[43] sums up the difference between the two groups. In contrast to the urgency of the productivists—who found in graphic design, exhibition design, and pedagogy an immediate escape from the autonomy of art—Maldonado argued that the proper reception of their works would be realized in the future, and posited this as the real litmus test for art. He wrote in 1946: "In the future the people will understand our works and many things more complicated than our works. Concrete artists bet on this. We are faithful to Lenin's maxim: give the best to the people. Concrete art is the best we can offer."[44]

Thus, the artists of the AACI seemed to have been anachronistically inspired by the Marxist revolution that motivated the Russian constructivists and not by the Argentine "revolution" of Juan Perón, with which they could not identify and indeed opposed. While this might be an oversimplification, the intention here is to highlight the incapacity of the Argentine cultural and political Left to consider (much less address) their domestic urban working class and the local political situation. Furthermore, in the writings of the AACI there is no mention of the specifics of the October Revolution or the Left Opposition with which the Soviet avant-garde identified in the early and mid-1920s. Nor do we find in AACI writings of the mid-1940s any sustained discussion of the politics of Russian constructivism or the Soviet avant-garde (whose main protagonists were known to the Argentines), its engagement with the Soviet state, or the official sanctioning of socialist realism in the early 1930s. The names of Marx, Lenin, Engels, and Stalin appear in Maldonado's essays in *Arte Concreto Invención* no. 1, and the AACI expressed its support for the Soviet state in an editorial in that issue of the magazine.[45] But by the 1920s, this same Soviet state had crushed all opposition while deploying a propagandistic "left turn" that produced a mirage of working-class Socialism, at home and especially abroad.[46] It is this complicated landscape of ideological mediations that shaped the Marxist and Communist alliances of the Argentine concretists in the mid-1940s and their attempt to produce works that drastically rethought the medium of painting and the role of art objects.

## SOURCES AND BEGINNINGS: THE CONCRETE, THE FRAME, AND THE OBJECT

Key notions of Marxist thought, particularly that of materialism, provided the theoretical basis for the aesthetic strategies that led the artists of the AACI to break the constraints of the frame. As Alfredo Hlito, a founding member of the AACI, cautioned in 1946: "Metaphysical systems have distinguished themselves . . . by not acknowledging the difference between the physical and historical world and the world of representation. In aesthetics, this amounted to ignoring the historical and practical nature of art, and consequently, to confusing . . . the properties of the natural object with those of the aesthetic object."[47] A Marxist materialist drive focused on concepts of action and change, which opposed the idealism of representation and contemplation, grounded the Argentine experiments in the reality of materials, in the actuality of the verifiable, and, arguably, in specific historical circumstances and practice. "For a materialist aesthetic . . . the aesthetic property resides in the concrete materiality of the work of art,"[48] continued Hlito, echoing European concrete art's emphasis on the plastic elements of art. The goal, for Hlito, was the transformation of the plasticity of the work of art into a concrete materiality with political possibilities. He rejected representation as "reflection" and subjective projection, and, appropriating Marxist language, he argued that representation (a mere reflection of the actual object) was equivalent to alienation from the objects of production.[49] Just as workers oppressed by capitalism were estranged from the products of their labor and the activity of production, so were representational artists oppressed by illusionism, which hindered their creative potential.

Thus, the paintings of the Argentine avant-garde emphasized the work's constituent elements to bring the viewer closer to the reality of things in the world. This strategy emerged from the profound desire of these artists to contribute to a Western trajectory of art that they perceived as an irreversible teleology at the very moment when the locus of that cultural tradition was immersed in an unimaginable calamity.[50] The vigorous texts and unconventional works produced between 1944 and 1946 by Carmelo Arden Quin, Tomás Maldonado, Lidy Prati, Gyula Kosice, Rhod Rothfuss, Manuel Espinosa, Edgar Bayley, Raúl Lozza, Alfredo Hlito, and Juan Melé (to name the most prominent figures working during those years) were shaped by a constellation of influences and antecedents in Europe and South America. These references were filtered through the complicated cultural and political landscape of Argentina and mediated by the cultures of exile that had shaped avant-garde art throughout the first half of the twentieth century.

One such crucial figure was the German-born photographer Grete Stern. She had studied with the photographer Walter Peterhans, privately and at the Bauhaus, in the early 1930s before settling in Argentina in 1935. Her knowledge of German avant-garde art and familiarity with the constructivist tendencies so influential at the Bauhaus earned her a special place among Argentine artists trying to develop radical models of cultural production. Gyula Kosice, for one, remembers that Stern shared seminal books written by or dedicated to key avant-garde figures such as László Moholy-Nagy, Paul Klee, Piet Mondrian, Kazimir Malevich, Walter Gropius, and others.[51] Tomás Maldonado recalled that immigrants displaced by the war brought to Argentina important documents that revealed the radical mutations that had taken place in Europe between the two wars and earlier: "documents already yellowed, picked up in Berlin, Cologne, Paris, Madrid, Budapest, Prague, Moscow, Milan. They were usually manifestos, pamphlets, books, magazines, catalogues that served as arguments or counterarguments to our feverish search for a new understanding of artistic practice."[52] According to Juan Melé, some of these magazines and catalogues were brought to Buenos Aires by the artists Juan del Prete (who had been a member of the Abstraction-Création group in Paris) and Antonio Berni.[53] In addition, the Uruguayan artist Joaquín Torres-García, an important reference for these artists, had firsthand knowledge of Parisian concrete art and was acquainted with key figures such as Theo van Doesburg, Piet Mondrian, and Georges Vantongerloo.

This exposure to advanced thought and artistic practice in Europe energized the Argentine artists, and in 1944 a group of poets, writers, and artists—including Tomás Maldonado, Gyula Kosice, Edgar Bayley, and the Uruguayans Carmelo Arden Quin and Rhod Rothfuss—founded a magazine called *Arturo* (plate 4) to promote abstraction and provide a platform for their ideas. One of the first editorial texts written for *Arturo,* by Arden Quin, "immediately sets a Marxist frame of reference":[54] "The material conditions of a society determine its ideological superstructures. Art, an ideological superstructure, is born and develops on the basis of the economic movements of society. This is the revelation that historical materialism makes about art."[55] In a desire to articulate their peripheral position vis-à-vis the advanced artistic experiments of Europe, the artists of *Arturo* found in this basic Marxist premise a justification for the eruption of abstraction (only vaguely represented in the magazine)[56] then taking place in the relatively undisturbed painterly landscape of Argentine bourgeois culture. By mobilizing this Marxist narrative, the artists of *Arturo* seemed to suggest that, until that moment, Argentina had been unable to produce advanced models of aesthetic production. The material conditions and productive practices of Argentine society—its technological, scientific, and economic structures and apparatuses—allowed for only certain developments and a corresponding ideological superstructure. Art and labor were forms of human action tied to the here and now via a movement that "does not explain practice from the idea, but explains the formation of ideas from material practice," as Marx and Engels wrote in a celebrated passage from *The German Ideology* (1845).[57] The authors go on to elucidate one of the basic premises for a "materialist conception of history": "By producing their means of subsistence, men are indirectly producing their material life. . . . [T]his mode of production . . . is a definite form of activity of these individuals, a definite form of expressing their life, a definite *model of life* on their part. As individuals express their life, so they are."[58] This passage suggests that the entire range of productive activities in which humans engage are forms of expression, creative endeavors that bind artistic activity to all other forms of production, all of which are constitutive of being.

It seems fair to suggest that Arden Quin thought of *Arturo* as a response to a new technical and economic horizon in Argentina that urgently needed a reconfigured superstructure—an idea later supported by Alfredo Hlito's elaboration of a "materialist aesthetic" in "Representación e invención" (Representation and Invention), his important essay of 1946. In this context, the act of inventing and the invention itself together formed a pivotal concept, one that was introduced by Arden Quin in his editorial for *Arturo* as a way of framing innovation and creativity. Against automatism and subjective expression (which the artists of *Arturo* rejected), invention was posited by Arden Quin as capable of shaping an artistic practice with strong relations to the activities undertaken in the technological field—an idea that would be reiterated throughout the writings of the AACI. Indeed, in the more precise prose of Hlito in 1946, invention was defined in opposition to fortuitous discovery and to alienation (the estrangement from one's own labor) and as a function of practical consciousness. "Inventing," Hlito wrote, "means INTRODUCING INTO THE WORLD BY MEANS OF EXPERIMENT AND INDUSTRY WHAT DID NOT EXIST UNTIL NOW."[59] *Invention* became such a key term in the Argentine avant-garde's linguistic arsenal that by 1945 they were calling their movement Invención, a title modified the following year in favor of the more explicative Asociación Arte Concreto Invención (Association of Concrete Art Invention).

The end of World War II had improved the economic realities of Argentina and the rest of South America, and the widespread expectation was that postwar reconstruction would increase international commercial traffic while South America would provide food and raw materials to the Old World.[60] In his seminal history of Latin America, Tulio Halperin Donghi analyzes how this expectation was challenged by the insuperable complexities of industrialization in the region and how the enthusiasm of many Latin American nations in 1945 soon dissipated into an effort to merely "secure the survival of an incurably primitive industry."[61] But to the artists of *Arturo,* the events and possibilities of 1944 seem to have suggested a point of no return, and they appeared to believe that their internationally leaning country was on the verge of social, economic, political, and cultural transformation. Using Marx's historical model, the Argentine avant-garde (Arden Quin's editorial suggested) could boldly leap into modes of artistic production that would respond to the economic (and technological) possibilities they contemplated. From an aesthetic point of view, however, it was primarily the attack on naturalistic and surrealistic modes of image production dominant in Argentina at the time—and, later, the engagement with the cutout frame theorized by Rhod Rothfuss in the pages of

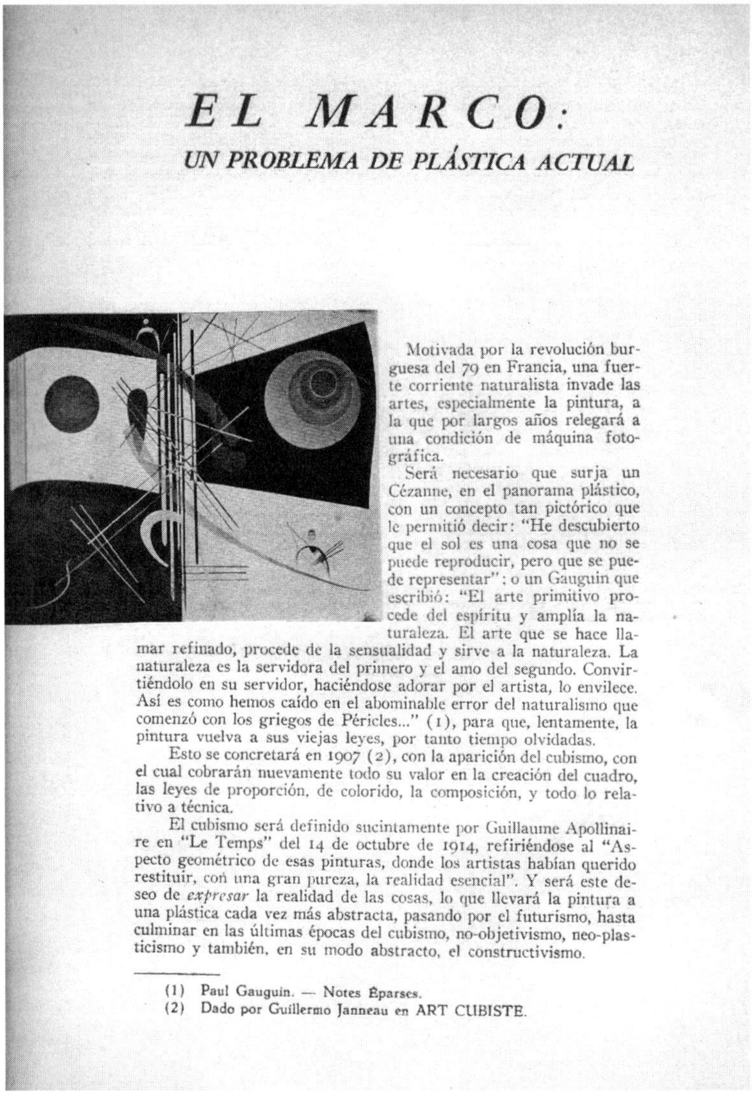

# EL MARCO:

## UN PROBLEMA DE PLÁSTICA ACTUAL

Motivada por la revolución burguesa del 79 en Francia, una fuerte corriente naturalista invade las artes, especialmente la pintura, a la que por largos años relegará a una condición de máquina fotográfica.

Será necesario que surja un Cézanne, en el panorama plástico, con un concepto tan pictórico que le permitió decir: "He descubierto que el sol es una cosa que no se puede reproducir, pero que se puede representar": o un Gauguin que escribió: "El arte primitivo procede del espíritu y amplía la naturaleza. El arte que se hace llamar refinado, procede de la sensualidad y sirve a la naturaleza. La naturaleza es la servidora del primero y el amo del segundo. Convirtiéndolo en su servidor, haciéndose adorar por el artista, lo envilece. Así es como hemos caído en el abominable error del naturalismo que comenzó con los griegos de Péricles..." (1), para que, lentamente, la pintura vuelva a sus viejas leyes, por tanto tiempo olvidadas.

Esto se concretará en 1907 (2), con la aparición del cubismo, con el cual cobrarán nuevamente todo su valor en la creación del cuadro, las leyes de proporción, de colorido, la composición, y todo lo relativo a técnica.

El cubismo será definido sucintamente por Guillaume Apollinaire en "Le Temps" del 14 de octubre de 1914, refiriéndose al "Aspecto geométrico de esas pinturas, donde los artistas habían querido restituir, con una gran pureza, la realidad esencial". Y será este deseo de *expresar* la realidad de las cosas, lo que llevará la pintura a una plástica cada vez más abstracta, pasando por el futurismo, hasta culminar en las últimas épocas del cubismo, no-objetivismo, neo-plasticismo y también, en su modo abstracto, el constructivismo.

(1) Paul Gauguin. — Notes Éparses.
(2) Dado por Guillermo Janneau en ART CUBISTE.

FIGURE 1.2

Rhod Rothfuss, "El marco: Un problema de plástica actual" (The Frame: A Problem in Contemporary Art) in *Arturo* magazine, summer 1944.

*Arturo*—that provided a united, if fleeting, front for the emerging abstractionists aiming at invention and experimentation.

Rothfuss's essay is without a doubt a cornerstone of the singular formal propositions that ensued. Entitled "El marco: Un problema de plástica actual" (The Frame: A Problem in Contemporary Art; fig. 1.2), it remains crucial to understanding the revolutionary aesthetic leap performed by these artists in the 1940s. The text suggests that the artists

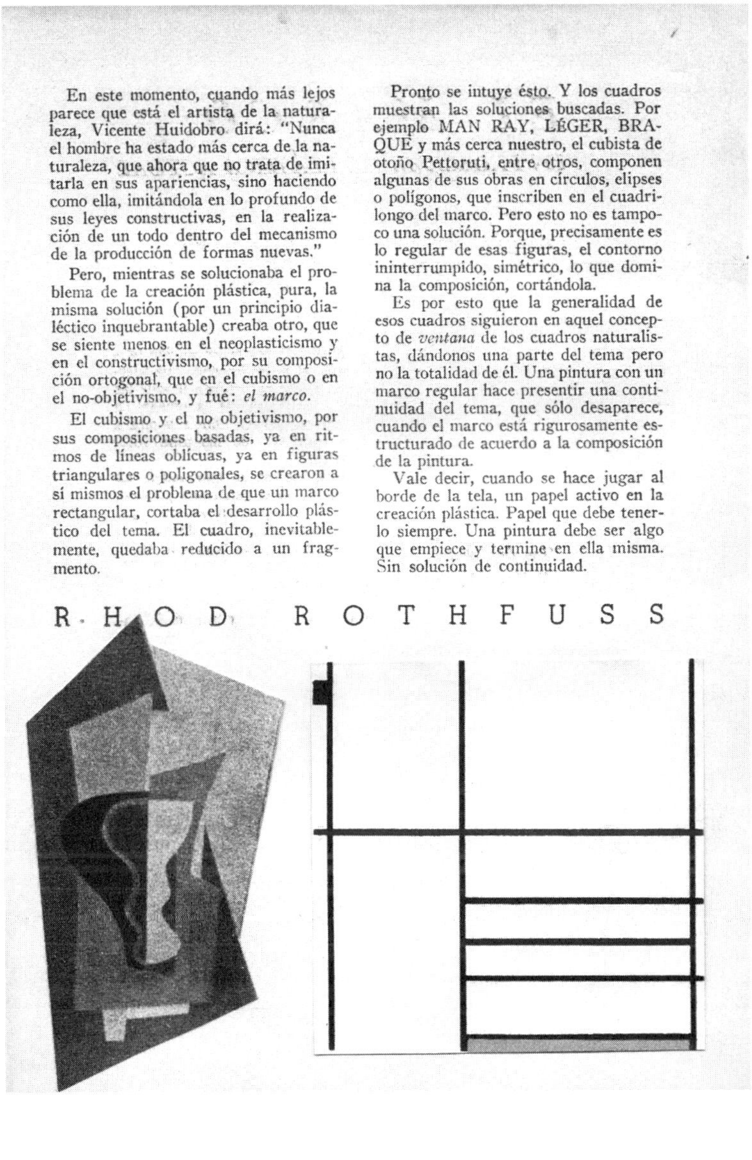

En este momento, cuando más lejos parece que está el artista de la naturaleza, Vicente Huidobro dirá: "Nunca el hombre ha estado más cerca de la naturaleza, que ahora que no trata de imitarla en sus apariencias, sino haciendo como ella, imitándola en lo profundo de sus leyes constructivas, en la realización de un todo dentro del mecanismo de la producción de formas nuevas."

Pero, mientras se solucionaba el problema de la creación plástica, pura, la misma solución (por un principio dialéctico inquebrantable) creaba otro, que se siente menos en el neoplasticismo y en el constructivismo, por su composición ortogonal, que en el cubismo o en el no-objetivismo, y fué: *el marco.*

El cubismo y el no objetivismo, por sus composiciones basadas, ya en ritmos de líneas oblícuas, ya en figuras triangulares o poligonales, se crearon a sí mismos el problema de que un marco rectangular, cortaba el desarrollo plástico del tema. El cuadro, inevitablemente, quedaba reducido a un fragmento.

Pronto se intuye ésto. Y los cuadros muestran las soluciones buscadas. Por ejemplo MAN RAY, LÉGER, BRAQUE y más cerca nuestro, el cubista de otoño Pettoruti, entre otros, componen algunas de sus obras en círculos, elipses o polígonos, que inscriben en el cuadrilongo del marco. Pero esto no es tampoco una solución. Porque, precisamente es lo regular de esas figuras, el contorno ininterrumpido, simétrico, lo que domina la composición, cortándola.

Es por esto que la generalidad de esos cuadros siguieron en aquel concepto de *ventana* de los cuadros naturalistas, dándonos una parte del tema pero no la totalidad de él. Una pintura con un marco regular hace presentir una continuidad del tema, que sólo desaparece, cuando el marco está rigurosamente estructurado de acuerdo a la composición de la pintura.

Vale decir, cuando se hace jugar al borde de la tela, un papel activo en la creación plástica. Papel que debe tenerlo siempre. Una pintura debe ser algo que empiece y termine en ella misma. Sin solución de continuidad.

R H O D R O T H F U S S

of *Arturo* were aware of the advances toward abstraction made by cubism, neoplasticism, nonobjectivity, and constructivism. Although they had not yet adopted the banner of concretism, their aesthetic predispositions are illuminated by Rothfuss's reference to the Chilean poet Vicente Huidobro's 1921 manifesto "La creación pura" (Pure Creation),[62] a work that that would be echoed by Huidobro's friend Jean Arp's conception of the artistic process in his writings on concrete art. Rothfuss quoted Huidobro: "Man has never been closer to nature now that he does not aspire to imitate its appearances, but to do as it does, imitating its constructive laws, in the realization of a whole, in the process of producing new forms."[63] Arp rehearsed Huidobro's principles of creacionismo (creationism) in a short essay published on the occasion of a 1944 exhibition entitled *Konkrete Kunst,* mounted in Basel and organized by Max Bill (who was at the time attempting to effect a smooth transition from prewar European concrete art to its postwar incarnation). Arp wrote: "We don't want to copy nature. We don't want to reproduce. We want to produce like a plant that produces a fruit and not reproduce. We want to produce directly and not through any intermediary. Since this art doesn't have the slightest trace of abstraction, we name it: concrete art."[64]

It was in the name of art's self-referentiality and against the illusionism of traditional pictorial paradigms that artists in Europe and Argentina embraced the notion of the work of art as an independent being growing from within its own structure—a view whose affiliation with the organic seems to favor causal and rational forms of development as well as the idea that parts of a work relate to each other meaningfully, with internal coherence and functional interdependence.[65] As the art historian Rosalind Krauss has pointed out, in abstract artistic circles of the 1930s in Europe, such as Cercle et Carré (founded by Joaquín Torres-García and Michel Seuphor) and Abstraction-Création (founded by Theo van Doesburg), "the sculptor was likened to a creator, to the original Creator, who did not replicate given objects, but added new ones to the repertory of nature."[66] For Krauss, the emblematic case is Arp, whose sculptures from the 1930s seem to capture a moment of functional and progressive growth associated with organic life (fig. 1.3). However, the materialist credo and art objects produced by the Argentine artists would problematize the principles of autonomy and organic functionalism posited by European concrete art, Parisian geometric abstraction in the 1930s, and Rothfuss's text. From the unpredictable configuration of Gyula Kosice's multipart *Röyi* (1944) and the open structure of Lidy Prati's *Untitled* (1945; plate 5), which resembles a Mondrian exploding into real space, to the coplanals, which incorporated the wall as a constituent element of the work, these objects did away with containment and dismissed the conventions of the medium, shattering as well notions of organic (functional) organization.

Unaware of the intermedial condition that the cutout frame would unleash, Rothfuss espoused the dictum of self-sufficiency proposed by Huidobro's creacionismo in his contribution to *Arturo.* For Rothfuss, the frame compromised the visual deployment of a painting and its composition; the frame sustained the impression that one is looking at a fragment of a whole. All paintings with orthogonal frames, he wrote, followed the illusionistic (and passive) concept of a window through which one contemplates a fragment of a theme. The only way to avoid this spectatorial passivity, Rothfuss argued, was by structuring the frame according to the composition of the painting. Aspiring to a continuity between internal composition and external frame—to an integration that would deliver a self-sufficient, self-generated pictorial organization—Rothfuss proposed

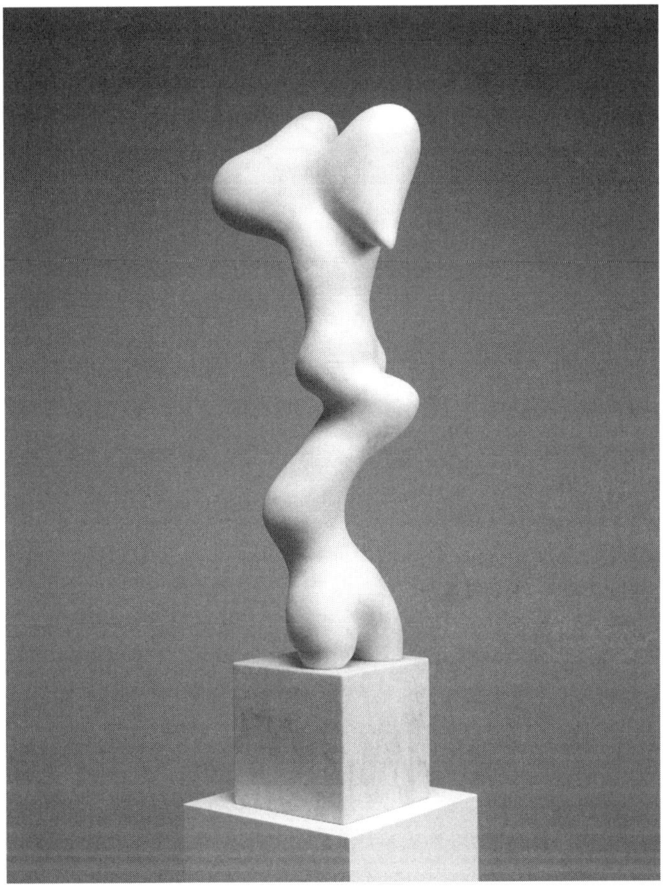

FIGURE 1.3
Jean Arp, *Growth,* 1938/60, marble, 43 × 17½ × 11 in.

abolishing traditional (symbolic, thematic, imagistic) approaches to painting. He concluded his essay with a paradoxical statement that threatened the painterly structure while at the same time protected the medium from extraneous figurative and narrative demands: The edge of the canvas, he wrote, plays "an active role in the work of art. A role it must always have. A painting should begin and end with itself."[67] Rothfuss was articulating here a sort of pictorial tautology, with the frame defining the shape of the support and echoing the internal composition of the work. Just as an organism reproduces, the frame, too, would beget form.

But the frame was also the painting's point of contact with the architectural wall—a fact to which Rothfuss didn't give any thought. By positing the frame as an active element of the composition, Rothfuss had attacked one of the most cherished conventions of painting: the frame as a limit that protected the ontology of the picture, the frame as that which confined painting. For Rothfuss, activating the frame asserted the autonomy of the pictorial signifier, a dynamic that ultimately exposed painting to the contingencies of real space and objects. The resulting cutout frame (*marco recortado*) overthrew the convention of the orthogonal frame, which is, as the Brazilian critic Ferreira Gullar would point out a few years later, a neutral zone where the conflict between real space and virtual space, between gratuitous work and the practical world, is extinguished.[68] By dismissing the traditional frame, Gullar wrote, "pictorial space evaporates [and] the surface of what was the 'picture' falls to the level of common things."[69] Although Gullar was addressing the elimination of the frame toward which Lygia Clark's work was moving in the mid-1950s, the argumentative force of his essay is relevant in thinking about the work of the Buenos Aires–based artists, which, despite Rothfuss's original intentions, moved toward pictorial dissolution by doing away with the orthogonal frame, insisting on the materiality (objecthood) of painting, and incorporating the wall as an element of the work. The abandonment of the frame and the commingling of these works with real space would bring the Argentine avant-garde to painting's edge.

The Uruguayan artist Joaquín Torres-García, a contributor to *Arturo,* was a key point of reference for the artists involved with that journal in their path toward a restructuring of painting. He was well known in the Argentine cultural milieu thanks to his regular articles for the newspaper *La Nación* and his various publications on art. He had personal knowledge of the European avant-gardes (his relationship to Theo van Doesburg in Paris is particularly relevant here), professed a disdain for surrealism, and had even suggested, via his encounter with European concrete art, an art in dialogue with everyday objects.[70] By the early 1940s Torres-García was pursuing a pictorial model that can be characterized as diagrammatic iconicity: emblematic pictographic symbols (fish, sun, anchor) inserted into gridlike structures that organized the pictorial surface. Back in Paris, however, under van Doesburg's influence, he produced some of the most abstract works of his career, systematically deploying the grid that De Stijl had inherited from cubism and redirected in its search for the basic elements of painting. This abstract work might not seem to have much to do with the experiments of the Argentines, but, as the art historian Nicolette Gast has observed, one early work by Torres-García merits attention.[71] This untitled work from 1929 (owned by van Doesburg at the time) is a figurative but simplified oil on canvas depicting the face and torso of a figure described with lines and blocks of color. Significantly, it features a thick wooden frame that extends beyond the canvas. Echoing the active role that frames had played in late medieval panel painting and acknowledging the incorporation of the frame in van Doesburg's own work, Torres-García painted over the frame and extended the composition beyond the support. This gesture suggested a more active role for the framing device—a recognition of its material plasticity related to the wood reliefs that Torres-García had been developing since 1924, first in Italy and then intensely in Paris between 1927 and 1933.[72]

It was in the early 1930s that the term *concrete art* gained currency in Paris. Van Doesburg had inaugurated a group and magazine with that name in 1930. (Torres-García expressed his intention to join the movement but soon backed out, unable to commit to the total abstraction the new alliance demanded.) The principles of the movement were published in the sole issue of *Art Concret* in April 1930. There, van Doesburg emphasized the need for a universal art entirely conceived in the mind before its execution. Self-referentiality was one of the cornerstones of European concrete art: the meaning of a work was to reside in the combination of its plastic elements, and its construction was to be "visually controllable."[73] The editors of the magazine took great pains to establish artistic creation as an intellectual activity tied to mathematics and geometry. And in a Neoplatonic tour de force, they demanded that the technical perfection of a work be equivalent to the perfection of the concept that gave it birth. Here we find those oft-quoted lines that clarify the difference between abstract and concrete art: "*Concrete* painting and not *abstract,* since nothing is more concrete, more real, than a line, a color, a surface. [Are] a woman, a tree, a cow on a canvas concrete elements? No. A woman, a tree, a cow are concrete in their natural state, but in the state of painting, they are abstract, illusory, vague, speculative; while a plane is plane, a line is a line; nothing less; nothing more."[74]

This emphasis on the literalness of the plastic elements of the work, which many abstract artists shared, was in Torres-García's work united with a renewed interest in the wood reliefs and constructions of artists influenced by Dada: Jean Arp, Sophie Taeuber-Arp, Kurt Schwitters, and Joan Miró. The art historian Agnès de Maistre points out that Torres-García's knowledge of recent developments in this vein can be deduced from his organization of *Exposició d'Art Modern Nacional i Estranger* in the fall of 1929 at Galeries Dalmau in Barcelona, featuring works by Arp, Taeuber-Arp, van Doesburg, Jean Hélion, Mondrian, Jean Xceron, and Georges Vantongerloo, among others.[75] While in Paris, Torres-García maintained close relationships with Arp and Vantongerloo, who seem to have pulled the Uruguayan artist toward three-dimensional work, which he had already explored in a series of transformable wooden toys of simplified shapes, initiated in 1917 and reprised in a set of small-format schematic wooden figurative sculptures in the late 1920s. Torres-García called these works, and several more made between 1929 and 1932, "plastic objects" or "constructions." Halfway between painting and sculpture, they asserted the physicality of their materials and exploited the ambivalent character of relief sculpture. Some of these objects are composed of colored pieces of wood juxtaposed and superimposed within a rectilinear frame, as in *Madera* (Wood Construction, 1929). Others are closer to assemblage, as in *Objet Plastique / Composition* (Plastic Object / Composition, 1931–34; plate 6), which features colored panels of different sizes and shapes organized around a central axis. Still others assert themselves as true antecedents of the Argentine avant-garde's experiments of the 1940s, including the minimal *Madera Planos de Color* (Wood Planes of Color, 1929), which, contra its title, features mostly brown, ocher, gray, and black areas distributed around incised rectilinear sections on an irregularly shaped wooden support.

Shortly after concluding this more or less systematic exploration of relief, Torres-García suggested a parallel between art and functional objects that later preoccupied the Argentine artists. In an essay written in 1934 (the year of his return to Montevideo)[76] titled "Funcionalismo" (Functionalism), he argued that "aesthetic unity" is the objective of every artist. Eager to articulate lessons learned abroad, he referred to the harmonious relation of parts to a whole (identified above with organic functionalism), a quality he associated with reason, sense, measure, clarity, and simplicity as well as the functionality of objects. Drawing a parallel with the productions of the "the humble man of work" (*hombre humilde del oficio*), he called the artwork a "plastic-object: painting-object, sculpture-object" and defined it as "work existing by itself, based on itself, thus independent; not work-reflection, not faux-nature, not illusionistic painting or sculpture but something concrete, like a telescope, a hat, or an umbrella. Aesthetic objects, like all these other objects, are useful."[77] Torres-García, like the artists of *Arturo* ten years later, was not remotely interested in submitting his artistic practice to the paradigm of the readymade (or the logic of mass production). His concern with concreteness and objecthood was directly linked to the functionalism (the harmonious relations of parts to a whole) that the art object must achieve if it aspires to a logic of its own—a functionalism analogous to the functionality of objects that respond to the primacy of purpose. The Uruguayan artist's allusion to utilitarian objects was informed by the comparison between art and the machine characteristic of the European avant-garde in the 1920s. "The machine," van Doesburg wrote in *De Stijl,* "is the phenomenon of spiritual discipline par excellence."[78] Arising from necessity and determined by rational planning, the technological/functional object was an exemplary form-giving (*Gestaltung*) device, resistant to the whims of decoration to which Torres-García, following a key constructivist dictum, also objected. As the architectural historian Detlef Mertins indicated in his invaluable mapping of these terms and debates in early-twentieth-century Germany: "Elementary form creation was to be guided by economy, a pure relationship between force and material, elementary means, order and lawfulness."[79] For Torres-García, reason was the structuring core of an art that could negotiate between the epochal and the individual—thus, its universality. A constructed art was to be achieved through "invention," not standardization, and proportion was underlined as what regulates and gives unity to the work, along with a harmonious relationship between structure and measurable form and the strict application of preestablished rules.

Embracing this idealist aesthetic, Torres-García was unstinting in his scorn for more literalist approaches to real, ordinary objects and the experimental freedom that this implied: "So much nonsense, also in modern times, has been spoken in the name of freedom: burning museums, painting with *pistolet,* making collective impersonal or madly personal art, murdering painting, absolute impersonal abstraction, moving sculpture, art based on real objects, noise music, collage, wire sculpture, sexual surrealist art, proletarian art, suprematism . . . ! From all this only one thing can save us: Reason."[80] This list of forbidden artistic strategies—a veritable compendium of key avant-garde experimental techniques—betrays Torres-García's profoundly conservative enterprise and helps to explain why the artists of the AACI, through the voice of Maldonado, ultimately condemned the Uruguayan artist.[81] Denying any destabilizing force

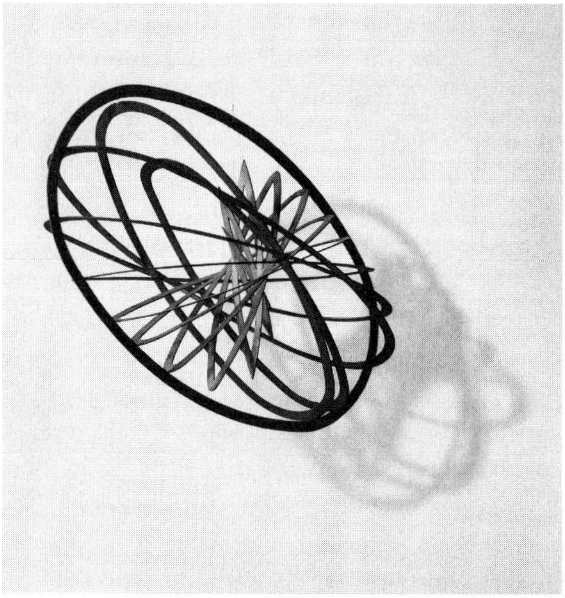

FIGURE 1.4
Alexander Rodchenko, *Spatial Construction no. 12*, ca. 1920, plywood, aluminum paint, and wire, 24 × 33 × 18½ in.

prompted by the work's use of concrete materials and proximity to the contingency of real space, Torres-García's words summarized a prescriptive modernism clearly founded on classicism: "functionalism based on measurement."[82]

Torres-García's comparison of art to everyday objects, however, signals a key paradox: in art's search for autonomy via an emphasis on functional relationships among its plastic (objective and material) elements, it grows close to the physicality and structural logic of concrete—that is, everyday and useful—objects and the mundane space they occupy. This tension between the ideational and the concrete evident in concrete art—a paradox that haunts Torres-García's essay—was refashioned by the Argentine artists who pursued a materialist approach and a more direct engagement with real space. This led to the increased instability of their paintings and marked an important difference from European concrete art, which remained focused on a priori compositionality and intellectual conceptualization. Notably, as early as 1944, the work that best embodied the traits of this paradox was not a painting but an object: Gyula Kosice's *Röyi* (1944; plate 7).

The work, which consists of rounded beams of wood connected by screws that allow the viewer to manipulate the position and final structure of the work, should be read in dialogue with this rapprochement between concrete materials and objects implicitly formulated by an abandonment of the orthogonal frame. Furthermore, *Röyi* has a mechanistic appearance, but its rather pointless movements elude any notion of functionalism in which there is a logical relationship between parts and whole—as in, for example, Alexander Rodchenko's *Spatial Constructions* (ca. 1920; fig. 1.4). In this sense, it is worth recalling, as Raymond Williams does, that the word *organic* was initially associated with *instrument*. In the sixteenth century, the word "followed first the sense of engine or tool. . . . [T]his is instructive in view of the later conventional contrast between organic and mechanical."[83] The common opposition of those terms was reconfigured in the 1920s by the European avant-garde, for whom *organic* bridged both realms and designated a purposeful "form-generating activity" common to art and industry.[84] Williams's etymology validates the association between the organic and the functional that traverses much writing about the status of the work of art vis-à-vis the constructivist tendencies of the 1920s and 1930s as well as the work of Vicente Huidobro and Torres-García. But, as the discussion of concrete/neoconcrete art in Brazil (chapters 2 and 3) and Gego's work in Venezuela (chapter 5) will show, the organic was to be a contested concept, constantly mobilized to defend or attack the systemic and rational dimension of geometric abstract works. In this regard, the organic may be associated with a causal development in which one can deduce the clear stages of a structure by analyzing the constituent relationships of a work or a system in which the organic "as an instrument of agency" is tied to organization; nevertheless, the same concept may also be used to account for more open, relational, and contingent interactions between form and environment.

Kosice's *Röyi* can be situated at the crux of these two understandings of the organic, as the work's aleatory performance conveys a playfulness that betrays its mechanistic look. Operating at the juncture of the organic and the mechanical, *Röyi* seems to anticipate key concerns in the Argentine reformulation of concretism: its objecthood, its embeddedness in real space, its nonhierarchical structure, and its attempt to involve the spectator. These issues were not addressed in the statements that accompanied the reproduction of a model of the work on the cover of *Invención*, a 1945 pamphlet edited by Kosice and dedicated to his work (fig. 1.5).[85] In sharp contrast to the militant writings of the AACI, Kosice (who would form Arte Madí in 1946 with Arden Quin and Rothfuss) wrote prose that was somewhat esoteric, making reference to the machine and invention as the conduit to eternity. Like Torres-García, Kosice saw the "law of permanence" (defined as "organic permanence"), which responds to the spatial concreteness of the object, as the foundation of the "invented organism" that harmonizes with its epoch.[86]

*Röyi*'s formal resolution is also in line with the concept of invention as variously mobilized by these artists between 1944 and 1946. It was around the term *invención*—as the publication on and by Kosice mentioned above confirms—that the artists associated with *Arturo* decided in 1945 to join together. Agnès de Maistre argues that "to differentiate themselves from Huidobro's creationism, Edgar Bayley proposed that their movement be called Invention. In opposition to the idealist conception of art that makes the artist a creator in the image of God, they [promoted] the materialism that attributes to man alone the power of invention."[87] For his part, Kosice characterized contemporary creation as a material invention in which the individual "penetrates into the world of physical realities" due to a "need in society."[88] Indeed, *Röyi* flirted with the image of tool, instrument, and machine that the concept of invention unleashed; due to its unambiguous three-dimensional status, it raised those associations to a greater extent than the

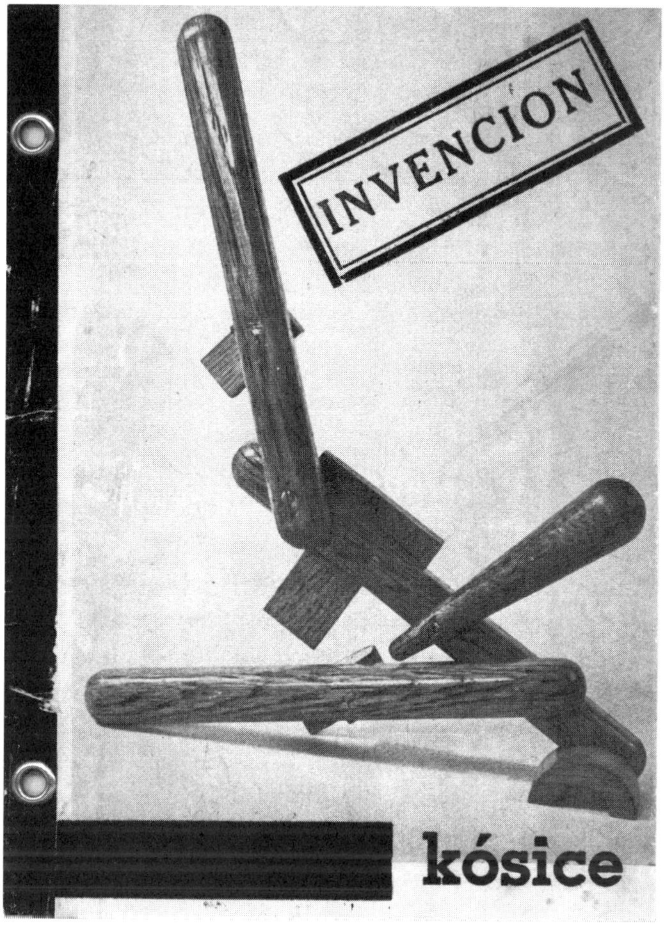


FIGURE 1.5
Gyula Kosice, *Röyi* maquette on the cover of *Invención*, 1945.

pictorial experiments that followed. Its solid physicality, manipulable structure, and arbitrary movements made it also an early example of the primacy of action in the work and thought of the Argentine avant-garde.

If understood dialectically (as Marx did, following Hegel), the material world is one of change and motion upon which humans act on the basis of their material conditions. Clearly, art, too, had to be revolutionized in accord with Marx's rejection of essences and the idealism of philosophy in favor of a historical materialism determined by circumstances. The philosopher of Communism argued that Ludwig Feuerbach, who influenced the development of materialism, "does not see how the sensuous world around him is, not a thing given direct from all eternity, remaining ever the same, but the product of industry and of the state of society; and indeed, [a product] in the sense that it is an historical product, the result of the activity of a whole succession of generations, each standing on the shoulders of the preceding one, developing its industry and its intercourse, modifying its social system according to the changed needs."[89]

This dialogue between material conditions and the activity of social actors would become, by 1946, a fundamental principle of invencionismo. Edgar Bayley, a central theoretician of this concept (as well as a poet), put it succinctly: "The invented concept, which is the basis of the new poetry, constitutes one of the paths toward revolutionary praxis. Through his invention, the poet is integrated into the world—that is, participates actively in the theoretical-practical task of transforming it."[90] Invention, in other words, was tied to human action upon the material world and implied an emancipatory process in which making, following Marx, was history itself.[91]

## CUTOUT FRAMES AND COPLANALS

The growing group of Argentine abstractionists loosely united under the invencionismo banner in 1945 had, by 1946, divided into two distinct groups.[92] Maldonado and Bayley led the group that was to become known as the Asociación Arte Concreto Invención; early members of this group included Lidy Prati (Maldonado's wife and a key contributor to *Arturo*), Manuel Espinosa, Alfredo Hlito, Alberto Molenberg, Oscar Nuñez, the Lozza brothers (Raúl, Rafael, and R. V. D.), Claudio Girola, and others, many of whom Maldonado knew from the Academia Nacional de Bellas Artes in Buenos Aires. Gyula Kosice, Carmelo Arden Quin, and Rhod Rothfuss were the core members of what became known as Arte Madí. However, prior to the creation of these two groups, the Arden Quin–Kosice–Rothfuss group exhibited twice in 1945.[93] The first exhibition took place in October at the house of Enrique Pichón-Rivière under the title *Art Concret Invention*—a French title that signals the artists' desire to establish a continuity with Parisian concrete art. The second show was held in December at Grete Stern's house and was titled *Movimiento de Arte Concreto Invención* (not to be confused with the Asociación Arte Concreto Invención, which would exhibit for the first time in March–April 1946).

Few documents remain as records of these two exhibitions. A photograph of the first shows a table with sculptures and the lower halves of three paintings. Identifiable on the table at right is a movable sculpture by Kosice made of curved, bent, and straight "brass pieces used to create the frame for handbags"[94] connected with small screws. The linear quality of the work seems predicated on the idea of an outline that has released its sculptural mass. In the background, the lower half of the painting on the left consists of a zigzagging frame; its interior appears to feature juxtaposed planes of color, and the line that separates them follows the shape of the frame. The painting in the center also obeys the strategy of the irregular frame, but its frame is wider, its materiality exalted rather than dissolved or integrated into the picture plane. The third work, on the right, is, according to Gabriel Pérez-Barreiro, attributed to Rothfuss.[95]

The exhibition at Stern's house was more elaborate. It signaled a multidisciplinary approach evident in the accompanying brochure, which listed participants under the followings rubrics: painting, sculpture, drawing, architecture and urbanism, photography, children's drawings, literature, music, and dance. In the background of a pho-

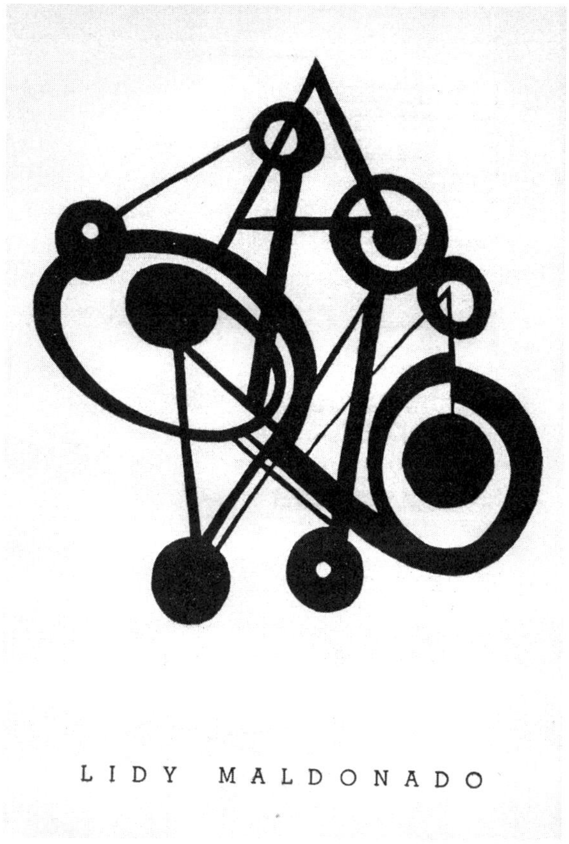


FIGURE 1.6
Lidy Prati (signed Lidy Maldonado), vignette in *Arturo* magazine, summer 1944.

tograph of the artists and members of the public who attended the opening are at least five unidentifiable paintings with irregular frames. It is easy, however, to deduce from the brochure that the event probably incorporated most of the works these young artists had produced during 1945, especially if we consider that only one work published in *Arturo*—by Rothfuss, appearing at the end of his article "El marco: Un problema de plástica actual"—shunned the orthogonal format. That unidentified work's skewed frame contained a color composition with curvilinear shapes so that there really was no correlation between the center and periphery of the painting, as Rothfuss calls for in the text. Interestingly, as Andrea Giunta has indicated, it is the group of vignettes designed by Lidy Prati (signing as Lidy Maldonado) scattered throughout the publication that constitute the most abstract statements in *Arturo* and seem, in their open, linear configuration, to plot the principles of the coplanals to come (fig. 1.6).[96]

The first official exhibition of the AACI took place from March 18 through April 3, 1946, at the Salón Peuser,[97] less than a month after the election of Perón as president. In a photograph of the event featuring the participating artists, five works appear in the background. Four of these, all made of wood, are identifiable, and they exemplify an object-based prac-

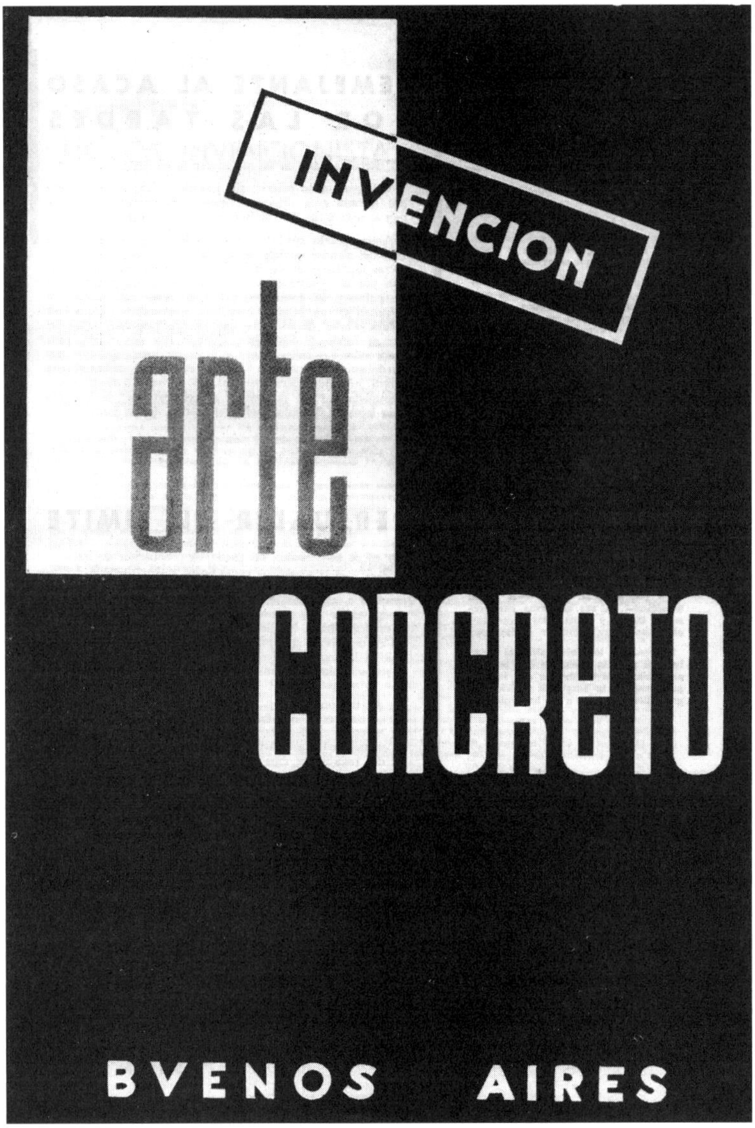


FIGURE 1.7
Tomás Maldonado, cover of *Arte Concreto Invención*, no. 1, August 1946.

tice approaching the medium of relief. One is Oscar Nuñez's *Sin título* (Untitled, 1946). It consists of rectilinear wooden panels painted in primary colors, black, and white that are locked together around a black backward-L-shaped piece, which—as in Prati's *Concreto* of 1945—functions as a core, a nucleus, that holds the "picture" in place, as if somehow substituting for the absent frame. Also visible is a work by Maldonado, later published without a title in *Arte Concreto Invención* no. 1 in August 1946 (fig. 1.7). The constituent elements of this work are linked through the use of diagonal or zigzagging forms, but the resulting structure seems unmotivated and not (as European concrete art demanded or as Rothfuss had required) mathematically or compositionally determined. However, the cutout technique displayed by this work advances the conception and forms of display of the coplanals, which, according to Maldonado, represented the epitome of these investigations in 1946.[98] Above Maldonado's work, a piece by Manuel Espinosa presents an irregular rectilinear panel featuring two cutout triangular shapes surrounded by areas of color that echo the contours of the work. Finally, a 1946 work by Antonio Caraduje entitled *Composición* (Composition) represents an idiosyncratic approach that features a whimsical format and an even more whimsical arrangement of internal shapes and cutouts.

These photographs, along with Espinosa's interview in *Contrapunto,* suggest that throughout 1945 and 1946 both the Arden Quin–Kosice–Rothfuss group (the basis of Arte Madí) and the artists surrounding Maldonado (soon to be members of the AACI) were committed to exploring the formal possibilities of the irregular frame. In their search for the fundamentals of painting—for an unmediated identification between container and content—they posed the paradox of an artistic practice predicated on the mutability of the frame and the arbitrariness of the cutout. Meant to correspond to the internal composition of a painting, the cutout was manifest in a number of strategies that were illustrated in *Arte Concreto Invención* no. 1 (fig. 1.8), the most comprehensive early record that we have of the AACI's activities, thoughts, and works. These works dismissed the frame and restructured the relation between the art object and the wall. The wall would subsequently be fully incorporated into the dismembered coplanals and would increasingly threaten the self-sufficiency of painting, exposing the contingency of its identity. At the moment that World War II was coming to an end and Argentina was undergoing one of its most severe political and social crises, this reformulation of the pictorial support emerged as a response to a crisis of representation, to the limits of pictorial orthogonality that Torres-García had associated with a "universal point of reference," a "physical law," a "sense that we [all] possess," and with "functionalism."[99]

Indeed, despite its geometric morphologies, use of the grid, and references to the golden section, the irregular frame and the dispersal of the support precluded an understanding of these elements as pure mental concepts (as demanded by van Doesburg's manifesto "Base de la Peinture Concrète" [The Basis of Concrete Art]) or as self-contained, autonomous pictorial entities (as required by Rothfuss's text). Instead, the strategies of the Argentine avant-garde elaborated an alternative semantic relationship to the wall and the surrounding environment through a formal configuration that was closer to relief sculpture than painting. These works obviously did not spring forth from the wall in the manner of classical reliefs, in which figures relate to the wall as actors relate to the backdrop on a theatrical stage. Rather, these object-paintings sat on the wall and allowed it to filter through the cutouts and irregular contours, thus dismantling the traditional frame and the picture plane. *Arte Concreto Invención* no. 1 featured all of

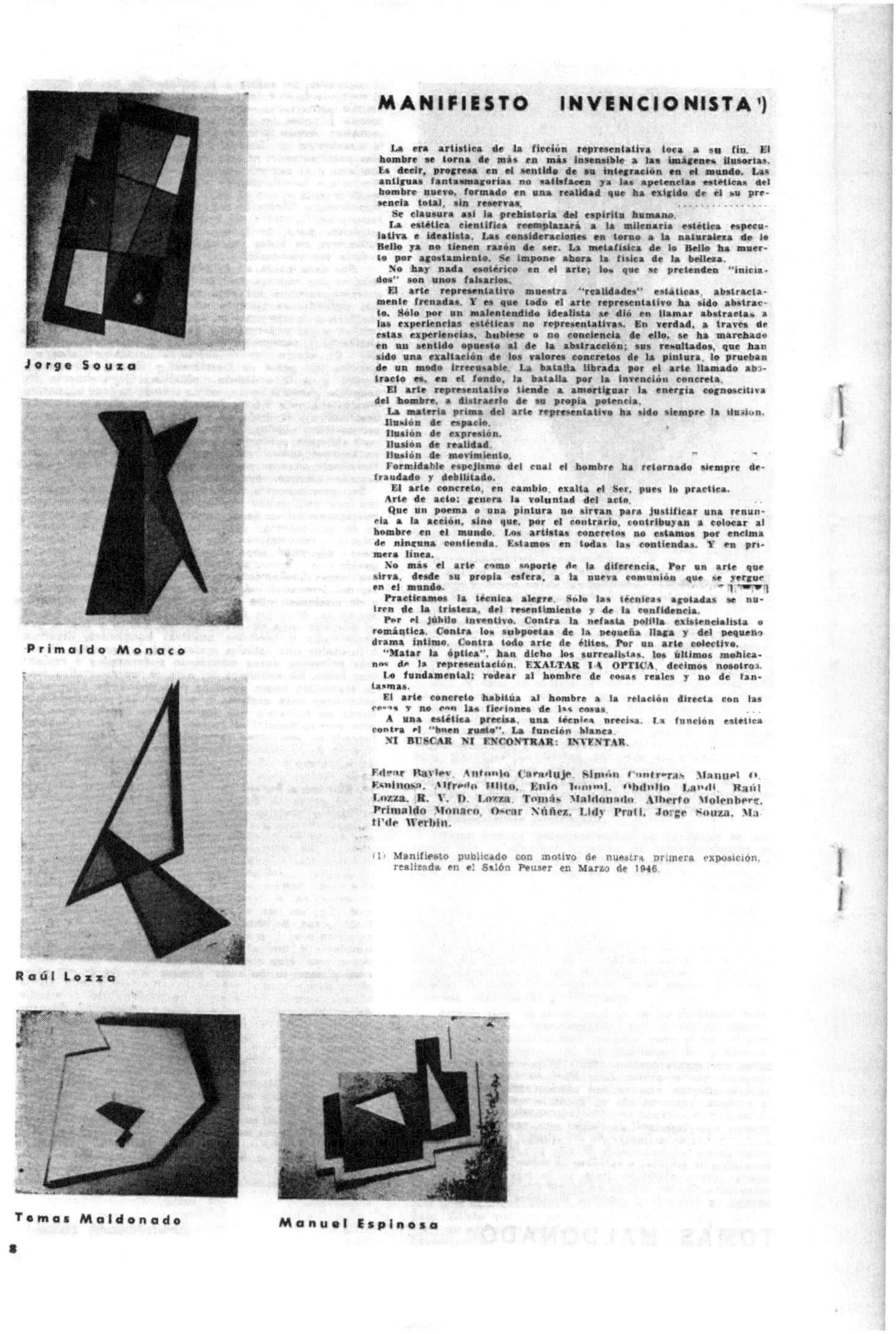

# MANIFIESTO INVENCIONISTA [1]

La era artística de la ficción representativa toca a su fin. El hombre se torna de más en más insensible a las imágenes ilusorias. Es decir, progresa en el sentido de su integración en el mundo. Las antiguas fantasmagorías no satisfacen ya las apetencias estéticas del hombre nuevo, formado en una realidad que ha exigido de él su presencia total, sin reservas.

Se clausura así la prehistoria del espíritu humano.

La estética científica reemplazará a la milenaria estética especulativa e idealista. Las consideraciones en torno a la naturaleza de lo Bello ya no tienen razón de ser. La metafísica de lo Bello ha muerto por agostamiento. Se impone ahora la física de la belleza.

No hay nada esotérico en el arte; los que se pretenden "iniciados" son unos falsarios.

El arte representativo muestra "realidades" estáticas, abstractamente frenadas. Y es que todo el arte representativo ha sido abstracto. Sólo por un malentendido idealista se dió en llamar abstractas a las experiencias estéticas no representativas. En verdad, a través de estas experiencias, hubiese o no conciencia de ello, se ha marchado en un sentido opuesto al de la abstracción; sus resultados, que han sido una exaltación de los valores concretos de la pintura, lo prueban de un modo irrecusable. La batalla librada por el arte llamado abstracto es, en el fondo, la batalla por la invención concreta.

El arte representativo tiende a amortiguar la energía cognoscitiva del hombre, a distraerlo de su propia potencia.

La materia prima del arte representativo ha sido siempre la ilusión.

Ilusión de espacio.

Ilusión de expresión.

Ilusión de realidad.

Ilusión de movimiento.

Formidable espejismo del cual el hombre ha retornado siempre defraudado y debilitado.

El arte concreto, en cambio, exalta el Ser, pues lo practica.

Arte de acto: genera la voluntad del acto.

Que un poema o una pintura no sirvan para justificar una renuncia a la acción, sino que, por el contrario, contribuyan a colocar al hombre en el mundo. Los artistas concretos no estamos por encima de ninguna contienda. Estamos en todas las contiendas. Y en primera línea.

No más el arte como soporte de la diferencia. Por un arte que sirva, desde su propia esfera, a la nueva comunión que se yergue en el mundo.

Practicamos la técnica alegre. Sólo las técnicas agotadas se nutren de la tristeza, del resentimiento y de la confidencia.

Por el júbilo inventivo. Contra la nefasta polilla existencialista o romántica. Contra los subpoetas de la pequeña llaga y del pequeño drama íntimo. Contra todo arte de élites. Por un arte colectivo.

"Matar la óptica", han dicho los surrealistas, los últimos mohicanos de la representación. EXALTAR LA OPTICA, decimos nosotros.

Lo fundamental: rodear al hombre de cosas reales y no de fantasmas.

El arte concreto habitúa al hombre a la relación directa con las cosas y no con las ficciones de las cosas.

A una estética precisa, una técnica precisa. La función estética contra el "buen gusto". La función blanca.

NI BUSCAR NI ENCONTRAR: INVENTAR.

Edgar Bayley, Antonio Caraduje, Simón Contreras, Manuel O. Espinosa, Alfredo Hlito, Enio Iommi, Obdulio Landi, Raúl Lozza, R. V. D. Lozza, Tomás Maldonado, Alberto Molenberg, Primaldo Monaco, Oscar Núñez, Lidy Prati, Jorge Souza, Matilde Werbin.

(1) Manifiesto publicado con motivo de nuestra primera exposición, realizada en el Salón Peuser en Marzo de 1946.

Jorge Souza

Primaldo Monaco

Raúl Lozza

Tomas Maldonado

Manuel Espinosa

8

FIGURE 1.8

Page 8 of *Arte Concreto Invención*, no. 1, August 1946.

the works described above and several more of these in-between (painting and relief) objects. Prati's object-oriented approach, for example, was represented by *Untitled* (1945; plate 5). The core of this piece is a T-shaped slab of wood that is painted black and runs diagonally from left to right. Three irregular polygons rest around this core: a red rectangle on top, a white trapezoid on the right, and an irregular quadrilateral on the left. The whole is initially reminiscent of a Mondrian painting, but because orthogonality has been replaced by a diagonal thrust and irregular polygons, and because the two-dimensional canvas has been replaced by three-dimensional wood, the effect is more nearly that of a Mondrian disintegrated by the active intervention of real space. This merging of art with real space, which Mondrian had envisioned as a future dissolution of painting into the environment, produces here a fragmented pictorial structure. The cutout frame, in which the artist eliminates the orthogonal frame and creates a closer identification between support (wooden panels, in this instance) and shape, was to become a crucial strategy that would problematize pictorial self-referentiality and favor a practice that employed concrete materials in space and opened up the art object toward other mediums, including the three-dimensionality of sculpture.[100]

In these object-paintings, the grid line that had bound color to support and perimeter to internal composition (in works such as Manuel Espinosa's *Pintura* [Painting, 1945; plate 3], for example) becomes a pure cut that delineates shape. It binds the monochromatic plane to its support tightly, while dislodging the picture plane and irremediably threatening the material and conceptual confines of painting. Here the cut was the defining mark-making operation, one that fully rejected the passivity of the picture plane and its function as a container. This testing of painterly conventions, which had been unthinkable in the Argentine artistic context a few years earlier, destabilized the medium at its core. Against the rectilinearity of the frame presumed by illusionistic models of representation, contra the containing ground of painting's support, in opposition to the delineational role of line, rejecting the use of descriptive color, and defying the traditional frontal-horizontal orientation of conventional painting, these works exemplified a dissolution of boundaries unprecedented in the local artistic milieu.

The cutout frame upset conventions and disrupted the window effect of traditional post-Renaissance painting, but—as Maldonado feared—it moved too close to the three-dimensionality of sculpture. A return to painting implied the pursuit of another paradoxical trajectory as the resulting coplanals advanced (more radically than the cutout frames) a passage from painting to wall, the fragmented support now sitting on and projecting away from the architectural wall on which it relied. Such a paradox would suggest that in this materialist inquiry, which had started as an affirmation of the autonomy of painting, the painting must be inextricably bound to the wall to remain legible as such. The eventual return to orthogonal formats by most of the artists of the AACI by 1947 seems to confirm that there could be no next step without abandoning this determining factor: the wall.

The "Manifesto Invencionista" accompanied the AACI's first exhibition in March 1946 and was later reprinted in *Arte Concreto Invención* no. 1 in August of that year.[101] The text stressed the necessity to eradicate all illusionism from the visual arts and advocated a scientific aesthetic that would replace idealism and speculation. Following the tenets of European concrete art, the artists argued that it was a mistake to define nonrepresentational art as abstract: nonrepresentational art exalts the concrete values of painting, they wrote, and is an art of action that generates a will for action in the viewer. The signatories of the manifesto situated themselves against existentialism, romanticism, and elitist or esoteric art: "A poem or painting does not serve to justify a renunciation of action, but, on the contrary, helps situate man in the world. We are not above any struggle. We are involved in all struggles. At the forefront."[102] And in defense of their object-oriented practice, they added: "Concrete art familiarizes man with a direct relation to things, and not with the fiction of things."[103] This materialist aesthetic—which echoed but moved away from European concrete art's commitment to logic, mathematics, geometry, objectivity, systems, and science (the ideational)[104]—aimed to enmesh viewers in the world of reality and action. Accordingly, an essay by Maldonado on the abstract and concrete in modern art (published in *Arte Concreto Invención* no. 1) delineates an impressive aesthetic genealogy for the Argentine experiments and draws on Naum Gabo and Antoine Pevsner's "Realistic Manifesto" (1920) to emphasize the link between art and reality.[105] A fundamental element of this movement toward the real is, according to Maldonado, the progressive abandonment of the orthogonal modality of the picture plane and a shift toward an "objective exaltation" that leads to "plastic structure." In Maldonado's view, previous investigations limited to the traditional plane were failures, since all were ultimately reliant on traditional composition and illusionistic space—as well as on contemplative modes of viewership. To wit, neither neoplasticism nor the incipient experiments with the irregular frame made by the Hungarian-born László Peri went far enough in questioning the traditional function of the picture plane. Even the most advanced pictorial propositions of the Swiss concretist Max Bill—whose work Maldonado would embrace with utmost devotion at the end of the decade—were deemed insufficient, as they failed to address the conventions of the "aesthetic structure."

Two coplanals—one by Raúl Lozza and another by Alberto Molenberg—illustrated Maldonado's essay "Lo abstracto y lo concreto en el arte moderno" (The Abstract and the Concrete in Modern Art) and suggest incipient experimentation with this modality. These spatial reliefs do away with the frame entirely, while the pictorial plane is broken down into irregular geometric shapes and held together against the wall by metal rods. This was the most explicit attempt so far to discard the pictorial surface as a static container, and it implied a move beyond the cutout frame by eliminating frame and continuous support altogether. Molenberg's *Función blanca* (White Function, 1946; fig. 1.9) is, in this sense, paradigmatic. Consisting of three zigzagging white wooden shapes connected by thin rods (later discarded), it radiates outward, casting shadows

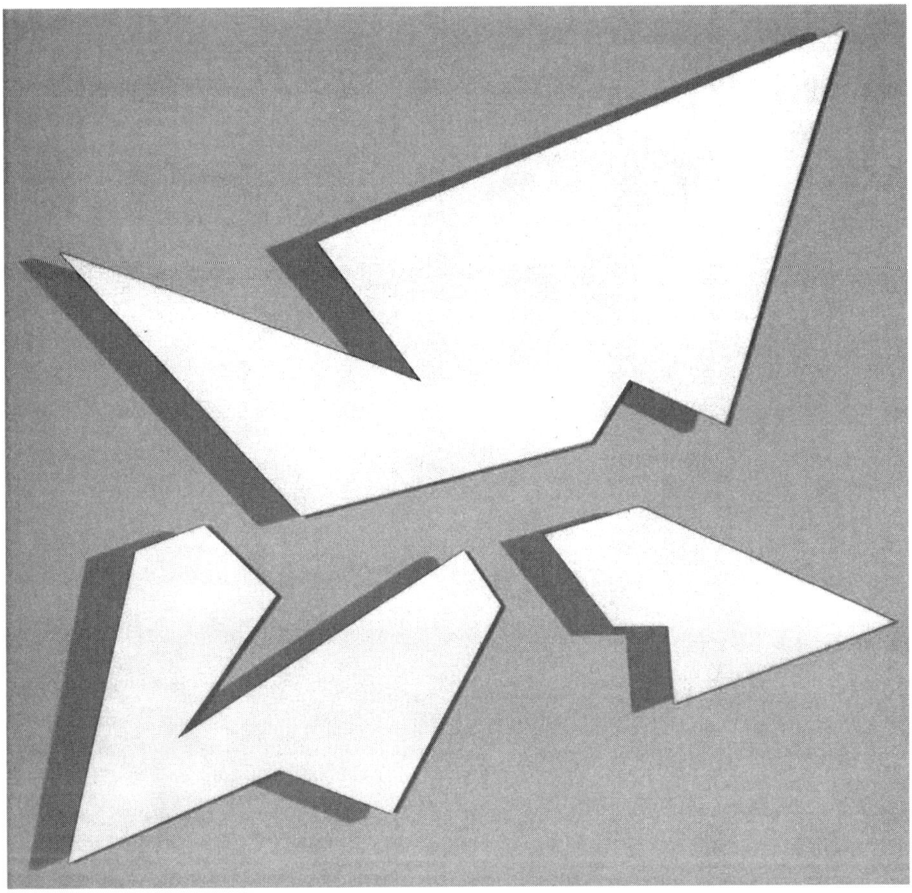

FIGURE 1.9
Alberto Molenberg, *Función blanca* (White Function), 1946, enamel on wood, 43 5/16 × 51 3/16 in.

and incorporating the space between the jagged forms into the overall structure of the piece. Here, the identification of shape and support is total: line as the graphic delineator of an internal composition exists as contour (the result of the cutout), and the multipart structure of the work accentuates the fragmented and relational quality of the violated pictorial support. The wall, whose stubborn materiality, architectural condition, and suggestive public nature would situate the coplanal outside the intimacy of contemplation, has been seized as part of the work. The choice of white as the unifying color of this shattered monochrome suggests a desire to focus exclusively on the new morphology of the coplanal, but it also establishes spatial and contextual contiguity with the wall, the architectural domain upon which the work relies for its now-diffusive legibility. Raúl Lozza's unidentified piece, illustrated in the magazine not by a photograph but by a print resembling a sketch, is more symmetrical and contained (fig. 1.10). This work may have

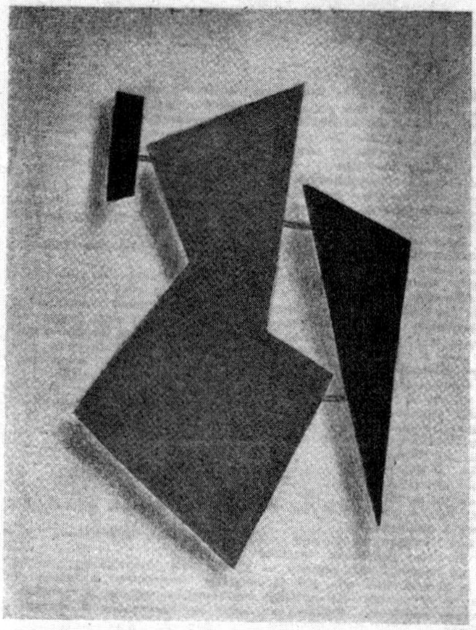

**Raul Lozza**

tistas no-representativos (1931-1940)— a quien su admiración por el pintor Joan Miró condujo, primero, a hacerle adoptar una actitud condescendiente para con la pintura superrealista y, posteriormente, a realizar obras donde subyace un notorio propósito expresionista-onírico. Los "móviles" de Calder son, con todo, un paso evidente hacia la liberación del objeto estético del barroquismo a que había sido llevado por Moholy Nagy, en su anhelo de ampliar y sutilizar la materia prima de este nuevo género artístico. Pero en lo que respecta a la estructura Calder insiste en el nefasto error de no inventar la estructura estética dinámica, sino que, por el contrario, se sujeta a la ordenación que le impone el motor o la fuente de energía. Y es en esta insuficiencia estructural —que no es en el fondo inventiva—, común a todas las manifestaciones del arte no-representativo donde debemos buscar el motivo, no sólo de la desviación de Calder, sino de todas las coincidencias posibles entre el arte no-representativo y el superrealismo o el expresionismo. Es evidente que cuando se renuncia a la voluntad de estructura se abandona irremisiblemente el campo de la invención y se pasa a una incontrolada "tierra de nadie", que, en última instancia, resulta ser la tierra del sueño, del subconciente, de la intuición pura, de la agorafobia, de las expresiones delirantes, de todos los matices posibles en la ilusión y de la representación.

. . . . . .

Por otra parte, en la pintura bidimensional se estaba en los mismos problemas: Kandinski y Bauer, la extrema derecha del arte no-representativo europeo, que defendieron siempre un escepticismo radical con respecto a la composición, exaltando el papel de la intuición y del automatismo geométrico ("expresionismo abstracto"), comenzaban a tener adictos en los EE. UU. En efecto, los no-objetivos norteamericanos siguiendo los pasos de Kandinski y Bauer retornan al cuadro y a la anécdota plástica. Generalmente, la anécdota consiste en un acento cromático (con alusiones musicales), una flecha (signo) o un zig-zag (suceso descriptivo), es decir, se vuelve al tema central de la composición clásica. Antes, era la "Virgen de las rocas" (Virgen, primer momento de la percepción—tiempo representado); ahora, es el "Acento Amarillo" de Kandinski (Acento amarillo, primer momento de la percepción—tiempo representado).

Es, precisamente, contra todas estas manifestaciones que implicaban una tendencia a extrañar al arte no-representativo de su verdadero destino: la conquista de lo concreto, que los militantes del movimiento concretista de la Argentina iniciamos hace algunos años nuestras tareas de investigación e invención, tratando de resolver sus problemas fundamentales y alejarlo así, definitivamente, del tremedal del expresionismo, del superrealismo o de cualquier otra forma artística idealista y representativa. Munidos del materialismo dialéctico, que es la filosofía viva de Marx, Engels, Lenin y Stalin, que confirmaba y confirma nuestras búsquedas, llegamos a formular una estética materialista o concreta. Nuestros primeros pasos estuvieron enderezados a replantear todos los poblemas del arte no-representativo desde Malevitch hasta nuestros días, buscando, claro está, soluciones más certeras y exhaustivas; comprendimos desde un principio que las mayores insuficiencias del arte no-representativo tenían su origen en no haberse logrado ni una nueva composición ni la liquidación definitiva de lo ilusorio. Empezamos, por ésto, quebrando la forma tradicional del cuadro (Rothffus, Maldonado, Arden Quin, Prati, Espinosa, y más tarde, Hlito, Mónaco y Souza); pero no nos quedamos allí (éste fué el error de Peri) sino buscamos comprender la utilidad y real trascendencia de esta conquista. Reparamos entonces que el "cuadro o marco recortado", como dimos en llamarlo, especializaba el plano; no podíamos ser indiferentes al hecho que de este modo abríamos las compuertas y que el espacio penetraba en el cuadro, participando como un elemento más, estéticamente beligerante. Al mismo tiempo, repetimos las experiencias de Nicholson y de Domela: materializamos figuras, las hicimos formas (Maldonado, Prati, Raúl Lozza, Antonio Caraduje). Pero a esta altura nos sorprendimos buscando una solución tridimensional al problema bidimensional: repetíamos el error... Y nos detuvimos. Nos propusimos firmemente que si salíamos al espacio iba a ser siempre después de una solución, nunca como desviación ante un escollo en lo bidimensional. Reiniciamos en profundidad el estudio del problema del "cuadro o marco recortado". Comenzamos por otorgarle más importancia al espacio penetrante que al cuadro mismo (Molenberg, Raúl Lozza Núñez). Y por este camino llegamos al descubrimiento máximo de nuestro movimiento: la separación en el espacio de los elementos constitutivos del cuadro sin abandonar su disposición coplanaria (Molenberg, Raúl Lozza). De este modo, el cuadro, como "organismo continente", quedaba abolido. Después de tantos años de lucha lo concreto había sido logrado y recién a partir de este instante la composición no-representativa podía ser una verdad, lo era ya de hecho.

Hoy, el arte no-representativo se encuentra, por primera vez, en la posibilidad de encarar el espacio y el movimiento desde un punto de vista absolutamente concreto.

TOMAS MALDONADO

7

FIGURE 1.10

Raúl Lozza, coplanal in *Arte Concreto Invención,* no. 1, August 1946.

existed only as a maquette at the time, which would have made Molenberg's coplanal the most emblematic work of the advanced thinking of the artists of the AACI.

This breakdown of the most entrenched conventions of painting—the frame and the pictorial support—was tantamount to the medium's deconstruction. This was necessary to unmask the fallacy of illusionism or, in Maldonado's words, painting as a "containing organism"—a designation that curiously echoes, contra Rothfuss, his 1944 proposition of pictorial self-generation. With the coplanal, wrote Maldonado, artists "began to give more importance to the space that penetrated the canvas than to the canvas itself. . . . This way we arrived at the ultimate discovery of our movement: the separation in space of the constituent elements of painting without abandoning their position on the same plane."[106] The earlier cutout frame and the more objectlike works that sought three-dimensional solutions—which Maldonado associated with a "materialization of form"—had failed to address the problem of painting. By contrast, the coplanal, which situated the fragmented support of the picture on a plane parallel to the wall, allowed the artists of the AACI to critically address the nature of the medium as it was being transformed, as its essence was being questioned, as it was exposed to change and contingency according to new historical and material circumstances. In this way, argued Maldonado, the coplanals remained within the realm of painting but attacked its cherished conventions, destroying its status as a self-sufficient, autonomous entity doomed to be the repository of an illusion. With the coplanals, Maldonado wrote, the "concrete had been accomplished."[107] In accord with Marx's materialist conception of history, this meant that painting had been not only purged of pictorial illusionism but also transformed. Its ontology—that is, its nature—had been altered by new relations among its materials, with the wall, with the spectator. The orthogonal frame's role as a universal, transhistorical marker that defined painting had been abandoned in favor of new relations staged through a practice that responded to a new horizon of material production. The spectator was confronted with a pictorial-relational device that defied the established essence of painting as defined by the frame and by the pictorial support as a container.

In the unambiguous editorial entitled "Nuestra militancia" (Our Militancy) that opened *Arte Concreto Invención* no. 1, the artists of the AACI pledged to pursue a dialectical relationship between creativity and political consciousness and insisted on the revolutionary imperative of their work: the transformation of quotidian reality via "the effective intervention of each reader or spectator in the aesthetic experience."[108] Former attitudes—here identified with the "old representative technique" and, thus, with the orthogonal frame that defined the illusionistic space of naturalistic painting—were rejected in favor of the following proclamation: "The artists of our movement are not indifferent to the everyday world or the problems facing the common man. Concrete artists are in solidarity with all the people of the world and with their great ally—the Soviet Union—in its efforts to preserve peace and stop imperialist plans to resuscitate Fascism."[109] This statement echoed contemporary Argentine Communist Party rhetoric. The AACI thus adopted what they believed was an internationalist, progressive, antifascist agenda, and yet they failed to address, or even acknowledge, the troubling association of Perón and the country's working masses. In other words, their political agenda was founded on a double blind spot that compromised their vision: they could not see that the Soviet Union, under Stalin, had become a totalitarian regime,[110] nor that the Argentine Communist Party had alienated the working masses who had become the base of Peronism.

Several other texts in this first iteration of the AACI's journal support the arguments outlined above. Simon Contreras, tangentially alluding to the productivist aesthetics of Russian and Soviet constructivism, argued for the creation of "new art objects that can act and participate in the life of the people and help to revolutionize their conditions of existence."[111] He called for the realization of new "natural, mechanical, or technical" elements, but, as we have seen, none of the works reproduced in the magazine suggest utilitarian or applied purposes; none, for that matter, even appear to be mechanical or to dialogue with the technological field in any way. Instead, one of their main achievements was to repudiate an illusionistic aesthetics associated with what Contreras called "reactionary individualism," while they were meant to promote "the formation of a new popular aesthetic consciousness."[112] In a second essay in the magazine, Maldonado insisted on reality as that which action can verify. Knowledge and praxis facilitate agency, he argued, and concrete art was poised to become the vehicle that would propel the Socialist art of the future. Defining concrete art as "invention" and "practice," Maldonado clarified that his use of the verb *invent* was intended "not in Bergson's sense, but in Marx's, meaning, PRACTICE, WORK."[113] In his key contribution to the magazine, Hlito invoked Marx's notion of change and "material intercourse" as fundamental to the essence of humans to justify the artists' transformative aesthetic project: "Art, like any activity that in its process 'changes constantly from the form of action to the form of being' . . . is verified concretely in the object. In the process of aesthetic invention, practice manifests itself as the production of new things, with new properties."[114] Thus, as Maldonado had forcefully put it, the artists of the AACI needed to remain within painting and not destroy it (as their unconventional production and political rhetoric might imply). They needed to test it, to bend it, to change it, to transform it according to a materialist aesthetic, which the cutout frame and coplanals adduced. Against the idealism of a fixed essence (painting circumscribed by a frame and the conventions of the pictorial plane), the coplanals reinvented the ontology of painting through a reorganization of its constituent material elements and exposure to real space that intimated art's contingency.

## RELATIONAL PAINTING

The AACI's emphasis on process, action, objectivity, and praxis is consistent with ideas posited by Marx in "Theses on Feuerbach" (1845), a key early text clearly known to the

Argentine avant-garde.[115] Not originally intended for publication, it consisted of short, enumerated statements that responded to Ludwig Feuerbach's work on "religious alienation," which Marx criticized for ignoring the fact that "'religious sentiment' is itself a *social product*."[116] The text conceived of "human activity as objective activity,"[117] calling for agency that would lead to revolutionary practice and change. It also addressed the relationship between theory and practice, an issue that preoccupied the members of the AACI in 1946 and that Marx expressed in the lapidary statement in the eleventh and best-known thesis: "Philosophers have only interpreted the world, in various ways; the point is to *change* it."[118] This call for action was accompanied by a rejection of what Marx termed "contemplative materialism," a propensity for conceiving of essences as abstractions instead of as "the ensemble of the social relations."[119] This focus on social relations, Étienne Balibar has argued, advocates multiplicity—the equating of human existence with "the multiple and active *relations* which individuals establish with each other (whether of language, labor, love, reproduction, domination, conflict, etc.)" and the acknowledgement "that it is these relations which define what they have in common, the 'genus.'"[120]

With the conceptualization of the coplanal and the new relations that it posited among its constitutive elements, the members of the AACI proposed a relational pictorial logic that defined the genus of painting as such—that is, as relational. Altering pictorial conventions in an effort to incorporate the relational premises of Marxism, these artists suspended the certainties upon which painting was predicated. The essential definition of painting had been partly secured by the frame but also by the containing quality of the picture plane, which had historically acted as the repository of a narrative or, in the most advanced forms of concrete art, as the receptacle for configurations of line, color, and form. The AACI had transformed painting's core through the concept of the coplanal, discarding the figure of containment and opening painting to the haptic as well as to the contingencies of real space signified by the incorporated wall. "What individuals are depends on the material conditions of their production," Marx and Engels wrote in *The German Ideology*. Clearly, artistic production had to be responsive to the here and now of the artist, to the "real life," the "actual world," the "life-process," to use Marx's vocabulary.[121] Production—understood in this context as a process of labor that has as its objective the creation of use value (rather than exchange value)—allows the individual to confront nature and adapt what it produces to his or her own needs. "By thus acting on the external world and changing it," wrote Marx in *Capital*, man "at the same time changes his own nature."[122] Likewise, concrete art "exalts 'Being' because it practices it," declared the AACI's manifesto.[123] The nature of being and the nature of painting, the AACI seemed to suggest, are equally determined by action and the change triggered by action, relations, and processes.

As both Alejandro Crispiani and Étienne Balibar point out, Marx alluded to Benjamin Franklin's definition of man as "a toolmaking animal," yoking production to "consciousness, reflection, experimentation and knowledge" and addressing "the question of the essence of man in things themselves."[124] In a parallel operation, these artists rejected the essence of painting as a fixed structure protected by the frame in favor of the medium subtended by relations among its elements and by relations between these elements and the surrounding space. The focus on a pictorial identity predicated solely on plastic values as posited by European concrete art was reoriented through the concept of invencionismo and Marx's materialism in favor of a relational identity.

The materialism of invencionismo suggested a displacement of the artwork by action, which the AACI articulated in terms of an ontology of relations that impinged on the medium specificity of painting and its contemplative aesthetics. In December 1946, Edgar Bayley posited concrete art as an instrument "that secures the spiritual fecundity of man," adding that "the new aesthetic cannot be legitimate if it is not founded on the daily struggle of man, if it is not integrated into the collective effort to change life, and in sum, if it does not contemplate the everyday need, common to all, of overcoming that which makes existence opaque and despicable."[125] A month later, on the occasion of a second exhibition of the AACI at the Sociedad Argentina de Artistas Plásticos (Argentine Society of Visual Artists) in Buenos Aires, an unsigned text attributed to Bayley defined the new painting as an "active revolutionary factor." This rebellious art, however, was not to be utilitarian, or to communicate directly or propel the viewer into immediate political action. It was, instead, conceived to "adapt the field of human sensitivity for the exercise of new faculties."[126] Such a goal was equivalent to making the artwork "a form of human practice," a sensorial device that exposed the viewer to alternative regimes of aesthetic material organization. By eliminating representation and its system of notation (perspective, figure-ground relations, line as delineation), by shattering the pictorial plane (as the repository of a story, a concept, and so forth), by disrupting the expected organization of pictorial elements, by giving equal value to positive and negative shapes, this art was to thrust the spectator into new relations of discontinuity and multiplicity that were hostile to the inertia of contemplation.

In *Arte Concreto Invención* no. 1, the members of the AACI took aim at the supporters of a realist art that claimed to side with the people: "In the end, they mistrust the people, whom they consider incapable of any mental enterprise."[127] By 1947 there was no doubt that this dubious friend of the people and supporter of realist art was the Argentine Communist Party, which was then under the full sway of the Soviet aesthetic creed.[128] In August of that year, Maldonado was expelled from the party after he categorically rejected realism at a meeting of Communist intellectuals convened by Rodolfo Ghioldi, and the precarious alliance between the AACI and the Communist Party came to an end.[129] Crispiani observes: "It is consistent with the history of *invencionismo* that in 1947, at the moment when . . . it became evident that the acceptance of its theories [and implicitly its art] by the leaders of the [party] was impossible, its artists would start doubting the coplanal and its qualities."[130] The result was a double farewell: to Communism and to the coplanal. In the end, neither the aesthetics of invencionismo nor Communism itself mobilized the people as Peronism had over the previous three years—

an astonishing temporal concurrence with the formal experiments of the Argentine avant-garde. As Carlos Altamirano has pointed out, the profound crisis of legitimacy that affected the dominant political order produced, through Peronism, an ideological configuration that offered expression and representation (precisely what the artists of the AACI so vehemently rejected) to the new proletarian masses. "How to escape the conclusion," he wrote, "that Perón, even through his words, helped produce the reality in the name of which he had explained the need for a new state action: the 'working masses' as political actor?"[131]

Starting in 1947, the artists of the AACI became increasingly interested in the European geometric abstract movements of the postwar period, particularly Swiss concrete art. An immediate effect on their work was a return to the orthogonal frame, a move justified in 1955 by Hlito, who argued that the question of whether to invest value in the image (as in representational art) or in the plane-object (as in the autonomous abstract aesthetics of the twentieth century) was academic. It is worth quoting Hlito at length:

> The required planarity, taken to its logical conclusion, led us to effect a disintegration of the plane. We considered in 1946 that neoplasticism was not an effective solution to the problem of space. As long as the picture consisted of a plane upon which forms were inscribed, space would continuously participate in it to create an ambiguous or illusory state. In order to get rid of this last remnant of space, we tried to embody the pictorial elements and abandon the canvas as a support. Some of our paintings of that time consisted of sets of colored planes, separated from one another in such a way that space actually participated in the composition of the work. But as those planes were located on the same level and the whole demanded to be seen as a picture, a new difficulty arose. The walls to which those paintings were fixed immediately assumed the optical function that the canvas had fulfilled before, so that the background reappeared again. These objects involved [the logic of] both painting and sculpture without arriving at a coherence of their own. If I mention this experience, which some of us gave up as unsatisfactory, it is because at least it served to prove that planarity could not be taken beyond certain limits without putting painting in a blind alley.[132]

Hlito added to this analysis: "The error of realism is the belief that one departs from an external model, and not from the modifications to which the plane is submitted to achieve that model. . . . The error of planarity is the belief that one departs from the plane, and not from the modifications to which the plane is submitted in order to express the artist's objective."[133] And in a statement of admirable lucidity—which has gone unnoticed as a clever alternative to the Greenbergian modernist *doxa* developing at the time in the United States—Hlito concluded: "The only observable property of the [pictorial] plane, the only generality, is that it can be modified. This property depends more on the conventions of the spirit and of culture than on its material nature."[134] While Hlito's suggestion that "the conventions of the spirit and of culture" determine the properties of painting is coherent with a "materialist conception of history" (*The*

*German Ideology*), isn't the wall—which these artists incorporated into their works—precisely the sort of cultural and social convention that made their experiments legible as paintings while problematizing the nature of painting?

Untheorized by these artists, the wall could be considered here as a hinge between painting and the historical material world that determines it. The wall, when incorporated into the relational nature of painting, was seen by Hlito as replicating the illusionism of the figure-ground relationship of conventional painting, and not as the architectural and material marker that made (to different degrees) the orthogonal pictorial plane, the cutout frame, and the coplanal legible as painting. Another blind spot, which echoes the AACI's inability to address its local political arena, can be identified here: these artists failed to recognize the wall as the institutional guarantor of artistic meaning that it is (the architectural support of the museum or the gallery space, and thus the institution of art). One could conclude that remaining within the specialized field of painting that Marx's critique of the division of labor sanctioned had its limits.

Maldonado effected a more drastic but also more coherent rupture with the artistic project of the AACI:[135]

> In the year 1948 our *splendid isolation* ends because we start to travel. . . . I come to Europe that year. In Italy I meet Max Huber, Bruno Munari, Piero Dorazio, Achille Perilli, Gianni Dova, Gillo Dorfles. In Zurich I establish contact with the main representatives of Swiss concretism: Max Bill, Richard P. Lohse, Camille Graeser, and Verena Loewensberg. In Paris, with Georges Vantongerloo. Back in Buenos Aires my artistic activity, and not only mine, begins to be influenced mainly by the Swiss concretists, Vantongerloo, and, in an indirect way, Vordemberge-Gildewart. In my specific case, I distance myself from the strongly experimental aspects that had characterized the previous period—the period, so to speak, of our heroic movement. It is precisely at this moment that I start to occupy myself with architecture and *design*.[136]

Maldonado would eventually abandon painting in favor of active engagement with modern architecture and design in the pages of the magazine *Nueva Visión*, which he founded in 1951. Three years later he left Argentina to serve first as a professor and later as the director at the Hochschule für Gestaltung in Ulm, Germany, founded under the leadership of the Swiss artist Max Bill in 1953. From then on, Maldonado's commitment to, and interest in, industrial design led him to expand and reconsider his political concerns in relation to a cultural practice of utilitarian dimensions and public service suitable to postwar modern society. By the 1950s the historical gestalt had changed profoundly, and Maldonado found himself confronting "productivism" head on, catching up with and surpassing what his Soviet antecedents had attempted by developing a techno-scientific, research-based, ultra-rational approach to industrial design. The Soviet avant-garde had delineated the foundations of this as-yet-unborn discipline in its desire to abandon art and to intervene in the daily life of society and play a role in the working-class revolution of their country. By contrast, and despite sharing an ideological core of Marxism/Communism and historical materialism with Soviet constructivism, the AACI had based its politics on art's autonomy while incapable of relating to Argentina's own working-class "revolution." The Soviet constructivists *departed* from a rejection of painting (and art) while the *concreto-invencionistas arrived* at its dissolution in an encounter with painting's contingency—its ontological instability, to rephrase Hlito's insight regarding the cultural conventions that determine the "essence" of painting.

For both groups of artists, however, the concrete materiality of their works (the laboratory-phase objects of the productivists in pursuit of practical application, and the coplanals of the AACI) aspired to deliver to spectators a new consciousness of their environment and reality. Both groups shared this fragile, revolutionary idea, which by the 1950s had been superseded by Max Bill's notion of "good form": objects of mass consumption at once beautiful and practical, with the potential to improve everyday life and the environment. But in the mid-1940s, despite all appearances of failure, the Argentine avant-garde managed to penetratingly address fundamental issues about the nature and conventions of art, artistic production at the periphery of global culture, and the impossibility of revolution at painting's edge.

# 2

# THE CONCRETE IDEA ON ITS WAY TO THE NONOBJECT, 1949–59

> Concrete art distinguishes itself by one characteristic:
> structure:
> the structure of the idea's construction
> the structure of the visual in reality
> reality as the structure of the idea
> the idea as the structure of reality.
>
> MAX BILL, "STATEMENT ON CONCRETE ART," 1960[1]

The Brazilian poet Ferreira Gullar's "Teoria do não-objeto" (Theory of the Nonobject) was published in December 1959 in the *Suplemento Dominical do Jornal do Brazil* (see fig. 0.1).[2] This short essay radically broke with the prevailing quest for a modernist pictorial identity, as was evident in concrete art's rejection of representational painting and its focus on the constitutive elements of the medium. It became a crucial conceptual tool for the Brazilian avant-garde, and it is fundamental to understanding Lygia Clark's and Hélio Oiticica's experiments with space and the spectator between 1959 and 1964. More forcefully than any other text in the Brazilian milieu, "Teoria do não-objeto" posited a rupture with the traditional modalities of the mediums of painting and sculpture, and with contemplative models of spectatorship. What was at stake during this period of intense artistic experimentation was an attack on the classical structure of representation (the artistic sign or object standing for something else, whether the artist's feelings or scientific rationalism). This structural critique of representation (and not just of representational painting) and its attendant abandonment of the object-based artwork was triggered by neoconcretism's interest in the phenomenological and affective dimension of the work of art. Gullar's theoretical contributions to this critique—and the intense exchanges between the poet, Clark, and Oiticica—opened up new avenues of investigation that profoundly upset the status of the art object (along with artistic production and reception) and radically expanded the artistic inquiries of neoconcretism as they were articulated in the notion of the nonobject.

This chapter addresses the theoretical underpinnings of concretism and neoconcretism. A dialogue with the constructivist and concretist traditions of Europe—specifically the ideas and works of the Swiss artist Max Bill, who, along with Alexander Rodchenko, Josef Albers, and Alexander Calder, was especially influential on the emerging geometric abstract artists working in the 1950s—was key to the advancement of modern art in Brazil during the postwar period. This transatlantic exchange had a strong philosophical component, evident in the Brazilian critic Mário Pedrosa's absorption of Gestalt psychology, which he developed in his 1949 dissertation "Da natureza afetiva da forma na obra de arte" (On the Affective Nature of Form in the Work of Art) and Gullar's interest in the phenomenology of the French philosopher Maurice Merleau-Ponty. These sources, along with Brazil's modernist cultural and institutional agenda, shaped the Brazilian concrete art movement of the 1950s and the neoconcrete rupture of 1959.

## EARLY LESSONS

The ample visibility of modern architecture and the industrialist aspirations that characterized postwar Brazil framed the emergence of geometric abstraction in the country.[3] The efforts of the government of President Juscelino Kubitschek (1956–61) to stimulate Brazil's lagging economic and cultural development led to a radical transformation of the urban environment. An earlier watershed in Brazilian modernism, however, was the 1939 construction in Rio de Janeiro of the Ministério da Educação e Saúde (Ministry of Education and Health, renamed the Ministry of Education and Culture in 1953; fig. 2.1).[4] Its design, reviewed by Le Corbusier during a visit to Brazil in 1936, was developed by a group of young architects led by Lúcio Costa.[5] Costa later oversaw the design of the country's new capital city of Brasília, which was constructed according to strict modern principles of urbanism that aspired to the organized integration of civic and governmental activities.[6]

Architecture provided the material basis for the transformation of the urban environment and the aesthetic radicalization of Brazilian culture, formally and conceptually stimulating the emergent avant-garde. Architecture's embeddedness in real space—its social dimension and unavoidable public mode of address—made it an appealing medium for artists interested in advancing both modernism and modernization via progressive cultural models of production. In a 1950 lecture on contemporary art in the Museu de Arte Moderna de São Paulo, the Argentine critic Jorge Romero Brest expressed an interest soon to be shared by others in Latin America: "From my point of view, the greatest art of our century is architecture, which, like sculpture, deals with real space."[7] Echoing the integrative ideas of the Bauhaus and De Stijl, Brest proposed an interlacing of painting, sculpture, and architecture as channeled through the concept of the synthesis of the arts that had been developed and propagated in Europe by Le Corbusier and later by André Bloc.[8] These ideas were influential within Brazil and encouraged a move toward a "constructive politics," as the Brazilian critic Ronaldo Brito defined the positivistic ethos that characterized the developmental strategies of

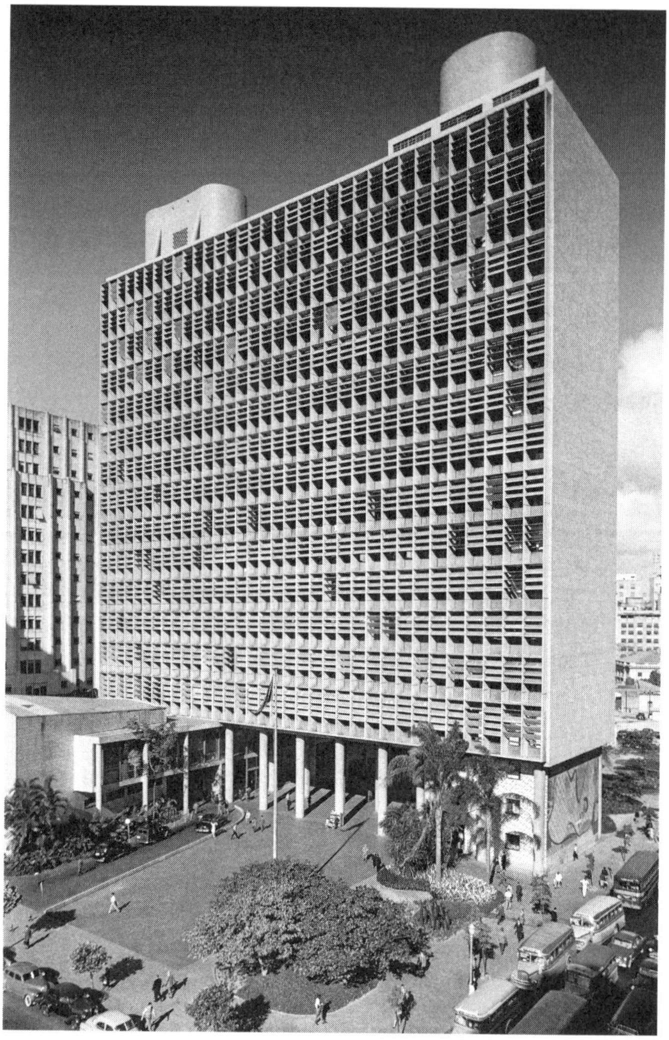

FIGURE 2.1
Marcel Gautherot (photographer), Ministry of Education and Health, Rio de Janeiro, ca. 1946.

the Kubitschek government and that provided a receptive environment for geometric abstraction in the 1950s.[9] According to another important Brazilian critic, Frederico Morais, there was a correspondence between the "constructive ideologies" of culture and the economic and political developmental agendas of the 1940s and 1950s. These were manifest in Kubitschek's plans for industrial development, which aimed to achieve economic independence for Brazil through, among other things, import substitution strategies, which would reduce dependence on foreign markets through the growth of domestic industries.[10] Accordingly, Brazilian artists—like their Argentine and Venezuelan colleagues—were eager to transcend the regional cultural discourses that had kept them at the margins of the modernist canon. These artists found in the aesthetic templates of the constructivist avant-garde, and particularly in the examples of concretism to which they were exposed early on, the vocabulary that would allow them to break away from the straitjacket of a nationalist imaginary.[11]

Brazilian exposure to European abstract art was advanced through two 1949 exhibitions: *A Nova Pintura Francesa e seus Mestres (De Manet a Nossos Dias)* (The New French Painting and Its Masters [From Manet to Today]), on view at the Ministry of Education and Health in Rio de Janeiro, and *Do Figurativismo ao Abstracionismo* (From Figuration to Abstraction) at the Museu de Arte Moderna de São Paulo. The São Paulo exhibition was organized by the museum's director, the French critic León Degand, and featured mostly European artists along with three Brazilian residents experimenting with abstraction: Cícero Dias, Samson Flexor, and Waldemar Cordeiro.[12] Also critical to Brazil's artistic development in that decade was the founding of the country's first museum, the Museu de Arte de São Paulo, in May 1947. This museum was the venue for important exhibitions by Alexander Calder (1948), Le Corbusier (1950), and Max Bill (1951). Brazilian artists initially encountered the Argentine concretist avant-garde (see chapter 1) through Jorge Romero Brest and the artist Tomás Maldonado, both of whom frequently lectured in Brazil, notably on the occasion of an exhibition of "modern" Argentine artists at the Museu de Arte Moderna do Rio de Janeiro in 1953.[13]

Augmenting the impact of these exhibitions were various other initiatives that promoted abstract art, advertising, design, and applied arts in general: the founding of the Bauhaus-inspired Instituto de Arte Contemporânea, the first school of industrial design in Brazil, and the first Salão de Propaganda (Advertising Salon), both based at the Museu de Arte de São Paulo.[14] The establishment of these institutions asserted the desire of the Brazilian elite to join the international artistic conversation and provided a locus for modernity and modernism, pointing to the presence of an urban class committed to re-signifying and substituting the popular national symbols that until then had defined Brazilian identity, and to asserting the regional presence of their country.[15] Moreover, as the art historian Aleca Le Blanc has observed, the Museu de Arte Moderna do Rio de Janeiro, the city's "first modern art museum, was a potent symbol of many of the democratic ideals that characterized the 1950s, such as entrepreneurship, initiative, creative freedom and education for the masses."[16]

The seminal event of the period, however—as most accounts agree[17]—was the first São Paulo Bienal, presented from October 20 to December 23, 1951, by the Museu de Arte Moderna de São Paulo—in the city that was becoming the industrial capital of the country. The Bienal brought to Brazil work from nineteen countries, including an important selection of works by the Swiss concretists Sophie Taeuber-Arp, Richard Paul Lohse, and Max Bill, among others.[18] Along with the abstract works of his Swiss colleagues, Bill's *Tripartite Unity* of 1948–49 (fig. 2.2)—the piece awarded the Bienal's first prize in sculpture—captured the imagination of the young Brazilian artists, including several who were already experimenting with geometric abstraction and had been included in the exhibition.[19] A three-part stainless-steel band that loops around itself, Bill's work alluded to his interests in topology and the continuous surface of the

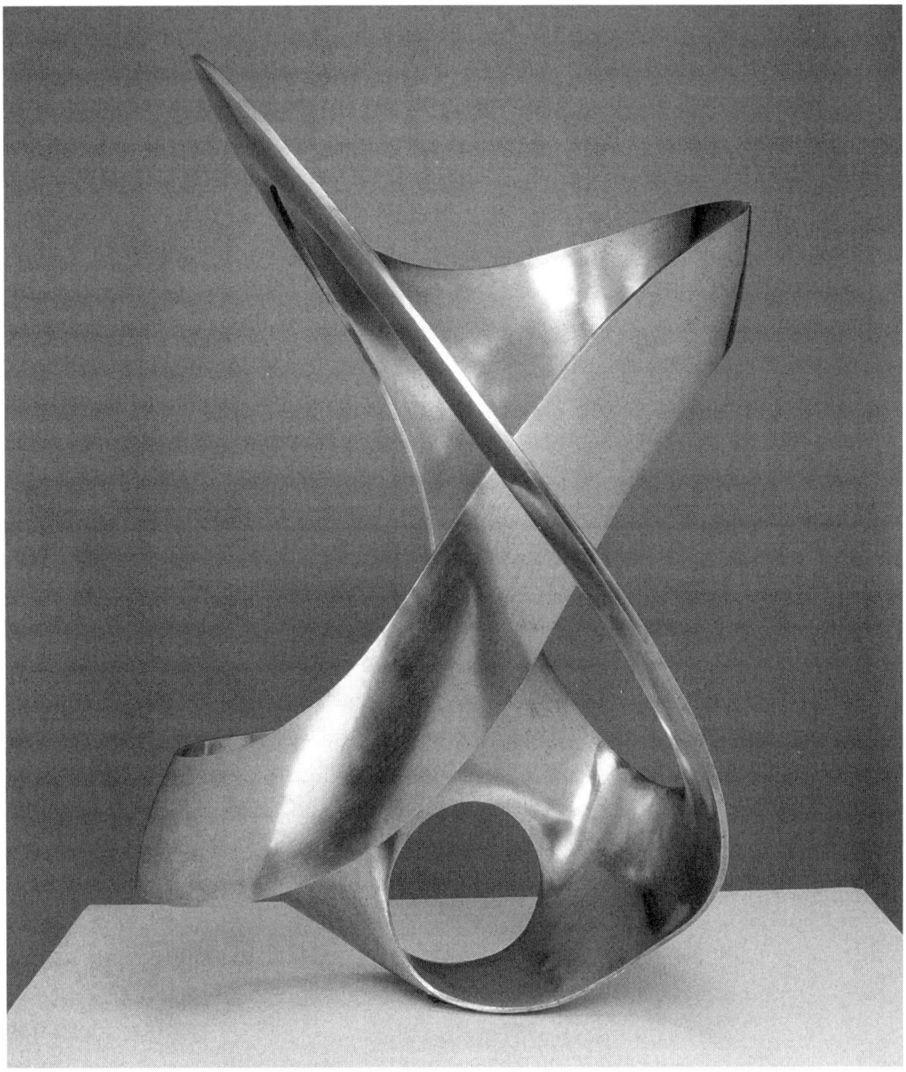

FIGURE 2.2
Max Bill, *Tripartite Unity*, 1948–49, stainless steel, 47⅞ × 34¾ × 38⅝ in.

Möbius strip. More than three feet high, with smooth and shiny surfaces, *Tripartite Unity* presented an open structure, incorporating space as a crucial plastic element of the work and suggesting the vitality of a modernity that had eluded Brazilian artists. The country's developmentalist agenda and its effects on the urban structure, as well as the emergence of cultural institutions such as the Bienal, framed the heroic reception and canonization of Bill's piece. Furthermore, Bill's rigorous version of concrete art; his multifaceted personality as a sculptor, graphic designer, and painter; and his embrace of a mathematical art were all deeply appealing to the young Brazilian artists.

Already interested in geometric abstraction and its self-referential vocabulary, they saw in European concrete art, and in Bill, an aesthetic model that would allow them to leap into modernity.[20]

For Bill, mathematics was not only a tool to apprehend objective reality, but also a system of relations that could help an artist aesthetically and effectively organize the visual. In the arts, he claimed, mathematics did not imply pure formalism but rather form as thought—an idea that resonated with the universal image sought by the emerging concrete artists in Brazil. "The more exactly thought is communicated," Bill wrote, "the more unitary the fundamental idea is, the closer we are to methodic thought, the closer we'll be to the primary structure. In its turn, art will become much more universal. More universal because in expressing itself without subterfuge it will be understood frankly, directly."[21] This call for honesty, with its ethical implications, was linked to the culture of reconstruction that infused the recovery of avant-garde practices in postwar Europe and would be further developed through the theoretical core of Bill's pedagogical practice: the notion of *die gute Form* (good form). This became the title of a 1949 traveling exhibition organized by Bill and sponsored by the Swiss Werkbund. Concerned with developing and producing for mass consumption functional, beautiful objects through which audiences would be exposed to goodness—"good because at once beautiful and practical"[22]—the exhibition emphasized the ethical dimension of Bauhaus concerns about the integration of industry and art. Bill argued for what he called a new humanism, one that would transform consumer goods into cultural goods.[23]

Bill had been a student at the Bauhaus and in 1953 became the founding director of the Ulm Hochschule für Gestaltung, the most prominent of all efforts in Europe to recover the legacy of the Bauhaus Dessau. At Ulm, he made "good form" the theoretical bedrock of the school. As the design historian Paul Betts has written, "Like most Werkbund members, Bill believed that genuine social and cultural reform began not with forced political training, but rather with reconstituting the very forms of the social environment, i.e., city planning, architecture, and the design of everyday objects."[24] Bill's ideas and art suited the progressive impulse that permeated the cultural milieu of Brazil in the 1950s. His presence, works, and writings were to be a direct influence on what became two distinct strands of concretism that formed at the beginning of the decade in São Paulo (Grupo Ruptura) and Rio de Janeiro (Grupo Frente). A reformulation of Bill's thoughts on art and form, together with a rejection of his commitment to the concept of gestalt as a compositional strategy and the intellectualism of his project, were to be crucial as well to the 1959 neoconcrete rupture led by Ferreira Gullar and the artists he supported in Rio de Janeiro.[25]

Bill's impact on abstract artists in Brazil was immense. In 1960—nine years after Bill's work had won accolades in the first São Paulo Bienal—Gullar saw *Tripartite Unity* and especially Bill's public sculpture *Continuity* (1946–47) as complicating dualities in ways that resonated with neoconcretism's interest in spatial ambiguities. "Truly," Gullar wrote regarding Bill's use of the enigmatic topological figure of the Möbius strip in these works, "the vision of those surfaces—that resolve in one [surface], that are one [surface] and two [surfaces at once]—in their unexpected unfolding, make us apprehend, without drama, the reality of a new space, precise and undetermined, coherent and ambiguous, clear and rich."[26] This assessment of Bill suggests that while the neoconcrete group came to reject the functionalism and ideational foundation of concrete art (in the art of Bill and of their São Paulo colleagues), the Swiss artist's interest in non-euclidian geometry nevertheless suggested a sense of spatial ambivalence that the Brazilian artists wished to prioritize.

Bill's own priorities were different. In 1949, in his well-known lecture for the Swiss Werkbund outlining the fundamentals of "good form" vis-à-vis social responsibility, he objected that "the initial impulse [in the artistic process] arises not so much from a conscious feeling of responsibility towards the user as from a sense of responsibility for the form, from the constant will to define a new expression."[27] It was precisely in the name of form—unmediated form and new expression—that the neoconcrete rupture would take place. These terms, and many others, were contested; they were subject to constant negotiation and local reformulation, despite the universalism to which Brazilian critics and artists aspired in the 1950s.

#### FUNCTIONAL BEAUTY = GOOD FORM (GESTALT)

Bill's aesthetic position generated productive readings and counterreadings in the Brazilian context. His first visit to Brazil—a May 1953 trip sponsored by the Brazilian Ministry of Exterior Relations—was one of his many excursions to the Americas, which throughout the years included stops in the United States, Argentina, Mexico, Peru, and Venezuela. The themes that concerned Bill during the early 1950s can be traced to his interest in beauty as the expression of harmonious form, a concept that increasingly permeated his understanding of the relationship between art and design and that led to his aspiration to create form that engaged "with the particular task at hand."[28] Art, he explained in a lecture delivered at the 1953 Aspen Design Conference, is ultimately "an order, a prototype of harmony. Every artist has to establish an order and a method for his expression."[29] Following a line of thought that can be traced back to El Lissitzky and De Stijl, Bill posited painting—a "field of tensions producing new forces like a power-station"—as a symbolic template of relations for efficient environmental design: "art, as pure art, is the forerunner of everyday design."[30]

The architectural historian Hans Frei has observed that Theo van Doesburg's concrete art and his attempt to define the rational basis of painting—a project that he articulated by distancing the medium from its historically representational task as well as from abstract art—were the sources for Bill's conception of function and beauty in the fields of both design and aesthetics.[31] Van Doesburg understood that whereas abstract art is the result of a diluted representation ultimately based on the real world, concrete painting is concerned with painting's own constituent elements. Following this self-referential dictum, Bill wrote in his foundational 1936 text "Concrete Design" that painting "makes a theme of its means and the rules that exist between them." In other words, painting develops rationally and functionally "from its own means and laws without having to borrow or derive these from external natural phenomena. Visual creation is therefore based on colour, form, space, light, and movement. Although every sort of creative work is stimulated by inspiration it cannot be completed without clear and precise form-giving."[32] The German title of this text, "Konkrete Gestaltung," suggests Bill's early assertion of a parallel between art and design as form-giving processes, a concept that would continue to interest him in the following years.[33] But form giving is also described by Bill as an endeavor through which works acquire "concrete form," through which "they are translated from their purely intellectual existence into facts, [thus becoming] objects of visual and intellectual use."[34] This rational formulation, with its commitment to the cerebral and to the singularity of vision, allowed Bill, as Frei notes, to "level out the differences usually made between the practical and the aesthetic,"[35] a notion that was anathema to Gullar and his circle as expressed in the "Manifesto Neoconcreto" and subsequent writings by the Brazilian poet.[36]

Bill's rational approach was visually articulated through references to Gestalt theory, seriality, permutational arrangements, linear and geometric themes, and calculated color compositions. In the hands of the Swiss artist—as well as those of the Brazilian concretists increasingly under his sway in the early and mid-1950s—these elements took the form of diagrammatic patterns that tested the laws of visuality while featuring precise forms of inscription (often through the use of geometric shapes) that sought the functional integration of the parts into a whole. A gouache-on-cardboard work by Bill from 1941 entitled *Design in 19 Squares* (plate 8) is characteristic of a template followed by the Brazilian concretists, especially those associated with Grupo Ruptura in São Paulo. Here, two concentric spirals unfold from the center of the composition. Instead of a continuous line, Bill used scalene triangles in black, green, orange, and violet to create the vectors of the two contiguous spirals. There is a clear subordination of parts to the whole, as the individual triangles that frame the quadrangular configuration create a complex unity, but Bill also injected dynamism through the interplay of the geometric figures and the white spaces between them. The focus on a central axis of rotation contributes to the effect of vanes propelled by a centrifugal force, making this force visible as the forms move rhythmically outward toward the edges of the picture frame. Secondary colors and black have been applied to the framing elements according to an alternating progression that contributes to the systematic, unifying effect. This reliance on clarity of structure and the ordering of form exemplifies Bill's aesthetic credo: "The special form of a work of art," he wrote twenty-four years later, "grows out of the general structure by means of a rhythmic order."[37]

Bill developed his understanding of gestalt (a concept against which Gullar often battled)[38] in his lectures on design in the early 1950s, employing it as a fundamental component of his theory of art and design and as a means of objectively and rationally framing his artistic production. He utilized the term to denote shape or form, or shape/form, as an attribute of things; this is the common meaning of *Gestalt* in German. It is obvious, however, that Bill borrowed from Gestalt theory and psychology (concerned mainly with the study of the perception of wholes) to articulate his concept of the term as a defining aspect of an aesthetic program that encompassed art and design.[39] Gestalt psychology had likely entered the pedagogical landscape of the Bauhaus by the time of Bill's arrival in 1927, when he enrolled in the architecture department to study with the Swiss architect Hannes Meyer. Meyer was known for his "technocratic determinism" and scientific approach to design, and he introduced psychology lectures at the Bauhaus in 1928.[40] Wassily Kandinsky's theories of form (as well as the search for the structural laws of form and vision by Walter Gropius, Paul Klee, and László Moholy-Nagy) have affinities with those proposed by Gestalt psychology, and the art historian Paul Overy, for one, noted that Gestalt theory, as the "newest theory of perception[,] . . . must have been a constant topic of discussion in the intellectual atmosphere of the Bauhaus."[41] Among the famous group of Bauhaus instructors, Josef Albers was certainly acquainted with, and his teaching was influenced by, Gestalt theory.[42]

Bill's concept of gestalt—identified with the ideal form of objects, their optimal resolution—echoed several principles proposed by Gestalt theory. Usually translated as "form," "configuration," or "structure" in psychology, *gestalt* refers to events (perceptions, experiences, thought processes) that cannot be described as the sum of their parts (sensations). Gestalt psychologists suggested instead that humans organize sensations into perceptive wholes that are discernible in figure-ground relationships. Fully established by the 1920s, Gestalt psychology advanced a number of principles that concerned perception and problems of recognition and form.[43] Lectures delivered in the summer of 1913 by the psychologist Max Wertheimer posited the basis of Gestalt psychology and asserted that human consciousness presents a characteristic "togetherness" that is hierarchically structured and "often 'comprehended' from an inner center"; that we grasp objects and their relational contexts as wholes; and that knowledge consists of a "process of 'centering,' of structuring, or of grasping that particular aspect that provides the key to an orderly whole, a unification of the particular individual parts that happen to be present."[44]

Gestalt theory's fundamental principle is that of *Prägnanz* (conciseness), which "maintains that grouping tends toward maximal simplicity and balance, or toward the formation of 'good form.'"[45] This condition would become the goal and basis of Bill's artistic philosophy as proposed in his 1949 exhibition *Die Gute Form,* which cut across disciplines or "form-giving" practices (design, art, architecture) to explore the "good" (that is, optimal or valid) form of things. Accordingly, "good form" was eventually replaced by "gestalt" in Bill's vocabulary. This is not surprising, since in Gestalt theory the principle of *Prägnanz* has an aesthetic dimension. Moreover, another founding figure of the discipline, Wolfgang Köhler, saw a correspondence between "the structural essence of physical Gestalten" (out there in the physical world) and psychological

Gestalten (inside the perceiving subject)—a condition called psychophysical isomorphism that allows the viewer to see "the beauty of natural order conceived as a unity."[46] Echoing this notion, Bill wrote, "When a landscape delights us it is as a whole, because of an underlying harmony in its grouping and proportions."[47] Indeed, according to Gestalt psychology, we tend to perceive and apprehend the geometric vectors that organize the exterior world, a process that favors regularity, symmetry, balance, and clarity. In conjunction with Gestalt theory's all-encompassing tendency toward organization, Bill suggested a privileging of vision and qualified the sensorial aspect of his artistic project: " [O]ur purpose is also to see, and to see clearly."[48] (Brazilian neoconcrete artists would vehemently reject this stance as an artificial isolation that ignored the totality of corporeal experience.)

From the existing press reports of Bill's visits to Rio de Janeiro and São Paulo in May and June 1953, it is not clear to what extent the concept of gestalt entered the conversations and public lectures that occupied him there. One article, reporting on Bill's presentations at the Museu de Arte Moderna do Rio de Janeiro on May 30 and June 3, focused on Bill's account of the history of the Bauhaus and mentioned gestalt in passing: "There were three or four professors, such as [Johannes] Itten and . . . [Lyonel] Feininger and later Kandinsky, Klee, and Moholy-Nagy, who sought to develop a new theory upon which art would have its foundation. The theory of Gestalt had not yet been formulated. Kandinsky and Klee, then, proposed a theory to organize space."[49] The anonymous writer of this article (a summary, not a transcription) indicated that Bill was not lecturing from notes, but these sentences suggest that Gestalt theory must have been introduced by Bill in his 1953 visit to Brazil as one of the main tools to provide an organized yet aesthetic foundation to the visual arts and design—a goal that resonated with Brazilian artists and critics at the time.

Furthering this agenda and clarifying the principles of the ideal form or gestalt that he aspired to achieve, Bill, in a lecture in Paris also given in 1953, was at pains to differentiate decoration from aesthetics and to define the latter as integral to design: "Beauty can indeed be the self-evident outcome of the unity of all functions." He also declared: "[T]he most audacious works of contemporary art act both conceptually and formally as standards for everyday goods and industrial objects." This dual track of beauty and function expands to merge aesthetics, functionality, and ethics into a composite in which "the aesthetic appearance is simultaneously the correct appearance, the expression of what is right." In this sense, "what is right" is that which provides the best solution (social and practical) to a particular task or problem. This, to Bill, is the main goal of form giving: "The form is not the basis of the things, but a result," he wrote. "It is the expression, the bringing together of the various functions, to which the quality of unity adheres. We then perceive this unity of all functions as a valid, typical form, as *gestalt*."[50]

Gestalt as Bill understood it thus encompasses the total identification between unity of means and ends to which the modernist artist/designer aspires. In Bill's lectures from 1953, this search for formal plenitude brought to the foreground two other concepts important to neoconcrete artists in Brazil: expression and organic form. Bill associated self-expression with an individualism that undermined the social role of the artist, and he was unwavering in his rejection of it. In his view, self-expression obscured the expression of the object in favor of the personality, subjectivity, and feelings of the artist—elements that had no place in Bill's aesthetic agenda. Gestalt—which he came to equate with organic form—was to suppress personal expression. In the search for a "unity of all functions" that would deliver "a neutral, *organic* and typical form" (emphasis added)[51] there is no place whatsoever for the whims of personal expression; all that matters is the "ideal" of functional form.[52] Echoing the creationist temper of concrete art best expressed in Jean Arp's declaration, "We want to produce like a plant that produces a fruit,"[53] Bill identified the process of form giving with the functional organic-ness conveyed by *Gestaltung*. As the architectural historian Detlef Mertins observed in his useful mapping of these debates in the German culture of architecture and design of the 1920s, "The term *Gestaltung* has multiple connotations that are not adequately registered by translating it as *design*. It refers both to form and to the process of formation or shaping, and it retains traces of the vital, creative energy of becoming in the concreteness of the resultant form. It also implies a figure or configuration that is a clear and individuated totality."[54]

The concept of the organic would become key to the neoconcretists, but they did not conceive of organic form as an ideal functional structure or as equivalent to the physical models of gestalt. Instead, Gullar alluded to the organic, in his characteristic nondefinitional language, as a "quasi-corpus" that transcends its objectivity and is not susceptible to rational analysis. He elaborated this formulation in 1960, arguing that the organic form is not, as in Gestalt theory (and in Bill's conception), reduced to its physical form (exterior to the individual) but instead is related to what the artist expresses. And what the artist expresses, he clarified, does not preexist its expression: "[T]he perfection of form is found at the same time as form: it is expression itself. Approaching form only as a physical phenomenon—which it undoubtedly also is—Gestalt theory relegates the problem of signification to the background."[55] For Gullar, perception was related to signification—a signification given in perception. Here, the Brazilian poet revealed the influence of the French philosopher Maurice Merleau-Ponty, who explained that "vital acts have meaning" and depend upon the "significance of situations" in which we often relate to others.[56] Thus, Gullar concluded, *signifying* form—rather than "typical" or "valid" form—is the true subject of the visual arts. Insisting on the importance of the signifying form in art, and rejecting rational and objectivist conceptions of time, space, and structure, Gullar would later write of "organic spatial-temporal structures" in which a dialogue between a work and its public takes place in the field of interior experiences and not merely in sensorial exteriority.[57] "Sensorial exteriority" concerned empiricism—or, per Merleau-Ponty, "sense experience [reduced to] the possession of a quality." As the French philosopher clarified: "[T]he pure *quale* would be given to us only if the world were a spectacle and one's own body a mechanism with which some impartial mind made itself acquainted. Sense experience, on the other hand, invests the quality with vital value, grasping it first in its meaning for us." This sense experience is charged with "affective and motor functions" that allow us to distinguish between a mere movement and an affectionate gesture.[58] Alluding to this formulation, Gullar described the organic form not as a functional organism but rather as a descent into the source of experience, with the resulting work charged emotionally and existentially.[59]

In 1953 Bill deployed the ideal good forms of gestalt to repress the body, contingency, arbitrariness, and change in favor of evolution, functionality, and identity. It can be argued that Bill aspired to find the identity of objects, their "type"—a normative, definitional project that was antagonistic to the neoconcrete embrace of medium indeterminacy unleashed by Gullar's concept of the nonobject. But before this counterterm, clearly dismissive of ontology, was formulated in 1959, concrete art and Bill's ideas flourished in the artistic milieus of São Paulo and Rio de Janeiro. The presence of concrete art would forever alter artistic production in these cities and stimulate debates about aesthetic processes, viewership, and the nature of the art object that shape Brazilian contemporary art to this day.

## IMAGE IDEA, IMAGE OBJECT, AND NONOBJECT

In concrete art, gestalt was evident in a plethora of geometric forms and visual exercises that tested the laws of perception posited by Gestalt theory. These invoked a process of "recentering," of achieving insight into the logical and functional workings of the represented formal configurations. Bill himself alluded to the satisfaction of "recentering" (a sort of epiphany that illuminates a situation) in his introduction to *Fifteen Variations on a Single Theme*, a group of lithographs published in Paris in 1938 and shown along with *Tripartite Unity* in a 1951 exhibition of Bill's work at the Museu de Arte de São Paulo. With this suite of images, Bill's goal was to facilitate a clear understanding of the "internal and external construction" of works of art, since "one is scarcely able to extract from them all the pleasure they can give without at least a little insight into the methods by which they have been evolved." He added that the purpose of his introductory text was "to give a glimpse of what a group of these methods consists of and to give anyone who takes the trouble to look at the plates the opportunity of following certain operations by means of the examples shown on them."[60] Bill explained that his method was not mathematical or geometric in nature, but rather involved the pure play of form and color intrinsic to art. Despite giving preeminence to form and color, Bill's strategy was expository: it allowed the viewer to unravel the concept that generated the work. This method was embraced by concrete artists such as Waldemar Cordeiro and Luís Sacilotto in São Paulo, but Gullar—and his mentor, the critic Mário Pedrosa—rejected the a priori idea that determines the resulting form. For them, a predetermined concept led to a situation in which "there is always an intellectual signification [behind plastic form] that will give us the key to understanding the beauty contained there."[61] Or, as

Gullar and the neoconcrete artists put it in the "Manifesto Neoconcreto," "We propose a reinterpretation of neoplasticism, constructivism, and other related movements on the basis of their expressive accomplishments and giving prevalence to the work over the theory."[62]

The "theme" of Bill's *Fifteen Variations on a Single Theme* is a spiraling linear configuration that begins in an open equilateral triangle and grows outward, delineating polygons whose vertices increase until a large, open octagon encloses the whole. Evolving from this source, the fifteen variations operate as a heuristic device probing the possibilities of the initial structure. It is this demonstrative trajectory, aided by the serial progression and graphic precision of the chosen medium, that disciplines the perceptual apprehension of the work of art. Here, art operates as a symbolic template for functional beauty but also emerges as the result of a systematic thought process, similar to that required in more practical domains such as industrial design. In true modernist fashion, the goal is to make form and means coincide, satisfying a dream of plenitude that represses the arbitrary and the contingent and equates form giving with knowledge. This logic—first systematically explored by a group of constructivist artists in Moscow in 1921—implied that, in the words of the German art historian Hubertus Gassner, the "artistic subject becomes as transparent as his creation. The previously impenetrable dark of his subconscious and body is illuminated and rendered transparent through the exposure of the logic of their functional models."[63]

This transparent and projective logic, by which the subject realized him- or herself in the defined form of the autonomous object, would be problematized by the Brazilian neoconcrete rupture and its phenomenological and affective interpretation of the concrete legacy. In particular, the folding plates, nooks and crannies, apertures, and gaps in the neoconcrete work of Lygia Clark and Hélio Oiticica (plate 9) bypassed the transparent logic implicit in the ideational form of the concrete image/object. In the Brazil of the 1950s, however, the transparent correspondence between subject and idea/object was to be the cornerstone of concrete art. Preoccupied with but not burdened by the practical demands imposed on the Soviet artists, concrete artists—in Brazil, as in Paris and Switzerland before them—could pursue an aesthetic project that equated a work's technical perfection with the perfection of the *concept* with which it originated.[64]

In Brazil this concurrence of concept and object evolved in different ways according to the distinctive approaches to art making of the two groups of abstract artists emerging in São Paulo and Rio de Janeiro in the early 1950s. This period saw the writing of manifestos, exhibitions, publications, and the prompt identification of these groups with European concrete art. The formation of the São Paulo–based Grupo Ruptura in 1952 was sealed by a manifesto signed by Geraldo de Barros, Lothar Charoux, Waldemar Cordeiro, Kazmer Féjer, Leopold Haar, Luís Sacilotto, and Anatol Wladyslaw and distributed on the occasion of their exhibition at the Museu de Arte Moderna de São Paulo. The text was printed in small caps, in a sans-serif font, and ordered in blocks of sentences throughout the page, recalling Bauhaus Dessau typographical experiments;

the text also played with font size to emphasize such dicta as "There is no more continuity!" The manifesto advocated artistic intuition characterized by "clear and intelligent principles" that could be developed in practice—ideas that resonated with Bill's own.[65] Most importantly, contra critics Mário Pedrosa and, later, Ferreira Gullar, art was to be a vehicle of knowledge deduced from "clear and intelligent" principles with possibilities for development in the practical realm of objects.[66]

In Rio de Janeiro, the year 1952 witnessed the first steps toward the formation of Grupo Frente. Some of its future members were then students of the artist Ivan Serpa, a close friend of the critic Mário Pedrosa, at the Museu de Arte Moderna do Rio de Janeiro. Through Serpa they were exposed to geometric abstraction, which he practiced in the late 1940s and 1950s.[67] In 1953 the Exposição Nacional de Arte Abstrata (National Exhibition of Abstract Art) was held in Petrópolis, Brazil (and was triggered in part by the vast presence of abstract art in the inaugural São Paulo Bienal in 1951); Max Bill arrived to participate in conferences at the Museu de Arte Moderna do Rio de Janeiro and at the Universidade de São Paulo. The year 1954 saw the first exhibition of Grupo Frente at the Brazil-USA Institute in Rio de Janeiro; according to the critic Frederico Morais, the participants included Ivan Serpa, Lygia Clark, and Lygia Pape as well as Serpa's students Aluísio Carvão, Vincent Ibberson, João José da Silva Costa, Carlos Val, and Décio Vieira.[68] Pape recalled that in the early 1950s, the group worked with a limited vocabulary of geometric forms and colors and—although they were aware of the Fibonacci sequence and had read Max Bill's and Georges Vantongerloo's pronouncements on art—took a rather intuitive approach to the application of mathematical principles to art making. Theoretical support for the group came from Gullar and Pedrosa, who wrote introductory essays for its exhibitions in 1954 and 1955, respectively.[69]

The second São Paulo Bienal took place from December 12, 1953, to February 28, 1954, and helped advance the abstract trends that were gaining momentum not only nationally but also regionally. As the art historian Adele Nelson has shown in her study of the early editions of the Bienal, the 1953 version also showcased the abstract experiments of artists from countries such as Argentina, Uruguay, Venezuela, and Cuba. Aside from the more familiar work of the Argentines (which had been exhibited earlier in 1953 at the Museu de Arte Moderna do Rio de Janeiro) and the well-known work of the Uruguayan Joaquín Torres-García and his school, the Bienal featured work by the Cubans Mario Carreño, Sandú Darié, and Luis Martínez Pedro and the Venezuelans Armando Barrios, Carlos González Bogen, and Mateo Manaure. The large Brazilian section reiterated the increasing relevance of geometric abstraction locally. The Bienal prominently displayed works by artists associated with the artist Samson Flexor's Atelier Abstração as well as those of the nascent Grupo Frente in addition to works by members of São Paulo's Grupo Ruptura.[70]

The principles of Paulista (from São Paulo) and Carioca (from Rio de Janeiro) concrete art and poetry were articulated in the pages of various publications that facilitated the circulation of works, ideas, and debates. In 1957, for example, the Paulista concrete poet Décio Pignatari echoed the ethos of the decade by allying himself with a "new world of serial industrial production," which he defined as "impersonal, collective, and rational" and which fully depended on "planning." Echoing Max Bill's notion of "good form," Pignatari called the union of usefulness and beauty a necessity. While practical applications in architecture, urbanism, design, advertising, cinema, and journalism were foreseen, the concrete object was to act as a symbol of an epoch that embodied "a general project of universal objectivity."[71] This idea resonated with aspirations of development and international integration in this period, specifically with President Kubitschek's goal of accomplishing "fifty years of progress in five" through national industrialization. In a later assessment of these groups and movements, however, the critic Ronaldo Brito argued that "Concretism was unable to think systematically about the political reason for its practice or to justify its insertion into the Brazilian cultural environment." As a result, "dominant idealism prevailed over materialistic culture."[72] This suggests that an explicit privileging of the object and its formal mechanisms led concrete art to operate primarily as a symbolic device that complemented the modernist rhetoric of the period.

If Max Bill could—not unproblematically, and partly because of Switzerland's role as a bystander in World War II—claim continuity with the avant-garde project that flourished at the Bauhaus,[73] in Brazil entirely different conditions of economic production and consumption disrupted the fallacy of a direct correspondence between the Kubitschek government's developmentalist plans and the concrete Paulistas' desire to effectively bridge art and industrial production. Instead, as Gullar pointed out at the time, the desire for objectivity and a materialist practice that contemplated the possibility of utilitarian work led Brazilian concrete artists to identify the notions of time, space, and structure in science with the manipulation of these elements in art.[74] This project was related to the stated aspiration of these artists to develop an artistic practice that would deliver epochal models of construction and formal laws that would contribute to the "formation of a common language of the times."[75] The European effort to retrace the steps of the various constructivist tendencies of the 1920s was in part a direct response to the will for cultural reconstruction that followed World War II.[76] In South America, the geometric abstract object, with its associations with technology, geometry, and mathematics, mostly facilitated a way out of the backwardness of nationalistic and mythological discourses, and the advancement of aesthetic models that concrete artists associated with a universal viewer.

This inquiry into the universal dimension of painting justified the "autonomous idea-object"[77] as art's most profound manifestation and validated the production of objects that, echoing the constructivist lineage described above, "formally create their own function, displaying the sensible idea that they embody."[78] These words by Pignatari were voiced in the context of a forcefully argued apology for the production of utilitarian works that would respond to a new world of serial industrial production. Pignatari argued, however, that the utilitarian object cannot absorb the "creative capacity of the arts."[79] Rather, the role of the artwork is to be a *forma mentis* that embodies an epochal sensibility. Here beauty is related to formal structures that are "objectively general and impersonal."[80] This privileging of the concrete artwork as an emblem of the mindset of an epoch was clearly linked to the desire of Brazilian intellectuals and artists to reposition their country vis-à-vis the realigned postwar global cultural landscape. As recent scholarship on the institutional and ideological makeup of Brazilian visual culture in the 1950s and 1960s has demonstrated, internationalism (and thus universalism) was closely linked to the aspirations of the political and economic elites of the country. Art, architecture, poetry, and culture in general were means for asserting Brazil's position within the international geopolitical arena.[81]

Despite limited engagement with industry, industry persisted as the background to the work produced by these concrete artists.[82] But the real common denominator of the visual production, advertising design, and poetry of the Paulista group was a treatment of geometry that obeyed the gestaltic maxim of simple forms and unified structure.[83] This is evident in works that feature a functional interdependence of parts predicated on repetition, alternation, or the progression of geometric shapes, lines, and virtual spaces. *Movimento contra movimento* (Movement Counter Movement, 1952; fig. 2.3), an early work by Grupo Ruptura member Geraldo de Barros, is a prime example. Over a black background the artist delineated a configuration of gray and off-white chevrons whose angles touch the midpoint of each side of the frame. Within, four increasingly smaller chevrons alternate from gray to off-white and echo the outer ones, while at the center they form a small diamond-shaped black void. The central points of all the polygons are perfectly aligned along the horizontal axis of the canvas. The sense of movement suggested by the title is produced by the alternating directionality of the chevrons. Moreover, the work alludes to the Gestalt principle of simultaneous contrast, which allows the viewer to shift focus from the shapes delineated by the chevrons to the virtual space, including the central diamond-shaped void.

A later painting by de Barros, done in enamel on Eucatex industrial board (a Brazilian brand popular in the 1950s and used by these painters as part of a wave of experimentation with materials), is entitled *Concreto* (Concrete, 1953; plate 10). The work displays an equally expository intention, a logic that viewers can follow, through repetition, inversion, and progression. On the black background of the orthogonal support the artist painted two white squares: one whose top, bottom, and left corners touch the edges of the canvas, and another, a quarter the size of the first and located to its right, whose upper corner alone contacts the top edge of the painting. Within each white square is inscribed a smaller colored square. Embedded in the right corner of the larger square is a red square half the size of the smaller white square to the right. That smaller white square repeats the square-within-a-square motif: here it is green, half the size of its red counterpart, and wedged in the lower corner of the white square. This logical design—facilitated by the repetition of a simple geometric form, measurable progressions, alternating elements, and contrasting and complementary colors; and proceed-

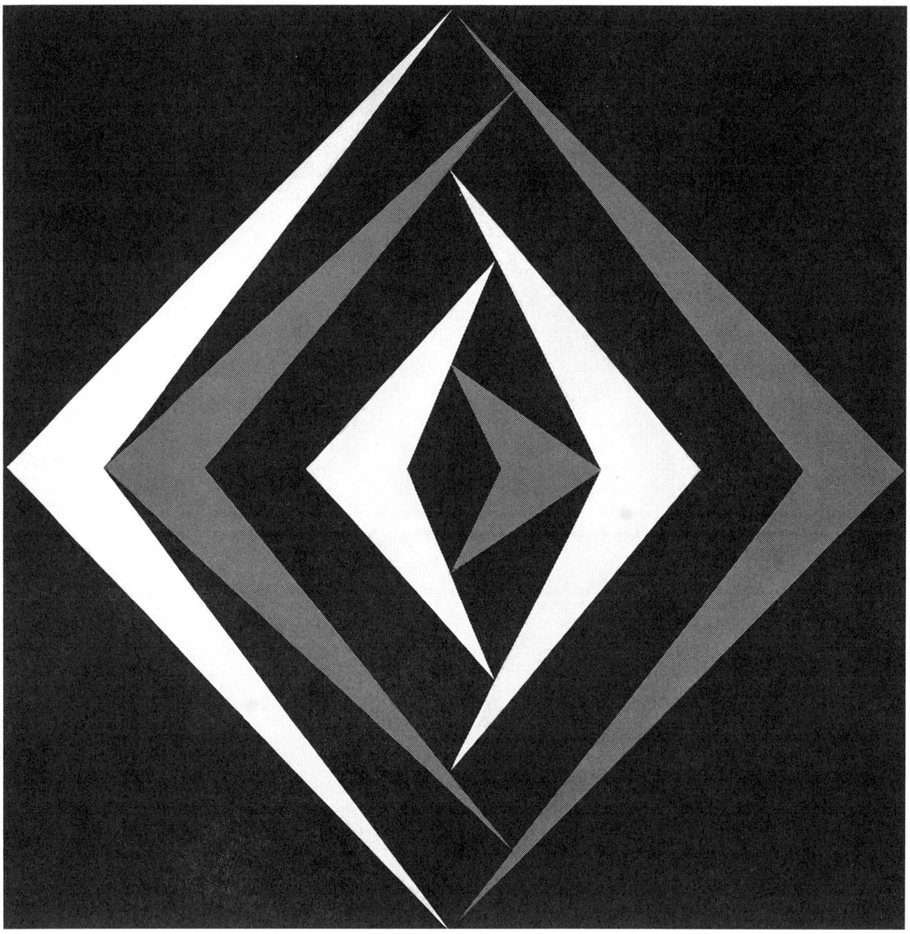

FIGURE 2.3
Geraldo de Barros, *Movimento contra movimento* (Movement Counter Movement), 1952, enamel on Kemlite, 23⅝ × 23⅝ in.

ing through the development and variation of an a priori structure—is consistent with what Waldemar Cordeiro, leader of Grupo Ruptura, called an *idéia visível* (visible idea). Cordeiro would give this title to a series of works conceived in the mid-1950s, but as early as 1949 he was advancing the notion of a legible art that, through information and understanding (instead of intuition and emotion), would reveal what is valuable in a work. In words that would later be echoed by Pignatari, Cordeiro wrote, "Only by objectivizing and depersonalizing form can one make it a matter of reflection, making the work comprehensible."[84]

## THE AFFECTIVE NATURE OF FORM

As has been amply observed and as the above examples demonstrate, Gestalt psychology was foundational to the conceptual and morphological modalities of concrete art that developed in Brazil in the 1950s. By contrast, it is rarely noted that Gestalt psychology was introduced in Brazil by the critic Mário Pedrosa (fig. 2.4), whose 1949 thesis, "Da natureza afetiva da forma na obra de arte" (On the Affective Nature of Form in the Work of Art), was submitted as part of the tenure process for a position in the department of the history of art and aesthetics at the Faculdade Nacional de Arquitetura (National School of Architecture) in Rio de Janeiro. The writing of Pedrosa's essay coincided with the emergence of abstract art in the country, which he increasingly defended against the figurative modernism of a cadre of well-known painters such as Cândido Portinari, Emiliano Di Cavalcanti, and Lasar Segall. Focused on national themes—the Brazilian landscape and its riches, its people, and its occupations—the modern realism privileged during the 1930s and 1940s as suitable to produce representations of Brazil was being contested by artists and critics by the late 1940s. This coincidence is relevant, since, as the art historian Sérgio Martins has observed, Gestalt theory gave Pedrosa the tools to highlight the universality and power of (good) form—form that is not necessarily attached to referential functions.[85] Pedrosa's study also introduced ideas and concerns that he and Gullar would later recalibrate vis-à-vis the divergent approaches to the art object and the artistic processes of concretism and neoconcretism.

Pedrosa had been exposed to Gestalt theory while a student of philosophy at the Freie Universität Berlin between 1927 and 1929.[86] Although his thesis was not published until 1979, the text circulated among friends and colleagues, and its ideas were surely discussed by the artists and intellectuals who frequented Pedrosa's household in Ipanema.[87] Focused on the affective response of the spectator to artistic form, Pedrosa's essay concerned organized initial perception as the basis of art's expressive force. Because artistic form alone mattered, the latter was undermined by analytical and external preoccupations of a different order: didactic, religious, scientific, personal. In other words, Gestalt theory allowed Pedrosa to focus on the art object's phenomenological and objective presence and not its content. With words that would be echoed by Gullar in the "Manifesto Neoconcreto" of 1959, he wrote that in cases in which these external factors (politics, the artist's feelings, and so on) are prioritized, art stops being an end and becomes a means of communicating contents.[88] To Pedrosa, the "global impression" (pure, primary, primitive) that is the basis of gestalt is not obliged to satisfy a need or respond to a function (he cites clusters of clouds and constellations as examples of "good form"). In his view, a unity emerges—and a figural whole has affective signification—because form has, first and foremost, preliminary existence as "sensible object."[89]

Pedrosa's field of inquiry positioned his investigation in a realm distant from Bill's precept of "beauty from function and as function." However, as with Bill and the Gestalt

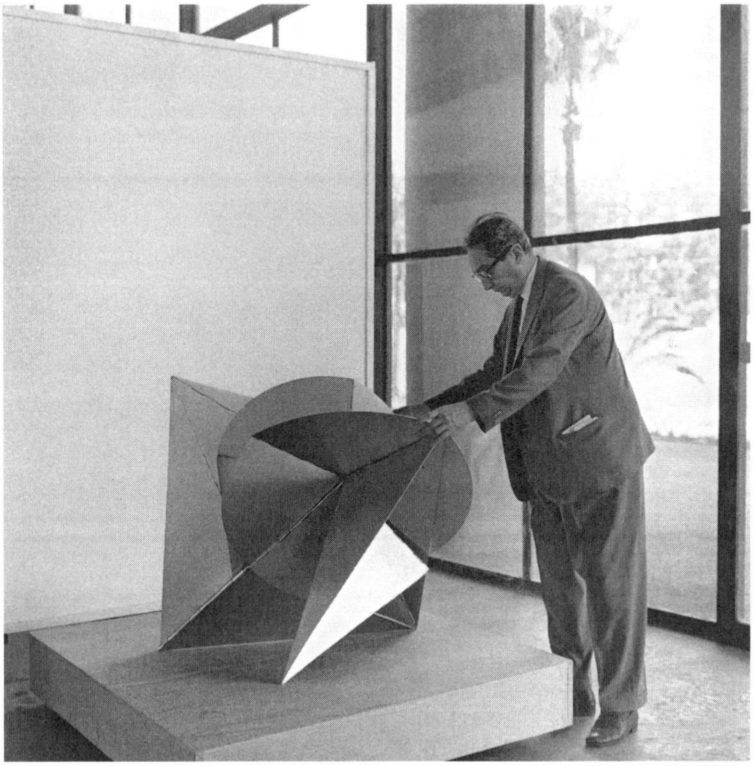

FIGURE 2.4
Thomaz Farkas (photographer), Mário Pedrosa manipulating Lygia Clark's *Bicho,* 1961.

psychologists, Pedrosa was delighted with the possibility of giving an objective foundation to the problems of form via Gestalt psychology, thus legitimizing the autonomous artistic phenomenon as an essential, universal human activity independent of scientific, religious, and political associations. This conceptualization of artistic form would resonate with the universalist aspirations of a generation of abstract artists coming of age precisely when Pedrosa was composing his text. Specifically, the objectivist parameters of Gestalt theory suited concrete art (Bill's own, as well as the nascent Brazilian versions that Pedrosa would support), given its emphasis on the internal laws of painting. Indeed, Gestalt theory allowed the Brazilian critic to focus on the intrinsic qualities of form and the viewer's perception of it. He thus bypassed approaches that privileged artistic technique or a subjectivism that located meaning in the unique experience of the artist—these were judged to be extrinsic to the artistic event and its distinctive communicability.[90]

Despite Pedrosa's detailed catalogue of the laws of structure and form in his rigorous analysis of the most recent literature on Gestalt theory and other studies on the structure of art and vision, he insisted on affective power as the strongest property intrinsic to form. He also favored the phenomenological matrix of Gestalt theory that gave primacy to perception and advanced a notion of the subject (key to phenomenology) as immersed in, and not separated from, the world.[91] Further, Pedrosa insisted on synesthetic perception (a subject that Gullar, invoking Merleau-Ponty's notion of a general symbolic of the body, would focus on in his neoconcrete writings), arguing, "It is necessary to see form not with what one knows, but simply with the senses. Eyes, movement, and touch participate in vision. . . . Motor phenomena, in effect, that accompany visual experience have their own spatial and temporal organization."[92] This suggests that Pedrosa was upholding Gestalt theory's original inclination to pursue an objective order that emanates from within the flux of experience. This dimension of Gestalt theory, which refuted the atomism of sensations, was influenced by Henri Bergson's notion of consciousness as a spatiotemporal continuum.[93]

In "Form and Expression," the last section of his thesis, Pedrosa turned to a theme that would become central to the "Manifesto Neoconcreto": the relationship between subject and object and the notion of expression (projection) beyond pure subjectivism. He explored this theme by borrowing the German psychologist Kurt Koffka's categories when he defined the work of art as phenomenologically objective and functionally subjective.[94] These two terms were synthesized by the author Bernard C. Heyl, quoted by Pedrosa, in the notion of relative objectivity which understands that "the properties [of the object] are objective in that they do not *belong to* the self, yet are relative in that they are *dependent upon* individual organisms."[95] This relativity, however, does not threaten the intrinsic specificity of the work of art but establishes a relationship between maker and viewer mediated by the object. More specifically, it is the object's intrinsic properties that produce affect, emotion, in the viewer. Pedrosa then turns his attention to the kind of relation that the work of art establishes between subject and object. In his view, the unifying quality of primary perception—the source of aesthetic organization, according to Gestalt psychology—facilitates a direct relation between object and ego thanks to a correspondence between the structure of perception and that of physical forms (defined by Gestalt theory as psychological isomorphism).[96] But unlike Bill, Pedrosa was concerned with the specifics that condition relations between the ego and the object, the possible situations in which ego and object are involved.[97] And Pedrosa viewed this dialogue between ego and object as expressive and moral: beings, objects, and situations are not apprehended as disembodied ideas but as meaningful wholes inserted in dynamic contexts in which the ego and the object interact. Thus, the Brazilian critic opened up a conversation around reception theory that would become increasingly important in Brazil and that, by moving beyond the purely physical properties of the work, retraced a crack in the concept of a strict correspondence between physical and perceptual structures (isomorphism) posited by Gestalt theory.

This crack imbued the encounter between subject and object with the situational, and was deepened by Gullar in his critique of the causality of Gestalt theory (via

Merleau-Ponty) when he objected to the discipline's identification between form as an event exterior to humans (subject to the laws of the field in which the form is situated) and form as a signification that humans apprehend.[98] In identifying the physical structure out in the world as homologous to the structure of perception, Gestalt theory makes the former the cause of the latter. Merleau-Ponty wrote that this amounts to saying that physical form defines humans and ignores the contextual, relational, and contingent nature of bodily perception.[99] As if responding to Merleau-Ponty's objection to Gestalt theory's isomorphism between physical structures and perception—a correspondence that depends, the French philosopher argued, on the objective (laboratory) conditions in which these correlations are studied—Pedrosa, following Koffka very closely here, emphasized the role of the affective field in which object and subject face off.[100] Thus, the Brazilian critic wrote, in a situation of embeddedness, determined by the subject's investment (emotional, material, aesthetic) in a particular situation, field and ego are united, and precision is diffused. Such is the case, for example, with a nature lover before a landscape that overwhelms him or her with emotion. Here, perception loses precision, and the situation is the opposite from that found in a laboratory, where the subject can keep a distance from the object perceived. Pedrosa posited, then, a very different scenario from the ideal transparency implicit in the heuristic templates of concrete art—a goal to which the work of van Doesburg, Bill, and Cordeiro implicitly aspired.

In a field of extreme differentiation, object and ego are distant, and the relationship between the subject and the object is vague and abstract, conceptual and utilitarian; one of Pedrosa's examples is the forest developer or speculator before that same landscape. The analytic approach that practicality implies, a sign of civilization associated with rationalism and science, has led to the impoverished life that Pedrosa recognized in contemporary Western culture.[101] Affect, he seemed to suggest, is displaced by functionality—precisely the quality upon which Bill based his own notion of gestalt. It is in the realm of art, Pedrosa concluded, that viewer and object are in a direct, close relationship, one that is not determined by its capacity to satisfy a need.[102] Utilitarian objects lose their total expression; a bridge, for example, or one of the many industrial objects Bill invoked to exemplify his notion of good form, is simply a means to an end, which the artwork is not. Bill's attention to the functional physiognomy of the designed object and the functional structure of the concrete artwork was certainly very different from a mere interest in the instrumental aspect of things. But for Pedrosa, there was no place for the invested approach in his quest to define the unique perceptual complexion of art. Furthermore, for the Brazilian critic, language—the "abstract concept" or the a priori idea—could interfere with, rather than enlighten, the apprehension of the work of art.[103] These various theoretical priorities help explain why Pedrosa would ultimately distance himself from the ideational basis of concrete art and its desire to illustrate intelligible structures.

This antifunctionalist imperative had previously been articulated by Pedrosa in his analysis of the work of Alexander Calder, whom he met in New York and about

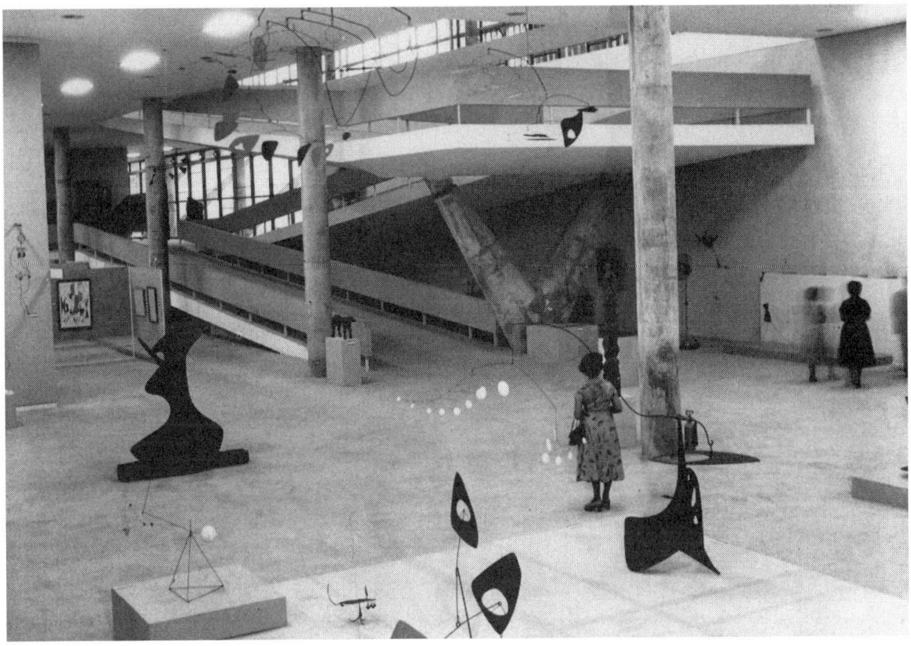

FIGURE 2.5
Installation view of Alexander Calder's exhibition at the second São Paulo Bienal, 1953–54.

whom he had written on the occasion of the American artist's exhibition at New York's Museum of Modern Art in 1943. In the playful work of Calder, with its skewed relation to a constructivist trajectory that referenced the world of modern functionality and the machine, Pedrosa recognized a plastic purity in which the engineer and the artist were fused "in perfect harmony."[104] This fusion in Calder's work was described by Pedrosa in gestaltic terms: "[W]hat sustains the cohesiveness and unity of the artistic group is the . . . affirmation of that total unity in strong contrast to the surrounding space. . . . Cohesion in Calder is not, thus, an organic or functional quality." In a conceptualization of the organic as functional, Pedrosa continued that "cohesion does not derive from the convergence of all parts to achieve a common end, external to the intrinsic nature, disinterested, of the object."[105] The "suggestive force" (*força sugestiva*) of the work is related instead to its plastic resolution, to the "pure gratuity of movement and the abstraction of its forms."[106] Indeed, the Brazilian critic insisted that Calder's objective was the creation of new forms.[107] He argued that these art forms violated functional mechanics in opposition to the prevailing American utilitarianism (fig. 2.5). Utilitarian objects implied the denaturalization of structure—a march toward pure objectivity, from the natural to formal abstraction—that is a constant of modern civilization. Interestingly, Pedrosa viewed the dividing line between artistic creation and industrial design in Calder's work as tenuous, despite the fact that the American artist subverted the materials and methods of practical domains such as design and engineering to create improvised, fantastic machines and gratuitous relations.

Pedrosa's attention to the experience of surprise that an artwork might provide, outside knowledge and habit but organized and objective, was indicated in his early interest in the art of children, so-called "primitive" art, and the art of the mentally ill. As the historian Otília Beatriz Fiori Arantes has pointed out, the critic's first texts for the newspaper *Correio da Manhã* in the mid-1940s coincided with his staunch support of art schools for children (*escolinhas da arte*) and an earnest enthusiasm for the art of the mentally ill. She stressed that the first more or less cohesive generation of abstract artists that formed in the late 1940s was also associated with these areas of interest. Ivan Serpa taught art to children and—with Pedrosa and the artists Almir Mavignier and Abraham Palatnik—collaborated with Dr. Nise da Silveira in her Centro Psiquiátrico Nacional Pedro II de Engenho de Dentro (National Psychiatric Center Pedro II at Engenho de Dentro) in Rio de Janeiro, which opposed aggressive psychiatric techniques such as electroshock.[108] The more direct, "primitive" art produced by children and psychiatric patients was considered by Pedrosa to be intuitive, strong, pure, affective, and analogous to the global impression of gestalt. It was at the Centro Psiquiátrico Nacional that Pedrosa considered the universality of pure form and its relation to modern art in a paper presented at a conference held on March 31, 1947, on the occasion of an exhibition of art by its patients. His text, entitled "Arte, necesidade vital" (Art, a Vital Necessity), referred to the French artist André Lhote's definition of the work of the modern artist as "affective," not reducible to a formula, obeying a "plastic" and "poetic rhythm"—aspects that the Brazilian critic saw as intimately linked to the eruption of the art of Oceania, Africa, India, and pre-Columbian America in the culture of the West.[109]

By 1953, the renewed perception and the nondeterministic dimensions of the art that interested Pedrosa was filtered through the phenomenology of the German philosopher Edmund Husserl. This was articulated in a short text on Paul Klee written for the newspaper *Tribuna da Imprensa*.[110] Here, Pedrosa invoked the Husserlian premise of astonishment required by the phenomenological reduction. Suspending habitual knowledge of the world, the phenomenological reduction aspires to experience the phenomenal world as if for the first time, with no preconceptions that deter us from apprehending the essence of things. Pedrosa identified in Klee—and in the impossibility of categorizing his art—a desire for ignorance, a divesting of knowledge in order to achieve a new understanding of the world. "Klee," the critic wrote, "methodologically strips away the conceptual past so as to be able to . . . situate himself wisely, naked and innocent as a child, before the object, [before] the sensitive thing so that it speaks with its proper language, by itself, without words."[111]

Four years later it would be words—specifically the language of the concrete poets—that would enable the liberation from preconception required by phenomenology. Concrete poetry had emerged forcefully and in tandem with concrete painting during the early 1950s.[112] Stressing the materiality of the word, its presentation, and the support on which it lays, concrete poetry refuted traditional verse and rhythm. The fissure between Paulista concretism and Carioca concretism in the visual arts and poetry, arguably caused by the excessive intellectualism of the São Paulo cohort, was manifest at the time of the first Exposição Nacional de Arte Concreta, which opened in December 1956 at the Museu de Arte Moderna de São Paulo and traveled to the Ministério de Educação e Cultura in Rio de Janeiro in February 1957.[113] In the exhibition, paintings, sculptures, and poems presented as posters were featured side by side to emphasize the close relationship between the visual arts and poetry, a situation reinforced by the active theorization of the movement by poets such as Gullar and Pignatari.

The clash between the ideational and rational stance of the Paulistas and the more intuitive approach of the Cariocas was recorded in two programmatic texts in the *Suplemento Dominical do Jornal do Brazil* in June 1957, one by Haroldo de Campos, entitled "Da fenomenologia da composição à matemática da composição" (From the Phenomenology of Composition to the Mathematics of Composition), and a riposte by Reynaldo Jardim, Ferreira Gullar, and Oliveira Bastos entitled "Poesia Concreta: Uma experiência intuitiva" (Concrete Poetry: An Intuitive Experience).[114] However, an earlier article by Pedrosa, dated February 16, 1957, and published in the recently created visual arts section of the *Jornal do Brasil*, had already delineated the distinctive theoretical fields with which both groups would become identified in future essays and manifestos (although here Pedrosa traced a dividing line between painters and poets more than Paulistas and Cariocas). This short article, entitled "Poeta e pintor concretista" (Concretist Poet and Painter), described the concrete poet's project as a radical decimation of conventional syntax and verse and its "cultivated, erudite, and conceptual" nature. Echoing ideas developed in his dissertation "Da natureza afetiva da forma na obra de arte" and various writings on modern art, Pedrosa argued that the concrete poets sought the "nakedness of perception, the virginity and purity of the initial blow, global, perceptive of gestalts."[115] Here, however, it was the phenomenological basis of Gestalt that Pedrosa invoked. The graphic-spatiality of the poem, he argued, gives it a substantial "formal nucleus" that facilitates the "formal-sensorial experience" of the "poem-object." Contesting the linguistic conventions of meaning, concrete poetry—that of the Paulista Pignatari as well as that of the Carioca Gullar—is "passionately phenomenological." And touching on a fundamental concern that Gullar would develop in his groundbreaking writings on the nonobject, Pedrosa insisted on the disconnecting logic of the concrete word: an object without definition, an object without name—"a composite of sounds and letters, phonemes and diphthongs, bereft of its immemorial logico-connotative functions, of its intrinsic conceptual nature."[116] What remains, he argued, sketching the premise of the Husserlian phenomenological reduction that would preoccupy neoconcretism, is a mere phenomenological object given to direct experience. As in Klee's approach to the sensual world, the concrete poem divested the word of history and conventional meaning. For Pedrosa, the concrete painters, especially the engineer-like calculations of the Paulistas, failed to achieve the perceptual astonishment that the concrete poets realized through their blighted words and spatial poems. He argued that concrete painting pursued "pure intellectuality," "a pure and perfect mental operation," "the precise exteriorization of visuality."[117]

This early assessment of the differences between poetry and painting as practiced by the Cariocas and Paulistas was founded on Pedrosa's rejection of the ideational and conceptual base of concrete painting and his embrace, following the work of the philosophers Ernst Cassirer and Susanne Langer, of intuitive knowledge and the emotional impact of created forms.[118] A series of essays written in 1954 (but not published until 1960) under the general heading of "Problems in Contemporary Art" delineated this broader theoretical horizon, which extended beyond Gestalt and furnished Gullar and the neoconcretists with a renewed understanding of traditional concepts such as expression, signification, and experience.[119] As Otília Beatriz Fiori Arantes has noted in her detailed account of Pedrosa's intellectual trajectory, Cassirer led the way out of gestalt and rejected it as being merely descriptive of representations. Pedrosa wrote that Cassirer was instead concerned with those spiritual processes that create new significations—symbols devoid of predetermined meaning, a synthesis of world and spirit—in which artistic form "presents itself . . . like an apparition that crystallizes into a finished structure, and that renews itself fully and always suddenly each time we enter into contact with it."[120] Breaking away from habit and recognition, the artwork recommences itself with each perception. "The novelty of modern art," concludes Arantes in her comments on Pedrosa and Cassirer, "would be in the fact that it has stopped being simple representation, be it figurative or not: it is in itself form-expression."[121] These are concerns familiar to any careful reader of Gullar's key neoconcrete texts—the "Manifesto Neoconcreto" (1959), "Teoria do não-objeto" (1959), and "Diálogo sobre o não-objeto" (Dialogue on the Nonobject, 1960)—and explain why the poet/critic and the young artists he supported, and who supported him, saw in Pedrosa an ally who supplied them with the tools to undermine the restrictions of Gestalt theory while remaining in dialogue with it.[122]

This rift between functionalism and affect that preoccupied Brazilian critics and artists involved with concretism in 1957 had been evident as early as 1953 during Bill's first visit to Brazil. As the art historian María Amalia García has demonstrated, Bill's state-sponsored trip to Brazil generated great expectations regarding the Swiss artist's opinions on the modern architecture of the country—a field in which Brazilians felt they had excelled, due to great international recognition.[123] But Bill's tripartite formula of form, function, and beauty did not correspond to the sinuous shapes, morphological freedom, decorative inclinations, and freely imported Corbusian grammar of the celebrated Ministério da Educação e Saúde building in Rio de Janeiro (1939–43) or the architectonic complex of Pampulha in Belo Horizonte (1942–44), among other buildings. For Bill, Brazil's failure to devote sufficient resources to the acute problem of social housing rendered these government and upper-class constructions national whims.[124] In response, García points out, Lúcio Costa and Oscar Niemeyer defended the plasticity

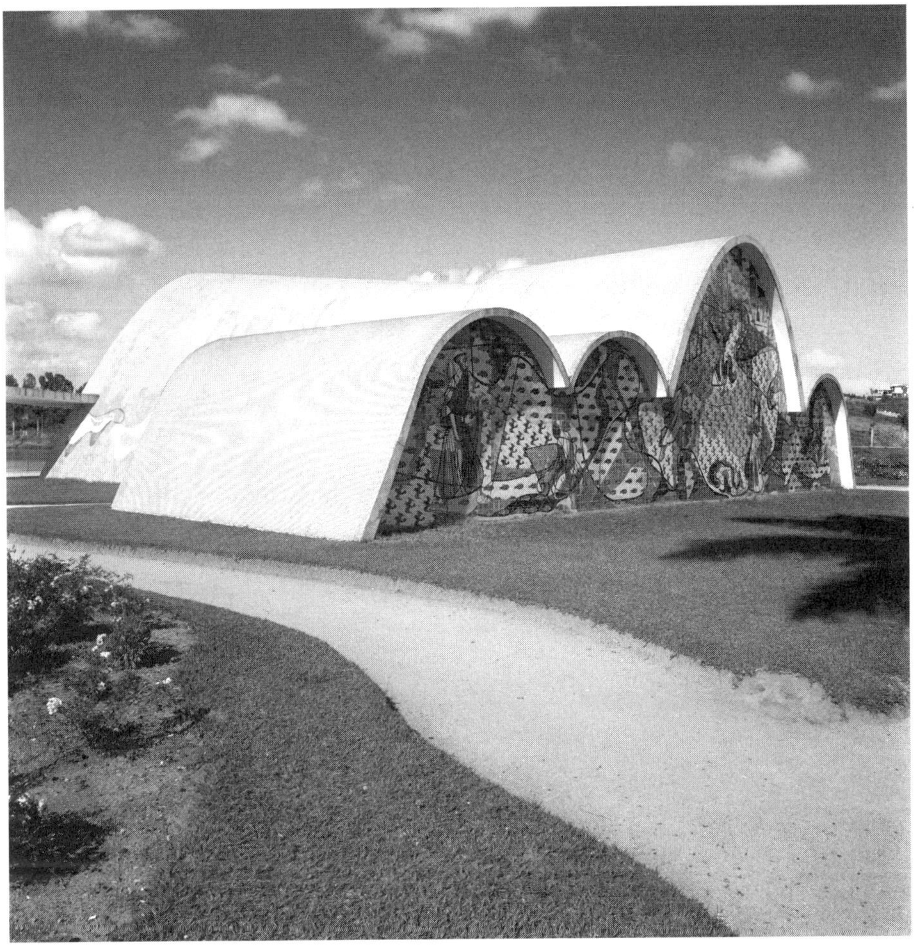

FIGURE 2.6
Marcel Gautherot (photographer), Oscar Niemeyer's Church of Saint Francis of Assisi, Pampulha, Brazil, 1942–44.

of their constructions. Costa in particular alluded to specific artistic elements that Bill had criticized—the blue tiles of the Ministério da Educação e Saúde and the "baroque" configurations of the Igreja de São Francisco de Assis (Church of Saint Francis of Assisi) in Pampulha (fig. 2.6)—as "affective" (the word is García's) negotiations among identity, history, and modern form.[125] As Gullar would a few years later, Costa put the accent on signification and, openly critical of Bill's abstract fascination with harmonious plasticity, argued that "the fundamental goal of art can't be limited to the realization of formal harmonies or *ideas linked or not to numbers*, but must be mainly to create meaningful forms as a function of a specific intention, whether interested or disinterested, and through which our 'human' passion manifests itself" (emphasis added).[126]

Summarizing the tenets of concrete art seven years later, Gullar would underline its ideational core. He cited Bill's notion of art as "the concretion of an idea" and also noted the Argentine artist Tomás Maldonado's procedural methodology: "The creative process of concrete art begins in the *image-idea* (*Bild-idee*) and culminates in the *image-object*."[127] Mathematics, science, and objectivity had become the foundational myth of concrete art, yielding paintings concerned with optical effects and perceptive facts. Thus, Bill's notion of painting as the production of fields of energy with the aid of color seemed to Gullar to generate only variations on "the same physical phenomenon,"[128] a condition that he found consistent with a gestaltic focus on physical form. It was this aesthetic field of the concrete—bracketed on the one hand by the image-object that displays its "sensitive idea" (in Pignatari's words), and on the other a mechanical (to use Gullar's word) approach to the aesthetic act that repressed human signification—that the "Manifesto Neoconcreto" and "Teoria do não-objeto" attacked.

# 3

# FROM WORK TO FRAME, IN BETWEEN, AND BEYOND

## The Topology of the Nonobject, 1959–66

Another dream: inside, which is outside, a window and me. Through this window I want to pass to the outside, which is the inside for me. When I wake up, the window of my room is the one from my dream; the inside I was looking for is the space outside.

LYGIA CLARK, "ABOUT THE ACT," 1965[1]

Inside and outside are inseparable. The world is wholly inside, and I am wholly outside myself.

MAURICE MERLEAU-PONTY,
*THE PHENOMENOLOGY OF PERCEPTION*, 1962[2]

The "Manifesto Neoconcreto" was published on the occasion of the neoconcretists' first exhibition at the Museu de Arte Moderna do Rio de Janeiro, March 19 to April 19, 1959, appearing in a small pamphlet that served as the show's catalogue. It was reprinted in the March 21–22 issue of the *Suplemento Dominical do Jornal do Brasil* (fig. 3.1), which was dedicated to artists active in the fields of painting, sculpture, theater, poetry, and printmaking.[3] The theoretical position of the manifesto was grounded in the value of experience. Neoconcretism rejected "a mechanistic notion of construction"[4] dependent on a unidirectional cause that produced an effect and in which the elements of the work could be traced back to a generative matrix that produced the form. Concomitantly, it postulated a notion of expression that countered the functionalist, rationalist, and theoretical references of much geometric abstraction and contested the preeminence of an objectivist vocabulary in the critical commentary on that body of work. The manifesto proposed "a reinterpretation of neoplasticism, constructivism, and other related movements on the basis of their expressive accomplishments and by prioritizing the work over theory."[5] Echoing Mário Pedrosa's focus on the affective quality of form in his 1949 dissertation "Da natureza afetiva da forma na obra de arte" (On the Affective Nature

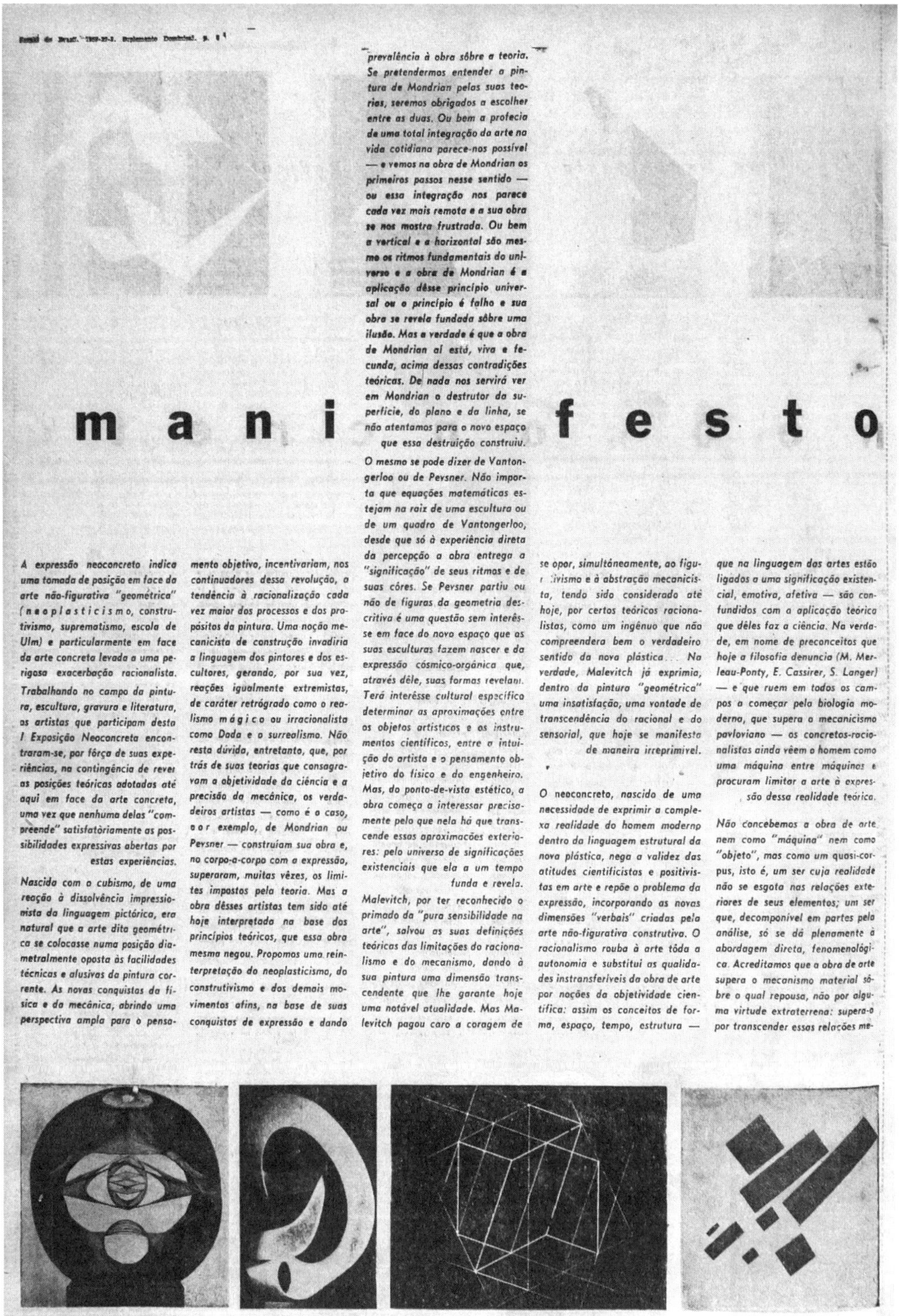

manifesto

A expressão neoconcreto indica uma tomada de posição em face da arte não-figurativa "geométrica" (n e o p l a s t i c i s m o, construtivismo, suprematismo, escola de Ulm) e particularmente em face da arte concreta levada a uma perigosa exacerbação racionalista. Trabalhando no campo da pintura, escultura, gravura e literatura, os artistas que participam desta I Exposição Neoconcreta encontraram-se, por fôrça de suas experiências, na contingência de rever as posições teóricas adotadas até aqui em face da arte concreta, uma vez que nenhuma delas "compreende" satisfatòriamente as possibilidades expressivas abertas por estas experiências.

Nascido com o cubismo, de uma reação à dissolvência impressionista da linguagem pictórica, era natural que a arte dita geométrica se colocasse numa posição diametralmente oposta às facilidades técnicas e alusivas da pintura corrente. As novas conquistas da física e da mecânica, abrindo uma perspectiva ampla para o pensamento objetivo, incentivariam, nos continuadores dessa revolução, a tendência à racionalização cada vez maior dos processos e dos propósitos da pintura. Uma noção mecanicista de construção invadiria a linguagem dos pintores e dos escultores, gerando, por sua vez, reações igualmente extremistas, de caráter retrógrado como o realismo m á g i c o ou irracionalista como Dada e o surrealismo. Não resta dúvida, entretanto, que, por trás de suas teorias que consagravam a objetividade da ciência e a precisão da mecânica, os verdadeiros artistas — como é o caso, p o r exemplo, de Mondrian ou Pevsner — construíam sua obra e, no corpo-a-corpo com a expressão, superaram, muitas vêzes, os limites impostos pela teoria. Mas a obra dêsses artistas tem sido até hoje interpretada na base dos princípios teóricos, que essa obra mesma negou. Propomos uma reinterpretação do neoplasticismo, do construtivismo e dos demais movimentos afins, na base de suas conquistas de expressão e dando prevalência à obra sôbre a teoria. Se pretendermos entender a pintura de Mondrian pelas suas teorias, seremos obrigados a escolher entre as duas. Ou bem a profecia de uma total integração da arte na vida cotidiana parece-nos possível — e vemos na obra de Mondrian os primeiros passos nesse sentido — ou essa integração nos parece cada vez mais remota e a sua obra se nos mostra frustrada. Ou bem a vertical e a horizontal são mesmo os ritmos fundamentais do universo e a obra de Mondrian é a aplicação dêsse princípio universal ou o princípio é falho e sua obra se revela fundada sôbre uma ilusão. Mas a verdade é que a obra de Mondrian aí está, viva e fecunda, acima dessas contradições teóricas. De nada nos servirá ver em Mondrian o destrutor da superfície, do plano e da linha, se não atentamos para o novo espaço que essa destruição construiu.

O mesmo se pode dizer de Vantongerloo ou de Pevsner. Não importa que equações matemáticas estejam na raiz de uma escultura ou de um quadro de Vantongerloo, desde que só à experiência direta da percepção a obra entrega a "significação" de seus ritmos e de suas côres. Se Pevsner partiu ou não de figuras da geometria descritiva é uma questão sem interêsse em face do novo espaço que as suas esculturas fazem nascer e da expressão cósmico-orgânica que, através dêle, suas formas revelam. Terá interêsse cultural específico determinar as aproximações entre os objetos artísticos e os instrumentos científicos, entre a intuição do artista e o pensamento objetivo do físico e do engenheiro. Mas, do ponto-de-vista estético, a obra começa a interessar precisamente pelo que nela há que transcende essas aproximações exteriores: pelo universo de significações existenciais que ela a um tempo funda e revela.

Malevitch, por ter reconhecido o primado da "pura sensibilidade na arte", salvou as suas definições teóricas das limitações do racionalismo e do mecanismo, dando à sua pintura uma dimensão transcendente que lhe garante hoje uma notável atualidade. Mas Malevitch pagou caro a coragem de se opor, simultâneamente, ao figurativismo e à abstração mecanicista, tendo sido considerado até hoje, por certos teóricos racionalistas, como um ingênuo que não compreendera bem o verdadeiro sentido da nova plástica... Na verdade, Malevitch já exprimia, dentro da pintura "geométrica" uma insatisfação, uma vontade de transcendência do racional e do sensorial, que hoje se manifesta de maneira irreprimível.

O neoconcreto, nascido de uma necessidade de exprimir a complexa realidade do homem moderno dentro da linguagem estrutural da nova plástica, nega a validez das atitudes cientificistas e positivistas em arte e repõe o problema da expressão, incorporando as novas dimensões "verbais" criadas pela arte não-figurativa construtiva. O racionalismo rouba à arte tôda a autonomia e substitui as qualidades instransferíveis da obra de arte por noções da objetividade científica: assim os conceitos de forma, espaço, tempo, estrutura — que na linguagem das artes estão ligados a uma significação existencial, emotiva, afetiva — são confundidos com a aplicação teórica que dêles faz a ciência. Na verdade, em nome de preconceitos que hoje a filosofia denuncia (M. Merleau-Ponty, E. Cassirer, S. Langer) — e que ruem em todos os campos a começar pela biologia moderna, que supera o mecanicismo pavloviano — os concretos-racionalistas ainda vêem o homem como uma máquina entre máquinas e procuram limitar a arte à expressão dessa realidade teórica.

Não concebemos a obra de arte nem como "máquina" nem como "objeto", mas como um quasi-corpus, isto é, um ser cuja realidade não se esgota nas relações exteriores de seus elementos; um ser que, decomponível em partes pela análise, só se dá plenamente à abordagem direta, fenomenológica. Acreditamos que a obra de arte supera o mecanismo material sôbre o qual repousa, não por alguma virtude extraterrena: supera-o por transcender essas relações me-

PEVSNER — MAX BILL — ALBERS — MALEVITCH

FIGURE 3.1
"Manifesto Neoconcreto" (Neoconcrete Manifesto) in *Suplemento Dominical do Jornal do Brasil*, March 21–22, 1959.

Jornal do Brasil. 1959-22-3. Suplemento Dominical. p. 5

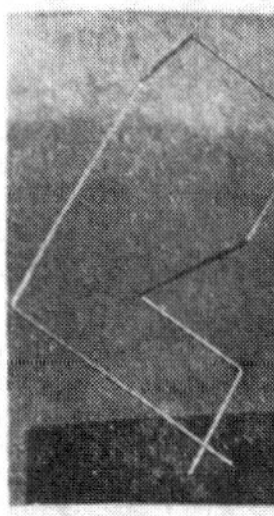

FRANZ WEISSMANN

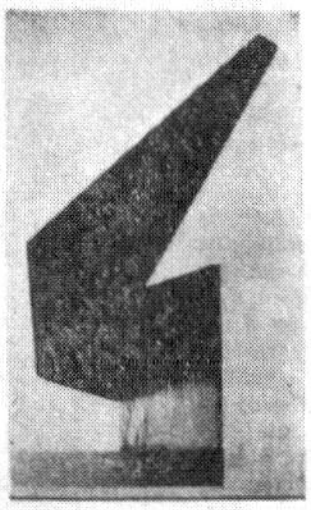

AMILCAR DE CASTRO

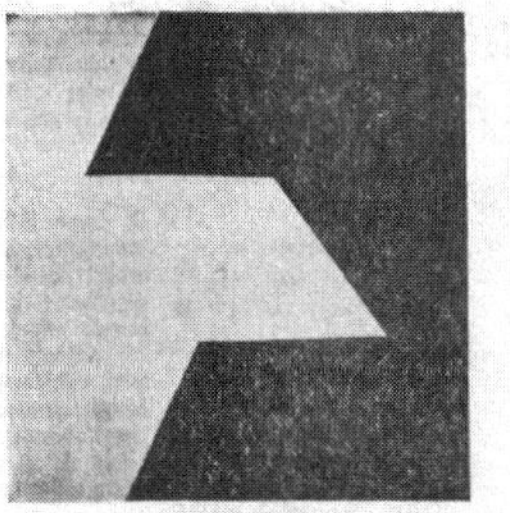

LYGIA CLARK

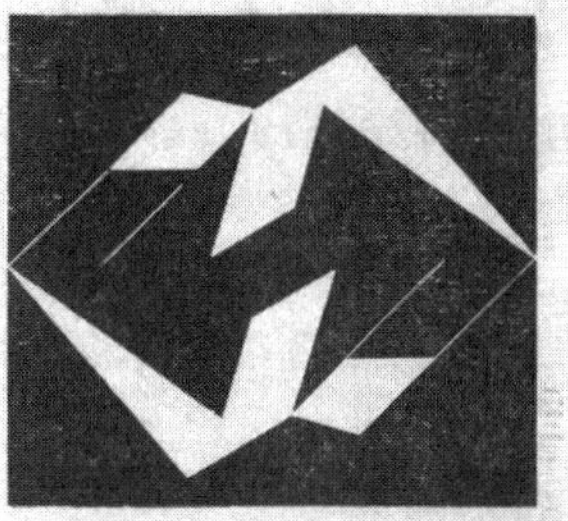

LYGIA PAPE

# n e o c o n c r e t o

*cânicas (que a Gestalt objetiva) e por criar para si uma significação tácita (M. Ponty) que emerge nela pela primeira vez. Se tivéssemos que buscar um símile para a obra de arte não o poderíamos encontrar, portanto, nem na máquina nem no objeto tomados objetivamente, mas como S. Langer e W. Wleidlé, nos organismos vivos. Essa comparação, entretanto, ainda não bastaria para expressar a realidade específica do organismo estético.*

*E' porque a obra de arte não se limita a ocupar um lugar no espaço objetivo — mas o transcende ao fundar nele uma significação nova — que as noções objetivas de tempo, espaço, forma, estrutura, côr, etc., não são suficientes para compreender a obra de arte, para dar conta de sua "realidade". A dificuldade de uma terminologia precisa para exprimir um mundo que não se rende a noções levou a crítica de arte ao uso indiscriminado de palavras que traem a complexidade da obra criada. A influência da tecnologia e da ciência também aqui se manifestou, a ponto de hoje, invertendo-se os papéis, certos artistas, ofuscados por essa terminologia, tentarem fazer arte partindo dessas noções objetivas para aplicá-las como método criativo.*

*Inevitàvelmente, os artistas que assim procedem apenas ilustram noções a priori, limitados que estão por um método que já lhes prescreve, de antemão, o resultado do trabalho. Furtando-se à criação intuitiva, reduzindo-se a um corpo objetivo num espaço objetivo, o artista concreto racionalista, com seus quadros, apenas solicita de si e do espectador uma reação de estímulo e reflexo: fala ao ôlho como instrumento e não ao ôlho como um modo humano de ter o mundo e se dar a êle; fala ao ôlho-máquina e não ao ôlho-corpo.*

*E' porque a obra de arte transcende o espaço mecânico que, nela, as noções de causa e efeito perdem qualquer validez, e as noções de tempo, espaço, forma, côr, estão de tal modo integradas — pelo fato mesmo de que não pré-existiam, como noções, à obra — que seria impossível falar delas como de têrmos decomponíveis. A arte neoconcreta, afirmando a integração absoluta dêsses elementos, acredita que o vocabulário "geométrico" que utiliza pode assumir a expressão de realidades humanas complexas, tal como o provam muitas das obras de Mondrian, Malevitch, Pevsner, Gabo, Sofia Taueber-Arp, etc. Se mesmo êsses artistas às vêzes confundiam o conceito de forma-mecânica com o de forma-expressiva, urge esclarecer que, na linguagem da arte, as formas ditas geométricas perdem o caráter objetivo da geometria para se fazerem veículo da imaginação. A Gestalt, sendo ainda uma psicologia causalista, também é insuficiente para nos fazer compreender êsse fenômeno que dissolve o espaço e a forma como realidades causalmente determináveis e os dá como tempo — como espacialização da obra. Entenda-se por espacialização da obra o fato de que ela está sempre se fazendo presente, está sempre recomeçando o impulso que a gerou e de que ela era já a origem. E se essa descrição nos remete igualmente à experiência primeira — plena — do real, é que a arte neoconcreta não pretende nada menos que reacender essa experiência. A arte neoconcreta funda um novo "espaço" expressivo.*

*Essa posição é igualmente válida para a poesia neoconcreta que denuncia, na poesia concreta, o mesmo objetivismo mecanicista da pintura. Os poetas concretos racionalistas também puseram como ideal de sua arte a imitação da máquina. Também para êles o espaço e o tempo não são mais que relações exteriores entre palavras-objeto. Ora, se assim é, a página se reduz a um espaço gráfico e a palavra a um elemento dêsse espaço. Como na pintura, o visual aqui se reduz ao ótico e o poema não ultrapassa a dimensão gráfica. A poesia neoconcreta rejeita tais noções espúrias e, fiel à natureza mesma da linguagem, afirma o poema como um ser temporal. No tempo e não no espaço a palavra desdobra a sua complexa natureza significativa. A página na poesia neoconcreta é a espacialização do tempo verbal: é pausa, silêncio, tempo. Não se trata, evidentemente, de voltar ao conceito de tempo da poesia discursiva, porque enquanto nesta a linguagem flui em sucessão, na poesia neoconcreta a linguagem se abre em duração. Conseqüentemente, ao contrário do concretismo racionalista, que toma a palavra como objeto e a transforma em mero sinal ótico, a poesia neoconcreta devolve-a à sua condição de "verbo", isto é, de modo humano de presentação do real. Na poesia neoconcreta a linguagem não escorre, dura.*

*Por sua vez, a prosa neoconcreta, abrindo um novo campo para as experiências expressivas, recupera a linguagem como fluxo, superando suas contingências sintáticas e dando um sentido novo, mais amplo, a certas soluções tidas até aqui equivocamente como poesia.*

*E' assim que, na pintura como na poesia, na prosa como na escultura e na gravura, a arte neoconcreta reafirma a independência da criação artística em face do conhecimento objetivo (ciência) e do conhecimento prático (moral, política, indústria, etc.).*

*Os participantes desta I Exposição Neoconcreta não constituem um "grupo". Não os ligam princípios dogmáticos. A afinidade evidente das pesquisas que realizam em vários campos os aproximou e os reuniu aqui. O compromisso que os prende, prende-os primeiramente cada um à sua experiência, e êles estarão juntos enquanto dure a afinidade profunda que os aproximou.*

***AMILCAR DE CASTRO FERREIRA GULLAR FRANZ WEISSMANN LYGIA CLARK LYGIA PAPE REYNALDO JARDIM THEON SPANUDIS RIO, MARÇO, 1959***

of Form in the Work of Art), the signatories of the manifesto denounced the reductive nature of all art that limits itself to representation. By this they meant not only figurative art but also art that stood for, that aimed to represent, rationality, objectivity, the nation, et cetera. Representation, in other words, was alien to neoconcretism, which was concerned with pure appearance—presentation rather than representation.

This chapter concerns the neoconcretist writings of the poet and critic Ferreira Gullar, and specifically his concept of the nonobject. This notion was forged in close dialogue with the work of Lygia Clark and Hélio Oiticica of 1958–61, as well as with the intellectual position staked out by Pedrosa during the preceding years. Neoconcretism distanced itself from earlier iterations of concrete art that emphasized the a priori conceptualization of the work of art and its identification with knowledge associated with mathematics, geometry, and Gestalt theory. The "Manifesto Neoconcreto" posited instead a reconceptualization of expression and the role of the viewer while raising questions about the nature of art and representation. This massive rewriting of the legacies of concrete and constructivist art was aided by the phenomenology of Maurice Merleau-Ponty, whose work, filtered through the poetics of the aesthetic object, led Gullar, Clark, and Oiticica to reject the idea in favor of affective perception. Turning away from the idealistic identification between subject and the object of knowledge claimed by concretism and represented in the concrete work of art, these artists and critics rethought the subject-object relation through the contingency of the perceiving body. They accomplished this, as had the Argentines before them, through a repudiation of the frame, a refutation of the pictorial support as the ground of representation, and a critical engagement with real space.

## UNTHINKING CATEGORIES: QUASI-CORPUS AND SPATIALIZATION

The contemporary writings of Gullar, Clark, and Oiticica make clear that they envisioned not a return to traditional conceptions of expression, but rather the affective reconfiguration of form, space, time, and structure to counter the intellectualism that they identified with recent developments in, and interpretations of, concrete art. Against the rational, scientific, and mathematical "concept" and "idea" manifested in the serial forms and demonstrative propositions of much concrete art, Gullar insisted on "direct perception" as the means of grasping signification. In so doing, he suggested the circumstantial embeddedness of both the work and the spectator in a social, somatic, and psychological matrix that implicitly took into account the work's structural relationship with culture and historical time. The signatories of the "Manifesto Neoconcreto" saw Piet Mondrian and Kazimir Malevich as paradigmatic artists who revealed a gap between the objectivist tenor of their geometric models and the perception of new spaces generated by their actual works. Gullar argued that the work of Malevich—his *Suprematist Painting: Eight Red Rectangles* (1915) was illustrated in the *Suplemento*'s reprint of the manifesto—"expressed a dissatisfaction, a will to transcend the rational and the sensory, that manifests itself in our time in an irrepressible way."[6] It was this dissatisfaction, prompted by the mathematically inspired organization and objectivism of much geometric abstract art, that neoconcretism sought to forestall through an emphasis on bodily perception, intuition, and affect. These concepts were to define the aesthetic matrix of neoconcretism and insisted that the work of art go beyond the material support on which it was grounded because it transcended mechanical relations and objectification. Neoconcretism aspired thus to mobilize geometric forms to generate new spaces and a new mode of expression; losing their objective character, these geometric forms were to become vehicles for the imagination.

Gullar had become familiar with the writings of Merleau-Ponty through Pedrosa, who opened his library to the young poet. The poet-turned-critic remembers reading the French philosopher's work on Paul Cézanne and soon thereafter plunging avidly into his philosophical essays, many of which were available in Spanish.[7] Most likely it was Pedrosa, too, who introduced Gullar to the theories of Ernst Cassirer and Susanne Langer. These three philosophers were seen by Gullar as opposing empiricism and rationalism, and the prejudice against bodily perception and the world of affect. Langer's ideas—expressed in her aesthetic treatise *Form and Feeling*, which Pedrosa regularly invoked in his writings of the 1950s—must have struck a chord among the young Brazilian artists. Her focus on nondiscursive symbolic systems, such as art, favored "significant form" as a manifestation of expression that bespoke the artist's "imagination of feeling." According to this understanding (here Langer was following Cassirer), an art mediated by symbols abstracted from experiential data and transformed by the mind was able to express "the forms of vital experience" better than language (which depends on fixed associations).[8]

To Gullar, Langer's emphasis on "vital function"—which suggested an equivalence between the logic of organic living structures and the life of the work of art—endorsed his rejection of the mechanistic conception of art that he associated with the "concrete-rationalists."[9] "Only life, once put in motion," wrote Langer, "achieves certain forms inevitably, as long as it goes on at all: the acorn becomes an oak, however stunted or varied, the sparrow's egg a sparrow, the maggot a fly."[10] Langer's examples echo the causative unfolding that guided the Swiss artist Jean Arp's *Concretions* of the 1930s, in which a generative set of principles (this time not geometric but morphologically inspired in nature) begets related forms. This perhaps explains why in the "Manifesto Neoconcreto" Gullar was careful not to completely identify the work of art with living organisms: "If we had to find a simile for the work of art, we would . . . not find it in the machine or in the object conceived objectively but, as S. Langer and W. Wleidlé do, in living organisms. This comparison, though, *is not sufficient* to express the specific reality of the aesthetic organism" (emphasis added).[11] Instead, the "aesthetic organism" was defined by Gullar as a *quasi-corpus*—a term that, like *nonobject*, stressed the indeterminacy that infused the Brazilian artists' aesthetic inquiry.

In "Arte Neoconcreta," an essay from 1960, Gullar interpreted the rapport between nature and concrete art in the following way: Theo van Doesburg established a correlation between pictorial forms and the forms of nature that undermined the quest for signification evident in the work of Malevich and Mondrian, a quest that transcended analysis of a work's constituent elements, the purely perceptual, and the privileging of vision. To Gullar, this correspondence between a work of art and, say, a tree posited an objectivist frame of reference that made the relationship between the artist and form equivalent to that between a scientist and nature: removed from a context of signification, the "realist" work of art (as real or as concrete as a tree) is analyzed just as matter is analyzed in a laboratory. Divested of everything imperceptible to vision "by an eye that wants to achieve the precision of a mechanical device, form is reduced to an act of pure perception, without historicity."[12] Clearly distancing the neoconcretist concept of the organic from van Doesburg's equivalence between the concreteness of painting and the concreteness of nature, Gullar wrote, "[H]ere the idealist foundation of concrete art is revealed, in the fact that it conceives of itself above the future, *outside history and contingency*" (emphasis added).[13]

Gullar was determined to reconfigure the organic for neoconcretism. The "Manifesto Neoconcreto" bypassed the organic functionalism of Max Bill's conception of form, which presupposed the functional relation of parts to a whole. Instead, Gullar defined the work of art as neither "a 'machine' nor an 'object,' but rather a *quasi-corpus*—that is, a being whose reality is not limited to the external relationships among its elements; a being that, disassembled through analysis, only delivers itself up wholly through a direct, phenomenological approach."[14] Gullar's "quasi-corpus" was thus opting for proximity with the phenomenal body, which did not correspond to the physical structures of the world (as Gestalt theory argued) but had immanent signification as something experienced by someone, lived rather than known.[15] And, nodding to lessons learned from Pedrosa's 1949 thesis, the "Manifesto Neoconcreto" emphasized the holistic aspect of an artwork's manifestation—that is, the integrated quality of its elements, which cannot be deconstructed or objectively analyzed.

Phenomenology provided Gullar with the vocabulary to convey the affective dimension of the work of art—the difference between the behavior of form in its physical environment and in relation to human perception. Gestalt theory (see chapter 2) usually considers perception under stable conditions. In contrast, Merleau-Ponty defined physical form not as an "element of the world but a limit toward which physical knowledge tends and which it itself defines."[16] Form, therefore, was understood not as a "physical reality" but as an "object of perception"[17] and signification, discontinuous and relational. This interest in the situatedeness of perception went hand in hand with an attempt to go beyond purely formal concerns and the objectivity of time, space, form, structure, and color that were the focus of concrete art. These elements alone, wrote Gullar, cannot account for the specificity of the work of art. They do not preexist the work, but rather are fully integrated within it and cannot be dissected as if they were in a scientific laboratory.[18]

Having dismissed Gestalt theory along with seriality, mathematical permutations, and other a priori methods of composition and construction (which they deemed simple illustrations of an objectivist discourse), the neoconcretists also condemned the sequential temporality and privileging of vision that these compositional strategies implied. The concretist work, says the "Manifesto Neoconcreto," "addresses itself to the eye as an instrument and not as a human way of grasping the world and of giving oneself to it. It addresses itself to the eye-machine and not to the eye-body."[19] In 1960, Gullar—summarizing the basis of neoconcretism—would insist on the interdependence of the sensory organs; that is, how the perception of one organ relied on the experience of others, a condition that produced signification in relation to a general perceptual symbology of the body.[20] This attack on the "eye-machine" and the privileging of vision was accompanied by the crucial concept of "spatialization" elaborated in the manifesto. Spatialization presumed a temporal unfolding of the work in space and highlighted the specific process through which the viewer apprehends the work: "What we mean by spatialization of the work is the fact that it is always making itself present, always recommencing the impulse that generated it and of which the work was the origin. And if this description also takes us back to the first—total—experience of the real, it's because neoconcrete art wants nothing less than to re-create this experience. Neoconcrete art founds a new, expressive 'space.'"[21]

This idealist quest to experience the work "as if for the first time" is an allusion to the phenomenological reduction. This concept, a cornerstone of the German philosopher Edmund Husserl's thinking, refers to the imperative to divest ourselves of conceptualized knowledge in order to experience the world with astonishment and therefore acquire a superior understanding of it. For Merleau-Ponty, since we are enmeshed in the flux of the world, and it is under those conditions that we carry our reflections, a complete reduction is impossible. Indeed, to the French philosopher, a locus from where we might see the world "spread out and completely transparent," an uninterrupted given instead of something that we apprehend situationally and in relation to others, is idealistic. Paralleling this objection was Merleau-Ponty's critique of analytical reflection that aims for "a return to the self" (a movement, he argued, that negates the inside-outside looping of perception). Instead, he proposed that, through reflection, we should discover ourselves in relation to others—we should discover a "weakness standing in the way of [our] being totally individualized: a weakness which exposes [us] to the gaze of others as a man among men or at least as a consciousness among consciousnesses."[22] Merleau-Ponty thus calls for intersubjectivity and historical situatedness, concepts that presided over the aesthetic projects of Clark and Oiticica and that informed the Heideggerian dictum of "being-in-the-world."[23] However, because we are interwoven with the world and others, the only way we can become aware of the world is by suspending our habitual knowledge and expectations, putting them "out of play," and seeing with "wonder."[24] From this, Merleau-Ponty observes, we gain no absolute knowledge, and so we are destined to perpetual beginnings, constant attempts to see anew.

According to this proposition, signification is produced from within the neoconcrete artwork; each encounter with the work would be a new encounter that shunned conventions and any suggested meanings that a techno-scientific discourse might impose on such elements as geometric form, space, line, color, time, and structure. Correspondingly, the "Manifesto Neoconcreto" had warned of "the difficulty of finding a precise terminology to express a world that cannot be reduced to formulae."[25] In sharp contrast to their North American counterparts, who in the 1960s arrived at geometric abstract art under the literalist motto of "What you see is what you see,"[26] neoconcrete artists proposed a multidimensional space that went against the realist premise of concrete art (aesthetic form = physical form) and the privileging of visuality.[27] As Pedrosa had suggested when writing about Paul Klee in 1953, the confrontation between subject and object requires conceptual nakedness and the innocence of a child.[28] This idealistic core of neoconcretism, which aspired to bypass all mediation, was to be shaken by the increased entanglement with real space and the body of the viewer in the works of Clark and Oiticica.

## THE "THREAD" OF SPACE

The "Teoria do não-objeto" (Theory of the Nonobject; see fig. 0.1) was a crucial conceptual tool for the emerging Brazilian avant-garde and is fundamental to understanding the experiments with space and the spectator that engaged Lygia Clark and Hélio Oiticica from 1959 on.[29] A text on Clark's work written by Gullar in 1958 posits the themes that he would develop in subsequent texts. In this landmark analysis, Gullar set out to chart the implications of Clark's treatment of the frame and the plane in works produced since 1954. A group of pieces entitled *Quebra da moldura* (Breaking the Frame, 1954) explored geometric form and compositional alternations and inversions associated with concrete art. These works, however, incorporated the frame into the composition through the use of color, extending it to the edge of the support-frame in a nonhierarchical fashion that threatened the center-periphery binary that characterizes conventional painting. This suggested a move outside the boundaries of the picture plane and a rejection of its traditional role as the container of a representation.

This simple gesture by Clark led Gullar to situate her efforts between two extremes: one affirming the surface as the foundational element of painting, and the other attempting to transcend its bidimensionality.[30] The tension between these poles, according to Gullar, led Clark to dismiss the surface—bracketed and protected by the neutral, mediatory frame—as a given element. In abandoning the frame, the boundary between the symbolic and the material was blurred, with form and expression thus emerging from the same source. In other words, the support of the painting was not treated as a container but as a material reality that had become the locus of creative work, now identified with the action of the artist. As a consequence, the formal-spatial experience realized in the painting was affected by the "relation [of the] artist [to the] world that is inherent in the act of painting."[31] Foreseeing the entanglement with everyday space that was to be essential to the nonobject, Gullar wrote, "[W]hen I break with the frame . . . pictorial space evaporates, the surface of what was 'painting' falls to the level of common things, and this particular pictorial surface becomes somehow equivalent with that of this door or that wall."[32] To Gullar, however, Clark's works from 1954–55 continued to operate on the painterly signifier (support and frame), as if this pictorial signifier "were a significant entity whose 'essence' [is] indissolubly linked to those [two] material elements."[33] Frame and support were still distinct in these works, and so, Gullar argued, a center/periphery relationship prevailed. It was only when the artist eliminated this material hierarchy that pure surface was restored—and traditional pictorial (fictional) space was defeated.

A subsequent group of works known as *Superfícies moduladas* (Modulated Surfaces, 1955–56) did away with frames entirely and continued this deconstruction of the center/periphery hierarchy. Early works in this series, such as the one reproduced in the catalogue of the second Grupo Frente exhibition, *Superfície modulada no. 4* (later known as *Superfície modulada no. 2,* 1955), involve rectilinear patterns of color that echo the shape of the support and visually dynamize the surface. A later work, *Superfície modulada no. 20* (1956; plate 11), features a modular configuration of angular rhythms delineated on a precut wooden surface, painted with industrial paint probably applied with a spray gun.[34] This work and others in this series feature patterns that echo the all-over decorative quality of textiles. To Gullar, the "line-space" that operated between frame and pictorial support in Clark's previous works—acknowledged in two works entitled *Descoberta da linha orgánica* (Discovery of the Organic Line, 1954)—was now the element that determined the structure of the picture, tracing or incising the wooden support from edge to edge. Indeed, in an analysis of this early phase of her work, Clark herself noted: "In 1956, I discovered the relationship between this line (which was not graphic) and the seams joining doors and frames, windows, and materials that make up a floor, etc. I called it the 'organic line' because it was real, it existed in itself, organizing space. It was a *line-space,* a fact that I would only come to understand later on. I took a job as an apprentice in a modeler's workshop and began to make models in which this line became the graphic-spatial module of a whole environment" (emphasis added).[35]

The decentering of the *Superfícies moduladas,* without frames or a central point around which representation coheres, removed these works from painting's function as container and enclosure; their dynamic patterns and play of colors appear closer to decorative mural painting than to easel painting. Moreover, as Gullar observed, this breakdown of boundaries emphasized "continuity between the space in which [the artist] realizes his or her work as a painter and the space in which the work of someone who paints a wall takes place."[36] In Clark's view, the two-dimensional surface was the support upon which the artist expressed something, whereas the *Superfícies moduladas* were constructed in order to express space itself. As early as 1956 she made a distinction between the expression of an individual artwork and the mode of expression articulated in the works (then called concrete) that occupied her at the time. The latter were defined by the organic line, which was associated with the patterns that structure materials such as wood and textiles and the functional seams between doors and walls, which, in her paintings, determined the various rhythms of the surface while aspiring to environmental integration realized in the context of architecture.[37]

Indeed, the modular, mural-like configurations of these paintings were influenced by the discourse on the integration of the arts, of which, according to Gullar, Clark, and Oiticica, Mondrian was a pioneer. The leap into real space made by Clark's works was, argued Gullar, a consequence of the visual literalness of concrete painting. With painting freed from its traditional representational role, painters could not reduce the medium to the tautological task of organizing and reorganizing pictorial elements and surface and thus indulging in a purely technical and formal activity. Instead, as a result of this representational crisis, the picture demanded to be integrated into real space.[38] Clark's works from the mid-1950s, then, must be seen in dialogue with three wooden models for interiors that she exhibited at the second Grupo Frente exhibition, which opened on July 14, 1955, at the Museu de Arte Moderna do Rio de Janeiro. In *Maquete para interior* (Maquette for Interior, 1955; fig. 3.2), for example, the walls feature abstract color schemes in modules that activate the surface of the enclosing partitions, which include two doorlike openings. The model's nonhierarchical geometric scheme evades analysis of form in relation to function. Clark's intention, she explained in 1956, was to transpose the individual expressive dimension of the artwork to the collective environmental space of architecture.[39] Concrete painting, devoid of the traditional representational function of the medium, could now achieve the harmonious rhythms of abstraction in real space. Instead of representing the individual expression of the artist, concrete painting existed in real space to make the "environment" "expressive in itself."[40] This notion of real, architectural space—charged with connotations of use, bodily interaction, and materiality—informed the role ascribed to the "line-space" as a mediating hinge between pictorial space and everyday space.

Clark's *Superfícies moduladas* and her subsequent *Planos em superfície modulada* (Planes on Modulated Surface, 1956–57) series were created in dialogue with the various compositional schemes explored by contemporary concrete artists in Brazil. Modular compositions and, later, complementary patterns formed the basis of Clark's plastic vocabulary, which by 1957, she explained, had rejected purely optical space in favor of what she called "ambivalent tensions."[41] An early group from the series *Planos em superfície modulada* features mesmerizing virtual volumes. Studies for these works were made in graphite and painted in with tempera. Another group of gouache-on-paper works systematically alternate the colors of the planes in two virtual cubic "reliefs," generating spatial ambivalences that destabilize the figure-ground relationship that is crucial to representation (plate 12).

Clark acknowledged that these works realized with industrial paint on wooden panels, and others from the same series conceived first as studies made of cut and pasted

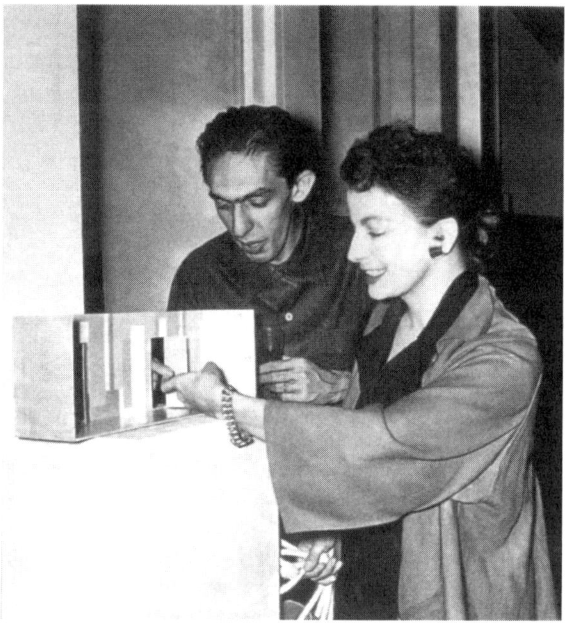

FIGURE 3.2
Lygia Clark and Ferreira Gullar with *Maquete para interior* (Maquette for Interior) at the second exhibition of Grupo Frente, 1955.

cardboard, were influenced by Josef Albers's *Structural Constellations* (initiated in 1949 and continued into the early 1960s), which she admired but found limiting due to their conventional presentation: a linear configuration centered in an open space rather than a composition extending to the edge of the support.[42] Albers's complex spatial structures were initially explored in drawings and prints, and their final material resolution—engraved on vinyl and Formica panels—dismissed many of the conventions of painting, including, as Brenda Danilowitz has observed, the frame (fig. 3.3).[43] In a review of Clark's works at the 1957 São Paulo Bienal, Pedrosa too argued that Albers's *Structural Constellations* preserved the centrality of the pictorial field and thus tacitly supported the role of the frame.[44] Likewise, Gullar wrote that, despite the "lucid graphicness"[45] of Albers's works, their axonometric play of space was achieved by delineating a central configuration over a background.[46] This was a key point: Clark, Pedrosa, and Gullar regarded the *Structural Constellations* highly but seemed to agree that they did not fully engage the overall pictorial surface and remained dependent on a figure-ground relationship. One of the *Structural Constellations* was illustrated in the "Manifesto Neoconcreto" (1959), and another appeared in a 1960 article on "Albers and Others" written by Gullar in the *Suplemento Dominical do Jornal do Brasil*.[47] Significantly, it is unlikely that Clark had seen these works firsthand. Had she encountered them, she would have seen that the incising line of the *Structural Constellations* echoed her own line-space. She would have also noticed that Albers's machine-engraved laminated plastic supports were backed with solid wooden boards, raising them off the wall slightly and into the space of the viewer. Instead, probably relying on available reproductions, Clark focused

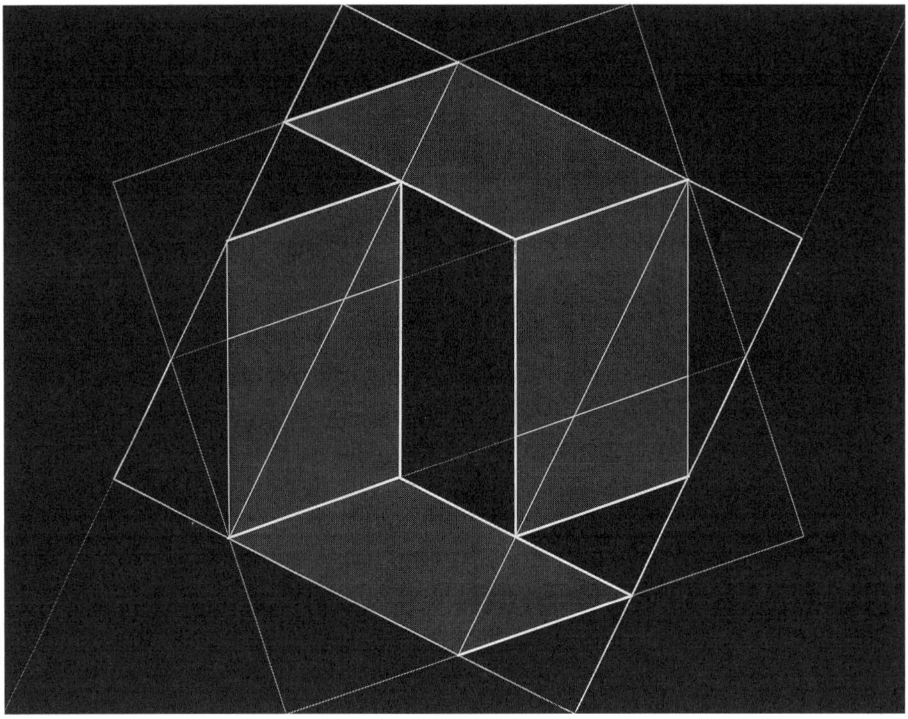

FIGURE 3.3
Josef Albers, *Structural Constellation, Transformation of a Scheme No. 12,* 1950, machine-engraved plastic laminate mounted on wood, 17 × 22½ in.

on the ambivalent "multidimensional" space generated by Albers's linear geometric constellations—"solids graphically hollowed out,"[48] as she called them.

The words of Frederick A. Horowitz regarding Gestalt theory's influence on Albers's teaching are instructive here, as they provide a larger context for Clark's own reading of Albers's work as multidimensional: "Motivated by Gestalt investigations into the figure-ground relationship, Albers led his students beyond thinking of a drawing or design only as the lines or shapes or colors they saw on a page, training them instead to recognize that the adjacent areas—the surrounds and in-betweens—were also a part of what they saw."[49] Responding to these investigations, Clark pursued the creation of ambivalent spaces through an "all-over" structure that made the edge of the painting a porous zone between inside and outside, pictorial space and real space.[50] For her, the dissolution of hierarchical composition through a treatment of the whole surface, an engagement with the edge of the canvas, and the incising line-space that structured these works were all strategies that resulted from her dismissal of the frame and her consequent interest in real space and the viewer. However, like Albers, she exploited the relational space suggested by Gestalt: the fluctuation of figure and ground and the eye's capacity to see volume where none existed.[51] Interestingly, in notes concerning her 1957 production under the heading "Albers's Influence," she wrote that the first *Superfícies moduladas* sprang from this virtual exploration of shape, which she understood not in Gestaltic terms but as a manifestation of a "topological-spatial equivalence between positive and negative space."[52] Indeed, rather than pursuing the clarity of figure over ground that the most important law of Gestalt postulates, Clark probed the ambivalence of shape and space through the equivalence of form. This was essentially a rejection of the space of representation, the background against which form emerges in all its clarity.

The twenty-four works presented by Clark in an exhibition at Galeria de Arte das Folhas of São Paulo in September 1958 included *Studo para superfície modulada no. 1* (Study for Modulated Surface no. 1, 1957), *Planos em superfície modulada nos. 2, 3, 5, 6, 7, 8,* (1957), *Planos em superfície modulada série B nos. 2–6* (1958), *Espaço modulado* (Modulated Space) *nos. 1–6* (1958), and *Unidades* (Units) *nos. 1–6* (1958). These works are made of plywood on Duratex (wooden panels made by the Brazilian company of that name) and industrial paint applied by spray gun, a technique that Clark introduced around 1955 or 1956, which further signaled her departure from traditional painting. The works of *Planos em superfície modulada série B* were widely reproduced at the time in the press and in exhibition catalogues. These pieces involve starkly simple jigsaw-puzzle-like arrangements of two complementary shapes in black and white (fig. 3.4). The resulting flat surface avoids the figure-ground problem and revolves around a mutual dependency between the black and the white forms.[53] With their graphic dynamism, pulsations, equivalence of form, and rejection of the frame and the support as containers for representation, these works were seen by Pedrosa, Gullar, and Clark herself as engaging (in contrast to most concrete painting) with the edge of the support and its surrounding space and suggested a move away from pure opticality and spectatorial distanciation that was key for the artist. Indeed, by 1957 Clark stated that she did not consider herself a concrete artist. Taking a stand against the serial configurations privileged by concrete art—which, to Clark, presupposed an external, part-by-part reading—she argued, prophetically, that her works demanded the direct participation of the spectator: "[One does] not see it (in the purely optical sense), but *feels* it."[54] Emphasizing what Clark had called a topological-spatial equivalence, Pedrosa argued that in these works perceptual tensions between what was inside the pictorial surface and what was outside caused space to expand and recede, to curve and grow. Advancing the conceptual matrix that would inform the "Manifesto Neoconcreto," he wrote that Clark's "painting, in opposition to the purely optical sensorial, reveals itself as a space composed of vectors that allow us to perceive it affectively and phenomenologically, and not just sensorially."[55]

The first piece listed in the catalogue for the exhibition at Galeria de Arte das Folhas was *Planos em superfície modulada no. 1* (Planes on Modulated Surface no. 1, 1957; fig. 3.5), a multipart wooden panel painted white. The central incising line that cuts diagonally across the surface is the indisputable axis of the work. Here, the line-space—the seam between the panels, Clark's "organic line"—acquires a more palpable physicality, a

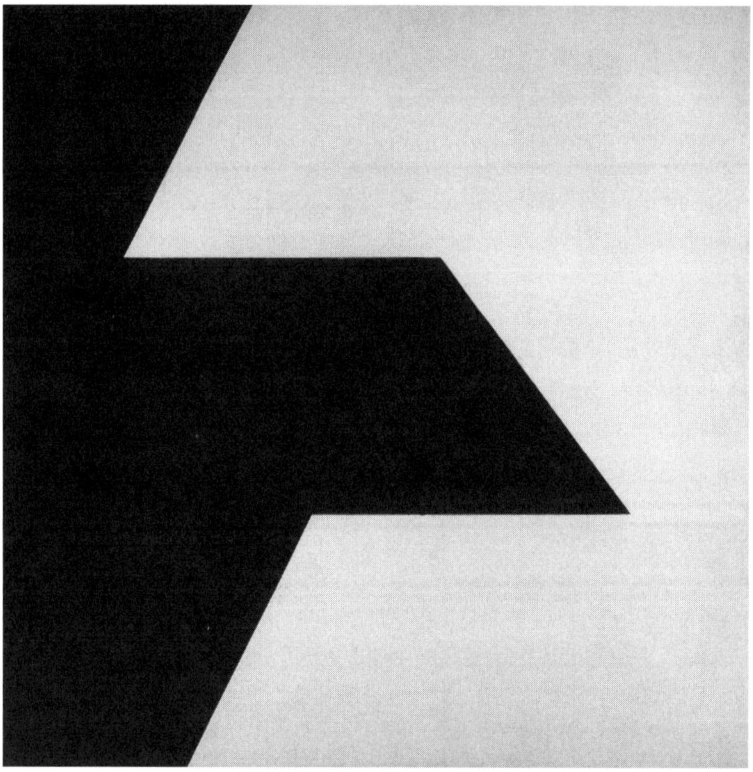

FIGURE 3.4
Lygia Clark, *Planos em superfície modulada B, no. 1* (Planes on Modulated Surface B, no. 1), 1958, industrial paint on wood, 33¹⁄₁₆ × 33¹⁄₁₆ in.

cut that asserts the spatial materiality of the line to a hitherto unexplored degree. In this work, the line-space renders the graphic operation of spatial delineation obsolete and announces the pictorial support of representation as a farce. The insertion of real space into the assembled work would, from this point on, signal the porous relationship between inside and outside in Clark's art and incorporated, in Gullar's words, a "temporal nucleus" that affects our perception of the work. Suggesting the concept of "spatialization" that would become a key concept in the "Manifesto Neoconcreto," Gullar stated that here space becomes a vehicle of time, while time reveals space.[56]

According to Gullar, this intertwining of time and space was most effective in two series realized by Clark in 1958 (both included in the Galeria de Arte das Folhas exhibition): *Espaço Modulado* (Modulated Space), consisting of quadrangular modules organized vertically in groups of three, and *Unidades* (Units), consisting of individual modules measuring thirty by thirty centimeters (fig. 3.6).[57] Initially conceived as maquettes on cardboard, the completed works of spray-painted wood feature backings that push them out from the wall and cast discreet shadows around the works[58]—a detail rarely

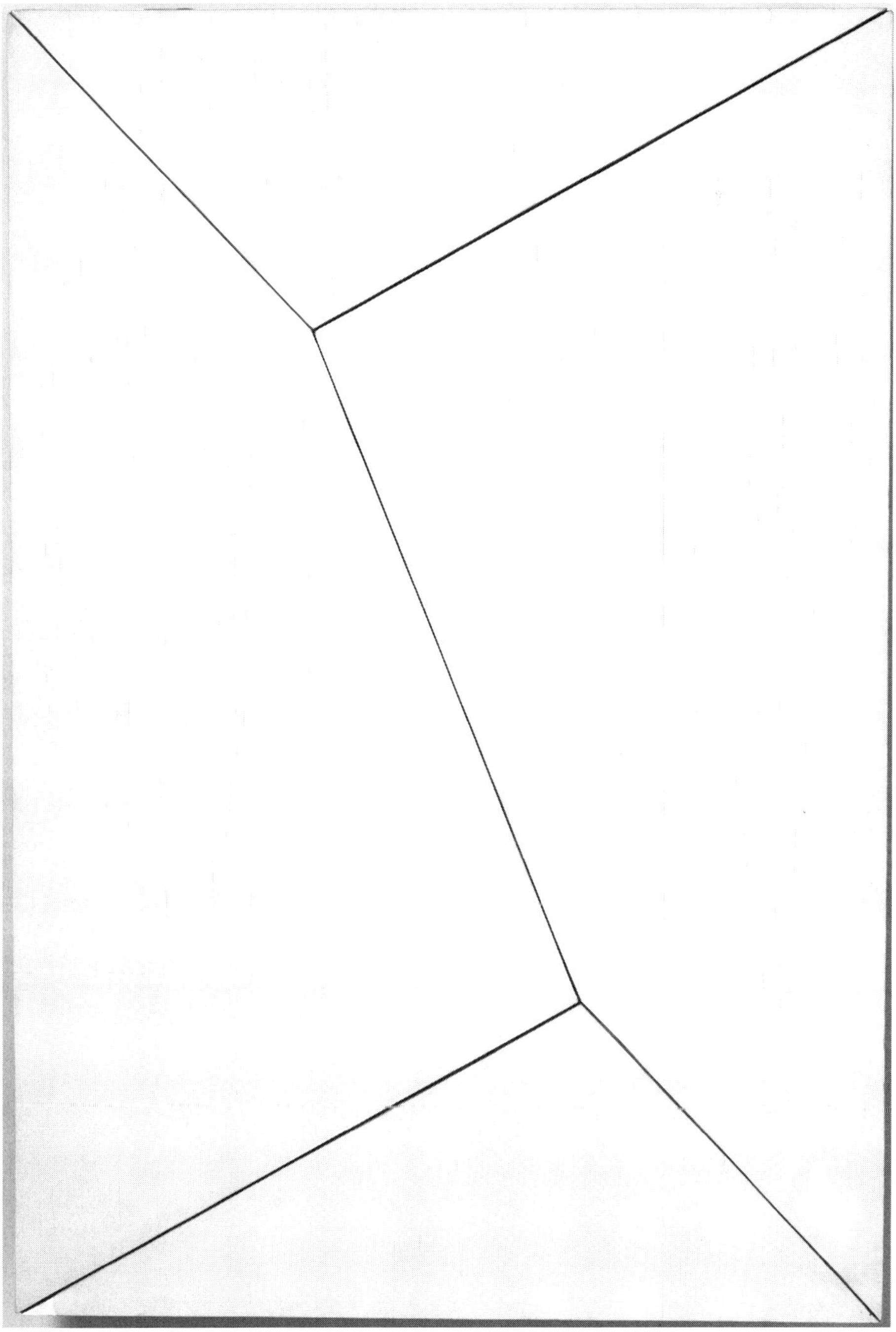

FIGURE 3.5
Lygia Clark, *Planos em superfície modulada no. 1* (Planes on Modulated Surface no. 1), 1957, industrial paint on wood, 43¼ × 23⁹⁄₁₆ × ⅜ in.

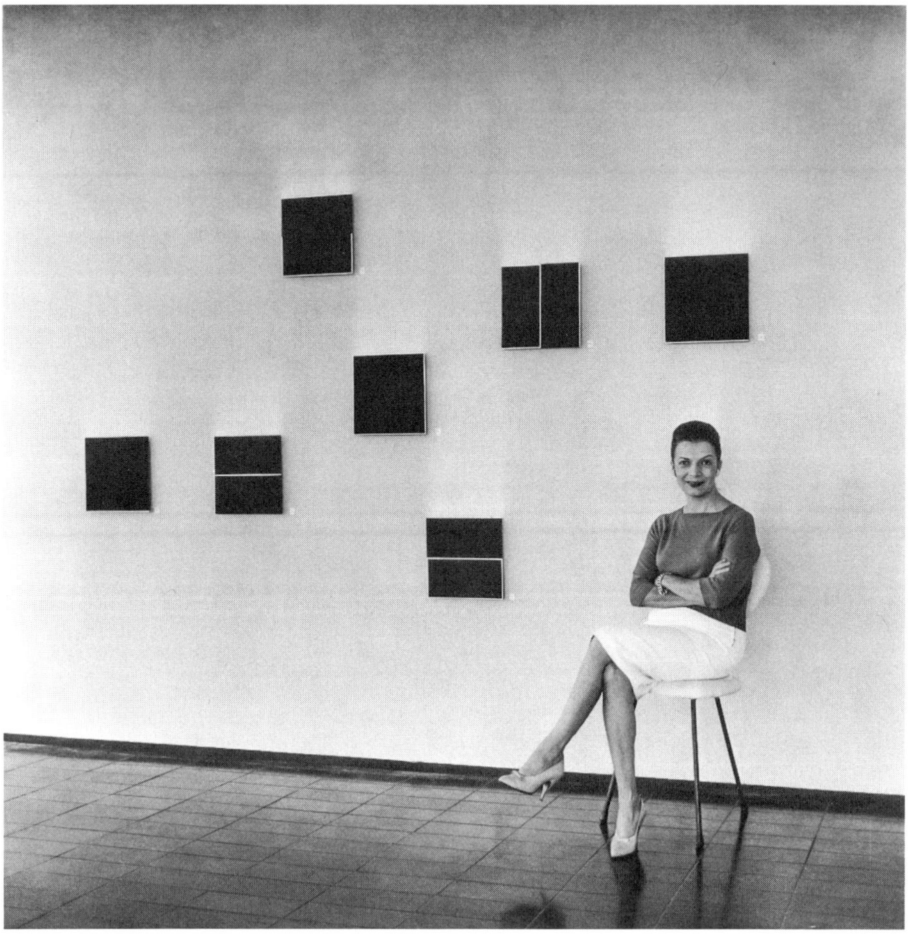

FIGURE 3.6
Lygia Clark with *Unidades no. 1–7* (Units no. 1–7), 1958, 11⅞ × 11⅞ each, depth varies.

evident in the photographic record. Of these works Gullar wrote, "This black canvas is the physical record of a precise duration that is the time in which that square was realized."[59] The work was thus identified with the action (in time) of the artist and suggested to Gullar a sort of plenitude, a longed-for identification between the creative act and the created work that was to be complicated by the inevitable contingency and ambiguity implied by the artwork's involvement with time and real space.[60]

Clark added a painted white line that defined the edges of the modules of the vertical surfaces of the *Espaço Modulado*; equivalent to the "line-space," here she called it "line-light"[61] or "line-time" (plate 13).[62] This line bisects or inscribes the border of the quadrilateral modules of the works, visually altering slightly the shape and size of these otherwise materially identical supports. Regarding these effects, Clark wrote: "An oblique tension automatically emerges when the external line penetrates the interior space of the surface, which is always black. Absolutely equal horizontal and vertical lines produce between them an oblique tension that distorts the square: the space is then revealed as a moment of the surrounding space."[63]

The perceptual ambivalences created by this white "line-time" fascinated Clark; the line broke down the invariable pace of a regular sequence of forms existing on the same level with respect to the pictorial plane. Clark identified the prescribed pace of a sequence of shapes or forms with seriality and associated it with mechanical time and a contemplative spectatorial position facilitated by the use of the pictorial surface as support and container: "Faced with a seriated composition, there is the spectator and the work. [The spectator] situates him/herself away from it and remains there . . . using each form as a starting point and a point of arrival."[64] In contrast, the modulated space Clark created in her works via the white "line-time" was a "time-space" that mediated the relation between form (black surface) and surrounding space—that is, this "line-time" altered form and stressed its porosity with the surrounding space while attempting to go beyond the static nature of the pictorial plane.[65]

To the Brazilian critic Ricardo Nascimento Fabbrini, writing one of the first monographs on Clark, the organic line—and by extrapolation the "line-time" or "line-light"—introduced difference, a rupture, rather than identity, as had been suggested by Gullar's desire for a correspondence between creative process and created work. To Fabbrini, the organic line was a spatial interval that celebrated incompleteness and withdrawal from the pretension of a "totalizing *logos*": "Inserting the outside inside, [the organic line] breaks with the unity of [the work's] material foundation. Like an ellipsis, it indicates an absence that marks the impossibility of self-presence in representation, of a plenitude of presence."[66] Suggesting the overlapping of the phenomenological with a critique of representation that is at the core of these aesthetic investigations, Fabbrini described the organic line as a trace that retains a loss. The penetration of real space into the work signified by the organic line hints at a suspension of the artist's presence in representation—problematizing not only the concept of the artwork as a stand-in for something else (such as an idea or a feeling) but also the projective nature of representation, the means by which the subject recognizes him- or herself in the object produced.

Indeed, a close reading of texts and works by Clark and Oiticica during this period reveals that one of the issues at stake was the dismantling of the classical structure of representation, a process triggered by a rejection of the ideation of concrete art and the conventions of painting and sculpture and by the neoconcretists' interest in the affective dimension of the work of art.[67] This attack on the logic of representation was pursued through the various formal and spatial reversals Clark and Oiticica employed in their works, including the interval and the fold (outgrowths of the "line-space")—strategies that mediated the relationship between the work and the viewer rather than facilitating identification between work and artist. In discarding the plane as a container, these works dismissed projection as the foundation of artistic subjectivity. Clark's well-known

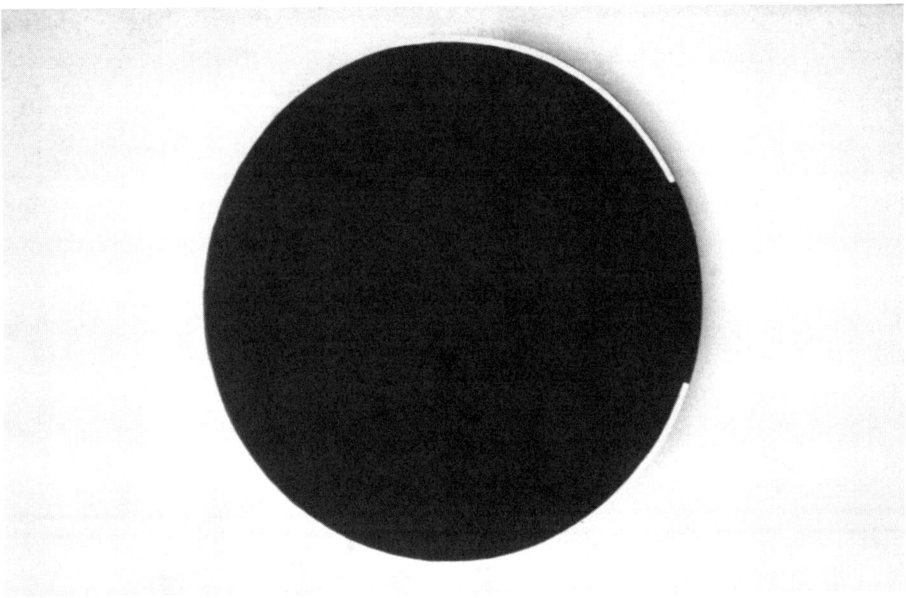

FIGURE 3.7
Lygia Clark, *Ovo linear* (Linear Egg), 1958, industrial paint on wood, 11⅞ × 11⅞.

*Ovo linear* (Linear Egg, 1958; fig. 3.7) operates heuristically, almost as a riposte to the Gestaltic exercises of the Paulistas, which remained dependent on the pictorial plane as the repository of an insightful visual/conceptual proposition. The work is also emblematic of Clark's grasp of topological space and her rejection of static form by deflecting attention from the plane and toward the edge of the painting.

Topology is defined by *Encyclopaedia Britannica* as a "branch of mathematics, sometimes referred to as 'rubber sheet geometry,' in which two objects are considered equivalent if they can be continuously deformed into one another through such motions in space as bending, twisting, stretching, and shrinking while disallowing tearing apart or gluing together parts. The main topics of interest in topology are the properties that remain unchanged by such continuous deformations."[68] The clearest image provided by the Britannica is of a doughnut that is transformed into a cup. Because both the doughnut and the cup have one hole (the doughnut's hole and the cup's handle), either one could, if they were made of malleable clay, be transformed into the other without cutting. The Möbius strip—an example as poetic as the cup-doughnut is prosaic—is another figure of topology. It is made by giving a rectangular strip of paper a half twist and fastening the ends together. The resulting continuous surface, with no inside and no outside, can be split into linked loops when cut down the middle. This spatial malleability attracted Clark to the figure of the Möbius strip, which she invoked as early as 1959 to explain her attack on the frontal plane of traditional painting. This figure of topology had gained great currency in the Brazilian artistic milieu with the visibility of Max Bill's *Tripartite Unity* (1948–49; see fig. 2.2) at the first São Paulo Bienal in 1951, and it allowed Clark to complicate spatial boundaries and form with radical consequences for her aesthetic enterprise.

In some ways *Ovo linear* is Clark's most didactic work. A black wooden circle is edged by a painted white line that is interrupted on the right side, suggesting the flow of the pictorial plane into real space. Elaborating on this visual metaphor, she wrote that *Ovo linear* was realized in real space by means of the line-space (or line-time), which merged with the white wall and distorted its edges, disrupting the perception of enclosed form. Once the background plane has been destroyed, she observed, what remains is "the thread of the space," or a "cut in real space."[69] This "cut in real space" implied an attack on the figure-ground foundation of representation—one equivalent to the twisting of the plane to create the Möbius strip. By bleeding into the wall instead of remaining on a pictorial background, *Ovo linear* could not obey Gestalt's law of closure, which states that we ignore gaps and complete broken contours to yield familiar forms. Clark considered the plane an arbitrary, false way of organizing space (the locus of representation), and she aimed to destroy it through this twisting that undid its false spatial coordinates. "A line," she wrote years later, allegorizing this abandonment of the plane of representation, "can only be the 'thread' of space when in contact with external space."[70] She continued, explaining the lessons derived from the Möbius strip, by asserting that time and space were one, and were only separated when the "thickness of space" (*espessura do espaço*) was considered a simple geometric form and not a "surface process" (*superfície-processo*). The twisting of the Möbius strip cuts through space and activates it, she argued.[71] In other words, if the pictorial plane is an abstract concept upon which the artist projects a static, ideal form that facilitates self transparent thought, then the Möbius strip destroys that plane with its false delimitations of high and low, front and back.[72] The "thread of space" now turned "surface process" categorically rejected the plane as a container and the projective nature of representation, thrusting Clark's work into the spatiotemporal dimensions of the nonobject and its antinominalist agenda.

## DISMEMBERED GEOMETRY

Gullar's writings on the nonobject—a term arguably prompted by one of Clark's works, which he described in the 1980s as a "dismembered picture"[73]—further delineated the aesthetic template that Clark and Oiticica embraced during this period of profound questioning of the status of the art object and the viewer. In this later interview Gullar also used the word *troço* to qualify the inspiring work, a slang term that in Portuguese signifies an undefined thing, something, stuff. He further explained that this *troço* was made of panels of layered wood, some white and some black.[74] It is unclear which specific work triggered Gullar's reflections, but by October 1959, when Gullar wrote in the press about an exhibition of neoconcrete art in Bahia, Clark had already embarked

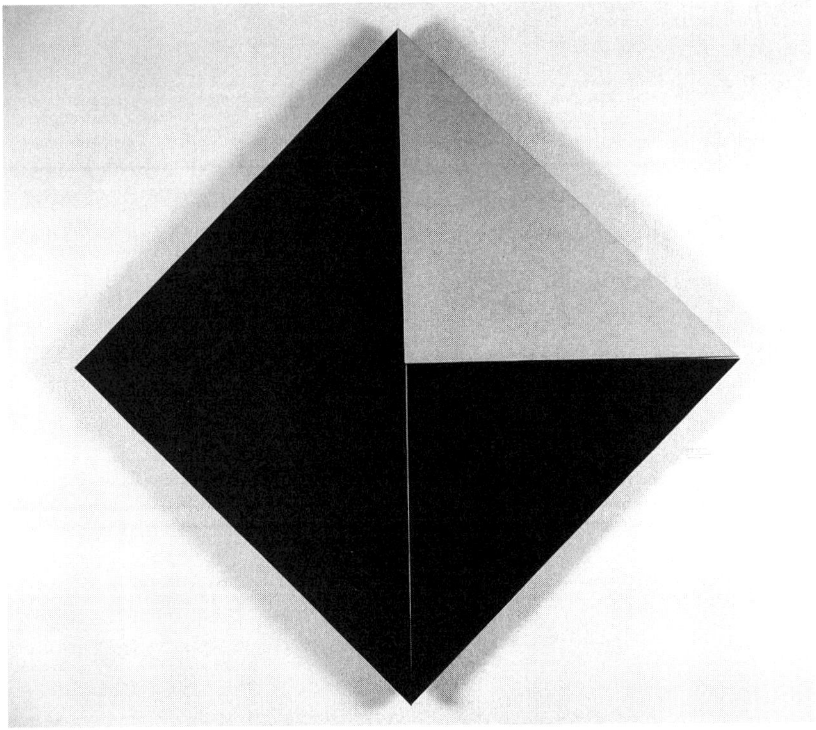

FIGURE 3.8
Lygia Clark, *Contra-relevo* (Counterrelief), 1959, industrial paint on wood, 55⅛ × 55⅛ × 1 in.

on works that the critic identified as neither painting nor relief nor sculpture.[75] He might have been referring to experiments that led to the *Contra-relevos* (Counterreliefs; fig. 3.8), works whose layered structure dismissed the unity and identity of the pictorial support and evaded definitions related to painting (flatness), sculpture (mass), and relief (which presupposes a background surface). Displayed in a lozenge-shaped configuration, the wooden panels of the *Contra-relevos* generate rectilinear configurations in black and white. They vary in scale (reaching sizes of more than a meter) and, when seen frontally, disclose little about their nature, rejecting as they do the planar dimension that structures traditional painting. Thus, as the critic Paulo Herkenhoff has written, the *Contra-relevos* demand a lateral reading that addresses the thickness of the support and discloses a tension between concealment and revelation.[76] This disruption of the surface is not only an attempt to undermine the notion of the pictorial support as a container (and the viewer's visual mastery of the object), but also a move beyond the boundaries of painting as a space of inscription and containment.[77]

Works by Marcel Duchamp, the neoconcrete sculptor Amilcar de Castro, and Lygia Clark (represented by the early *Superfície modulada no. 1* of 1955) were reproduced in "Teoria do não-objeto" when it was published in 1959. Why the inspiring "dismembered picture" was not reproduced with these other works is an intriguing question, as two months before the essay was published, Gullar had described works from the Bahia exhibition in "nonobject" terms. Moreover, Gullar's October 1959 review of the Bahia show is consistent with comments made by Clark in a letter to her friend Luiz de Almeida Cunha, a diplomat and critic, of October 7, 1959, where she was at pains to convey her artistic trajectory, calling her current work "modulated reliefs" (*relevos modulados*), which, she clarified, had everything to do with her own research and nothing to do with traditional conceptions of that medium. In these pieces, Clark wrote, she had returned to color; she mentioned reliefs that were all red, all white, and black and white and "made of cut wood and 'piled up' on top of each other"—a technique that suggests the material and technical specificities of the *Contra-relevos*.[78] The line-time of the *Espaços modulados* and *Unidades*, she added in this letter, "moves in these reliefs to the edge of the surface."[79] And, echoing Tomás Maldonado's hesitations about a leap from painting into sculpture, she continued: "I am one step away from sculpture, but I'll only go into it after exploring to the fullest what the surface can give me."[80] Confirming this flirtation with sculpture, Gullar's only footnote in the "Teoria do não-objeto" clarifies that the term *nonobject* had been adopted by Clark to "designate her last works that are constructions built directly in space."[81]

The period of late 1959 and early 1960 was a conceptual turning point for Clark—one that Gullar had perceptively captured in his writings of the period. The "Teoria do não-objeto," for one, closely approximated the spatial logic Clark pursued in her work of this period: nonrepresentational painting and sculpture (devoid of mass) approximates common objects by abandoning the frame and the base, respectively, and relinquishes the privileged space of traditional representation. Painting and sculpture converge at a point distant from their origins, and this convergence ultimately leads to the rejection of traditional artistic mediums, which Gullar associated with a dismissal of representation. Following the phenomenological thread introduced in the "Manifesto Neoconcreto," Gullar described the nonobject as free of all significations unrelated to its own manifestation. This proposition revealed the idealist dimension of neoconcretist theory, which designated the nonobject as an event that appears as if for the first time—a presentation instead of a re-presentation, unmediated and free from the conventions of use and language. Transparent to perception—or, to use Gullar's concluding words, a "primary formulation"—the nonobject was to be understood in light of phenomenology's idealist plenitude. But it should also be seen as a response by the neoconcretists to the rigid categories of meaning and interaction that were manifested, via the notion of art as idea and product, in the work of the concrete artists. Indeed, Gullar's essay is partly a response to the artist Waldemar Cordeiro's 1956 essay "O objeto" (The Object), which posited art as product, specifically a product of its time. Cordeiro's formulation, according to Gullar, established a correlation between individual mechanism and social mechanism: in other words, the work of art is the result of an isomorphism between the individual and society.[82]

Gullar's follow-up to "Teoria do não-objeto," entitled "Diálogo sobre o não-objeto" (Dialogue on the Nonobject; fig. 3.9) and published three months later, in March 1960,

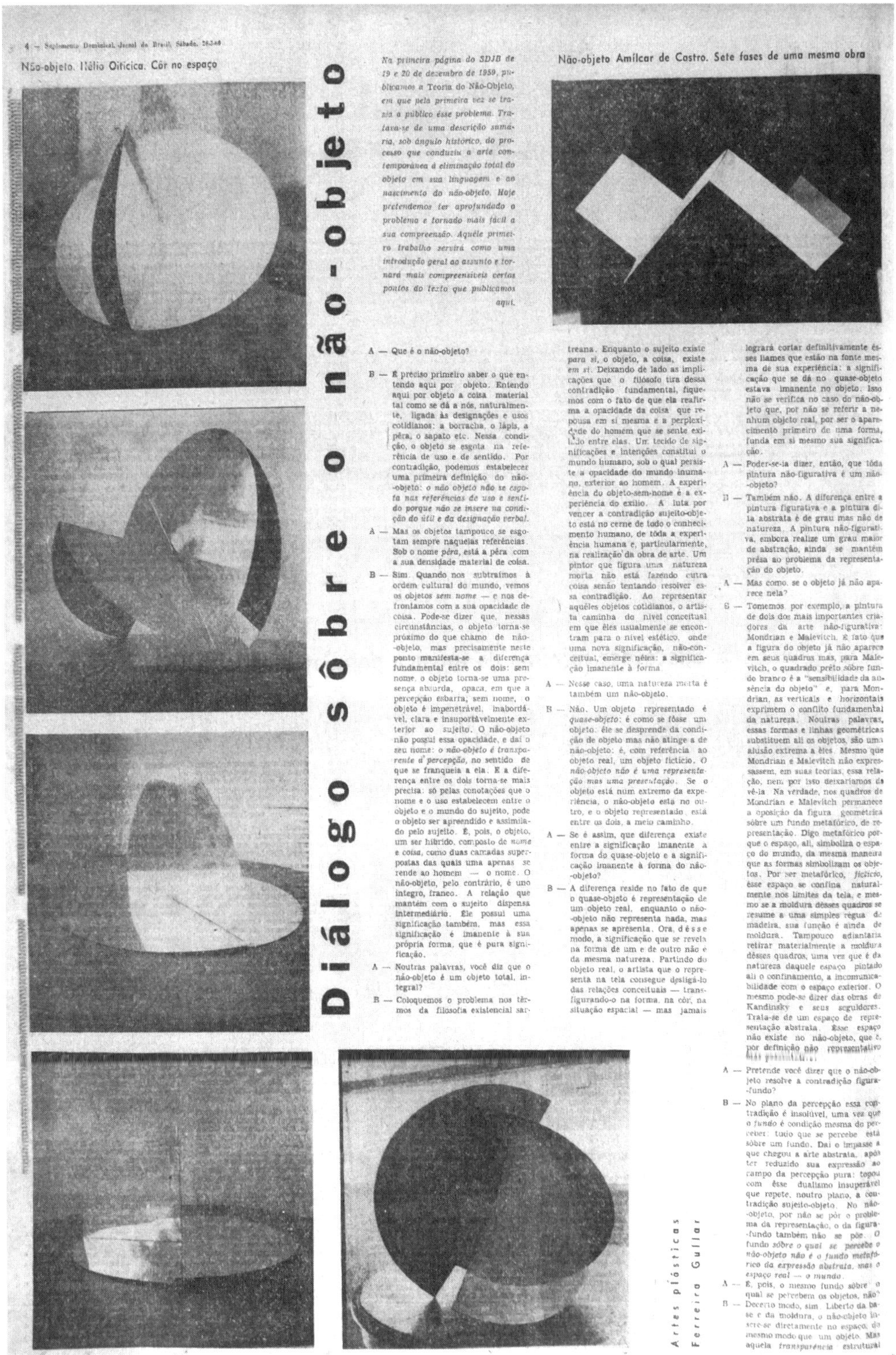

4 — Suplemento Dominical, Jornal do Brasil, Sábado, 26-3-60

Não-objeto. Hélio Oiticica. Côr no espaço

Não-objeto Amílcar de Castro. Sete fases de uma mesma obra

# Diálogo sôbre o não-objeto

Artes plásticas

Ferreira Gullar

*Na primeira página do SDJB de 19 e 20 de dezembro de 1959, publicamos a Teoria do Não-Objeto, em que pela primeira vez se trazia a público êsse problema. Tratava-se de uma descrição sumária, sob ângulo histórico, do processo que conduziu a arte contemporânea à eliminação total do objeto em sua linguagem e ao nascimento do não-objeto. Hoje pretendemos ter aprofundado o problema e tornado mais fácil a sua compreensão. Aquêle primeiro trabalho servirá como uma introdução geral ao assunto e tornará mais compreensíveis certos pontos do texto que publicamos aqui.*

A — Que é o não-objeto?

B — É preciso primeiro saber o que entendo aqui por objeto. Entendo aqui por objeto a coisa material tal como se dá a nós, naturalmente, ligada às designações e usos cotidianos: a borracha, o lápis, a pêra, o sapato etc. Nessa condição, o objeto se esgota na referência de uso e de sentido. Por contradição, podemos estabelecer uma primeira definição do não-objeto: *o não objeto não se esgota nas referências de uso e sentido porque não se insere na condição do útil e da designação verbal.*

A — Mas os objetos tampouco se esgotam sempre naquelas referências. Sob o nome *pêra*, está a pêra com a sua densidade material de coisa.

B — Sim. Quando nos subtraímos à ordem cultural do mundo, vemos os objetos *sem nome* — e nos defrontamos com a sua opacidade de coisa. Pode-se dizer que, nessas circunstâncias, o objeto torna-se próximo do que chamo de não-objeto, mas precisamente neste ponto manifesta-se a diferença fundamental entre os dois: sem nome, o objeto torna-se uma presença absurda, opaca, em que a percepção esbarra; sem nome, o objeto é impenetrável, inabordável, clara e insuportàvelmente exterior ao sujeito. O não-objeto não possui essa opacidade, e daí o seu nome: *o não-objeto é transparente à percepção*, no sentido de que se franqueia a ela. E a diferença entre os dois torna-se mais precisa: só pelas conotações que o nome e o uso estabelecem entre o objeto e o mundo do sujeito, pode o objeto ser apreendido e assimilado pelo sujeito. É, pois, o objeto, um ser híbrido, composto de *nome* e *coisa*, como duas camadas superpostas das quais uma apenas se rende ao homem — o nome. O não-objeto, pelo contrário, é uno íntegro, franco. A relação que mantém com o sujeito dispensa intermediário. Êle possui uma significação também, mas essa significação é imanente à sua própria forma, que é pura significação.

A — Noutras palavras, você diz que o não-objeto é um objeto total, integral?

B — Coloquemos o problema nos têrmos da filosofia existencial sartreana. Enquanto o sujeito existe *para si*, o objeto, a coisa, existe *em si*. Deixando de lado as implicações que o filósofo tira dessa contradição fundamental, fiquemos com o fato de que ela reafirma a opacidade da coisa que repousa em si mesma e a perplexidade do homem que se sente exilado entre elas. Um tecido de significações e intenções constitui o mundo humano, sob o qual persiste a opacidade do mundo inumano, exterior ao homem. A experiência do objeto-sem-nome é a experiência do exílio. A luta por vencer a contradição sujeito-objeto está no cerne de todo o conhecimento humano, de tôda a experiência humana e, particularmente, na realização da obra de arte. Um pintor que figura uma natureza morta não está fazendo outra coisa senão tentando resolver essa contradição. Ao representar aquêles objetos cotidianos, o artista caminha do nível conceitual em que êles usualmente se encontram para o nível estético, onde uma nova significação, não-conceitual, emerge nêles: a significação imanente à forma.

A — Nesse caso, uma natureza morta é também um não-objeto.

B — Não. Um objeto representado é *quase-objeto*: é como se fôsse um objeto: êle se desprende da condição de objeto mas não atinge a de não-objeto: é, com referência ao objeto real, um objeto fictício. *O não-objeto não é uma representação mas uma presentação.* Se o objeto está num extremo da experiência, o não-objeto está no outro, e o objeto representado está entre os dois, a meio caminho.

A — Se é assim, que diferença existe entre a significação imanente à forma do quase-objeto e a significação imanente à forma do não-objeto?

B — A diferença reside no fato de que o quase-objeto é representação de um objeto real, enquanto o não-objeto não representa nada, mas apenas se apresenta. Ora, dêsse modo, a significação que se revela na forma de um e de outro não é da mesma natureza. Partindo do objeto real, o artista que o representa na tela consegue desligá-lo das relações conceituais — transfigurando-o na forma, na côr, na situação espacial — mas jamais logrará cortar definitivamente êsses liames que estão na fonte mesma de sua experiência: a significação que se dá no quase-objeto estava imanente no objeto. Isso não se verifica no caso do não-objeto que, por não se referir a nenhum objeto real, por ser o aparecimento primeiro de uma forma, funda em si mesmo sua significação.

A — Poder-se-ia dizer, então, que tôda pintura não-figurativa é um não-objeto?

B — Também não. A diferença entre a pintura figurativa e a pintura dita abstrata é de grau mas não de natureza. A pintura não-figurativa, embora realize um grau maior de abstração, ainda se mantém prêsa ao problema da representação do objeto.

A — Mas como, se o objeto já não aparece nela?

B — Tomemos por exemplo, a pintura de dois dos mais importantes criadores da arte não-figurativa: Mondrian e Malevitch. É fato que a figura do objeto já não aparece em seus quadros mas, para Malevitch, o quadrado prêto sôbre fundo branco é a "sensibilidade da ausência do objeto" e, para Mondrian, as verticais e horizontais exprimem o conflito fundamental da natureza. Noutras palavras, essas formas e linhas geométricas substituem ali os objetos, são uma alusão extrema a êles. Mesmo que Mondrian e Malevitch não expressassem, em suas teorias, essa relação, nem por isso deixaríamos de vê-la. Na verdade, nos quadros de Mondrian e Malevitch permanece a oposição da figura geométrica sôbre um fundo metafórico, de representação. Digo metafórico porque o espaço, ali, simboliza o espaço do mundo, da mesma maneira que as formas simbolizam os objetos. Por ser metafórico, *fictício*, êsse espaço se confina naturalmente nos limites da tela, e mesmo se a moldura dêsses quadros se resume a uma simples régua de madeira, sua função é ainda de moldura. Tampouco adiantaria retirar materialmente a moldura dêsses quadros, uma vez que é da natureza daquele espaço pintado ali o confinamento, a incomunicabilidade com o espaço exterior. O mesmo pode-se dizer das obras de Kandinsky e seus seguidores. Trata-se de um espaço de representação abstrata. Êsse espaço não existe no não-objeto, que é, por definição não representativo [illegible]

A — Pretende você dizer que o não-objeto resolve a contradição figura-fundo?

B — No plano da percepção essa contradição é insolúvel, uma vez que o *fundo* é condição mesma do perceber: tudo que se percebe está sôbre um fundo. Daí o impasse a que chegou a arte abstrata, após ter reduzido sua expressão ao campo da percepção pura: topou com êsse dualismo insuperável que repete, noutro plano, a contradição sujeito-objeto. No não-objeto, por não se pôr o problema da representação, o da figura-fundo também não se põe. *O fundo sôbre o qual se percebe o não-objeto não é o fundo metafórico da expressão abstrata, mas o espaço real — o mundo.*

A — É, pois, o mesmo fundo sôbre o qual se percebem os objetos, não?

B — Decerto modo, sim. Liberto da base e da moldura, o não-objeto insere-se diretamente no espaço, do mesmo modo que um objeto. Mas aquela *transparência* estrutural

FIGURE 3.9
Ferreira Gullar, "Diálogo sobre o não-objeto" (Dialogue on the Nonobject) in *Suplemento Dominical do Jornal do Brasil*, March 26, 1960.

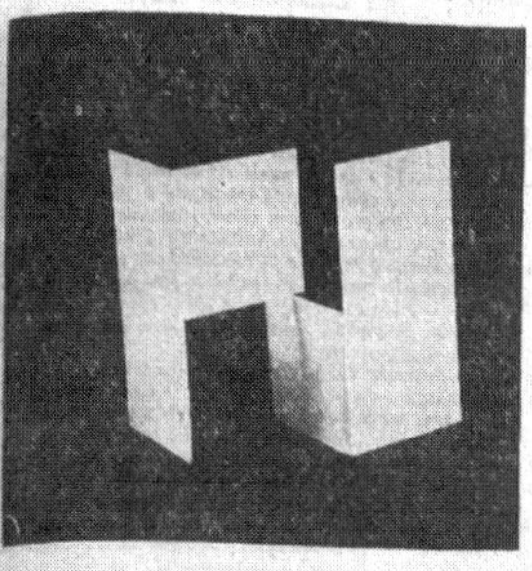

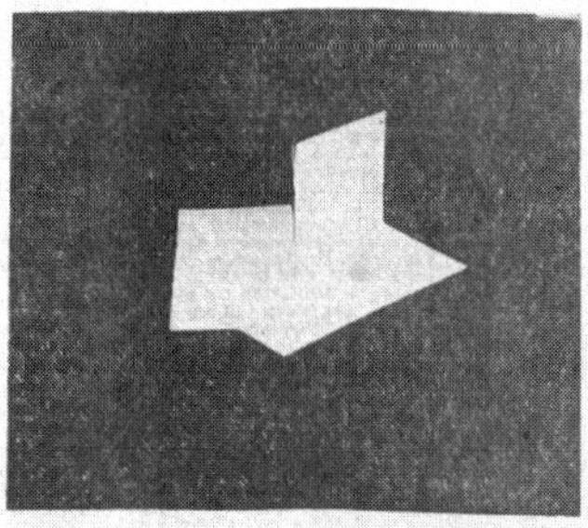

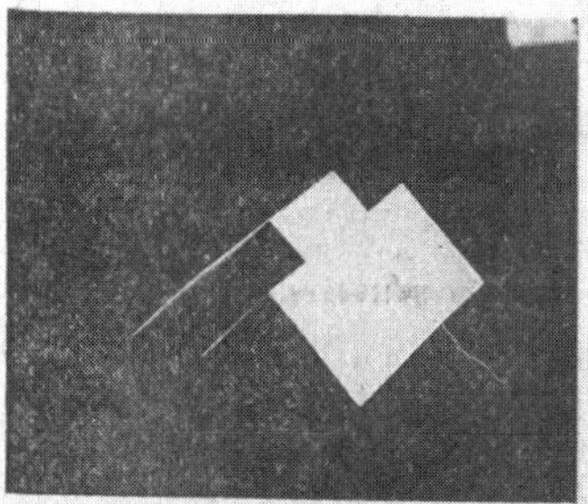

do não-objeto, que o distingue do objeto, permite-nos dizer que êle transcende o espaço, e não por iludi-lo (como faz o objeto), mas por nêle se inserir radicalmente. Nascendo diretamente no e do espaço, o não-objeto é ao mesmo tempo um trabalhar e um refundar dêsse espaço: o renascer permanente da forma e do espaço. Essa transformação espacial é a própria condição do nascimento do não-objeto.

A — Você falou em moldura e base. Basta eliminar êsses elementos para fazer um não-objeto?

B — Não, da mesma maneira que não bastava eliminar a figura para fazer um bom quadro abstrato. Não se trata da presença ou ausência material da moldura ou da base. Trata-se de criar sem o apoio dêsses elementos. A moldura e a base, na pintura e na escultura respectivamente, condicionam a expressão do artista e são, também, os marcos de uma determinada posição em face da arte. O que importa, pois, não é fazer um quadro sem moldura ou uma escultura sem base, mas resolver os novos problemas que se põem quando a expressão já não conta com aquêles elementos.

A — Que significam a moldura e a base?

B — Significam que a linguagem da obra é representativa, mesmo se as formas são abstratas (falo da base e da moldura como elementos pressupostos na expressão). Quando o problema da representação é ultrapassado, a moldura e a base perdem a função. Mas não basta simplesmente retirá-las da obra. No caso da escultura, a base indica uma posição privilegiada, e se a escultura não possui base (materialmente falando) mas detém aquêle privilégio, o problema da base continua inerente a ela. Não se trata, portanto, de um não-objeto.

A — Conclui-se daí que a não-representação é um caráter básico do não-objeto. É êle ainda pintura ou escultura?

B — As considerações a que nos obriga o aparecimento do não-objeto, conduziu-nos a ver a representação como elemento inerente à pintura e à escultura. Ao contrário do que se vem afirmando há pelos menos 50 anos, só em alguns casos excepcionais a arte contemporânea ultrapassou o problema da representação. Essas exceções — os contra-relevos de Tatlin, as *arquiteturas*, suprematistas de Malevitch — estão fora das definições do que seja pintura, escultura, arquitetura. O mesmo se dá com os trabalhos do grupo neoconcreto — e daí o nome de não-objeto. Acredito que uma arte realmente não-representativa repele as noções acadêmicas de gênero artístico. O próprio conceito de arte vacila, se não o tomamos na acepção fundamental de *experiência primeira*.

A — Quer dizer que, na sua opinião, pintura e escultura acabaram...

B — Ou talves nunca tenham, de fato, existido. Pelo menos na época moderna, todo artista trabalha no limite de sua arte, tentando ultrapassá-lo. Trata-se sempre de uma *antiarte*. O que importava para Brancusi — quer êle o soubesse ou não — não era fazer escultura, mas *a escultura*. Contraditoriamente, para fazer *a escultura*, êle se distanciava cada vez mais de tudo o que se conhecia como escultura. O mesmo pode-se dizer de Pevsner, de Vantongerloo, de Picasso, de Mondrian, de Kandinsky, de Malevitch, de Pollock etc. O artista busca, na pintura ou na escultura, a experiência primeira do mundo, mas a própria pintura (ou escultura) já é um mundo *conceituado*, que é preciso ultrapassar. E finalmente chegou-se ao momento atual, em que o artista já não se preocupará em *fazer pintura* ou *escultura*, para através delas reencontrar a experiência primeira do mundo: tenta precipitar diretamente essa experiência. É uma redescoberta do mundo: as firmas, as côres, o espaço não pertencem a esta ou àquela linguagem artística mas, antes, ao mundo mesmo, à experiência viva e indeterminada do homem. Lidar diretamente com êsses elementos, fora dos quadros institucionais da arte, é lidar diretamente com o mundo, é formulá-lo pela primeira vez. E aqui, observa-se outra diferença fundamental entre um quadro e um não-objeto: aquêle nasce de um esfôrço do artista para, gradativamente, romper o mundo já conceitual da linguagem artística — vem-se de fora para dentro, da significação usual para uma nova significação; o não-objeto irrompe de dentro para fora, da não-significação para a significação.

A — Dentro da teoria do não-objeto, como se coloca precisamente o problema da poesia?

F — Também o poeta busca a experiência primeira do mundo, também êle trabalha no limite da linguagem poética. Na época moderna, vimos a destruição das formas fixas de estrofe, de verso, para chegar-se ao verso livre. Mas, depois, o verso livre também tornou-se um instrumento estereotipado: rebentou-se a sintaxe e chegou-se à palavra como elemento primeiro. Da mesma maneira que a côr libertou-se da pintura, a palavra libertou-se da *poesia*. O poeta tem a palavra mas já não tem um quadro estético preestabelecido onde colocá-la hàbilmente. Êle se defronta com ela desarmado, sem nenhuma possibilidade definida mas com tôdas as possibilidades indefinidas. O que importa não é fazer um poema — nem mesmo fazer um não-objeto — mas revelar o quanto de mundo se deposita na palavra.

A — Você já escreveu que, no que se refere à poesia, o não-objeto é a procura de um *lugar* para a palavra. Que quer dizer isto?

B — É que a palavra ou está na frase — onde perde sua individualidade — ou no dicionário, onde se encontra sòzinha e mutilada, pois é dada como mera denotação. O *não-objeto verbal é o antidicionário: o lugar onde a palavra isolada irradia tôda a sua carga*. Os elementos visuais que ali se casam a ela têm a função de explicitara, intensificar, concretizar a multivocidade que a palavra encerra.

A — Há, então, uma fusão de pintura, relêvo, escultura e poesia?

B — Creio que não. Planos, formas, côres, são elementos da realidade, antes de serem elementos de uma linguagem artística. No não-objeto os elementos plásticos não são usados com o mesmo sentido que na pintura ou na escultura. Já são escolhidos segundo um propósito *verbal*, isto é: da mesma maneira que um poeta tradicional elabora seu poema convocando e repelindo palavras, o poeta neoconcreto convoca, além das palavras, formas, côres, movimentos, num nível em que a linguagem verbal e a linguagem plástica se interpenetram. Ninguém ignora que nenhuma experiência humana se limita a um dos cinco sentidos do homem, uma vez que o homem reage com uma totalidade e que, na "simbólica geral do corpo" (M.-Ponty), os sentidos se decifram uns aos outros.

A — O não-objeto deve ter movimento?

B — Nessa altura, cabe esclarecer que não digo *como deve ser* o não-objeto, mas apenas defino o que já existe, o que está feito. A maioria dos não-objetos existentes implicam, de uma forma ou de outra, no movimento sôbre êle do espectador ou do leitor. O espectador é solicitado a *usar* o não-objeto. A mera contemplação não basta para revelar o sentido da obra — e o espectador passa da contemplação à ação. Mas o que a sua ação produz é a obra mesma, porque êsse *uso*, previsto na estrutura da obra, é absorvido por ela, revela-a e incorpora-se à sua significação. O não-objeto é concedido no tempo: *é uma imobilidade aberta* a uma mobilidade aberta *a uma imobilidade aberta*. A contemplação conduz à ação que conduz a uma nova contemplação. Diante do espectador, o não-objeto apresenta-se como *inconcluso* e lhe oferece os meios de ser concluído. O espectador age, mas o tempo de sua ação não flui, não transcende a obra, não se perde além dela: incorpora-se a ela, e dura. A ação não consome a obra, mas a enriquece: depois da ação, a obra é *mais* que antes — e essa segunda contemplação já contém, além da forma vista pela primeira vez, um passado em que o espectador e a obra se fundiram: êle verteu nela o seu tempo. O não-objeto reclama o espectador (trata-se ainda de espectador?) não como testemunha passivo de sua existência mas como a condição mesma de seu *fazer-se*. Sem êle, a obra existe apenas em potência, à espera do gesto humano que a atualize.

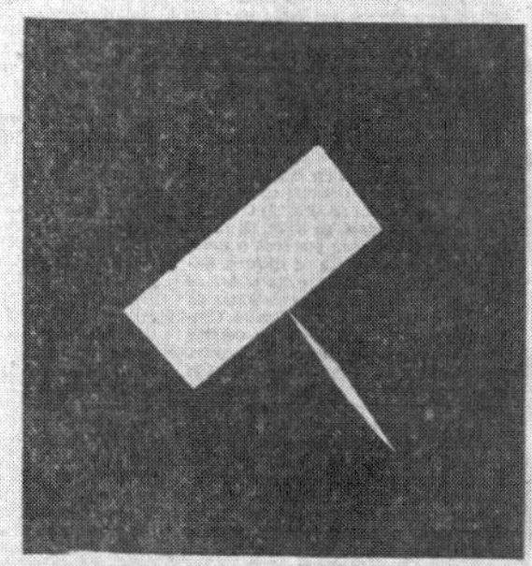

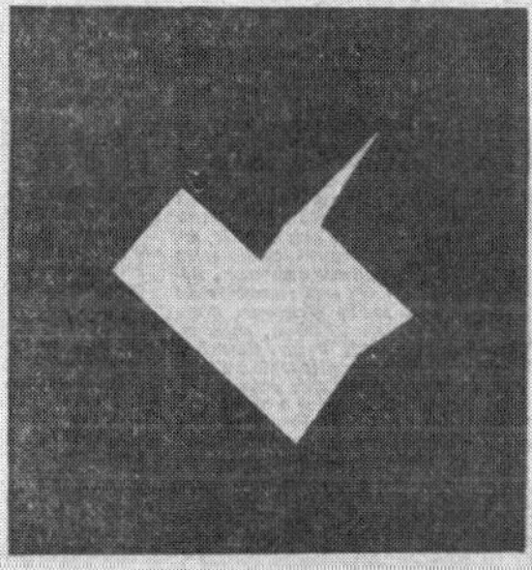

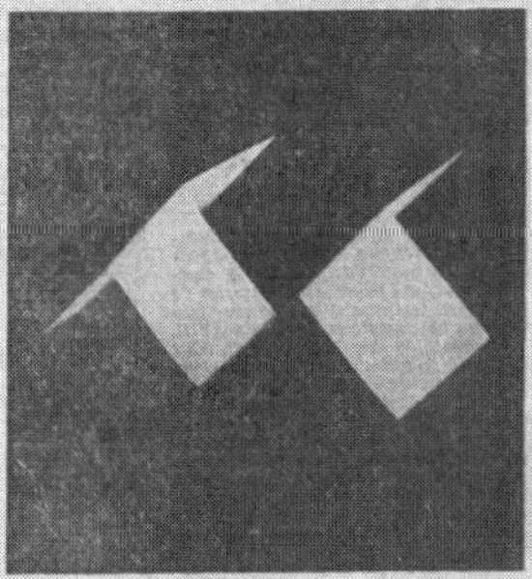

Não-objeto. Amilcar de Castro. Seis fases de uma mesma obra

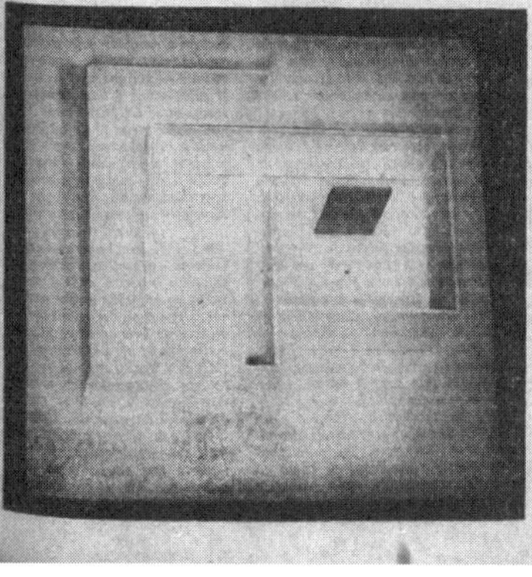

took the format of an imaginary interview. It further clarified what its author meant by the term *nonobject*.[83] *Pace* Cordeiro, Gullar refuted the object's utilitarian dimension, which requires language to be conceptually assimilated by the subject, in favor of the indeterminacy of the nonobject, which is not limited by references of use and meaning. The nonobject requires no linguistic mediation and, according to the existential tenor that informed neoconcretism's investigations, its "signification [is] immanent in its own form";[84] neither meaning nor form takes precedence over the other, but rather they coexist. Gullar argued that the traditional work of art, like language, is part of a fabric of significations that renders familiar the opacity of things. It sheds light, thanks to its semantic constitution, on our world, mediating between us and the world; it dwells in the realm of representation. According to this logic, pictorially represented objects are quasi-objects (*quasi-objetos*). While they lack the materiality of the things that surround us, their referential nature renders them "fictitious objects"—extensions, albeit transfigured, of the familiar objects of the world. In contrast, the nonobject was to be a "presentation," unrelated to the encoded meaning that dictates our apprehension of objects. Its meaning is not referential; it does not send us back to familiar things and codified meanings but is a new form—a first form—and thus inaugurates its own signification.

Gullar emphasized that the matrix of the nonobject is real space and not the metaphorical field of abstract art, which, he argued, still operated on the principle of representation ("metaphorical because space [in those works] symbolizes the space of the world, in the same way that the forms symbolize objects").[85] Since the nonobject is a categorical rejection of representation, it discards the figure-ground configuration (the plane as the container of form) present at the heart of much geometric abstract pictorialism. The nonobject's background, like that of any ordinary object, is the world. Both the object and the nonobject assert themselves directly in space, but the nonobject facilitates a permanent rebirth of form and space (spatialization), and as such it eludes the stagnant task of linguistic and visual representation, of systematized denomination, inherited by traditional (art) objects. This semantic renunciation is accompanied by an abdication of medium specificity, a convention that Gullar deemed academic now that art attempted to go beyond itself and thus flirted with anti-art—that is, with ordinary objects. A crucial reference in this regard was Constantin Brancusi, whose blunt incorporation of the base into his sculptures the Brazilian poet saw as prefiguring the nonobject. Implicit in Brancusi's art was the intermedial quality of the nonobject that avoided identifiable pictorial and sculptural iterations.[86] In Gullar's view, both painting and sculpture were fully conceptualized worlds that had to be transcended by the artist if he or she was to "reencounter the first experience of the world."[87]

The contentious challenge of fully circumventing mediation between viewer and artwork would lead to an impasse in Gullar's theorization of the nonobject, while prompting Clark and Oiticica to radicalize it. In 1959–60, however, the ruptures proposed by the neoconcretists in the field of art opened up new avenues of investigation and revolutionary symbolic models of cultural and social meaning. Gullar wrote: "It is a rediscovery of the world: forms, colors, space do not belong to this or that artistic language, but to the living and indeterminate experience of man. To deal directly with these elements, outside the institutional frame of art, is to reformulate them as if for the first time."[88]

Aspiring to sever the nonobject from the conventions of representation, Gullar conceptualized an aesthetic proposition that, dissociated from use and language, would confront the viewer directly. Presciently, he even foresaw the nonobject operating outside the institutional framework of art—the museum, the gallery—and addressing the increasingly relevant theme of viewer participation that would come to preoccupy these artists. He wrote (likely with Clark's *Bichos* in mind): "The viewer is asked to *use* the nonobject. Mere contemplation is not enough to reveal the sense of the work—and the viewer moves from contemplation to action. But what the viewer's action produces is the work itself, because that use, anticipated by the structure of the work, is absorbed by the work, revealed and incorporated into its signification. The nonobject is conceived in time. . . . The nonobject presents itself as *incomplete* and offers the viewer the means to complete it."[89]

## THE BODY OF COLOR

This neoconcretist inquiry into the nature of representation would be incomplete without an assessment of Hélio Oiticica's participation in these debates. No doubt Clark's and Oiticica's artistic practices of the period embodied more poignantly than any other body of work produced by a neoconcrete artist the crisis of the art object that the nonobject unleashed. Oiticica's intense artistic dialogue with Lygia Clark began in 1957, when he initiated his *Metaesquemas* (Metaschemes) series, works in which he covered the surface of paper with tilted and mirrored geometric patterns or irregular shapes that were outlined or filled with a strong color; he favored black, red, and blue.[90] Oiticica's interest in destabilizing the spatial conventions of concrete painting and its dependence on preconceived compositional structures—especially the seriated form and the heuristic structure or progression favored by concrete artists—is evident in these works. The *Metaesquemas* are boldly graphic thanks to the pristine technique of the precocious artist (he was barely twenty years old at the time). A group of black and white *Metaesquemas* (1958; fig. 3.10), each measuring approximately twenty-nine by thirty-eight centimeters, bear an immediate resemblance to collages from Clark's *Planos em superfície modulada* (1957), although in Oiticica's works the ground generally remains white while the figure is articulated through irregular rectilinear black shapes that defy exact geometric definition.

A subsequent group of paintings called *Série Branca* (White Series; fig. 3.11) invokes Clark's organic line through internal tracings produced with a black line that furrows the surface. Oiticica's writings on these works, however, focused on the issue of "color-light." This concept allowed him to move painting away from representation and into the realm of the environmental by calling attention to the instability of color in space.

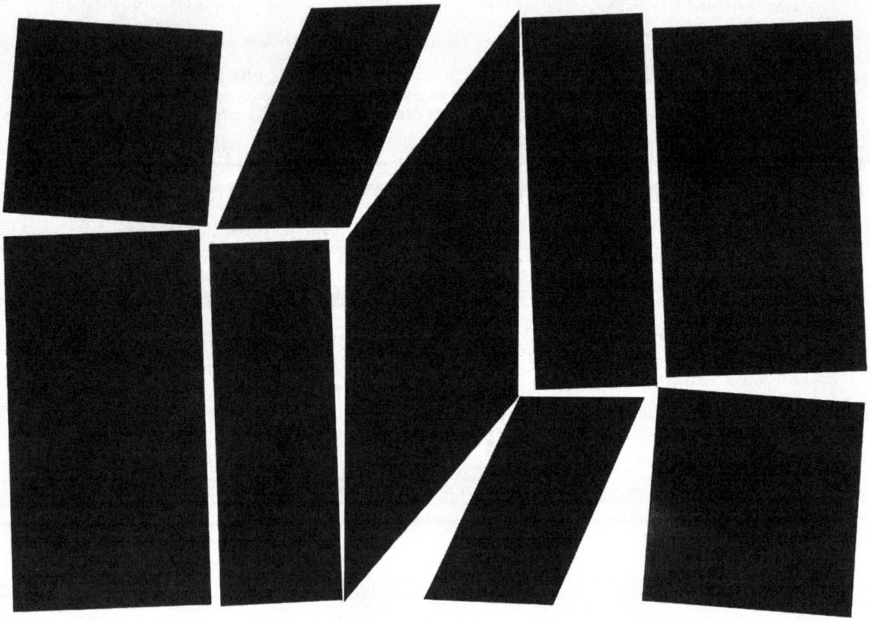

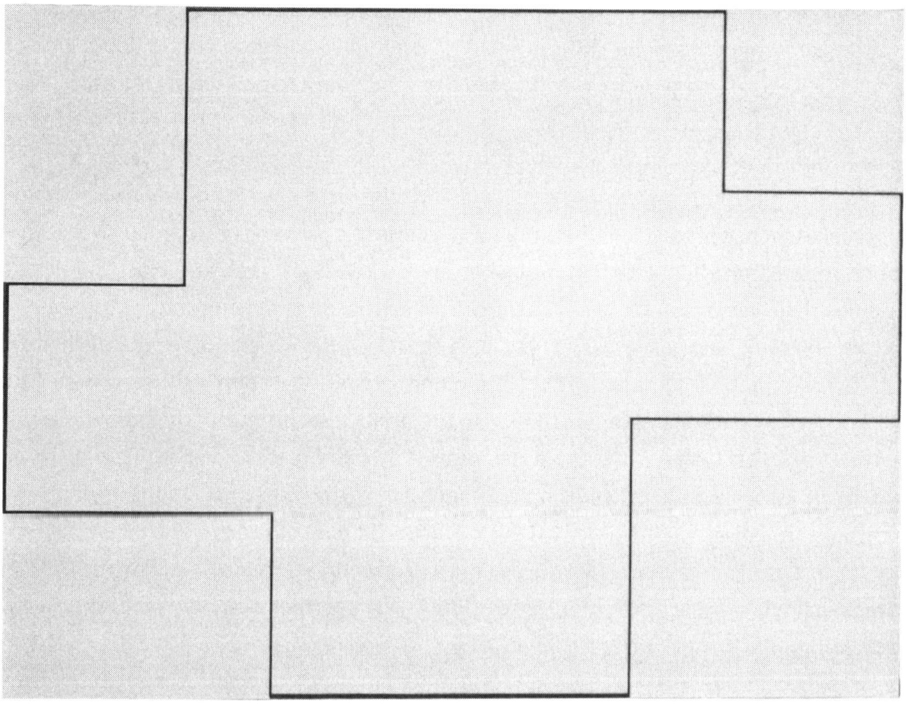

FIGURE 3.10 *(top)*
Hélio Oiticica, *Metaesquema* (Metascheme), 1958, gouache on cardboard, 19⁵⁄₁₆ × 26¹¹⁄₁₆ in.

FIGURE 3.11 *(bottom)*
Hélio Oiticica, untitled work from the *Série Branca* (White Series), 1959, oil casein emulsion on wood fiberboard, 35⅞ × 48 in.

Indeed, for Oiticica, the temporalization of chroma grounded his neoconcrete experiments in the realm of painting (specifically its metaphysics, as he called it at the time) even as he destroyed painting's conventions, structure, and support. If color, applied in layers and in different directions or in two different tones, revealed the qualitative differences of "active color-light," it also, he argued, made painterly structure immanent. Following one of neoconcretism's dictums, he wrote, "There is no 'a priori' structure, it builds itself from the action of color-light."[91] In other words, color does not refer to other things, but simply is itself.

In 1959 Oiticica initiated a series of monochrome works that occupied him until 1962: small wooden panels, thirty centimeters square, in a range of reds that shade into pink, yellow, and orange, with color conceived as embodied rather than represented light. The curator Carlos Basualdo has convincingly argued that Oiticica's use of color in these monochromatic works, titled *Invenções* (Inventions), which released chroma from its material boundaries, was not a "completely objective" pictorial element. Here, he wrote, "color is a sort of *entredeux* . . . [that] exists in the object although its presence is not defined in itself but in relation to the perception of the viewer, to light, to the physical nature of its surroundings."[92] Following Oiticica's call to release painting from its support, Basualdo argued that liberating color was the only way to overcome the figure-ground hierarchy on which representation is based. As Oiticica put it, when "color is no longer tied to the rectangle, nor to any representation on this rectangle, it tends to embody itself; it becomes temporal, creates its own structure, so the work becomes the 'body of color.'"[93] Like the Argentine concretists, Oticica's goal was to redefine the material circumstances of painting in order to overcome representation.

Alluding to this environmental dispersal of painting that concerned him in 1959, Oiticica quoted (in English) Mondrian's words in the context of his own meticulous diaristic writings: "[T]here is no escape for the nonfigurative artist; he must stay within his field and march toward the consequence of his art. This consequence brings us, in a future perhaps remote, toward the end of art as a thing separate from our surrounding environment."[94] In citing this passage, was the twenty-two-year-old Oiticica contemplating the possibility that the future envisioned by Mondrian was materializing in the development-against-all-odds environment of Brazil in the 1950s? To be sure, the massive urban reconfiguration, democratic aspirations, and industrialist policies of President Kubitschek (1956–61)—along with the construction of a new capital city, Brasília, which imported the latest urban standards to the country's remote plains—seemed to indicate as much. The late 1950s were a time of political, economic, and cultural prosperity that coincided with intellectuals' optimism regarding the creation of a stable public sphere and a solid civic society. These conditions grounded Brazil's internationalist and modernist agenda, framed the utopian geometric-abstract enterprise of the concretists (who saw their work as operating in dialogue with the industrializing efforts of the period), and fueled the relentless faith in modernity of the neoconcretists, for whom art was to become a participatory, potentially transformative event of aesthetic agency.

Gullar's writings in the *Suplemento Dominical do Jornal do Brasil* reveal the extent to which neoconcretism was understood as the epitome of a modernist trajectory that began with cubism.[95] Indeed, a week after the publication of the "Manifesto Neoconcreto" in March 1959, Gullar initiated a series of weekly articles on the European avant-garde that continued through October 1960. Highly idiosyncratic and selective, the articles aimed to establish a narrative in which the total rejection of pictorial representation was achieved in neoconcretism through the nonobject's materialization and sustained engagement with real space.[96] This rigorous teleology, the art historian Irene Small has argued, yielded "remarkable resonances with the developmentalist mandates of the time."[97] Economic development was to be accompanied by social and cultural modernization.

Indeed, in the late 1950s, the critic Mário Pedrosa often said that Brazilians were "condemned to be modern" (*condenados o moderno*). This maxim, an ideological proposition that loomed large over artists and intellectuals at the time, was voiced in the context of his writings on Brazilian architecture and Brasília and alluded to what seemed an endless capacity to embrace the new.[98] For Pedrosa, Brazil, a country devoid of a history of ancient civilization, provided modernism's ideal tabula rasa, a place of endless new beginnings.[99] This desire resulted in the artificiality of Brasília, more than six hundred miles away from the metropolitan hubs of Rio de Janeiro and São Paulo, along with the utopian plan of its architect, Lúcio Costa, who believed in the self-sufficiency of the frontier region while remaining keenly aware of the incongruity of an urbanistic program in such a location.

In 1959, on the occasion of the International Congress of Critics taking place in the as-yet-unfinished Brasília—and despite doubts he raised the previous year in a short article entitled "Nuvens sobre Brasília" (Clouds Over Brasília)[100]—Pedrosa endorsed the transformative potential of the "cidade nova" (new city), with its capacity to enlarge the national market through "the creation of true and new regions in the center of the country, around the new capital."[101] Certain that such an urban utopia could not be built without a socialist project to counteract the inequities of the market, he continued: "[We] will not be able to re-equip or equip those territories without the agrarian reform of which we speak more and more in Brazil. In sum, Brasília supposes a geographic, social, and cultural remodeling of the whole country."[102]

This utopian élan was accompanied by the reinstitution of the aesthetic dimension in public life and suggests that the neoconcrete project was intimately related to the urban chimera of Pedrosa, for whom Brasília was the ultimate collective work of art. Indeed, it was only a few months after the publication of the "Manifesto Neoconcreto" in March 1959—and only three months before "Teoria do não-objeto" appeared in December 1959—that Pedrosa wrote about the ideal modern city's capacity to restore "lost social cohesion."[103] It is obvious that the close-knit group of intellectuals and artists around Pedrosa were attracted to this notion of urban collective agency that looked forward optimistically: away from backwardness and the merciless dynamics of capitalism (a key concern of Pedrosa's) and toward the possibilities of radicalizing international avant-garde culture.

## AN ARCHITECTONIC VISION OF COLOR

Oiticica's small "paintings" of 1959, titled *Invenções* (Inventions), were hung from walls but pushed forward slightly by wooden supports, casting shadows that destabilized their self-sufficiency (similar to Clark's *Espaços Modulados* and *Unidades* from 1958).[104] According to Oiticica (echoing Clark and Gullar), the painterly, layered surfaces of these small canvases attempted to express the act of painting, an operation emphasized by the multidirectionality of his brushwork, a record of the duration of the artist's action. This surface-work denied depth (but not thickness) and rejected the illusionistic space of representation while asserting its environmental materiality, thrusting painting into real space and operating, as did Clark's works of this period, between mediums: The work "closes upon itself and refuses to belong to the wall or to turn into relief," wrote Oiticica in a 1962 article in *Habitat*. There he also claimed that it was pure color, the kernel of painting, that forced him into three-dimensional space.[105]

This testing of the limits of the medium was also carried out in works that aspired to overcome the plane—"that old element of representation," so defined because of its "a priori sense of a surface to be painted."[106] Influenced by the neoconcretist debates, Oiticica's attack on the integrity of the pictorial support was further realized in a series of shaped canvases painted in a range of whites entitled *Bilaterais* (Bilaterals), initiated in 1959 (fig. 3.12).[107] These double-faced panels are hung from the ceiling, thereby dispersing painting throughout real space and encouraging apprehension from various points of view. These works sought to disrupt passive contemplation and to trigger a multidimensional experience in accord with the participative aims of neoconcretism and the breakdown of boundaries among the senses. Without back or front and positioned away from the wall, the *Bilaterais* were intended to mobilize, in Gullar's words, an "architectonic vision of color."[108] This logical step in Oiticica's work signified a plunge into space that claimed the intermedial reliefs of Vladimir Tatlin and Alexander Rodchenko and the suprematist architecture of Malevich as antecedents.[109] Indeed, despite his attentive theorization of color, Oiticica increasingly saw real space (experienced temporally) as the undeniable path away from the restrictions of the medium of painting and the conventional task of representation.[110] His *Bilateral Equali* (1959) consists of five two-toned, double-faced, superimposed wooden panels hanging in space—essentially a deconstructed cube whose dispersed layout was defined by Oiticica as architectonic.[111] Aggressively incorporating real space and suggesting collective modes of reception, *Bilateral Equali* announced Oiticica's concerns with what he would come to call *programa ambiental* (environmental program).

A key text by the young Oiticica, written in close dialogue with the aesthetic preoccupations of Gullar and Clark, was published in 1960 in the *Suplemento Dominical do*

FIGURE 3.12
Hélio Oiticica, *Bilateral Clássico* (Classic Bilateral), 1959, oil casein emulsion on wood fiberboard, 39¾ × 45⅝ × ½ in.

*Jornal do Brasil* as "Côr, tempo e estrutura" (Color, Time, and Structure). The transformation of the plane, a sedentary surface upon which representation depends, was to be pursued through a fusion of color, structure, space, and time—an organic unity, he called it, that was detached from the wall and did not function as background but as an "unlimited," "foreign," albeit necessary, element. This transformed plane was to activate color-light, facilitating the plane's integration into space while rejecting contemplative space and mechanical time. This mechanical time was defined by Oiticica as the virtual time that in painting relates one figure to another, or a figure to perspectival space. By this he meant the temporality of representational painting, of pictorial signs resting on the support as a container of representation.[112] Clearly interested in color theory, Oiticica attempted to justify this most pictorial element, color, in relation to the core concerns of the "Manifesto Neoconcreto": real space, affect, and the participatory role of the viewer. The notion of structure was to be key in this endeavor, as it allowed Oiticica to think anew about relations between the various plastic elements. In 1962 he wrote, "[C]onstructive artists are those who establish new structural relations in painting (color) and in sculpture and open up new perceptions of space and time."[113] This notion of structure, as a recombination of plastic elements that defied the conventions of the medium, also facilitated Oiticica's irregularly shaped canvases that hung from the ceiling and triggered a noncontemplative role for the viewer: "The structure, then, is taken into space, turning 180 degrees on itself. This is the definitive step in the encounter of the [structure's] temporality with that of color; here the viewer not only sees one side [of the structure], in contemplation, but is encouraged to act, turning around it, completing its orbit in a multidimensional perception of the work."[114]

Multidirectionality and multidimensionality were further pursued in Oiticica's *Relevos espaciais* (Spatial Reliefs) of 1960 (plate 14), which furthered the disintegration of the picture plane. Brightly painted in reds and yellows applied with a spray gun, the works consist of rectilinear shapes based on a combination of triangular and quadrilateral panels, layered wooden boards whose gaps, nooks, and crannies reconfigure the support and disturb the viewer's habitual perception of painting. Like the *Bilaterais* before them, the *Relevos espaciais* were to be hung from the ceiling—a practice that seems to have been tested earlier without much note by another member of the neoconcrete cohort, Aluísio Carvão, in the second exhibition of Grupo Frente (1955).[115] Oiticica explained in 1961 that the gap between the two superimposed panels that formed some of the *Bilaterais* needed to be dynamized, so he created new planes by "raising" the wooden panels, thereby producing an effect of folded planes.[116] As suggested by Clark's *Contra-relevos,* the thickness of the support, emphasized by stacked layers of wood, instigates alternative forms of engagement with the disjunctive pictorial plane. As a result, in both Clark's *Contra-relevos* and *Casulos* and Oiticica's *Relevos espaciais,* layers and gaps open up the surface as if revealing the fictitious nature of the support of painting, the plane's false flatness disclosed by real space. Neither painting nor sculpture, the work produced by Oiticica between 1959 and 1960 complied with the intermediatic condition of the nonobject. In regard to these spatial investigations and referencing the *Bilaterais,* he wrote: "When the plane of the canvas began to function actively, a sense of time had to emerge as the principal new factor in nonrepresentation. Thus, the concept of the *nonobject* was born, a term invented and explained by Ferreira Gullar, and one more appropriate than *picture,* given that the structure was no longer unilateral (as in painting) but multidimensional."[117]

Oiticica's—and neoconcretism's—antirepresentational stance must be understood in light of the Brazilian avant-garde's rejection of the traditional modes of pictorial representation that had been favored by the national rhetoric of Brazilianness of the 1930s and 1940s. Prone to an iconography of the popular and the land, the modernism of that period was seen as stagnant. But this inquiry into the limits of figural representation had profound implications. In opening the artwork to real space and in considering the spectator, Clark and Oiticica unleashed a profound questioning of the status of the object and the subject of representation, shattering in the process the contemplative position of the viewer and the identity of the art object. This antirepresentational position was thoroughly elaborated in Gullar's "Diálogo sobre o não-objeto," but the conversation that Clark and Oiticica initiated through the common structure of the fold was instrumental in positioning the viewing subject at the intersection of representational and real space.

Writing about the initial assault on the pictorial support that she launched in the late 1950s, Clark wrote: "Arbitrarily defining the limits of space, the plane gives us an entirely false and rational idea of reality. Hence, the opposing concepts of high and low, front and back—which contribute to the destruction of our sense of wholeness."[118] To Clark, such idealistic wholeness implied a merging of subject and world, an "organic whole." Rejecting subjective projection—the projection of the artist's ego onto the surface of the painting, where he/she recognizes herself—and the consequent transcendence of the surface and the ego, Clark proposed the vulnerability of a nonrational space. In words that clearly evoke lessons learned from Malevich, she wrote, "We plunge into the totality of the cosmos"[119]—a statement whose spatial resonance opposes the positionality that constitutes the modern subject in representation, which elsewhere Clark associated with the "old idea of continuing to express the world."[120]

Writings by Gullar, Clark, and Oiticica during this period manifest a concern with these enduring philosophical preoccupations. Skepticism toward science, objectivity, objectification, and the imagistic transformation of the world into a picture points to the neoconcretists' radical break with the entire concept of representation.[121] Consider these words by Oiticica, critical of the contemplative relationship between subject and object that he was attempting to overcome in his work: "[T]he viewer looked to ideal form, outside him/herself, for internal coherence. . . . Form was then anxiously sought and sculpted to produce something eternal, infinite, and immovable within the finite, changing world of phenomena. . . . The 'picture' would thus be the support for the contemplative expression in which the viewer achieved his/her desire for synthesis between what is indeterminate and mutable (the world of objects) and his/her aspiration to infinity through the imagistic transposition of these very objects onto the level of formal ideas."[122]

The a priori idea and the clear structure that had been favored by concrete art and the "spatial forms" of constructivism[123] were rejected by Gullar, Clark, and Oiticica in favor of the experiential dimension of the nonobject unfolding in time. Clark and Oiticica's engagement with time and space (classical constructivist elements that were taken to their logical extremes in their work), the concomitant unfolding of the support into the environment, and their concern with the viewer led modernist painting to an imminent collapse. Contra the pictorial self-referentiality that European concrete art had proposed, the neoconcrete destruction of representational space suggested the impossibility of a pictorial ontology and triggered its consequent "nonobjectification." It is worth quoting Oiticica's complete statement on this point: "The painting of our century passes through a disintegration of its own former characteristics and assumes others to the point where we cannot call certain works 'painting.' A main characteristic of painting's interrelationship with other mediums is the destruction of representational space and its consequent nonobjectification."[124]

By 1961, overcoming representation led to an impasse for Gullar. He articulated his concerns in two articles published in the *Suplemento Dominical do Jornal do Brasil* in consecutive weeks in February 1961. In the first, entitled "O lugar da obra" (The Place of the Work), Gullar departed from Mondrian's utopian aspiration to merge and dissolve art with/in the environment, arguing instead that the conflict posed by the insertion of the work into real space pointed toward a larger crisis involving the artist and society. If the "economic and political complex" did not evolve to facilitate Mondrian's ideals, rendering an integration of the arts impossible, then the art object could not restore its old identity. It became instead a body in transition, integrated not into architecture but—as was evident in the work of Clark—into space, making "its own place" (*o seu próprio lugar*). The fact that this new work, which created its own place, had to reside in a museum, a domestic setting, or a public building was a contradiction, a negation of this temporal creating of place. Gullar attempted to resolve this contradiction by interpreting the social role of art making in terms of a "critical-creative activity"—that is, as a "perpetual reworking of our sensorial experiences." As to the material manifestation of the nonobject, this was conceived by Gullar as a historical shell, a residue, its signification ephemeral.[125]

A second article, "O tempo e a obra" (Time and the Work), confirmed this grounding of the work of art in its "own place" and contradicted the move into the environment implicit in the nonobject and its participatory dynamics as it was being enunciated in the work of Clark and Oiticica. Gullar hinted at this contradiction when he wrote that in order to negate reality (the mundane reality of habit), a work had to assert reality. This conflict kept the work alive, outside categories and mediums. Its recognition as art implied its death. This was intimately linked to the temporal dimension of modernity whereby time implied constant change, instability. Gullar used as an example impressionism's depiction of time as a sequence of instants, each annulling the validity of the last as representations of a constantly changing reality. This divorce from reality asserts the autonomy of painting. Gullar argued that the work of art—now relieved of its representational task and detached from the appearance of things—deploys a self-reflexive trajectory. This process was facilitated by two operations: one in which creative work (the action of the artist) and created work coincide, and another in which the viewer's action is absorbed by the work.[126] Clarifying what this gesture of self-reflexiveness meant, he wrote that the artwork "has to be the authentic manifestation of the interior reality of the artist. That reality will be more authentic when more individual, more individual when more interior, more interior when least contaminated by exterior reminiscences."[127] These words repressed the outgoing course of the nonobject and returned to an extreme subjectivism, one that identified the temporality of the creative act with the created (non)object. Aspiring to bypass mediation and insisting on the desire for plenitude that the "Manifesto Neoconcreto" had introduced through the notion of spatialization, Gullar foreclosed historicity. As in the "Teoria do não-objeto," he here relied on a teleological narrative that favored not the abandonment of the frame but painting's self-reflexiveness, a move not toward real space but toward interiority. It is evident that the nonobject's exposure to real space and the world of objects posed insurmountable contradictions for Gullar, ones that defied his desire for an unmediated experience of the work and implied the abandonment of the nonobject. This was confirmed by Clark and Oiticica's radicalization of the nonobjectual implications of the nonobject, their overt entanglement with the "outside" of art. As Gullar confirmed many years later, if the work of art is pure signification, and the object is a nonobject, ephemeral and temporal, what remains of it after our encounter with it is a "material shell" (*casca material*).[128]

Shortly after the appearance of these articles, Gullar resigned as editor of the visual arts page of the *Suplemento Dominical do Jornal do Brasil* to lead the Fundação Cultural Brasília, where he became increasingly concerned with popular art and the political dimension of culture as a rejection of the aesthetic solipsism he had theorized in these texts.[129] The conception of the neoconcrete work as a manifestation of the artist's interiority had gained the upper hand in Gullar's neoconcrete thinking as a consequence of his categorical rejection of pictorial representation and the attendant self-reflexiveness of the nonobject. In contrast, Clark's and Oiticica's work gestured toward the outside and leaped toward the other (the viewer) and the environment instead of remaining entrenched in self-reflexivity or searching for an alternative artistic ontology.

## THE INSIDE IS THE OUTSIDE

Clark's and Oiticica's complex attack on the pictorial surface—and later on the institutions of art—constituted a critique of the classical scheme of representation realized in the art object conceived as the support for subjective artistic projection. The works that incorporated the fold, morphologically and structurally, posited the nonobject (and its antinomian premise) as an alternative to the logic of representation implied by the pictorial plane while staging a continuous loop between the work and the world. Rejecting projection and exteriorization, Clark and Oiticica stressed a more fluid and pliant relationship between inside and outside. In questioning the extreme objectification deployed by concrete art, they submitted the art object to a foundational examination. This was accomplished by rethinking the relationship between subject and object via phenomenology's emphasis on embodied experience.

The dissolution of the traditional support reached a climax in Clark's *Contra-relevos* and was further pursued via the bursting of folds in her *Casulos* (Cocoons), shown in the second exhibition of neoconcrete art in November 1960.[130] In these small-format works, Clark executed a series of folds on the metal surface, extending it toward the viewer. When seen frontally, these works reveal little of their spatial acrobatics. But when the *Casulos* are seen laterally or up close, when the viewer approaches the work and is forced to look into it, the folds bulge; when the work is approached laterally or from below, one discovers the airy thickness of the support, the disintegrating trajectory of the pictorial plane, and the oscillating tension between form and emptiness. Three of these lozenge-shaped metal structures, each measuring approximately forty-two centimeters square and painted black and white, were reproduced in the London-based *Signals* magazine in a 1965 issue devoted to Clark (fig. 3.13). The photographic layout featuring the three works embodies a pulsation from closed to open to closing. Advancing Clark's preoccupations with the spatiotemporal dimension of the "thread of space," the *Casulos* literalize the notion of "surface as process."[131]

Around the same time, Clark developed her famous *Bichos* (Critters), a large selection of which was shown in her solo exhibition at Galeria Bonino in Rio de Janeiro in October 1960. These polymorphic works consist of triangular, rectilinear, and circular plates of aluminum and, origami-style, are folded and articulated by hinges that facilitate manipulation by the viewer-participant. The range of kinetic possibilities explored by Clark in the *Bichos* rendered the plane multidirectional, transitional, processual, and temporal, and its manipulation implicated the viewer-participant in different ways: some are pocket size, while others were conceived as "fantastic architectures."[132] The small pieces, ranging from twenty to twenty-six centimeters in width when extended, are easy to handle, while larger ones, measuring more than a meter, involve a more cumbersome and threatening interaction, as their spiky blades refuse easy manipulation. Initially modeled from balsa wood, Clark made the first maquettes in aluminum and planned the production of works in three sizes: small, medium, and large.[133]

A small hexagonal *Bicho* from 1960 called *Metamorfose I* (Metamorphosis I) is often reproduced in different positions, following a transformative sequence suggested by the artist (fig. 3.14).[134] These photographs document the unfolding of an initially symmetrical structure into unpredictable, unsuspected configurations—a metamorphosis that leads from normative "good form" to nonnormative formlessness consistent with neoconcretism's phenomenological critique of prescribed plastic structure.[135] Such experiments weaken the stable relation between the viewer and the art object. Through the inconclusive explorations and unpredictable quality of the *Bichos*, subjective projection on the part of the spectator is frustrated. Furthermore, what Clark called the "dialogue" between the *Bichos* and the viewer-participant is illusory. The exchange is mostly predicated on an ambiguity that hinders understanding. Folded flat, a *Bicho* may be perceived as symmetrical and geometrical, but unfolded, folded, or refolded, its identity is unstable and avoids permanence, despite its structural precision.

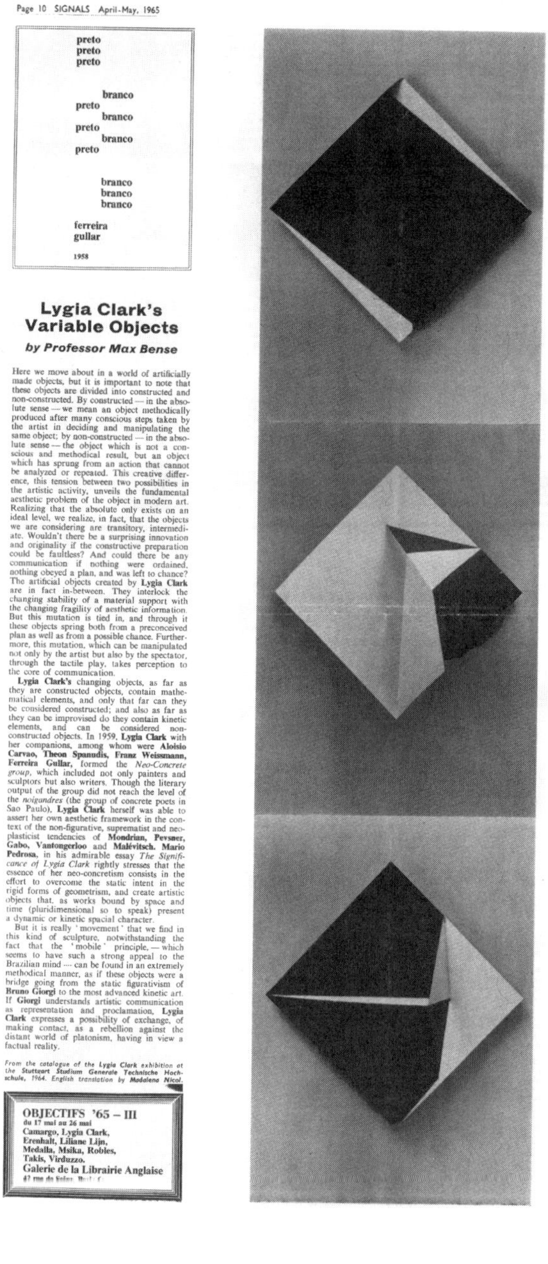

Page 10 SIGNALS April-May, 1965

preto
preto
preto

branco
preto
branco
preto
branco
preto

branco
branco
branco

ferreira
gullar

1958

## Lygia Clark's Variable Objects

***by Professor Max Bense***

Here we move about in a world of artificially made objects, but it is important to note that these objects are divided into constructed and non-constructed. By constructed — in the absolute sense — we mean an object methodically produced after many conscious steps taken by the artist in deciding and manipulating the same object; by non-constructed — in the absolute sense — the object which is not a conscious and methodical result, but an object which has sprung from an action that cannot be analyzed or repeated. This creative difference, this tension between two possibilities in the artistic activity, unveils the fundamental aesthetic problem of the object in modern art. Realizing that the absolute only exists on an ideal level, we realize, in fact, that the objects we are considering are transitory, intermediate. Wouldn't there be a surprising innovation and originality if the constructive preparation could be faultless? And could there be any communication if nothing were ordained, nothing obeyed a plan, and was left to chance? The artificial objects created by **Lygia Clark** are in fact in-between. They interlock the changing stability of a material support with the changing fragility of aesthetic information. But this mutation is tied in, and through it these objects spring both from a preconceived plan as well as from a possible chance. Furthermore, this mutation, which can be manipulated not only by the artist but also by the spectator, through the tactile play, takes perception to the core of communication.

**Lygia Clark's** changing objects, as far as they are constructed objects, contain mathematical elements, and only that far can they be considered constructed; and also as far as they can be improvised do they contain kinetic elements, and can be considered non-constructed objects. In 1959, **Lygia Clark** with her companions, among whom were **Aloisio Carvao, Theon Spanudis, Franz Weissmann, Ferreira Gullar,** formed the *Neo-Concrete group*, which included not only painters and sculptors but also writers. Though the literary output of the group did not reach the level of the *noigandres* (the group of concrete poets in Sao Paulo), **Lygia Clark** herself was able to assert her own aesthetic framework in the context of the non-figurative, suprematist and neoplasticist tendencies of **Mondrian, Pevsner, Gabo, Vantongerloo** and **Malévitsch. Mario Pedrosa**, in his admirable essay *The Significance of Lygia Clark* rightly stresses that the essence of her neo-concretism consists in the effort to overcome the static intent in the rigid forms of geometrism, and create artistic objects that, as works bound by space and time (pluridimensional so to speak) present a dynamic or kinetic spacial character.

But it is really 'movement' that we find in this kind of sculpture, notwithstanding the fact that the 'mobile' principle, — which seems to have such a strong appeal to the Brazilian mind — can be found in an extremely methodical manner, as if these objects were a bridge going from the static figurativism of **Bruno Giorgi** to the most advanced kinetic art. If **Giorgi** understands artistic communication as representation and proclamation, **Lygia Clark** expresses a possibility of exchange, of making contact, as a rebellion against the distant world of platonism, having in view a factual reality.

*From the catalogue of the Lygia Clark exhibition at the Stuttgart Studium Generale Technische Hochschule, 1964. English translation by Madalena Nicol.*

**OBJECTIFS '65 – III**
**du 17 mai au 26 mai**
**Camargo, Lygia Clark, Erenhalt, Liliane Lijn, Medalla, Msika, Robles, Takis, Virduzzo.**
**Galerie de la Librairie Anglaise**

FIGURE 3.13
Lygia Clark, *Casulos* (Cocoons), 1959, in *Signals* 1, no. 7, April–May 1965.

Encouraging a temporal apprehension that disturbs the work's geometric references and the precision of its calculations, the hinge situates the *Bichos* between two opposing paradigms—the organic and the formless—that deliver the uncertainty of the quasi-corpus proposed by the "Manifesto Neoconcreto" (see fig. 3.1). However, the organic metaphor and the dialogic relation between spectator and artwork have been privileged in interpretations of the *Bichos*.[136] Not only were discussions of the organic character of

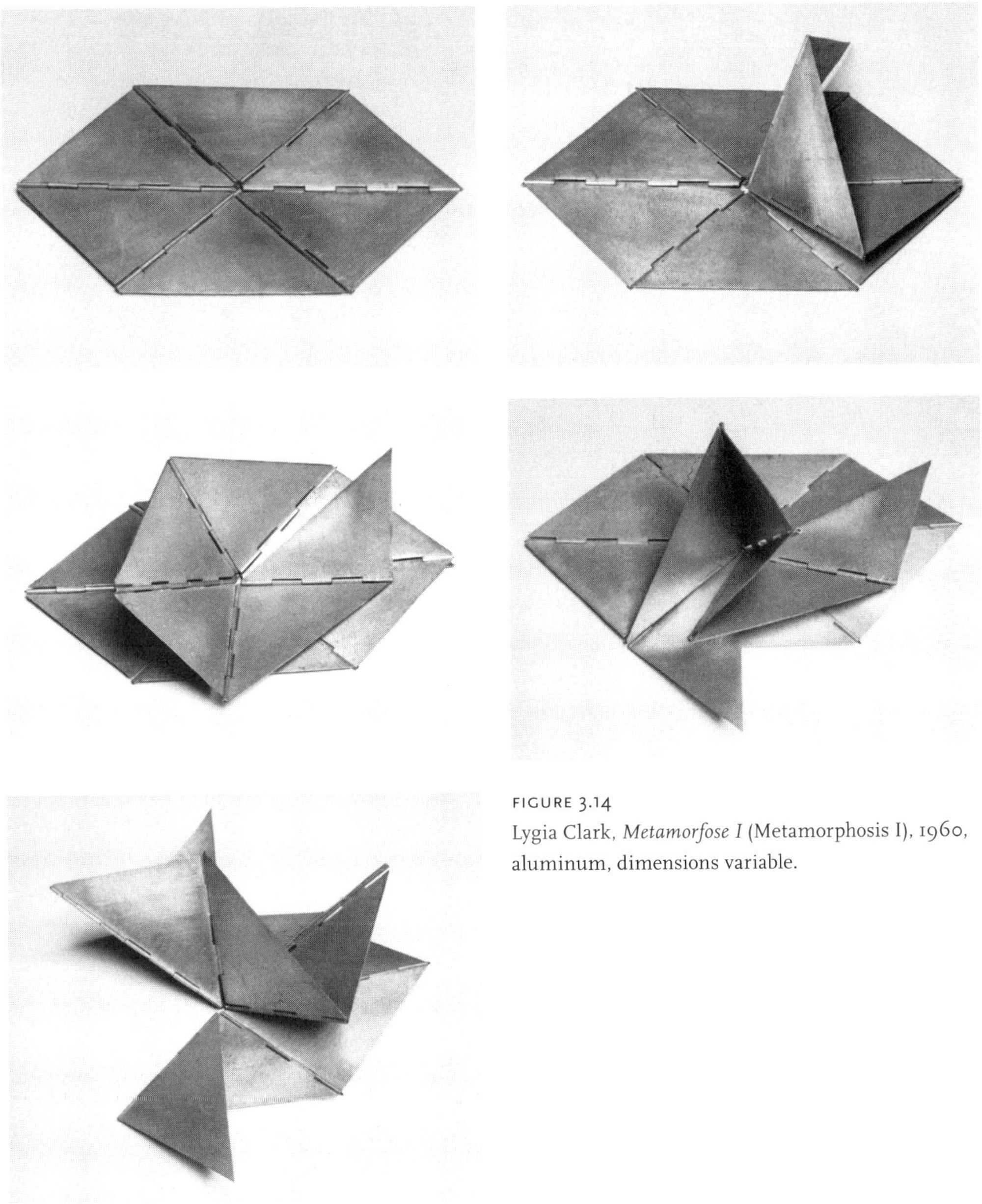

FIGURE 3.14
Lygia Clark, *Metamorfose I* (Metamorphosis I), 1960, aluminum, dimensions variable.

the pieces common at the time, but Clark herself posited a vitalist reading of the *Bichos* that echoed concrete art's creationism as well as Max Bill's functionalism. In the catalogue of her 1960 exhibition at Galeria Bonino, she noted that "each 'bicho' is an organic entity . . . a living organism, an essentially active work. . . . [T]he 'bicho' has very well defined responses to the spectator's stimuli." Later in this introductory text, she added that the *Bicho* "is not composed of still, independent forms that can be manipulated indefinitely at one's will, as in a game. On the contrary, its parts work together harmoniously as in a real organism, and the movements of these parts are interdependent."[137]

The functional mode implicit in this conception of the organic—mobilized years later by Gullar, who referred to the *Bichos* as if they had been born to the *Casulos*[138]—is interrupted by the unforeseeable morphologies adopted by these works, which, due to their unpredictability, frustrate conceptual transparency (plate 15). In this sense, the critic's 1962 assessment of the *Bichos* is telling and indicative of an unresolved understanding of these works. At that time Gullar did not allude to the organic or to nature, but instead referred to a perturbing first impression of interpenetrating planes of different shapes—suggesting contradictory directions—that elude form and apprehension. When we interact with these works, he wrote, "our job is to analyze and to separate in order to apprehend, but the movement we make [with our hands] with the intention of unraveling a specific form, if indeed it makes that form explicit, hides other [forms], and thus results in that sensation of slipping away that we observe in the 'bichos.'"[139] Pedrosa also alluded to this opacity and sense of slippage; as he indicated in a 1960 article, the *Bichos* are constructed according to given structural laws, but the eye cannot predict their evolution.[140] Operating according to a process opposite to that of Waldemar Cordeiro's "visible idea," the complex topography of these objects still baffles us today, in person and in photographs.

The impact of the *Bichos* on the Brazilian artistic milieu of the period cannot be overstated.[141] Oiticica seems to have been responding to these works when he assembled his *NC1 Pequeno Núcleo no. 1* (NC1 Small Nucleus no. 1, 1960; plate 9), a structure composed of five wooden panels that incorporates a mirror, onto which the crevices and crannies of the work are reflected, making them visible to the viewer but also affirming the incorporation of outside space and the viewer as crucial components of the piece. With this work, the self-sufficiency of the art object is suspended, and the work becomes dependent on exterior contingencies, both human and environmental (to use a word that would soon become key in Oiticica's vocabulary).

A peculiar *Bicho* from 1963 entitled *O dentro é o fora* (The Inside Is the Outside), of which several versions exist, announced an interest in malleability and relinquished the calculations and systematic traits of the geometric *Bichos,* which performed according to a limited set of possibilities (fig. 3.15). *O dentro é o fora* was cut from a single sheet of thin, pliant stainless steel rather than constructed from articulated geometric planes. Its curvilinear pattern followed the trajectory of the Möbius strip by encouraging the twisting of the plane. This configuration determined the topological dynamics of the work: no inside, no outside, no front, no back. Elastic and "deformable," as Clark herself described it, the piece impressed her because it transformed her perception of herself and her body: "It changes me," she wrote, "I am formless, elastic, without definite physiognomy. . . . 'Inside and Outside': a living being open to all possible transformations. Its internal space is an affective space." In the same text she added: "[I]n its dialogue with my 'Inside and Outside' the acting subject encounters its own precariousness. The subject, like the

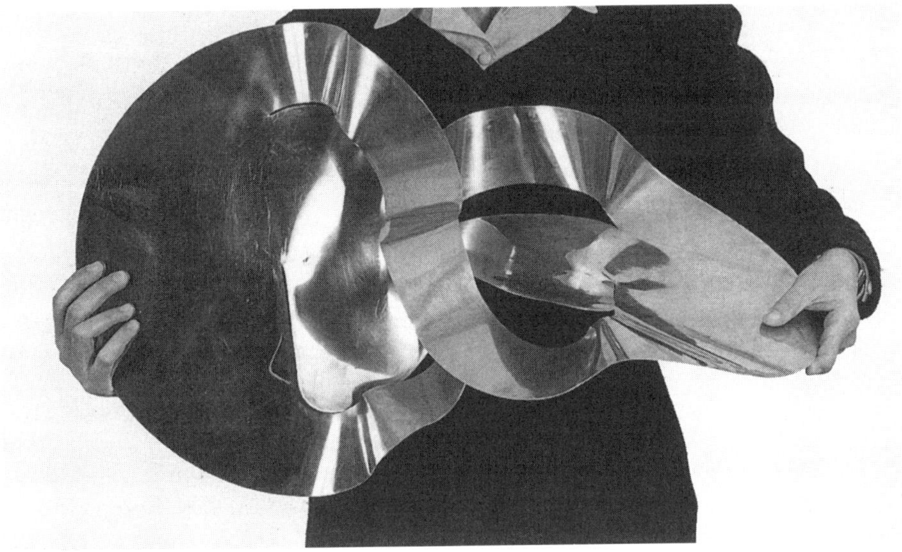

FIGURE 3.15
Lygia Clark, *O dentro é o fora* (The Inside Is the Outside), 1963, stainless steel, dimensions variable.

*Bicho,* has no self-defining, static physiognomy. It discovers the ephemeral in contrast to every type of crystallization. Space is now a kind of time continuously metamorphosed through action. Subject and object identify with each other in the act."[142]

In this text and in *O dentro é o fora,* Clark linked the spatial indeterminacy of the Möbius strip to subjective precariousness, a condition that mobilized "an affective space" and dissolved the preeminence of form in space, stable identity.[143] Indeed, 1963 was a landmark year in Clark's work and writings, as she initiated a dedicated reflection on and around subjectivity in which the art object became one more element in a relational (temporal) scheme structured around the relationship of the self to the world. This brought instability to the art object and the subject of reception, and thrust Clark into an intimate rapport with the body-subject of phenomenology. In words that recall Clark's own allusion to the precarious self, the philosopher Jack Reynolds reminds us that Maurice Merleau-Ponty made time one of the determining aspects in his conception of subjectivity:

> According to Merleau-Ponty, ambiguity prevails both in my perception of things, and in the knowledge I have of myself, primarily because of our temporal situation which he insists cannot but be ambiguous. . . . It is because of this temporal alterity that Merleau-Ponty asserts that we can never say "I" absolutely. Rather, he suggests, "I know myself only insofar as I am inherent in time and in the world, that is, I know myself only in my ambiguity." Elsewhere in *The Phenomenology of Perception* he goes on to imply that the subject is time and time is the subject.[144]

The temporal had been activated in Clark's work through the "surface process" of the Möbius strip, and the topological looping between inside and outside that it produced. When posed vis-à-vis the question of the subject, this topological condition signaled a spilling of the self toward the world (and back). This spatiotemporal circuit was symbolized in a dream of Clark's, which she positioned as the origin of her pliant *O dentro é o fora* and which suggested that time and space were not objects of knowledge, but dimensions of being.[145] Recounting the dream, Clark wrote: "[I]nside, which is outside, a window and me. Through this window I want to pass to the outside, which is the inside for me. When I wake up, the window of my room is the one from my dream; the inside I was looking for is the space outside. The *Bicho* that I called 'Inside and Outside' was born from this dream. . . . ([I]mmediately before 'Inside and Outside,' I made a *Bicho* without hinges that I called 'Before What Comes After.')" Poeticizing the lessons of phenomenology and topology, Clark added: "I am the before and the after, the future and the present. I am the inside and the outside, the right side and the reverse."[146]

Clark's engagement with the temporal and the spatial reversals of the Möbius strip facilitated her attack on the plane and prompted her complete abandonment of "good form." This withdrawal from the certainty of form led the artist to initiate what she called "propositions," in which she used humble objects as mediators of ephemeral actions that further explored this hinge between self and world. These propositions advanced the intertwining of subject and object, inside and outside, announced by her *Bichos* and furthered what we might call a topological conception of the subject. An action, which the artist entitled *Caminhando* (Walking, 1963), unleashed these "propositions." It was produced by repeatedly cutting through a paper Möbius strip to generate a series of interconnected loops until no further cuts were possible without breaking the chain. Clearly operating outside the boundaries of conventional art (as Mário Pedrosa observed in an early article discussing the work),[147] *Caminhando* was a frontal attack on form and mediums—on the normative treatment of the Möbius strip as symbolized by the heroic granite, brass, and marble sculptures Max Bill made of it starting in the 1930s. As Clark herself wrote, "[T]his expression starts where Max Bill's ends. Evidently I didn't depart from him but from the 'bicho' without hinges. It is the beginning of the end."[148] *Caminhando,* as is clear from the artist's diary entries of 1963, was the epitome of a fascination with space and time that was aesthetic but mostly existential and signaled the end of a certain notion of art. Reacting against the rigidity of Bill's concrete monuments—which, fixed in plastic form, betrayed the spatial ambivalences of the Möbius strip (its quality of "surface-process")—Clark aspired to a fusion of space and time through the act, an undertaking that ended in an entanglement of strips of paper, with no beginning or end, no form or shape.

Most importantly, in close dialogue with her previous investigations into the "surface process," Clark's exploration attested to the impossibility of representing artistic expression and subjectivity, which, according to Merleau-Ponty, is never completely constituted.[149] Indeed, traditional expression suggested a transcendental operation that would betray the desire for a coexistence of art and life implicit in the post-neoconcretist agenda elaborated by these artists and prolonged in Clark's "propositions" of the mid-1960s. The word *immanence* enters Clark's diary notes around 1963. It usually appears over the crossed-out word *transcendence,* an indication that she attempted to revise her writings to incorporate her philosophical discussions with colleagues (at this point mostly Oiticica and Pedrosa). It seems fair to suggest that sometime in the early 1960s *transcendence* became entangled in Clark's thinking with the exterior object of representation (form) and representation as such, while *immanence* better accounted for the privileging of experience, temporality, and the coexistence of art and life that rejected the analytical distanciation of the subject from the world.[150] Accordingly, for Clark, all that counted was the act, the temporality of the gesture that shook the subject out of social habit in a search for alternative modes of subjectivity and aesthetic agency. In close dialogue with the critique of mechanization, rationality, and objectivity voiced in the "Manifesto Neoconcreto," Clark invoked the automatization of labor and wrote that she sought to restore the artisan's loss of expression through the gratuitous gesture of *Caminhando.*[151] Against the ontological stability of the art object, Clark insisted on the participant's action and choice as the expression of "life experience" (*vivência*): "*Caminhando* carries within it all the possibilities attached to action itself: it allows for choice, for the unpredictable, for the transformation of the virtual into a concrete undertaking."[152] Clark told viewers how to accomplish this concreteness: "[W]hen you have gone around the Möbius strip, choose whether to cut to the left or to the right of the cut you've already made. This idea of choice is decisive. The only meaning of this experience resides in the act of doing it. . . . There is a single type of duration: the act. The act is what produces *Caminhando.* There is nothing before, nothing after."[153]

This focus on perception as propulsion toward action, and the rejection of time as a succession of moments, echoed Merleau-Ponty's arguments for flux and transience, for an "overlapping of past and future through the present," whose image is "the landscape seen through a railway carriage window."[154] Curiously invoking a similar metaphor—most likely not drawn from a close reading of *The Phenomenology of Perception* but from her own poetic interpretation of discussions with fellow artists and critics—Clark mirrored the philosopher's insight in conjuring the idea of immanence that so preoccupied her at the time: "*Caminhando* . . . only took on meaning for me when, crossing the countryside by train, I experienced each fragment of the landscape as a temporal totality, a totality in the process of forming, of producing itself before my eyes, in the immanence of the moment. The moment was the critical thing."[155]

In this imaginary dialogue between Clark and Merleau-Ponty, the latter would surely have endorsed Clark's intuitions and replied: "In the present and in perception, my being and my consciousness are one." However, he would likely have added—complicating the perceptual transparency envisioned by the "Manifesto Neoconcreto" and the fusion of self and world to which Clark aspired[156]—"My being is not clearly set out before me; on the contrary, perception is opaque." Merleau-Ponty's subject is a being *in* the world and not *in front* of the world: "We hold time in its entirety, and we are present to ourselves because we are present to the world."[157] Or, in another felicitous statement that resonates with the aesthetic projects that concern us here: "[C]onsciousness needs to unfold itself into a multiplicity," and it must be manifest "to open itself to an Other and to go forth from itself."[158] *Caminhando* and the subsequent propositions suggested such openness and dispersal, a bursting and shattering of form that eroded the compartmentalized ideals of time and space (as well as of subject and object). These were treated as elements to be analyzed by concrete art and negated as clear-cut dualities by neoconcretism and phenomenology. The organic, too, was recast in the *Caminhando*: instead of being conceived as a functional unity, the work was "organically structured, since it carries within itself infinite possibilities."[159]

Echoing Gullar's "material shell," *Caminhando* materialized in a formless interlacing of paper that hinted at the impossibility of ascertaining self-presence in representation. Indeed, in diary notes from 1963, Clark characterized *Caminhando* as the end of a position vis-à-vis the problem of contemporary expression (*expressividade contemporânea*). Within this scheme, the old form in art operated according to a mechanism of transference that the art object called for.[160] Transference was replaced in Clark's own idiosyncratic philosophy with an idealistic image of totality facilitated through perception. "Since there is no longer any power in transference," she wrote, humans "experience art itself by becoming part of its totality."[161] However, as Merleau-Ponty had suggested toward the end of *The Phenomenology of Perception,* casting doubt on the possibility of this fusion and totality longed for by Clark, "since the lived is thus never entirely comprehensible, what I understand never quite tallies with my living experience; in short, I am never quite at one with myself."[162]

*Caminhando* led to the relinquishing of mastery that the heuristic concrete artwork cherished. The topological configuration appropriated by the artist—the entanglement with the outside and the temporality of the action—rendered the act and the work, the subject and the object, a complicated affair irreducible to objective form. The twisting, the cutting, the coiling of paper, and the resulting shreds and remnants were traces of an impossible setting forth (of the world, the self, perception) in front of oneself. "The world is what I perceive," wrote Merleau-Ponty, suggesting the apparent but false identity that would problematize neoconcretism's search for the first experience and the transparency of the nonobject, as well as Clark's desire for a fusion of subject and object. But, Merleau-Ponty continued, "as soon as we examine and express its absolute proximity, it also becomes, inexplicably, irremediable distance."[163] Clark was aware of this "distance," which she perceived as a loss, a sense of subjective precariousness accompanied by the end of the object of art and the certainty of representation.

Clark's writings registered this crisis, which had been elicited by the abandonment of the object in favor of action and the temporal, triggered by her rejection of the frame and the pictorial plane as the support of a representation. In her texts from the early and mid-1960s, phenomenology did not deliver the subject of self-presence but the vulnerable and diffused body of perception. "I am inhaled by others. Perception so powerful that I feel myself torn up from my roots. Unstable in space. I feel as though I were in the process of disintegrating. To live perception, to be perception."[164] A mutual emphasis on the continuous destabilization of the body as a fixed entity and on the ephemeral opened up precariousness not only as a paradigm of production, but also as a means to understand the impermanence of the self, the uncertainty of the cogito shaken by this encroachment of the inside on the outside. Echoing the elusive language that Gullar had mobilized in his neoconcrete writings, Clark referred to these oscillations, this undoing of polarities, in terms of a complementary difference defined as "empty-plenitude" (*vazio-pleno*), something she had conceptualized around 1960: "this totality of the interior, of the exterior that I always talk about."[165]

This shattering of boundaries complicates what Clark, in the same diary entry, called an identification of subject and object within the act that preoccupied her in *Caminhando* and that would yield a feeling of totality.[166] Yet, hesitantly, she wrote: "Where is the *Bicho*—myself? I become an abstract existence. I sink in real depths, without connection to my work—which looks at me from a distance, outside of myself. 'Is it I who did that?' Upheavals. Delirious escape. Only a thread holds me fast. My body abandoned me—'walking' [*caminhando*]."[167] And in a diary entry from October 28, 1963, Clark asked herself, "[H]ow can I feel a total unity if precariousness, constant movement, is the essence of my work, and has therefore become my essence as well? The 'moment' remains the fixed element within the precariousness. . . . I am crying over what is fixed and no longer has meaning instead of accepting the precarious with the greatest joy, as a concept of existence."[168]

In 1966 Clark plunged into the sensorial explorations of her "propositions." The first sustained series of these works was poignantly called *Nostalgia do corpo* (Nostalgia of the Body). In some of these propositions, bodily sensations are evoked through the manipulation of humble materials, attempting a suspension, in Husserlian phenomenological fashion, of our cognitive habits. In one example, *Pedra e ar* (Stone and Air), a plastic bag is filled with air, sealed, tied with an elastic band, and a small pebble is set upon it and wobbles as pressure is applied to the bag. The impression of a breathing organism led Clark to define the work metaphorically as a living thing: a body without frame, limits, or delineation. Such attempts at a prereflective enterprise dwelled on the disruptive effects of the gratuitous gesture of the participant, which bracketed habitual perception of the body: "I feel the nostalgia of normality, and I am afraid of madness,"[169] she wrote in 1972, long after her dismissal of the object. In this and other texts, Clark would both relish and fear the loss of form and boundaries, the effacement of the unity of the body, the loss of isomorphic correspondence with the world around us.[170]

## IN BETWEEN

A proposition entitled *Diálogo de mãos* (Hand Dialogue, 1966; fig. 3.16), made by Clark in collaboration with Oiticica, summarizes the radical aesthetic practices that these artists developed and the contradictory philosophical implications of their explorations. The proposition required two participants, a wrist of each enclosed in the loops of an elastic Möbius strip. This work again renounced the concrete-constructivist object—an object produced by the subject of rationality and presence and that concerned the concurrence of cognition and object. In *Diálogo de mãos* the intertwining of hands, of the touched and the touching, alluded to a spatial configuration dear to Merleau-Ponty, who described the looping of inside and outside as the foundation of subjectivity and signification. In his last, unfinished book, *The Visible and the Invisible* (begun, according to the handwritten manuscript found after his death, the same month and year the "Manifesto Neoconcreto" was published), he continued to explore the relationship between self and world, subject and object, mind and body, understood in terms of intertwining and divergence and mediated through the notion of the flesh. For Merleau-Ponty, this "carnality of the visible" acts as connective tissue between the subject and the perceptible and renders the world visible and the subject (part) of this world. But this image of the flesh also alludes to the figure of chiasma: a figure of intersection that undoes dualisms and also opposes identification and fusion, since the dilution of the seer and the seen would cause vision to "vanish at the moment of formation."[171] The key concept here is reversibility of subject and world, inside and outside. It is to this figure of reversibility, previously posited in *The Phenomenology of Perception*, that Merleau-Ponty returns in his final text: "[M]y right hand touches my left hand while it is palpating the things, where the 'touching subject' passes over to the rank of the touched, descends into the things, such that the touch is formed in the midst of the world and as it were in the things."[172] This "double belongingness" of the body—to the "order of the 'object' and to the order of the 'subject'"[173]—led the French philosopher to invoke a spatial trajectory that closely resembles that of the Möbius strip: "[I]t would be better to say that the body sensed and the body sentient are as the obverse and the reverse, or again, as two segments of one circular course which goes above from left to right and below from right to left, but which is but one sole movement in its two phases."[174] Categorically refuting the positionality of the subject in front of the world, who conceives the world as a picture, Merleau-Ponty's figure of reversibility posits our bodies as part of the "full spectacle."[175]

"The handshake too is reversible," Merleau-Ponty wrote, proposing that this common interface of the flesh allows a transitive communication between oneself and others: "[W]e situate ourselves in ourselves *and* in the things, in ourselves *and* in the other, at the point where, by a sort of *chiasm,* we become the others and we become the world."[176] Subjectivity, thus, is not located inside or outside, in the mind or in the body, but forged at the intersection of self and world, self and other. The topological handshake Clark and Oiticica enacted in *Diálogo de mãos* produced just such an attempt at figuring forth the

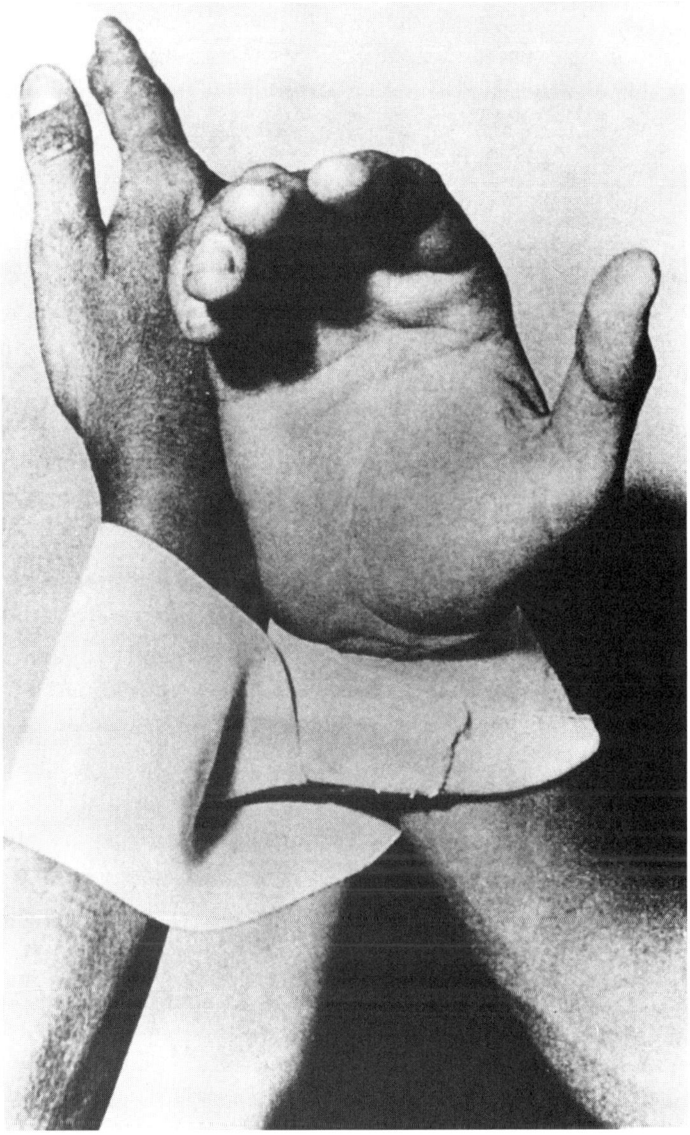

FIGURE 3.16
Lygia Clark and Hélio Oiticica, *Diálogo de mãos* (Hand Dialogue), 1966, elastic fabric, dimensions variable.

elliptical relation between self and other, the intertwining of one into the other, their encroachment but also their difference. Once inside the loop, however, the twisting (rather than shaking) of the hands produced a feeling of irresolution and noncoincidence—not fusion but discontinuity. This "dialogue" silenced traditional expression and delivered the perceptual transparency to which the nonobject aspired: a pointless struggle of the hands. In the poignant words of a critic: "If the 'dialogue' is continued long enough, a moment comes when the impression is born that the hands are carrying out a kind of autonomous dance and that, in their false symmetry, they are separated from the body."[177] Correspondence, coincidence, and identity are frustrated, as "touching and touched" are not identical and therefore can "never fully coincide."[178]

Indeed, frustrating the looping figure of continuity on which he had labored and insisting instead on a lack of coincidence, Merleau-Ponty warned that reversibility is "always imminent and never realized in fact."[179] We cannot, in other words, touch and feel ourselves touching, or hear ourselves as we hear others. Rather, there is a gap, a hinge, a space, a hiatus between touching and touched that amounts to the impossibility of superimposing one experience on top of the other. The concepts of divergence, difference, deflection, fission, and dehiscence were variously used by Merleau-Ponty to refute perceptual presence, positing instead a fundamental ambiguity at the heart of this encounter between self and world: "My flesh and that of the world therefore involve clear zones, clearings, about which pivot their opaque zones."[180]

In their critique of representation, motivated by a rejection of the art object as a rational structure, Clark and Oiticica eroded aesthetic subjective projection: the principle of certitude, the identity of thought and object, to which concretism aspired. But the works discussed here also invalidated the phenomenological idealism—Husserlian in kind—that aspires to the coincidence of perception and self, immediacy, astonishment, and transparency that the "Manifesto Neoconcreto" and the nonobject had longed for. Consequently, the phenomenological reduction these artists initially sought to achieve did not salvage the subject of artistic production and reception but rather perilously repositioned it. The mid-1960s saw an exploration of the ramifications of this demise of the art object that took the artists in radically different directions: Clark's bodily and participatory propositions (which reached their culmination in her nonverbal relational therapy) and the collective, environmental matrix of Oiticica's post-neoconcrete work. For both artists, this move outside the artwork, and also beyond the self, was a return to the inside and the world of affect—an oscillation that, in the end, knew no beyond, but only the spacing of the interval, the hinge, the fold.

# 4

# FORMS OF AFFECT

## Hélio Oiticica's *Parangolés*, 1964–65

> As it unfolds, the work establishes and recognizes intercorporeal space. It is made for that space, and we cannot expect a sense of totality from it, as if it were merely a work situated in an ideal time-space that may or may not require the spectator's participation.
>
> HÉLIO OITICICA, "ANOTAÇÕES SOBRE O PARANGOLÉ," NOVEMBER 1964[1]

> With affect, a body is as much outside itself as in itself—webbed in its relations—until ultimately such firm distinctions cease to matter.
>
> GREGORY J. SEIGWORTH AND MELISSA GREGG, "AN INVENTORY OF SHIMMERS," 2010[2]

The years 1963 and 1964 signaled an important period in the work of Lygia Clark and Hélio Oiticica, one that brought neoconcretism's lessons on form and structure to the space of bodily and social interaction. The move by Clark and Oiticica outside the institutions of art and into the world seemed to signal the end of an era of unrelenting faith in development and coincided with the beginning of political and cultural conflict in Brazil. This chapter maps Oiticica's work as it unfolded into the environment through his *Parangolés,* initiated in 1964 and developed in close dialogue with the artist's involvement with samba and the favela (shantytown) of Mangueira, located in the north region of Rio de Janeiro. The *Parangolés* were, in Oiticica's careful conceptualization, the epitome and true manifestation of environmental art (*arte ambiental*). This art resulted from the abandonment of the conventions of painting and sculpture and involved the creation of environments and the participation of the spectator in accord with Oiticica's interest in the social, political, and ethical dimensions of his work.[3] The *Parangolés*—which primarily took the form of banners, tents, and capes made of layers of plastic

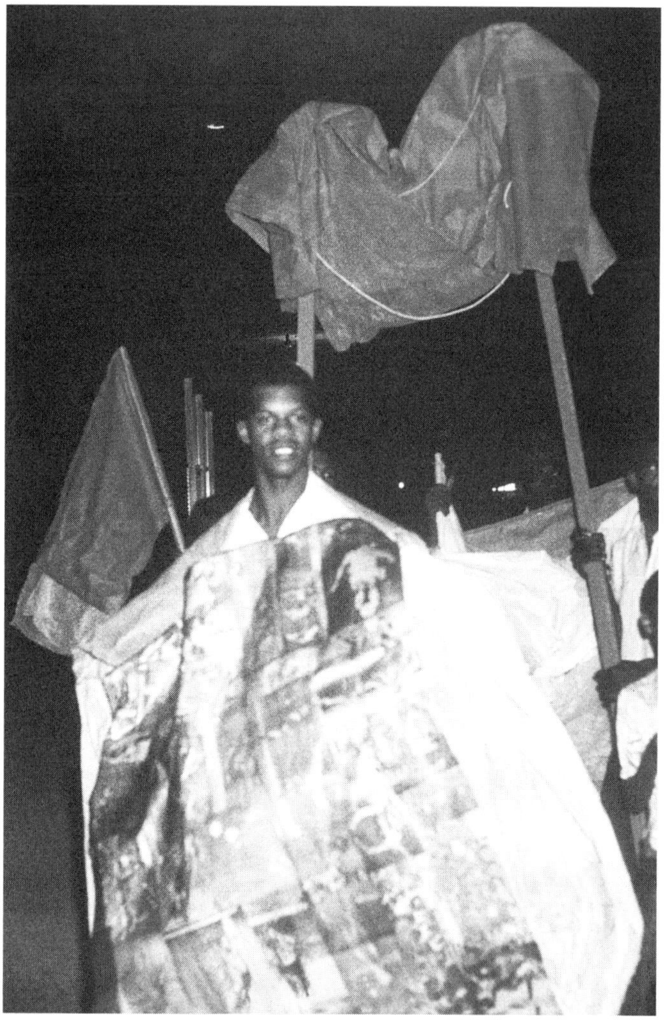

FIGURE 4.1
Miro da Mangueira wears *P6 Parangolé capa 3 "Pedrosa"* (Hélio Oiticica, 1964–65) at the opening of *Opinião 65*, Museu de Arte Moderna do Rio de Janeiro, August 12, 1965.

and cloth painted in bright colors, but also included photographs and text—represented a rupture with the neoconcrete project that preceded them (fig. 4.1). But these works also sustained an engagement with key concerns of neoconcretism—structure, time, space, color, affect, participation—that had allowed Oiticica (along with Lygia Clark and Ferreira Gullar) to displace the ontological (modernist) definition of the work of art advocated by concretism. Grounded in the neoconcrete experience, the *Parangolés* aspired to articulate *forms of being* in the world as opposed to *representations of things* in the world.[4] In so doing, these works actualized and problematized many of the aspirations posited in the theoretical program of 1959–61 (see chapter 3).[5] Through Oiticica's reformulation of space, color, materials, and aesthetic reception, the *Parangolés* crystallized neoconcretism's thinking on subjectivity, affect, and participation.

## *QUAL É O PARANGOLÉ?*

The word *parangolé* lacks a precise meaning. The writer Waly Salomão, a friend of Oiticica, noted that the term was slang from the favela and had multiple meanings. Salomão wrote that "Qual é o parangolé?" was a very common expression at the time and essentially meant "What's going on?" "What's up?" or "What's the deal?" Brazilian dictionaries confirm that *parangolé* was slang for pointless conversation, insincere banter, bragging, loquacity, idle chatter, and a jumble of words.[6] The term could also indicate confusion, the popular excitement that contrasts with normative behavior or formal situations—a pertinent association given the *Parangolés'* origin in the context of the favela. Like Gullar, who described one of Clark's works using the slang term *troço* (an undefined thing: something, stuff); like Clark herself, who called one of her series *Bichos* (critters or animals); and like the German-Venezuelan artist Gego, who likewise called her antisculptural production *bichos,* which in Spanish alludes to bugs as well as amorphous and heterogeneous things—like all of these figures, Oiticica clearly sought in the plasticity of language a way to bypass rigid definitions by using words that encompassed the intermedial, even ephemeral status of these unconventional works.

Oiticica himself recalled seeing the word *parangolé* written across a piece of burlap that formed the wall of a shack; he first noticed it while riding a bus on his way to work at Rio's Museu Nacional.[7] His description of the shack (fig. 4.2) is quite detailed, a clear indication of how important the spatial and environmental qualities—and the precarious and improvisational nature—of these makeshift constructions found in the urban landscape would become for him. He wrote that the shack was formed by four wooden posts and included a "virtual wall" made of strings, from which hung pieces of plastic of various colors. A piece of burlap attached to one of the posts created the effect of a tent, inside of which someone slept (as Oiticica later verified). He ended the short note describing this encounter with the word *parangolé* by lamenting his failure to photograph the structure, which was dismantled soon thereafter.[8] This brief, handwritten text contains the elements of a mythic origin: a chance encounter, a revelation, a significant identification. It also hints at the *Parangolés'* axiomatic references—the shelter, spatial interaction, the body—as these were articulated in the works' three main iterations: *Parangolé tenda* (Parangolé Tent), *Parangolé estandarte* (Parangolé Banner), and *Parangolé capa* (Parangolé Cape).[9]

Interpretations of the *Parangolés* have been based on the understanding that their development coincided with Oiticica's regular visits to the favela of Mangueira beginning in late 1963 and early 1964.[10] However, as early as 1962, in a short note on his *Penetráveis* (Penetrables)—colored wooden panels assembled to encourage the viewer to enter the structure they formed—Oiticica argued for works that were responsive to their surroundings and could be experienced and comprehended in relation to their site. In so doing, he announced a key point for an understanding of site specificity that would be developed in the coming years by artists in North America and Europe.[11] The

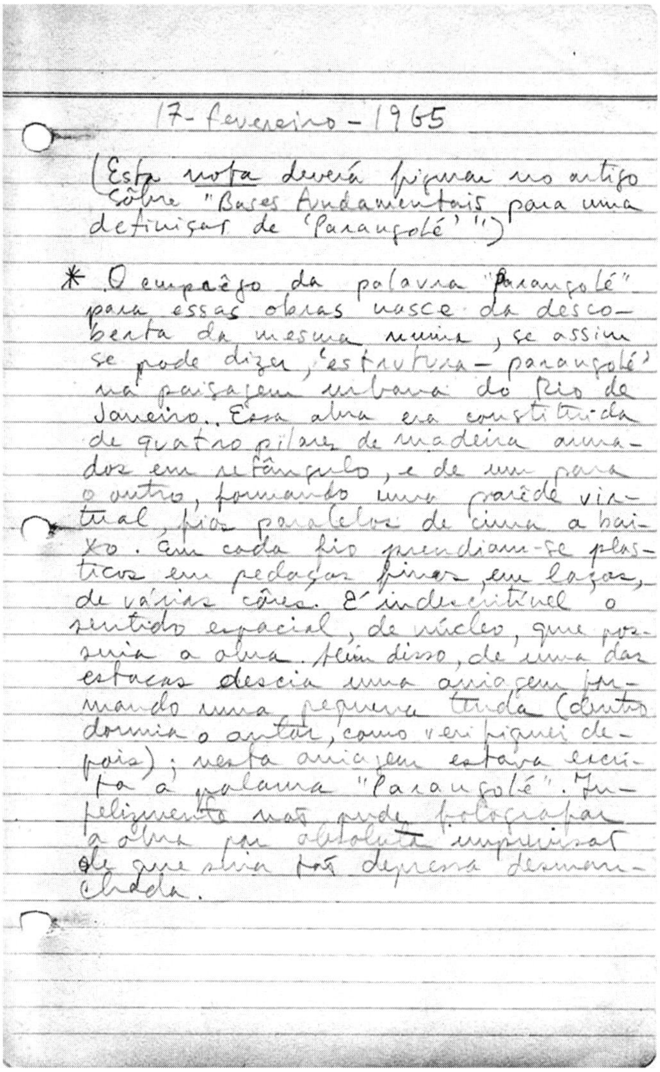

17-fevereiro-1965

(Esta nota deverá figurar no artigo sôbre "Bases Fundamentais para uma definição de 'Parangolé'")

* O emprêgo da palavra "Parangolé" para essas obras nasce da descoberta da mesma numa, se assim se pode dizer, 'estrutura-parangolé' na paisagem urbana do Rio de Janeiro. Essa obra era constituída de quatro pilares de madeira armados em retângulo, e de um para o outro, formando uma parede virtual, fios paralelos de cima a baixo. Em cada fio prendiam-se plásticos em pedaços finos em laços, de várias côres. É indescritível o sentido espacial, de núcleo, que possuía a obra. Além disso, de uma das estacas descia uma aniagem formando uma pequena tenda (dentro dormia o autor, como verifiquei depois); nesta aniagem estava escrita a palavra "Parangolé". Infelizmente não pude fotografar a obra por absoluta imprevisão de que seria tão depressa desmanchada.

FIGURE 4.2
Hélio Oiticica, note, February 17, 1965.

*Parangolés,* therefore, were clearly conceived and produced with Mangueira serving as more than a catalyst or backdrop.

In late 1963 the artist Jackson Ribeiro, who was assisting Amilcar de Castro in creating decorations for the 1964 carnival parade of the Escola de Samba Estação Primeira de Mangueira (Samba School of the First Station of Mangueira), invited Oiticica to help out. Oiticica then became a regular in this urban and social fringe of northern Rio de Janeiro.[12] The artist quickly embedded himself in the daily life of Mangueira: he made friends with inhabitants and outlaws (a gesture that should be understood in the context of his embrace of marginality in the face of cultural stagnation); he became familiar with the local drug culture; and, most importantly, he became a *passista* (lead dancer) of the local samba school, participating for the first time in this capacity in the carnival festivities of 1965. These experiences were fundamental to the creation of the *Parangolés,* allowing Oiticica to refine his previous investigations into the structure of the nonobject and the relationship between subject and object.

The transformation of the nonobject into the *Parangolé* was also, however, mediated by Oiticica's engagement with the ideas and activities of the critic and poet Ferreira Gullar and the Brazilian cultural Left.[13] By 1962 Gullar had fully broken with the experimental project of the Brazilian avant-garde to involve himself with the Centros Populares de Cultura (Centers for Popular Culture, or CPC), an organization devoted to the development and promotion of a national culture of popular roots. Gullar served as director of the CPC's Rio de Janeiro chapter from 1962 to 1964. Though unwilling to relinquish the nonrepresentational thrust of his artistic enterprise, Oiticica advanced his practice through a vernacular filter that was relevant to the cultural Left at the time and paralleled Gullar's commitment to popular culture.[14] The temporal unfolding into space of the *Relevos espaciais* (Spatial Reliefs), *Nuclei,* and *Penetráveis* subsequently implied the enmeshment of Oiticica's work in a politicized cultural agenda that valued collective participation and the communicative power of popular culture. This was facilitated by the specific spatial matrix of the *Parangolés*: the urban and social fringes of Mangueira.

The CPC was founded in Rio de Janeiro in 1961, operated branches throughout the country, and was dissolved in 1964. It developed courses in theater, cinema, visual arts, and philosophy and produced films, plays, and publications. The CPC was one of several Brazilian projects at the time that were preoccupied with popular art, revolutionary art, and art for the masses. These themes were key to a larger discussion about national and popular culture that responded to long-standing issues of economic and cultural dependency. Both the União Nacional dos Estudantes (National Student Union) and the CPC (which operated under it) were part of what the Brazilian critic Roberto Schwarz called an "intelligent" moment in the country's history—one in which ideas of revolution resulted in economic and political reforms that were clearly leftist in tenor.[15] As the Brazilian writer Heloísa Buarque de Hollanda wrote, this impetus fueled political enthusiasm and activism that gained the support of artists and intellectuals and brought into focus "at the center of their preoccupations a commitment to social participation."[16]

The CPC's principles were articulated in a 1962 text written by the sociologist Carlos Estevam Martins, the organization's first director. The document, openly Marxist in nature, called for a revolutionary art that would affect the material foundations of society. Martins had previously been associated with the Instituto Superior de Estudos Brasileiros (Superior Institute of Brazilian Studies), which as early as the 1950s had espoused an agenda for national development and economic autonomy that responded to the developmentalist ideology that defined the decade.[17] Accordingly, the CPC document sprang from a programmatic assessment of the Brazilian situation, which was fraught with contradictions, for example between developing and backward forces of production, between working social classes and those who owned the means of production, between a nation eager to achieve its economic potential and global imperialism.[18] Martins argued that these facts demanded new forms of artistic engagement. Warning against banal novelty and subjectivity and invoking objectivity and the laws of science, he declared: "What is new is the people, and the new is where the people are, and only where the people are."[19] This prioritizing of the people established the main thrust of Martins's manifesto and led to a discussion of the social position of artists, their need to identify with the public, and the perils of their petit bourgeois origins. In the face of the conflict between what is required of the engaged artist in the struggle and what ensues spontaneously as the expression of an individuality allied with a bourgeois ideology, Martins argued for the necessity of imposing limits on creative activity. This censorship was not compelled by the CPC, he clarified, but rather was the result of a subjective adjustment—artistic self-control, as it were—that grew out of the artist's commitment to communicating with the people.

Following this train of thought, Martins defined two problematic categories: "art of the people," in which the artist is not an agent differentiated from the masses that consume the products of the artist's making (for example, folk art), and "popular art," in which the masses are the unproductive receptors of art created by specialists who have no control over the circulation of their products in the market (TV soap operas, for example). Martins declared that both of these practices were incapable of achieving the status of art in bourgeois culture (that is, Art with a capital *A*) and that they also lacked the imperative of shaping revolutionary subjects. This incapacity was due to naïveté (arguably of its producers) in the case of the "art of the people" and to ingrained escapism in the case of "popular art," and both categories were compromised because of their audiences' complacency with the status quo and the hierarchy that separates them from the high art of the elites. Elite art remained the paradigm around and against which Martins proposed a third, politicized alternative: a "popular revolutionary art" that sprang from the artist's careful reflection on power relations within a society of classes. The goal of this committed art, he suggested, was the production of agency, the creation of a subject in control of his or her own destiny. Martins argued that this third option could only be achieved through a collective entity whose organized political activity was to be its sole "path to redemption."

Martins's text was the most complete articulation of the artistic principles of the CPC, and it exercised an undeniable influence on Brazilian culture and art of the early 1960s.[20] As Buarque de Hollanda indicated in her recollection of the period: "Despite its failure as a political and poetic term, ['revolutionary popular art'] succeeded, in its context, in a high level of mobilization among the younger generation of artists and intellectuals to the point where its effects can still be felt today."[21] Several concepts mobilized by the CPC manifesto resonate with concerns that guided the aesthetic inquiry traced by Oiticica in 1964: popular culture, the favela, collective participation. The Brazilian artist Carlos Zilio observed that, in practice, the CPC almost completely dismissed form in favor of content and that, in the end, it had no option but to embrace the "art of the people" (which Martins in his manifesto had spurned due to its purported naïveté) since what mattered most was to reach the largest audience with the "best possible ideological content."[22] By 1964, though, members of the CPC found limiting the prospect of developing a mass audience to the detriment of the quality of the artwork.[23] This would suit Oiticica just fine: while popular revolutionary art was certainly an epochal reference in the development of the *Parangolés,* the CPC's reliance on representation and content and its concomitant rejection of formal experimentation and expression were anathema to the young artist.

Many of Martins's condemnations regarding bourgeois art could have been targeting neoconcretism, though no style, movement, or artist is mentioned by the author. Against what he simply calls the "art of the elites"—with its limitless expressive resources, its creative freedom, its search for new forms, its individualism, and its aestheticism—Martins proposed an art that recycles strategies, that is disrespectful of unitary style, that is communicative, and that, most importantly, is made for "the other."[24] It is hard not to see the *Parangolés* as a negotiation of these various cultural and political dictums: a rejection of the representational imperatives of the CPC's manifesto (specifically its moratorium on formal experimentation) and, at the same time, an embrace of its communicative and collective aspirations, predicated on the artist's identification with the people. Indeed, for Martins, the popular revolutionary artist had to belong to the cultural community to which he or she spoke—in this case, the disenfranchised classes to which "the people" of the manifesto referred. This requirement helps contextualize Oiticica's attempt to integrate himself into the life of Mangueira, a complex intervention that was fraught with contradictions.

Gullar, too, wrote about the value of art as a medium of collective communication in his 1965 book *Cultura posta em questão* (Culture in Question).[25] The book was less the final word on contemporary culture than an analysis of Gullar's personal intellectual trajectory vis-à-vis Brazil's recent cultural history, and in it the poet suggested lines of thought that could have been interpreted as—or redirected toward—less dogmatic resolutions than the CPC manifesto had offered. For example, he spoke of the artwork as a type of "action upon social reality" (*ação sôbre a realidade social*), as the result of a continuity with local cultural experience, and he noted that no individual exists outside a situation (a nod to phenomenology). Certainly, Gullar's acute analysis of architecture as a utilitarian structure with socioeconomic implications, of the end of painting, and of the determining role of the art market—as well as his sustained, if vague, references to participation—must have recommenced and redirected a fruitful, albeit interrupted (due to Gullar's rejection of avant-garde practices in 1961–62) intellectual relationship between Oiticica and the critic.[26]

### THE STRUCTURE OF THE FOLD

Oiticica's *Parangolé capas*—constructed around a pliant materiality of folds and protrusions and designed to be worn by the artist and others—thus emerged at a specific cultural and historical juncture: on the one hand, in relation to the phenomenological and participatory potentialities of the nonobject, and on the other, in relation to the politicized collective precepts of the Brazilian Left. As defined by the CPC manifesto, the elite artist avoided conforming to the impersonal idiom of the masses and thus was happy to occupy the margins of history. In contrast, the revolutionary artist's priority was not the immanence of form but engagement with the people of the public. Consequently, Martins condemned "the ideal of absolute spontaneity, the Bergsonian ambition of overcoming the evil of mediation."[27] It is remarkable that Martins not only mentions one of Oiticica's favorite philosophers but also associates one of neoconcretism's greatest aspirations—the bypassing of the mediation of representation—with elite art's most palpable ideal. Gullar, too, questioned the idealism of his own neoconcretist position in its search for the pure state of poetry, its desire for a total identification between experience and expression, and its longing for a language of pure signification.[28] However, the detailed analysis that Gullar devoted to his poetical-experimental trajectory (and that of contemporary art) in *Cultura posta em questão* suggests that his previous experiences were too important to be totally rejected. With words that could be extrapolated from Gullar's text to describe the border-crossing practices of Clark and Oiticica in 1963–64, he wrote regarding the boundaries of literary practices: "The experience of the avant-garde, whose nonconformism is limited to the realm of literary forms, when taken to its logical conclusion, exceeds the limits of the literary realm and reinstates the existential and political problem."[29] Here Gullar implicitly addressed the impasse at which the nonobject had arrived. By abandoning artistic conventions that questioned the intrinsic notion of art, the nonobject went beyond the artistic realm, and the resulting dissolution of boundaries—boundaries between mediums disrupted by the elliptical relation between self and world that phenomenology had encouraged—rendered the art object (the nonobject) a mere "material shell" (*casca material*) incapable of engaging with that same world that shattered its self-sufficiency.[30]

If Martins's text was a blueprint for the politicized artistic practices of the 1960s,[31] then we can identify in the genesis of the *Parangolés* a series of elements that clearly engage with the theoretical framework delineated by the CPC. Did Oiticica find in samba and the favelas a model of collective organization—and subjectivity—that resonated with the politicized and vernacular priorities of the culture of the period? Could the bodies of samba, appropriated by the artist as the support of the first *Parangolés*, facilitate his entry into the communal life of the favela? According to Martins, "Having chosen the people as its public, revolutionary popular art has nothing to do, in its contents, with the art of the people or popular art, but it needs to approach their forms since it is with these forms that one develops the language that communicates with the people."[32] Oiticica redirected this proposition in his foundational text of 1964, "Bases fundamentais para uma definição do 'Parangolé'" (Fundamental Basis for a Definition of the *Parangolé*) not to defend "popular revolutionary art" but to argue for his own strain of experimental art. In this text he clarified that despite the origin of the word *parangolé* in folkloric slang (*gíria folclórica*), the work does not imply a fusion of folklore with the artist's experience.[33] Instead, like the word *Merz* in Kurt Schwitters's practice, *Parangolé* defined an experimental position; it did not refer to a final meaning but rejected it in favor of a structural approach to reality.

Oiticica's rejection of a referential appropriation of the "art of the people" (so called in CPC jargon) was reiterated by the firm grounding of the *Parangolés* in his neoconcretist artistic practice. He cited his earlier neoconcrete *Penetráveis* and *Nuclei* series and the *Bólides* (Fireballs or Meteorites; plate 16) as the immediate context for the *Parangolés* and insisted on the antirepresentational, antireferential nature of these new works. The *Parangolés* were not about a "transposed objective apprehension" (*apreensão objetiva transposta*) of their materials ("plastics, clothes, mats, screens, ropes, etc.") nor about the objects to which they related ("tents, banners, etc.").[34] What mattered to Oiticica was the "first intention" of the work, thus aligning the process of production that characterized the *Parangolés* with the manipulation of colored pigments in the *Bólides*. The appropriated objects in these works became part of the total work: they were not to be apprehended as parts but as a total phenomenon that should be "direct." Following principles of defamiliarization key to the experience of astonishment necessary for the phenomenological reduction proposed by the "Manifesto Neoconcreto," the reapprehension of the objects and materials employed in these works produced a "relation . . . that transforms what was already known into new knowledge."[35] The rest, that which we do not know, were those aspects of the work that remained open to the imagination. Acknowledging Gullar's efforts to rethink the art object through the nonobject, Oiticica described these dynamic processes as "transobjectivity" and the work as an ideal "transobject."[36]

The term *transobject* had been coined by Mário Pedrosa in 1960 but was fully theorized by Oiticica in a 1963 text on the *Bólides*.[37] These works consisted of painted boxes with compartments and sliding doors that incorporated materials such as pebbles, pigments, mirrors, and pieces of mesh fabric. They also included glass vessels and bottles that contained shells, pigments, and colored liquids. In this 1963 text Oiticica referred to a displacement of the enigmatic condition of the object to the work of art, a process that had been delineated by Gullar in his "Diálogo sobre o não-objeto": the everyday object without a name, removed from its everyday cultural order, becomes opaque and foreign. Like the nonobject, this nameless object is pure materiality, divorced from reference and use. But while this nameless (formerly everyday) object is an absurd presence that collides with perception, the nonobject (which, in its classic neoconcrete manifestation, rejected the readymade)[38] is transparent and integral, its meaning immanent in its form—a form that is pure signification. Merging the experiential potentialities of the nonobject (its condition as pure signification divorced from function and use) with the paradoxical proximity to quotidian space (the space of objects) of his *Bólides,* Oiticica insisted on a total identification between the structure of the appropriated objects and the structure of the resulting artwork. Writing about the perceptual dynamics of the *Bólides,* which he described in terms of a child's first experience of the qualities of objects, Oiticica explained that their purpose was "a matter of stripping existing objects, whether utilitarian or not, of their connotative qualities in order to leave them in their primitive purity. Clearly, earlier perceptions cannot be erased, but new perspectives can be gained through a new aesthetic experience, allowing for the extraction of new possibilities from an object or a given solid form."[39] As an example he pointed to the boxes used in his *Bólides*: these were known objects that might be reapprehended, experienced anew, through a new spatial valorization of the color and elements they contained. In the *Bólides,* dislocation and recontextualization advanced the "primary formulation" of the nonobject, articulated now through everyday materials subsumed within the overall structure and the "new experience" (*nova vivência*) of the work.

According to Oiticica, by the mid-1960s the neoconcrete nonobject had degenerated into a proliferation of objects, boxes, reliefs, and mixed-media work that he deemed academic—just one more category that undermined the experimental vibrancy of the best art. In 1968 he criticized these developments as banal and clarified that, beyond a simple rejection of established categories such as painting and sculpture, what was at stake in that repudiation of conventional mediums was the very *being* of art—its *whys and wherefores,* its modes—which in the truly experimental work of the period produced an interest in "action on the environment," in propositions, in the search for experiences (*vivências*).[40] Almost ten years after the "Manifesto Neoconcreto," Oiticica's interests clearly reflected the influence of phenomenology and the tenets of neoconcretism. The move away from painting and sculpture initially indexed by the nonobject was to be superseded, in true experimental art, by "a discovery of the world in each moment." Oiticica added that the object "does not exist as a 'work' established 'a priori,' but is [instead] a creation of whatever we want it to be."[41] Echoing Lygia Clark's description of her proposition *Caminhando* (Walking, 1963), he called the object not a resolved work but an "OBJECTact" (*OBJETato*)—"the object of the moment, which exists as it is experienced and can't be repeated."[42] To conclude, he referred to the writer and graphic designer Rogério Duarte's contribution to the debate: the notion of *probjeto.* As Oiticica explained in detail in another text, this invented concept refers to the "probabilities of the object," or, better yet, the object *as* a probability. "Not the result of one probability," he clarified, "but the potentiality for a probability."[43] This idea was in accord with the artist's distrust of the "work of art," with its traditional manifestation as the "realization of an idea." In contrast, Oiticica posited the primacy of *vivências*—a word whose common meaning is *experiences,* but which, he wrote (in English), "I translate sometimes as feelings,"[44] insisting in this way on the affective force that the nonobject had aspired to unleash in 1959.

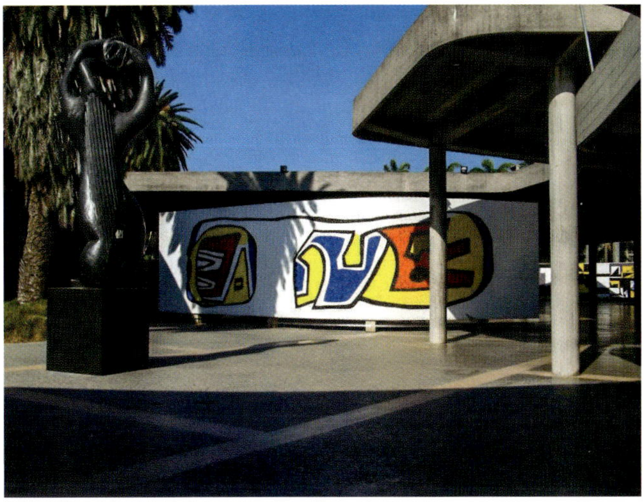

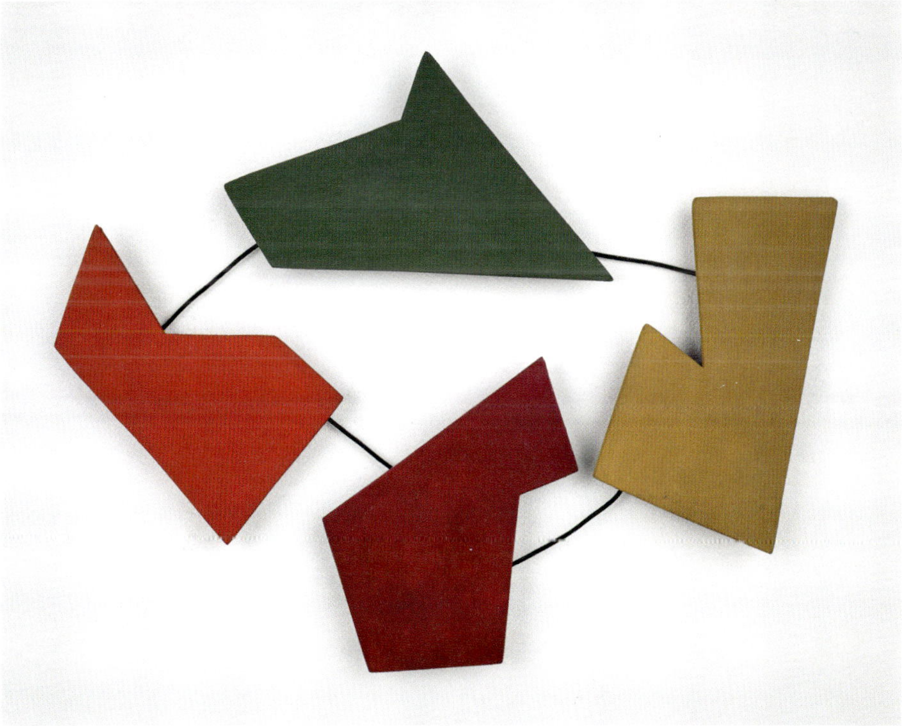

PLATE 1 *(top)*. Carlos Raúl Villanueva, Plaza Cubierta (Covered Plaza), 1953, showing Fernand Léger's *Bimural* (1954) and Henri Laurens's *Amphion* (1953), Ciudad Universitaria de Caracas.

PLATE 2 *(bottom)*. Raúl Lozza, *Relieve #30* (Relief #30), 1945, oil on plywood and metal, 16½ × 21⅛ × 1¹⁄₁₆ in.

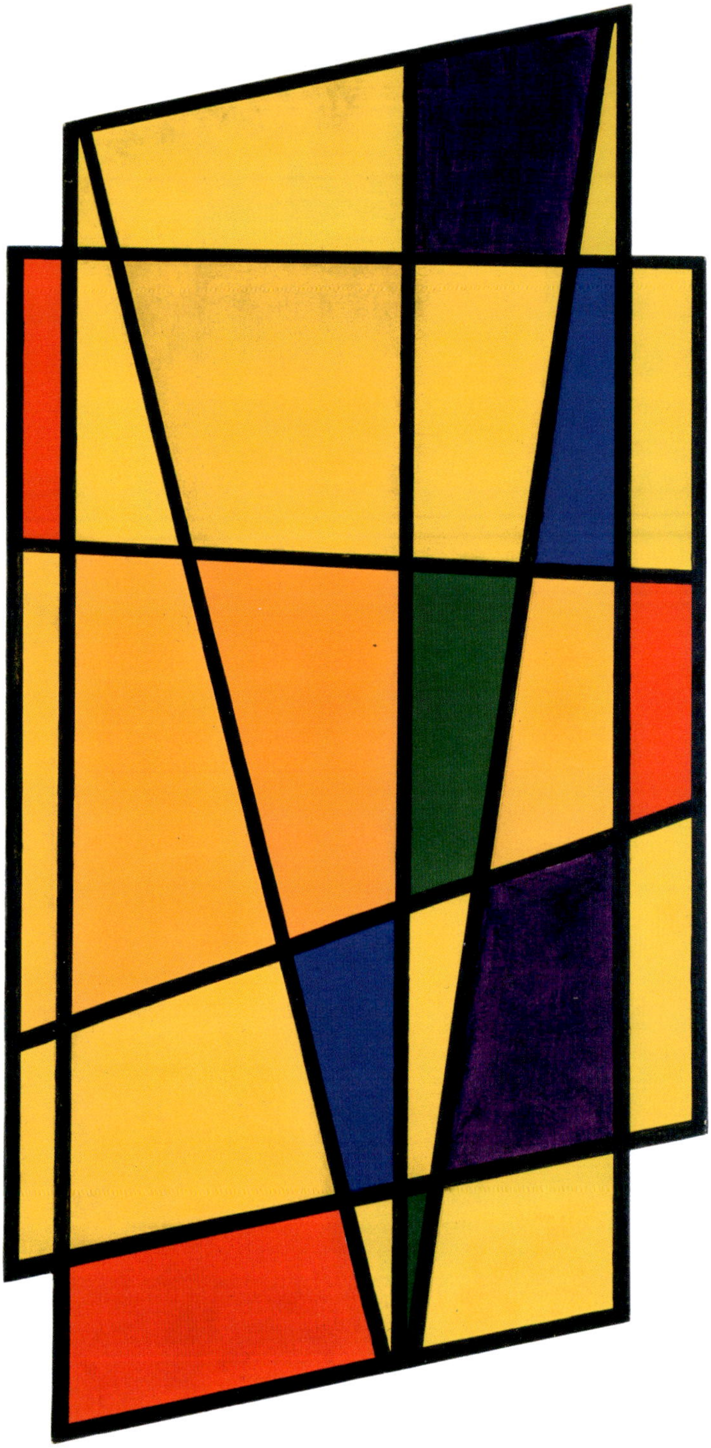

PLATE 3. Manuel Espinosa, *Pintura* (Painting), 1945, oil on wood, 34⅝ × 18½ in.

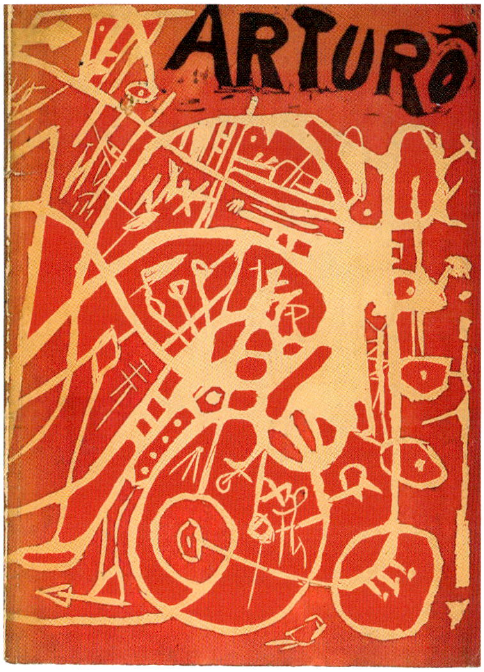


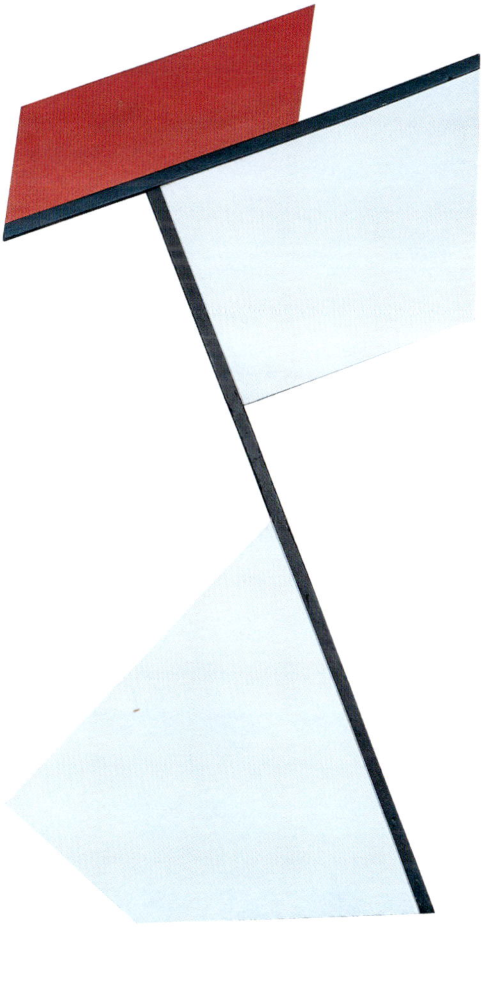

PLATE 4 *(top)*. Tomás Maldonado, cover of *Arturo* magazine, summer 1944.

PLATE 5 *(bottom)*. Lidy Prati, *Untitled*, 1945, oil on wood, 24 3/8 × 18 7/8 in.

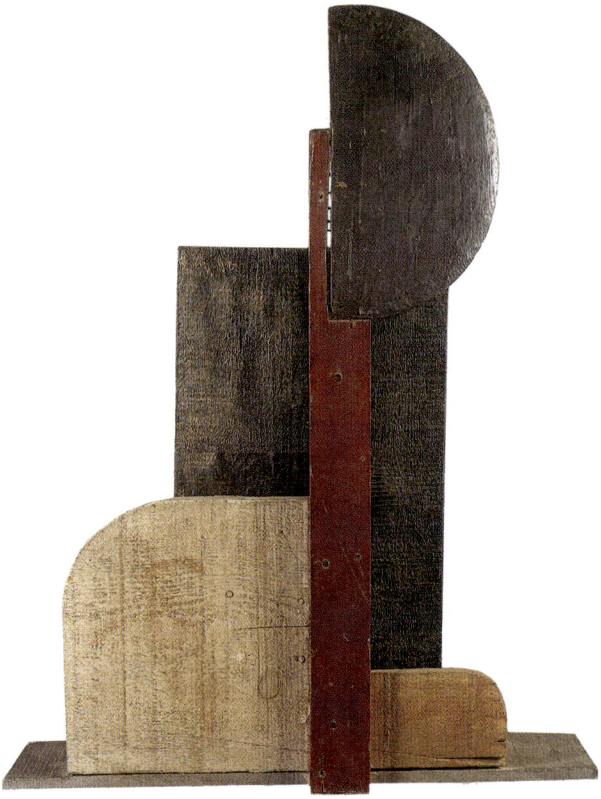

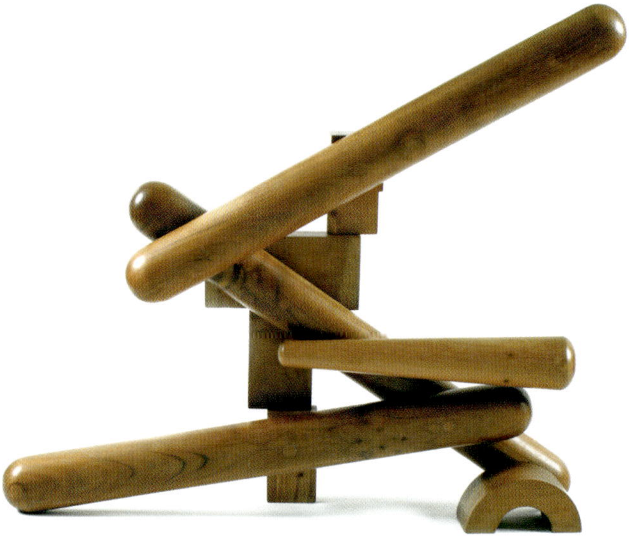

PLATE 6 *(top)*. Joaquín Torres-García, *Objet Plastique/Composition* (Plastic Object/Composition), 1931–34, oil, nails, and wood, 20¼ × 16⅜ × 3½ in.

PLATE 7 *(bottom)*. Gyula Kosice, *Röyi no. 2,* 1944–93, wood, dimensions variable.

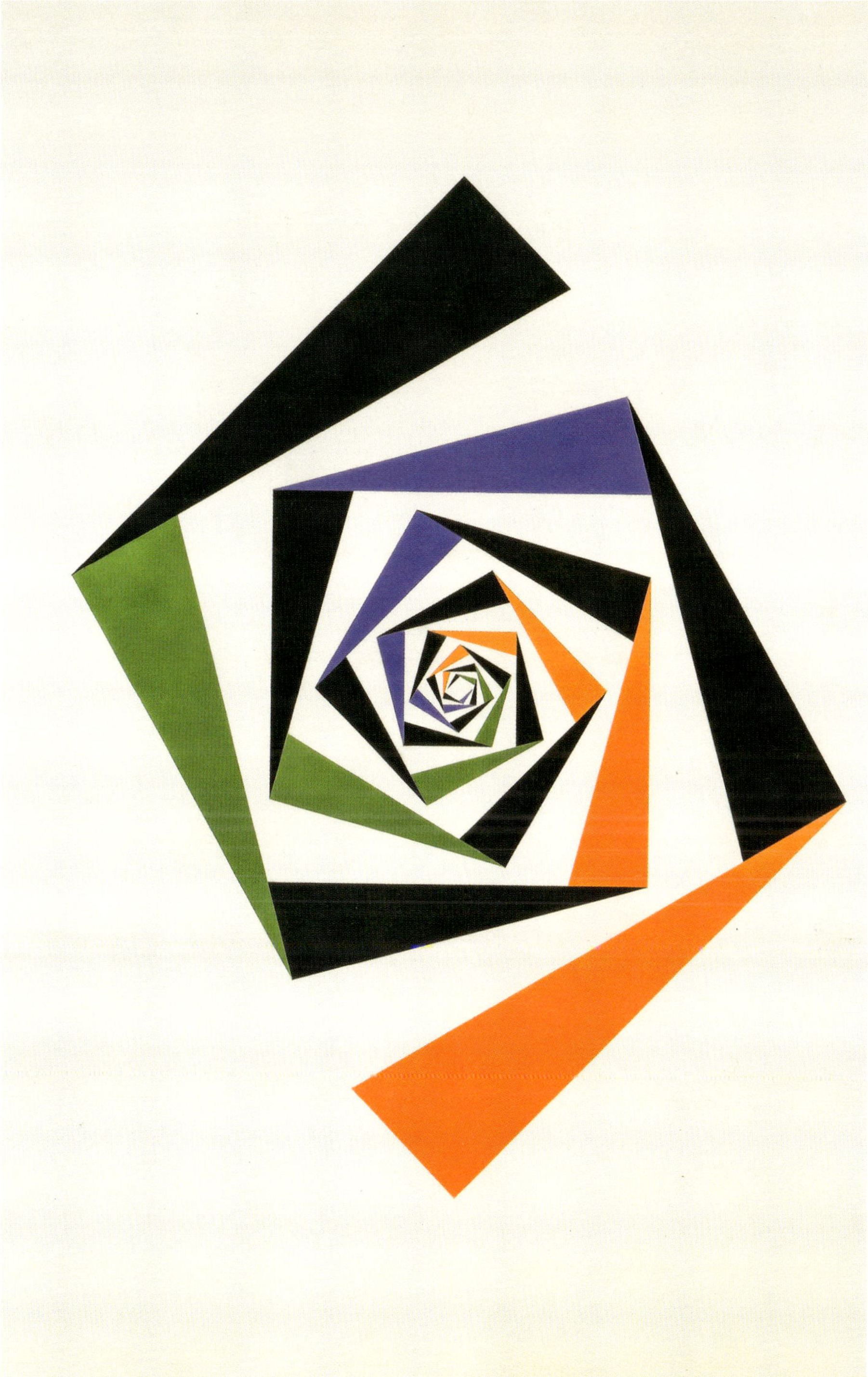

PLATE 8. Max Bill, *Design in 19 Squares,* 1941, bodycolor on cardboard, 40⅛ × 28⅝ in.

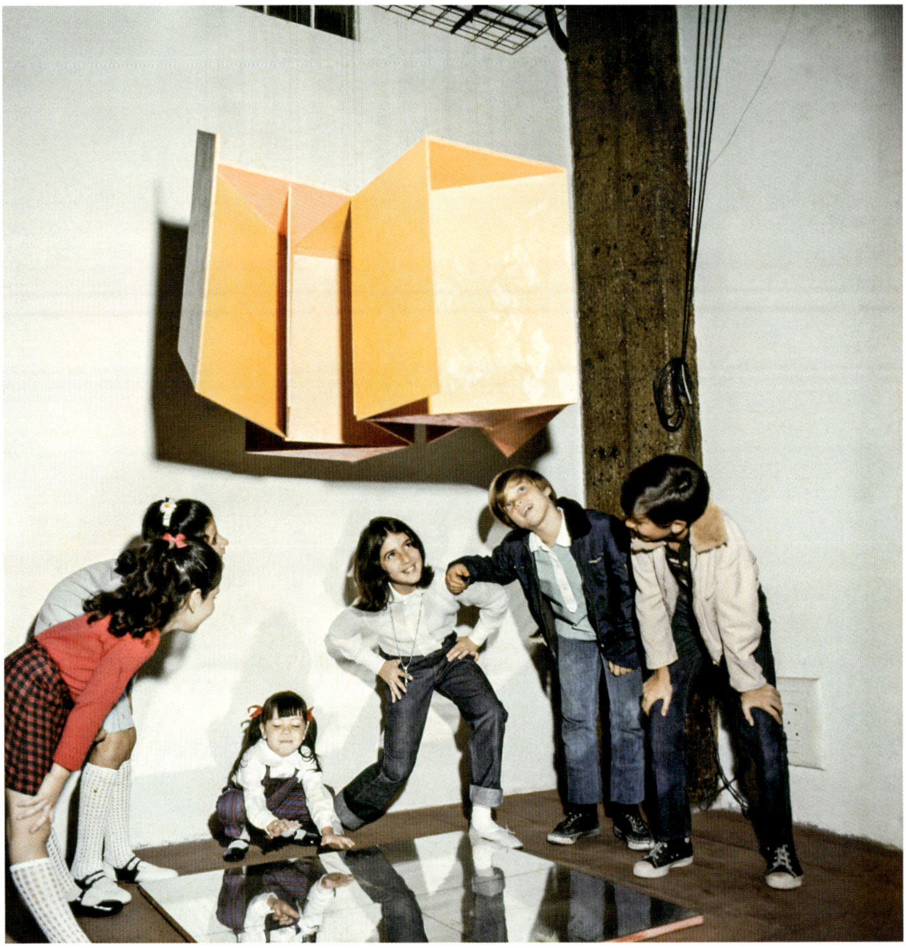

PLATE 9. Hélio Oiticica, *NC1 Pequeno Núcleo no. 1* (NC1 Small Nucleus no. 1), 1960, synthetic resin on wood fiberboard, mirror, 20½ × 14½ × 14½ in.

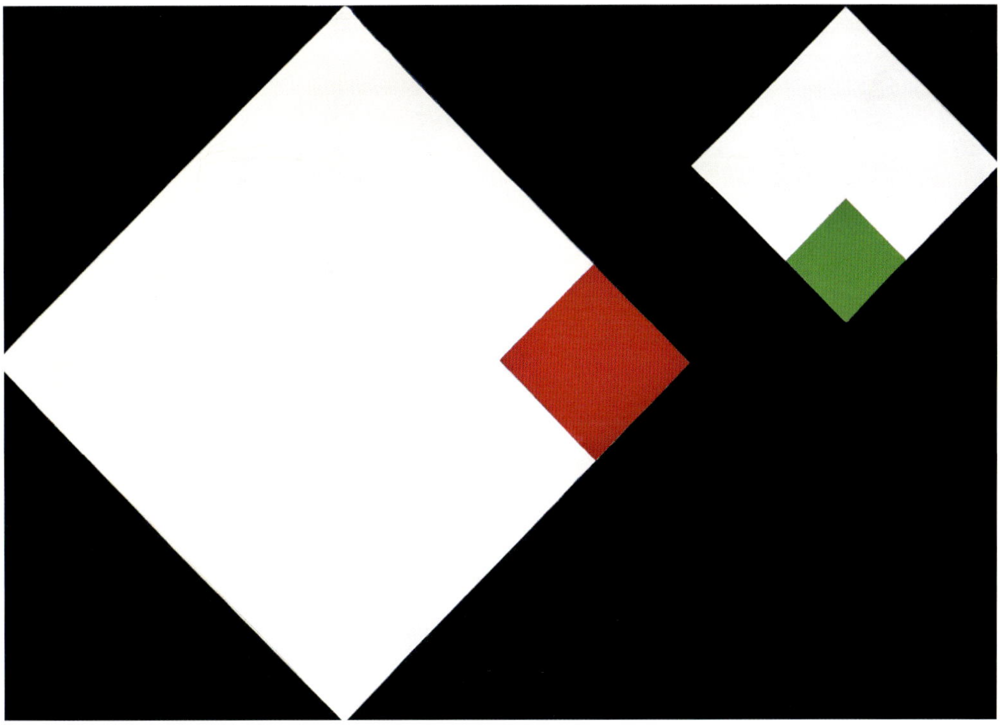

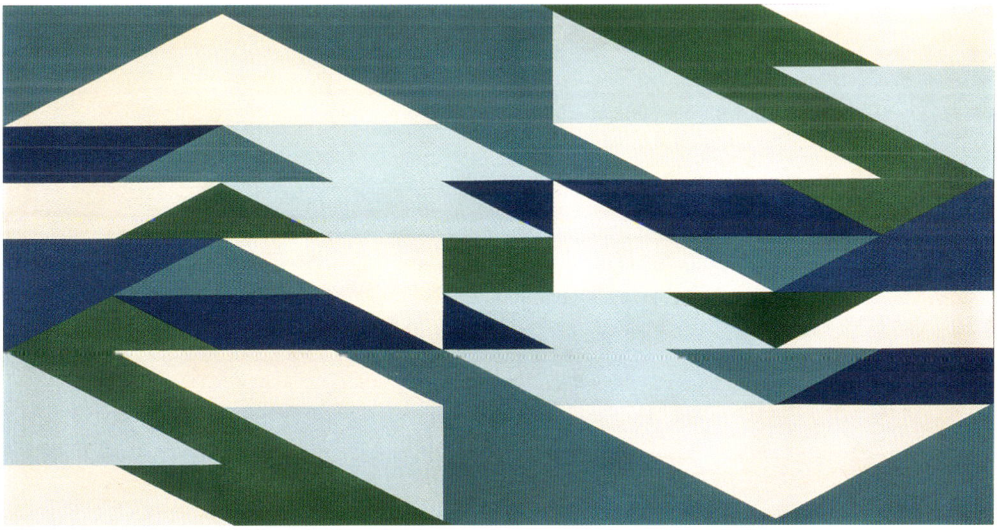

PLATE 10 *(top)*. Geraldo de Barros, *Concreto* (Concrete), 1953, enamel on hardboard, 19⅜ × 27¹⁵⁄₁₆ in.

PLATE 11 *(bottom)*. Lygia Clark, *Superfície modulada no. 20* (Modulated Surface no. 20), 1956, industrial paint on wood, 23⅝ × 47⅝ in.

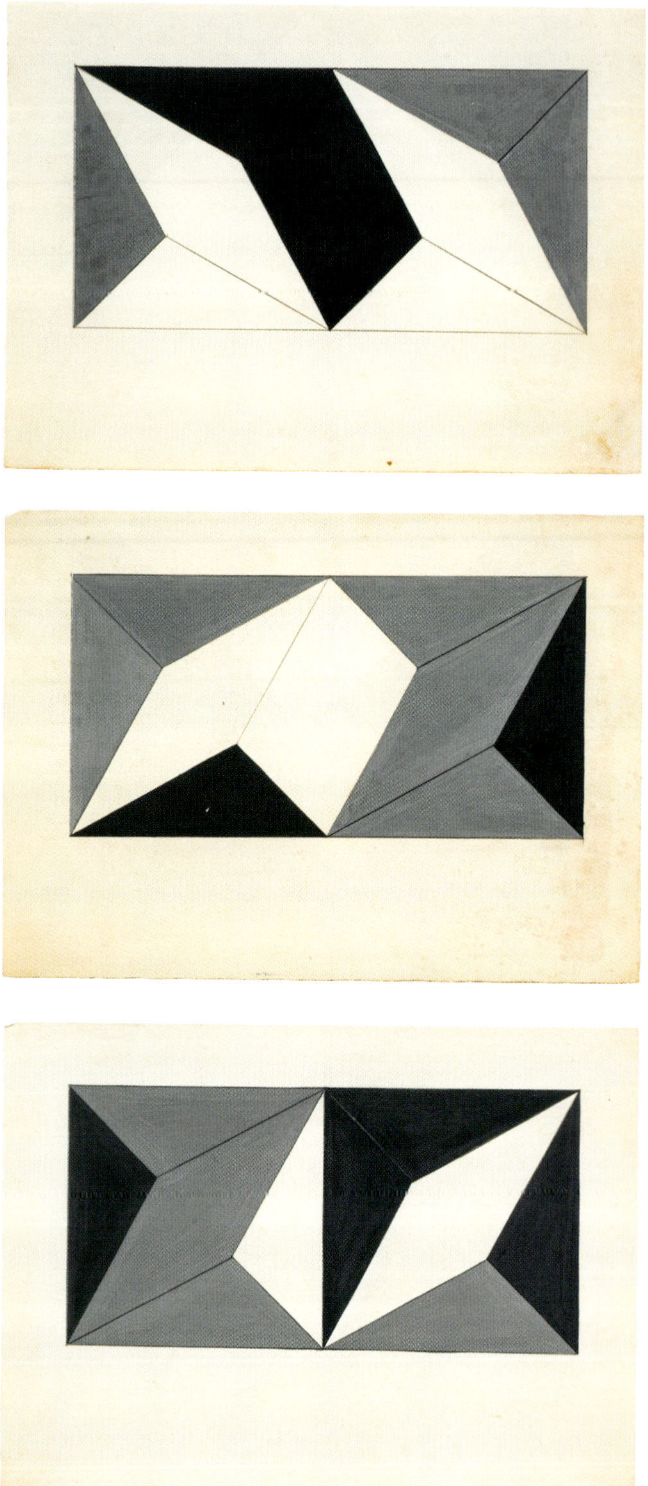

PLATE 12. Lygia Clark, studies for the series *Planos em superfície modulada* (Planes on Modulated Surface), 1957, gouache on paper, 9⅞ × 13¾ in. each.

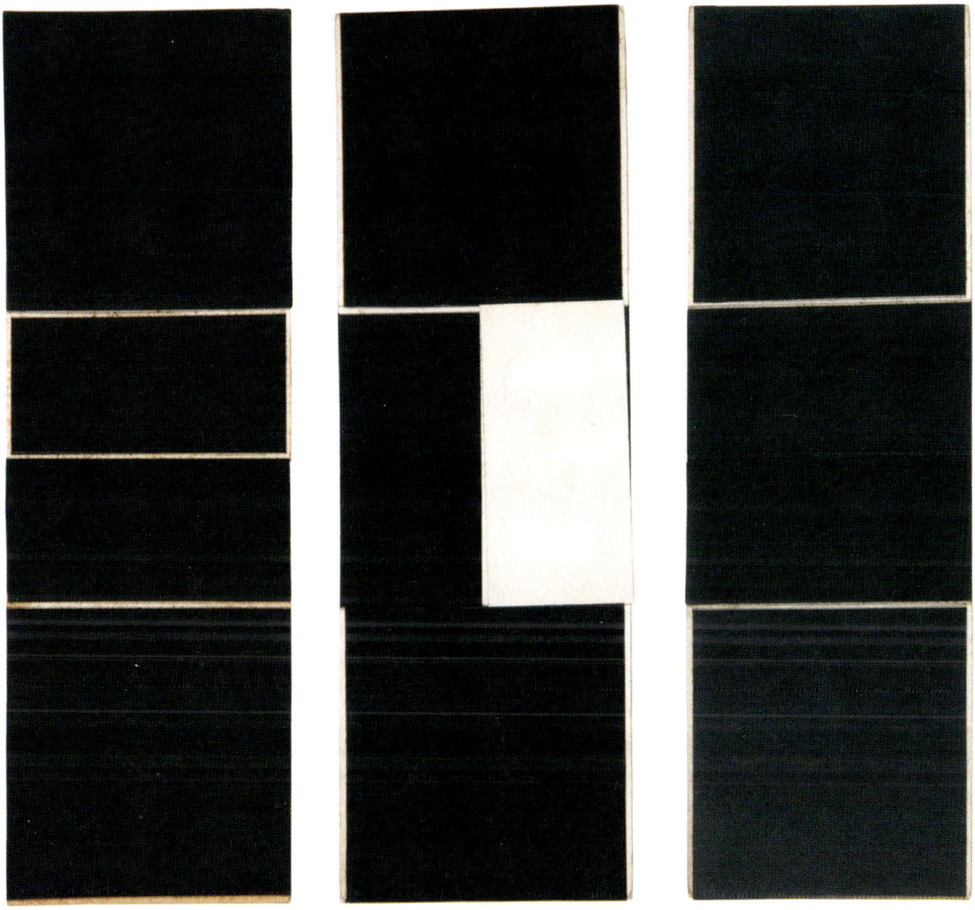

PLATE 13. Lygia Clark, studies for *Espaço modulado* (Modulated Space), 1958, cut and pasted colored paper on paper, approx. 4 × 11¾ in. each.

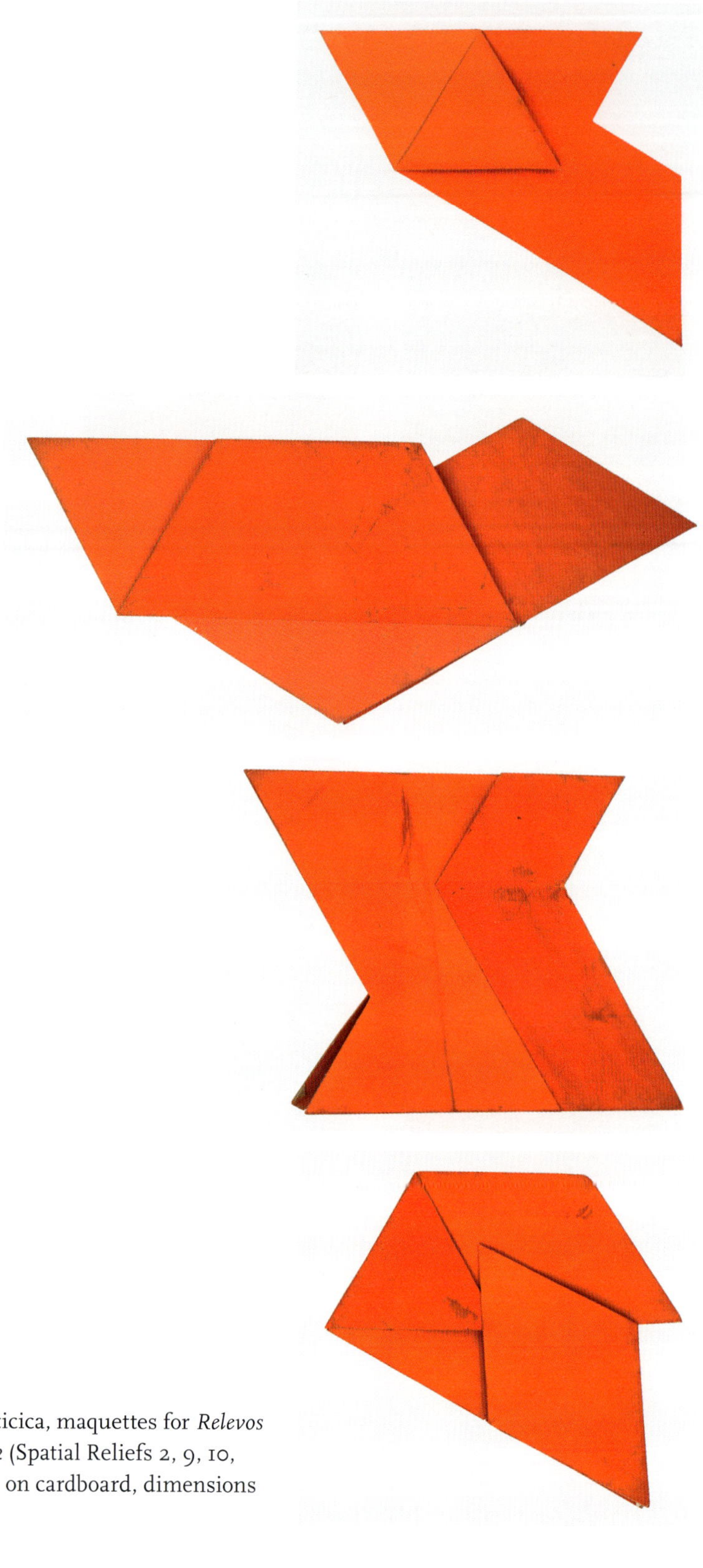

PLATE 14. Hélio Oiticica, maquettes for *Relevos espaciais 2, 9, 10, 12* (Spatial Reliefs 2, 9, 10, 12), 1960, gouache on cardboard, dimensions variable.

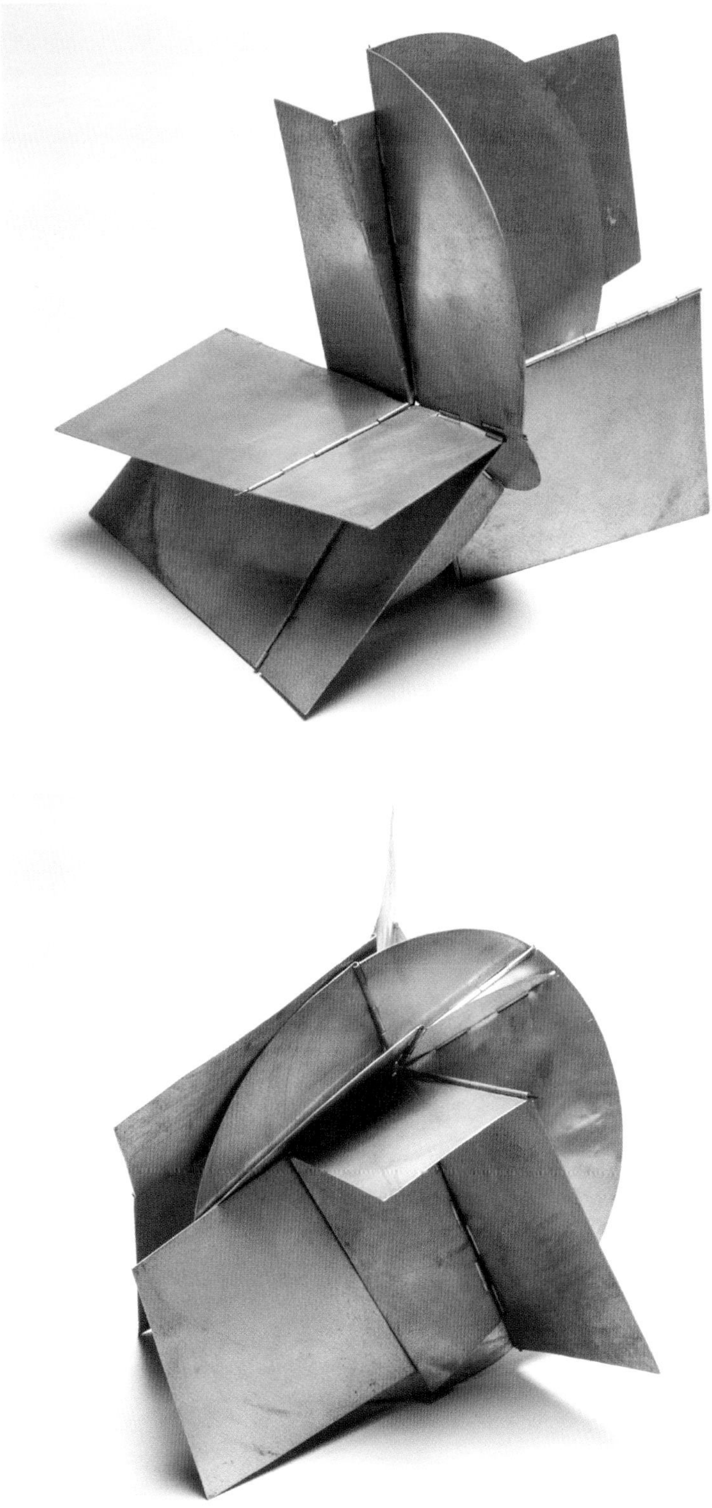

PLATE 15. Lygia Clark, *Bicho* (Critter), ca. 1960, aluminum, dimensions variable.

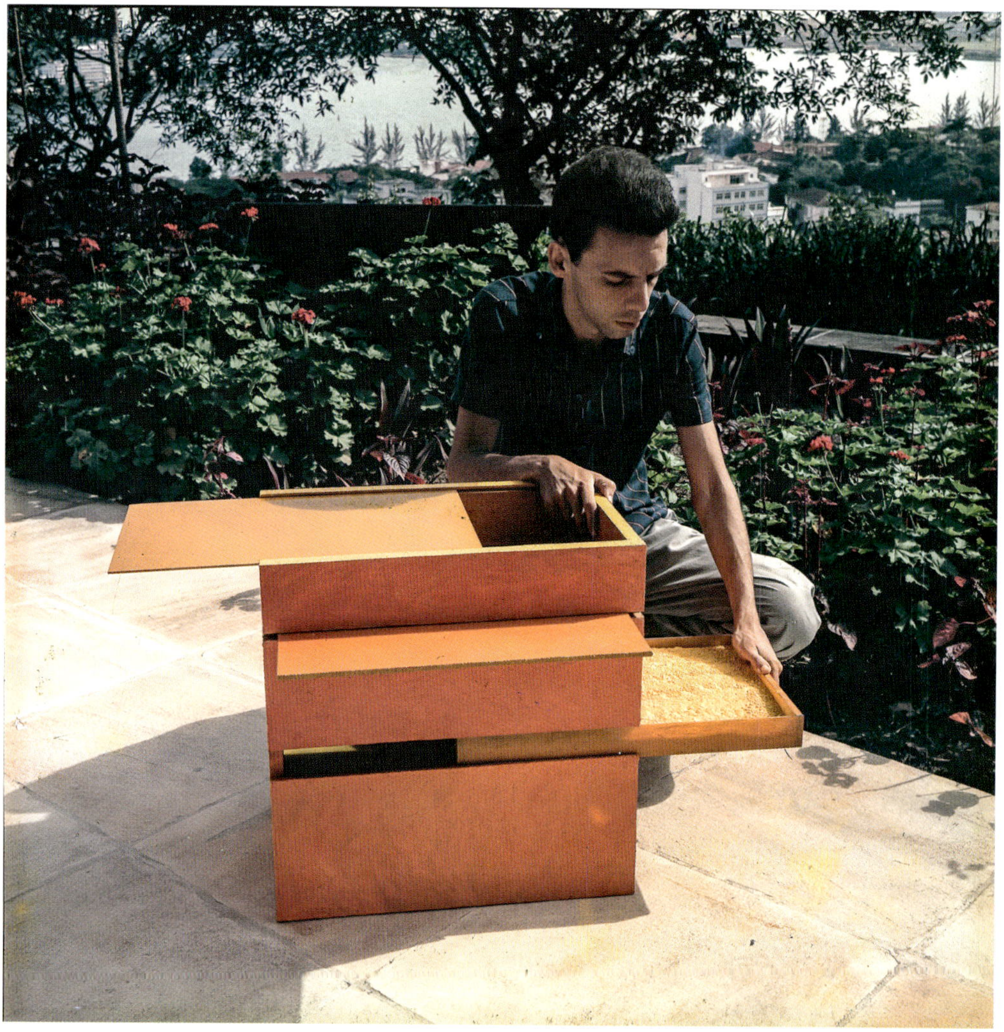

PLATE 16. Hélio Oiticica manipulating *B11 Bólide Caixa 9* (B11 Box Bólide 9), 1964.

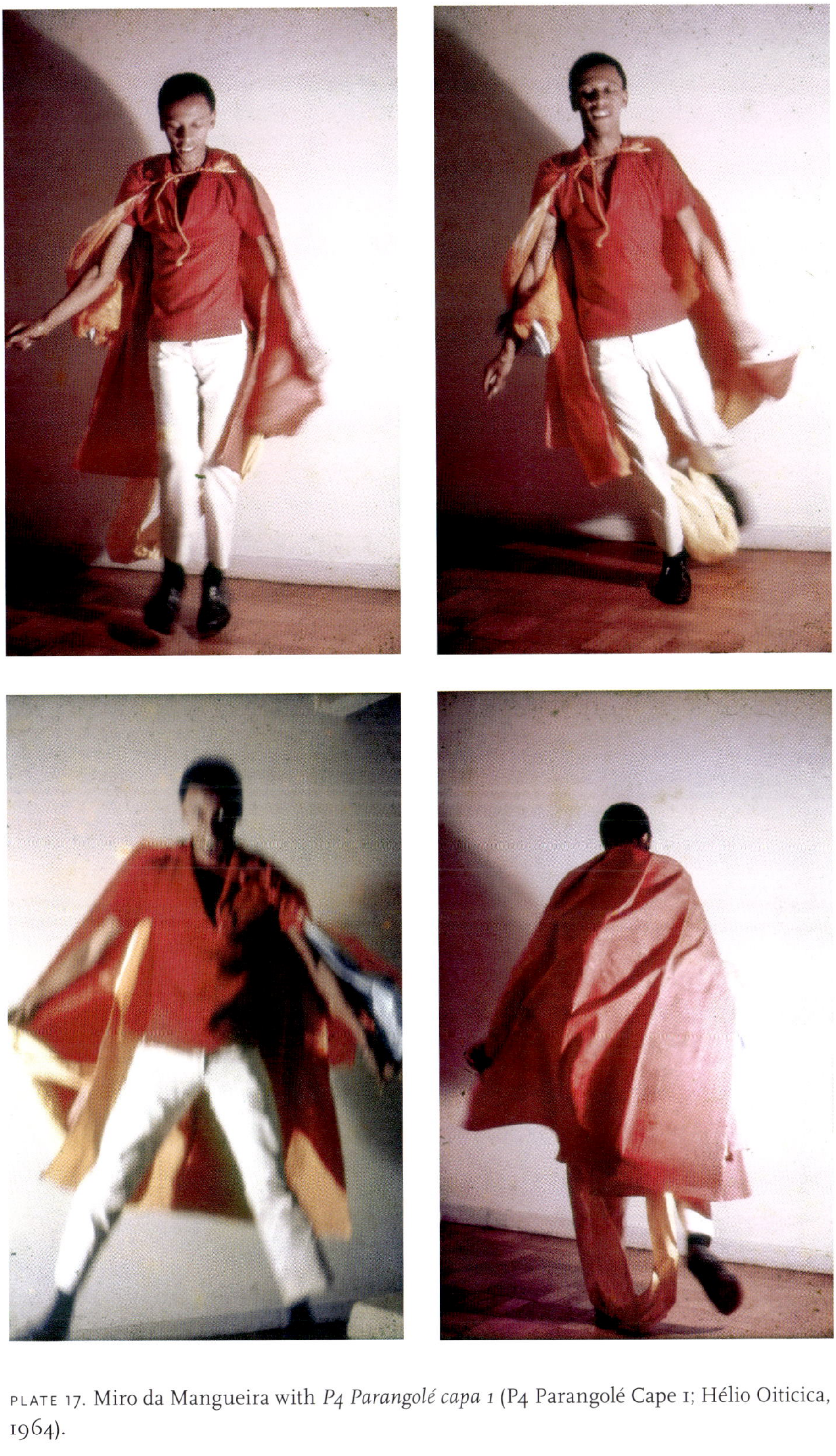

PLATE 17. Miro da Mangueira with *P4 Parangolé capa 1* (P4 Parangolé Cape 1; Hélio Oiticica, 1964).

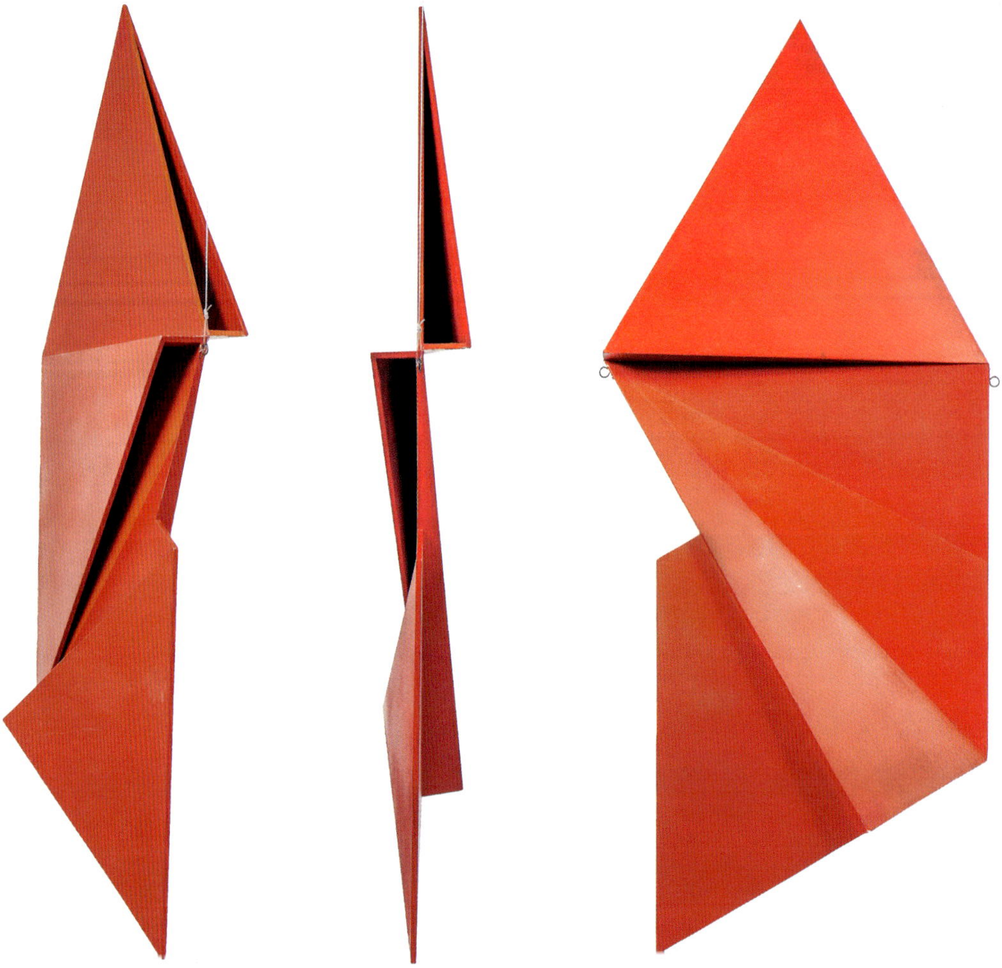

PLATE 18. Hélio Oiticica, *Relevo espacial (vermêlho)* (Spatial Relief [Red]), 1960, polyvinyl acetate resin on plywood, 59 1/16 × 24 7/16 × 6 1/8 in.

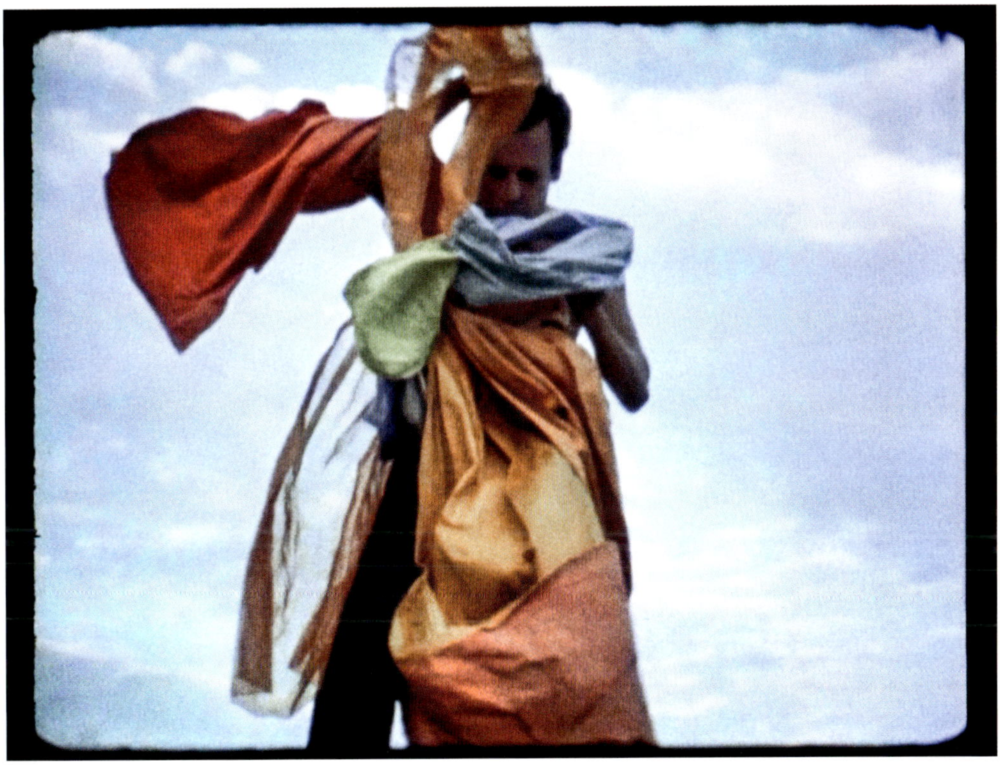

PLATE 19. Hélio Oiticica with *P4 Parangolé capa 1* (1964), still from *H. O.*, a film by Ivan Cardoso, 1979.

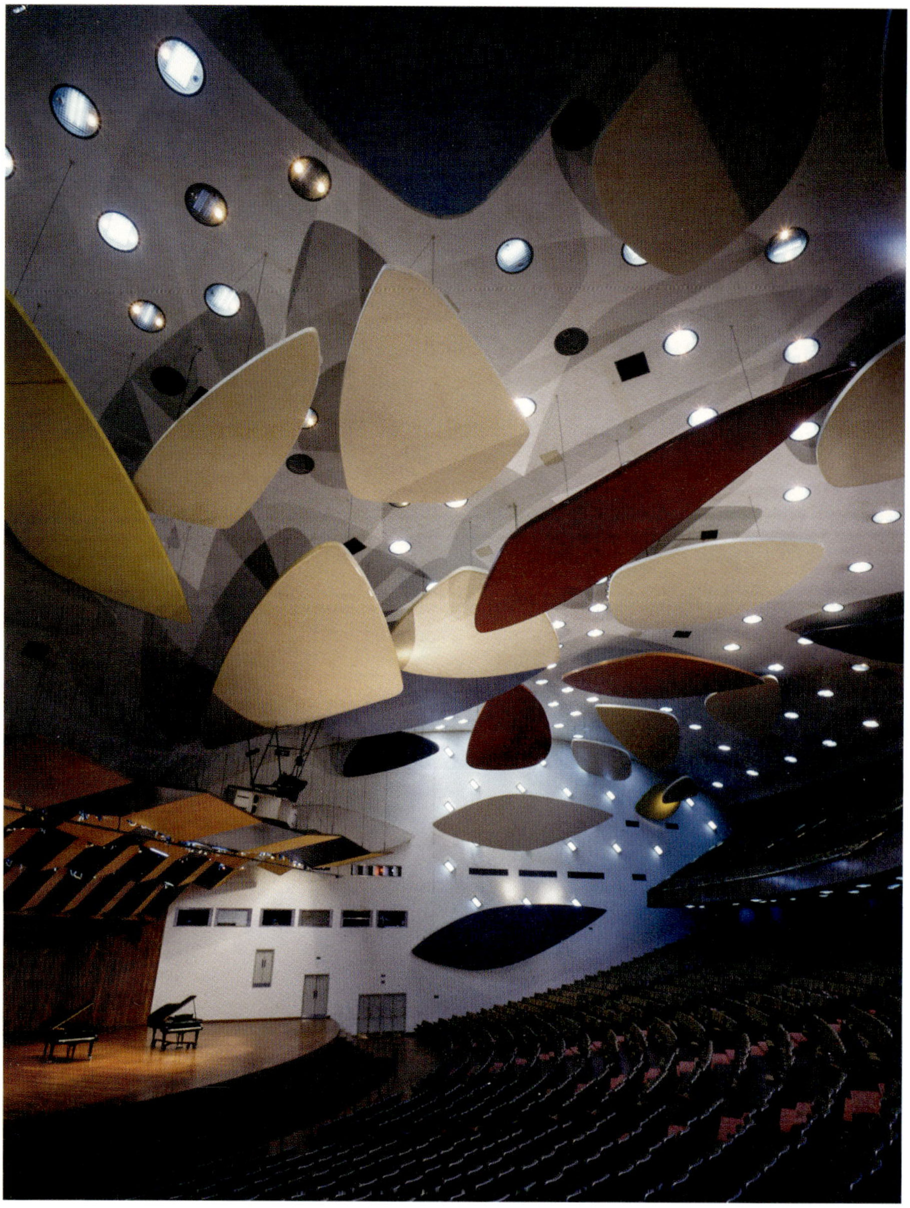

PLATE 20. Carlos Raúl Villanueva and Alexander Calder, Aula Magna auditorium, Ciudad Universitaria de Caracas, 1952.

The *Parangolés* explored these preoccupations, grounded as they were in the defeat of the traditional categories of painting and sculpture and the emergence of a "new structure of the object-art."[45] These works were concerned with environmental action and processual activity: "life processes," explained Oiticica, to clarify the affective and experiential dimensions of the imagination and the experimental. The lessons he drew from constructivism—the jump into real space facilitated by the example of artists such as Vladimir Tatlin, Alexander Rodchenko, Kazimir Malevich, and Piet Mondrian—and his ever-present interest in structure (concomitant with a rejection of representation) impeded Oiticica's embrace of language and objects/images as the transparent communicable vehicles demanded by the strictures of the CPC.

Indeed, Oiticica's notion of structure proves fundamental to an understanding of the relationship between his works and the world of objects, the architecture of the favelas, the rituals of samba, and the "other." In "Côr, tempo e estrutura" (Color, Time, and Structure), published in 1960,[46] the artist referred to time as the element that activated color and structure beyond the conventional support of the picture. He reprised this formulation in 1962 when he stated that "an art based on structural transformations is always in opposition to the passive state of the support."[47] Liberated from its traditional format and location (the wall), painting now existed in real time and space, and color could be "embodied," in Oiticica's famous formulation. In this context he alluded to his *Bilaterais* (Bilaterals, 1959; see fig. 3.12), light-colored wooden panels that hung from the ceiling. He described these works as structures that are thrust into space, each "turning 180 degrees on itself," which confront the spectator, who "is encouraged to act, turning around it, completing its orbit, in a multidimensional perception of the work."[48] Structure became not only a substitute for painting but also a spatial device that mediated the viewer's nonreferential relationship with the surrounding world.[49] Rejecting the unilateral task of representation and following the logic of the nonobject, Oiticica saw structure as unleashing a multidimensional apprehension that demanded action and movement on the part of the viewer. This was developed further in the artist's *Nuclei*, specifically *Núcleo médio no. 1 (NC3)* (1961), which was originally composed of twelve rectangular colored wooden panels of various sizes that hung from a gridlike structure and created a "labyrinthine sense" that required the spectator to circulate through its interior.[50] In August 1961 Oiticica described the work, which existed as a model in his studio, using language that had begun to abandon the spiritual overtones of previous diary entries marked by references to the cosmic and sublime dimension of color: "The orthogonal colored panels, overlapping in three levels, do not intersect when projected onto a plane surface, not from one side or the other, and [they] are as important as the space. The construction of this nucleus . . . is architectural par excellence, not only for its levels of panels but for its orthogonality."[51]

The *Nuclei* were conceived with the participation of the spectator in mind, as indicated in a diary entry from December 27, 1961, in which the artist referred to the installation in his studio of an "improvised *Nucleus*" (*núcleo improviso*) and the *Núcleo médio no. 1 (NC3),* the third work in the series, but the first medium-size example after two smaller ones).[52] A text entitled "O problema da mobilidade pela participação do espectador na obra" (The Problem of Mobility by the Participation of the Viewer in the Work), written the following day, identified an earlier *Penetrável* (Penetrable) conceived with rotating panels (never realized) as the kernel of these investigations.[53] It is an index of Oiticica's fluid thinking at this time, however, that he had previously referred to the movement of the spectator around the *Nuclei* vis-à-vis the architectonic scale of the *Penetráveis* (then unrealized maquettes), which invite penetration.[54]

The most complex of these experiments with architectonic space was a group of integrated *Penetráveis* entitled *Projeto cães de caça* (Hunting Dogs Project), shown as a maquette at the Museu de Arte Moderna do Rio de Janeiro in November and December 1961 but conceived earlier that year.[55] Named after an astral constellation,[56] the work consisted of five interconnected *Penetráveis*—semiarchitectural, labyrinthine structures and chambers that invited the spectator to pass through corridors and movable walls painted in bright colors. Conceived as a public garden project[57] that also included Ferreira Gullar's *Poema enterrado* (Buried Poem) and *Teatro Integral* (Integral Theater) by the poet and editor (of the *Suplemento Dominical do Jornal do Brasil*) Reynaldo Jardim, *Projeto cães de caça* advanced the neoconcrete preoccupation with in-between mediums and the participation of the spectator.

*Poema enterrado* was derived from so-called spatial poems in which Gullar utilized simple panels of wood to occlude and reveal a word, the sole linguistic nucleus of the poem. The "reader" entered a chamber and manipulated three nested boxes until the word *rejuvenesça* (rejuvenate) appeared. Jardim's contribution, a cubic chamber in which a rotating platform held a chair for a one-person audience, proposed a space of defamiliarization in which the manipulation of light would enhance the spectatorial experience of the play. As Oiticica, Jardim, and Pedrosa all observed, the purpose of these works was to disconnect the viewer "from the conventional world,"[58] to liberate the spectator from quotidian space so as to produce that sought-after "first experience."[59] Here, for Oiticica, space and everyday experience would be reintegrated as "human sublimation"—a goal that was to become increasingly at odds with the architectonic (and implicitly public) dimension his work was clearly acquiring.[60]

By March 1962 the "nuclear development of color" that Oiticica theorized in these works was defined not simply as an exploration of tonal color but as an attempt to "virtually move color, in its very structure."[61] This implied a "return to the nucleus of color—its intrinsic, virtual, interior luminescence"[62] and its subsequent unfolding in space. This progression into space correlated with the architectural dimension of the *Penetráveis* and the *Nuclei,* whose projected shadows and supporting materials (Oiticica mentioned specifically the strings of nylon used to hang the painted panels) were welcomed spatial elements.[63] An article by Oiticica published that year in *Habitat,* "A transição da cor do quadro para o espaço e o sentido de construtividade" (The Transition of Color from the Painting Into Space and the Meaning of Construction; fig. 4.3), summarized his thoughts on color; it also alluded to the "constructive" as an expanded category in his effort to rethink the validity of the term in contemporary art—that is, as a "structural technique." Referring to the Russian constructivism he clearly admired, Oiticica wrote: "I consider, then, constructive artists those who establish new structural relations in painting (color) and in sculpture, and open new perceptions of time and space."[64] In this reconsideration of the meaning of *constructive,* Oiticica (echoing the logic of the nonobject) discussed experiments in relief that explore the "spatial-structural problem, in a halfway between painting and space."[65] Among the many artists who exemplified this expanded definition of the constructive for Oiticica—a panoply of key American and European pre- and postwar artists—he singled out Lygia Clark for the "transformable structure" of her *Bichos,* pioneering works that delivered "a new form of expression." This new expression, quite different from the subjective projection of feeling that neoconcretism associated with traditional artistic expression, was produced through the "structural transformation and the temporal dialogue between the spectator and the work."[66] Here, "structure" also referred to the artwork's transition into three-dimensional space, either through its spatial/architectonic/environmental expansion (as in the case of Jackson Pollock) or through monochromatic reduction (as in the case of Yves Klein). Ultimately, structure allowed Oiticica to keep the objectification of representation at bay. Alluding to action and the consequent shattering of contemplation, Oiticica argued that structure disturbed the process through which the spectator searched for the "ideal form," a form that would resolve the classical opposition between subject and object: "Form was then anxiously sought and sculpted to produce something eternal, infinite, and immovable within the finite, changing world of phenomena."[67]

Rejecting an "imagistic transposition" (*transposição imagética*) of the world of objects to the picture plane of idealized forms, Oiticica's notion of structure embraced a more processual approach to form. The following reference to Clark's *Bichos* stands as a good summary: "When a sculptor such as Lígia Clark, for example, articulates triangles, circles, or sections of circles and squares, her concern . . . is to seek a structure that develops in space and in time, and form is apprehended as long as those elements enter into action, linked in this case to the participation of the spectator. Triangles, circles, and squares are not the 'formal outcome' of the sculpture, but elements that create a structure that, as it develops in space and in time, becomes form."[68] Indeed, Clark's *Bichos*—whose impact on the Brazilian avant-garde was decisive—had already been identified by Oiticica as a foundational influence on his investigations of movement and spectator participation in the *Nuclei* and *Penetráveis.*[69] For both artists, structure allowed a revision of the key constructive elements of time and space, a possibility indicated by Clark when she wrote in her diary that in order to say something new, the artist had to create a structure.[70]

This background provides a better understanding of Oiticica's dialogue with the

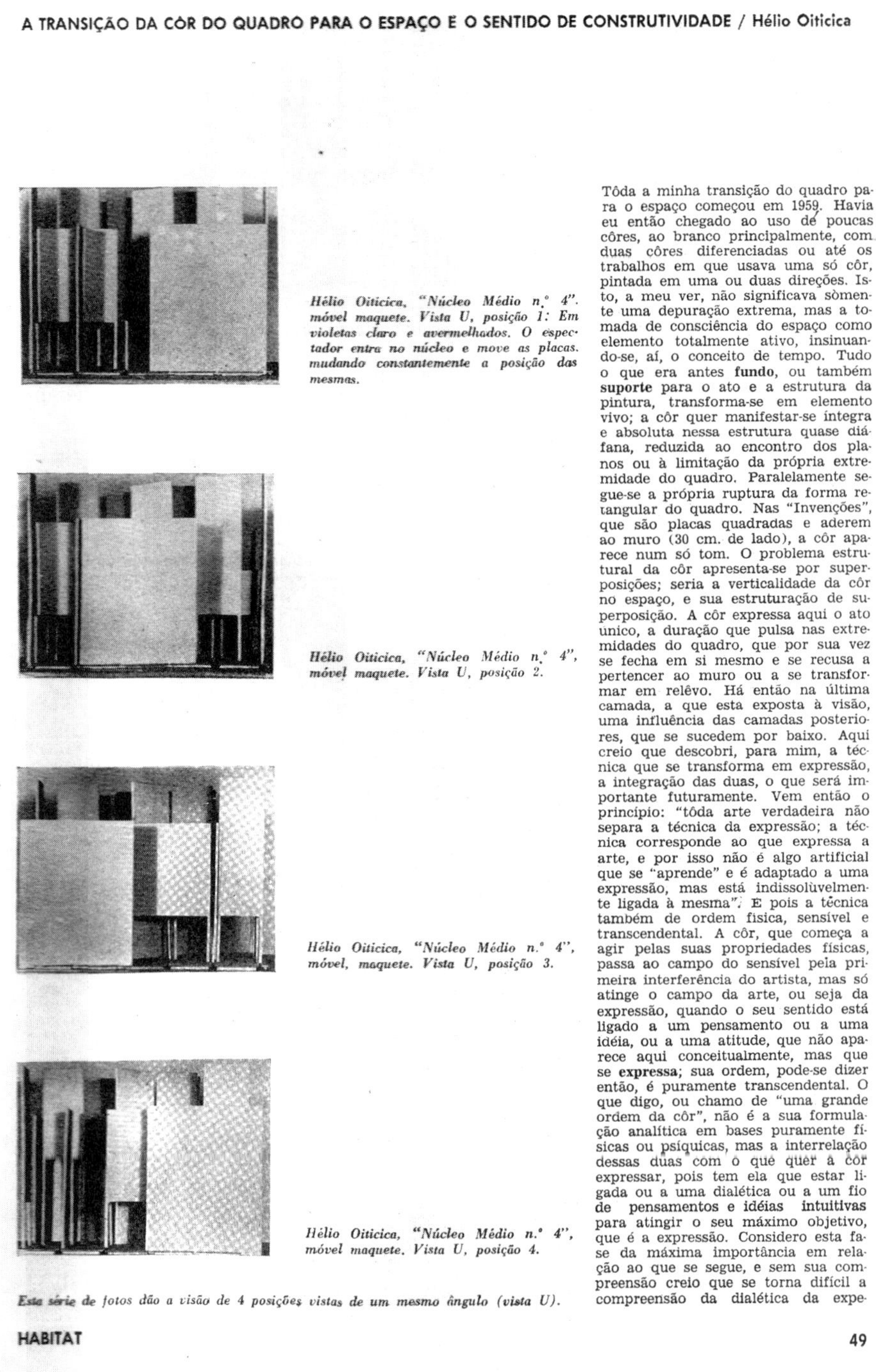

A TRANSIÇÃO DA CÔR DO QUADRO PARA O ESPAÇO E O SENTIDO DE CONSTRUTIVIDADE / Hélio Oiticica

*Hélio Oiticica, "Núcleo Médio n.° 4". móvel maquete. Vista U, posição 1: Em violetas claro e avermelhados. O espectador entra no núcleo e move as placas. mudando constantemente a posição das mesmas.*

*Hélio Oiticica, "Núcleo Médio n.° 4", móvel maquete. Vista U, posição 2.*

*Hélio Oiticica, "Núcleo Médio n.° 4", móvel, maquete. Vista U, posição 3.*

*Hélio Oiticica, "Núcleo Médio n.° 4", móvel maquete. Vista U, posição 4.*

*Esta série de fotos dão a visão de 4 posições vistas de um mesmo ângulo (vista U).*

Tôda a minha transição do quadro para o espaço começou em 1959. Havia eu então chegado ao uso de poucas côres, ao branco principalmente, com duas côres diferenciadas ou até os trabalhos em que usava uma só côr, pintada em uma ou duas direções. Isto, a meu ver, não significava sòmente uma depuração extrema, mas a tomada de consciência do espaço como elemento totalmente ativo, insinuando-se, aí, o conceito de tempo. Tudo o que era antes **fundo**, ou também **suporte** para o ato e a estrutura da pintura, transforma-se em elemento vivo; a côr quer manifestar-se íntegra e absoluta nessa estrutura quase diáfana, reduzida ao encontro dos planos ou à limitação da própria extremidade do quadro. Paralelamente segue-se a própria ruptura da forma retangular do quadro. Nas "Invenções", que são placas quadradas e aderem ao muro (30 cm. de lado), a côr aparece num só tom. O problema estrutural da côr apresenta-se por superposições; seria a verticalidade da côr no espaço, e sua estruturação de superposição. A côr expressa aqui o ato único, a duração que pulsa nas extremidades do quadro, que por sua vez se fecha em si mesmo e se recusa a pertencer ao muro ou a se transformar em relêvo. Há então na última camada, a que esta exposta à visão, uma influência das camadas posteriores, que se sucedem por baixo. Aqui creio que descobri, para mim, a técnica que se transforma em expressão, a integração das duas, o que será importante futuramente. Vem então o princípio: "tôda arte verdadeira não separa a técnica da expressão; a técnica corresponde ao que expressa a arte, e por isso não é algo artificial que se "aprende" e é adaptado a uma expressão, mas está indissolùvelmente ligada à mesma". E pois a técnica também de ordem física, sensível e transcendental. A côr, que começa a agir pelas suas propriedades físicas, passa ao campo do sensível pela primeira interferência do artista, mas só atinge o campo da arte, ou seja da expressão, quando o seu sentido está ligado a um pensamento ou a uma idéia, ou a uma atitude, que não aparece aqui conceitualmente, mas que se **expressa**; sua ordem, pode-se dizer então, é puramente transcendental. O que digo, ou chamo de "uma grande ordem da côr", não é a sua formulação analítica em bases puramente físicas ou psíquicas, mas a interrelação dessas duas com o que quer a côr expressar, pois tem ela que estar ligada ou a uma dialética ou a um fio de **pensamentos e idéias intuitivas** para atingir o seu máximo objetivo, que é a expressão. Considero esta fase da máxima importância em relação ao que se segue, e sem sua compreensão creio que se torna difícil a compreensão da dialética da expe-

HABITAT

49

FIGURE 4.3
Hélio Oiticica, "A transição da cor do quadro para o espaço e o sentido de construtividade" (The Transition of Color from the Painting Into Space and the Meaning of Construction), in *Habitat*, no. 70, December 1962.

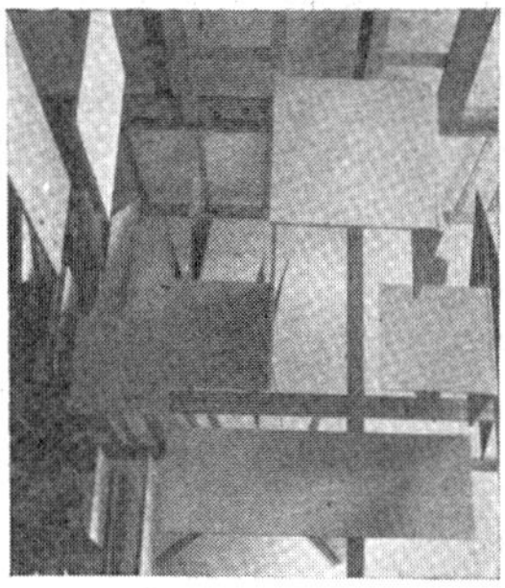

*O atelier de Hélio Oticica. Ângulo do "Núcleo Médio", nº 1, em detalhe.*

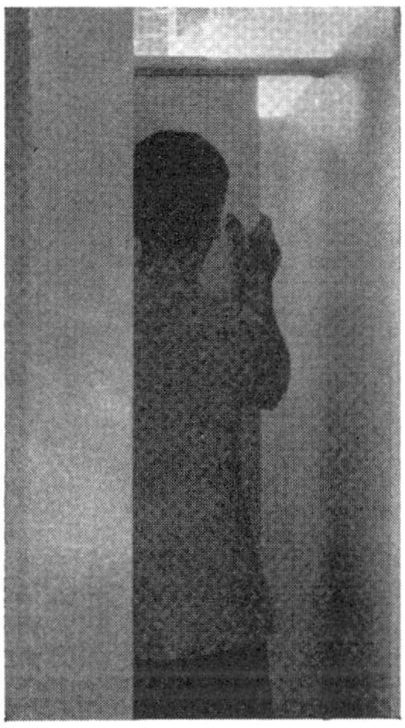

*Um detalhe de um "penetrável". As placas se movem, permitindo a entrada do espectador.*

*Vista do ateliê de Hélio Oiticico, vendo-se em primeiro plano o "Núcleo Médio n.º 1", em laranjas e amarelo escuro que aparece em detalhe.*

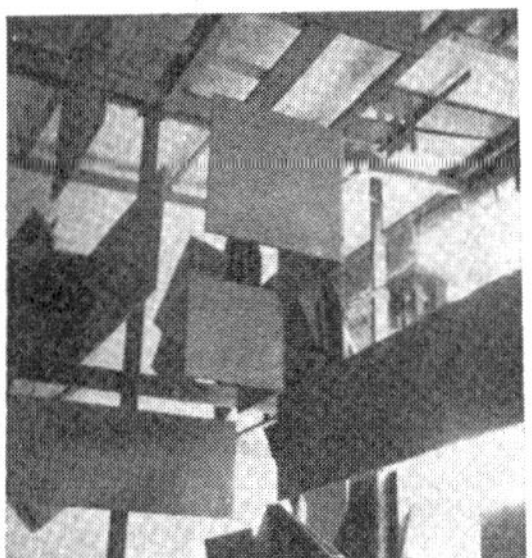

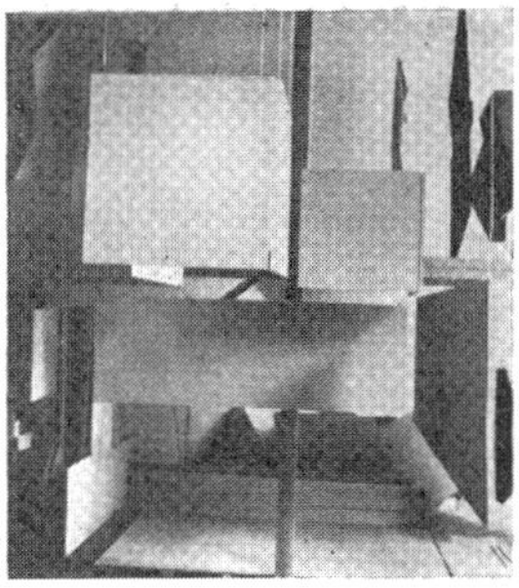

*Outra vista do ateliê de Hélio Oiticica, vendo-se o "Núcleo Médio n.º 1", em outro ângulo, mas também em detalhe pois que as outras placas estão escondidas.*

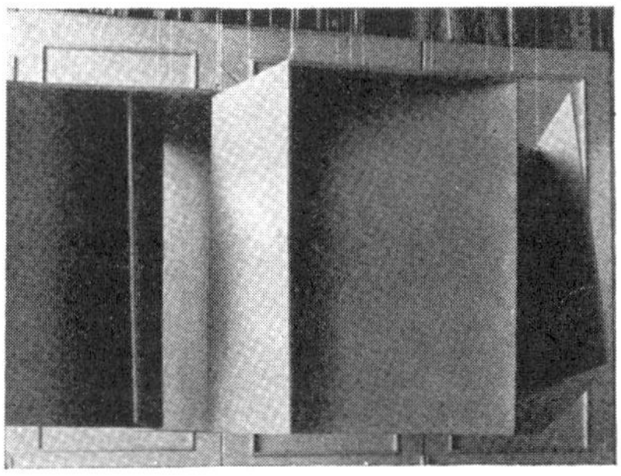

*Hélio Oitica, "Núcleo Pequeno n.º 1". Em amarelos, rosa e laranja. 1960-1962.*

*Hélio Oiticica, "Núcleo Médio n.º 3", maquete, em amarelos e esverdeados. No tamanho real, permite a entrada do espectador por entre as placas.*

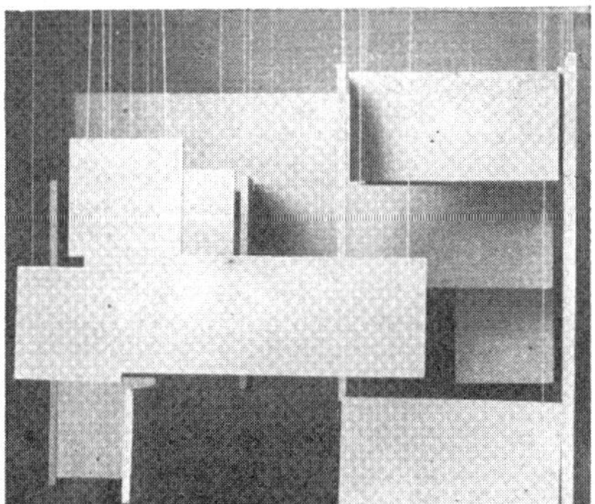

favela, samba, and carnival, as well as with the popular realm of festivals, fairs, shacks, and decorations that he invoked in his seminal 1964 essay "Bases fundamentais para uma definição do 'Parangolé.'" As he stated toward the end of that text:

> Finding *Parangolé* elements in urban or rural landscapes or the like is also part of the "establishment of structural-perceptive relationships" between those elements that grow within the *Parangolé*'s structure (representing here the general character of the color-structure within the environmental space) and those "found" in the environment. One of the *Parangolé*'s features is implicit in the architecture of the favela, one example of which may be seen in the organic quality of the elements that constitute its structures, their internal circulation, and the external disjointedness of those constructions, there being no abrupt passages from "room" to "living room" or "kitchen," only an essential definition of each part as it connects to the next part in continuity.[71]

Oiticica's structural (nonreferential) relationship with the favela would materialize in what he called the "work-environment" (*obra-ambiente*), characterized by the experience of "collective participation."[72] These "environmental totalities" would be created and explored in all their dimensions, "from the infinitely small to architectonic, urban space, etc."[73] Further, they suggested an increased concern with "site specificity," upon which Oiticica reflected when he pondered the loss of the base in sculpture and the relevance of location for his *Penetráveis*. Hinting at issues that would be raised with the *Parangolés* and moving away from the rather aesthetic concerns of the *Projeto cães de caça*, Oiticica argued in 1962 for an integration of work and site that would avoid gratuitousness: "What would the work gain in possessing 'unity' if that unity was lost in a locality where it not only did not fit as an idea, but also where there was no possibility of its full experience and comprehension?"[74]

In this sense the *Parangolé tenda* was an exemplary structure, as it articulated key concerns of the period: the architectural, the environmental, the specificity of site. Like the simplest of constructions (a hut, a hovel), the *Parangolé tenda* (1964; fig. 4.4)—initially called *Penetrável-Parangolé* (fig. 4.5)—was a precarious structure, an architectural skeleton that protected the body and mediated the subject's material interface with place. Constituting a basic rectangular structure approximately 262 by 120 centimeters, the open facade of this stall featured a wooden surface, which, like the humblest of entablatures, framed the entrance to the tent. Its sides were covered with colored panels of canvas, layered and tied in knots, clearly alluding to the unfinished and fraying strata of the shanty as well as to the disunified layers of the *Parangolé capas*. Orange straw matting, a blue nylon screen, and plastic sheeting haphazardly covered the wooden structure and amplified the antiarchitectural effect of the tent, which alluded, in its elemental poverty, to the basic function as shelter for the body recognized in the homes of the favelas.[75]

Structure thus became key in a complex negotiation of material and artistic elements

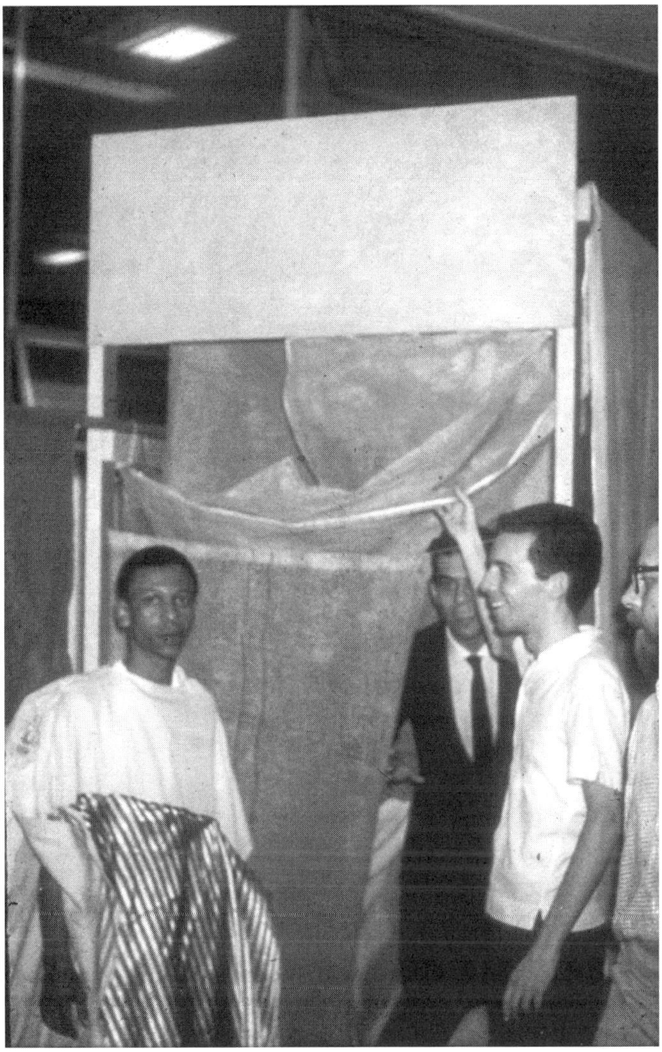

FIGURE 4.4
Left: Nildo da Mangueira wearing *P8 Parangolé capa 5 "Mangueira"* (Hélio Oiticica, 1965); right: Cesar Oiticica, Hélio Oiticica, and Reynaldo Jardim with *P3 Parangolé tenda 1* (Hélio Oiticica, 1964) at the opening of *Opinião 65*, Museu de Arte Moderna do Rio de Janeiro, August 12, 1965.

that insisted on an antirepresentational treatment of reality via the categories of the environmental and the participatory. The nonobject had returned to the world of objects, and these everyday objects were to be the "objective genesis of the work" (*gênese objetiva da obra*), the foundation of its "direct perceptual molding" (*plasmação direta perceptiva*), a sort of structural template that informed the work's behavior and the participatory dynamics to which it aspired.[76] In 1964 and 1965 the crux of the *Parangolés* was the arbitration of political, social, artistic, and philosophical positions and conditions that were manifested in the works' structural engagement not only with the world of objects, the favela, and the leftist politics of the 1960s, but also with the immanence of form and affect.

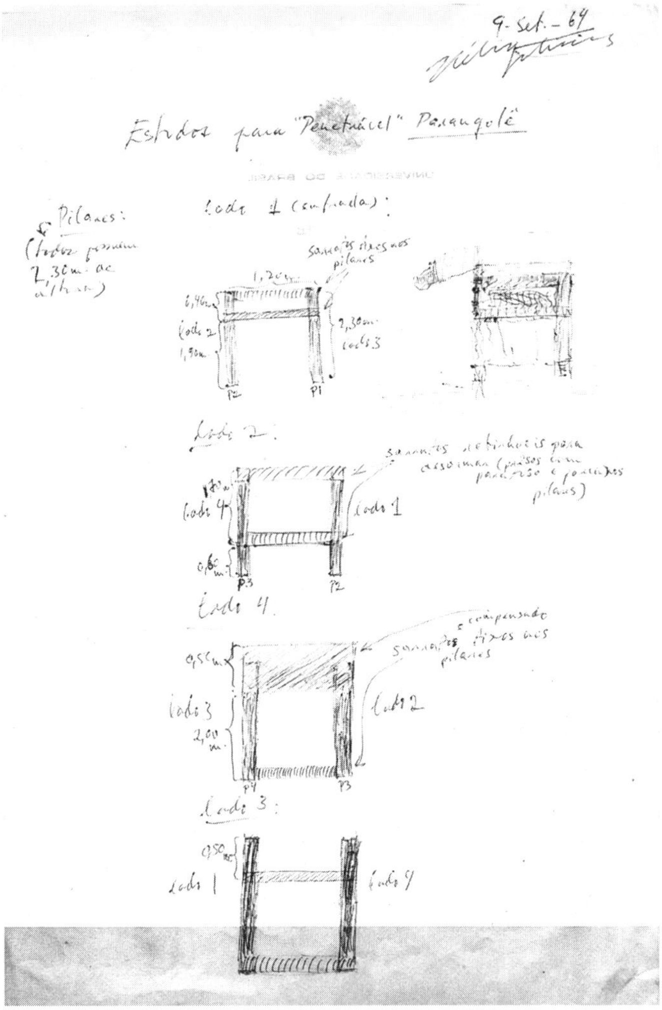


FIGURE 4.5
Hélio Oiticica, study for *Penetrável-Parangolé*, September 9, 1964.

## CULTURAL MEDIATORS AND SYNCRETIC SITUATIONS

The first setting of the *Parangolés*—the favela—was the locus of many of Oiticica's concerns during the mid-1960s. *Favela* is the toponym used by Brazilians to refer to the squatter settlements that since the 1930s have proliferated in major Brazilian cities. By the 1960s these urban configurations housed roughly a third of the population of Rio de Janeiro.[77] Although readily identified as marginal—in their construction, population, and social habits—the favelas are home to resourceful communities whose precarious but organized dwellings feature innovative constructions in challenging terrain considered too steep for urban development. Ultimately hastened by the abrupt and poorly planned economic programs that occupied the Brazilian state in the 1950s—which, while promoting the growth of industrial markets, led to the stagnation of agricultural sectors and failed to develop a solid middle class capable of acquiring newly available goods and services—the growth of the favelas was the result of migrations from rural areas to the cities, where urban modernity beckoned. As Janice Perlman has demonstrated in her important study on the topic, the favelas were widely seen in Brazilian political, social, and cultural circles in the 1960s as the ultimate borderline site. Generally associated with the poor, the jobless, migrants, deviants, and other (racial, ethnic, cultural) minorities, the category of the "marginal" was employed in official documents and sociological reports to explain the favelas and their inhabitants. Characterized by "family breakdown, anomie, lack of trust and cooperation, secularization, rampant crime, violence, and promiscuity," the favela represented the quintessence of the "other."[78] A precarious fringe of housing settlements that surrounded the city, the favela was marked by constructive instability and insufficient infrastructure.

Oiticica shared in the more romantic vision of the belief system that posited the favela as marginal, as indicated by his embrace of the figure of the outcast: the rebellious, nonconformist type embodied in the figure of the artist, the criminal, and the revolutionary set on rejecting the mainstream or dominant culture. His *Bólide caixa 18, Poema caixa 02 "Homenagem a Cara de Cavalo"* (Box Bólide 18, Poem Box 02 "Homage to Horse Face," 1966)—which featured a photograph of his friend, the deceased Mangueira criminal Cara de Cavalo, posed as if crucified—clearly stated this embrace of marginality. As articulated in his writings at the time, Oiticica aspired to an experience fundamentally different from the life of regulated society (ruled as it is by rationality and cultural conditioning). In his well-known 1965 text "A dança na minha experiência" (Dance in My Experience), which specifically addressed the artist's "vital need for deintellectualization" (*necessidade vital de desintelectualização*), Oiticica associated his encounter with Mangueira and samba with "marginalization"—a condition that to him was natural to the artist and which he defined as a "total 'lack of social place.'"[79]

The no-man's-land of the favela was thus identified with social marginalization, and it became a base from which to launch attacks on preconceptions, stereotypes, bourgeois conditioning—a social version, if you will, of the phenomenological experience of astonishment that informed the "Manifesto Neoconcreto." Against the a priori knowledge that conditions our apprehension of the world, phenomenology in its most idealistic version aspired to access the world of essences, uncontaminated by theoretical presumptions. In 1959 the "spatialization" of the artwork that so preoccupied Gullar, Clark, and Oiticica was related to the desire for the nonobject to constantly make itself present, returning viewers to the first experience, an experience of plenitude. In 1965, dance, specifically samba, would provide that experience through the frenzy of its practice—a fluency, argued Oiticica, that obscured the intellect: "Dance is the search for the direct expressive act par excellence, for the immanence of that act." He added, "Dance does not propose an 'escape' from that immanent world, but reveals it in all its plenitude."[80]

Expression and experience remained key concerns in Oiticica's writings of the 1960s, and these concepts were always articulated in relation to his expanded interest in a practice of environmental dimensions. "Life experience" (*vivência*) was a key concept in the artist's phenomenological arsenal: it could be associated with the experience of nuclear color, as when he argued in 1962 that the temporal diffusion of his monochromatic *Invenções* (Inventions) expressed a *vivência*;[81] or it could refer to his own experience of Mangueira, as when he wrote with dismay in 1968 about the Brazilian bourgeoisie's domestication and celebration of the favela, samba, and the marginal. Indeed, in this latter text Oiticica rejected the objectification of facile images of the favela and warned about the consumption of these images: "[D]on't forget that there are elements there that cannot be consumed by this bourgeois voracity: the direct experiential element that goes beyond the problem of the image."[82]

Although Oiticica did not completely bypass a romantic view of the favela and its inhabitants, he did reject a purely ocular and superficial relationship to them—specifically the practice then common among artists of venturing temporarily into these urban fringes to dress its dwellers for the carnival, creating seasonal excitement around the favela, and then withdrawing.[83] As the anthropologist Hermano Vianna has pointed out, by the mid-1960s the favelas were an object of curiosity for many middle-class Cariocas: anthropologists, artists, and social figures were lured by the otherness of this unruly and "deformed urban space," as an official document defined the favela in 1968.[84] During this same period, singers and composers brought samba into the well-to-do South Zone of Rio, where the middle class was appropriating this popular music and dance, so intimately linked to the life of the favelas, as essentially Brazilian. In contrast, Oiticica's collaborators (the wearers of his first *Parangolés*) were humble inhabitants of Mangueira: youths, men, and women rarely identified in contemporary photographs (fig. 4.6) by more than a nickname (such as Mosquito) or a first name (Luiza, Nildo, Roberto, Bidu).[85] The tensions and complex arbitrations among these social classes and cultural spaces, between subjects inside and subjects outside, helps account for the material, formal, and conceptual constitution of the layered, heterogeneous, and unresolved structure of the *Parangolé capa*.

The samba schools had provided models of community empowerment for the marginalized inhabitants of the favela since the 1930s, when samba Carioca first became identified with Brazilian carnival, as noted by Hermano Vianna in his book *The Mystery of Samba*. Analyzing the political, cultural, and social conditions that facilitated samba's conversion into a national symbol, Vianna traces the discourse surrounding miscegenation in Brazil in the context of the work of the anthropologist Gilberto Freyre. Author of the seminal book *The Masters and the Slaves* (1933), Freyre argued for mixed (*mestiço*) culture as a critical element of Brazilian identity and delineated a concomitant revalorization of all things popular and native. This national identity was crystallized in Freyre's social ideal of "Luso-tropicalism," which had its antecedents in the Portuguese experience as a bridge between Europe and Africa and, in Freyre's view, contributed to Brazil's penchant for diversity and mixture, change and adaptability.[86] The Brazilian

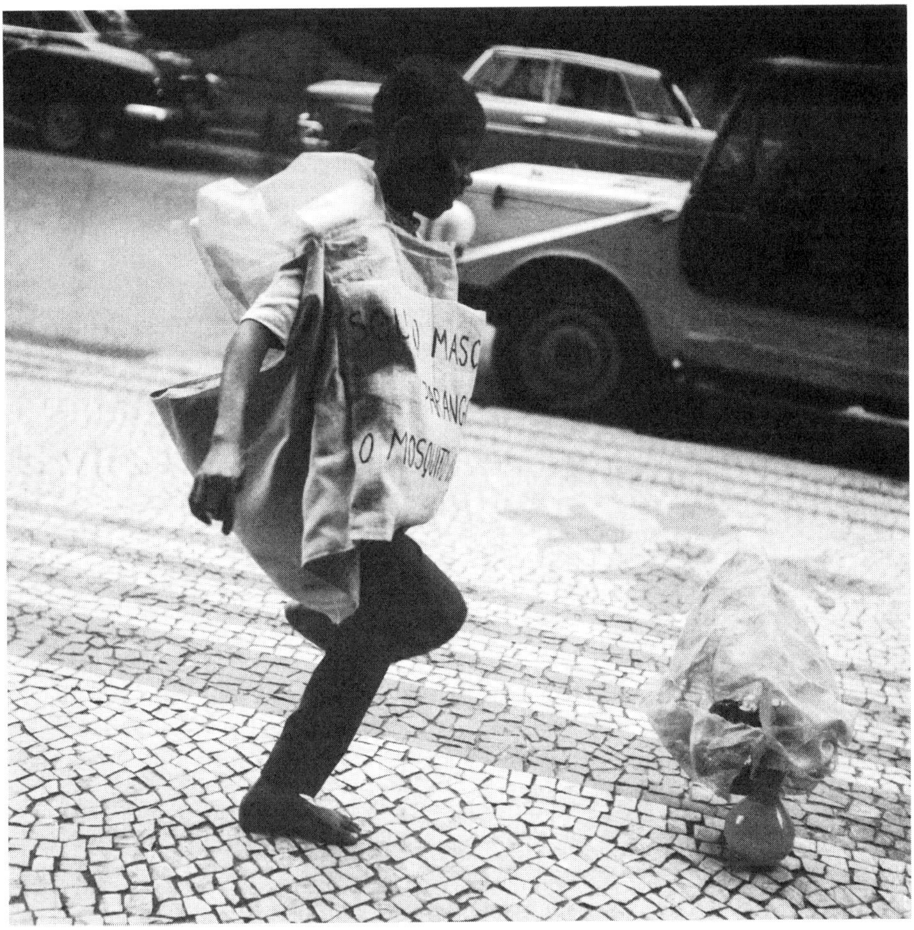

FIGURE 4.6
Mosquito de Mangueira with *P10 Parangolé capa 6 "Mosquito"* (Hélio Oiticica, 1965) and *B17 Bólide vidrio 5 "Homenagem a Mondrian"* (B17 Glass Bólide 5, "Homage to Mondrian"; Hélio Oiticica, 1965).

modernist poet Oswald de Andrade had articulated a similar ethos in his foundational 1928 "Manifesto Antropófago" (Anthropophagic Manifesto), in which the "other" (in this case, the European avant-garde) is incorporated critically into an impure native identity through a symbolic cannibalism that absorbs the colonizer. In Vianna's discerning words: "Everything would be mixed, perpetually the beginning of something different. That essential instability became the chimera of Brazilian modernists."[87]

The 1940s saw not only a political revolution against the Brazilian coffee oligarchy, but also urban restructuring in the main cities of the country that implied the development of material and technological innovations, which in turn facilitated the shaping of images and ideas identified with a Brazilian nationalism advocated by the dictatorial regime of Getúlio Vargas (1930–45). Popular music, specifically samba, increasingly served the new government's agenda, but it also functioned, according to Vianna, as a mediator between the cultural elites and the people of growing favelas such as Mangueira, where most of the sambistas lived.[88] Not surprisingly, the terms *favela samba* and *samba de morro* (samba from the hills) emerged at this time, establishing a tight link between Rio's favelas and the samba of the carnival.[89] It is samba's role as a "cultural mediator" that interests Vianna: the composers and middle-class intellectuals who moved back and forth between city and favela to facilitate the symbolic identification of samba with Brazilian identity. The anthropologist Maria Laura Viveiros de Castro Cavalcanti also focuses on the constant social, cultural, and racial "traffic" that informs carnival and that had its clearest expression in the figure of the *carnavalesco,* or parade designer, in the 1960s. This role originated in the late 1950s, when samba schools began to outsource the design of their floats and costumes used for the juried parade competition that awarded the winner a title. What began as an occasional involvement became a recognized profession with the work of Fernando Pamplona for the Escola de Samba Acadêmicos do Salgueiro. A leftist stage designer for the Theatro Municipal do Rio de Janeiro, Pamplona had been a member of the União Nacional dos Estudantes (National Student Union, affiliated with the CPC) and had studied and later taught in the school of fine arts of the Universidade Federal do Rio de Janeiro. He was friendly with artists and intellectuals and contributed important innovations in the use of materials and the development of parade themes staged by the samba schools for the carnival.[90]

The first of the themes developed by Pamplona in 1960 proposed to interrupt the litany of white narratives that had traditionally been celebrated by the samba schools in favor of a tribute to Zumbi dos Palmares, a black military leader who in the late seventeenth century defended the refugee black community of Quilombo dos Palmares in northeastern Brazil against Portuguese colonizers. The story Pamplona staged, however, was one of conflicting sociocultural differences and expectations. In order to communicate the story elegantly and authentically, Pamplona asked members of the samba school to dress as slaves from Palmares. The simple costumes he proposed had nothing to do with the flamboyant and richly decorated *fantasias* (costumes) that *favelados* eagerly anticipated wearing on the day of the parade. Dismayed by Pamplona's proposal, Salgueiro's blacks threatened to abandon the parade. The samba chronicler Sérgio Cabral observed: "In the end, the people of the samba schools, unemployed or poorly paid in their jobs, were already slaves the entire year. Why also be a slave at carnival?"[91]

Two years later, this collision of interests was confirmed when the artist Niltón de Sá, regretting his own participation in the above event, declared that the intervention of artists and intellectuals in popular culture had led to the latter's corruption.[92] But in 1963 the Escola de Samba Acadêmicos do Salgueiro triumphed in the carnival parade thanks to the innovations and general professionalization introduced by Pamplona and fellow stage designer Arlindo Rodrigues. Other schools soon followed suit, notably the Estação Primeira de Mangueira, which asked the neoconcrete sculptor Amilcar de Castro to design one of its floats for the carnival of 1964—a commission that resulted, Sérgio Cabral reports, in an obelisk whose abstract character precluded any possible identification with the school or its members.[93] While assiting de Castro in this commission, presumably at the end of 1963, the artist Jackson Ribeiro invited Oiticica to visit Mangueira. Thus, Oiticica's encounter with the popular world of the favela, samba, and carnival was informed by this complex landscape of constant mediations. His arrival at the favela coincided, too, with the expansion of Mangueira's samba school, which, thanks to a growing membership and audience, had moved into a new building, the Quadra Antiga.[94] The conditions were ripe for Oiticica to initiate the kind of process that CPC director Carlos Estevam Martins had warned against in his antiexperimentalist manifesto: in seeking models, symbols, and the aesthetic criteria of validity among the popular classes, the artist engaged in a sort of sociological research, a kind of fieldwork, in which the collection of material for his or her practice might lead to findings that could generate radical formal innovations in the context of experimental art.[95] Yet it could not have been otherwise for the structurally oriented Oiticica, whose antirepresentational practice embodied rather than represented the syncretic process of racial, cultural, social, and artistic exchange that characterized the samba and the favelas in the early 1960s.

In fact, Oiticica's entire relationship to the favela, carnival, and samba was mediated by the notion of structure, which was in turn closely linked to his aesthetic investigation into the material and conceptual consequences of the nonobject and the constructive. As Vianna points out, while the artist's incursion into the culture of Mangueira was clearly facilitated by the consolidation of the samba schools as symbols of national identity in the imaginary of middle-class Cariocas, Oiticica never functioned as a *carnavalesco* charged with orchestrating the school's narrative, look, and staging for the carnival parade. Consistent with his rejection of representation and his interest in the structural conditions of the object in a situation, Oiticica's intent would never be to "represent" Mangueira or its inhabitants in the way that Pamplona, for example, aspired to be "truer" to the people of the favela through his homage to Zumbi dos Palmares. The materiality of the *Parangolés* indicates as much. Rejecting stylistic unity and conceptual resolution, as well as referentiality, the *Parangolés* mobilized the interval, the fold, the in-between spaces, the processual as complementary to and constitutive of the capes' layers, pockets, protrusions, attachments, and material heterogeneity, their lightness and weight. Asked why he never dressed the dancers of Mangueira for the carnival with his *Parangolés*, Oiticica replied: "No, that's not interesting. Now, to connect with one person or another, to connect with the thing, that's my thing, what I want, I can't disguise myself."[96]

## POLITICAL AMBIGUITY AND THE STRUCTURE OF DISPLAY

The first public presentation of the *Parangolés* was preceded by Oiticica's appearance as one of Mangueira's *passistas*, or leading dancers, in the March 1965 carnival, which commemorated Rio's four hundredth anniversary. Oiticica's membership in the local samba school was clearly an effort to integrate himself into Mangueira's social texture at a moment when middle-class intrusion had sharpened the differences between sympathizers and spectators and *componentes* (people who participated in the parade).[97] In turn, Oiticica appropriated the carnival-parade format for the first public staging of the *Parangolés*, at the *Opinião 65* exhibition at the Museu de Arte Moderna do Rio de Janeiro in August 1965. As if acknowledging the ties between the *Parangolés'* genesis and the artist's introduction to the favela, carnival, and samba, Oiticica's procession enacted a different trajectory, as the *favelados* dancing samba and wearing the *Parangolés* made their way from the favela toward the museum. This pattern of intersections between favela and city was complicated by political events. The enthusiasm of the Brazilian Left for popular and democratic reforms collapsed abruptly in April 1964 with a military coup that deposed President João Goulart.[98] Oiticica's arrival in Mangueira, therefore, coincided with the forced transformation of the revolutionary effervescence of Brazilian society and its institutions. While the coup interrupted the progressive momentum of the early 1960s, it also influenced the political background against which Brazilian culture constituted itself as a "pocket of resistance" that in the mid-1960s paradoxically enjoyed ample visibility.[99]

*Opinião 65*[100] was a crucial event in the post-1964 cultural program proposed by intellectuals, artists, and students. The inaugural *Opinião* event in December 1964 had been a concert featuring the music of the sambista Zé Kéti, the composer João do Vale, and the bossa nova singer Nara Leão, and it delineated the popular, denunciatory, festive, and expressive temper of the contemporary cultural Left. Although the organizers were close to the now-defunct CPC, the event coalesced around more experimental and expressive tendencies, as well as "the idea that art is 'much more expressive' when it has an 'opinion,' that is, when it becomes an instrument for the communication of political content," observed Heloísa Buarque de Hollanda and Marcos A. Gonçalves.[101] For Brazilian artists and intellectuals eager to repress their unrealized revolution and to distance themselves from the military power that had shattered it, "a new imperative emerged: to talk, to sing, to manifest."[102] And to dance, but also to explore unorthodox modes of protest against dominant political and social formations.

At the August 1965 opening of *Opinião 65*, Oiticica presented his *Parangolés* in their three different configurations—banners, capes, and tents—and explained his new order (as he called his various aesthetic projects) in two mimeographed texts: "Anotações sobre o Parangolé" (Notes on the Parangolé, written in November 1964) and "Bases fundamentais para uma definição do 'Parangolé.'" Several photographs of the event show the first work in the series, *P1 Parangolé estandarte 1* (P1 Parangolé Banner 1), consisting of a piece of cloth painted bright red and looped around two wooden shafts (fig. 4.7); others show an adult and a child carrying *P2 Parangolé bandeira* (P2 Parangolé Flag), a flag made of two pieces of cloth, one red and one yellow, sewn together and attached to a pole (fig. 4.8). This "iconography" is relevant in light of the elusive or dislocated referentiality that

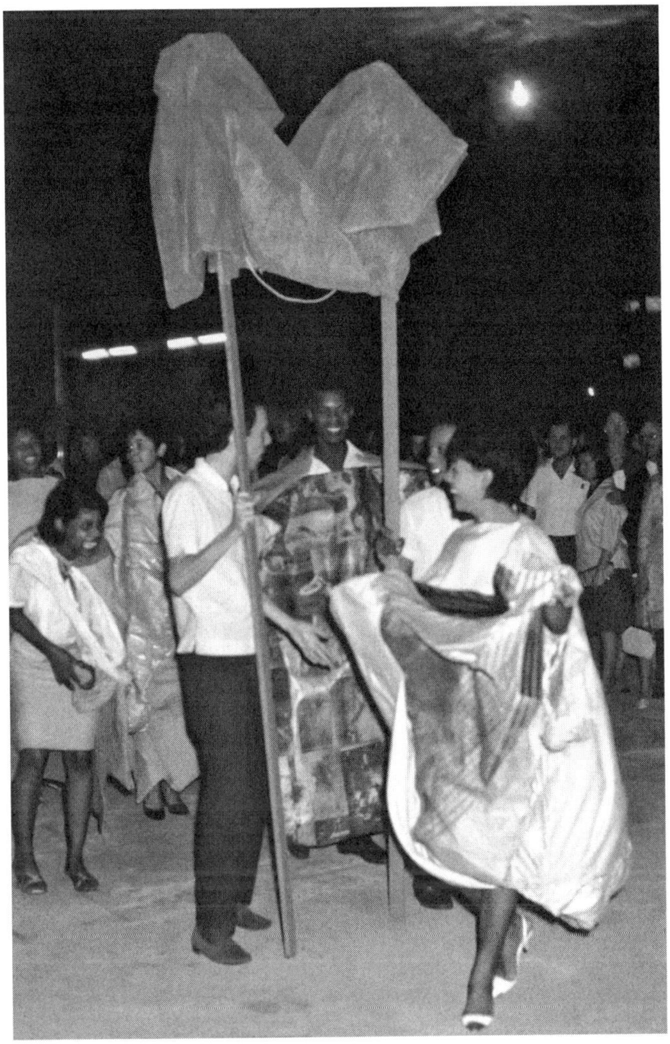

FIGURE 4.7
Hélio Oiticica with *P1 Parangolé estandarte 1* (Hélio Oiticica, 1964) and Maria Helena with *P8 Parangolé capa 5 "Mangueira"* (Hélio Oiticica, 1965) at the opening of *Opinião 65*, Museu de Arte Moderna do Rio de Janeiro, August 12, 1965.

known objects were to acquire in Oiticica's practice and in the environmental program that he was keen to develop from these various spatial practices. As Oiticica had written at the beginning of "Bases fundamentais para uma definição do 'Parangolé'": "The relationship between 'appearances' and preexisting things exists but is not essential to the genesis of the idea, or maybe it could be from a different point of view: the 'why' of that relationship verifiable in the realization of the work, its formation."[103] The answer to that question—the why of that (structural) relationship between the work and things in the world, like the opinions the artwork was to give voice to—was to remain crucial but uncodified, an imageless symbol attempting to articulate the political imperatives of the moment via the affective dimension of the *Parangolés*. Oiticica's banner and flag were borne by the procession-cum-manifestation at the *Opinião 65* opening just as the

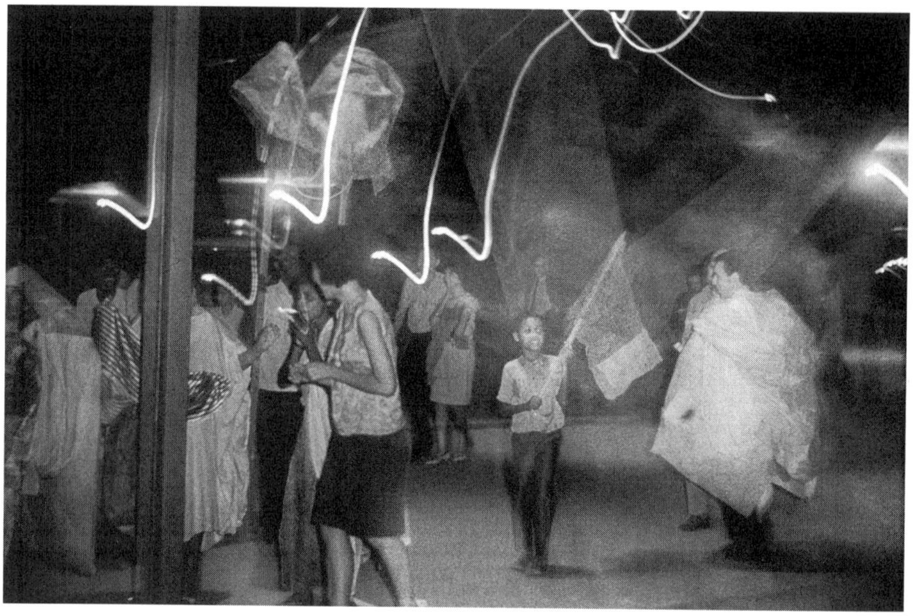

FIGURE 4.8
Hélio Oiticica wearing *P4 Parangolé capa 1* on the grounds of the Museu de Arte Moderna do Rio de Janeiro on the occasion of the opening of the exhibition *Opinião 65*, 1965. Also visible from left to right are *P9 Parangolé capa 5 "Mangueira,"* 1965; P1 *Parangolé estandarte 1*, 1964; and P2 *Parangolé bandeira 1*, 1964.

*porta-bandeira* (flag-bearer) and *mestre-sala* (master of ceremonies) carried them in the carnival parade. These *Parangolés* enacted their proclamatory roles but withdrew from declaration and identifying imagery to embrace the opacity of the object. Like Gullar's absurdist object without name, the literal meaning of these declaratory *Parangolés* was obscured while the manifestation articulated a processual and environmental economy of affect that channeled the ambivalent political imperatives of 1965. The flag belonged to no nation, no school, no movement, no party.[104] Here, the nonobject—or, rather, the transobject—enmeshed in the contingency of social space, delivered ambiguity instead of plenitude and radicalized the transition from work to action, from viewing to carrying, from one to many that the neoconcrete experience had triggered.

According to the local press, Oiticica and his Mangueira collaborators were prevented from entering the museum by its director.[105] So they performed outside, to the celebratory approval of a group of attendees of the opening. The event defined the anti-institutional status of the *Parangolés* (which supplemented their representational nullity) and served well their reception in the Brazil of the 1960s.[106] Assessments of this and related exhibition events of the period confirm that artists were expected to pursue a politicized art that was attuned to the reality of the nation; artists were asked to express their "opinions" and to implicitly abandon the aesthetic concerns of the geometric and informal abstract art that had preceded it.[107] But the post-1964 artistic intelligentsia turned enthusiastically toward forms of spectacle, as if "the issues of the moment required new mediums, more efficient in uniting the public," as Buarque de Hollanda has indicated.[108] The concept of the Festive Left (*esquerda festiva*), she adds, emerged around this time, partly as a response to the serious and self-righteous tone of the CPC generation. The Festive Left mobilized an economy of ambiguity at the heart of the uncertainties of post-1964 Brazil, a less combative aesthetic that did not lack a critical dimension.

It is easy to see the *Parangolés* emerging at the crux of these various cultural negotiations among politics, art, and the popular. In this sense, the works actualized the affective and participatory ambitions of neoconcretism through their "structural" assimilation of the syncretic nature of the favela and carnival. At the same time, the *Parangolés* remained in dialogue with the collectivization of culture that had been paramount for the CPC and the festive, ritualistic tenor of what followed, as represented in the temper of the *Opinião* events. But while the figures of the mediator and the interval and references to syncretism and heterogeneity might help explain the material ambiguity and conceptual unsettledness of the *Parangolés,* this does not mean that they were a tool of emancipation, as some interpretations suggest.[109] In his 1982 study entitled "Da antropofagia à tropicália" (From Cannibalism to Tropicália), Carlos Zilio observed that the encounter between popular and elite culture staged by the *Parangolés* on that night in August 1965 revealed aspects of both in a relationship that would "never be of harmony, since [the *Parangolé*'s] social insertion is designed to sharpen tensions. The relationship is one of estrangement, since the sambista wears a special costume in a specific place, like a museum, an art gallery, or a public artistic event."[110]

The scandal, in other words, had only partly to do with the anti-aesthetics of the work and more to do with a provocation, a "tension between different symbolic universes":[111] that of the museum and that of the favela. This was Oiticica's own perception of the event as he reported it to the Filipino artist David Medalla in a letter written shortly after the opening of *Opinião 65*. In it he expressed disappointment about the outcome of the event:

> [U]nfortunately it hasn't been a great thing concerning the "participation" of the public—even the most intelligent ones haven't understood the necessity of this participation. It has been, on the other side some sort of scandal among the "habitués" of exhibits, and it was almost necessary in the opening in the Museum for them to call the police, for I had introduced the PARANGOLÉ with a participation of dancing (the Brazilian "samba" with components of Mangueira one of the greatest Samba Schools of which I am also a component, as a matter of fact a "passist," that is, the one who makes improvisations throughout the dance). The Museum directors didn't like it for they see the Museum as a very "solemn" thing to abide such heresies as "samba" or the kind of people that make it: the ones from Rio's "favelas" (slums).[112]

Three years later, writing about *Tropicália,* a group of *Penetráveis* from 1967 that incorporated pebbles, sand, a parrot, and a television monitor, Oiticica explicitly addressed the issue of Brazilian identity. In this text he focused on racial (rather than social) difference, which he now conceptualized as a hybrid, as "the *myth of miscegenation*—we are blacks, Indians, whites, all at the same time" (emphasis added).[113] If *Tropicália* negotiated heterogeneous images of Brazil, the *Parangolés'* intermedial dimension embraced a multifarious materiality that resonated with the syncretic origins, ethnic miscegenation, and mediated realities of the favela. That is, they staged dissonance and difference by way of the fold that structured the relationship between inside and outside so crucial in the neoconcrete work that preceded them.

## THE BEHAVIOR OF THE FOLD

In a 1968 text titled "A obra, seu caráter objetal, o comportamento" (The Work, Its Object Character, Its Behavior), Oiticica underlined context—and the behavior of the work in a particular context—as fundamental to the meaning of his work. By way of example he cited the work of Piet Mondrian, whose presentation in museums—behind glass, framed, and hung in impeccable galleries—aestheticizes a practice that seems much more alive when seen in photographs of the artist's studio. If we want to be faithful to the Dutch artist's thought, Oiticica asked, why not re-create his environments through the study of photographs? This suggests that Oiticica saw the photographic record of his own work as an element capable of conveying something about the way he wanted it to operate. For Oiticica, a new art of environments and experiential participation posed the question of the "work-site" (*recinto-obra*) or the "place-site-context-work open to participation" (*lugar-recinto-contexto-obra aberto à participação*).[114] This environmental art was based on a specific context and could not simply be relocated to the museum.

Photographs of the *Parangolés*—particularly the first and most photographed cape in the series, *P4 Parangolé capa 1* (1964)—reveal aspects of their behavior. In some of the earliest images, taken that year by Oiticica's friend Desdemone Bardin, Miro da Mangueira wears the cape while dancing in a sequence of at least four photographs (plate 17). The casual backdrop, bare walls, and parquet floor suggest a middle-class setting (probably a room in the artist's house). A harsh light coming from a single source casts strong shadows and creates a peculiar mood. At the center of these pictures Miro dances, his feet barely touching the floor, his eyes shut, his figure distorted by the movement caught by the camera. The cape itself is made of layers of various pieces of canvas painted red, orange, and yellow (blue is visible in other images). Beneath the stiff outer shell, gauze and strips of plastic—one long yellow strip touches the floor, as if the inner organs of this painterly body were being ejected—evoke the tensions between outer layers and inner spaces so masterfully articulated in Oiticica's *Relevos espaciais* (Spatial Reliefs) of 1960.

The enigmatic layering of the red *Relevo espacial* (plate 18) could only be grasped by circling around the work and looking through breaches in the wooden panels that exposed the false flatness of the support, as real space diffused volume through gaps and folds. Likewise, the heterogeneous materials, colors, and forms of behavior encouraged by this first *Parangolé capa* coalesced around the structure of the interval—spatial and temporal, and now embodied. This temporal and spatial embodiment describes the difference between the *Relevos espaciais* and the *Parangolés*. Within the museum, gallery, or exhibition space we can more or less replicate the conditions, expectations, and rules of engagement that define our interactions with the more contained works. The *Relevos espaciais* modified that interaction, and the subsequent *NC1 Pequeno Núcleo 1* of 1960, an assemblage of five yellow wooden panels that further complicated the expanding structure that characterized these nonobjects, advanced that intention by incorporating a mirror into the work—an extension of the material conundrum offered by the work that also incorporates the reflection of the viewer. However, the *Parangolé capa* so clearly defies the conventions of exhibition—a challenge with which curators are still trying to come to terms—that replicating its participatory requirements might simply be impossible within a structure of museological display.

In "Anotações sobre o Parangolé," Oiticica further mapped the constellation of references of the *Parangolé* by focusing on its performative aspect. Here he argued that the spectator's actions (carrying, dancing, running) and interactions with the work revealed the "expressive act" (*o ato expressivo*). This dynamic was clearest in the capes worn by spectators. Consisting of layers of cloth that unfold to reveal such varied elements as colored strips of plastic and tulle (*P4 Parangolé capa 1*, 1964), a plastic pouch with powdered pigment (*P5 Parangolé capa 2*, 1965), or newspaper photographs (*P6 Parangolé capa 3 "Homenagem à Mário Pedrosa,"* 1964–65), these works demanded "direct corporeal participation" (*participação corporal direta*) that, according to Oiticica, implied "a corporeal-expressive transmutation of the spectator," which he associated with dance.[115] These words are key to understanding the processual dimension of the capes as they extended the "surface-process" of Lygia Clark's *Caminhando* to encompass a model of identity (of the subject and the object) that was fluid and contingent. Dependent on the movement required of the wearers of the *Parangolés* and the morphological reorganization of their elements, the capes avoided any ideal resolution and negated the possibility of fixed form. Furthermore, the layered and heterogeneous composition of the capes, their bulky structure and stiff surfaces—which invited tactile interaction—frustrated any attempt to think of these works as one would think of represented, fixed images or objects.

Oiticica further explained that when the capes unfolded, an intercorporeal space was created that split our very sense of being. These works were designed not for an ideal space-time (the museum, the wall, the frame), but for an in-between space, and thus, as he said, "[W]e cannot demand a sense of totality from it."[116] This sense of incompleteness is, paradoxically, what constituted, through wearing, the "experiential totality of the work" (as opposed to watching, which was necessary but secondary). Upon the works' unfolding, the spectator experienced the spatial transmutation that was operative in the *Parangolés* and defined their poetics of alterity. The capes performed "the experiential unfolding of that intercorporeal space,"[117] a somatic equivalent of the gaps and folds of the *Relevos espaciais* from four years earlier. But the capes also echoed the transformative logic of the carnival, where the self is encouraged to stage an "other,"[118] and where enacting the collective frenzy of dance points to that place where individual consciousness is replaced by the collective, libidinous body. In this sense too, the favela—a place that is no place, a place where the rationality of the public sphere metamorphoses into ephemeral communal encounters and strategies of collective survival—helped define the performatics of the cape: transmutation as an operation that disregarded the integrity of the body and the subject and dismissed identity (of the spectator and the work) as a self-sufficient or ideal unit.[119]

Dance provided a model in which process, action, expression, time, space, the body, the other, and participation were all elements at work. In "A dança na minha experiência" from 1965, Oiticica focused on what he referred to as the Dionysian dimension of dance, which in samba translates to a dedicated repetition of lyrics, rhythm, and steps—a veritable act of endurance, an "immersion in the rhythm, a vital identification of the gesture, of the act, with the rhythm."[120] This euphoric performativity was antagonistic to the static image, to representation—elements that Oiticica categorically rejected—and provided the link between collective and individual expression. This connection was evident not only in the choreographed efforts of the samba schools as they rehearsed before the carnival, but also in the related yearlong efforts of composers, dancers, singers, artists, dressmakers, and organizers, all of which downplayed a classical notion of authorship while providing a sense of collective participation that culminated in the carnival parade and informed the everyday texture of life in the favela.[121] Only this blurring of the individual within the collective, an unfolding in between the structures of the environment, could guarantee the "total experience" predicated on incompleteness and transformation. In a statement that betrayed the persistent influence of the neoconcrete experience and phenomenology on his thinking, Oiticica argued that dance would reveal the world of immanence (a favorite word of both Oiticica and Lygia Clark at the time) in all its plenitude.[122] Or, as he declared in 1966 in an effort to clarify the notion of creation through a corporeal act founded on a principle of uninterrupted transformation, dance revealed "the immanent gesture of the corporeal expressive act, which transforms itself continuously."[123]

## FORMS OF AFFECT

A pair of black-and-white photographs juxtaposed by Oiticica and distributed along with "Anotações sobre o Parangolé" and "Bases fundamentais para uma definição do 'Parangolé'" on the occasion of *Opinião 65* sheds more light on the operational possibilities of the cape (fig. 4.9). Oiticica's scholar, Irene Small, describes them as "photolithographic

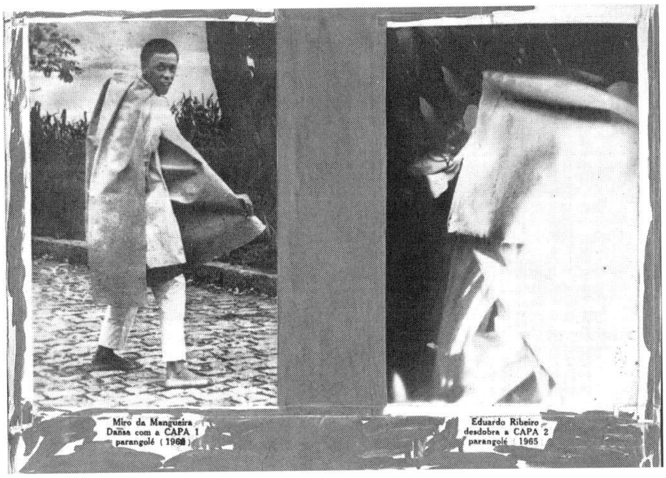


FIGURE 4.9
Left: Miro da Mangueira dances with *P4 Parangolé capa 1* (Hélio Oiticica, 1964); right: Eduardo Ribeiro unfolds *Parangolé P5 capa 2* (Hélio Oiticica, 1965).

reproductions aligned horizontally on a page" that served as a "printer's mock-up for a pamphlet."[124] The image on the left, captioned "Miro da Mangueira Dansa com a CAPA 1 parangolé (1964)" (Miro from Mangueira Dances with CAPE 1 Parangolé (1964)" features a young black man, nearly all of his body but his face turned away from the camera. He stands barefoot in the street that separated Oiticica's house from the ebullient center of the neighborhood down the hill in the Jardim Botânico area. Miro is posing more than dancing, his outstretched right arm extending the upper layer of the cape, its stiffness almost palpable in the wrinkled surface exposed to the camera. In this image, clearly conceived as documentation of the work's usage, the *Parangolé* seems to connect Miro to the landscape of the city, implied by the indistinct hills in the background, the trees and vegetation, and the cobblestone street. The body and the *Parangolé* are situated in the environment, in context, and the allusion to dancing and Miro's expressive face suggest the "affective alliance" that the cape aspired to articulate. That term was coined by the scholar Lawrence Grossberg to describe "an organization of concrete material practices and events, cultural forms and social experience which both opens up and structures the space of our affective investments in the world."[125] Layered and complex, contingent and contextual, unstable and disruptive, these alliances may displace dominant expectations, behaviors, and meanings to suggest different configurations of "desire and pleasure" that dismiss the congealed status of identities. Affect, in other words, is posited in the *Parangolés* as materially grounded in specific bodies and places while thwarting normative legibility and conventional semantic regimes via the structural—we could also say *transobjectual*—relation to the popular universe of the favela and samba.

What in 1959 began as a rejection of ideation, rationalism, and objectivism through an attempt to produce forms of affect, in 1964–65 delivered the body-subject in flux and proposed an alternative subjective and social economy vis-à-vis the authoritarian models of representation advocated by the CPC and normative society at large. The *Parangolés* aspired to generate phenomenologically constituted forms of affect founded by the material stratum of context as well as by the social, economic, and cultural configurations that define the moment of immanence. Against a privileging of reason, the idea, and the subject of cognition over that of affect, the philosopher Maurice Merleau-Ponty proposed "an understanding of embodied intentionality [as] a rejection of both the empirical subject—the subject understood as mere body—and the idealist subject—the subject of pure mind"—thus his usage of the term *body-subject*. This assessment of Merleau-Ponty's work is articulated in the context of an understanding of affect as a turning away from the "philosophical separation of mind and body" and as the privileging of "movements in between, particularly between mind and body . . . between the rational and the affective,"[126] and also as an oscillation between the body-subject and the world.

Conceptually syncretic and materially heterogeneous, a movement between affect and the social: this is the most explicit gesture of the *Parangolés*, one we can trace in the photographic record of the works—a drifting across subjects, across neighborhoods, across situations, attempting to negotiate differential and nonnormative relations between subjects and places. Whereas in Clark's *Bichos* the hinge articulated a relationship between the viewer and the work, the *Parangolés* were themselves hinges between the body-subject and the environment, a tool of mediation between city and favela, fine art and popular art, self and other. The unresolved materiality of the *Parangolés* suited their intervallic nature, which revealed the subject caught in the unstable gap between the suspension of habit and regulated behavior: suspension is determined by the action of carrying the *Parangolé*, its disunified logic conducive to a rejection of identity and scattered among lookers and wearers, while the normative is dictated by context, the social environment through which all subjects navigate (even those in the favela). As such, the *Parangolés* disturbed and resignified the subject and its context through a fluctuation that delivered, if only momentarily, alternate but also ambiguous and conflicting states of being in the world. Acknowledging the camera, displaying the *Parangolé*, and set within the mundane landscape, Miro demonstrated the work's task of articulation and the body as the locus of endless interfaces between the social and the affective, the environment and the body-subject.

Two days before the *Parangolés'* first public presentation, the journalist Esther Emílio Carlos wrote (under Oiticica's direction) about the work's three iterations: banners, capes, tents. As the journalist explained in a note, they indicated different "spatial positions" (*posições espaciais*) in the relationship of work to spectator. With the tent, the participant "penetrates" it to uncover "the spatial color-structure of the work." In the case of the banners, the structure is related to the act of carrying by the participant. The cape involves three stages: an initial participant wears the cape; a second participant watches the first wear the cape; and the wearing reveals its color-structure.[127] No doubt the spectator, the subject, the body, constituted the fulcrum of Oiticica's *Parangolés*, the "quasi-corpus" of the nonobject now replaced by the "total body" of the participant. However, this was an "empty-full" totality, to use Lygia Clark's term, or a totality predicated on incompleteness, on a splitting of being, in Oiticica's words. This was a totality verifiable in the relationship between the work and the participant (previously the spectator), the work and the environment, the inside and the outside. It is not by chance that some of the capes cling to the body, mirroring the enigmatic topological figure of the Möbius strip.

Participation, then, was conceived in relation to the environment, the other, and experience (*vivência*), with an awareness of the ocular economy of display in which both the subjects of carnival and works of art participate. Indeed, Oiticica identified two modalities of participation: one in which, by looking at (watching) the unfolding of the cape, we become aware of its objective—spatial and temporal—constitution, and another in which participation is of an experiential-subjective nature (wearing). The two modes are important for the completion of a cycle (wearing-watching) that is defined as an "intermediary" stage arguably superseded by a plurality of participants (that is, more than one pair of subjects interacting). Oiticica continued: "Here, environmental space-time transforms into a 'work-environment' totality."[128] But, like the heterogeneous layers of materiality of the *Parangolés* and the gaps between those layers, the body-subject of the participant was an incomplete totality that experienced the self in the spaces between itself and the other (the work, the other, the world). This establishment of relations between the *Parangolé* and the outside, mediated via the concept of structure, determined the "total experience of the work." In keeping with the phenomenological discourse that informed neoconcretism, Oiticica made *vivência* the core concept of an artistic practice now filtered through the environmental and the collective. "These work-participant nuclei," Oiticica wrote, introducing the plural, "when related in a particular environment (in an exhibition, for example), create an 'environmental-system' *Parangolé*, which in turn can be watched by other external participants."[129]

The morphology of the *Parangolés*, with their emphasis on diverse materials and sensations, flowing surfaces and heavy pockets, opaque canvases and transparent gauzes, photographs and colors, as well as on the action of the body in the environment, actualized the nonobject's affective aspirations. *P4 Parangolé capa 1* (1964) was just such an affective (non)object; it suspended habit and dislocated obvious relations among the body, the work, the environment, and the other because it set them in motion, in flux, susceptible to Clark's logic of "the inside is the outside."[130] As Oiticica firmly stated, however, this pliancy was embedded in the environmental. Thus, the situational structure that the *Parangolés* embodied was tied to the material specificity of the bodies and places it encountered. Recent writing about affect underlines the foundational nature of encounters for a processual subjectivity that the *Parangolés* so insistently figured forth. In practice, Gregory Seigworth and Melissa Gregg write, "affect and cognition are never fully separable—if for no other reason than that thought is itself a body, embodied. Cast forward by its open-ended in-between-ness, affect is integral to a body's perpetual becoming (always becoming otherwise, however subtly, than what it already is), pulled beyond its seeming surface-boundedness by way of its relation to, indeed its composition through, the forces of encounter. With affect, a body is as much outside itself as in itself—webbed in its relations—until ultimately such firm distinctions cease to matter."[131]

## OPACITY

The second photograph, next to the one of Miro described above, counteracts the evidentiary quality of the first. Labeled "Eduardo Ribeiro desdobra a CAPA 2 parangolé (1965)" (Eduardo Ribeiro Unfolds CAPE 2 Parangolé [1965]) it is in every way its opposite. Cropped and overexposed, the diffuse image of a young white man is taken from above. His upper body is completely covered by the layers of the cape, and his face is obscured as he looks down and away from the camera. The photograph reveals almost nothing of the subject or the action that he is performing, and the *Parangolé* here is a formless wrapper that occludes the individual beneath. The *Parangolé,* this image seems to suggest, is not meant to channel individual expression, nor is it meant to reveal the self within. But here another gap emerges more clearly than in other images of the *Parangolés*: that is, the gap between the situation that the photographs attempt to convey and the unrepresentable dimension of *vivência* and affect, as the other, the onlooker, and context itself is absent from this image. Tellingly, in the opening scenes of a 1979 film on Oiticica, the artist dons his first *Parangolé capa* (plate 19) and gently moves under the layers that envelop him. Oiticica's voice-over declares: "The series of works makes what I am intelligible, I become [*sic*] to know myself better through what I do. Actually, I don't know what I am because if it is an invention, I am not able to know it."[132] Ambiguously verbalizing the operations of the *Parangolé*—its emphasis on action over identity and the uncodified imperatives of invention—Oiticica here describes the work as a positivity and a negativity, ultimately a nonrevelatory structure, opaque to knowledge and certainty.

The *Parangolés* made affect the central motor of the artwork, a preoccupation that by the late 1960s was characterized by Oiticica as an attempt to transform "art process into life feelings," "to integrate all visual structures into 'felt' ones," and to achieve a "total affective experience."[133] The *Parangolés* embodied what Seigworth and Gregg have defined as affect's in-betweenness: "the capacities to act and be acted upon" as a consequence of clashes that result from "the body's . . . ongoing immersion in and among the world's obstinacies and rhythms, its refusals as much as its invitations."[134] In the context of the neoconcretist debates, *affect* refers to that unrepresentable surplus that the "Manifesto Neoconcreto" understood as repressed in an aesthetic discourse that valued rationalism above all and certitude articulated in geometric configurations organized according to prescribed premises. But affect also informed the unsettled relation between self and environment, self and other, that the *Parangolés* underscored. Most importantly, affect, as a guiding concept, threw Gullar, Clark, and Oiticica back to the body. As Gullar wrote many years later in assessing the impact of Merleau-Ponty on the "Manifesto Neoconcreto," the problem was one of signification, not merely perception, and since perception happens in time, it was necessary to integrate thought in this temporal flux, to "think with the body" (*pensar com o corpo*).[135] If the "nonobject" and the "quasi-corpus" had the task of destabilizing and uncategorizing the work of art, their afterlife in the *Parangolés* foregrounded their processual and participatory dimension, unleashing a nonnormative rapport with the other and the outside. Predicated on action and a hybrid materiality that related structurally (not referentially) to its surrounding environment, the *Parangolés* furthered the uncertainty of the "nonobject" and the "quasi-corpus," the formlessness of their non-ontology.

The *Parangolé capas,* in other words, figured forth the body as a locus of encounters that are syncretic, ambiguous, processual, mediatory, always on the go, and hostile to the prescriptions of bourgeois identity and representation, which Oiticica rejected. These encounters impinge on the subject, the body-subject, whose capacities and modalities are sustained and intersected by the "field or context of its force-relations."[136] While the *Parangolés* were evidently the result of an artistic-phenomenological inquiry into the body's perceptual operations, they also probed a phenomenological situatedness in which relations, encounters, interfaces, confrontations, and mediations, materially deployed and allegorized by the fold and the interval, blatantly undermined the satisfaction of identity, the unified subject, and the reassuring stability of objects with a name.

# 5

# ANOTHER GEOMETRY

## Gego's *Reticulárea*, 1969–77

> And if, slightly tired, the viewer abandons the discovery of the constructive character of the forms, leaving the work to rest and abandoning the perception of the modes in which it was configured, so that something other is shown there . . . then, in that moment of rest, emerges an always inconclusive configuration, always in the making, a work prone to error, a sincere trace of the meandering gaze.
>
> HANNI OSSOTT, *GEGO*, 1977[1]

In Gego's artistic trajectory, only the spatial displacement of the geometric plane, the increasing materialization of the line, and her interest in experimental engineering hints at the radical leap represented by her *Reticulárea*. The Spanish word *retícula* refers to a network of lines or a net, and this work—first exhibited in June 1969 at the Museo de Bellas Artes de Caracas (fig. 5.1) and reinstalled and re-created several times thereafter—consisted of metal meshes and nets connected and dispersed irregularly within a room. The *Reticulárea* rehearsed a paradigm of artistic production that, in its refusal of the conventions of sculpture (mass, volume, surface), made line and space the means for a critique of architectural enclosure and sculptural monumentality. In its systematic undoing of the calculated geometries and gridlike structures favored by postwar geometric abstraction, Gego's work interrogated idealized models of representation and their illusory reflection of a modernized urban space. Her "weaving" of nets—as she called the production process implied by the design of the *Reticulárea*—was part and parcel of the constructive ethos that had fueled Venezuela's artistic imaginary in the 1950s but which by the late 1960s had been domesticated by the government and the economic elite as a symbol of the country's wealth and international aspirations.[2] In its attack on form and cubic spatiality, Gego's *Reticulárea* went against the grain of standard sculptural bodies to engage marginal spaces—such as the peripheries of rooms that she was at pains to activate in her installations—and to respond to the erratic urban landscape of Caracas. This chapter argues for the relevance of the *Reticulárea* in the context of a continental postwar crisis of geometric abstraction that questioned the

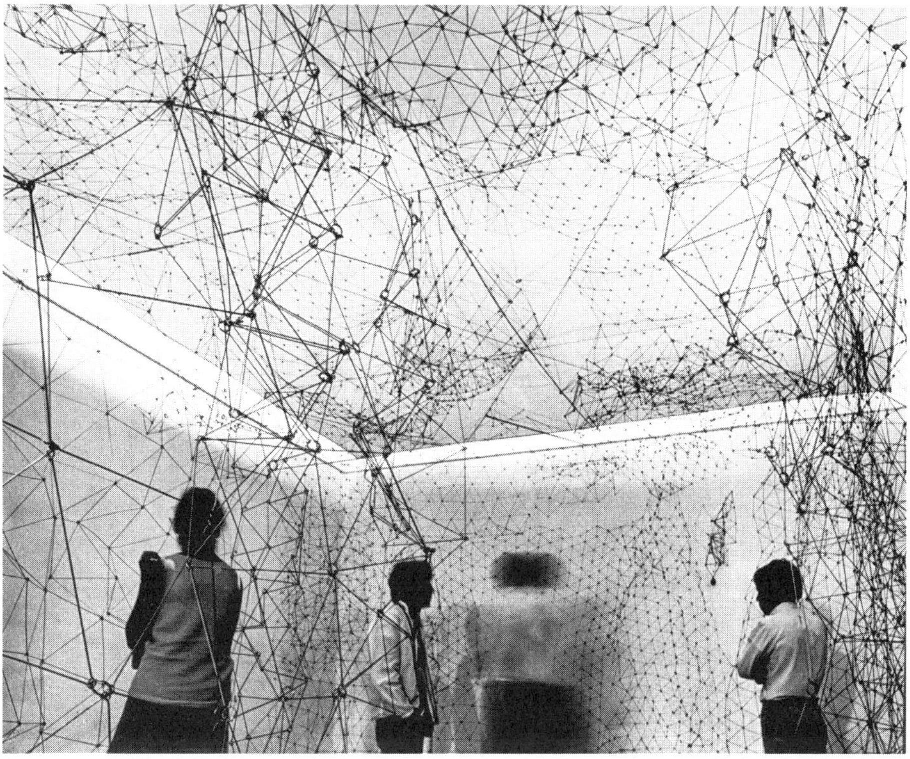

FIGURE 5.1
Gego, *Reticulárea*, Museo de Bellas Artes de Caracas, 1969.

conventions of mediums. It also pays close attention to how Gego's geographical and professional displacements (from Germany and from architecture; to Venezuela and to the visual arts) informed the intermedial aspect of her practice.

## ARCHITECTURAL CONSTRUCTION, MONUMENTAL STRUCTURES: AN EDUCATION AND A LEGACY

Gego (Gertrude Goldschmidt), born in Hamburg in 1912, was a niece of the art historian Adolph Goldschmidt (who taught the likes of Alexander Dorner, Erwin Panofsky, and Rudolph Wittkower at the University of Berlin). In the winter semester of 1932–33, she began her studies in architecture and engineering at the Technische Hochschule of Stuttgart under the tutelage of Paul Bonatz. Bonatz was one of the main exponents of the modernist masonry style that emerged in Germany between the wars. He had been influenced by Theodor Fischer's masonry buildings and had put into practice a modernized version of his mentor's approach in the railroad station of Stuttgart, which Bonatz designed in collaboration with F. E. Scholer from 1911 to 1928. But Bonatz also favored more traditional forms and methods of construction and was a major advocate of the so-called *Heimatstil* (regional style), which was derived from the rural German vernacular architecture of the nineteenth century.[3] Under his leadership, the Technische Hochschule put in place reforms that emphasized a practical attitude toward architecture. As a consequence, the school expanded its courses in elementary construction and required all students to have six months of experience at a construction site before entering the program. Halfway through their studies, following their second year, students worked in an architect's office for a full year. Bonatz described this "comprehensive education for young architects" as one in which students had a fixed curriculum during the first half of their studies and free choice of courses and professors only in the second part of their training.[4] Under Bonatz, the school emphasized group work as a means for arriving at standard solutions to architectural problems, and all professors were involved in the critique of final projects, reducing the risk of unfair evaluation. Gego earned a double degree in architecture and engineering from the Technische Hochschule, and with that credential and experience from one of the few institutions among Germany's polytechnics structured as an architecture school, she arrived in the port of La Guaira, Venezuela, in August 1939.

The country that Gego encountered, although undeveloped from an urban and cultural perspective, was undergoing rapid transformation. Indeed, her arrival coincided with the presentation of the Plan Rotival (Monumental Plan), the first professional proposal to remake Caracas into a modern and regulated urban space.[5] The twenty-seven-year dictatorship of Juan Vicente Gómez had ended with his death in 1935, unleashing an era of dependency on the oil industry that came to define the country's identity, politics, and economy—as it has to this day. Venezuela thus became a rentier state whose economy grew exponentially from the policies of and concessions granted to foreign oil companies. By the late 1930s, Standard Oil and Shell had come to control 85 percent of the oil extraction in the country,[6] and the Venezuelan government had become a "distributor of oil wealth."[7] The death of the dictator also fueled a public debate on democracy, foreign interests, and national wealth. A generation of young intellectuals and professionals, some of whom had experienced exile, argued that a democratic government would allow Venezuela to reclaim its natural resources to the benefit of the social progress of the nation while at the same time fighting imperialism. This groundswell led to a coup in 1945, fashioned as revolutionary and pro–universal suffrage, that brought the Acción Democrática (AD) party to head the government until 1948. As the Venezuelan historian Fernando Coronil observed, during this brief democratic experiment AD was able to expand its social base, which now included the lower and middle classes. Profiting from its control of the oil industry, however, the party (like the dictatorships it followed and preceded) became centralized and hierarchical. Most importantly, Coronil adds, "carved by the flow of oil wealth, an unusual social edifice was being built in Venezuela, one modeled after the Western ideals which Venezuela sought to attain: a productive civil society and a representative state, although with inverted structural elements in which the top supported the base. With the continuous expansion of the oil industry, an increasingly wealthy state, financially independent from domestic agents, was making the people dependent on it."[8]

The democratic government orchestrated by AD proved to be precarious: after the 1945 coup, the AD's candidate, the novelist Rómulo Gallegos, was elected president in 1947 but remained in power for only nine months. A military junta followed in November 1948, with its leaders seeking to restore order and control the popular political expansion that AD had encouraged. The transition to dictatorship was swift, abetted by politicians' resentment of AD and by a society subject to those in control of the state apparatus (and, thus, its oil wealth). Venezuela's government—under the various military and civilian juntas and during the interregnum of Acción Democrática—established a pattern in which the political and economic claims of the state were not backed up by substantial development in the areas of industry and social services. Later, the main goal of the dictatorship of Colonel Marcos Pérez Jiménez (1952–58) was to be the transformation of the country's urban environment. As a result, under the aegis of his increasingly strict regime and within a discredited political environment, the country witnessed urban transformation that had no historical precedent. Revenues from the oil industry and, to a lesser degree, the iron industry, paired with the monumental aspirations of the Pérez Jiménez government, transformed the capital of Caracas into an urban center featuring modern architecture and infrastructure for approximately eight hundred thousand inhabitants.

Office buildings, residential centers, low-income housing, hotels, commercial centers, military installations, theaters, and highways changed the face of the city (fig. 5.2). As noted by the minister of internal relations during Pérez Jiménez's dictatorship: "If anything characterizes the current political regime in Venezuela, it is the bulldozer. . . . The bulldozer is the best collaborator of the government, the most precise interpreter of the elevated and noble objective to transform the physical environment. . . . The current government believes that the majority of our problems can be solved by engineering. Housing, water, communications are demands that technicians must analyze and satisfy. The new national ideal is based on rationally oriented work."[9] This correlation between material construction, progress, and rationality pervaded the carefully constructed and managed image of modernity that Pérez Jiménez sought to establish. The ideological program under which this technocratic agenda was set forth, called Nuevo Ideal Nacional (New National Ideal), articulated "the regime's fetishistic vision of modernity as a collection of grand material achievements," as Coronil puts it.[10]

Indeed, in 1954 *Architectural Forum* described Caracas as "the buildingest city in South America" and "one of the fastest growing cities in the world,"[11] and a few years later *Architectural Record* published an article entitled "Highlights of Venezuela's Burgeoning New Architecture."[12] In 1956 the Paris journal *L'Architecture d'Aujourd'hui*[13] dedicated fifty-four pages to commercial and residential buildings throughout Venezuela (fig. 5.3). Stressing the problems produced by uncontrolled rural migrations and the

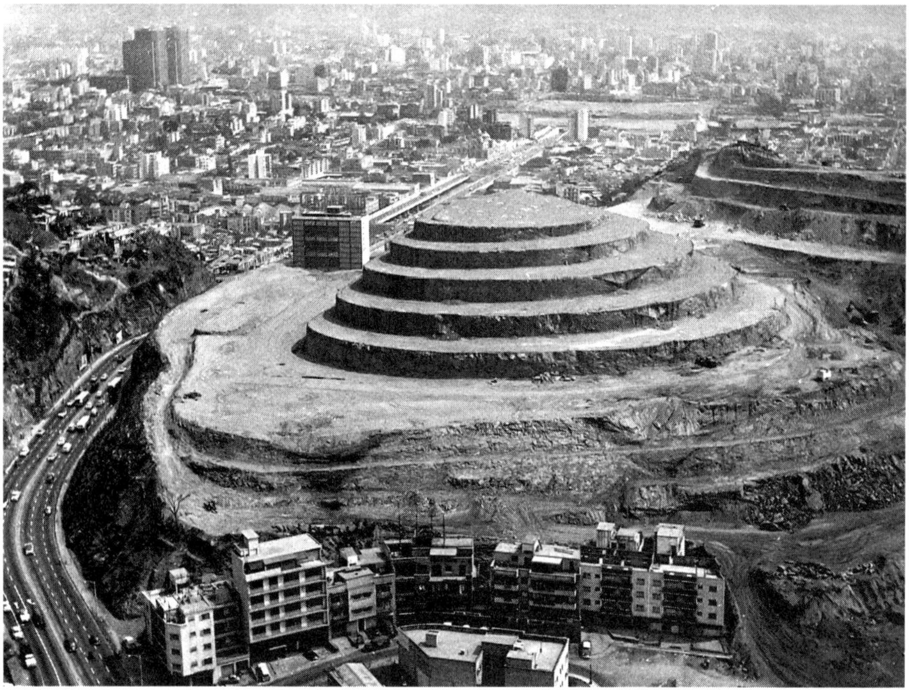

FIGURE 5.2
Construction of El Helicoide, Caracas, ca. 1956.

chaos of unplanned construction,[14] the magazine described the virtues of new buildings that would provide all sorts of services to the new communities of rural migrants. In time, it concluded, Caracas would be an exemplary case of habitat planning. That was surely one of the aspirations of the Nuevo Ideal Nacional espoused by Pérez Jiménez, whose focus on the physical transformation of the country was an updated version of the ideal of order and progress that characterized regimes throughout the continent. Influenced by nineteenth-century positivism, this program aimed to transform the natural habitat (the cause of underdevelopment in the view of the government) and, through rationality and planning, to dominate the whims of nature. But if the urban and architectural achievements of the regime—with its emphasis on professional planning and embrace of architectural and design experimentation—were to make Venezuela a "continental reference of functionalist modernism," they also exposed a tendency to uncritically appropriate foreign models, and poor planning that contributed to the rapid spread of a periphery of shantytowns—a "belt of misery"—whose growth was accelerated by the promise of city lights.[15]

Gego's architectural and engineering training in Stuttgart predisposed her toward an architectural reading of sculptural space and an awareness of the urban contradictions of the built environment she observed in Caracas during its phase of rapid moderniza-

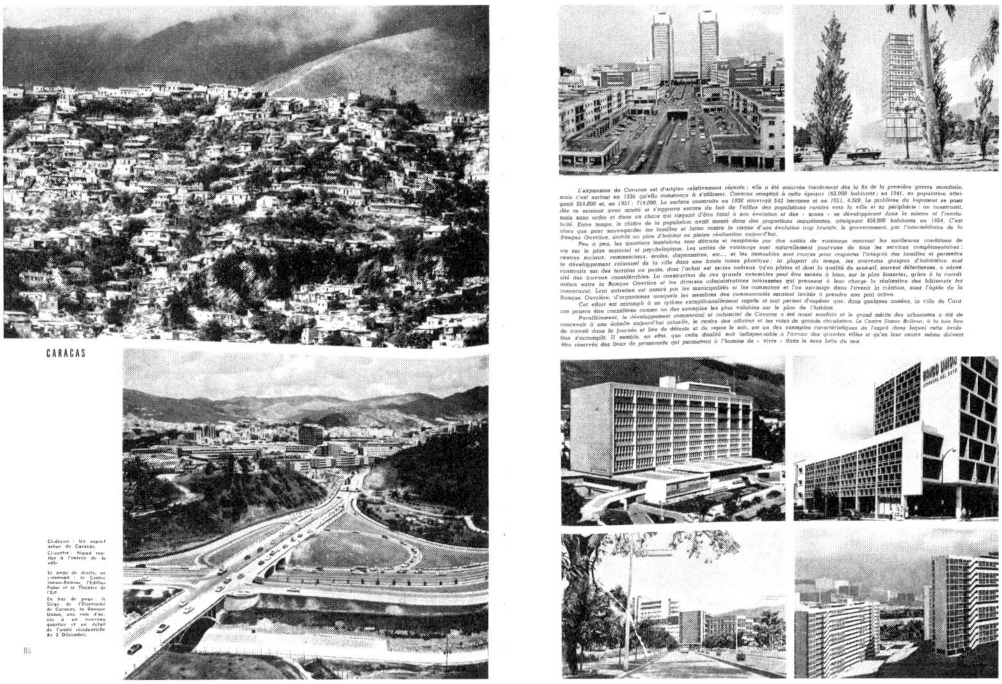


FIGURE 5.3
*L'Architecture d'Aujourd'hui* nos. 67–68, October 1956, special feature on Venezuelan architecture.

tion in the 1950s and beyond. Influenced by the polemics surrounding the downfall of modern architecture and avant-garde culture in Nazi Germany, and later the optimistic presence of geometric abstraction in Venezuela in the 1950s and 1960s, Gego was eager to embrace a sculptural practice that would recapture, and later redefine, sculpture's use of real—architectural—space. It seems only logical that at some point she would go beyond an object-based art practice to engage more complex situations through works that would develop modes of public address in which viewers collectively confronted a spatiotemporal field organized according to the matrix of spatial and material dedifferentiation that can also be recognized in the work of Eva Hesse, whose *Right After* (fig. 5.4) came to fruition in 1969, the same year Gego's *Reticulárea* was first shown.

Scholars have observed that *Reticulárea* bears the influence of the American engineer Buckminster Fuller, particularly his geodesic domes—spherical, lightweight structures based on a tetrahedral module. As early as 1969, the Venezuelan art critic and historian Lourdes Blanco, in her short, insightful text on the *Reticulárea,* mentioned Fuller and Alexander Calder as influential antecedents for the work.[16] For Gego (and a whole generation of artists in the 1960s), engineering, like architecture, was a compelling field in which radical reconceptualizations and experiments with structures and urban space were taking place. Gego's 1968 work *Flechas* (Arrows)—commissioned by the Estudio

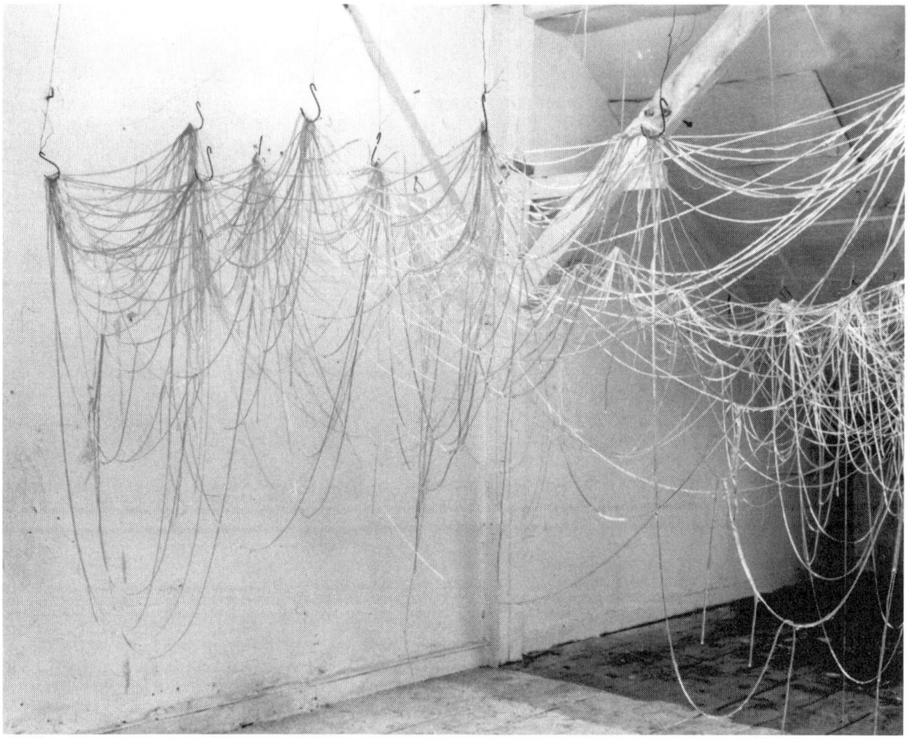

FIGURE 5.4
Eva Hesse, *Right After,* 1969, fiberglass, polyester resin, and wire, 60 × 214 × 48 in., three sections.

Actual art gallery for an interior courtyard of the Centro Comercial Chacaito (Chacaito Mall) in Caracas—was suspended in the open space between two floors (fig. 5.5). It generated a matrix of triangles made of metal tubes that were echoed by triangular metal blades and connected by nylon ropes. The work's technique relied on "tensegrity," a structural system in which compression elements (here, metal rods) are linked through tensioned members (in this case, ropes and wires) and attests to Gego's training and interest in engineering. Tensegrity was developed in 1948 by the American artist Kenneth Snelson during a seminar with Fuller at Black Mountain College, and, according to Michael John Gorman, it "demonstrated that tension structures could be extended in all directions to create networks of forces that counterbalanced each other."[17] A small sculpture made by Snelson at the end of 1948 titled *Early X-piece* rudimentarily but aptly demonstrates the system (fig. 5.6). Its vertical configuration—two X-shaped wooden pieces, one suspended on top of the other through an axial course of nylon cords—likely inspired the radial structure of Fuller's geodesic domes, which relied on the modular multidirectionality suggested by the sculpture.[18]

Fuller's masterpiece was a geodesic dome seventy-six meters in diameter built on the occasion of the 1967 Universal Exposition in Montreal for the American Pavilion. This

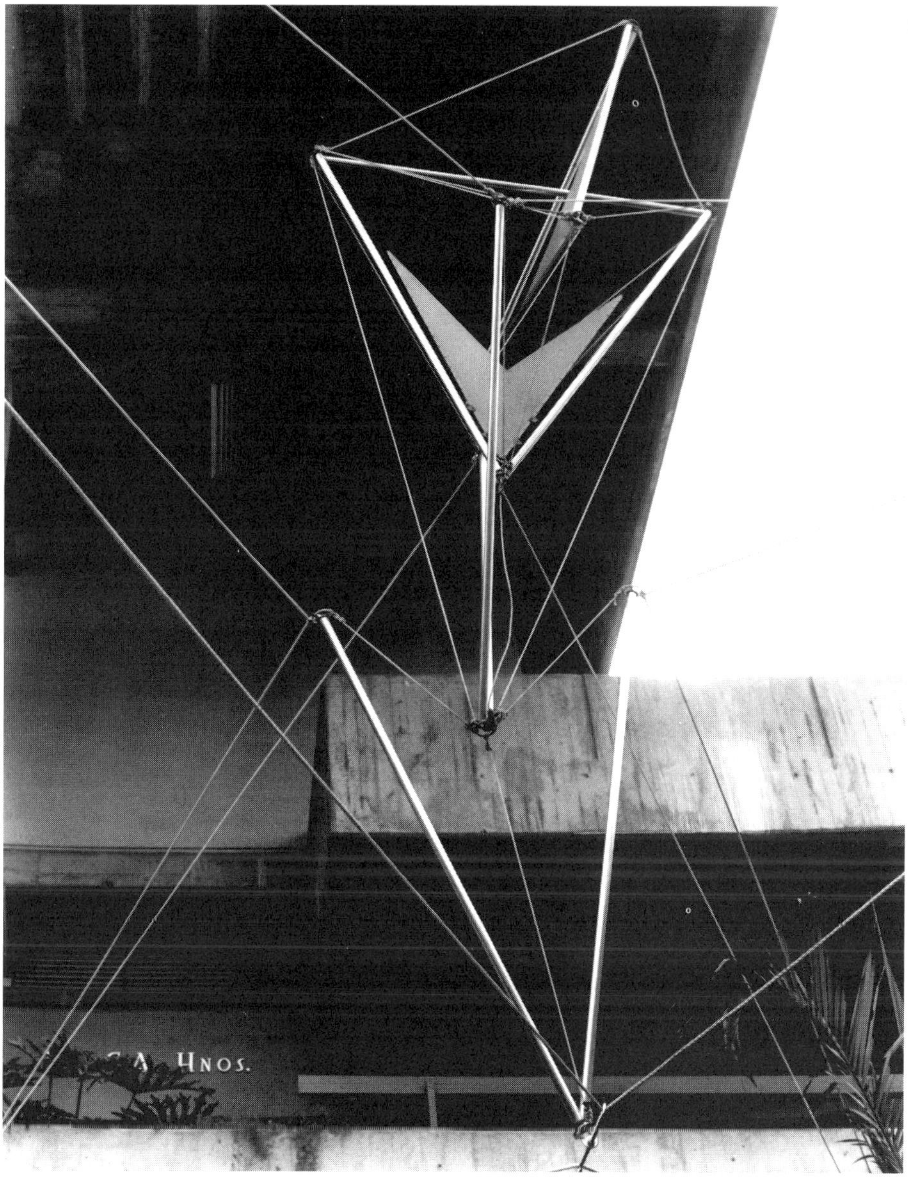

FIGURE 5.5
Gego, *Flechas* (Arrows), 1968, aluminum and nylon ropes, 354 × 354 in.

work (of which Gego was probably aware) embodied a "futuristic optimism"[19] directly connected to the new structural and spatial challenges of the period. Geodesic domes, along with other lightweight structures that offered an alternative to mainstream modernist architecture, were widely publicized in architectural magazines during the 1950s and 1960s. Fuller's work also found its way into art venues: from September 1959

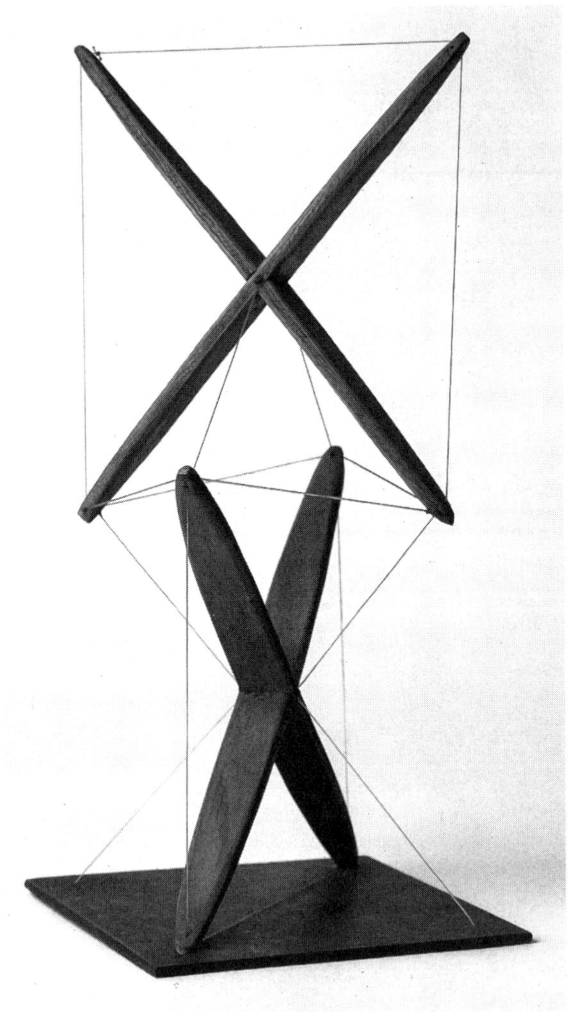

FIGURE 5.6
Kenneth Snelson, *Early X-piece*, 1948, wood and nylon, 11 ½ × 5⅜ × 5⅜ in.

through 1960, the Museum of Modern Art in New York mounted *Three Structures by Buckminster Fuller*, which featured a geodesic radome, an octet truss, and a tensegrity mast.[20] Gego could have seen the MoMA exhibition when she and her partner, the Lithuanian-Venezuelan artist and designer Gerd Leufert, visited New York that year (the presence of the exhibition brochure in the artist's home library in Caracas suggests this). Two years later, in 1962, the editor of *L'Architecture d'Aujourd'hui*, the artist André Bloc—who had widely publicized Carlos Raúl Villanueva's Universidad Central in Caracas (1945–58), where Gego was a professor in the school of architecture—published an issue on *architectures fantastiques*, which featured many experimental projects that reconceived the city dweller's relationship to the urban metropolis. These projects shared a fluid conception of space in which structural systems characterized by open modularity encouraged "unpredictable patterns of living"[21] and, according to the architectural historian Mark Wigley, were indebted to the pioneering work of Buckminster Fuller and Konrad Wachsmann. Both men were associated with the Institute of Design in Chicago,[22] and their work must have been familiar to Gego due to her interest in experimental engineering and her growing interest in the Bauhaus pedagogy and its legacies. This interest was prompted by the opening of a new building for the school of architecture at the Universidad Central in Caracas in 1957–58, where Gego taught a course on the foundations of composition from 1959 to 1966.[23] It was precisely in 1962, when talk of spatial architectures and space frames was at its peak in France, that Gego spent a year in the United States and Europe to study various first-year architecture programs.

As an architecture student in Stuttgart, Gego must have been acquainted with the Bauhaus—or at least the debates on rationalization, standardization, internationalism, and tradition it had provoked and the work it produced and inspired. And she would surely have been familiar with the Weissenhof Settlement, the exhibition of experimental housing built on a hill overlooking Stuttgart in 1927. This groundbreaking complex of buildings featured the work of such prominent modernist architects as Ludwig Mies van der Rohe, Le Corbusier, Walter Gropius, J. J. P. Oud, and Bruno Taut, among others.[24] The ambitious exhibition was organized by the German Werkbund—an association of architects and designers founded in 1907 to promote modern industrial design—and sponsored by the city of Stuttgart. The project was intended to demonstrate the advantages of the Neues Bauen (or New Building, a term that increasingly defined the modern architectural movement of the 1920s in Germany) and its methods of rationalization and standardization. The *Siedlung*, however, proved extremely controversial, as it cast light on tensions between internationalism and localism, experimentalism and tradition. These negotiations were relevant, as the Weissenhof Settlement was part of an effort by the city of Stuttgart to boost its national prominence. Friction between the indigenous and the international would be replayed in Venezuela, though on very different terms. Modern architecture and the variants of geometric abstraction that circulated in the Caracas of the 1950s and 1960s would highlight the stresses between local culture and what was perceived as its total opposite: a universalism generally associated with the canonical artistic trajectories of European art since the nineteenth century.

Gego's familiarity with Bauhaus pedagogy was evident in her teaching at the architecture school of the Universidad Central. The foundation course she taught there in the 1960s introduced students to concepts such as line, space, volume, form, structure, and texture, and the basics of spatial representation. This course was known as the orientation cycle; it was followed by an analytic cycle, concerned with the human element and the habitat; and the series concluded with a synthetic cycle, which investigated and studied "architectonic groups that respond to topics of urban and/or rural planning."[25] Photographs of her students' work at both the Universidad Central and the Instituto de

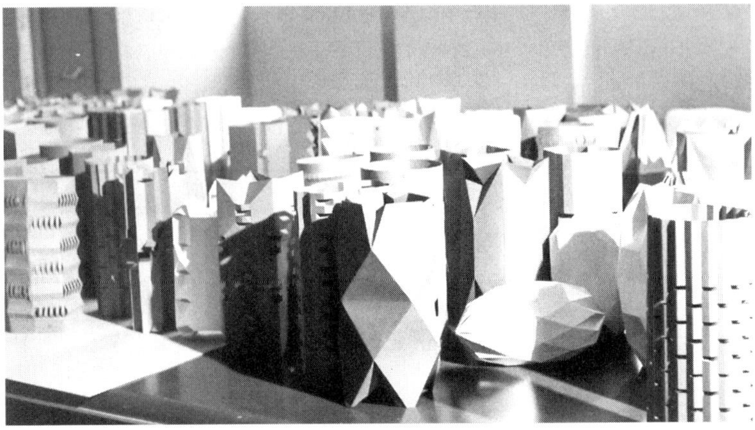

FIGURE 5.7
Student work from Gego's seminar on three-dimensional form at Instituto de Diseño, Fundación Neumann, Caracas, 1967.

Diseño, Fundación Neumann, where she began to teach in 1964 (fig. 5.7),[26] demonstrate that by the 1960s Gego had become steeped in the pedagogic practices of the Bauhaus's *Vorkurs* (the foundational course that was the school's most distinctive educational feature) as well as in the more contemporary iterations and exercises associated with preliminary courses in Bauhaus-influenced institutions (fig. 5.8). These photographs show an impressive range of student work that encompasses Bauhaus-inspired interest in modularity as well as more recent experiments with tensegrity. For example, a 1968 tensegrity mast made by a student at the Universidad Central attests to knowledge of this fascinating structure (fig. 5.9).

Gego seems to have been attracted to the aesthetic possibilities of these Bauhaus-related exercises and expansive, netlike morphologies of space frames during these years of intense teaching. And given the fact that neither her *Flechas* nor the *Reticulárea* were meant to enclose or cover space as Fuller's geodesic domes did, it is tempting to see Gego's work as a morphological and structural riposte to the German architect Konrad Waschmann's large metal space frames of the early 1950s. Based on a modular system of standardized elements that allow for multiple combinations, Waschmann's structures revolve around a "universal connector," which consists of a node from which up to twenty secondary tubular elements can radiate in any direction, allowing for unlimited adaptability to all possible geometric systems.[27] A similar configuration was used as a connecting device by Gego in the *Reticulárea,* where she attached metal rods to a large ring. While her nets echo the multidirectional network of Fuller's geodesic domes, they also invoke the infinite modularity and open quality of Waschmann's space frames (fig. 5.10).

Yet Gego's work clearly behaved in a radically different manner. While she utilized

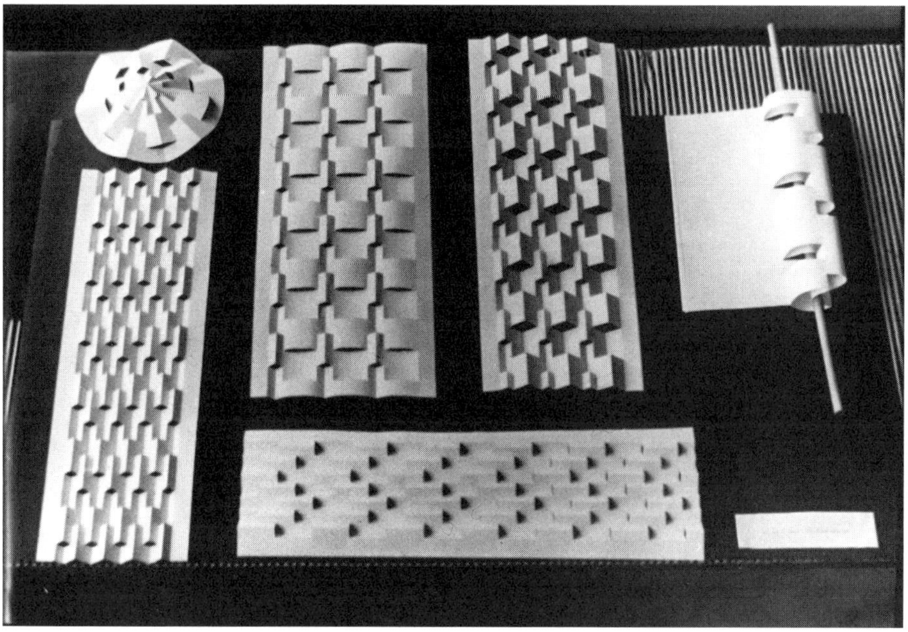

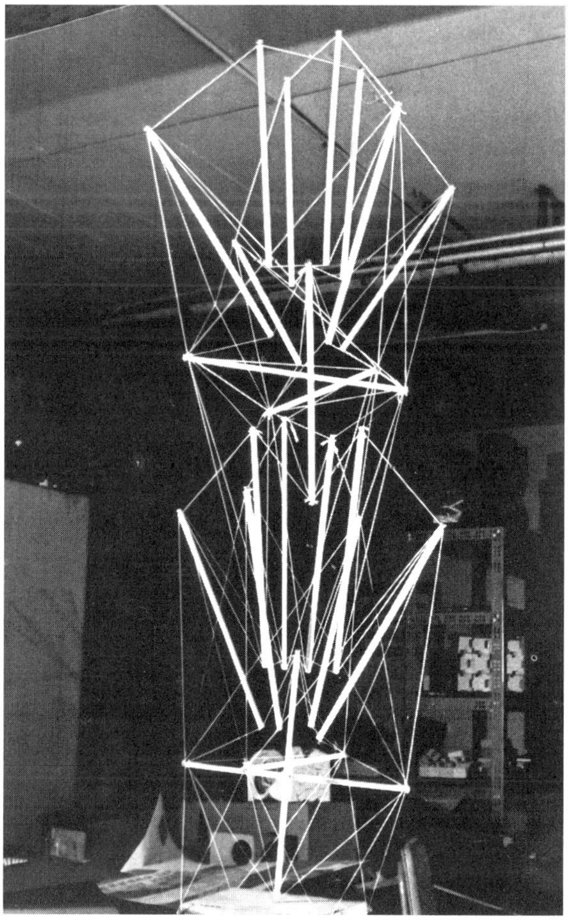

FIGURE 5.8
Student work from Josef Albers's preliminary course: studies in the three-dimensional use of paper, ca. 1927.

FIGURE 5.9
Student work from Gego's basic composition workshop, Universidad Central de Venezuela, Caracas, 1968.

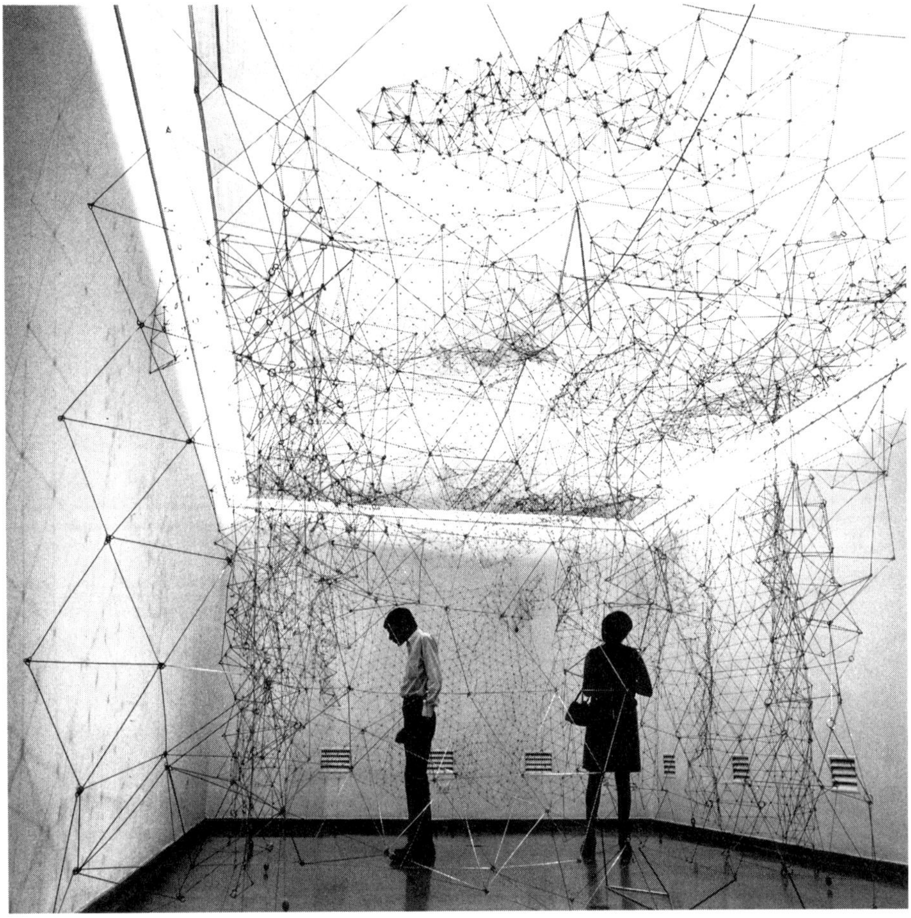

FIGURE 5.10
Gego, *Reticulárea,* Museo de Bellas Artes de Caracas, 1969.

a variation of the "key components of the space frame—node and connecting bar,"[28] the *Reticulárea* bypassed its functional concerns (rigidity and strength) as well as its monumentality. Moreover, while these international references were important to Gego, more pliant and poetic treatments of space and structure had been available to the artist in Venezuela since the early 1950s in the form of an architectural and engineering tour de force at the Universidad Central in Caracas: the architect Carlos Raúl Villanueva's Plaza Cubierta (Covered Plaza, 1953) and the linked Aula Magna auditorium, the latter designed in collaboration with Alexander Calder (plate 20). Gego's spatial and architectural sensibilities and her involvement with the Universidad Central—of which the Aula Magna and Plaza Cubierta are the cultural, social, and aesthetic heart—must have prompted her to absorb the airiness, pliancy, and distinctive spatiotemporality that this architectural complex embodied. Moreover, not only was the university the locus of an

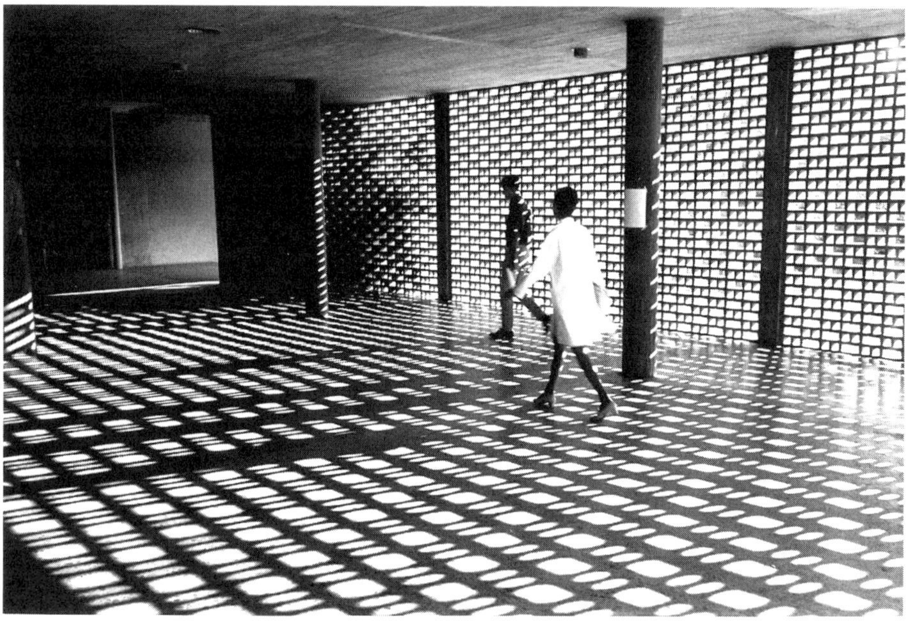

FIGURE 5.11
Carlos Raúl Villanueva, corridor leading to Plaza Cubierta, Ciudad Universitaria, Caracas, 1950s.

important experiment in the integration of the arts, architecture, and urban design, but it was also the site of an exchange between local and international aesthetic models that gave ample visibility to the constructivist trends of the postwar period that would influence and flourish among a number of Venezuelan artists in the 1950s.

The Universidad Central was and still is one of the most important interventions in the urban fabric of Caracas. Despite its primary role as an educational institution, it has been the public site for numerous cultural, social, and political encounters, debates, and conflicts. Commissioned in 1944 by the administration of the Venezuelan president Isaías Medina Angarita, the project was fully supported by and came to be identified with the Pérez Jiménez regime and its desire to rapidly "modernize" Caracas and project a positive international public image.[29] It was the government's eagerness to finish the core of the Universidad Central—the Aula Magna and surrounding Plaza Cubierta—for the Inter-American Conference in March 1954 that guaranteed funding for the involvement of the artist Alexander Calder in the design of the Aula Magna as well as for the many murals and sculptures that fill the Plaza Cubierta.[30]

Conceived as a public space topped by a roof to protect students and passersby from sun and rain, the Plaza Cubierta is flanked by perforated concrete screens that fragment the sunlight (fig. 5.11). It is punctuated by free-standing murals, patios bursting with tropical vegetation, and ramps leading to the Aula Magna. The Venezuelan architectural historian William Niño Araque characterized the Plaza Cubierta as an open plan that

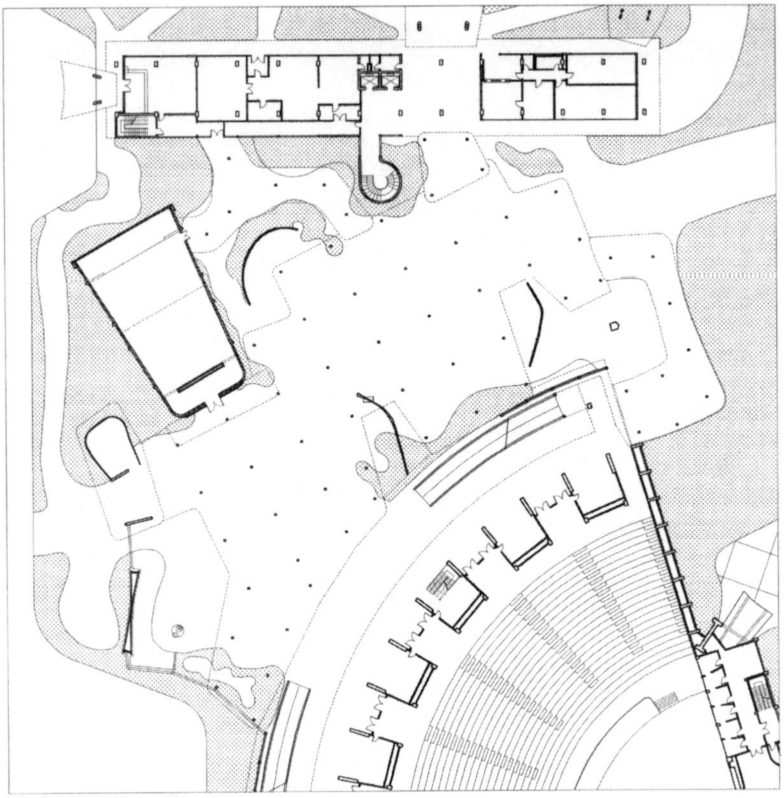

FIGURE 5.12
Carlos Raúl Villanueva, plan for Plaza Cubierta, n.d.

does not comply with the rigid scheme associated with the stasis and holistic organization of classical architecture.[31] The resulting ambiguous space is predicated on a very simple post-and-lintel structure, in which an irregularly shaped concrete roof is supported by simple columns distributed on an orthogonal grid that meets, but does not correspond to, a grid of concrete bands on the floor of the plaza.

The Plaza Cubierta links the most significant buildings of the university: a rectory, a concert hall, a main library, a hall of honor, and the Aula Magna. A plan of this grouping (fig. 5.12) reveals an unusual flexibility in the treatment of architectural demarcation and conveys a disunified feeling of dispersal. Like a formless mass spreading among—at times embracing and connecting—buildings and interstitial spaces, the slab of concrete that forms the roof of the plaza facilitates multiple apertures and virtual boundaries created by the sunlight. The topological figure of the "inside is the outside," exemplified by the Möbius strip, is embodied in the Plaza Cubierta by an intimate public space that daylight alters, disorienting the visitor. The passerby moves, wrote the architectural historian Sibyl Moholy-Nagy, from "low shelter areas to lofty halls, from narrow passages through dense vegetation to generous plazas, inviting public assembly."[32] The fickleness of the space is accentuated by the small gardens, murals, and works of art scattered throughout. The continuous shifting of boundaries is accentuated by the light that passes through the screens of perforated concrete that border the outer edge of the plaza and by the ramps that lead toward the auditorium. The patterned projections of light on the ground and the repetition of columns transform architecture into weightless space. The unregulated coordinates of this environmental treatment of architecture—an architecture that disperses itself through the crucial elements of sunlight and the void—was a counterpoint to the skyscrapers rising in Caracas at the time as a manifestation of the achievements of the dictatorial regime.[33]

Villanueva's Universidad Central has been hailed as an unprecedented example of the integration of the arts, and its influence on a generation of Venezuelan artists—Gego among them—has yet to be properly assessed. By placing abstract art in dialogue with his dynamic architecture, Villanueva helped to fortify the constructivist path that art was taking in Venezuela.[34] This art was integrated into the different buildings and areas of the university in diverse ways, with some instances more effective than others. Freestanding sculptures such as Jean Arp's *Cloud Shepherd* (1953) interact with Mateo Manaure's *Mural* (1954), while freestanding curved murals such as Fernand Léger's glass mosaic *Bimural* (1954) and Victor Vasarely's *Homage to Malevich* (1954), done in enameled ceramics, punctuate the fractured space of the plaza. Other murals cover the walls of the buildings, such as the one on the facade of the school of engineering by Alejandro Otero (1954). Also incorporated into the architecture are floor-to-ceiling stained-glass windows by Léger (in the Central Library) and Otero (in the school of engineering). Internal areas feature figurative murals, mostly by Venezuelan and other Latin American artists, and earlier commissions from 1950 feature allegorical sculptures by Francisco Narváez, with whom Villanueva had collaborated on previous projects. Although this figurative component has been considered a compromise on Villanueva's part, it is also an indication of the divided artistic terrain in which geometric abstraction was developing.[35] Moreover, the greatest achievement of Villanueva's campus—and of the Plaza Cubierta—lay not in its individual works of art but in the perceptual and spatial richness of the site.

In the Aula Magna—designed in collaboration with the acoustical engineer Robert B. Newman and Alexander Calder—Villanueva paralleled the spatial complexity of the Plaza Cubierta. The fan-shaped auditorium has a large vaulted ceiling and curved rear walls. Special acoustic panels distribute sound evenly throughout the vast space. These reflecting elements were designed by Calder and are sometimes referred to as "flying saucers" or "clouds" in the rich epistolary dialogue between the architect and the artist. Their correspondence from June 1952 reveals the uncertainty of Calder's participation, but by November 1952, detailed technical drawings of the ceiling panels were being redrafted in Newman's office. In these drawings, twenty-nine acoustic panels are classified as flat, convex, or concave. In the end, a total of thirty-one panels (nine on the walls, twenty-two on the ceiling) consisting of steel frames covered by metal lath and gypsum plaster were distributed irregularly along the space of the auditorium.[36]

The fusion of artistic effect and functionality, surprise and practicality, art and industry achieved in the Aula Magna provided Villanueva with an opportunity to rethink decoration under the auspices of a synthesis of the arts that aspired to combine architecture, painting, and sculpture. But beyond intermedial plasticity, the auditorium project sustained an effective integration of form, function, and site based on a "more profound structural connection between plastic activity in general and the techno-scientific social base."[37] This integration was extended through the architectural continuum created between the Aula Magna and the Plaza Cubierta. From the open, dilated space of the plaza, visitors to these spaces could access the radial auditorium and experience the kinetic pulsations of the acoustic "clouds"—which conveyed a sense of lightness despite their large size—and the constantly shifting views of the space, all of which echoed the dynamic parallax of the Plaza Cubierta.

The acoustic panels thus achieved a tripartite effect: they were fully functional in meeting the acoustical requirements of the auditorium; they emphasized the oblique trajectories of the space and thus shattered geometric stasis; and they complemented the dissolving quality of the Plaza Cubierta—the exterior equivalent of the Aula Magna. The dynamism triggered by the arched surfaces and irregular shapes of the "clouds," their scattered organization and fragmented effect (which the acoustic engineers celebrated for functional reasons), invited synesthetic apprehension of the space. The "clouds"—perceivable from everywhere, comprehensible from nowhere—complemented the open and generous space of the tiered seating area and emphasized the democratic access to the stage appropriate to a public theater. Accordingly, the auditorium feels limitless (without dimension or direction, in Villanueva's words) despite the enclosure that acoustic requirements demand.

While the Aula Magna is the pulsating heart of the architecture of the Universidad Central, the surrounding Plaza Cubierta radiates and spreads out, counteracting and complementing the latent kineticism of the vault structure of the auditorium. Acknowledging this relationship between the inside and the outside, Villanueva wrote, "In the covered plaza . . . it was necessary to prepare the environment of the auditoriums; color had to be spatial and it had to be composed with movement (space-time)."[38] The spatial radiance of Calder's "clouds" spreads throughout the Plaza Cubierta, where space-time unfolds in a contingent dialectic between the movements of passersby and the specific environmental effects of the site.

It is hard not to see a relationship between this architectural complex and important experiments with environmental sculpture in Venezuela during the 1960s and 1970s: Jesús Rafael Soto's *Penetrables,* Alejandro Otero's public sculptures with wind-propelled vanes, Carlos Cruz-Diez's *Cromosaturaciones,* and Domingo Álvarez's *Corridors,* among others. But despite the rapid advances of Venezuelan abstract art during the 1950s and an interest in more spatial and public work during the 1960s and 1970s, not until 1969 with Gego's *Reticulárea* did there emerge a sculptural project analogous to the Plaza Cubierta and the Aula Magna in its manipulation and defiance of orthogonal space and geometric form. Discernible in Villanueva's and Gego's unorthodox and radical treatment of architectural and sculptural space, respectively, is a parallelism grounded in their attention to local site, material specificities, and bodily (as opposed to optical) apprehension of space.

As a professor in the school of architecture at the Universidad Central, Gego was exposed to Villanueva's space on a daily basis; for many years she was the active passerby these spaces demanded. It is not surprising that next to the words "elements to analyze" on a handout for her students entitled "Analysis of an Urban Space," Gego wrote, by hand: "Changes of perception during circulation. Movement in space."[39] This spatio-temporal dimension would be crucial to Gego's *Reticulárea*; like the Plaza Cubierta, the *Reticulárea* rejected enclosures, welcomed discontinuous material intersections, and explored in-between mediums, operating not as an idealized, stable structure but as a contingent spatial body vulnerable to the inflections of site and viewer.

## THE IN-BETWEEN LINES

If the spatial experiments in architecture and engineering of Villanueva, Calder, Fuller, and others provided Gego with material to develop her (anti-)sculptural practice—which she defined in relation to its dismissal of volume and mass—she circumvented their spectacularity, grandiosity, structural precision, functional efficiency, and industrial optimism through strategies that favored precariousness and bespoke the contradictions of technology. Ironically, it was through drawing—a medium associated in art as in architecture with preliminarity—that she was able to break free from the containment of the sculptural object.

Indeed, Gego seems to have found in the endless iterability of the line the basis for an artistic practice in which the ideality of geometric abstraction was suspended in the dialectics between the spatial and temporal registers operative in the displacement of line from its pictorial support into real space. Her drawings and prints from the 1950s and 1960s stress line and medium—pen and ink, graphite, crayon—to deploy, through repetition and disruption or through minimal interventions on the white page, nonsystematic modes of inscription that advanced her radical attacks on the sculptural object of the late 1960s and early 1970s. None of Gego's drawings is like another. Their insubordinate force is twofold: they produce a literal disruption of form and gesture, and they reveal as obsolete any kind of stylistic categorization and/or encoding of line. Indeed, browsing through a fraction of the more than three thousand works on paper that the artist produced during her lifetime, including etchings, lithographs, collages, handmade books, watercolors, and drawings, it is amazing to see the diversity of approaches toward form, material, and technique. The one thing these works on paper share is the use of the white surface of the support to celebrate the interstices, the in-betweenness of

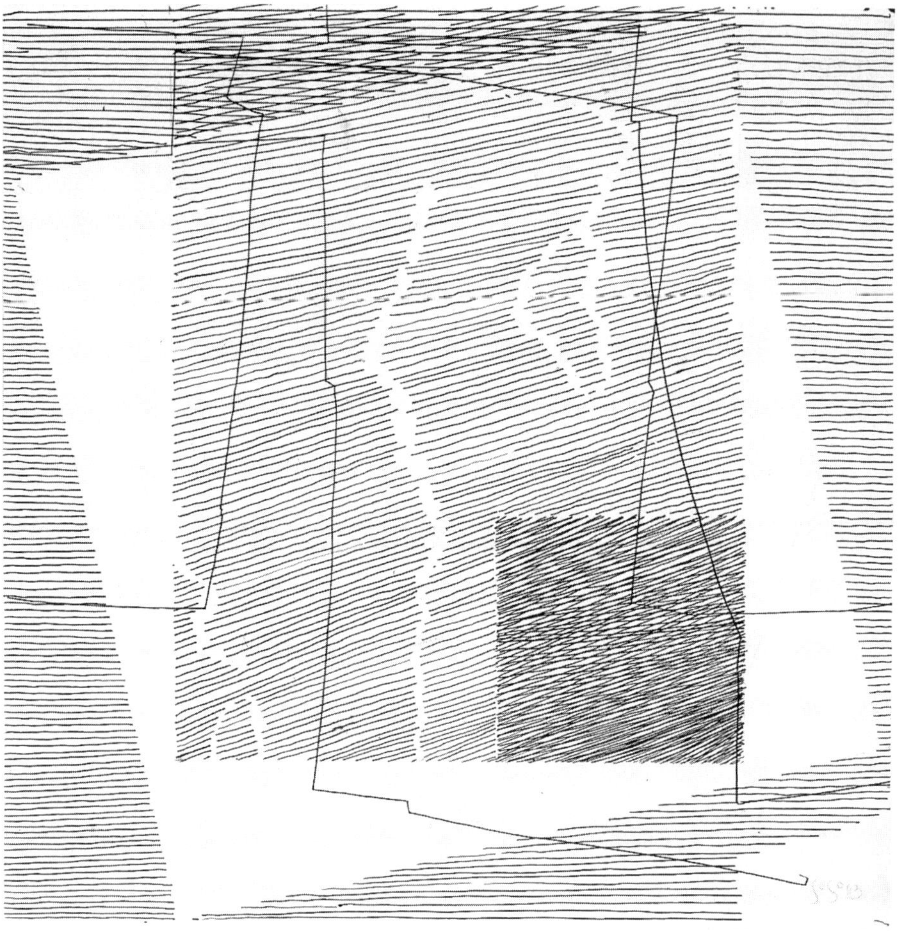

FIGURE 5.13
Gego, *Untitled,* 1963, ink on paper, 11⅛ × 11⅛ in.

the lines, which on the one hand undoes the self-sufficiency and semantic transparency of the line, and on the other underscores the necessarily contextual nature of meaning. While it is the protagonist in all her drawings, the line shifts dramatically within individual works and from one work to the next, producing modes that oscillate between, while at the same time undoing, the gestural and the mechanical (fig. 5.13).

Drawing provided Gego with strategies of diffusion and disruption befitting the marginal character of the medium. Her prolific work on paper delivers the liberating effect evident in the *Reticulárea* of 1969 and the small works that preceded it. In much of her graphic work, Gego explored the boundless possibilities of line, combining structures, moods, and inflections that disrupted preconceived order and discrete form. In 1968,

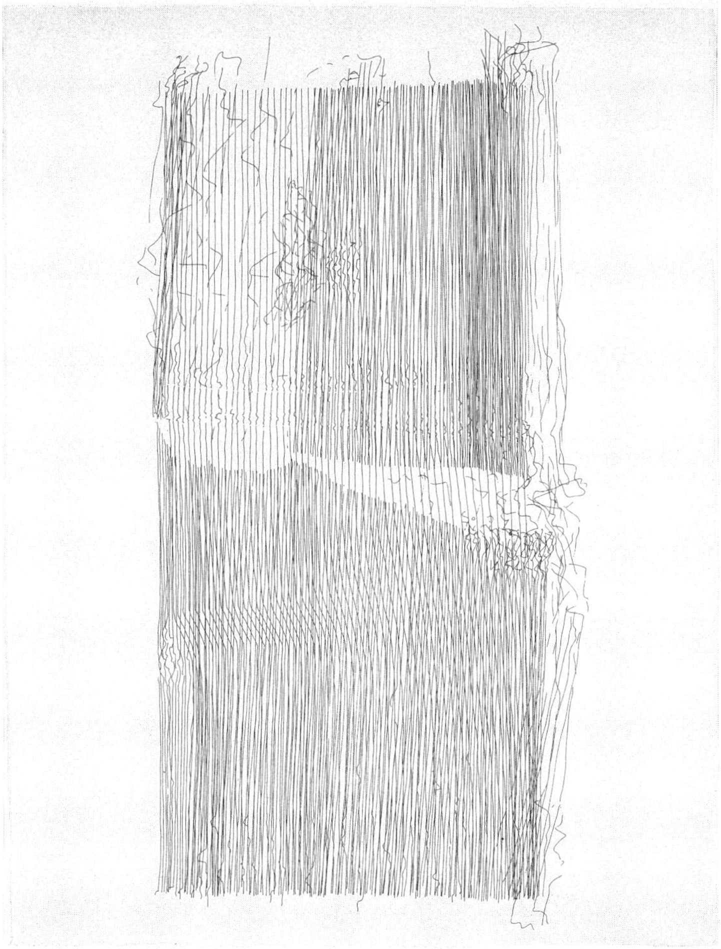

FIGURE 5.14
Gego, *Untitled*, 1967, ink on paper, 25⅞ × 19⅞ in.

aware of this rebellious quality emerging in Gego's drawings, Lourdes Blanco wrote: "[T]his kinship with sculpture takes place when lines break away from their parallel formation and twist in playful disarray in and out of the stated plane." She added, "The lines in Gego's drawing will just as soon submit to a controlled parallel rhythm as to a playful fussy form. And just as she realizes and gives importance to the thickness of a line, Gego knows precisely what the white unmarked space can mean and how it can be brought into a totalling relationship with line."[40] An untitled ink drawing from 1967 (fig. 5.14) exemplifies a threefold approach to line that echoes Blanco's description: it mobilizes repetition and proximity to create transparencies and densities, it incorporates the empty space of the paper surface, and it defies regularity by combining straight and twisting lines. Line does not delineate the boundaries of forms, nor does it self-reflexively map the materiality of the support. Instead, the support is incorporated and actively utilized to generate visual modalities that defy analysis and description while attesting to the unparalleled pliancy of line. Here, line runs from top to bottom, uniformly, and then bends slightly, stopping at various points, curling, and coiling. A line can undo form as fast as it can create it.

A 1969 series of untitled drawings in black, red, violet, and gray ink rehearsed the structural system deployed by the *Reticulárea* (fig. 5.15). The density of the modules and the thickness of the lines vary, at times suggesting volumes, at times emphasizing flatness. In this series, an irregular triangular net covers the white or cream paper. Continuity with real space is suggested by reference to a modernist trajectory that sought to incorporate the frame (Georges Seurat) or dismiss it (Piet Mondrian), an operation that led to the displacement of line into space and into the ever-expanding web of the *Reticulárea.* In Gego's case, this beyond-the-frame quality encouraged in her work and installations a logic of connectivity and transformation, a process of becoming that would permeate much of her work after 1969. It is likely that these drawings were produced in conjunction with, or maybe slightly before, the individual pieces that constituted the large *Reticulárea* of 1969. Blanco identified this peculiar symbiosis among drawing, sculpture, and space taking place in Gego's work: "[H]er line on paper took on an entirely different character: it became radial, it traced triangles, hexagons. The step into spaces was made with linear elements such as florist and stainless steel wire—clipped to manageable lengths—with which she could draw freely in space, delineating volume without confining it."[41]

Gego's unwillingness to confine space and form generated an investigation into the in-betweenness of lines that can be traced back to her early sculpture of the late 1950s. "Parallel lines" is how Gego defined the structural system that governs these pieces,[42] a system in which geometric planes dissolve into parallel lines that turn, slide, fold, or spiral to complicate the source shape—identified by titles such as *Sphere* (1959), *Ocho cuadrados* (Eight Squares, 1961), and *Cubo en esfera* (Cube Within Sphere, 1966). In an undated manuscript, Gego typed out a short chronology of her work, most likely for herself and the poet Hanni Ossott in preparation for her retrospective exhibition of 1977 (the chronology stops in 1976). According to this chronology, in 1957 she was searching for transparency and the integration of space on both sides of the linear matrix that constituted the work. The kinetic effect created through the superimposition and intersection of linear planes was not her original goal, wrote Gego, but an unavoidable result of her investigations into the dissolution of the plane and enclosed space. This observation signals an effort on Gego's part to distance herself from the kinetic art (cinetismo) to which her earlier work was indeed indebted.

By the late 1960s (and certainly by the 1970s) kinetic art was identified in Venezuela with government and corporate commissions and with a visible monumentality that punctuated the urban noise of the city.[43] Thus, Gego's preferred term to define the

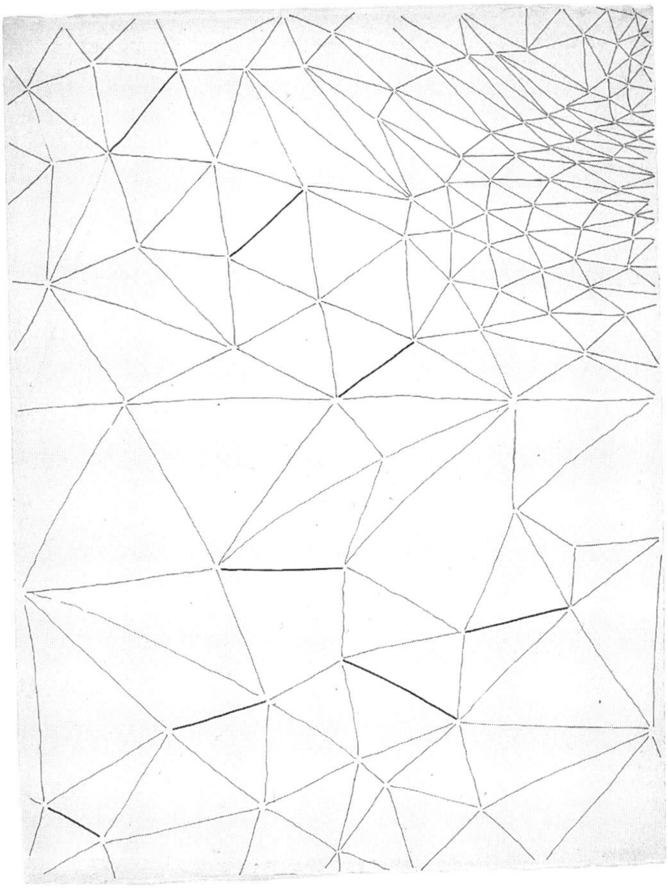

FIGURE 5.15
Gego, *Reticulárea,* 1969, ink on paper, 25¾ × 19⅞ in.

vibrating effect produced in these object-bound, geometric-abstract works was "parallactic charm," a phrase coined by Alfred H. Barr Jr., the first director of New York's Museum of Modern Art, to describe the transformations of the visual field caused by the spectator's movement in relation to the artist's work.[44] However, thanks to the "parallactic charm" of which she was so fond during this period (1957–67), the object-bound nature of Gego's work could not help but be related to the kinetic works of Jesús Rafael Soto. Many of the kinetic vibrations produced by Soto's work relied precisely on the minute perceptual changes produced by "binocular parallax." In the words of the critic James Smith Pierce:

> This small disparity in viewpoint between the eyes is enough to set nearby objects into apparent motion, if we do no more than close one eye, then close the open eye, and open

> the closed one. This will set up what psychologists call the "phi phenomenon," as the object appears to shift from one point to another. This alternate closing and opening of the separate eyes is often enough to activate the simple forms of "parallactic art" (i.e., works which encourage observation from more than one point of view). The smaller "polyphonic tableaux" of Agam or Soto's striped boxes will begin to work this way, but more movement will be induced by tilting the head from side to side, or by walking past the work, the tempo and sequence of the transformations being directly dependent upon the movement of the perceiver.[45]

In these "rigidly prescribed" works, as Smith Pierce describes them, the visual effect is determined by the narrowly defined lateral reading that they demand. The result is a limited, characteristically formulaic visual configuration—one that, as the art historian Luis Enrique Pérez-Oramas observed, is determined by a linear reading "from left to right (or vice versa), as if we were reading a 'text.'"[46] This is not strictly the case with Gego's early work, which can be viewed from different perspectives and encourages viewers to circle around objects. Parallactic effects are part of these works—they occur where linear planes intersect—but their structural complexity is just as important. Certain pieces, such as *Vibración en negro* (Vibration in Black, 1957; fig. 5.16), favor the creation of virtual volumes. This hanging piece is made of approximately forty bands of black-painted aluminum that spiral in on themselves at the base and fold onto themselves at the top, Möbius strip–like, creating optical vibrations where the bands visually intersect—an effect enhanced by the rotation of the piece and the movement of the viewer.

A piece such as *Vibración en negro* can be compared to Alexander Rodchenko's *Spatial Constructions* (ca. 1920; see fig. 1.4), but in Gego's work the geometric shape is replaced by a linear structure that curves and folds, actions that obscure the transparency of the geometrical model. If Gego's early work relied on "parallactic charm" and was connected to the optical effects of kinetic art, then the turns and foldings of her linear planes were obviously related to her interest in line as a malleable element—an element that facilitates spatial inversions and that, in her drawings, undermined the limits of form-shape. Gego's explorations in this area, heavily limited in the 1950s and 1960s by her use of welding and iron, reached their full realization in the airy weaving of nets that constituted the *Reticulárea*.

In the late summer of 1959 Gego accompanied Gerd Leufert to the United States, where he had been awarded a fellowship at Iowa State University. The following year they spent some time in New York and, after visiting Gego's family in California, returned to Caracas in August 1960. These were productive trips, highlighted by encounters with artists engaged with abstraction.[47] In May 1960 Gego exhibited work at David Herbert's gallery in New York in a group show entitled *Recent Sculpture*. That year Gego and Leufert also met Betty Parsons, who in turn invited them to show in her *New Names* exhibition from December 20, 1960, to January 7, 1961. Here, Gego showed two metal

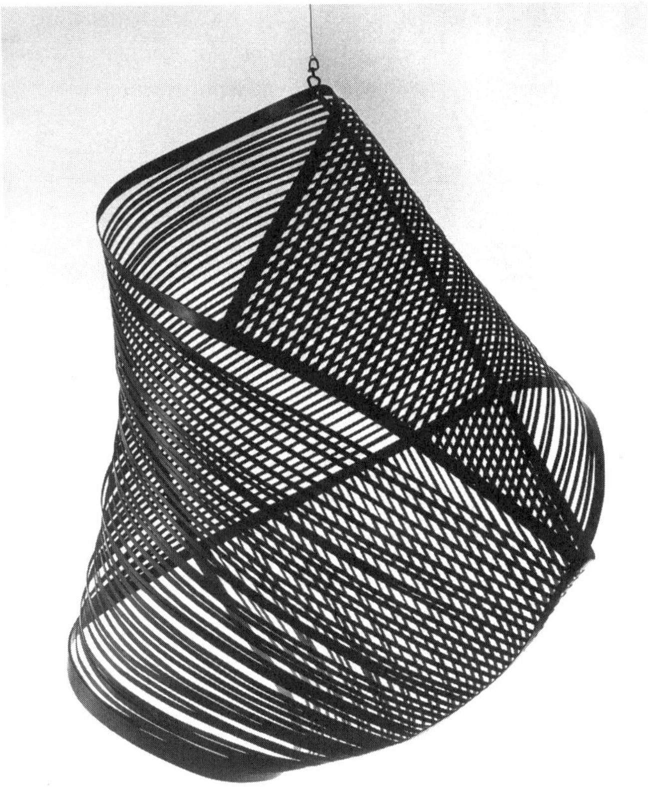

FIGURE 5.16
Gego, *Vibración en negro* (Vibration in Black), 1957, aluminum, 34⅝ × 23⅝ × 17 in.

pieces in the spirit of her 1959 *Sphere*. This work suggested its titular form by means of intersecting semicircular linear planes of black iron organized around three different inclined axes—a strategy Gego employed again in her *Three Folded Triangles* of 1960, one of the pieces she probably shipped to New York for the *New Names* show.[48] Little in these welded works prepares us for the weblike disfigurations of her nets of the late 1960s.

## DEFYING STRUCTURES: THE *RETICULÁREA* OF 1969

Gego started working on the three-dimensional nets that formed the *Reticulárea* probably during the first half of 1969,[49] but their ultimate environmental scope was influenced by Miguel Arroyo's invitation to exhibit at the Museo de Bellas Artes de Caracas in June of that year. Arroyo, an artist as well as the director of the museum, was a strong presence in Venezuelan cultural life and a supporter of the constructivist-influenced artistic trends that had swept the country in the 1950s and 1960s. He was also Gego and Leufert's next-door neighbor and was fully involved in following and supporting the artistic careers of his friends and colleagues. A small brochure published by Gego's gallery, Galería Conkright,[50] after the inaugural installation of the *Reticulárea* defined the piece as an environmental installation done by Gego in collaboration with Arroyo. He observed in a later interview that Gego was very much on her own when planning the layout of the piece,[51] as the floor plans and installation drawings left by the artist prove. Nevertheless, the dialogue with Arroyo was evidently intense enough that Gego chose to officially acknowledge her friend's input in this publication.

Several small pieces made in 1969 based on the triangular module that we identify in the larger nets of the environmental *Reticulárea* seem to have served as prototypes for the pieces that formed the core of the June installation. Arroyo owned one of these small pieces (known today as *Appliqué for Reticulárea*), in which Gego relished in an artisanal modularity that denied mechanical techniques and pristine finishes.[52] This unusual standing piece is made of thin florist wire: a transparent, irregular structure of interconnected triangles. A similar work attaches to the wall and includes a hanging wire with a ball of lead (fig. 5.17); despite its small size, it enters the viewer's space aggressively, exploring the geometrical deformations for which the *Reticulárea* would be known. This effect is produced by the different sizes of the triangular modules and the precarious quality of the florist wire, which is easily deformed.

Between 1962 and 1967 Gego produced small-scale works in which she increasingly incorporated assembling, a technique that allowed her to manipulate her materials more freely. Several of these are made of elements of steel, iron, and plastic. These pieces resemble doodles, sketches, remnants, idle scribbling, and graffiti, and are closely allied to the playful contortions of the line in Gego's graphic repertoire.

She further explored assemblage in a series of works from 1969, probably produced just before or at the same time as work on the pieces that made up the *Reticulárea* started. In these works—called *Líneas* (Lines) or *Serie de Nueve* (Series of Nine) or left untitled—millimeter-thick steel wires (the same type of wire would appear in the *Reticulárea*) are threaded through holes in transparent acrylic boxes (or simply sit on them). Some of these works present a U-shaped configuration, while others twist and zigzag upward. Most are thirty-five centimeters in height. The small scale of the works and their rejection of volume, mass, delineation, and form in favor of linear irregularity facilitated the displacement of drawing into space that had become a trademark of Gego's work.

After more than a decade of interest in geometric abstraction, Gego managed—in dialogue with her architectural and engineering training and her interest in linear unruliness—to undo its rigidness and idealism from within. The small *Reticuláreas* described above were the first works in which the artist explored the structural system of spatial demarcation that would allow her to perform a dramatic attack on Cartesian space and Euclidean geometry, those traditional conceptual pillars of geometric abstraction. The reticular system that facilitated this rupture was carefully described by Hanni Ossott, in close dialogue with Gego, in the artist's retrospective exhibition book-catalogue of 1977: "Its name was given by the art critic Roberto Guevara. 'Reticule' designates a weaving in the form of a net. Reticule-area: area of nets. These [nets]

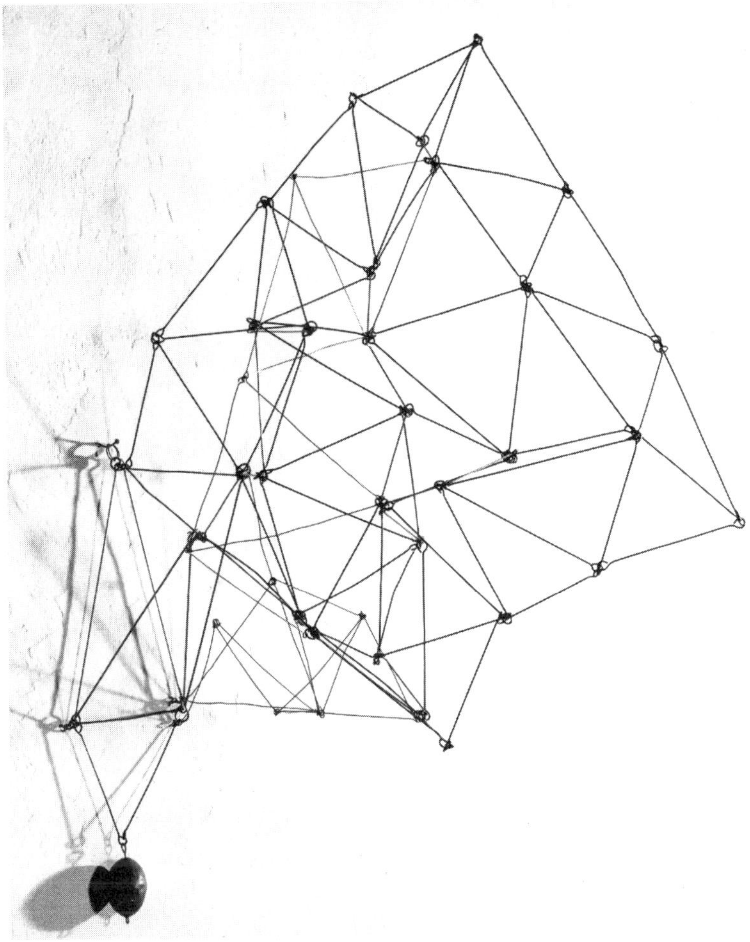

FIGURE 5.17
Gego, *Untitled (Appliqué Reticulárea)*, 1969, stainless steel wire and lead, 21⅝ × 21⅝ × 11⅞ in.

emerge from the liberation of the scheme of parallel, or almost parallel, lines that Gego had developed since 1956. The drawing of crisscrossed lines forming nets and planes of nets led to the concept of the three-dimensional triangular modules and the different configurations of nets."[53]

Roberto Guevara confirmed in an interview that the name *Reticulárea* had been suggested by him in a studio visit prior to its presentation to the public.[54] Gego met Guevara not long before the opening to discuss the work and brainstorm a title. Guevara named the grouping of nets according to its latticelike structure and appearance. Undated notes (using English and Spanish) found in Gego's files show the artist playing with the word *reticule* by adding prefixes and suffixes—including *room, multi,* and *poly,* among

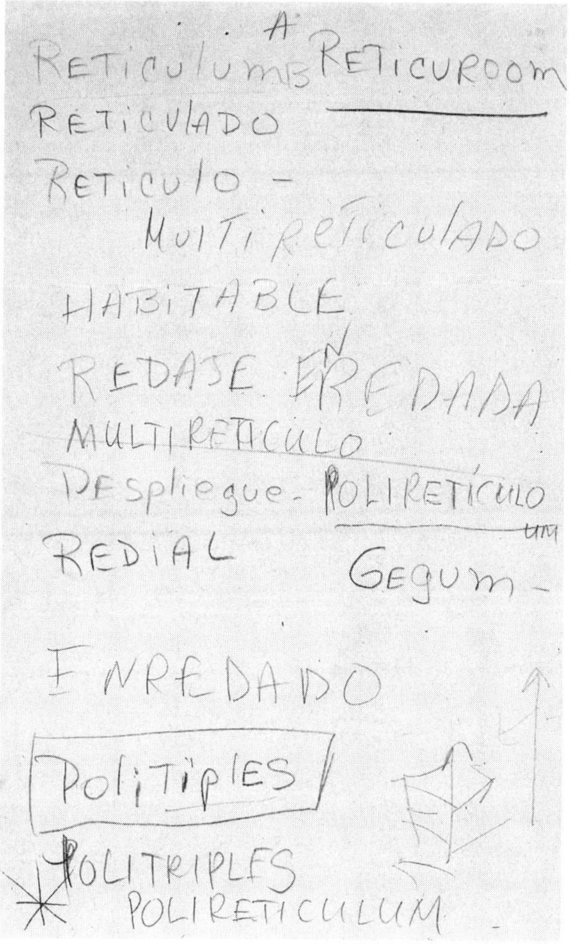


FIGURE 5.18
Gego, working notes on the naming of the *Reticulárea*, ca. 1969.

others—to amplify its meaning. Words such as *habitable, entangled,* and *deployment* were also noted by Gego and suggest that she was interested in the conceptual, and not merely morphological, resonances of the work (fig. 5.18).

The *Reticulárea* was installed in Gallery 8 of the Museo de Bellas Artes, a rectangular space measuring approximately eight and a half meters long, four and a half meters wide, and four and a half meters high, and which could be accessed from Galleries 9 and 7. Photographs, checklists, and sketches that Gego produced for the installation name the constitutive pieces according to their orientation in relation to the ceiling and walls: "columns," "screens," "horizontals," and "appliqués."[55] "These terms distinguished the various triangular-hexagonal modular nets made of florist wire, stainless steel, and aluminum wire that hung from the ceiling and were distributed irregularly throughout the gallery space. The individual pieces (there were thirty-six, according to one of Gego's checklists) varied in density, size, materials, and color, and while enumerated and described, they were never titled. Checklists state that the "screens" referred to the larger, more two-dimensional nets that Gego situated at irregular intervals around the perimeter of the room. The "columns" hung from the ceiling vertically and were given stability through plumb lines attached to the bottom of the structures. The "appliqués" and "horizontals" designated smaller pieces that were attached to the wall or hung parallel to the ceiling like "clouds" or "beehives," to use Ossott's terminology.[56]

These sources offer approximate documentation of the work, and the nomenclature used to describe the pieces is not consistent. Gego's notes and sketches reveal her habit of organizing and recording all aspects of her work while also mirroring the unregulated way in which she distributed the nets in the space. In subsequent installations, contingency went hand in hand with the unpredictable metamorphosis and fluid boundaries of the work. Its identity was constantly destabilized, not only by the different spaces in which it was shown and by its dismissal of conventional supports, but also because the constitutive pieces changed—some accidentally destroyed, some sold, some given away, some made anew to adequately occupy the corresponding space.[57]

Indeed, Gego's sketches and checklists, like the *Reticulárea* itself, were constantly being transformed. Words and instructions were crossed out; new units, new shapes, and new positions were added; and various modes of organization for the piece were rehearsed. Despite Gego's detailed planning, everything about these documents indicates the fluid structure of the work. The documents oscillate between an orientational plan and the diagrammatic representation of a zone of indeterminacy that testifies to Gego's irresolute attempt to bridge the gap between idea and representation, knowledge and understanding. In introductory notes for one of her courses, she stated, "Doing is one thing, and understanding is another. But one understands only when one knows and one knows when one has experienced, lived."[58] The ability to tie knowing to making had been key to Gego's architectural training (and to the Bauhaus *Vorkurs* that she had assimilated into her teaching), but her attempt to tie knowing to life experiences resonated with the affective aesthetic projects of her Brazilian neighbors. In Gego's hands, art, in its postwar geometric abstract incarnation, would not function as a template for harmony between the techno-rational and the artistic. Order, as advocated by Gego's rigorous architectural training, proved unsustainable in the context of the *Reticulárea* as it plunged into excess and disarray: terms, diagrams, and sketches could not map, project, or rationalize the spatial and linear inversions at work in Gego's practice. The decentralized, antihierarchical, layered, and manifold logic of the *Reticulárea* defied a priori order and knowledge in favor of affect and perception, advancing the rhizomatic associations that the work would later generate.

Preliminary sketches indicate that Gego first designed a frame for the ceiling. This frame, measuring approximately seven and a quarter by three and a half meters, was enveloped by two pieces of fabric sewn along a vertical axis to create a suspended ceiling from which most of the pieces hung; others were secured to the walls of the gallery. Gego employed different forms of linkage in the *Reticulárea*. In one of the most

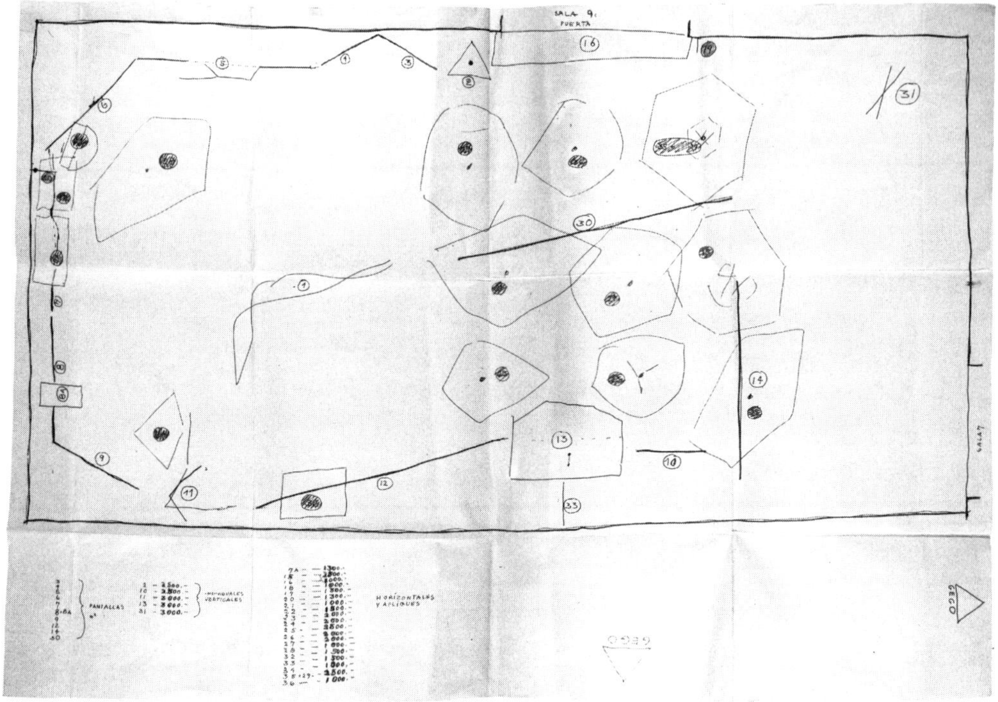

FIGURE 5.19
Gego, sketch "A," 1969.

common, steel wires ending in loops were hooked together, making the resulting nets partially or totally collapsible. The loops were created with pliers, a process that required intense labor. In another type of joint—the one most visible in pictures of the 1969 *Reticulárea*—the wires and steel rods were hooked to rings of various sizes, allowing these nets to bend and modulate in space. A version of this connecting structure ties rods to a circle with internal hoops; as a result, deformation of the triangular grid structure was not only possible but desirable. The steel rods within each net tended toward material uniformity, but at times Gego introduced a discordant note through the random incorporation of metal tubes, painted rods, or the doubling of wires, which further inflected the open configuration of the piece. Similarly, the airy quality of the *Reticulárea* was countered by small lead weights that hung at the bottom of some nets, pulling them toward the floor.

Several sketches lay out the distribution of the nets of the 1969 *Reticulárea* and show an irregular organizational pattern marked by fluidity and determined by the spatial relaxation that the artist was interested in producing. One large sketch ("A") on brown wrapping paper numbers and classifies the pieces as "screens," "individual verticals," and "horizontals and appliqués" (fig. 5.19). A complementary sketch made on the same

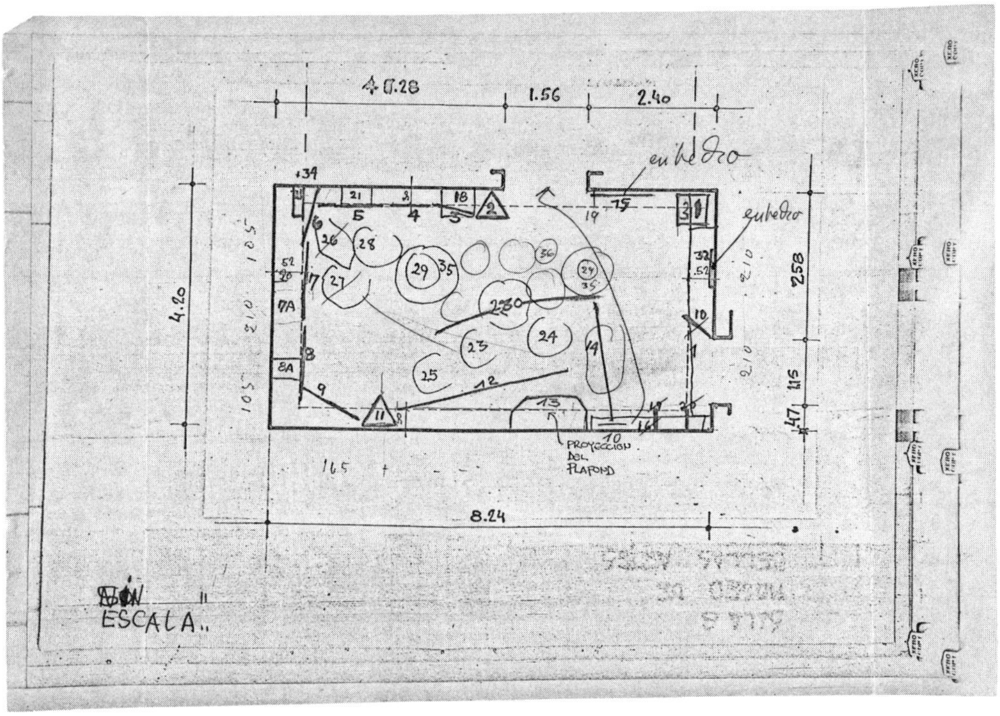


FIGURE 5.20
Gego, sketch "B," 1969.

kind of paper indicates the approximate shape of each piece, its price, notations on configuration (in Spanish and German), and in some cases the size of the pieces and how they were to intersect, since Gego sometimes envisioned pieces within pieces.

The plan proposed by the above sketch suggests a configuration in which the artist delivered an enveloping effect that encouraged the viewer to apprehend the relational space produced by the individual pieces. The xerox of a second sketch ("B") echoes the layout described above but locates the dense area of the horizontal pieces to the right of the entrance adjacent to Gallery 9, and not only in front of this entrance (fig. 5.20). It also activates further the perimeter of the room by adding pieces along the two walls of the corner that is framed by the two entrances. Here, Gego included in red ink corrections to the xeroxed sketch and, pointing to two screens hanging parallel to the wall, she wrote twice the word *enredo* (tangle).

One of the large nets of the *Reticulárea* was photographed approximately two months before the exhibition opened, probably sometime in April 1969 (fig. 5.21). It shows Gerd Leufert in a corner behind a large modular screen of woven wires. The screen is firmly fastened to the two walls and the floor. The triangular net is irregular; some triangles are smaller than others; they curve and bend. The effect, at once precise and indeter-

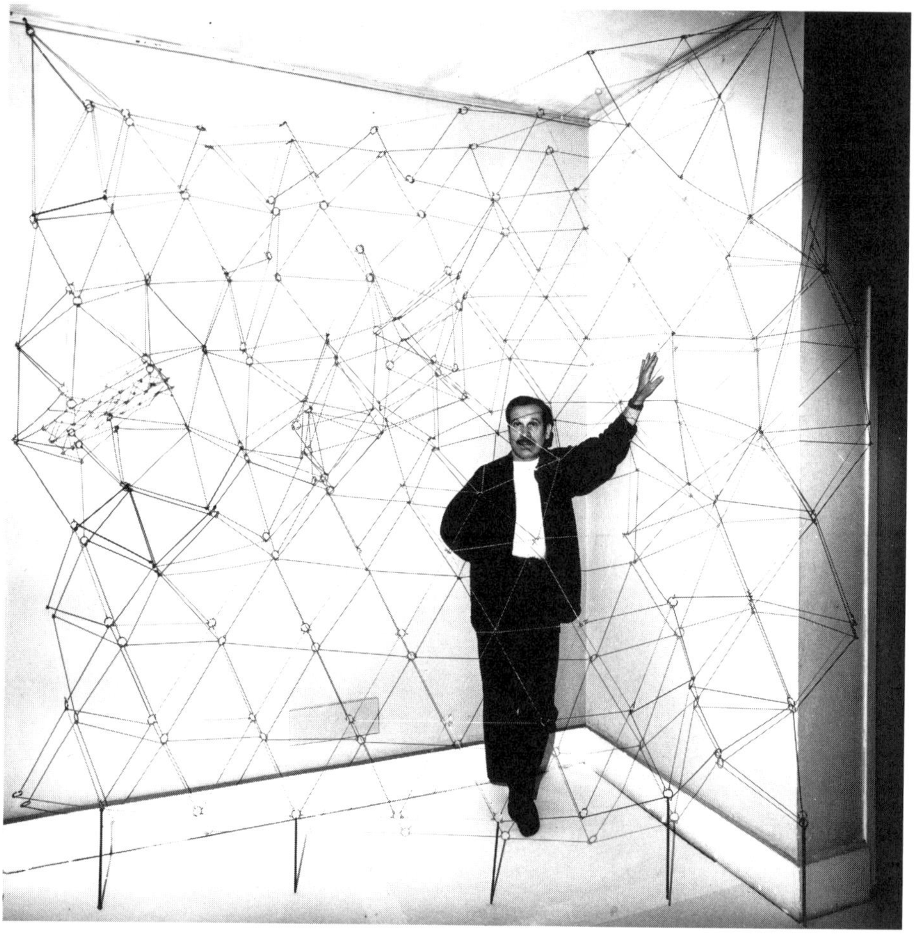

FIGURE 5.21
Gerd Leufert with screen for *Reticulárea*, ca. 1969.

minate, is intensified by the linear doubling of the net produced by the shadows created by the strong light the photographer used. The enveloping aspect of the work, its architectural dimension, is suggested in this photograph, which posits the body as an unavoidable reference. Accordingly, the *Reticulárea* unleashed the effect of an enveloping spider's web: "Walking into the *Reticulárea* as it was arranged in Caracas's Museo de Bellas Artes is like entering the domain of a friendly giant spider," wrote Lourdes Blanco in her introductory essay to a small pamphlet published on the occasion of the show.[59] Similar references were made by reviewers of the exhibition, who alluded to the mode of bodily address articulated by the piece.[60]

While sketch "A" locates the dense area of horizontal pieces directly in front of the gallery entrance, sketch "B" has them to the right of the entrance. Sketch "B" actually seems to be the earlier sketch, since it includes corrections in red pen that match the plan laid out in sketch "A." In any event, an assessment of the individual pieces, as well as any attempt at an analysis of their distribution, is a far cry from the diffusive effect deployed by the work itself, as the group of pieces that constituted the *Reticulárea* of 1969 defied precise description. Even some of the most symmetrical screens enhanced the irregularity and formlessness of the whole through their pliancy, which deformed the modularity of the web. Several of the horizontal pieces, located parallel to the ceiling, created three-dimensional clusters of metal that have been defined as "clouds," "nests," or "beehives" but really do not correspond to any shape or form, either natural or human-made. Despite its basic triangular configuration, the *Reticulárea*'s most obvious operation was to dismantle the ideational quality of geometry, the "ideal realm of construction." In the words of Hanni Ossott, "[W]here in Gego's work the most rigorous ordering of the elements is present, she also mocks the number, measurement. And if there an eye thinks, another part of [the eye] is devoted to erasing all knowledge. Error means here willingness to err."[61] Indeed, Gego's exacting training in architecture and engineering might have drawn her to the geometric and mathematical universe of constructivism and its legacies. But by the late 1960s the pliancy of the line in her drawings, the spatial reversals of her sculptures, the pseudo-weaving technique introduced with the *Reticulárea,* and the perceptual inconsistencies generated by the line in space placed the experiential body-subject—that of the artist and that of the viewer—at the center of her work. Error and failure, Ossott seemed to imply, were not excluded from Gego's artistic process; rather, they had been embraced by the diffused forms of her nets and the meanderings of her webs. An inconsistent, formless, "other" geometry emerged, one in which defined form was replaced by flexible and unpredictable connections. Discontinuity, disjunction, heterogeneity, and fragmentation were woven into the *Reticulárea* to produce a space that disregarded the unambiguous internal coherence of cubic architectural environments and self-contained sculptural bodies. Most important, the performative dimension of the *Reticulárea*—the work's shifts from two-dimensional to three-dimensional, from object to environment, from collapsible net to field, from art to event—embodied a pliant logic rather than an organic one.

Assessments of Gego's work have often privileged the word "organic" to describe her precarious geometries. In 1977 the Argentine critic Marta Traba defined what she called "organic constructivism" in relation to Gego's work: "Gego thinks that appropriate forms correspond to functions that exist in nature. She thus establishes a homology between the real and dynamic *existence* of that vast organic ensemble [i.e., nature], and the *aspect* that covers each one of its components. Things live, in other words, they function, with an end and a goal: such a necessary and functional logic is what determines form. For Gego it is crucial to understand the structures of the organic form, the internal order that is verified in nature, the appropriate relations of the parts to the whole."[62] Despite Gego's continuous interest in and references to nature and the organic, however, the behavior of the *Reticulárea*—transitional and marginal, peripheral and supple, pliant and twisted—defied the functional logic of organic-ness invoked by Traba, with its significant relationships among parts and its emphasis on functionality and coherence.

A more fitting description of the work's behavior came from the German architect Christian Thiel, who helped Gego install her last *Reticulárea* at the Alte Oper in Frankfurt in 1982. In a brief letter dated November 12, 1983, Thiel wrote with urgency to Gego, a year after their collaboration, that he had come across Gilles Deleuze and Félix Guattari's essay "Rhizome" (in their recently published *Mille Plateaux* (A Thousand Plateaus, 1980) and felt that her work seemed to operate according to a rhizomatic logic. *Rhizome,* from *rhizoma,* is a botanical term that refers to an underground stem that grows continuously and horizontally and puts out lateral shoots and accidental roots at intervals (Oxford English Dictionary). In Deleuze and Guattari's narrative, the term was used to deploy a critique of Western philosophy and its quest for truth that was popular among architects.[63] The authors observed in "Rhizome," the introduction to their book, that in classical thought, the tree is the image of the world—an image that corresponds to "the classical book, as noble, signifying, and subjective organic interiority (the strata of the book)." They added: "[W]henever we encounter this formula, even stated strategically by Mao or understood in the most 'dialectical' way possible, what we have before us is the most classical and well reflected, oldest, and weariest kind of thought. Nature doesn't work that way: in nature roots are taproots with a more multiple, lateral, and circular system of ramification, rather than a dichotomous one."[64] Clearly, to Thiel, the connection between the rhizome and Gego's oeuvre was inspired by her work's open and dysfunctional demeanor. Primarily, however, the *Reticulárea*'s arachnoid morphology must have evoked the interconnectedness and multiplicity figured forth by the concept. In contrast to the binary logic of classicism, multiplicity operates with a frank disregard for systems that rely on a strong principal unity. Dismissive of idealized structures (social, visual, conceptual, linguistic, and so on), rhizomatic performance undoes Platonism and favors heterogeneity, antihierarchical connections, and an affective materialism that is mutable and transitory. It changes its nature as it increases its connections. There are no positions in it, only lines.[65]

Gego's weblike configurations are also antagonistic to centralized structures.[66] They not only lack a center, a top, or a bottom, but disrupt the homogeneous quality of a space organized according to Cartesian coordinates. This capacity to occupy interstitial spaces was exploited by the *Reticulárea,* whose nets could be expanded infinitely while welcoming disruptions and broken lines, creating a space of dedifferentiation that dismissed ideas of unity and identity. Instead of treating her nets as objects, Gego wove the margins of the room, celebrating the spatial connectivity of the work. The implications of this scattered configuration are clear: it undermines the authority of the autonomous sculptural object and of the monument; it is attentive to circumstances and context (the situational relation of elements that define its production and reception) through its ephemeral transformation of abstract space into marked place; and it problematizes recognition and representation by being dismissive of identity (of fixed artistic categories such as sculpture, architecture, and drawing) and conceptual transparency. Accordingly, the work undoes fixed boundaries—between drawing and sculpture, volume and space, virtuality and reality—in favor of a mutational process of aesthetic production that acts as a symbolic figuration of the historical, material, and affective situation that Gego, her work, and its viewers occupied.

Indeed, in her substitution of a pliant geometry for the geometric abstract object, Gego did away with conventional hierarchies that rule spatial apprehension: inside and outside, up and down, left and right—in short, *point of view*. Thus, the *Reticulárea* manages to deliver a subtle critique of classical rationalism and the fixed structures upon which it is predicated by decentering the viewer's positionality and frustrating the artificial separation of the spatiotemporal registers upon which objective analysis depends. As the German social theorist Niklas Luhmann observed, European rationality, as a unified semantic, is characterized by its use of distinctions. At stake is a "narrator who stages the narration—whether of the novel or of world history—in which he no longer appears," an observer who draws distinctions, who remains unobserved, who distinguishes what he or she observes from everything else that remains as "unmarked space," and who observes from this "unmarked space."[67]

That Gego's work would embody a spatial field of multiple connections among its constitutive units—morphologically elusive, structurally discontinuous, and visually inconsistent, but materially and historically specific—would suit her position as a female Jewish émigré who produced her most radical work at the age of fifty-seven. She thus challenged expectations about hegemonic cultural production and male artistic supremacy, as well as the myth of a youthful avant-garde, while embracing a "politics of location" and contingency. Borrowing Luhmann's words in his critique of the false unity of rationalism, one could say that Gego's *Reticulárea* embodies a model of spectatorship in which the observer reenters observation and "constitutes [herself] in [her] own field—and thereby necessarily in the mode of contingency, that is, with an awareness of other possibilities."[68] Further, this attention to the situational as vital to the perception of the work goes hand in hand with the artist's sensitivity to her unique "sociosymbolic positioning"[69] and suggests a localized viewer, not only in space but within the symbolic order, who countered the universal subject presupposed by the geometric abstract work that many of Gego's male peers practiced. It had been in the name of this universal subject that Los Disidentes, working from Paris against the stagnant visual arts of the Venezuela of the 1940s, had embraced the geometric abstract path that would eventually lead to kinetic art and its accompanying fetishizing of international recognition.

How important the observer and his or her positioning within the work was to the meaning of the *Reticulárea* is evident in the photographic record of its various installations. Most of the photographs feature visitors interacting with the work and point to the *Reticulárea*'s capacity to address not one but many spectators (fig. 5.22). Peter Hönig, who was in charge of photographing the work in Germany on the occasion of its 1982 installation, wrote to Gego that he could not conceive of the work without people;

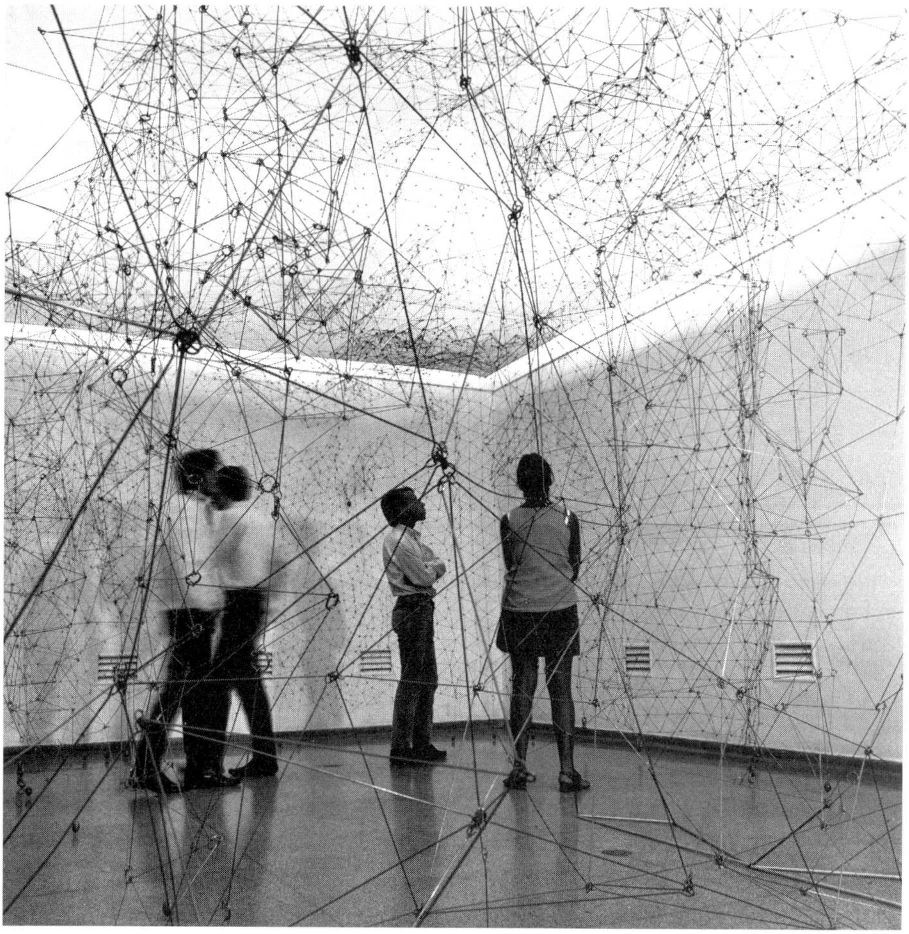

FIGURE 5.22
Gego, *Reticulárea*, Museo de Bellas Artes de Caracas, 1969.

he had the impression that it could not be considered without taking into account the close relationship between observer and work.[70] The position of these observers within the work is also important in understanding the mode of spectatorship encouraged by the *Reticulárea*. Unable to distance themselves from the work, viewers cannot occupy a point in space from which it can be fully described. Local reviewers emphasized the enveloping quality of the environment, which could not be apprehended in its entirety but instead had to be experienced; the dynamic was one of fusion with the work rather than analytical observation of it. Roberto Guevara, one of the *Reticulárea*'s most careful observers, wrote that "the drawing of lines has jumped into real space, the environment, to surround the spectator in a new and effective experience." In lieu of a single space, the viewer was in the presence of a thousand fused spaces in "discontinuous equilibrium," he wrote, using the visual figure of a drawing in space: "It is as if we walked inside one of Gego's drawings, suddenly materialized, making real space its own." Against the static quality of object-bound works of art, Guevara emphasized that "each corner, each objective change in vision, each precise mental perception of [what has been] observed means a new vision, a different aspect, unique in its own. From one spectator to the other, from one attitude to the other, the work also transforms itself, varies, fluctuates, develops." The temporal sequencing and dedifferentiated field that characterized the *Reticulárea* had to be sustained by the viewer, he clarified, "because we become part of it, because once inside, outside feeling is inconceivable."[71] Guevara attributed the "discontinuous equilibrium" of the *Reticulárea* to the interruptions in material, scale, form, and structure posed by the work, which generated a multiplicity of spaces that could not be submitted to any kind of overarching scheme. Inside the *Reticulárea* the effect was one of all-overness, formlessness, diffuse boundaries, uncharted fields in which the line demarcates but never delimits space.

The dispersed body of the *Reticulárea* is woven into space itself, part and parcel of our apprehension of it—not as an idealized, homogeneous entity but as a circumstantially inflected field. The viewer, too, is woven into the *Reticulárea* and the surrounding space; one sees oneself as observer, reenters the process of observation, and destabilizes the authority of the omnipresent observer. What is observed is always different, always partial, always fragmentary, never whole. At times it might appear structural, and at times linear; at times clear, and at times messy; at times geometrical, but generally formless. As Ossott put it: "And if, slightly tired, the viewer abandons the discovery of the constructive character of the forms, leaving the work to rest and abandoning the perception of the modes in which it was configured, so that something other is shown there . . . then, in that moment of rest, emerges an always inconclusive configuration, always in the making, a work prone to error, a sincere trace of the meandering gaze."[72] The *Reticulárea*'s implicit boundlessness, intermedial quality, and defiance of structure embodied the crisis of geometric abstraction that also concerned Oiticica and Clark. Against the idealism of the universalizing geometries and grids that populated the techno-rational imaginary of Gego's colleagues, the *Reticulárea* gave way to a radical materiality that profoundly altered the conventions of production and reception of the geometric abstract object.

## MONSTROUS BODIES AND ARCHITECTURES: THE *RETICULÁREA* OF THE 1970S

Five years after the *Reticulárea*'s first installation, Gego had the opportunity to increase its rhizomatic potential and further its sculptural disintegration, arriving at a sort of nothingness that would frustrate the illusory culmination of the 1969 environment. In 1974 the *Reticulárea* was installed in Gallery 1 of the new building of the Museo de Bellas Artes de Caracas (fig. 5.23). There, the piece acquired a more sculptural qual-

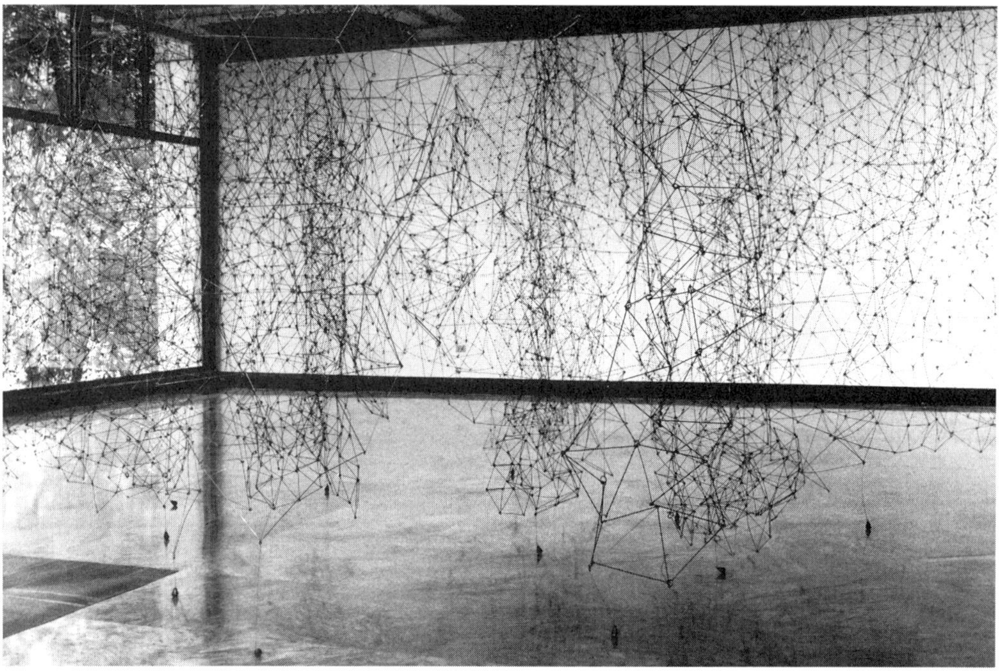

FIGURE 5.23
Gego, *Reticulárea,* Museo de Bellas Artes de Caracas, Gallery 1 (new building), 1974.

ity, since it could be read as a volume—albeit a semitransparent and indescribable one—that hung from a metal grid, measuring approximately three and a half by five and a half by five meters.[73] The ceiling pieces and "appliqués" of the 1969 iteration were apparently gone, and the large screens were hung close to each other, further undoing any kind of structural transparency. In photographs, the resulting configuration resembles a big knot, a cluster of entangled metal, formless and imprecise. Some of the tightly grouped columns and screens touched the floor, while other pieces were suspended between ceiling and floor. In photographic details of the work, the original triangular structure is barely discernible, so that any geometric reference seems to have been replaced by a maze of lines. This effect was produced by the proximity of the nets and meshes, which now literally followed the principle of accumulation and agglomeration loosely rehearsed in the 1969 installations. As a consequence of this absolute disregard for structure, any trace of clarity gave way to opacity, and the resulting abandonment of linearity, precision, contour, boundary, and form favored fusion, flux, and flow. Although less dispersed and more "sculptural" than the environmental *Reticulárea* of 1969, the elusive "volume" of the 1974 work—which could be walked around but not, as in the 1969 work, penetrated—allowed no identification between viewer and work. Unable to grasp the underlying logic of this amorphous object, the spectator had to be satisfied with only surfaces and comply with the structural opacity of this "big nothing."[74]

At the end of 1976, the *Reticulárea*—along with the entire collection of Venezuelan art of the Museo de Bellas Artes—became part of the collection of the Galería de Arte Nacional in Caracas, where it was installed at the beginning of 1977. Once again, the work mutated into a disfigured body that could not be penetrated or walked through. The large scale of the galleries in the museum and the work's relation with other works on display emphasized the fuzzy and indeterminate outlines of this version of the *Reticulárea*. In both installations of the 1970s, the calligraphic quality that Guevara had recognized in the work as early as 1970—when he defined its behavior as "zigzagging writing"—was exploited to its fullest, in favor not of meaning but of the release that one associates with doodles, graffiti, and "automatic writing."[75] Written bodies in which legibility was dramatically obliterated, the 1970s versions of the *Reticulárea* were direct attacks on organic notions of the sculptural body as whole, unified, and standard, to be replaced by a deformable mass irreducible to delineation.

That these clustered configurations of the 1970s were relevant to Gego is evident from two 1977 sketches for a future permanent installation of the *Reticulárea* (fig. 5.24). As soon as the work became part of the collection of the Galería de Arte Nacional, plans were made to house it permanently in one of the galleries. Sketches for this installation show proposals to install the work in a tent. This time Gego placed the majority of the nets in a central area while a smaller group of hanging pieces was located to the right of the entrance to the room. The central grouping was approximately four and a half by four meters, with visitors circulating around the conglomeration of nets. It is obvious that Gego was thinking of the recent installations of the *Reticulárea* as a viable if crucially different model of undoing spectatorial stasis and sculptural equilibrium.

If the 1969 *Reticulárea* rejected the transcendentalism and universal character of geometry and Cartesian space, these later installations resisted the very idea of a sculptural body and related notions of shape, proportion, and interiority. The work's distorted and amorphous effects were partly the result of unpredictable connections between drawing and sculpture, space and line, structure and cluster. In this hybrid approach, the work advanced the concept of *bicho,* the term increasingly used by Gego to refer to all of her three-dimensional work, probably in an effort to avoid a conventional terminology associated with sculpture and the fine arts. The word, found on the cover of the three notebooks that record all of Gego's three-dimensional work from 1957 to 1989, first appears in reference to a small piece entitled *Perro invisible o bicho* (Invisible Dog or Critter) from 1965. This piece (subsequently destroyed accidentally) was a rare referential work, though sketchy and freely made with strands of thin, easily manipulated metal. In Spanish, *bicho* means "animal," "critter," and most commonly "bug." In Venezuelan usage, *bicho* is also a colloquial interjection of rejection, a pejorative designation, while a related word such as *bichero* is often used to refer to groupings of heterogeneous animals or objects. The word *bicho*—along with the English word *messy*—recurs throughout

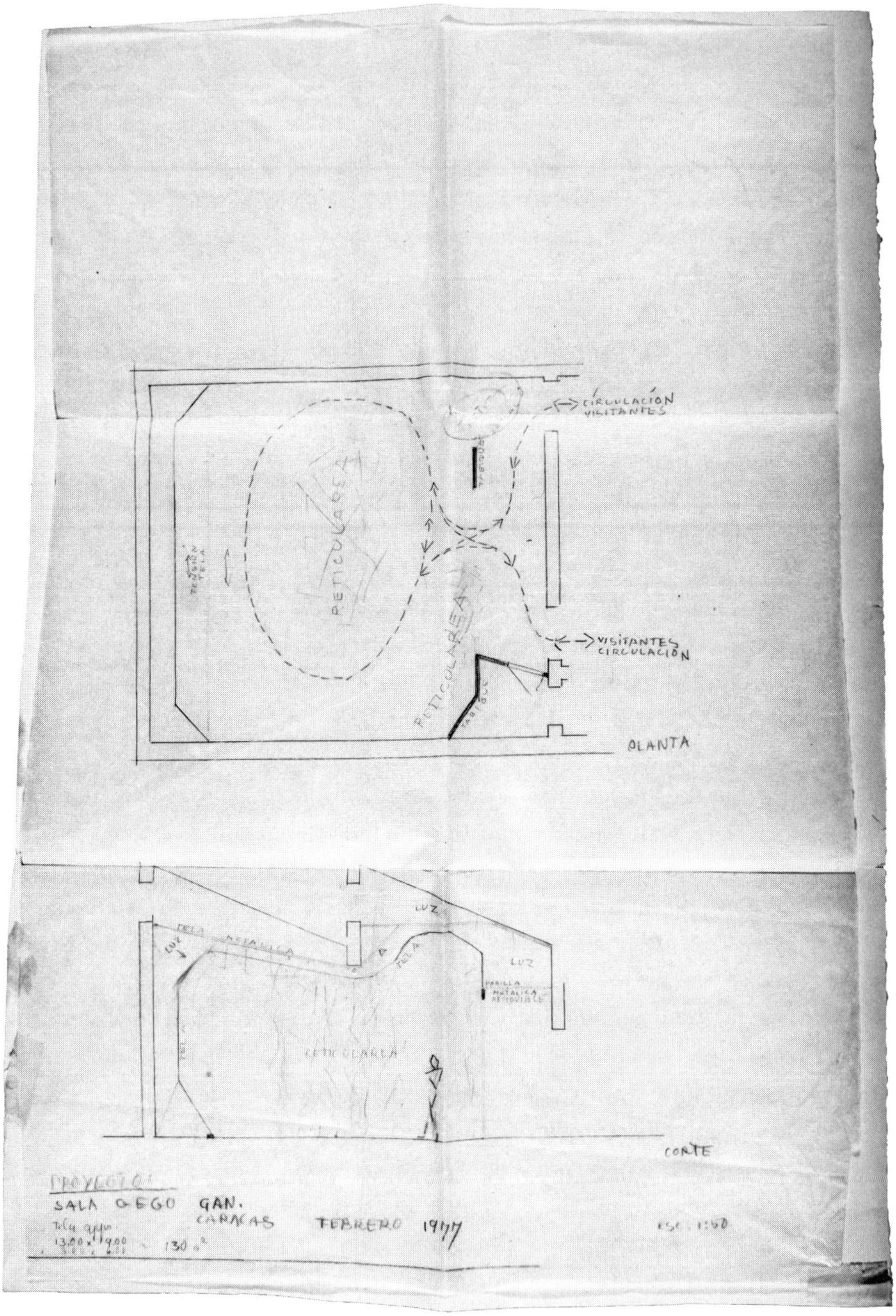

FIGURE 5.24

Gego, project for permanent installation of *Reticulárea* at the Galería de Arte Nacional, Caracas, 1977.

Gego's lists and descriptions of her work and is evidence of the artist's disdain for tectonic legibility, structural precision, and medium specificity. Curiously enough, according to the dictionary of the Royal Spanish Academy, *bicho* also refers to a person whose appearance is absurd, and/or a person with bad intentions. While it is likely that Gego was appropriating the humble and anti-ideal connotations of the word, it is interesting to note that installations of the *Reticulárea* in the 1970s did resemble a huge, disfigured, deformed sculptural body—a sculptural *bicho,* one might say.

The flow between space and body that these versions of the *Reticulárea* incarnated has been addressed by the architect Greg Lynn in his discussion of "the proportional correspondence between a temple and a *well shaped man*."[76] Against the notion of body and architecture as a closed (organic) system of proportional orders and functional relations among constituent parts, Lynn argues for bodily deformations through the deployment of local alliances and connections of base matter. This rhizomatic model of "continuous transformation" proposes that bodies "emerge through processes of differentiation, yielding varying degrees of unity based on specific affiliations and mutations."[77] Borrowing from the feminist writer Luce Irigaray, Lynn suggests an alternative bodily scheme, one ruled by the condition of viscosity. Thus, he notes, "Viscosity is a quality of being mutable or changeable in response to both favorable and unfavorable situations that occur by vicissitude."[78] Or, again, referring to Irigaray's exploration of the fluid quality of the feminine: "The viscous [is] the model for relations of the '*near and not the proper.*'"[79]

In its improper use of geometry, its attack on gestalt and organic integrity, its deployment of a deformative matrix and dismissal of proportions, symmetry, and delineation, the *Reticulárea* of the 1970s advanced the idea of *bicho,* of residue and disfiguration, used by Gego to counteract the authority of the sculptural signifier. In its dismissal of the notion of self-identity and in its mutational capacity, the more bodily *Reticuláreas* of the 1970s rejected the correspondence between the ideality of geometries and the ideality of bodies, of the "human as measure of all things," of "human" as the standard ideal. Hence, these installations of the 1970s, in their tacit dialogue with central geometric abstract works of the period such as the monumental abstract works that populated Caracas, rebelliously embraced a certain monstrosity.

For the writer and philosopher Brian Massumi, "monstrosity,"[80] following the rhizomatic logic of Deleuze and Guattari, is associated with processes of becoming and mutation. "Becoming-other" responds to a desire to escape fixation, sameness, bodily limitation, and idealized abstraction in the face of constraints that the body-in-becoming transforms into opportunities. The body-in-becoming undoes habitual patterns of action and preestablished organization and boundaries, and it is always singular in its mutational capacity to challenge the standard. Accordingly, the feminist writer Rosi Braidotti refers to the idea of monstrosity as a deviation from the norm.[81] A closer reading of the term in relation to the feminine body led her to unearth disturbing but by now expected historical associations. In literature, Western philosophy, scientific discourse, and psychoanalysis, "woman" is the negative term of the binary logic that rules classical thought. Furthermore, Braidotti writes: "The woman's body can change shape in pregnancy and childbearing; it is therefore capable of defeating the notion of fixed *bodily form,* of visible, recognizable, clear, and distinct shape as that which marks the contour of the body. She is morphologically dubious." And later she adds, "Woman/mother is monstrous by excess; she transcends established norms and transgresses boundaries. She is monstrous by lack: woman/mother does not possess the substantive unity of the masculine subject. Most important, through her identification with the feminine she is monstrous by displacement: as sign of the in between areas, of the indefinite, the ambiguous."[82]

In-betweenness, indefiniteness/infinitude, and ambiguity are, of course, tropes that describe the spatial behavior of the 1969 *Reticulárea*. And if it seems appropriate to displace these tropes onto a bodily reading of the 1970s installations of the work, it is because they posit the (sculptural) body as something that must come under attack. Opaque and impenetrable, clustered and unruly, the *Reticulárea* was the "other" set in opposition to the virtual linear and geometric configurations of kinetic art, which by the 1970s had become the "standard" in the Venezuelan urban landscape.[83]

A text by the philosopher Elizabeth Grosz links feminist concerns about monstrosity with an architecture of excess.[84] She proposes, through a confrontation with structures of waste (Alphonso Lingis's community of outcasts and the marginalized, Georges Bataille's notion of "unproductive expenditure," and Luce Irigaray's maternal-feminine), to destabilize the authoritarian, monumental, and bureaucratic structure of architecture by positing a feminine economy of surplus as a radical alternative to patriarchal notions of space and time. Here the Irigarayan interval is the operative term: "undecidably spatial and temporal," the interval embodies a passage, an in-betweenness that displaces the conventional opposition between externalized feminine spatiality and interiorized masculine duration—a dialectical configuration that posits the maternal feminine as the ground, the place, the space that underlies male identity and its structured systems of spatial and material organization. Grosz asks: could the interval—excess left by the weaving of space and time, the "site of their difference and their interchange"—become foundational to an architecture "in which the 'more' is not cast off but made central, in which expenditure is sought out, in which instability, fluidity, the return of space to the bodies whose morphologies it upholds and conforms, in which the monstrous and the extra-functional, where consumption as much as production, act as powerful forces?"[85]

The utter dysfunctionality, anti-organicism, and linear excess deployed by the deformed body of the *Reticulárea* was produced by its antiarchitectural stance and lawless incontinence. This unrestrained quality referred to the work's paradoxical combination of dispersed and sheltering effects, infinite and erratic, defying the conquering gaze of the observer. Was this pulsation of the work between entrapment and infinite release, accumulation and dispersal, an effort to imagine a "monstrous architecture"? Or was it a symbolic riposte to the monstrous architecture of Caracas in the 1960s, which the Venezuelan authors Graziano Gasparini and Juan Pedro Posani connected to organic dysfunctionality and eclecticism as a system?[86] Or perhaps Gego's work was irremediably informed by the example of that *other* monstrous architecture, the one that disturbed the urban "normalcy" of the city and was consistently thematized as the residue of modernity, the marginal site par excellence, literally the land of the outcast: the shantytown.

Indeed, if there is a "monstrous architecture"—an architecture of the "near and not the proper," a sheltering architecture that grows at the margins of the city, not only on the hills that surround it or on abandoned lots, but literally in between well-to-do, even rich, neighborhoods, in between commercial and residential areas, in public plazas and underneath bridges and highways—it is the shanty. Totally unrepresentable, obliterated from official visual discourse (shantytowns were not marked on maps), these urban structures are still defined as informal, irregular, uncontrolled, subnormal, spontaneous, and illegal. Eliminating this residual urban structure was central to all modern Venezuelan political programs. Oblivious of efforts to think of the shantytown as a peculiar urban formation that required specific ways of integration into the life of the metropolis, past governments and economic elites postulated it as the quintessential negative space.[87]

In Venezuela, crucial steps were taken in the late 1940s and 1950s to develop a housing policy that would repress the explosion of shantytowns that had been accelerated by rural migrations to the city that began in the 1940s. The key organization here was the Banco Obrero (Workers' Bank), a state public-housing agency created in 1928, which, during the brief stint of a modernizing government with democratic aspirations (1945–48), set out to develop an organized and informed housing plan for overcrowded cities, particularly Caracas. The projected plan for workers' residences was the responsibility of the architect Carlos Raúl Villanueva, whose successful residential development of El Silencio in Caracas had become a continental model for public housing. But a combination of factors—poor infrastructure, the limitations of the private construction industry, housing policies that privileged middle-class needs—doomed these efforts.[88] What followed, with the coup of 1948 and the establishment of a military junta, was one of the most commented-upon episodes in Venezuelan urban history. Under the aegis of a developmentalist agenda, the military, with its reputation for discipline and role as guarantor of national security, oversaw the most aggressive battle against the shanty in its history. This battle was waged through public monies, which in turn facilitated the transfer of oil income to the private sector while the interests of the working class were rhetorically invoked by the government.[89]

In the early 1950s there were more than fifty thousand shanties in Caracas alone. To eradicate them, the Banco Obrero utilized models based on the German *Siedlung* movement of the 1920s and abandoned the single-family or detached house model in favor of simplified multilevel units. As the architectural historian Manuel López Villa wrote: "[T]he Caracas *Siedlungen* [were to] fulfill their ideological role as examples of organization, hygiene, and morality, and of 'social pact' promoted by the dictatorial regime."[90] Under the leadership of Villanueva, the Taller de Arquitectura (Architecture Workshop) of the Banco Obrero was staffed by a group of young architects who proposed the *superbloque* (residential block) as the cure for the maladies of the impoverished urban population. The large low-cost housing developments of Le Corbusean extraction that erupted in the Caracas of the 1950s would, however, suffer drastic reformulations that ignored the needs of their constituents.[91] As a consequence, after the collapse of the military regime in 1958, the shanty persisted as the only housing alternative for the poor in the face of societal indifference and contempt.

It should be no surprise, then, that some of Elizabeth Grosz's suggestions for a "monstrous" architecture coincide with the unorthodox, fluid, and rhizomatic nature of the shanty. With no intention of idealizing or decontextualizing the plight of those who have no choice but to resort to "self-help" housing, it should nevertheless be noted that the shanty grows and divides itself by adapting to the needs of its inhabitants; has multiple entrances; is alterable; establishes circumstantial connections between heterogeneous spaces; never obeys a master plan; multiplies and decomposes at the same time; and collapses public and private spaces, labor and leisure, family and community, micropolitics and life. Accordingly, Grosz argues for an architecture shaped by the events, objects, and people who inhabit it: a heterogeneous space capable of housing multiplicity, an architecture of passage, of domestic and social mobility (that last, admittedly, is rarely available to shantytown dwellers). Returning to an association between the maternal body and the sheltering function of architecture, she posits as central to the radical project of a monstrous architecture "an economy of pure gift" and "of immense expenditure . . . of excessive generosity."[92] Doesn't the *Reticulárea*—in its embodiment of a "crisis" (of geometric abstraction, of linearity, of urban space), in its aggregational logic, in its antisculptural stance—pronounce itself as residue and margin, as nonfunctional space outside architecture, as pure excess . . . as gift? Is it possible to read in the tensions between the dispersed space and monstrous body of Gego's *Reticulárea* the becoming and ephemerality of shelter, with its emphasis on covering the body as opposed to building permanent architectural forms?

In the isolation of its sculptural parameters, the singularity of its diffused morphologies, and its peculiar historical position (as the work of a Jewish émigré, a woman, and an artist from the periphery), Gego's work stood in critical relation to the urban disarray of Caracas and the public spectacularity of Venezuelan kinetic art (its monumental spatiality and universalist aspirations). The *Reticulárea*'s recurrent deformation of the grid and erratic tectonics embraced the (ideal) world of geometries, systems, and organization only to undermine it from within. In its dialogue with the legacy of geometric abstraction, the functionalist language of architecture and engineering, and the building of a country characterized by extremes of wealth and poverty, the work is both a symptom of and a model for the discontinuous modernist fabric of the country. Is the work's emphasis on layering, accumulation, eidetic opacity, dispersal, and formlessness, then, a response to the supple and precarious urban situation that characterized the South American postwar metropolis?

Aside from some scattered notes, there is no larger record of Gego's discursive engagement with the cultural and social issues of her time. But the 1960s were polemical, and the rhetoric of progress and development in the 1950s—the ground from which a new modern and technologically advanced society, based on the riches of the oil economy, would be constructed—was replaced in the 1960s by increasing clashes between a wealthy state and its erratic urban and social politics. One should assume that the complexity of contemporary historical situations permeated Gego's work and that a network of nuanced mediations infused its semiotic constitution.

Through Gego's relationship to line and space (urban, architectural, and sculptural), the *Reticulárea* was able to generate a series of questions that problematized the smooth grids embraced by, on the one hand, an inconsistent project of construction and urbanism oblivious to local conditions and, on the other, the dematerializing morphologies of kinetic art. Indeed, while espousing an architectural language and developing architectural paradigms of production and reception (spatial contextuality, attack on the contemplative mode of spectatorship, environmental scale), Gego's work celebrated linear, geometric, and spatial inconsistency and undermined the principles of organization, containment, and structure that rule architecture. In a short manuscript entitled "Gego: Drawings for Projects" written in 1976 for a small exhibition at the Instituto de Diseño, Fundación Neumann in Caracas, Hanni Ossott observed that the architecture students of the 1930s had to adjust to the point of view imposed by the professor and that experimentation was only possible outside the classroom: "Gego, like us, despised the demands and the premises dictated by the architecture professors."[93]

Indeed, there is a line of thinking that draws attention to the authoritarian dimension of architecture: its reliance on ideal geometries, on boundaries, and on notions of wholeness, unity, and harmony.[94] In Venezuela, during the period of urban planning and modernization in the 1950s and through the social and urban decline that followed in the 1960s, architecture stood for self-containment, progress, and order. It was to be the means by which the amorphousness of the city, its semirural and precarious shape and its increasingly marginal population and uncontrolled riches, were to be regulated and systematized. But by the end of the 1960s, despite previous government efforts to eradicate it, the shanty—that ubiquitous icon of underdevelopment and the Venezuelan urban landscape—was a stronger presence than ever. The shanty's antiarchitectural stance—its formlessness, its precariousness, its ever-expansive structure—was everywhere present. The modern dream of a self-contained urban grid quietly nurtured by the wealth of the national oil industry was only political rhetoric.

To Gego, the shanty seems to have been not so much a peripheral, outsider construction but integral to the urban ecology. Like the hut built since immemorial times, the shanty was a refuge, the shelter necessary for survival. Thus, in notes for one of her lectures, Gego asked her students to imagine themselves assembling a shelter in what was becoming one of the most populated shanty areas outside Caracas: the hills along the Caracas–La Guaira highway, which was constructed between 1950 and 1953 and inaugurated around the time that the Aula Magna and other landmark works of Venezuelan architecture and engineering were being built: "I suppose that each of you . . . knows that in that region there are hills, vacant lots, dry streams, or [streams] with water. Imagine that you have to erect a refuge there without any access to civilization! What materials can you find there that could help [you reach] your goal? How are you going to combine these materials? What are their dimensions, and what are the dimensions of the refuge?"[95]

It is worth noting that the words Gego used in Spanish are immediately recognizable to any Venezuelan as characteristic of the shantytown: for example, for *hills* she used *cerros,* and not *colinas,* which has a more pastoral connotation. *Cerros* is the toponym for shantytowns in Venezuela, and to urban dwellers, the *cerros* are stripped of their topographic meaning and are instead identified with the shantytown. *Baldíos* (vacant lots) are abandoned areas, the common site for precarious constructions that grow randomly according to the immediate necessities of the inhabitants who appropriate them. And *quebrada* (streams) is the final crucial word, not only because streams provide water where plumbing is lacking, but also because the streams can rise and flood, producing fatal mudslides that regularly put the population of the *cerros* at risk.

Gego's exercise, designed to generate intuitive responses from her students (she asked them to write down everything that crossed their minds in relation to these questions and not to use their ignorance on the matter as an excuse), revealed her emphasis on local conditions and contextual contiguity. Here she pressed students to think of a particular situation, the local demands of a place, rather than an ideal construction site. She dismissed imported cultural models and cautioned her students to learn from them only if local necessities were not overlooked: "Because in many cases," she wrote, "the result is an unsatisfactory copy."[96] This critique was most pertinent in light of inconsistent urban planning policies prone to favoring foreign models, ideas, and procedures that were uncritically assimilated or adapted—especially, as we have seen, in regard to the development of public housing.[97] The fact that Gego was intimately familiar with those foreign models that attracted architects in her adopted country only sharpened her critical stance.

In Gego's artistic work and from her scattered notes on architecture and art, one can perceive a growing skepticism toward ideal urban, geometric, and sculptural organizations. In this context the *Reticulárea* can be understood as a conflictive linear geometric body whose behavior was a dialogical response to Gego's sociocultural constitution and the local material conditions in which she was working. One of the outstanding gestures of the *Reticulárea* was its capacity to mutate, to fluctuate, to change in relation to the spaces and circumstances in which it operated, while at the same time upsetting the notion of architectural space as a container and of line as the boundary of bodies. In opposition to the logic of the monument, which occupies and memorializes a unique space (and to which traditional sculpture is undeniably related), the *Reticulárea* embraced a logic of displacement limited by the built-in precariousness of the pieces and by Gego's age—the incapacity of her body to re-create and reinstall the work as she would wish.[98] Unfortunately, the resources that would have allowed a continuous mutation of the work, even after her death, were not available to the artist: today the *Reticulárea* is poorly installed (after undergoing a restoration in the mid-1990s) in a permanent space in the Museo de Bellas Artes de Caracas. But for more than a decade after its inaugural exhibition, the *Reticulárea* was on the move. Furthermore, many of its premises migrated into other important projects made by Gego in the years that followed, and her work has become an exemplary template for critically thinking about form for subsequent generations of artists at home and abroad.

# NOTES

Unless otherwise indicated, all translations are my own. For alternate English translations of many of the writings by Lygia Clark and Hélio Oiticica quoted throughout, see *Lygia Clark*, exh. cat. (Barcelona: Fundació Antoni Tàpies, 1998); Cornelia H. Butler and Luis Enrique Pérez-Oramas, *Lygia Clark: The Abandonment of Art, 1948–1988*, exh. cat. (New York: Museum of Modern Art, 2014); and Mari Carmen Ramírez and Luciano Figueiredo, *Hélio Oiticica: The Body of Color*, exh. cat. (Houston: Museum of Fine Arts; London: Tate Modern, 2007). When the term "man" or "men" has been used to refer to humanity in general, I have retained the original due to the historical nature of the texts. I use "he/she" when the masculine third person is used to refer to an unspecified gender subject.

## INTRODUCTION: THEORIES OF THE NONOBJECT

1. Lygia Clark, "Capturar um fragmento de tempo suspenso," reprinted in English as "To Capture a Fragment of Suspended Time," in *Lygia Clark*, exh. cat. (Barcelona: Fundació Antoni Tàpies, 1998), 187. This undated text appears to have first been published in this exhibition catalogue. I couldn't locate the original in the archives of the Associação Cultural "O Mundo de Lygia Clark" in Rio de Janeiro, which I used in most cases when citing Clark. I've modified slightly the English translation.
2. Hélio Oiticica, "A transição da cor do quadro para o espaço e o sentido de construtividade," *Habitat*, no. 70 (December 1962): 52.
3. Fernando Cocchiarale and Anna Bella Geiger, eds., *Abstracionismo geométrico e informal: A vanguardia brasileira nos anos cinqüenta* (Rio de Janeiro: Funarte, 1987), 98.

4. "It concerns a series of constructions of superimposed planes in space." Ferreira Gullar, "Exposição Neoconcreta na Bahia," *Suplemento Dominical do Jornal do Brasil,* October 31, 1959.
5. Pioneering studies and compilations of documents still consulted today include: Aracy A. Amaral, ed., *Projeto construtivo brasileiro na arte: 1950–1962* (São Paulo: Funarte, 1977); Ronaldo Brito, *Neoconcretismo: Vértice e ruptura do projeto construtivo brasileiro,* trans. Lia Alvarenga Wyler and Florence Eleanor (Rio de Janeiro: Funarte / Instituto Nacional de Artes Plásticas, 1985); Nelly Perazzo, *Arte Concreto en la Argentina* (Buenos Aires: Gaglianone, 1983); Fernando Cocchiarale and Anna Bella Geiger, *Abstracionismo Geométrico e Informal*; and Hanni Ossott, *Gego* (Caracas: Museo de Arte Contemporáneo, 1977).
6. On geometric abstract art in Europe after the war, see Jean-Paul Ameline, *Denise René: L'intrépide—une galerie dans l'aventure de l'art abstrait, 1944–1978,* exh. cat. (Paris: Éditions du Centre Pompidou, 2001). For a general overview of the cultural situation in France, see Serge Guilbaut, "Postwar Painting Games: The Rough and the Slick," in *Reconstructing Modernism: Art in New York, Paris, and Montreal, 1945–1964* (Cambridge, MA: MIT Press, 1990), 30–79. On geometric abstraction specifically, see Serge Guilbaut, "Squares and Stains: The Impossible Mix in Cold-War Paris," in *The Geometry of Hope: Latin American Art from the Patricia Phelps de Cisneros Collection,* exh. cat., ed. Gabriel Pérez-Barreiro (Austin: Blanton Museum of Art, University of Texas at Austin, 2007), 62–73.
7. Alfredo Hlito, "Notas para una estética materialista," *Arte Concreto Invención,* no. 1 (August 1946): 12.
8. Lygia Clark, "1960.1," Diário-2 folder, Archives of the Associação Cultural "O Mundo de Lygia Clark," Rio de Janeiro.
9. Ferreira Gullar, "Teoria do não-objeto," *Suplemento Dominical do Jornal do Brasil,* December 19–20, 1959, reprinted as "Theory of the Non-Object," in *Cosmopolitan Modernisms,* ed. Kobena Mercer, trans. Michael Asbury (London: Institute of International Visual Arts; Cambridge, MA: MIT Press, 2005), 170–73. A facsimile of the essay in English (along with several other articles concerning neoconcretism from the *Suplemento Dominical do Jornal do Brasil*) was published as Michael Asbury, Caroline Menezes, Laura Barbi, and German Alfonso Nunez Adaid, eds., *Neoconcrete Experience,* exh. cat., trans. Michael Asbury, Luciana Dumphreys, Nadia Kerecuck, and Michael Marsden (London: Embassy of Brazil in London, 2009), 12.
10. [O. G.] Carlsund, [Theo van] Doesburg, [J.] Hélion, [L.] Tutundjian, and [M.] Wantz, "Base de la Peinture Concrète," *Art Concret* (Paris), no. 1 (April 1930): 1, reprinted in *The Tradition of Constructivism,* ed. Stephen Bann (New York: Da Capo Press, 1974), 193.
11. Works by Malevich and Tatlin were reproduced in "Teoria do não-objeto." Ferreira Gullar referred to the intermedial quality of Tatlin and Rodchenko's spatial experiments in "Cor e estrutura-cor," *Suplemento Dominical do Jornal do Brasil,* October 29, 1960.
12. Ferreira Gullar, "Teoria do não-objeto."
13. Ferreira Gullar, "Diálogo sobre o não-objeto," *Suplemento Dominical do Jornal do Brasil,* March 26, 1960. A facsimile of the essay in English appears in *Neoconcrete Experience,* 18–19.

14. These were published in the December 3–4, 1960, issue of the *Suplemento Dominical do Jornal do Brasil* and reprinted in Aracy A. Amaral, *Projeto construtivo brasileiro na arte: 1950–1962*, 88–89.
15. Ferreira Gullar, "Diálogo sobre o não-objeto."
16. For the most recent exhibition and publication in accord with this model, see Osbel Suárez, ed., *Cold America: Geometric Abstraction in Latin America (1943–1973)*, exh. cat. (Madrid: Fundación Juan March, 2011).
17. Donald Preziosi, "Epilogue: The Art of Art History," in *The Art of Art History* (New York: Oxford University Press, 2009), 488.
18. Aside from numerous exhibitions presented in the Americas and more recently in Europe, the CPPC has sponsored numerous symposiums, conferences, events, and publications.
19. Gabriel Pérez-Barreiro, introduction to *The Geometry of Hope*, 13.
20. Ibid.
21. Luis Enrique Pérez-Oramas, "Caracas: A Constructive Stage," in *The Geometry of Hope*, 79.
22. Marta Traba, "Gego. Caracas 3000," *7º Dia*, no. 11 (April 11, 1973): 11.
23. Juan Ledezma, *The Sites of Latin American Abstraction*, exh. cat. (Miami: Cisneros Fontanals Art Foundation, 2007), 29–43. This exhibition too was based on a private collection, that of Ella Fontanals Cisneros.
24. See Celso Favaretto, *A invenção de Hélio Oiticica* (São Paulo: Editora da Universidade de São Paulo, 1992); Maria Alice Milliet, *Lygia Clark: Obra-trajeto* (São Paulo: Editora da Universidade de São Paulo, 1992); and Ricardo Nascimento Fabbrini, *O espaço de Lygia Clark* (São Paulo: Atlas, 1994).
25. *Lygia Clark*, exh. cat.; and Guy Brett et al., *Hélio Oiticica*, exh. cat. (Rotterdam: Witte de With; Minneapolis: Walker Art Center, 1992).
26. Here, by *nonobject* I refer not specifically to Gullar's proposition but to the abandonment of traditional material supports pursued, for example, in Clark's "Propositions," initiated in 1963, and in Oiticica's *Parangolés* of 1964 and subsequent work—a gesture that is consistent with the move away from painting and sculpture that the Gullarian nonobject mapped.
27. Mari Carmen Ramírez et al., *Gego: Between Transparency and the Invisible*, exh. cat. (Houston: Museum of Fine Arts, 2006), 23; and Mari Carmen Ramírez and Luciano Figueiredo, *Hélio Oiticica: The Body of Color*, exh. cat. (Houston: Museum of Fine Arts; London: Tate Modern, 2007). As I finish revisions to the manuscript of this book, Cornelia H. Butler and Luis Enrique Pérez-Oramas, *Lygia Clark: The Abandonment of Art, 1948–1988*, exh. cat. (New York: Museum of Modern Art, 2014) has just been published to accompany the retrospective exhibition of the artist at MoMA.
28. Like Gullar, Mário Pedrosa is a key figure in understanding the theoretical alliances and cultural configurations that facilitated concrete and neoconcrete art in Brazil. After the end of World War II and the dictatorship of Getúlio Vargas, Pedrosa returned from exile to write art criticism for the prestigious newspaper *Correio da Manhã* (owned by Paulo Bittencourt, future founder of the Museu de Arte Moderna do Rio de Janeiro). During the 1950s, Pedrosa was involved with the São Paulo Bienal, the Museu de Arte Moderna do Rio de Janeiro, and the international congress of the association of art

critics in Brasília (which explored the theme of the synthesis of the arts) and was a key supporter of the constructivist tendencies and geometric abstract art that proliferated in Brazil during the decade.

29. See my "Displaced Boundaries: Geometric Abstraction from Pictures to Objects," *Art Margins* 3, no. 2 (June 2014): 101–17.
30. I borrow the term from Sérgio B. Martins's recent assessment of these debates as they concerned the Brazilian avant-garde, *Constructing an Avant-Garde: Art in Brazil 1949–1979* (Cambridge, MA, and London: MIT Press, 2013), 1–2.
31. A small sampling of the diverse studies that posit minimalism as the source of the experimental artistic practices that characterized the art of the 1960s, 1970s, and sometimes 1980s includes: Miwon Kwon, *One Place After Another: Site-Specific Art and Locational Identity* (Cambridge, MA: MIT Press, 2002); Frazer Ward, *No Innocent Bystanders: Performance Art and Audience* (Dartmouth, NH: Dartmouth College Press, 2011); Martha Buskirk, *The Contingent Object of Contemporary Art* (Cambridge, MA: MIT Press, 2005); Nancy Spector, *Felix González-Torres* (New York: Guggenheim Museum, 1995); Gill Perry and Paul Wood, *Themes in Contemporary Art* (New Haven, CT, and London: Yale University Press in association with the Open University, 2004); Hal Foster, "The Crux of Minimalism," in *The Return of the Real* (Cambridge, MA: MIT Press, 1996), 35–71; and Andrea Fraser, "It's Art When I Say It's Art, Or . . . ," (1995) in *Museum Highlights: The Writings of Andrea Fraser,* ed. Alexander Alberro (Cambridge, MA: MIT Press, 2005): 36–44.
32. A sampling would include Guy Brett, "Fait sur le corps: Le Parangolé de Hélio Oiticica," *Les Cahiers du musée national d'art moderne,* no. 52 (Spring 1995): 32–45; Simone Osthoff, "Hélio Oiticica's Parangolés: Nomadic Experience in Endless Motion," in *Diaspora and Visual Culture: Representing Africans and Jews,* ed. Nicholas Mirzoeff (London and New York: Routledge, 2000), 234–35; Paula Braga, "Hélio Oiticica and the Parangolés: (Ad)dressing Nietzsche's Übermensch," *Third Text* 17, no. 1 (2003): 43–52; Anna Dezeuze, "Tactile Dematerialization, Sensory Politics: Hélio Oiticica's Parangolés," *Art Journal* 63, no. 2 (Summer 2004): 59–71; Renato Rodrigues da Silva, "Hélio Oiticica's *Parangolé* or the Art of Transgression," *Third Text* 19, no. 3 (May 2005): 213–31; Michael Asbury, "Hélio Couldn't Dance," in *Loose Threads: The Art of Hélio Oiticica,* ed. Paula Braga (São Paulo: Perspectiva, 2008); Sérgio B. Martins, "Hélio Oiticica: Mapping the Constructive," *Third Text* 24, no. 4 (July 2010): 409–22; and Hermano Vianna, "Não quero que a vida me faça de otário! Hélio Oiticica como mediador cultural entre o asfalto e o morro," *Overmundo* (Brazil), January 15, 2007, http://www.overmundo.com.br/banco/helio-oiticica-como-mediador-entre-asfalto-e-morro.
33. One important omission, for example, has been concrete and neoconcrete poetry. Ferreira Gullar was a renowned poet, and his neoconcrete experiments with poetry advanced the notion of the nonobject that he elaborated in relationship to Clark's work.
34. See for example Paulo Herkenhoff, "Divergent Parallels: Toward a Comparative Study of Neo-concretism and Minimalism," in Yve-Alain Bois et al., *Geometric Abstraction: Latin American Art from the Patricia Phelps de Cisneros Collection,* exh. cat. (Cambridge, MA: Harvard University Art Museums, 2001); Luis Enrique Pérez-Oramas, "La poética del Penetrable y la escena Minimalista: Las paradojas de la absorción absoluta," lecture

delivered at the Fogg Museum, Harvard University, Cambridge, Massachusetts, March 3, 2001; Mónica Amor, "Between Spaces: The Reticulárea and Its Place in History," in *Gego, 1955–1990*, exh. cat., ed. Iris Peruga (Caracas: Museo de Bellas Artes, 2003), 312–26; Michael Asbury, "Neoconcretism and Minimalism: Cosmopolitanism at a Local Level and a Canonical Provincialism," in *Cosmopolitan Modernisms*, ed. Kobena Mercer (London: Institute of International Visual Arts; Cambridge, MA: MIT Press, 2005), 174–89; and Anna Dezeuze, "Minimalism and Neoconcretism," paper delivered as part of the October 2006 talks series "Brazil: A Site and Subject for Sculpture," Henry Moore Institute, Leeds, England, http://www.henry-moore.org/hmi/online-papers/papers/anna-dezeuze.

35. Donald Judd, "Specific Objects," *Arts Yearbook* 8 (1965): 74–82.
36. Ibid., 122.
37. Ibid., 119.
38. Ibid., 120.
39. Ibid.
40. Lygia Clark, "Lygia Clark e o espaço concreto expressional," *Suplemento Dominical do Jornal do Brasil*, July 2, 1959.
41. Robert Morris, "Notes on Sculpture, Part 2," *Artforum* (October 1966): 20–23, reprinted in Robert Morris, *Continuous Project Altered Daily: The Writings of Robert Morris* (Cambridge, MA: MIT Press, 1993), 11–21 (subsequent page citations refer to this reprinted version). An earlier essay, "Notes on Sculpture, Part 1," is an introduction to the issues that preoccupied artists at the time, engaged as they were in contesting or complying with the modernist paradigm put in place mainly through the formalist art criticism of Clement Greenberg. A preoccupation with defining the terms and the nature of the new sculpture runs throughout the essay. Morris looks back at constructivism and mentions Vladimir Tatlin, Nikolaus Pevsner, and Georges Vantongerloo as producers of a "non-imagistic sculpture," a condition "essential" to the sculpture of the time in which Morris was writing. In a gesture that evoked the emphasis on self-referentiality in much constructivist sculpture and particularly in concrete art's stress on the use of concrete materials in the 1930s, Morris posited the autonomous and the literal as prerequisites to the type of sculpture that he represented. See Robert Morris, "Notes on Sculpture, Part 1," *Artforum* (February 1966): 42–44, reprinted in Robert Morris, *Continuous Project Altered Daily*, 1–8.
42. In the same year that Morris published his three-part "Notes on Sculpture," addressing the viewer's bodily engagement with the new sculpture (see note 41 above), Rosalind Krauss explored the phenomenological reading of Judd's work in "Allusion and Illusion in Donald Judd," *Artforum* (May 1966): 24–26. During the 1960s, phenomenology emerged as a model of spectatorship identified with the new work through an implicit dialogue with Michael Fried's notion of "theatricality," which referred negatively to the antipictorial stance of minimalism, its use of real space, and its lack of disciplinary specificity. See Annette Michelson, "Robert Morris: An Aesthetics of Transgression," in Robert Morris, *Robert Morris*, exh. cat. (Washington, DC: Corcoran Gallery of Art; Detroit: Detroit Institute of Arts, 1969); and Michael Fried, "Art and Objecthood," *Artforum* (June 1967), reprinted in Gregory Battock, ed., *Minimal Art: A Critical Anthology*

(Berkeley: University of California Press, 1995). During the 1970s, Krauss's writings were instrumental in securing this association between minimalism and phenomenology, particularly an essay entitled "Sense and Sensibility: Reflections on Post '60s Sculpture," *Artforum* (November 1973): 149–56; and her book *Passages in Modern Sculpture* (Boston: MIT Press, 1977). More recent phenomenologically inflected readings of Judd (who was not particularly interested in such approaches) include Yve-Alain Bois, "The Inflection," in Yve-Alain Bois, *Donald Judd: Sculpture 1991,* trans. Gregory Sims (New York: Pace Gallery, 1991); Briony Fer, "Judd's Specific Objects," in *On Abstract Art* (New Haven, CT: Yale University Press, 1997); and Alex Potts, "Objects and Spaces," in *The Sculptural Imagination: Figurative, Modernist, Minimalist* (New Haven, CT: Yale University Press, 2000).

43. Robert Morris, "Notes on Sculpture, Part 1," 6.
44. Ibid.
45. This piece, made of wooden cubes covered by Plexiglas mirrors, was first shown at Green Gallery in New York in 1965. The mirrored cubes reflected the gallery's floors and walls, works hanging nearby, and viewers. The work merged and reflected its surroundings while dissolving the geometric precision of the cube.
46. This potential suspension of a more bodily interaction with the work that we've come to associate with minimalism was also elaborated in the reception of so-called minimalist work. The critic Barbara Rose, for example, in a 1969 essay on the new sculpture, summed up the desire for "immediacy of impact": "From wherever we first approach a Judd, a Bell, or a Morris, we can immediately (without necessarily walking around it) understand that we are looking at a certain kind of known three-dimensional shape. Unlike sculpture 'in-the-round' which requires a sequence of acts of looking, we can experience transparent or familiar forms *immediately* as gestalts. It takes us much less time, in other words, to process the information regarding such forms because we either see or can sense them all at once." Barbara Rose, "Sculpture, Intimacy and Perception," in Martin L. Friedman et al., *14 Sculptors: The Industrial Edge,* exh. cat. (Minneapolis: Walker Art Center, 1969), 8.
47. Robert Morris, "Notes on Sculpture, Part 2," 15.
48. This turn away from the immediacy that the known gestalt (the cube) could trigger correlated to the spatiality articulated in Morris's solo exhibition at Green Gallery in New York in 1963–64 (see fig. 0.4). In that exhibition, seven different geometric volumes made of painted plywood engaged the space of the gallery in ways that undermined the independent identities of object, viewer, and space. The placement of the works—either resting on the floor, hanging from the ceiling, or wedged into corners—problematized the self-sufficiency of the object and foregrounded its interdependence with architectural space in ways that recall Oiticica's colorful, labyrinthine *Nuclei* made three years earlier. The architectural dimension of these works coincided with a move away from traditional sculpture and contemplative modes of viewing, leading Morris and Oiticica to actively engage with situational practices.
49. See for example Mário Pedrosa, "Reflexões em torno da nova capital," *Brasil, Arquitetura Contemporânea* (Rio de Janeiro), no. 10 (1957); "Introdução à Arquitetura Brasileira—I," *Jornal do Brasil* (Rio de Janeiro), May 23–24, 1959; and "Brasília, a Cidade Nova," *Jor-*

*nal do Brasil,* September 19, 1959. All are reprinted in Mário Pedrosa, *Dos Murais de Portinari aos Espaços de Brasília* (São Paulo: Editora Perspectiva, 1981), 303–16, 321–27, 345–53.

50. See Mário Pedrosa, "Reflexões em torno da nova capital."
51. "Invención Integral," *Arte Concreto Invención,* no. 1 (August 1946): 10.
52. See Afredo Hlito, "Representación e invención," *Boletín de la Asociación de Arte Concreto Invención,* no. 2 (December 1946): 7.
53. Carlos Altamirano, *Bajo el signo de las masas* (Buenos Aires: Grupo Editorial Planeta, 2001), 42–43.
54. Ana Longoni and Daniela Lucena (2004), "De cómo el júbilo creador se trocó en desfachatez: El pasaje de Maldonado y los concretos por el Partido Comunista, 1945–1948," *Políticas de la memoria* (Buenos Aires), no. 4, CEDINCI, 118–28; María Amalia García, "La construcción del arte abstracto: Interconecciones entre el internacionalismo cultural paulista y la escena artística Argentina, 1949–1953," and María Cristina Rossi, "En el fuego cruzado entre el realismo y la abstracción," both in María Amalia García, María Cristina Rossi, and Luisa Fabiana Servidio, *Arte argentino y latinoamericano del siglo XX: Sus interrelaciones* (Buenos Aires: Fundación Espigas, 2004), 17–54, 85–125; María Amalia García, *El arte abstracto: Intercambios culturales entre Argentina y Brasil* (Buenos Aires: Siglo Veintiuno Editores, 2011); and Alejandro Crispiani, *Objetos para transformar el mundo: trayectorías del arte concreto-invención, Argentina y Chile, 1949–1970* (Buenos Aires: Universidad Nacional de Quilmes, 2011).
55. See María Amalia García, "Max Bill on the Map of Argentine-Brazilian Concrete Art," in *Building on a Construct: The Adolpho Leirner Collection of Brazilian Constructive Art at the Museum of Fine Arts,* exh. cat., ed. Mari Carmen Ramírez and Héctor Olea (Houston: Museum of Fine Arts; New Haven, CT, and London: Yale University Press, 2009), 53–68; María Amalia García, "Tensiones entre tradición e innovación: las críticas de Max Bill a la arquitectura moderna brasileña," *Concinnitas,* Universidad do Estado do Rio de Janeiro, año 11, vol. 1, no. 16 (June 2010): 148–63; Aleca Le Blanc, "Palmeiras and Pilotis: Promoting Brazil with Modern Architecture," *Third Text* 26, no. 1 (January 2012): 103–16; and Adele Nelson, "Monumental and Ephemeral: The Early São Paulo Bienais," in *Constructive Spirit: Abstract Art in South and North America, 1920s–1950s,* exh. cat., ed. Mary Kate O'Hare (Newark, NJ: Newark Museum of Art; Fort Worth: Amon Carter Museum, 2010), 139, note 8. García's essay "Max Bill on the Map" is also particularly useful in understanding Bill as a link between the AACI and concrete and neoconcrete art in Brazil.
56. Ferreira Gullar et al., "Manifesto Neoconcreto," *Suplemento Dominical do Jornal do Brasil,* March 21–22, 1959. Though signed and conceptualized by Amilcar de Castro, Ferreira Gullar, Franz Weissmann, Lygia Clark, Lygia Pape, Reynaldo Jardim, and Theon Spanúdis, the manifesto was actually written by Gullar. A facsimile of the essay in English appears in *Neoconcrete Experience,* 6–7.
57. Ferreira Gullar et al., "Manifesto Neoconcreto."
58. This project was delineated by Oiticica in 1962 through a reference to Pedrosa's notion of a "new constructivism." See Hélio Oiticica, "A transição da cor do quadro para o espaço e o sentido de construtividade," *Habitat,* no. 70 (December 1962): 54.

59. To Gullar, concrete art's reduction of form to a "pure act of perception" ignored historicity. This revealed the idealist dimension of the movement, which conceived of itself as above history and contingency. See Ferreira Gullar, "Arte Neoconcreta," *Suplemento Dominical do Jornal do Brasil,* October 2, 1960.
60. Ferreira Gullar et al., "Manifesto Neoconcreto."
61. Merleau-Ponty himself saw the reduction as part of an attempt, on the part of Husserl, to grasp essences based on our concrete experiences and to consider essence as contingent as the fact. See Maurice Merleau-Ponty, "Phenomenology and the Sciences of Man," in *The Primacy of Perception and Other Essays on Phenomenological Psychology, the Philosophy of Art, History and Politics,* ed. James M. Edie (Evanston, IL: Northwestern University Press, 1964), 72.
62. Ferreira Gullar, "O Tempo e a Obra," *Suplemento Dominical do Jornal do Brasil,* February 18, 1961.
63. On the meaning of the word *parangolé,* see chapter 4, p. 139.
64. "We do not conceive of a work of art as a 'machine' or 'object' but as a quasi-corpus; that is, a being whose reality is not exhausted in the external relationships among its elements, a being that, disassembled through analysis, only delivers itself up wholly through a direct, phenomenological approach." Ferreira Gullar et al., "Manifesto Neoconcreto."
65. Gego spoke Spanish with a heavy accent and never displayed a full command of the language. Although the handsome publication of her working notes—see María Elena Huizi and Josefina Manrique, eds., *Sabiduras y otros textos de Gego* (Houston: International Center for the Arts of the Americas, Museum of Fine Arts; Caracas: Fundación Gego, 2005)—might suggest otherwise, these, to my view, are notations that invite interpretation but are very different from the discursive muscle displayed by the Argentine and Brazilian artists.

## 1. AT PAINTING'S EDGE: *ARTE CONCRETO INVENCIÓN*, 1944–46

1. *Boletín de la Asociación de Arte Concreto Invención* (Buenos Aires), no. 2 (December 1946): 7. The Asociación Arte Concreto Invención published two issues of this magazine in 1946: one in August called *Arte Concreto Invención,* no. 1, and one in December called *Boletín de la Asociación de Arte Concreto Invención,* no. 2. Subsequent citations in the notes and the main text retain this wording.
2. Tomás Maldonado, "Los Artistas Concretos, el 'realismo' y la realidad," *Arte Concreto Invención,* no. 1 (August 1946): 10.
3. Edgar Bayley et al., untitled text, *1a Exposición de la Asociación Arte Concreto Invención,* exh. cat. (Buenos Aires: Salón Peuser, 1946), reprinted as "Manifesto Invencionista," *Arte Concreto Invención,* no. 1 (August 1946): 8. Citations will be from this latter version of the text.
4. Many artists who participated in *Arturo* went on to become members of the AACI and Arte Madí, which became discrete movements by the end of 1945 or early 1946. A third group grew out of the AACI called perceptismo; it was founded in 1949 by Raúl Lozza, who remained its only member. In the mid-1940s the artists of the AACI drew on European concrete art as a source; by the 1950s they identified with it unreservedly.

5. Classic accounts include Jorge B. Rivera, *Madí y la vanguardia Argentina* (Buenos Aires: Paidos, 1976); Gyula Kosice, *Madí* (Buenos Aires: Ediciones de Arte Gaglianone, 1982); and Nelly Perazzo, *El arte concreto en la Argentina en la década del 40* (Buenos Aires: Ediciones de Arte Gaglianone, 1983). In the 1990s, Agnès de Maistre, "Les Groupes d'Abstraction Géométrique: Art Concret–Invention et Madí, Buenos Aires, 1940–1948" (PhD diss., Université de Paris IV–La Sorbonne Institut d'Art et d'Archéologie, 1994) and Gabriel Pérez-Barreiro, "The Argentine Avant-Garde, 1944–1950" (PhD diss., University of Essex, UK, 1996) expanded these earlier accounts and clarified the development of events and artistic production during the movement's active period. Most recently, this project has been refined in such works as Andrea Giunta's "El arte moderno en los márgenes del Peronismo" in her book *Vanguardia, internacionalismo y política: Arte Argentino en los años sesenta* (Buenos Aires: Paidós, 2001), 45–83; Ana Longoni and Daniela Lucena (2004), "De cómo el 'júbilo creador' se trastocó en desfachatez: El pasaje de Maldonado y los concretos por el Partido Comunista, 1945–1948," *Políticas de la memoria,* no. 4 (Buenos Aires, CEDINCI): 118–28; María Amalia García, "La construcción del arte abstracto: Interconecciones entre el internacionalismo cultural paulista y la escena artística Argentina, 1949–1953," and Maria Cristina Rossi, "En el fuego cruzado entre el realismo y la abstracción," both in María Amalia García, María Cristina Rossi, and Luisa Fabiana Servidio, *Arte argentino y latinoamericano del siglo XX: Sus interrelaciones* (Buenos Aires: Fundación Espigas, 2004), 17–54, 85–125; María Amalia García, *El arte abstracto: Intercambios culturales entre Argentina y Brasil* (Buenos Aires: Siglo Veintiuno Editores, 2011); and Alejandro Crispiani, *Objetos para transformar el mundo: trayectorías del arte concreto-invención, Argentina y Chile, 1949–1970* (Buenos Aires: Universidad Nacional de Quilmes, 2011).
6. Alejandro Crispiani, *Objetos para transformar el mundo,* 84.
7. Crispiani mapped the philosophical makeup of this early, humanist Marx (translated into Spanish in the 1920s and early 1930s) that influenced the Argentine artists and that would be rejected by the Stalinist state and more orthodox forms of Marxism in the 1950s. This so-called humanist Marx is particularly relevant in the context of the AACI, as it addresses the creation of objects and highlights the liberating capacity of creative production. Many of Marx's texts, Crispiani wrote, were reprinted in Argentina in a volume entitled *Carlos Marx y Federico Engels: sobre arte y literatura,* trans. Jean Freville (Buenos Aires: Problemas, 1940). Another text that could have been an important reference to the young artists was Rodolfo Mondolfo, *Feuerbach y Marx: La dialéctica y el concepto marxista de la historia* (Buenos Aires: Claridad, 1933). And in 1946, Alfredo Hlito explicitly discussed Marx's "Theses on Feuerbach" (1845) in "Representación e invención" (see note 1 above). However, 1845 marked a turning point in Marx's work, one that Étienne Balibar defines as a distancing from his earlier "theoretical humanism." This shift was caused, says Balibar, by a series of "political experiences: in particular, [Marx's] encounter with the German and French proletariats . . . and [his] active re-entry into social struggles (which has a direct counterpart in [his] exit from academic philosophy)." Étienne Balibar, *The Philosophy of Marx* (London: Verso, 1995), 7. For Crispiani's mapping of the AACI's theoretical makeup, its reading of Marx, and contemporary references available to these artists, see Alejandro Crispiani, *Objetos para transformar*

*el mundo,* 91–114. For a detailed account of how the aesthetic dimension influenced Marx's early propositions on the nature of unalienated labor and production, see William Adams, "Aesthetics: Liberating the Senses," in *The Cambridge Companion to Marx,* ed. Terrell Carver (Cambridge, New York, and Melbourne: Cambridge University Press, 1991), 246–74.

8. Étienne Balibar, *The Philosophy of Marx,* 1–2.
9. According to *Orientación,* the official publication of the Argentine Communist Party, the artists who joined the party were Edgar Bayley, Manuel Espinosa, Claudio Girola, Alfredo Hlito, Tomás Maldonado, and Aldo Prior. "Artistas adhieren al comunismo: Los artistas y escritores del movimiento arte concreto se afilian al partido comunista," *Orientación,* September 19, 1945, cited in Ana Longoni and Daniela Lucena, "De cómo el 'júbilo creador' se trastocó en desfachatez," 118; and Alejandro Crispiani, *Objetos para transformar el mundo,* 91. While these texts trace the relationship between the Argentine concrete artists and the Communist Party, they do not address the relationship of the party to contemporary political events.
10. William Adams, "Aesthetics: Liberating the Senses," 249. Here Adams discusses Marx's *Economic and Philosophical Manuscripts* (1844), which delineate the economic theory that concerned him throughout his oeuvre. The writings of the AACI (by Tomás Maldonado, Edgar Bayley, and Alfredo Hlito, to name the most prolific members) do not always refer to specific texts, but ideas and concepts elaborated by Marx in the *Economic and Philosophical Manuscripts,* "Theses on Feuerbach" (1845), and *The German Ideology* (1845) resonate throughout their manifestos, declarations, and articles written between 1944 and 1946.
11. J. L. Romero, *Latinoamerica: Las ciudades y las ideas* (Buenos Aires: Siglo XX editores, 1986), 327.
12. Carlos Altamirano, *Peronismo y cultura de izquierda (1955–1965),* Latin American Studies Center Series, no. 6 (College Park: University of Maryland, 1992), 30–38.
13. Flavia Fiorucci, *Intelectuales y Peronismo, 1945–1955* (Buenos Aires: Editorial Biblos, 2011), 20. On the early alliance between Argentine nationalists and Perón, see Carlos Altamirano, *Bajo el signo de las masas (1943–1973)* (Buenos Aires: Grupo Editorial Planeta, 2001), 21–22.
14. Flavia Fiorucci, *Intelectuales y Peronismo,* 23.
15. Jorge Abelardo Ramos, *Revolución y contrarevolución en la Argentina: Historia de la Argentina en el siglo XX,* vol. 2 (Buenos Aires: Editorial Plus Ultra, 1965), 565; and Flavia Fiorucci, *Intelectuales y Peronismo,* 23.
16. See for example Américo Ghioldi's editorials for the Socialist newspaper *La Vanguardia,* collected in *Palabras a la nación: A través de los editoriales de "La Vanguardia"* (Buenos Aires: Editorial de La Vanguardia, 1945).
17. Tomás Maldonado, "A dónde va la pintura?," *Contrapunto: Literatura-crítica-arte* (Buenos Aires), no. 3 (April 1945): 10.
18. Manuel Espinosa, "A dónde va la pintura?," *Contrapunto,* no. 5 (June 1945): 11.
19. Gabriel Pérez-Barreiro, "The Argentine Avant-Garde, 1944–1950," 103.
20. See Andrea Giunta, "El arte moderno en los márgenes del Peronismo," 45–83; and Flavia Fiorucci, *Intelectuales y Peronismo,* 11–63.

21. Andrea Giunta, "Nacionales y populares," in *Tras los pasos de la norma: Salones nacionales de bellas artes (1911–1989)*, ed. Marta Penhos and Diana Wechsler (Buenos Aires: Jilguero-CAIA), 159–60.
22. Ibid., 48.
23. See for example Karl Marx, "Theses on Feuerbach" (1845), in Karl Marx and Friedrich Engels, *The German Ideology* (Amherst, New York: Prometheus Books, 1998).
24. Jorge Abelardo Ramos, *Revolución y contrarevolución en la Argentina*, 484. This view was also put forward by Ángel Perelman in his openly biased account of the period, *Cómo hicimos el 17 de Octubre* (Buenos Aires: Ediciones Coyoacán, 1961), 31–35, 59. According to Rodolfo Puiggrós, a member of the Communist Party until his expulsion in 1946 (due to his desire to redirect the party's position toward Perón), the Argentine Communist Party's indifference to local realities was long-standing and had been associated since the 1920s with a Moscow-based power structure that did not tolerate dissent. See Rodolfo Puiggrós, *Historia crítica de los partidos políticos Argentinos* (Buenos Aires: Editorial Argumentos, 1956), 167–76. Alberto Ciria summarizes the situation: "Of course, all tactical and fundamental interpretations followed the international line that guided local Communism. This line joined the fate of the Soviet Union under Stalin's command too closely (and not exactly dialectically) to our own fate, without realizing that the problem was exactly the opposite: from the particular to the universal, and that the 'national question' was what was urgent and had priority." Alberto Ciria, *Parties and Power in Modern Argentina (1930–1946)*, trans. Carlos A. Astiz with Mary F. McCarthy (Albany: State University of New York Press, 1974), 141.
25. Juan Carlos Torre, *La vieja guardia sindical y Perón: Sobre los orígenes del peronismo* (Buenos Aires: Editora Sudamericana, 1990), 71.
26. On the various interpretations of the proletarian base that supported Perón in the Argentine imaginary, see Federico G. Neiburg, *Los intelectuales y la invención del peronismo* (Buenos Aires: Alianza Editorial, 1988), 122–32. For rigorous historical accounts, see Juan Carlos Torre, *La vieja guardia sindical y Perón*, 71–72; and Carlos Altamirano, *Bajo el signo de las masas*, 19–49. Perón summarized the goals and accomplishments of the newly created Secretaria de Trabajo y Previsión (Secretariat of Labor and Social Security) in a radio address on Workers' Day (May 1) in 1944; see Juan D. Perón, "Trabajamos para todos los argentinos, mensaje a los trabajadores el 1º de Mayo de 1944," reprinted in Carlos Altamirano, *Bajo el signo de las masas*, 117–23.
27. Carlos Altamirano, *Bajo el signo de las masas*, 42–43.
28. Maria Cristina Rossi, "En el fuego cruzado entre el realismo y la abstracción," 85–125; and Maria Cristina Rossi, "Mirando al futuro: Maldonado entre las voces emergentes," in *Tomás Maldonado: Un moderno en acción*, ed. Mario H. Gradowczyk (Buenos Aires: Eduntref, Editorial de la Universidad Nacional de Tres de Febrero, 2009). As is well known, by the early 1930s, socialist realism had become the official aesthetic doctrine in the Soviet Union, so it is not surprising that in matters of aesthetics Maldonado would look west to Paris.
29. Tomás Maldonado, "Sobre humanismo," *Boletín de la Asociación de Arte Concreto Invención*, no. 2 (December 1946): 6.
30. Ibid.

31. Ibid.

32. Serge Guilbaut, "Postwar Painting Games: The Rough and the Slick," in *Reconstructing Modernism: Art in New York, Paris, and Montreal, 1945–1964* (Cambridge, MA: MIT Press, 1990), 34. However, a tenuous association between the Communist Party and modern artists was still possible in 1947, resulting in part from a shared anti-American attitude. Thus, intellectuals such as Tristan Tzara, Roger Vailland, Louis Aragon, Paul Éluard, Pablo Picasso, and Fernand Léger, among others, remained close to the French Communist Party. Ibid., 43.

33. Tomás Maldonado, "Picasso, Matisse y la libertad de expresión," *Orientación* (Buenos Aires), no. 418 (November 19, 1947): 7.

34. Edgar Bayley, "Sobre arte concreto," *Orientación*, no. 327 (February 20, 1946): 9.

35. Ibid.

36. Ibid.

37. Américo Ghioldi, "'La Vanguardia,' los socialistas y el coronel Perón," *La Vanguardia*, March 6, 1945, reprinted in Américo Ghioldi, *Palabras a la nación*, 260.

38. Ibid., 260. On Américo Ghioldi's humanist conception of the "producer" as "man" above all (i.e., as civic "citizen"), the primacy of education in Socialism, and his critique of Perón's populism, see "Productores y Ciudadanos," *La Vanguardia*, November 28, 1943; "¿Productivismo?," *La Vanguardia*, January 5, 1944; and "¿Mates vacíos o cabezas llenas?," *La Vanguardia*, March 13, 1945, reprinted in Américo Ghioldi, *Palabras a la nación*. Ghioldi's brother, Rodolfo, was a prominent leader of the Argentine Communist Party who would become editor of the Communist publication *Orientación* in 1947.

39. In 1946, Raúl Lozza declared: "In the developed and learned countries of the world, the most modern artists, in all their manifestations and in different aesthetic tendencies, are contributing their efforts to the progressive and democratic cause." Raúl Lozza, "Carta abierta a M. Lobato," *Boletín de la Asociación de Arte Concreto Invención*, no. 2 (December 1946): 5. That this was the condition to which the Argentine artists aspired cannot be doubted. In this text Lozza was specifically dismissing parallels drawn between modern art and Fascism by the Brazilian writer José Bento Monteiro Lobato in the newspaper *El Mundo* (November 1946).

40. For a different point of view, see Daniela Lucena, "Arte y diseño Argentino: Vínculos entre la vanguardia concreta y el constructivismo ruso," *Cuartas Jornadas de Jóvenes Investigadores* (Buenos Aires, Instituto de Investigaciones Gino Germani, Facultad de Ciencias Sociales, Universidad de Buenos Aires), September 2007, http://www.iigg.fsoc.uba.ar/Jovenes_Investigadores/4Jorandasjovenes/principal.htm. The First Working Group of Constructivists was formed in Moscow, within Inkhuk (the Institute of Artistic Culture) in March 1921. For a concise account of the group, see Christina Lodder, "The Transition to Constructivism," in Paul Wood et al., *The Great Utopia: The Russian and Soviet Avant-Garde, 1915–1932*, exh. cat. (New York: Guggenheim Museum, 1992), 267–81.

41. Among the institutions that provided a platform of intervention for the Soviet avant-garde were Izo-Narkompros (Department of Fine Arts of the People's Commissariat of Enlightenment), a government agency based in Petrograd; Vkhutemas, the state art and technical school; and the First Working Group of Constructivists at Inkhuk, the last

two based in Moscow. The Academy of Arts and Ginkhuk (the State Institute of Artistic Culture) in Petrograd also welcomed avant-garde artists.

42. Alexander Rodchenko, "Program of the Production Section of the Inkhuk Constructivist Group," in Alexander Rodchenko, *Experiments for the Future: Diaries, Essays, Letters, and Other Writings*, ed. Alexander N. Lavrentiev (New York: Museum of Modern Art, 2005), 145.
43. Paul Wood, "The Politics of the Avant-Garde," in *The Great Utopia*, 12.
44. Tomás Maldonado, "Sobre humanismo," 6.
45. Tomás Maldonado, "Lo abstracto y lo concreto en el arte moderno" and "Los Artistas Concretos, El 'Realismo' y la 'Realidad,'" in *Arte Concreto Invención*, no. 1 (August 1946): 5–7, 10.
46. This history is relevant in light of what can be construed as avant-garde naïveté (in the case of the Argentines) or complicity (in the case of the Soviets). Paul Wood warns: "One of the points which needs to be borne in mind here is the class position of artists and designers, not to mention theorists. They were not proletarians. They would not have experienced the sharp end of the exploitation mounting in the factories and mines. Quite the contrary: the misery in the countryside and the superintensification of productivity in industry would all have been mediated through the terms of the very propaganda campaign whose articulation *was* the site of the contribution of the designers (unless one wants to postulate mendacity of a degree which seems highly unlikely)." Paul Wood, "The Politics of the Avant-Garde," 20.
47. Alfredo Hlito, "Notas para una estética materialista," *Arte Concreto Invención*, no. 1 (August 1946): 12.
48. Ibid.
49. See Alfredo Hlito, "Representación e invención," 7. A critique of alienation is elaborated by Marx in his *Economic and Philosophical Manuscripts* (1844).
50. As the art historian María Amalia García argued in her important study on geometric abstraction in postwar Argentina and Brazil, *Arturo* proposed a regional alternative to a Europe in decline, one whose time had come to contribute to international culture. See María Amalia García, *El arte abstracto: intercambios culturales entre Argentina y Brasil* (Buenos Aires: Siglo Veintiuno Editores, 2011), 52–53.
51. Gyula Kosice, "Gyula Kosice, la memoria y el proyecto," interview with Jorge López Anaya, in *Kosice: Obras, 1944 1990* (Buenos Aires: Museo Nacional de Bellas Artes, 1991), 10, cited in Gabriel Pérez-Barreiro, "The Argentine Avant-Garde, 1944–1950," 124.
52. Tomás Maldonado, interview with Giacinto Di Pietrantonio, *Flash Art* 151 (Summer 1989), reprinted in Tomás Maldonado, *Escritos preulmianos* (Buenos Aires: Ediciones Infinito, 1997), 121.
53. Juan Melé, *La vanguardia del cuarenta en la Argentina: Memorias de un artista concreto* (Buenos Aires: Ediciones cinco, 1999), 74.
54. Derek Harris and Gabriel Pérez-Barreiro, *The Place of* Arturo *in the Argentinian Avant-Garde* (Old Aberdeen, Scotland: University of Aberdeen, 1994), 5. See also the detailed account of the birth of *Arturo* in María Amalia García, *El arte abstracto*, 25–53.
55. Carmelo Arden Quin, *Arturo*, no. 1 (Summer 1944). In Marx's model, the base (what

Arden Quin calls the "material conditions of a society") encompasses the material forces of production—that is, the raw materials and tools that produce human sustenance—and the social forces of production, which refers to how society organizes itself around these productive activities. It is out of this social organization that class divisions stem, making class struggle, as Marx and Engels write in the *Communist Manifesto* (1848), a key historical determinant.

56. As has been widely observed, the visual component of the magazine was varied, ranging from the mosaic-like figurative gouaches of the Brazilian artist Maria Helena Vieira da Silva to the fully abstract vignettes of Lidy Prati. For a detailed analysis of the visual and textual components of *Arturo,* see María Amalia García, *El arte abstracto,* 27–53; and Gabriel Pérez-Barreiro, "*Arturo* 1944," chapter 2 in "The Argentine Avant-Garde," 42–82.
57. Karl Marx and Friedrich Engels, *The German Ideology,* 61. In a parallel formulation, Marx wrote: "It is not consciousness that determines life, but life that determines consciousness," 42.
58. Ibid.
59. Alfredo Hlito, "Representación e invención," 7. The conception of invention as opposing alienation and as a function of practical consciousness echoed Marx, for whom productive activities define human nature and, in a nonalienated world, bind the maker to the thing made and to others. See William Adams, "Aesthetics: Liberating the Senses," 250–52.
60. Tulio Halperin Donghi, *Historia contemporáneo de América Latina* (1969) (Madrid: Alianza Editorial, 1997), 444.
61. Ibid., 449.
62. Alejandro Crispiani's account of the connections between Argentine invencionismo (from *invención*) and Vicente Huidobro's creacionismo is the most exhaustive and comprehensive to date. He calls attention to the Argentine writer Juan-Jacobo Bajarlía's construction of the relationship between creacionismo and invencionismo in the 1950s and traces Huidobro's relationship to abstraction and concrete art. See Alejandro Crispiani, *Objetos para transformar el mundo,* 54–69; and Alejandro G. Crispiani, "Frutos de la invención," in *Tomás Maldonado: Un moderno en acción; Ensayos sobre su obra,* ed. Mario H. Gradowczyk (Buenos Aires: Eduntref, 2009), 49–55.
63. Vicente Huidobro, "La creación pura," in *L'Esprit Nouveau* (Paris), April 7, 1921, quoted in Rhod Rothfuss, "El marco: Un problema de plástica actual," *Arturo,* no. 1 (Summer 1944). *L'Esprit Nouveau* was edited by Le Corbusier.
64. Jean Arp, "Art Concret," in *Konkrete Kunst,* exh. cat. (Basel: Kunsthalle Basel, 1944), 11–12, reprinted in Jean Arp, "Concrete Art," in *Arp on Arp,* ed. Marcel Jean, trans. Joachim Neugroschel (New York: Viking, 1972), 139.
65. See Raymond Williams, *Keywords: A Vocabulary of Culture and Society* (New York: Oxford University Press, 1976), 229.
66. Rosalind Krauss, *Passages in Modern Sculpture* (Boston: MIT Press, 1977), 140.
67. Rhod Rothfuss, "El marco: Un problema de plástica actual."
68. Ferreira Gullar, *Lygia Clark: Uma experiência radical (1954–1958)* (Rio de Janeiro: Departamento de Impresa Nacional, 1958).

69. Ibid.

70. Torres-García contributed an essay to *Arturo* entitled "Con respecto a una futura creación literaria" (Regarding a Future Literary Creation); a poem, "Divertimento"; and a drawing from 1932. Arden Quin claimed to have met Torres-García in 1935 and to have visited—with Maldonado, Prati, Kosice, and Rothfuss—the artist in the early 1940s. See "Chronology, 1934–1942," and "Chronology, 1943–1967," in Mari Carmen Ramírez and Cecilia Buzio de Torres, *La Escuela del Sur: El taller Torres-García y su legado*, exh. cat. (Madrid: Museo Nacional Centro de Arte Reina Sofía, 1991), 45, 48, 158. Torres-García's work was exhibited in Buenos Aires at Müller Gallery in 1942 and at Comte de Ignacio Pirovano Gallery in 1944 (as part of the Salón de pintores modernos uruguayos).

71. Nicolette Gast, "Torres-García in Paris," in Jorge Garcia et al., *The Antagonistic Link: Joaquín Torres-García, Theo van Doesburg* (Amsterdam: Institute of Contemporary Art, 1991), 72.

72. For the most detailed recent study of this body of work, see Mari Carmen Ramírez et al., *Joaquín Torres-García: Constructing Abstraction with Wood* (New Haven, CT: Yale University Press, 2009). See also see Thierry Dufrêne, "El pequeño panel de Madera de Torres-García," in Joaquín Torres-García et al., *Joaquín Torres-García: Un mundo construido*, exh. cat. (Madrid: Museo Colecciones ICO, 2002), 155–75.

73. Otto Gustaf Carlsund, Theo van Doesburg, Jean Hélion, Léon Tutundjian, and Marcel Wantz, "Base de la Peinture Concrète," *Art Concret* (Paris) (April 1930): 1.

74. Ibid., 2.

75. Agnès de Maistre, "Les Groupes d'Abstraction Géométrique," 5–6.

76. Torres-García left Uruguay in 1891 and returned in 1934, embarking on an intense pedagogical campaign that promoted what he called Universalismo Constructivo (Universal Constructivism), in which he aspired to create a dialogue between abstraction and figuration, the local and the international. Publication of the journal *Circulo y cuadrado* (Circle and Square), which promoted his ideas and the artists of La Escuela del Sur (School of the South), was initiated in 1936 in French and Spanish and continued until 1943. The magazine also published articles and statements by Mondrian, van Doesburg, Amédée Ozenfant, Jean Hélion, Jean Gorin, Georges Vantongerloo, and others, thus facilitating circulation of the ideas of the Parisian avant-garde of the 1920s and 1930s in the region.

77. Joaquín Torres-García, "Funcionalismo" (1944), in *Universalismo Constructivo* (Madrid: Alianza Editorial, 1984), 101. The book compiled lectures given by Torres-García between 1934 and 1943.

78. Theo van Doesburg, "Der Wille zum Stil (Neugestaltung von Leben, Kunst und Technik)," part 2, *De Stijl* 5, no. 3 (March 1922): 33, translated and quoted by Detlef Mertins in the introduction to Walter Curt Behrendt, *The Victory of the New Building Style* (Los Angeles: Getty Research Institute for the History of Art and the Humanities, 2000), 47. Mertins's essay is an excellent analysis of this intersection of the organic and the mechanical in German culture of the late nineteenth and early twentieth centuries.

79. Ibid., 49.

80. Joaquín Torres-García, "Funcionalismo," 102.

81. As Mari Carmen Ramírez has observed in her recent study of Torres-García's wood

reliefs, the objecthood of these works is related to the larger project of engaging "in the spiritual process of abstracting essential features from individuals and ordinary objects to synthesize them into concrete, three-dimensional signs." In her view, even the most abstract reliefs "celebrate the paradoxical traits of a form of abstraction that does not abandon the human referent." This clearly would not have suited the Argentine concretists' enterprise, as Maldonado's 1946 attack on Torres-García's attachment to figuration attests. But their likely early introduction to Torres-García's reliefs would have exposed them more directly to the visual, formal, and technical qualities of these remarkable works rather than to their "meaning." See Mari Carmen Ramírez, "A Constructed Precariousness: Abstraction Against the Grain," in Mari Carmen Ramírez et al., *Joaquín Torres-García,* 32–49 (quotes from pp. 36 and 45). See also Tomás Maldonado, "Torres-García contra el arte moderno," *Boletín de la Asociación de Arte Concreto Invención,* no. 2 (December 1946): 1–2.

82. Joaquín Torres-García, "Funcionalismo," 105.
83. Raymond Williams, *Keywords,* 227.
84. Detlef Mertins in *The Victory of the New Building Style,* 44.
85. Gyula Kosice, *Invención* (Buenos Aires), no. 1 (1945). Texts by Kosice in English, French, and Spanish accompanied the cover image of *Röyi.* A second issue of *Invención,* also published in 1945, was dedicated to Edgar Bayley, while a third, to focus on the work of Tomás Maldonado, was never realized. As Pérez-Barreiro observed: "The fact that these three names appear linked together in this fashion suggests that the concept of Invention was still enough to hold these artists together, although by the end of 1945, when we can assume Maldonado's issue was to appear, there had been a split into the two groups which would eventually lead Kosice, Arden Quin and Rothfuss into the Madi Movement and Bayley, Maldonado and Prati into the Asociación Arte Concreto-Invención." Gabriel Pérez-Barreiro, "The Argentine Avant-Garde, 1944–1950," 89. For a detailed description of *Röyi,* see ibid., 92.
86. Gyula Kosice, *Invención,* no. 1.
87. Agnès de Maistre, "Les Groupes d'Abstraction Géométrique," 41. Alejandro Crispiani points out that for Huidobro, as well as for his friend and collaborator Jean Arp, the poet is an "absolute creator," an "artist-God," and, as such, is the "irreducible expression of an exceptional individuality"; the creator is, however, separate from and parallel to the artistic creation, which is entrenched in its own world. See Vicente Huidobro, "La creación pura," in *Obra poética,* ed. C. Goic (Madrid: ALLCA XX, Ediciones Crítica, Colección Archivos, 2003), 1310, quoted in Alejandro Crispiani, *Objetos para transformar el mundo,* 66–67.
88. Kosice, *Invención,* no. 1 (text originally in English).
89. Karl Marx and Friedrich Engels, *The German Ideology,* 45.
90. Edgar Bayley, "Sobre invención poética," *Arte Concreto Invención,* no. 1 (August 1946): 13. The concept of *invention* was conceived as an alternative to *concrete;* Bayley's aesthetic proposal did not emphasize the mathematical and compositional a priori elements that were paramount for the European iteration of concretism. "IT IS NECESSARY TO REBUILD THE WORLD," he had written the year before in his essay "La batalla por la invención" (The Fight for Invention). He concluded this text by introducing a concept

that would be critical for the Brazilian neoconcretists Lygia Clark and Hélio Oiticica—that of *vivencia* (life experience): "[T]he replacement of a life experience with any other kind of reality is impossible, and any attempts to do so will only lead to the weakening of the life experience, or its complete annihilation." Edgar Bayley, "La batalla por la invención," *Invención,* no. 2 (1945).

91. For a concise and helpful account of Marx's concept of a "materialist conception of history," see Terence Ball, "History: Critique and Irony," in *The Cambridge Companion to Marx,* ed. Terrel Carver (Cambridge, New York, Melbourne: Cambridge University Press, 1991), 124–42.
92. It is possible that the initial rupture within the Invención group was based on personal differences as well as the level of political commitment expressed by the artists who formed the AACI. As Agnès de Maistre points out, the rift occurred at the precise moment when Maldonado, Bayley, Espinosa, Hlito, Claudio Girola, and Aldo Prior joined the Communist Party. See Agnès de Maistre, "Les Groupes d'Abstraction Géométrique," 50.
93. A post-*Arturo* exhibition seems to have taken place in early 1945 at the Comte Gallery in Buenos Aires. See Agnès de Maistre, "Le Mouvement Madí," in Alain Sayag et al., *Art d'Amerique latine, 1911–1968,* exh. cat. (Paris: Centre Georges Pompidou, 1992), 339; and Gabriel Pérez-Barreiro, "The Argentine Avant-Gárde, 1944–1950," 86–89.
94. Gabriel Pérez-Barreiro, "The Argentine Avant-Garde, 1944–1950," 110.
95. Ibid., 109.
96. Andrea Giunta, "Retratos de la originalidad" lecture at the symposium Auge y reinvención de la abstracción latinoamericana en el discurso del arte actual, Museo Nacional Centro de Arte Reina Sofía, Madrid, March 3, 2012.
97. This exhibition was apparently preceded by a smaller one in Maldonado's atelier in November 1945 that included works by Maldonado, Enio Iommi, Claudio Gírola, Alfredo Hlito, and Lidy Prati. See "Aclaración," *Boletín de la Asociación de Arte Concreto Invención,* no. 2 (December 1946): 2.
98. Tomás Maldonado, "Lo abstracto y lo concreto," 7.
99. Joaquín Torres-García, "Funcionalismo," 102.
100. Maldonado would object to this rapport with sculpture; see Tomás Maldonado, "Lo abstracto y lo concreto," 7.
101. Edgar Bayley et al., "Manifesto Invencionista," 8.
102. Ibid.
103. Ibid.
104. See *Art Concret* (Paris), no. 1 (April 1930).
105. Tomás Maldonado, "Lo abstracto y lo concreto," 7.
106. Ibid. A similar trajectory was rehearsed by Bayley in a presentation at the Centro de Profesores Diplomados de Buenos Aires on September 5, 1946, published as Edgar Bayley, "Introducción al arte concreto," *Boletín de la Asociación de Arte Concreto Invención,* no. 2 (December 1946): 3–4.
107. Tomás Maldonado, "Lo abstracto y lo concreto," 7.
108. Edgar Bayley et al., "Nuestra militancia," *Arte Concreto Invención,* no. 1 (August 1946): 2.
109. Ibid., 2.

110. European and American intellectuals had been growing increasingly disillusioned with the Soviet Union since the Moscow Show Trials of the 1930s. Reports of a culture of terror and oppression, the Nazi-Soviet nonaggression pact of 1939, and the Soviet invasion of Finland in 1940 led to a disenchantment that was only alleviated by the role of the Soviet Union in defeating Nazism between 1941 and 1945.
111. Simon Contreras, "Sobre las artes aplicadas a la necesidad revolucionaria y el arte de la invención concreta," *Arte Concreto Invención*, no. 1 (August 1946): 4.
112. Ibid.
113. Tomás Maldonado, "Los Artistas Concretos, el 'realismo' y la realidad," 10.
114. Alfredo Hlito, "Notas para una estética materialista," 12.
115. Alfredo Hlito referred to "Theses on Feuerbach" in his 1946 article "Representación e invención," 7.
116. Karl Marx, "Theses on Feuerbach," 574.
117. Ibid., 572.
118. Ibid., 574.
119. Ibid., 573.
120. Étienne Balibar, *The Philosophy of Marx*, 30.
121. Karl Marx and Friedrich Engels, *The German Ideology*, 25–28.
122. Karl Marx, *Capital: A Critique of Political Economy* (New York: Cerf and Klopfer, 1906), 198.
123. Edgar Bayley et al., "Manifesto Invencionista," 8.
124. Étienne Balibar, *The Philosophy of Marx*, 28. Alejandro Crispiani, *Objetos para transformar el mundo*, 109. Marx's reference to Franklin can be found in chapter 7 of *Capital*, 200.
125. Edgar Bayley, "Introducción al arte concreto," 4. These ideas had already been expressed in the editorials of *Arte Concreto Invención*, no. 1: see "Nuestra militancia," 2; and "Invención Integral," 10.
126. [Edgar Bayley], "El arte concreto constituye la culminación de un proceso estético," in *Exposición de Arte Concreto Invención* (Buenos Aires: Sociedad Argentina de Artistas Plásticos Galería de los Artistas, 1946).
127. Edgar Bayley et al., "Los amigos del pueblo," *Arte Concreto Invención*, no. 1, (August 1946): 2.
128. See Ana Longoni and Daniela Lucena, "De cómo el 'júbilo creador' se trastocó en desfachatez"; Maria Cristina Rossi, "Mirando al futuro"; and Alejandro Crispiani, *Objetos para transformar el mundo*, 137–40.
129. Ana Longoni and Daniela Lucena, "De cómo el 'júbilo creador' se trastocó en desfachatez," 126. The authors report that the meeting was meant to promote a realist canon and reject modern tendencies.
130. Alejandro Crispiani, *Objetos para transformar el mundo*, 140.
131. Carlos Altamirano, *Bajo el signo de las masas*, 28. This working mass, as Juan Carlos Torre pointed out in his study of the relationship between traditional unions and Perón, was usually portrayed as anomic and politically naive. But Torre has argued that traditional and established unions (formed by urban workers of foreign origin), as well as contingents of workers newly arrived from rural areas, were united by their dissatisfac-

tion with their status as second-class citizens. The social constellation that emerged between 1943 and 1946 was the result of a rational process. Torre wrote regarding the unions that facilitated this process: "Its positive response to Perón's call must be understood, then, not as the consequence of a phenomenon of collective anomie or cronyism, but as the result of a process of national deliberation that opposed the disadvantages of the previous social and political order [and embraced] the new opportunities that a new order had begun to offer to the working sectors through Perón." Juan Carlos Torre, *La vieja guardia sindical y Perón*, 14.

132. Alfredo Hlito, "El tema del espacio en la pintura actual," *Nueva Visión* (Buenos Aires), no. 8 (1955): 11.
133. Ibid., 13.
134. Ibid.
135. On the issue of continuity and rupture in Maldonado's postconcrete phase, see Daniela Lucena, "Arte concreto y *Nueva Visión*: Una lectura en clave política," *Aurora* 10 (2011), accessed May 20, 2012, http://www.academia.edu/5183843/Arte_concreto_y_Nueva_Visi%C3%B3n_una_lectura_en_clave_pol%C3%ADtica.
136. Tomás Maldonado, interview with Giacinto Di Pietrantonio, in Tomás Maldonado, *Escritos Preulmianos*, 123.

## 2. THE CONCRETE IDEA ON ITS WAY TO THE NONOBJECT, 1949–59

1. Max Bill, "Afirmação sobre a arte concreta," página Invenção, *Correio Paulistano*, July 17, 1960, reprinted in João Bandeira, ed., *Arte Concreta Paulista. Documentos* (São Paulo: Cosac & Naify, 2002), 60.
2. The *Suplemento Dominical do Jornal do Brasil* was the Sunday supplement of the Rio de Janeiro–based newspaper that between 1956 and 1961 became a key instrument in the promotion of concrete and neoconcrete art in Brazil. Ferreira Gullar, "Teoria do não-objeto," *Suplemento Dominical do Jornal do Brasil*, December 19–20, 1959. The *Suplemento* was one of several publications created in the 1950s to promote and discuss the art and architecture of the period. Others included *Habitat: Revista das artes no Brasil* (1950–55); *Módulo: Revista de arquitetura e artes visuais no Brasil* (1955–65); and *Arquitetura é Decoração* (1953–58), published by the studio of the architect Oscar Niemeyer.
3. This link to architecture was voiced early on by Mário Pedrosa in his "O Paradoxo Concretista," *Jornal do Brasil*, June 24, 1959, reprinted in Mário Pedrosa, *Mundo, homem, arte em crise*, ed. Aracy A. Amaral (São Paulo: Editora Perspectiva, 1986), 26–27. Pedrosa's copious writings on international architecture, Brazilian architecture, and Brasília are key to understanding the profound impact of this practice on the artistic imaginary of the young artists at that time. See also Mário Pedrosa, *Dos murais de Portinari aos espaços de Brasília*, ed. Aracy A. Amaral (São Paulo: Editora Perspectiva, 1981), 251–411.
4. The institution itself was conceived by the government of Getúlio Vargas, who was in power from 1930 to 1945, then was democratically elected in 1950 and remained president until 1954.
5. Le Corbusier's early and active presence in Brazil—his first visit took place in 1929—ignited the flame of modern architecture that contributed to the progressive intellectual

milieu of the 1950s and solidified links with European modernism. On Le Corbusier's visits to Brazil, see Fernando Pérez Oyarzún, *Le Corbusier y Sudamérica: Viajes y proyectos* (Santiago: Ediciones de la Escuela de Arquitectura–Pontificia Universidad Católica de Chile, 1991). The architects in charge of adapting Le Corbusier's architectural language for this important building included Affonso Reidy, Oscar Niemeyer, Jorge Moreira, Ernâni Vasconcellos, Carlos Leão, and Lúcio Costa. On the significance of the Ministry of Education and Health building, see Yves Bruand, *Arquitetura contemporânea no Brasil* (São Paulo: Editora Perspectiva, 1997), 81–93. For a contemporary view of the emergence of modern architecture in Brazil, see Mário Pedrosa, "Introdução à arquitetura brasileira—I–II," in Mário Pedrosa, *Dos murais de Portinari aos espaços de Brasília,* 321–35. And for a detailed account of the institutional cultural terrain of the 1940s, especially in São Paulo, see Adele Nelson, "The Monumental and the Ephemeral: The São Paulo Biennial and the Emergence of Abstraction in Brazil, 1946–1954" (PhD diss., New York University, 2012), 9–58.

6. Brasília was inaugurated in 1960 and became a clear symbol of the ambitions of the Kubitschek administration. For a classical account, see James Holston, *The Modernist City: An Anthropological Critique of Brasília* (Chicago: University of Chicago Press, 1989). On the role of architecture in Brazil's modernist and developmentalist agenda, see Aleca Le Blanc, "Palmeiras and Pilotis: Promoting Brazil with Modern Architecture," *Third Text* 26, no. 1 (January 2012): 103–16, and her dissertation "Tropical Modernisms: Art and Architecture in Rio de Janeiro in the 1950s" (PhD diss., University of Southern California, 2011). For an excellent account of Costa's and Niemeyer's conception of synthesis of the arts in Brasília, see Guilherme Wisnik, "The City as Sculpture," paper presented at a meeting of the Latin American Studies Association, San Francisco, May 24, 2012.

7. Jorge Romero Brest, "A arquitectura é a grande arte de nosso tempo—1948: Romero Brest em São Paulo," *Folha da Manhã* (São Paulo), December 17, 1950, reprinted in Aracy A. Amaral, ed., *Projeto Constructivo Brasileiro na Arte (1950–1962)* (Rio de Janeiro: Museu de Arte Moderna; São Paulo: Pinacoteca do Estado, 1977), 98. According to Pedrosa, it was Brest, along with Tomás Maldonado, who brought the discussion of concrete art to Brazil. See Fernando Cocchiarale and Anna Bella Geiger, eds., *Abstracionismo geométrico e informal: A vanguardia brasileira nos anos cinqüenta* (Rio de Janeiro: Funarte, 1987), 105. On Brest's first visit to São Paulo, recorded as having taken place in 1948 but probably not occurring until 1950, see María Amalia García, "La construcción del arte abstracto: Impactos e interconexiones entre el internacionalismo cultural paulista y la escena artística argentina, 1949–1953," in María Amalia García, María Cristina Rossi, and Luisa Fabiana Servidio, *Arte Argentino y Latinoamericano del siglo XX: Sus interrelaciones* (Buenos Aires: Fundación Espigas, 2004), 33–34. This chronology is confirmed in *Abstracionismo geométrico e informal,* 35.

8. The engineer-turned-artist André Bloc was a founder of the Group Espace and publisher of *L'Architecture d'Aujourd'hui,* launched in Paris in 1930. The magazine strongly supported the geometric abstract tendencies of the period and was attentive to international architectural developments, including those in South America. The Museu de Arte Moderna do Rio de Janeiro hosted an exhibition of artists associated with the

group entitled *Grupo Espaço de Paris* in 1955. See Aleca Le Blanc, "Tropical Modernisms," 250.

9. One of the first substantial critical analyses of concrete and neoconcrete art in Brazil was Ronaldo Brito's 1975 essay "Neoconcretismo: Vértice e ruptura do projeto construtivo brasileiro." The study was not published until 1985, when it was translated into English. See Ronaldo Brito, *Neoconcretism: Peak and Rupture of the Brazilian Constructivist Project,* trans. Lia Alvarenga and Florence Eleanor (Rio de Janeiro: Funarte, 1985). The architectural imaginary was so strong in Brazil that it remained a crucial reference in the neoconcrete and post-neoconcrete work of Clark and Oiticica. Clark, for example, speaking about the spatial dimension of her *Bichos* (Critters) of 1960–64 and her *Caminhando* (Walking) of 1963, stated: "When space [became] truly architectural, it completely revolutionized me viscerally. . . . How different it is to do a painting or a sculpture and think in terms of architecture! It is there that the collective thing might appear, since now it is not me alone who counts but fundamentally *everyone.*" Lygia Clark, "1963.4," Diário-2 folder, Archives of the Associação Cultural "O Mundo de Lygia Clark," Rio de Janeiro.

10. Frederico Morais, "Vocação construtiva (mas o caos permanece)," in *Artes plásticas na América Latina: do transe ao transitório* (Rio de Janeiro: Editora Civilização Brasileira, 1979), 88. For a detailed study of the rapport between import substitution industrialization and Brazilian concrete art, see Aleca Le Blanc, "Tropical Modernisms," especially chapters 1 and 4.

11. As Otília Beatriz Fiori Arantes recounts, "We could not conceive of cultural activity that was not in the service of the *figuration* of the country, that was not [an] instrument of knowledge and consolidation of the *image* of a country still very uncertain of itself; painting was to help discover it, to build in sections a nation diminished by the colonial complex." Otília Beatriz Fiori Arantes, *Mário Pedrosa: Itinerário crítico* (São Paulo: Cosac Naify, 2004), 62. Artists who were identified with the project of nation building through art, such as Cândido Portinari and Emiliano Di Cavalcanti, had grown close to the government of Getúlio Vargas through public commissions and were therefore problematic in the view of the influential Trotskyist critic Mário Pedrosa, an early and vocal supporter of concrete art.

12. For more on the exhibition, which opened on March 8, 1949, and León Degand's presence in Brazil, see Adele Nelson, "The Monumental and the Ephemeral," 58–95.

13. The exhibition, entitled *Grupo de artistas modernos argentinos,* took place between August 6 and 23, 1953, and included the concrete artists Tomás Maldonado, Alfredo Hlito, and Lidy Prati. For more on Maldonado's influence during the early 1950s, see the recollections by the artists João José and Décio Vieira in Frederico Morais, "Grupo Frente—a primera turma," in *Ciclo de exposições sobre arte no Rio de Janeiro,* vol. 2 (*Grupo Frente, 1954–1956*); and vol. 3 (*I Exposição nacional de arte abstrata, Hotel Quitandinha, 1953*) (Rio de Janeiro: Galeria de Arte BANERJ, 1984), n.p.

14. The artist Antônio Maluf, designer of the well-known poster for the first São Paulo Bienal, declared in an interview that he was introduced to the notion of art as product at the Instituto de Arte Contemporânea. In drawing and printmaking courses, he was also exposed to concrete art and geometric abstraction. "Antônio Maluf em depoimento

a Mayra Laudanna, Jun. 2002: O conceito de arte concreta a partir de meu trabalho," in *Arte concreta Paulista: Documentos*, ed. João Bandeira (São Paulo: Cosac & Naify, 2002), 41. At the Museu de Arte Moderna do Rio de Janeiro, the director Niomar Moniz Sodré tried unsuccessfully to establish the Escola Técnica da Criação (Technical School of Creation) with the assistance of Tomás Maldonado. Despite this failed effort, the museum offered an active educational program with a range of studio and art history courses, lectures, and conferences. Classes led by the artist Ivan Serpa at the museum, initiated in 1952, were instrumental in introducing concrete art and geometric abstraction to young artists in Rio de Janeiro, and Waldemar Cordeiro in São Paulo had, since the late 1940s, been acquainted with Italian avant-garde groups such as Forma and the Art Club of Rome. See Aleca Le Blanc, "Tropical Modernisms," 215–21; and Adrian Anagnost, "Internationalism, *Brasilidade*, and Politics: Waldemar Cordeiro and the Search for a Universal Language," *Hemisphere: Journal of the Americas* 3 (2010): 23–41. For more on the Instituto de Arte Contemporânea, see Adele Nelson, "The Monumental and the Ephemeral," 121–28.

15. Founded in 1947, the Museu de Arte de São Paulo was the project of the media tycoon Assis Chateaubriand and its first director, Pietro Maria Bardi; the Museu de Arte Moderna de São Paulo was founded in 1948 by the industrialist Francisco (Ciccillo) Matarazzo Sobrinho; and the Museu de Arte Moderna do Rio de Janeiro was conceived by Paulo Bittencourt, owner of the Rio de Janeiro–based newspaper *Correio da Manhã*, and officially opened in 1948.

16. Aleca Le Blanc, "Tropical Modernisms," 33. For a concise analysis of these institutions and their role in the formation of concrete poetry in Brazil, see Gonzalo Aguilar, *Poesía concreta brasileña: Las vanguardias en la encrucijada modernista* (Rosario: Beatriz Viterbo Editora, 2003), 57–62. For the most recent scholarship on the subject in English, see Aleca Le Blanc, "Tropical Modernisms," and Adele Nelson, "The Monumental and the Ephemeral."

17. See for example Mário Pedrosa, "A primeira Bienal—I," *Jornal do Brasil*, October 27, 1951, reprinted in Mário Pedrosa, *Dos murais de Portinari aos espaços de Brasília*, 39–42; Ferreira Gullar, "Arte Concreta," *Suplemento Dominical do Jornal do Brasil*, June 25, 1960; and Aracy A. Amaral, "The Advent of Geometric Abstraction in Brazil," in *Arte construtiva no Brasil: Coleção Adolpho Leirner*, ed. Aracy A. Amaral (São Paulo: DBA Artes Gráficas, 1998), 29–63. As recent scholarship indicates, while abstraction was well under way in Brazil, the Bienal catalyzed concrete art locally and nationally. Adele Nelson observes: "In the two years between the first and second biennials, local artists established two new abstract artistic groups, the Grupo Ruptura (Rupture Group) and Atelier Abstração (Abstraction Studio), and virtually every month brought a new exhibition of abstract art." Adele Nelson, "The Monumental and the Ephemeral," 111; see also her chapter 3, "Creating History: The Definition of Modernism at the Second São Paulo Biennial," for the crucial role this second iteration of the event had on the concrete groups emerging at the time (1953–54) in São Paulo and Rio de Janeiro.

18. After the war, Swiss artists most energetically rehabilitated the legacy of concrete art, thanks in part to Bill's efforts in this realm. Since the 1930s, adept artists in the movement—including Richard Paul Lohse, Verenea Loewensberg, Camille Graeser, and Bill

himself—had produced and exhibited works in a geometric abstract style. In 1944 an exhibition of concrete art (*Konkrete Kunst*) took place at Kunsthalle Basel under Bill's supervision. See Willy Rotzler, "Incubation and Radiation," in *Constructive Concepts: A History of Constructive Art from Cubism to the Present* (New York: Rizzoli, 1977), 137–60. It is important to note, as María Amalia García has done, that Bill was not part of the Swiss delegation to the Bienal; rather, he had received a personal invitation to participate from the organizing committee. For an excellent account of the reception of Bill's work in Brazil, see María Amalia García, "Ações e contatos regionais da arte concreta," *Revista USP*, no. 79 (September–November 2008): 196–204.

19. Early in 1951 Bill had exhibited at the new Museu de Arte de São Paulo, but the event lacked the resonance of the Bienal, at least in the press. For a clarification on dates regarding this show, mistakenly thought to have taken place in 1950, see Adele Nelson, "Monumental and Ephemeral: The Early São Paulo Bienals," in *Constructive Spirit: Abstract Art in South and North America, 1920s–1950s*, exh. cat. (Newark, NJ: Newark Museum of Art; San Francisco: Pomegranate Press, 2010), 139, note 8. See also María Amalia García, "La construcción del arte abstracto," 18, note 22; and Lorenzo Mammi et al., *Concreta '56: A raiz da forma / Concrete '56: The Root of Form*, exh. cat. (São Paulo: Museu de Arte Moderna de São Paulo, 2006), 22–50. Tomás Maldonado's journal *Nueva Visión* (first published in 1951) also would have been a source of information for the young Brazilian artists. Bill published several essays in *Nueva Visión*, and in 1955 Maldonado edited a monograph on Bill (part of the Nueva Visión series of books that he published with Alfredo Hlito). Bill first visited Brazil in 1953 for three weeks and returned to serve on the jury of the São Paulo Bienal the following year. On his first trip to the country he participated in conferences and gave interviews that contributed to his status as a crucial influence in the Brazilian artistic context. The Brazilian artists Ivan Serpa and Abraham Palatnik were also awarded prizes for their abstract works in the first Bienal, a testament to the early endorsement of the new artistic tendency by the jury, which included the Argentine critic Jorge Romero Brest. For more on the presence of Brazilian abstraction in the first São Paulo Bienal, see Adele Nelson, "The Monumental and the Ephemeral," 161–78.

20. According to Fernando Cocchiarale and Anna Bella Geiger, initial experiments with abstract art in 1948 can be attributed to Ivan Serpa, Abraham Palatnik, and Almir Mavignier and were associated with the critic and historian Mário Pedrosa in Rio de Janeiro. In São Paulo, Waldemar Cordeiro became the founder of the Art Club in 1949 and joined Luís Sacilotto and Lothar Charoux to constitute the first group of abstract concrete–oriented artists in Brazil. See *Abstracionismo geométrico e informal*, 11.

21. Max Bill, "Die mathematische Denkweise in der Kunst unserer Zeit," *Werk* (Bern) 36, no. 3 (March 1949): 86–91. This essay appeared as "El Pensamiento Matemático en el Arte de Nuestro Tiempo" *Ver y Estimar*, no. 17 (May 1950), and was reprinted in German, Spanish, English, and French in Tomás Maldonado, ed., *Max Bill* (Buenos Aires: Editora Nueva Visión, 1955), 36–43. I cite this English translation, by Veronica Kleiber.

22. Max Bill, "The Bauhaus Ideas from Weimar to Ulm," in *Architects Yearbook*, vol. 5, ed. Morton Shand (London: Elek Books, 1953), 29–32, as cited in Paul Betts, "Science, Semiotics and Society: The Ulm Hochschule für Gestaltung in Retrospect," *Design Issues*, no.

2 (Summer 1998): 72. See also Bill's essay "Form, Function, Beauty" in *Max Bill*, ed. Tomás Maldonado, 119, where he wrote: "Since form means 'the sum of all functions in harmonious unison,' and since 'Form = Art = Beauty,' the obvious conclusion is that Art as well as Beauty may also be defined as the 'sum of all functions in harmonious unison.'" The same idea had been put forward in another essay by Bill, "Form and Art," which introduced his book *Form: A Balance Sheet of Mid-Twentieth Century Trends in Design* (Basel: Verlag Karl Werner, 1952), 7–11. This tripartite concept of form/beauty/function was first theorized by Bill in his lecture at the Werkbund's meeting in Basel in October 1948, and was published as "Schönheit aus Funktion und als Funktion," *Werk* 36, no. 8 (August 1949): 272–74; see the preface and acknowledgments in his book *Form*, page 5. This essay was also published in Brazil as "Beleza provida da função e como função," *Habitat* 2 (January–March 1951): 61–65, and reprinted as "Beauty from Function and as Function," in Max Bill, *Form, Function, Beauty = Gestalt*, trans. and ed. Pamela Johnston (London: Architectural Association London, 2010), 32–41 (subsequent citations are to this last reprinted version).

23. Max Bill, "Continuity and Change," in *Form, Function, Beauty = Gestalt*, 77–80.
24. Paul Betts, "Science, Semiotics and Society," 68.
25. Neoconcrete artists previously involved with the Grupo Frente include Lygia Clark, Lygia Pape, Franz Weissmann, and Amilcar de Castro.
26. Ferreira Gullar, "Max Bill," *Suplemento Dominical do Jornal do Brasil*, July 23, 1960.
27. Max Bill, "Beauty from Function and as Function," 32.
28. Ibid., 34.
29. Max Bill, "A, B, C, D . . . ," in *Form, Function, Beauty = Gestalt*, 47.
30. Ibid., 47, 55.
31. On the notion of "transversal" thought in the work of Max Bill, see Hans Frei, "Max Bill's Transversal," *2G* (Barcelona) "Max Bill Architect" special issue, nos. 29–30 (2004): 20–29.
32. Max Bill, "Konkrete Gestaltung," in *Zeitprobleme in der Schweizer Malerei und Plastik*, exh. cat. (Zurich: Kunsthaus, 1936). An English translation of this essay was recently published as "Concrete Design" in the "Max Bill Architect" special issue of *2G*, page 255. It is from this version that I quote. Bill revised the essay and retitled it "Concrete Art" for *Zürcher Konkrete Kunst: Max Bill, Lanfranco Bombelli Tiravanti, Heinrich Eichmann, Hans Fischli, Camille Graeser, Vreni Loewensberg, Richard Paul Lohse*, exh. cat. (Stuttgart: Galerie Lutz und Meyer, 1949). Other important influences from the fields of design and architecture acknowledged by Bill include Henry van de Velde, Adolf Loos, and Walter Gropius. See Max Bill, *Form, Function, Beauty = Gestalt*.
33. On the term *Gestaltung* in German, see note 54 below.
34. Max Bill, "Concrete Design," 255.
35. Hans Frei, "Max Bill's Transversal," 23.
36. See for example Ferreira Gullar, "Arte Concreta," *Suplemento Dominical do Jornal do Brasil*, June 23, 1960.
37. Max Bill, "Structure as Art? Art as Structure?," in *Structure in Art and Science*, ed. György Kepes (New York: Braziller, 1965), 150.
38. See for example Ferreira Gullar, "Os Neoconcretos e a Gestalt," *Suplemento Dominical do Jornal do Brasil*, March 15, 1959.

39. Interestingly, Kurt Koffka, one of the German founders of Gestalt theory, wrote in 1940: "[M]uch as we may be interested in the artist, we are not, or certainly not in the same way, interested in the artisan. . . . I do not want to say that the psychology of furniture, of tools, of products of engineering may not at one time become a definite and valuable object of enquiry. . . . But even so it remains true that the psychology of art has preceded all such endeavors and that the creator will play a very different role in those other fields from the one he has in the psychology of art. In a work of art the artist speaks to the spectator, but no such relationship exists between the engineers and the buyers and drivers of motor cars." Kurt Koffka, "Problems in the Psychology of Art," in *Art: A Bryn Mawr Symposium* (Lancaster, PA: Bryn Mawr College, 1940), 200. Discussions of Gestalt/gestalt in debates concerning art, design, and architecture in Germany in the 1920s attest to the liveliness of Gestalt theory across material practices. See Detlef Mertins's introduction to Walter Curt Behrendt, *The Victory of the New Building Style* (Los Angeles: Getty Research Institute for the History of Art and the Humanities, 2000), 53–54.
40. See Hans M. Wingler, *Bauhaus: Weimar, Dessau, Berlin, Chicago* (Boston: MIT Press, 1969), 159. Detlef Mertins writes that "before his dismissal as director of the Bauhaus, in 1930, [Hannes Meyer] had planned to introduce courses in sociology and Gestalt psychology. . . . Visual training for psychic well-being went hand in hand with social reorganization and the organic way of living that was to be made possible through advances in industry and science." Detlef Mertins, "Hannes Meyer: German Trade Unions School, Bernau 1928–1930," in *Bauhaus, 1919–1933: Workshops for Modernity*, exh. cat., ed. Barry Bergdoll and Leah Dickerman (New York: Museum of Modern Art, 2010), 260. This holistic approach would be echoed by Bill in his goal for a design practice that ranged "from plastic tea-cups to the planning of better towns." Max Bill, "Form and Art," 11.
41. Paul Overy, *Kandinsky: The Language of the Eye* (New York: Praeger, 1969), 49.
42. Frederick A. Horowitz traces Albers's relationship to Gestalt theory and how it influenced his concept of design in "Albers the Teacher," in *Josef Albers: To Open Eyes: The Bauhaus, Black Mountain College, and Yale* (London and New York: Phaidon Press, 2006), 73–272.
43. For an excellent and nuanced account of Gestalt theory and its institutional background, see Mitchell G. Ash, "Gestalt Psychology: Origins in Germany and Reception in the United States," in *Points of View in the Modern History of Psychology*, ed. Claude E. Buxton (San Diego, CA: Academic Press, 1985), 295–344.
44. Ibid., 308.
45. Solomon E. Asch, "Gestalt Theory," *International Encyclopedia of the Social Sciences*, vol. 6 (New York: Macmillan, 1968), 160. The law of "good form," which alludes to strongly organized forms, was formulated by Max Wertheimer in 1914.
46. Mitchell G. Ash, *Gestalt Psychology in German Culture, 1890–1967: Holism and the Quest for Objectivity* (New York: Cambridge University Press, 1995), 185–86.
47. Max Bill, "Form and Art," 7.
48. Max Bill, "Continuity and Change," 75.
49. Max Bill, "Visita ao Brasil do famoso escultor modernista," *Boletim do Museu de Arte Moderna do Rio de Janeiro*, no. 9 (July 1953): 5.

50. Max Bill, "The Basis and Aims of Aesthetics in the Machine Age," in *Form, Function, Beauty = Gestalt,* 62–66. This lecture was delivered in Paris on the occasion of the first international conference on industrial aesthetics, organized by L'Institut d'Esthétique Industrielle.
51. Ibid., 67.
52. Hans Frei has observed, "In Max Bill's view 'Concrete design' could easily be transferred to organic forms and sculptures if they were developed 'out of their own means and laws.'" Hans Frei, "Max Bill's Transversal," 23.
53. Jean Arp, "Concrete Art," in *Arp on Arp* (New York: Viking, 1972), 139.
54. Detlef Mertins, introduction to *The Victory of the New Building Style,* 31. *Gestaltung* was a key concept in the architectural critic Walter Curt Behrendt's forging of the term *Baustil* (building style), the subject of Mertins's essay. Behrendt's intellectual background, which he shared with such architectural luminaries as Walter Gropius, Ludwig Mies van der Rohe, Le Corbusier, Sigfried Giedion, and Adolf Behne, sheds light on German intellectual discussions on art, architecture, and design of the interwar period to which Bill was clearly indebted. For example, Mertins writes, "[T]he key instrument in the battle for a new style as utopia was the principle of direct, unmediated, and unimpeded organic expression operative at the level of material means and life functions and at the higher level of spirit. Its signs were 'good form'—self-identical and self-determined, the outer expression of inner formative forces—and 'quality,' the elusive ideal of the Werkbund to restore the spiritual effect of the craft object under the conditions of mechanical reproduction. Embracing packaging and marketing, as well as the design and production of objects, good design became the guarantor of quality. All this was incorporated in the idea of *Gestaltung,* at once form, formation, form creation, and configuration—verb as well as noun, process as well as product, force as well as form. *Gestaltung* was the form-generating activity of all organic beings and of life itself. It was the process of actualizing forces, *Gestaltungskräfte.* As such, *Gestaltung* was the form of activity through which style, organicity, and unity were to be achieved in a struggle against the conflictive nature of the present period of transition. Moreover, the activity of *Gestaltung* promised to resolve the antinomies of modernity, for it was the principle of nature's own self-fashioning creativity, as well as the regulative principle in art and technology. In art, it served to spiritualize living substance *(lebender Stoff).* It marked the activity of life itself understood as ceaseless self-generation. Offered as the antithesis of imitation, it reestablished mimesis in terms of process rather than form." Detlef Mertins, introduction to *The Victory of the New Building Style,* 44–45. It is beyond the scope of this book to unpack the rich interweavings between aesthetic theory and design theory that informed Bill's own theories. But, as can be grasped from the above citation, it is clear that the Swiss artist's notions of beauty, harmony, good form, the organic, et cetera were clearly indebted to this constellation of references. He was surely exposed to these concepts of form and style—first while at the Bauhaus through Hannes Meyer's own holistic approach to material culture, and later as a member of the Swiss Werkbund.
55. Ferreira Gullar, "Arte concreta 6; Tentativa de compreensão," *Suplemento Dominical do Jornal do Brasil,* September 10, 1960.

56. Maurice Merleau-Ponty, *The Structure of Behavior,* trans. Alden L. Fisher (Boston: Beacon Press, 1963), 159, 161. Ferreira Gullar explicitly engaged with this early (1942) book by Merleau-Ponty in his essay "Arte concreta 6."
57. Ferreira Gullar, "Da arte Concreta a arte Neoconcreta," *Módulo* (Rio de Janeiro), no. 13 (March 1959): 31, reprinted in *Suplemento Dominical do Jornal do Brasil,* July 7, 1959.
58. Maurice Merleau-Ponty, *The Phenomenology of Perception* (1962), trans. Colin Smith (London: Routledge, 1995), 52, 55.
59. Ferreira Gullar, "Da arte Concreta a arte Neoconcreta," 31.
60. Max Bill, *Fifteen Variations on a Single Theme,* 16 lithographs (Paris: Editions des Chroniques du Jour, 1938); text reprinted in Max Bill and James N. Wood, *Max Bill,* exh. cat. (Buffalo, NY: Buffalo Fine Arts Academy and Albright-Knox Art Gallery, 1974), 54.
61. Mário Pedrosa, "Da natureza afetiva da forma na obra de arte," in *Arte/forma e personalidade* (São Paulo: Kairos, 1979), 23.
62. Ferreira Gullar et al., "Manifesto Neoconcreto," *Suplemento Dominical do Jornal do Brasil,* March 21–22, 1959.
63. Hubertus Gassner, "The Constructivists: Modernism on the Way to Modernization," in *The Great Utopia: The Russian and Soviet Avant-Garde, 1915–1932* (New York: Guggenheim Museum, 1992), 317. I am referring to the construction/composition debate held at Inkhuk led by the General Working Group of Objective Analysis. There, Alexander Rodchenko and his colleagues spent four months debating the nature of construction, an exercise that would help them rethink the role of art in postrevolutionary Russia. While for Bill art was to sustain its functional autonomy vis-à-vis the practical utilitarianism of design, to the constructivists this aesthetic functionality was to be a transitional phase in a trajectory that implied a move away from painting toward product. See Hubertus Gassner, "The Constructivists," 312–16.
64. Otto Gustaf Carlsund, Theo van Doesburg, Jean Hélion, Léon Tutundjian, and Marcel Wantz, "Base de la Peinture Concrète," *Art Concret* (Paris), no. 1 (April 1930): 1, reprinted in *The Tradition of Constructivism,* ed. Stephen Bann (New York: Da Capo Press, 1974), 193. Two principles in this important document regarding the identification between work and concept are worth quoting. Point 2 reads in part: "The work of art must be entirely conceived and formed by the mind before its execution." Point 4 reads: "The construction of the picture, as well as its elements, must be simple and visually controllable."
65. The year 1952 also saw the publication of Max Bill's book *Form: A Balance Sheet of Mid-Twentieth Century Trends in Design* (see note 22), which likely circulated in Brazil and Argentina. The publication featured a grid-based layout; six-point sans-serif typography; multilingual text (English, German, and French); a square format; and a minimalist cover in blue with the title, in black, centered just above the lower edge of the book. As Bill stated in his preface and acknowledgments, the book included all the pictures in the exhibition *Die Gute Form* as well as images of cars, works of art, furniture, domestic wares, natural formations, toys, jewelry, architecture, bridges, urban dwellings, and landscaping. It built on earlier publications concerned with typologies of building and industrial structures, for instance Walter Gropius's "Monumentale Kunst und Industriebau," a lecture given at the Folkwang-Museum in Hagen on April 10, 1911; Paul

Schultze-Naumburg, *Kulturarbeiten,* a series of nine books published from 1901 to 1917 (Munich: Callwey) addressing the structures of the built environment; and Werner Lindner, *Die Ingenieurbauten in ihrer guten Gestaltung* (Berlin: E. Wasmuth, 1923). See Detlef Mertins, introduction to *The Victory of the New Building Style,* 34–35, 48. In 1955 Tomás Maldonado published a book on Bill that included several important works and texts by Bill and echoed all of the graphic features mentioned above. The title on the cover reads *Max Bill,* but inside it is twice printed as *Tomas Maldonado: Max Bill* [*sic*] as if to establish a direct connection between author and artist. See Tomás Maldonado, *Max Bill* (Buenos Aires: Ediciones Nueva Visión, 1955). That year Maldonado went to Ulm, Germany, to work with Bill (see chapter 1).

66. Lothar Charoux, Waldemar Cordeiro, Geraldo de Barros, Kazmer Féjer, Leopoldo Haar, Luís Sacilotto, and Anatol Wladyslaw, "Manifesto Ruptura," reprinted in Aracy A. Amaral, *Projeto Constructivo Brasileiro na Arte,* 69. On Grupo Ruptura, see Ana Maria Belluzzo, "Rupture and Concrete Art," in *Arte construtiva no Brasil,* 95–141; and Erin Aldana, "Mechanisms of the Individual and the Social: Arte Concreta and São Paulo," in *The Geometry of Hope: Latin American Art from the Patricia Phelps de Cisneros Collection,* exh. cat., ed. Gabriel Pérez-Barreiro (Austin: Blanton Museum of Art, University of Texas at Austin, 2007), 39–49.
67. The group that coalesced around Serpa at the time met at his house on weekends. These gatherings, according to recollections recorded by Frederico Morais for an exhibition organized for the Galeria de Arte Banerj in 1984, also took place in the houses of artists Vincent Ibberson, Lygia Pape, and Décio Vieira. See Frederico Morais, "Grupo Frente."
68. Ibid. Grupo Frente had a total of four exhibitions between 1954 and 1956.
69. Ibid.
70. Adele Nelson, "The Monumental and the Ephemeral," 234–36. This second Bienal, which coincided with the celebration of the fourth centennial of the city of São Paulo, took place in a newly constructed complex of modernist buildings in Ibirapuera Park designed by the architect Oscar Niemeyer.
71. Décio Pignatari, "Forma, função e projeto geral," *Arquitetura e Decoração* (São Paulo), no. 24 (July–August 1957), reprinted in Aracy A. Amaral, *Projeto Constructivo Brasileiro na arte,* 76–77. Originally a member of the São Paulo–based Noigandres group of poets founded by the brothers Haroldo and Augusto de Campos, Pignatari was one of nine poets to participate in the inaugural Exposição Nacional de Arte Concreta (National Exhibition of Concrete Art ) in 1956–57, which brought together the groups from São Paulo and Rio de Janeiro. A close dialogue between poetry and the visual arts characterized Brazilian concretism. Poems printed as posters were shown, along with paintings and sculptures, at the Exposição Nacional de Arte Concreta of 1956–57.
72. Ronaldo Brito, *Neoconcretism,* 104.
73. Contemporary objections to this continuity between the Bauhaus and the Ulm Hochschule für Gestaltung were raised by, among others, the Danish artist Asger Jorn, who proposed a counterimaginist Bauhaus, and Reyner Banham, who referred to Max Bill as an "advocate of a bygone era." Hans Frei, "Max Bill's Transversal," 20. To his critics, Bill's "good form" and its integration into the world of commodities was the consum-

mation of a pervasive danger in prewar constructivist artistic practices, which risked full integration into the prevailing economic system of their time. Capitalism and the highly developed market of consumption in postwar Germany provided the conditions, despite Ulm's anticommercial stance, for a transformation of Bill's "moral idealisms of 'good form' into highbrow product advertising." Paul Betts, "Science, Semiotics and Society," 74.

74. As Décio Pignatari later declared, "The objectivity of concrete art was profoundly linked to a Marxist revolution." Quoted in Décio Pignatari, "Entrevista," in *Abstracionismo geométrico e informal,* 72. For Ferreira Gullar, see his "Da arte Concreta a arte Neoconcreta," *Módulo* (Rio de Janeiro), no. 13 (March 1959), 31.

75. Décio Pignatari, "Forma, função e projeto geral," 76.

76. For an assessment of geometric abstract art in Europe in the years following the end of the war, see Véronique Wiesinger, "Mouvements et marchés de l'abstraction: De la Libération de Paris à la 'Documenta II' de Casel (1944–1959)" and "L'art cinétique dans la guerre des marchés: De l'hommage à New York à l'ouverture du Centre Georges Pompidou, 1960–1977," in *Denise René, l'intrépide: Une galerie dans l'aventure de l'art abstrait, 1944–1978,* exh. cat. (Paris: Éditions du Centre Pompidou, 2001), 43–53, 129–41.

77. Décio Pignatari, "Forma, função e projeto geral," 76.

78. Ibid.

79. Ibid.

80. Ibid., 77.

81. See for example Aleca Le Blanc, "Tropical Modernisms"; Adele Nelson, "The Monumental and the Ephemeral"; and Irene Small, "Exit and Impasse: Ferreira Gullar and the 'New History' of the Last Avant-Garde," *Third Text* 26, no. 1 (January 2012): 91–101.

82. See Décio Pignatari, "Entrevista," in *Abstracionismo geométrico e informal,* 71–83. This applies to Grupo Frente as well. As its members stated in 1955: "Our group intends to make of art a practical activity with the objective of integrating it completely with life and contemporary society . . . . [Art] must intervene in the production of modern industry, so that those objects created by industry become works of art, in a perfect synchronization between form and function." Frederico Morais, "Grupo Frente." Lygia Pape recalled in an interview published in 1987 that artists in São Paulo and Rio de Janeiro—herself included—developed parallel work in graphic design; see *Abstracionismo geométrico e informal,* 157. On these links between art and design, see Daniela Name and Felipe Scovino, *Diálogo Concreto: Design e construtivismo no Brasil* (Rio de Janeiro: Caixa Cultural, 2008).

83. On links with poetry, which are ripe for investigation, see Claus Clüver, "The Noigandres Poets and Concrete Art," *CiberLetras* (City University of New York), no. 17 (July 2007), http://www.lehman.cuny.edu/ciberletras/v17/cluver.htm; Gonzalo Aguilar, *Poesía concreta brasileña,* 69–79; and Sérgio Martins, *Constructing an Avant-Garde: Art in Brazil 1949–1979* (Cambridge, MA: MIT Press), 31–40. On concrete poetry and gestalt, see Gonzalo Aguilar, *Poesía concreta brasileña,* 212–27; and João Bandeira, "Words in Space: Poetry at the National Exhibition of Concrete Art," in *Concreta '56: a raiz da forma,* 121–41. On design and the concrete artists, see Alexandre Wollner, "The Emergence of Visual Design," in *Constructive Art in Brazil: Adolpho Leirner Collection,* ed.

Aracy A. Amaral (São Paulo: DBA Artes Gráficas, 1998), 222–59; Daniela Name and Felipe Scovino, *Diálogo Concreto*; and Aleca Le Blanc, "Tropical Modernisms," 264–66.

84. Waldemar Cordeiro, "Ainda o abstracionismo," *Revista dos Novíssimos* 1, no. 1 (January–February 1949): 27–28, reprinted in *Waldemar Cordeiro: Uma aventura da razão* (São Paulo: Museu de Arte Contemporânea da Universidade de São Paulo, 1986), 43.
85. Sérgio Martins, *Constructing an Avant-Garde*, 24.
86. See Otília Beatriz Fiori Arantes, preface to Mário Pedrosa, *Arte/forma e personalidade* (São Paulo: Kairos, 1979), 2. Arantes observes that Pedrosa represents a rare early attempt to deal with Gestalt theory in the field of art and aesthetics. The canonical text on the topic, Rudolf Arnheim's *Art and Visual Perception*, was first published in London in 1941. Prior to that, she argued, only Gestalt theory founder Kurt Koffka (cited by Pedrosa throughout his own study) had addressed the topic in "Problems in the Psychology of Art," 180–272. In fact, Gestalt psychology was influential throughout the highly advanced art critical discourse of Germany in the 1920s and 1930s. Frederic Schwartz has written recently on the art historian Hans Sedlmayr's use of Gestalt psychology in his work of the 1930s and has referred to the impact of the Gestalt psychologist Karl Bühler on art historians in Vienna. See Frederic J. Schwartz, *Blind Spots: Critical Theory and the History of Art in Twentieth-Century Germany* (New Haven, CT: Yale University Press), 153–67, 186–87.
87. For a recollection of the regular "salons" held by Pedrosa and his wife, Mary Houston, see Luciano Martins, "A utopia como modo de vida. Fragmentos de lembrança de Mário Pedrosa," in *Mário Pedrosa e o Brasil*, ed. José Castilho Neto (São Paulo: Editora Fundação Perseu Abramo, 2001), 33–36. Lygia Pape also confirmed that in the early 1950s, young artists experimenting with geometric abstraction in Rio de Janeiro (soon to become Grupo Frente) visited Ivan Serpa's house as well as Pedrosa's; see Frederico Morais, "Grupo Frente." Pape also indicated that Pedrosa's thesis was relevant to the emergence of geometric abstraction in Brazil. See Lygia Pape, "Entrevista," in *Abstracionismo geométrico e informal*, 153.
88. Mário Pedrosa, "Da natureza afetiva da forma na obra de arte," 13.
89. Ibid., 16.
90. Ibid., 24.
91. See Mitchell G. Ash, *Gestalt Psychology in German Culture*, 2.
92. Mário Pedrosa, "Da natureza afetiva da forma na obra de arte," 47.
93. Mitchell G. Ash, "Gestalt Psychology," 299–300. Bergson would become a key influence on Oiticica, as is evident in his writings. See Mari Carmen Ramírez, "The Embodiment of Color—'From the Inside Out,'" in *Hélio Oiticica: The Body of Color*, exh. cat., ed. Mari Carmen Ramírez (Houston: Museum of Fine Arts; London: Tate Modern, 2007), 27–73.
94. "Psychology," Koffka argued, "is concerned with the totality of experience, its objective no less than its subjective side." Kurt Koffka, "Problems in the Psychology of Art," 194. In Pedrosa's formulation, then, form is the universal element we all perceive, but each of us perceives it subjectively—differently and situationally.
95. Mário Pedrosa, "Da natureza afetiva da forma na obra de arte," 56.
96. In the view of Koffka, whose text Pedrosa follows closely, "the emotional reaction is an intelligible, not a purely contingent, result of the properties of the object: the sub-

lime commands awe and admiration, the horrible repels and makes us feel horror, the funny gives us that complex emotion that expresses itself in laughter, and the beautiful attracts us and stirs in us an emotion which we may well call love." Kurt Koffka, "Problems in the Psychology of Art," 208.

97. Early criticism of Gestalt theory's weak treatment of the subject of perception points to a topic close "to the heart of the Gestalt theorists' position and concerns," wrote Ash. "This critique can be summarized in William Stern's (1928) slogan 'No Gestalt without a Gestalter.' Stern maintained that continuing references to the dependence of perception on the state of the organism at a given time were not sufficient to account for the specifically human aspects of experience." Mitchell G. Ash, "Gestalt Psychology," 323. A thorough critique of the discipline would be undertaken by Maurice Merleau-Ponty in *The Structure of Behavior* (1942; see note 56).

98. Ferreira Gullar, "Arte concreta 6."

99. Maurice Merleau-Ponty, *The Structure of Behavior,* 136. Form, Merleau-Ponty insisted, "is not a physical reality, but an object of perception"; it "cannot be defined in terms of reality but in terms of knowledge." Conceived as a unity, form is constructed for science according to an artificial (positivist) conception of causality that ignores dispersion, discontinuities, and interferences—to wit, "the ambivalence of time and space at the level of perceptual consciousness" (143–44). Here, Merleau-Ponty follows Edmund Husserl, for whom Gestalt theory considered consciousness as a form among others (corresponding to the gestalts found in nature—psychological isomorphism). "As Husserl sees it," wrote Merleau-Ponty, "the very fact that one uses the same term 'Gestalt' to designate the unity of consciousness and that of the lamp justifies the conclusion that Gestalt psychology naturalizes consciousness. It defines consciousness as other objects can be defined, and does not see that it is the subject for every possible object." Maurice Merleau-Ponty, *The Primacy of Perception, and Other Essays on Phenomenological Psychology, the Philosophy of Art, History and Politics,* ed. James M. Edie (Evanston, IL: Northwestern University Press, 1964), 57.

100. It is unlikely that Pedrosa was aware while writing his dissertation (1947–49) of Merleau-Ponty's strong critique of Gestalt theory as put forward in *The Structure of Behavior* (1942). While it is beyond the scope of the present project, a comparison of the two texts would be fascinating. As a result of Pedrosa's emphasis on affect and, implicitly, *signification*—a term that allowed the French philosopher to foreground his rejection of the mechanism of Gestalt—we find strong points of coincidence between the two authors: a rejection of atomist psychology, an emphasis on milieu as a field of action for the phenomenal body, the cruciality of signification for Merleau-Ponty and of affect for Pedrosa. Merleau-Ponty found common ground with Gestalt theory, both ultimately being concerned with the perceived world, though Merleau-Ponty thought Gestalt ignored human signification. Gullar, too, would underline the value of Gestalt theory and recognize the complexity of its investigations. See for example Ferreira Gullar, "Debate sôbre arte Concreta," *Suplemento Dominical do Jornal do Brasil,* December 10, 1958, in which the tenets of the "Manifesto Neoconcreto" had already been laid out; and Ferreira Gullar, "1a Eposição Neoconcreta," *Suplemento Dominical do Jornal do Brasil,* March 15, 1959.

101. Pedrosa, it should be pointed out here, was a former Trotskyist who was mainly a political activist during the 1920s. His noninstrumental conception of art, first posited in "Da natureza afetiva da forma na obra de arte," responds to a desire to conceive of art outside the sphere of instrumentalized capitalism.
102. Again, Pedrosa is rephrasing Koffka: "We live in a civilization with a relatively high degree of field-differentiation and ego-isolation. Therefore our world will be poor in physiognomic characters compared with fields of persons in other, more 'primitive' civilizations, and other qualities will be dominant in our fields." Kurt Koffka, "Problems in the Psychology of Art," 225.
103. Mário Pedrosa, "Da natureza afetiva da forma na obra de arte," 80–82.
104. Mário Pedrosa, "Calder, escultor de cata-ventos," *Correio da Manhã,* December 10–17, 1944, reprinted in *Mário Pedrosa: Modernidade cá e lá,* ed. Otília Beatriz Fiori Arantes (São Paulo: Editora da Universidade de São Paulo, 2000), 65.
105. Mário Pedrosa, "Tensão e coesão na obra de Calder." This text, originally published in *Correio da Manhã* in 1944, was reworked in 1948 for a lecture entitled "Calder e a Música dos Ritmos Visuais" at the Ministério da Educação of Rio de Janeiro and at the Museu de Arte de São Paulo. It was published in Mário Pedrosa, *Arte, necesidade vital* (Rio de Janeiro: Casa do Estudante do Brasil, 1949), 108–29, and reprinted in *Mário Pedrosa: Modernidade cá e lá,* 75–78.
106. *Mário Pedrosa: Modernidade cá e lá,* 78.
107. Mário Pedrosa, "A máquina, Calder, Léger e outros," *Política e Letras* (Rio de Janeiro) (September 1948), reprinted in *Mário Pedrosa: Modernidade cá e lá,* 81–90. Calder's work would be showcased again in 1953–54 as the U.S. submission to the second São Paulo Bienal.
108. Otília Beatriz Fiori Arantes, *Mário Pedrosa: Itinerário Crítico* (São Paulo: Cosac Naify, 2004), 58–59. In 1952 Serpa organized an exhibition of children's art entitled *Exposição Infantil do Museu de Arte Moderna do Rio de Janeiro.* The exhibition was introduced by Mário Pedrosa in a text entitled "Arte Infantil." In 1954 the museum offered art courses for children under the direction of Ivan Serpa.
109. Mário Pedrosa, "Arte, necessidade vital," paper presented at the Centro Psiquiátrico Nacional, sponsored by the Associação dos Artistas Brasileiros, March 31, 1947, published in *Correio da Manhã,* April 13 and 21, 1947, and reprinted in *Mário Pedrosa: Forma e Percepção Estética,* ed. Otília Beatriz Fiori Arantes (São Paulo: Editora da Universidade de São Paulo, 1996), 45.
110. Otília Beatriz Fiori Arantes observed that this allusion to Husserl bespeaks the increasing attraction that phenomenology exerted on the critic. *Mário Pedrosa: Modernidade cá e lá,* 17.
111. Mário Pedrosa, "Klee, ponto de partida," *Tribuna da Imprensa,* January 31, 1953, reprinted in *Mário Pedrosa: Modernidade cá e lá,* 192. Klee would be amply represented in the second São Paulo Bienal, which opened at the end of 1953. Pedrosa was a member of the Bienal's artistic committee. To fulfill this job, he moved to Europe for about eight months starting in March 1953 and dedicated great effort to ensure Klee's presence in the Bienal. See Adele Nelson, "The Monumental and the Ephemeral," 200, 211–14.
112. In 1952, Haroldo de Campos, Augusto de Campos, and Décio Pignatari formed the São

Paulo–based Noigandres group. The name was taken from Ezra Pound's *Cantos* (Pound had borrowed it from the medieval troubadour Arnaut Daniel) and was appealing as a word whose meaning the members of the group ignored (on the word's signification as invention, see Antonio Risério, *Cores Vivas* [Salvador, Brazil: Fundação Casa ed. Jorge Amado, 1989], 94–95). Dialogue was established between the concrete poets from São Paulo and the Rio de Janeiro–based poets Ferreira Gullar and Oliveira Bastos through an invitation to publish jointly in the *Suplemento Dominical do Jornal do Brasil.* See "Grupo Noigandres," in *Arte concreta Paulista: Documentos,* ed. João Bandeira (Rio de Janeiro: Cosac & Naify, 2002), 62–84.

113. As Lorenzo Mammi has indicated, the strict geographic division between the Paulistas and the Cariocas is simplistic, as demonstrated by the participation of São Paulo natives Willys de Castro, Hércules Barsotti, and Theon Spanúdis in the neoconcrete movement based in Rio de Janeiro. See Lorenzo Mammi, *Concreta '56: a raiz da forma,* 22.

114. Haroldo de Campos, "Da fenomenologia da composição à matemática da composição," and Reynaldo Jardim, Ferreira Gullar, and Oliveira Bastos, "Poesia Concreta: Uma experiência intuitiva," both in *Suplemento Dominical do Jornal do Brasil,* June 23, 1957.

115. Mário Pedrosa, "Poeta e Pintor concretista," *Artes Visuais, Jornal do Brasil,* February 16, 1957. A second article, dated February 19, 1957, traces the divide across both cities: São Paulo and Rio de Janeiro. In it Pedrosa delineates the opposition between the intellectualism of the Paulistas and the sensorial dimension of the Cariocas. Paulistas such as Cordeiro and Sacilotto, writes Pedrosa, transpose the idea to the canvas; like designers, their use of color is in the service of creating visually dynamic patterns, and form is centrally located in such a way that hierarchical composition is retained. The Cariocas, instead, prioritize the support, last point of contact with the physico-sensorial dimension of matter. Mario Pedrosa, "Paulistas e Cariocas," *Artes Visuais, Jornal do Brasil,* February 19, 1957.

116. Mário Pedrosa, "Poeta e Pintor concretista." It is interesting to note Pedrosa's use of the term "poem-object," which would be employed by Gullar to define his neoconcrete poetic practice and is related to his concept of the nonobject. As João Bandeira indicates, the "poem-object" genre had already been introduced by Décio Pignatari and Wladimir Dias-Pinto at the time of the first Exposição Nacional de Arte Concreta. See João Bandeira, "Words in Space," 136.

117. Mário Pedrosa, "Poeta e Pintor concretista."

118. See Susanne K. Langer, *Feeling and Form: A Theory of Art* (New York: Scribner's, 1953); and Ernst Cassirer, *The Philosophy of Symbolic Forms,* trans. Ralph Manheim (New Haven, CT: Yale University Press, 1955).

119. Mário Pedrosa, "Das formas significantes à lógica da expressão (Problemática da Arte Contemporánea)," written in 1954 and published in *Suplemento Dominical do Jornal do Brasil,* July 23, 1960, then reprinted in Mário Pedrosa, *Mundo, Homem, Arte em Crise,* 61–71.

120. Mário Pedrosa, "Problemática da sensibilidade I," in *Mundo, Homem, Arte em Crise,* quoted by Otília Beatriz Fiori Arantes in *Mário Pedrosa: Itinerário Crítico,* 80.

121. Otília Beatriz Fiori Arantes, *Mário Pedrosa: Itinerário Crítico,* 97.

122. In an effort to clarify his position vis-à-vis that of the concrete poets from São Paulo,

Gullar wrote in 1957, soon after the first Exposição Nacional de Arte Concreta: "The concrete poet will not confuse creative objectivity—the indispensable control in the creation of a poem whose reading is the apprehension, by the reader, of the functionality of its gestalt—with the scientific objectivity that presupposes an observer exempt from circumstantial factors." In Reynaldo Jardim, Ferreira Gullar, and Oliveira Bastos, "Poesia Concreta: Uma experiência intuitiva." The following year, summarizing a discussion on concrete art at the Galeria das Folhas in São Paulo (on the occasion of an exhibition by Lygia Clark, Lothar Charoux, and Franz Weissmann), Gullar sided with Gestalt theory: "Gestalt comprehends the autonomy of the various perceptual fields; it recognizes its [own] specific laws and, instead of fabricating particular conditions to explicate visual phenomena, prefers to examine them in their natural, everyday context, attempting to understand the nature of perception instead of judging it according to an ideal model." In Ferreira Gullar, "Sôbre arte Concreta: Visão e realidade," *Suplemento Dominical do Jornal do Brasil,* October 12, 1958. By 1959 Gullar's position regarding Gestalt theory was more critical, influenced by his exposure to Maurice Merleau-Ponty. The critic clearly stated that his intention was not to negate Gestalt theory—"whose discoveries concerning the laws of perception are definitive—but, adopting Merleau-Ponty's point of view, to negate the theoretical interpretation of the principles it has discovered." In Ferreira Gullar, "Arte concreta 6."

123. María Amalia García, "Tensiones entre tradición e innovación: Las críticas de Max Bill a la arquitectura moderna brasileña," *Concinnitas* 1, no. 16 (June 2010): 148–63.
124. The architectonic complex of Pampulha was commissioned by Juscelino Kubitschek (then mayor of Belo Horizonte) and designed by Oscar Niemeyer; it consisted of a nightclub, a yacht club, a casino, and the Igreja de São Francisco de Assis.
125. María Amalia García, "Tensiones entre tradición e innovación," 159–60.
126. Lúcio Costa, "A nossa arquitetura moderna: oportunidade perdida," *Manchete* (Rio de Janeiro), no. 63 (July 4, 1953), reprinted in *Depoimento de uma Geração,* ed. Alberto Xavier (São Paulo: Cosac & Naify, 2003), 181–82.
127. Ferreira Gullar, "Arte Concreta," *Suplemento Dominical do Jornal do Brasil,* June 26, 1960.
128. Ferreira Gullar, "Arte concreta 6."

## 3. FROM WORK TO FRAME, IN BETWEEN, AND BEYOND: THE TOPOLOGY OF THE NONOBJECT, 1959–66

1. Lygia Clark, "1965: Do ato," Diário-2 folder, Archives of the Associação Cultural "O Mundo de Lygia Clark," Rio de Janeiro.
2. Maurice Merleau-Ponty, *The Phenomenology of Perception* (1962), trans. Colin Smith (London: Routledge, 1995), 407.
3. Ferreira Gullar et al., "Manifesto Neoconcreto," *Suplemento Dominical do Jornal do Brasil,* March 21–22, 1959. Other articles in that issue included Ferreira Gullar, "Lygia Clark: Uma experiência radical" and "Livro-Poema"; Lygia Pape, "Gravura: Depoimento de Lygia Pape"; Reynaldo Jardim, "Ballet experiência visual" and "Duas formas no tempo"; Theon Spanúdis, "Poesia Neoconcreta"; and interviews with the artists Amilcar de Castro, Lygia Pape, and Franz Weissmann, and the composer Gabriel Artusi. An

article by Gullar in the previous week's issue had introduced the exhibition, the artists, and the manifesto to readers of the *Suplemento Dominical do Jornal do Brasil,* where he was the primary art critic. See Ferreira Gullar, "1a Exposição Neoconcreta," *Suplemento Dominical do Jornal do Brasil,* March 15, 1959.

4. Ferreira Gullar et al., "Manifesto Neoconcreto."
5. Ibid. Between March 1959 and October 1960, Gullar published a series of short articles devoted to modern art in the *Suplemento Dominical do Jornal do Brasil.* As he wrote in the preface to a compilation of these essays, he was attempting to situate neoconcretism as heir to the most radical artistic experiences of the century. Clearly teleological and pedagogical in nature (his synthesis and analysis of individual artists and works is accompanied by a general assessment of the various movements), these texts show a clear command of the recent literature on modern art and its main formal and theoretical issues. See Ferreira Gullar, *Etapas da arte contemporânea: Do cubismo à arte neoconcreta* (Rio de Janeiro: Editora Revan, 1985). The first of these articles, on cubism, appeared a week after "Manifesto Neoconcreto."
6. Ferreira Gullar et al., "Manifesto Neoconcreto."
7. Ferreira Gullar, email to the author, December 11, 2010. Otília Beatriz Fiori Arantes, who has written extensively about Pedrosa's work, indicates that Pedrosa never fully developed a critique of Gestalt theory, even as he increasingly incorporated concepts from phenomenology into his writings. However, according to Arantes, it was Pedrosa who introduced Maurice Merleau-Ponty's *The Phenomenology of Perception* to the neoconcretists and thus facilitated the rift with concrete art and Gestalt psychology. See Otília Beatriz Fiori Arantes, *Mário Pedrosa: Itinerário crítico* (São Paulo: Editora Página Aberta, 1991), 61. Both Gullar and Oiticica cite Spanish editions of Merleau-Ponty's books: see for example Ferreira Gullar, "Cor e estrutura-cor," *Suplemento Dominical do Jornal do Brasil,* October 29, 1960; and Hélio Oiticica, "Sept. 13, 1960," unpublished doc. no. 0121.60, p. 25, Archives Hélio Oiticica / Projeto Hélio Oiticica, Rio de Janeiro. In a 1968 interview Oiticica mentioned as formative the works of Kurt Koffka and Wolfgang Köhler, Susanne Langer, Merleau-Ponty, and Ernst Cassirer (Vera Pedrosa, "Aprender a ver," *Correio da Manhã* [Rio de Janeiro], October 19, 1968). These discussions concerning phenomenology seem to have involved the work of Edmund Husserl, to whom Pedrosa (although not Gullar) referred in his writings: see for example Mário Pedrosa, "Klee, ponto de partida," *Tribuna da Imprensa,* January 31, 1953, reprinted in *Mário Pedrosa: Modernidade cá e lá,* ed. Otília Beatriz Fiori Arantes (São Paulo: Editora da Universidade de São Paulo, 2000), 192; and Mário Pedrosa, "A obra de Lygia Clark," *Suplemento Literario* in *O Estado de São Paulo,* December 28, 1963, reprinted in *Mário Pedrosa: Acadêmicos e modernos,* vol. 3, ed. Otília Beatriz Fiori Arantes (São Paulo: Editora da Universidade de São Paulo, 1998), 348.
8. Susanne K. Langer, *Feeling and Form: A Theory of Art Developed from Philosophy in a New Key* (New York: Scribner's, 1953), 32.
9. Ferreira Gullar et al., "Manifesto Neoconcreto."
10. Susanne K. Langer, *Feeling and Form,* 89.
11. Ferreira Gullar et al., "Manifesto Neoconcreto."
12. Ferreira Gullar, "Arte Neoconcreta," *Suplemento Dominical do Jornal do Brasil,* October 2,

1960. This was the last article in a weekly series dedicated to modern art that delineated a trajectory that culminated in neoconcrete art. Gullar's argument had first emerged in a 1957 article about Waldemar Cordeiro, who, à la Theo van Doesburg, had claimed concrete painting to be as real as an apple. See Ferreira Gullar, "Do quadro e da maçã," *Suplemento Dominical do Jornal do Brasil,* August 31, 1957.

13. Ferreira Gullar, "Arte Neoconcreta."
14. Ferreira Gullar et al., "Manifesto Neoconcreto."
15. Merleau-Ponty's systematic critique of Gestalt was first voiced in *La structure du comportement* (1942), whose terms are invoked in the "Manifesto Neoconcreto." The French philosopher argued against Gestalt's "law" of good form and in favor of a consideration of the context in which the organism finds itself: "[T]he organism is not a machine governed according to a principle of absolute economy. For the most part preferred behavior is the simplest and most economical *with respect to the task in which the organism finds itself engaged.*" Reacting against positivism, Merleau-Ponty insisted that the laws posited by the theory of form are only possible within isolated, stable, ideal conditions that have no meaning outside "the dynamic structure considered." Maurice Merleau-Ponty, *The Structure of Behavior* (1942), trans. Alden L. Fisher (Boston: Beacon, 1963), 147. This inquiry would continue to occupy Merleau-Ponty in *The Phenomenology of Perception,* 138, 147, 149, 150.
16. Maurice Merleau-Ponty, *The Structure of Behavior,* 142.
17. Ibid., 143.
18. Ferreira Gullar et al., "Manifesto Neoconcreto." See also Ferreira Gullar, "Arte Neoconcreta."
19. Ferreira Gullar et al., "Manifesto Neoconcreto."
20. Ferreira Gullar, "Arte Neoconcreta."
21. Ferreira Gullar et al., "Manifesto Neoconcreto." This actualization of space and time was carefully elaborated in the "Diálogo sobre o não-objeto" (Dialogue on the Nonobject), where Gullar spoke of the nonobject as "unfolding radically in that space." He added: "Emerging directly in and of the space, the nonobject is at once a working through and recasting of that space: it is the permanent rebirth of form in space." Ferreira Gullar, "Diálogo sobre o não-objeto," *Suplemento Dominical do Jornal do Brasil,* March 26, 1960.
22. Maurice Merleau-Ponty, preface to *The Phenomenology of Perception,* xii.
23. Ibid., xiii.
24. Ibid.
25. Ferreira Gullar et al., "Manifesto Neoconcreto." Merleau-Ponty had warned: "To treat the physical world as if it were an intersecting of linear causal series in which each keeps its individuality, as if it were a world in which there is no duration, is an illegitimate extrapolation; science must be linked to a history of the universe in which the development is discontinuous." Maurice Merleau-Ponty, *The Structure of Behavior,* 139.
26. The famous statement is by the artist Frank Stella in Bruce Glaser, "Questions to Stella and Judd," in *Minimal Art: A Critical Anthology,* ed. Gregory Battcock (Berkeley: University of California Press, 1995), 158.
27. The anti-literalist core of Gullar's writing had been elaborated as early as 1957 in an

essay entitled "Do quadro e da maçã" (The Frame and the Apple), in which Gullar objected to Waldemar Cordeiro's claim that concrete painting was as real as an apple. Gullar instead argued, per Susanne Langer, for art's symbolic dimension.

28. Mário Pedrosa, "Klee, ponto de partida."
29. The first issue of *Malasartes,* a short-lived magazine published in Rio de Janeiro between September 1975 and June 1976 by some of the most important artistic names of that decade, reprinted the "Teoria do não-objeto" with this brief introduction: "It is the intention of *Malasartes* to publish historical texts fundamental to a critical understanding of Brazilian art. This important text . . . concerns one of the most intelligent theoretical productions of Brazilian art and literature, and its reading . . . helps foster our discussions about art." *Malasartes,* no. 1 (September–October–November 1975): 26.
30. Ferreira Gullar, *Lygia Clark: Uma experiência radical (1954–1958)* (Rio de Janeiro: Departamento de Impresa Nacional, 1958), n.p., reprinted in *Suplemento Dominical do Jornal do Brasil,* March 22, 1959. Gullar's essay was published on the occasion of an exhibition of works by Clark, Franz Weissmann, and Lothar Charoux held at Galeria de Arte das Folhas in São Paulo in the context of an award competition entitled Prêmio Leirner de Arte Contemporânea, São Paulo. The exhibition, as indicated in the catalogue, opened on September 23, 1958. For another detailed analysis of Clark's works of the mid-1950s, see Ricardo Nascimento Fabbrini, *O espaço de Lygia Clark* (São Paulo: Editora Atlas, 1994), 28–55.
31. Ferreira Gullar, *Lygia Clark: Uma experiência radical.*
32. Ibid.
33. Ibid.
34. Clark describes the making and materials of these works in "Ligia Clark busca na pintura a expressão do proprio espaço," *Folha da Noite* (São Paulo), September 22, 1958. In the catalogue for the second Grupo Frente exhibition at the Museu de Arte Moderna do Rio de Janeiro, the medium for *Superfícies moduladas nos. 4, 5,* and *6* is listed as "duco on plywood" (*duco sobre madeira compensada*). Duco is an automobile lacquer developed in the 1920s. A detailed analysis of Clark's materials remains to be carried out, and inconsistencies in the archive need to be clarified. For example, the catalogue for the 1955 São Paulo Bienal lists the medium for Clark's *Superfícies moduladas nos. 1, 2,* and *3* as oil paint.
35. Lygia Clark, "Lygia Clark e o espaço concreto expressional: Depoimento concedido a Edelweiss Sarmento," *Suplemento Dominical do Jornal do Brasil,* July 2, 1959. Interestingly, this text was published after the first exhibition of neoconcrete art, but its title retained the word *concrete,* although modified by the adjective *expressional,* which had also appeared in the "Manifesto Neoconcreto." The recurrence of the term is odd, since Clark had already dissociated herself from the aims of concrete art in notes dated 1957; see Lygia Clark, "1957," Diário-4 folder, Archives of the Associação Cultural "O Mundo de Lygia Clark." Clark proposed the organic line as the center of her investigations in a talk given in 1956 at the School of Architecture in Belo Horizonte, her hometown. The text of her talk, published in a local newspaper, associated the organic line with the spaces between functional architectural elements but also with "patches of materials, fabrics, etc." See "Pintora mineira (Ligia Clark) descobre novas linhas orgânicas nas artes plásticas," *Diário de Minas* (Belo Horizonte), January 27, 1957. This later theoriza-

tion of the organic line is preceded by two works titled *Descoberta da linha orgânica,* dated 1954.

36. Ferreira Gullar, *Lygia Clark: Uma experiência radical.*
37. "Pintora mineira (Ligia Clark) descobre novas linhas orgânicas nas artes plásticas."
38. Ferreira Gullar, *Lygia Clark: Uma experiência radical.*
39. "Pintora mineira (Ligia Clark) descobre novas linhas orgânicas nas artes plásticas"; and Lygia Clark, "Lygia Clark e o espaço concreto expressional."
40. Lygia Clark, "Lygia Clark e o espaço concreto expressional."
41. Lygia Clark, "Ligia Clark busca na pintura a expressão do proprio espaço."
42. Lygia Clark, "1957," Diário-4 folder, Archives of the Associação Cultural "O Mundo de Lygia Clark." The artist and architect Flavio de Carvalho included a group of works on paper by Albers in the third Salão de Maio exhibition in 1939; see Aracy A. Amaral, "The Advent of Geometric Abstraction in Brazil," in *Arte construtiva no Brasil: Coleção Adolpho Leirner,* ed. Aracy A. Amaral (São Paulo: DBA Artes Gráficas, 1998), 50. The German painter had also participated in the 1957 São Paulo Bienal, but no *Structural Constellations* were included. Clark apparently communicated with Albers through her friend the Brazilian diplomat and writer Luiz de Almeida Cunha. In a letter dated December 12, 1960, she thanks de Almeida for his article on Albers and tells him of Pedrosa's interest in including Albers in the next São Paulo Bienal. Lygia Clark, "07–12–1960 Carta a Luiz de Almeida Cunha," Correspondências enviadas diversas folder, Archives of the Associação Cultural "O Mundo de Lygia Clark."
43. Brenda Danilowitz, "Josef Albers: From North Carolina to Mexico and Beyond," paper presented at the "Dialogues in South and North American Abstraction" symposium, Newark Museum, New Jersey, April 10, 2010.
44. Mário Pedrosa, "Lygia Clark, ou o fascínio do espaço" (1957), in *Mário Pedrosa: Acadêmicos e modernos,* vol. 3, 289–90. He reiterated this point in his presentation of Clark's work at the Galeria de Arte das Folhas in 1958. See Mário Pedrosa, introduction to *Ligia Clark, Franz Weissmann, Lothar Charoux: Galeria de arte das "Folhas," Premio Leirner de arte contemporânea,* exh. cat. (São Paulo: Impresa, 1958) n.p.
45. Ferreira Gullar, *Lygia Clark: Uma experiência radical.*
46. Gullar raised this objection to geometric abstract painting in general in "Diálogo sobre o não-objeto." The pictorial background of a painting was associated with the fictional space of representation whenever a figure-ground relationship was sustained.
47. Ferreira Gullar, "Albers e outros," *Suplemento Dominical do Jornal do Brasil,* July 30, 1960.
48. Lygia Clark, "1957," Diário-4 folder, Archives of the Associação Cultural "O Mundo de Lygia Clark."
49. Frederick A. Horowitz, "Albers the Teacher," in Frederick A. Horowitz and Brenda Danilowitz, *Josef Albers: To Open Eyes: The Bauhaus, Black Mountain College, and Yale* (New York: Phaidon, 2006), 92.
50. Mário Pedrosa put it succinctly in a review of Clark's work at the 1957 São Paulo Bienal. Discussing her relationship to Albers, he wrote that Clark's "line is no longer content, however, with unfolding at the center of the modulated surface, but, cutting the edge, it seems to want to project itself outside the limits of the picture and return." Mário Pedrosa, "Lygia Clark, ou o fascínio do espaço."

51. "Albers introduced his students to the all-important figure-ground relationship and had them create patterns that had a fluctuating figure-ground relationship. To bring about a figure-ground fluctuation, both figure and ground had to be acknowledged as partners, equally 'serving and served,' and their placement precisely calculated. The exercise thrust the students directly into the perceptual and relational issues that to Albers were at once vital and vitally intertwined." Frederick A. Horowitz, "Albers the Teacher," 118.
52. Lygia Clark, "1957," Diário-4 folder, Archives of the Associação Cultural "O Mundo de Lygia Clark."
53. Lygia Clark, "Ligia Clark busca na pintura a expressão do proprio espaço."
54. Ibid. In 1955 Clark seems to have begun to keep notes organized by year. The few pages that survive from that year, however, lack the precision of her working notes from 1957. Those later notes include a document of ten typewritten pages that enumerates all the important issues Clark addressed in her work during the mid-1950s. Whether these notes were written during 1957, at the end of the year, or later is unclear, as the cover page only features a handwritten "1957." Some of the themes in this document are mentioned by Clark in newspaper notes published in 1957, 1958, and 1959, suggesting that they were indeed written in 1957 or soon after, in close dialogue with Pedrosa's and Gullar's analyses of her work.
55. Mário Pedrosa, *Ligia Clark, Franz Weissmann, Lothar Charoux.*
56. Ferreira Gullar, *Lygia Clark: Uma experiência radical.*
57. The relationship between these works and Oiticica's *Invenções,* initiated in 1959, was acknowledged by the artist himself when he described the *Invenções* as tending toward three-dimensional space. See Hélio Oiticica, "A transição da côr do quadro para o espaço e o sentido de construtividade," *Habitat* (Rio de Janeiro), no. 70 (December 1962): 52.
58. Oiticica would employ a similar effect in his own colored monochromes of 1959, entitled *Invenções.*
59. Ferreira Gullar, *Lygia Clark: Uma experiência radical.*
60. Gullar reiterated this point in a 1960 article on the artist. Clark's *Unidades,* he wrote: "encompassed . . . the creation of the painting as an existing material reality: painting and expression were born of the same generative movement." Ferreira Gullar, "Do quadro ao não-objeto," *Suplemento Dominical do Jornal do Brasil,* October 16, 1960. This sentiment was echoed by Clark, most forcefully in a short text from 1960 titled "A morte do plano" (Death of the Plane). Reacting against the artistic projection that the plane invites, she argued that its destruction would facilitate a sense of totality. Lygia Clark, "1960—A morte do plano," Diário-2 folder, Archives of the Associação Cultural "O Mundo de Lygia Clark."
61. See Lygia Clark, "Ligia Clark busca na pintura a expressão do proprio espaço"; and Lygia Clark, "Lygia Clark e o espaço concreto expressional."
62. Lygia Clark to Luiz de Almeida Cunha, October 7, 1959, Correspondências enviadas diversas folder, Archives of the Associação Cultural "O Mundo de Lygia Clark."
63. Lygia Clark, "Ligia Clark busca na pintura a expressão do proprio espaço."
64. Lygia Clark, "Lygia Clark e o espaço concreto expressional."
65. Clark's series produced in the late 1950s have yet to be fully catalogued. It is important

to clarify that many of these works were intended as studies on cardboard to be realized later as paintings.

66. Ricardo Nascimento Fabbrini, *O espaço de Lygia Clark,* 41.

67. Clark insisted on the affective dimension of art even during this period of rigorous investigation into the materiality of the pictorial plane and the surrounding space: "My vision is not purely optical but is viscerally linked to my experience of feeling." Lygia Clark to Luiz de Almeida Cunha, August 5, 1959, Correspondências enviadas diversas folder, Archives of the Associação Cultural "O Mundo de Lygia Clark."

68. *Encyclopaedia Britannica Online,* s.v., "topology," accessed January 10, 2012, http://www.britannica.com/EBchecked/topic/599686/topology.

69. Lygia Clark, "Lygia Clark e o espaço concreto expressional."

70. Lygia Clark, Livro-Obra Folder (Versão de Luxo), n.d., p. 4, Archives of the Associação Cultural "O Mundo de Lygia Clark."

71. Ibid.

72. See Lygia Clark, "1960—A morte do plano," Diário-2 folder, Archives of the Associação Cultural "O Mundo de Lygia Clark."

73. "Ferreira Gullar," in *Abstracionismo Geométrico e Informal: A vanguardia brasileira nos anos cinqüenta,* ed. Fernando Cocchiarale and Anna Bella Geiger (Rio de Janeiro: Funarte, 1987), 98.

74. Ibid.

75. "It concerns a new series of constructions made of superimposed planes in space. . . . These new works by Lygia Clark escape the characteristics of painting, nor do they fit the designations of 'relief' or 'sculpture.'" In Ferreira Gullar, "Exposição Neoconcreta na Bahia," *Suplemento Dominical do Jornal do Brazil,* October 31, 1959. The exhibition opened in November 1959 and included works by Aluísio Carvão, Amilcar de Castro, Willys de Castro, Lygia Clark, Carlos Fernando Fortes de Almeida, Ferreira Gullar, Reynaldo Jardim, Claudio Mello e Souza, Hélio Oiticica, Lygia Pape, Theon Spanúdis, and Franz Weissmann. A small brochure accompanying the exhibition included a reprint of the "Manifesto Neoconcreto" from March of that year. For a more recent account of this epiphanic moment, by now charged with the aura of myth, see Weydson B. Leal and Ariel Jiménez, *Ferreira Gullar in Conversation with Ariel Jiménez* (New York: Fundación Cisneros / Colección Patricia Phelps de Cisneros, 2012), 52–53.

76. Paulo Herkenhoff, "Lygia Clark," in *Lygia Clark,* exh. cat. (Barcelona: Fundació Antoni Tàpies, 1999), 41.

77. The earliest *Contra-relevo,* currently in the Patricia Phelps de Cisneros Collection (New York), is dated 1958. I question this date, however: I have not encountered documentation before 1959 indicating the existence of these works. Clark does not mention them in her lengthy interview with Edelweiss Sarmento from July 1959, which ends with a discussion of the *Espaços Modulados* (1958), nor are the works alluded to by Pedrosa or Gullar before 1960. The first photographic record that I have been able to locate of the *Contra-relevos* (and its first documented appearance in an exhibition) was in the catalogue of the inaugural exhibition of Galeria Bonino in Rio de Janeiro (May 19–June 5, 1960), which reproduces an imposing lozenge-shaped relief, measuring a meter square and dated 1960. The brochure for the neoconcrete exhibition in Bahia from

October 1959, where the intermedial works mentioned by Gullar were shown, does not include a list of works but could conceivably have featured *Contra-relevos* or precursors to the *Contra-relevos*. In a 1960 article on Aluísio Carvão and Hélio Oiticica, Gullar defined the *Counter-reliefs* of Valdimir Tatlin and Alexander Rodchenko as intermediary expressions between painting and sculpture (Ferreira Gullar, "Cor e estrutura-cor"). In 1962, Hélio Oiticica, in a reassessment of the term *constructive*, highlighted new experiments with relief that "continue to explore the spatial-structural problem, in a half-term between painting and space." He mentions the work of several artists, including the *Contra-relevos* and *Casulos* of Clark (Hélio Oiticica, "A transição da côr do quadro," *Habitat* [1962]). In 1965, an all-Clark issue of *Signals* magazine (on the occasion of Clark's show at London's Signal Gallery) referred to *Superfície modulada no. 8* and three *Casulos* (Cocoons, all 1959) as counterreliefs, while *Ovo linear,* one of the *Unidades,* and one of the *Superfícies moduladas* (all 1959) were called reliefs. Clearly, the word *relief* best accounted for the intermedial explorations that concerned these artists at the time.

78. See the letter from Lygia Clark to Luiz de Almeida Cunha, October 10, 1959, in which Clark mentions these works as her current preoccupation and as following the *Unidades* and *Espaços Modulados*. In the Correspondências enviadas diversas folder, Archives of the Associação Cultural "O Mundo de Lygia Clark."
79. Ibid.
80. Ibid.
81. Ferreira Gullar, "Teoria do não-objeto," 3. The *Casulos* were also developed around this time, although like the *Contra-relevos,* they, too, rest on the wall. Gullar's assertion that these "last works" of Clark (not identified in the essay) were constructed directly in space suggests that neither the *Contra-relevos* nor the *Casulos* directly triggered the term.
82. Waldemar Cordeiro, "O objeto," *Revista Arquitetura e Decoração* (São Paulo) (December 1956), reprinted in *Projeto construtivo brasileiro na arte (1950–1962),* ed. Aracy A. Amaral (Rio de Janeiro: Funarte, 1977), 74. Gullar issued a critique of this text before the publication of his "Teoria do não-objeto" in "Da Arte Concreta à Arte Neoconcreta," *Módulo,* no. 13 (April 1959): 31–34, reprinted in *Suplemento Dominical do Jornal do Brasil,* July 18, 1959.
83. A small brochure featuring both "Teoria do não-objeto" and "Diálogo sobre o não-objeto" was published by the *Suplemento Dominical do Jornal do Brasil* to accompany the second exhibition of neoconcrete art at the Ministry of Education and Culture, Rio de Janeiro, November 21–December 20, 1960.
84. Ferreira Gullar, "Diálogo sobre o não-objeto."
85. Ibid.
86. Ferreira Gullar, "Brancusi e o problema da base na escultura," *Suplemento Dominical do Jornal do Brasil,* April 9, 1960.
87. Ferreira Gullar, "Diálogo sobre o não-objeto."
88. Ibid.
89. Ibid.
90. This relationship and influence were acknowledged in Oiticica's diary entry of August 13, 1961. See Hélio Oiticica, "13 de agosto de 1961," in *Aspiro ao grande labirinto,* ed.

Luciano Figueiredo, Lygia Pape, and Waly Salomão (Rio de Janeiro: Rocco, 1986), 33. Oiticica met Clark, Pedrosa, and Gullar around 1954 or 1955 and participated in the second Grupo Frente exhibition at the Museu de Arte Moderna do Rio de Janeiro in July 1955.

91. Hélio Oiticica, "Dezembro 1959," in *Aspiro ao grande labirinto,* 17.
92. Carlos Basualdo, "Algunas anotaciones suplementarias sobre el Parangolé" (unpublished manuscript). I am citing the original unpublished manuscript, translated and published as "Quelques annotations supplémentaires sur le Parangolé," in *L'art au corps: Le corps exposé de Man Ray à nos jours,* ed. Véronique Legrand and Philippe Vergne (Marseille: Mac, galeries contemporaines des Musées de Marseille, 1996), 256–73.
93. Hélio Oiticica, "5 de outubro de 1960," in *Aspiro ao grande labirinto,* 23.
94. Hélio Oiticica, "Natal de 1959," in *Aspiro ao grande labirinto,* 17.
95. An excellent analysis of the construction of this discourse is provided by Irene Small, "Exit and Impasse: Ferreira Gullar and the 'New History' of the Last Avant-Garde," *Third Text* 26, no. 1 (2012): 91–101.
96. Ferreira Gullar, *Etapas de arte contemporânea: Do cubismo à arte neoconcreta* (Rio de Janeiro: Editora Revan, 1998).
97. Irene Small, "Exit and Impasse," 94.
98. See for example Mário Pedrosa, "Reflexões em torno da nova capital," *Brasil, Arquitetura Contemporânea* (Rio de Janeiro), no. 10, 1957; "Introdução à arquitetura brasileira—I," *Jornal do Brasil* (Rio de Janeiro), May 23–24, 1959; and "Brasília, a cidade nova," *Jornal do Brasil,* September 19, 1959. Each is reprinted in Mário Pedrosa, *Dos murais de Portinari aos espaços de Brasília,* ed. Aracy A. Amaral (São Paulo: Editora Perspectiva, 1981), 303–16, 321–27, 345–53.
99. See Mário Pedrosa, "Reflexões em torno da nova capital."
100. Mário Pedrosa, "Nuvens sobre Brasília," *Jornal do Brasil,* May 21, 1958, reprinted in Mário Pedrosa, *Dos murais de Portinari aos espaços de Brasília,* 337–39.
101. Mário Pedrosa, "Brasília, a cidade nova," 351.
102. Ibid.
103. Mário Pedrosa, "Crescimento da Cidade," *Jornal do Brasil* (Rio de Janeiro), September 16, 1959, reprinted in Mário Pedrosa, *Dos murais de Portinari aos espaços de Brasília,* 299.
104. Oiticica sketched Clark's *Unidades* in a diary entry dated August 13, 1961. He admiringly referred to these works as epitomizing a concern with the spatiotemporal dimension of painting. Oiticica also drew an all-black *Unidade* and rotated it 45 degrees to produce a diamond-shaped surface. This pivoting of the plane was effected by Clark in her *Contra-relevos* and *Casulos* and was seen by Oiticica in this text as the first step into real space. Hélio Oiticica, doc. no. 0187.61, p. 37, Archives Hélio Oiticica / Projeto Hélio Oiticica, Rio de Janeiro. While Clark referred to the space articulated by the *Espaços Modulados* and *Unidades* as "vertical space"—that is, time-space as opposed to mechanical time (the distance between one object and another)—Otiticia used the term "vertical color" to allude to the effect of layers just under the surface in his *Invenções.* See Lygia Clark, "Lygia Clark e o espaço concreto expressional"; and Hélio Oiticica, "A transição da côr do quadro," 49.
105. Hélio Oiticica, "A transição da côr do quadro," 49.

106. Hélio Oiticica, "Côr, tempo e estrutura," *Suplemento Dominical do Jornal do Brasil,* November 26, 1960.
107. This theme of an attack on a fixed, passive space and on mechanical, serial, linear notions of time was common among neoconcrete artists and poets, and it routinely alluded to the spatiotemporal. Aside from Pedrosa, Gullar, Clark, and Oiticica, the poet Theon Spanúdis also pondered these themes; see for example Theon Spanúdis, "Nova realidade espacial: A pintura de Lygia Clark," *Suplemento Dominical do Jornal do Brasil,* July 4–5, 1959.
108. Ferreira Gullar, "Cor e estrutura-cor."
109. Ibid.
110. Indeed, by 1962 all previous investigations were seen as facilitating a direct intervention in space: "My transition from picture to space started in 1959." Hélio Oiticica, "A transição da côr do quadro," 49.
111. Hélio Oiticica, "Côr, tempo e estrutura."
112. Ibid.
113. Hélio Oiticica, "A transição da côr do quadro," 52. In 1962 Oiticica also clarified the role of structure: "An art based upon structural transformations is always opposed to the passive role of the support, and the conflict reaches a point where there can be no evolution unless it is resolved. In truth, whoever represents *upon* something will better represent *through* something. There is the intermediary between the sense of space and the structure, and the spectator who receives the idea. Evidently, the creator needs the means by which to express himself, but the means should be direct, or, better, will have to be so, to the extent that the expression is structural and abstract." Hélio Oiticica, "6 de fevereiro de 1962. Suporte," in *Aspiro ao grande labirinto,* 38.
114. Hélio Oiticica, "Côr, tempo e estrutura," 5.
115. See Mário Pedrosa, *Grupo Frente: Segunda Mostra Coletiva,* exh. cat. (Rio de Janeiro: Museu de Arte Moderna do Rio de Janeiro, 1955), n.p. Pedrosa referred to Carvão's experiments involving a flat surface and a three-dimensional object that he hung in space in an attempt to exchange the restrictions of a frontal view for a "multiplicity of plastically alive colored surfaces." Three works in wood by Carvão—*Construção* (Construction) *nos.* 4, 5, and 7—were included in the catalogue, suggesting that they were indeed precursors to Clark's and Oiticica's own intermedial experiments. However, when Gullar discussed Carvão and Oiticica together five years later, he analyzed the former's use of color but made no reference whatsoever to innovations in the display of his work. Instead, he discussed Oiticica's hanging structures in detail and saw them as intrinsic to the arist's experiments with color-form in space. Gullar linked Clark and Oiticica through their common effort to construct directly into space. Ferreira Gullar, "Cor e estrutura-cor," 3.
116. Vera Martins, "Oiticica: Transformação dialética da pintura," *Suplemento Dominical do Jornal do Brasil,* May 20–21, 1961.
117. Hélio Oiticica, "Côr, tempo e estrutura," 5.
118. Lygia Clark, "1960—A morte do plano," Diário-2 folder, Archives of the Associação Cultural "O Mundo de Lygia Clark." A series of texts, with titles preceded by the year in which a particular concept or topic was elaborated in her work, exist in various versions

and explicate Clark's work of the 1960s. These are based on diary notes that appear to have been reworked for future publication in *Livro obra* (an artist's book published in 1983) and typewritten on letterhead of the Rio de Janeiro newspaper *O Globo*. I am citing these texts here.

119. Ibid.

120. Lygia Clark, "1960.1," Diário-2 folder, Archives of the Associação Cultural "O Mundo de Lygia Clark."

121. A good summary of this mechanism of objectification is Martin Heidegger, "The Age of the World Picture," in *The Question Concerning Technology, and Other Essays*, trans. William Lovitt (New York: Harper & Row, 1977), 115–54.

122. Hélio Oiticica, "A transição da côr do quadro," 54. In her notes from 1963, Clark also rejects the artistic process of transference by which form is invested with expression; see for example Lygia Clark, "1963.5," Diário-2 folder, Archives of the Associação Cultural "O Mundo de Lygia Clark."

123. In this sense it is interesting to note that Tatlin and Malevich—who are not constructivist artists proper—that is, not members of the First Working Group of Constructivism (as Alexander Rodchenko and Karl Ioganson were)—are the Russian artists most often mentioned in texts by Clark, Oiticica, and Gullar of this period. The Brazilian artists found greater affinity with the tactile and spatial structures of Tatlin (especially his *Corner-counter-reliefs*, 1915) and Malevich (*Arkitektons*, 1920s). Ferreira Gullar addressed the influence of Malevich and Tatlin on neoconcretism in "Tentativa de Compreensão," *Suplemento Dominical do Jornal do Brasil*, November 28, 1959. On constructivism's "spatial forms," see Maria Gough, "In the Laboratory of Constructivism: Karl Ioganson's Cold Structures," *October* 84 (Spring 1998): 90–117.

124. Hélio Oiticica, "Junho 1960," in *Aspiro ao grande labirinto*, 19.

125. Ferreira Gullar, "O lugar da obra," *Suplemento Dominical do Jornal do Brasil*, February 11, 1961.

126. The first point had been proposed earlier in Gullar's essay on Clark; see Ferreira Gullar, *Lygia Clark: Uma experiência radical*. He expressed the second point in "Diálogo sobre o não-objeto," arguing that with the nonobject "the spectator goes from contemplation to action. But what his/her action produces is the work itself, because that use, anticipated in the structure of the work, is absorbed by it, revealed and incorporated into its signification." Ferreira Gullar, "Diálogo sobre o não-objeto," 4.

127. Ferreira Gullar, "O tempo e a obra," *Suplemento Dominical do Jornal do Brasil*, February 18, 1961.

128. See Ferreira Gullar, "Depois do Neoconcretismo," in Ferreira Gullar, *Experiência Neoconcreta* (São Paulo: Cosacnaify, 2007), 68.

129. See the interview with Vera Martins, "Gullar e a Fundação Cultural de Brasília," *Suplemento Dominical do Jornal do Brasil*, June 11, 1961.

130. The exhibition was on view at at the Ministry of Education and Culture from November 21 to December 10, 1960, and included works by Hércules Barsotti, Amilcar de Castro, Willys de Castro, Aluísio Carvão, Lygia Clark, Osmar Dillon, Ferreira Gullar, Reynaldo Jardim, Claudio Mello e Souza, Hélio Oiticica, Lygia Pape, Roberto Pontual, and Décio Vieira.

131. See Lygia Clark, "Lygia Clark e o espaço concreto expressional."
132. Although the generic term *Bicho* is common in discussions of these pieces, Clark gave individual titles to most works in the series. These more poetic titles convey the existential themes that preoccupied her at the time, for instance *Em si* (In Itself) of 1962 and *O antes é o depois* (The Before Is the After) and *O dentro é o fora* (The Inside Is the Outside) of 1963. Titles of earlier works allude to their morphology: *Bicho Ponta* (Pointed Critter, the first and simplest in the series), *Prisma* (Prism), and *Constelação* (Constellation), all from 1960; *Caranguejo* (Crab) of 1960–63; and *Máquina* (Machine) of 1962. According to records in the Clark archives, three *Bicho*-like models are dated 1963 and titled *Arquitetura fantástica* (Fantastic Architecture).
133. Lygia Clark, "L'art, c'est le corps," *Preuves: cahiers mensuels du Congrès pour la liberté de la culture* (Paris), no. 13 (1973), 139.
134. This instructive layout was photographed by Sérgio Zalis, staff photographer at Paço Imperial in Rio de Janeiro, where Clark exhibited along with Oiticica in the Salão de Artes Plásticas in 1986, two years before her death.
135. Regarding the neoconcrete rupture, the critic Ronaldo Brito wrote, "We might say that the proposal was to activate an intense circulation of the observer's (participant's) desire, by means of a fight to break away from the conventions [of] work-spectator." Ronaldo Brito, *Neoconcretismo: Vértice e ruptura do projeto construtivo brasileiro,* trans. Lia Alvarenga Wyler and Florence Eleanor (Rio de Janeiro: Funarte / Instituto Nacional de Artes Plásticas, 1985), 112.
136. See for example Guy Brett, "Lygia Clark: The Borderline Between Art and Life," *Third Text* 1, no. 1 (Autumn 1987): 80; Paulo Herkenhoff, "Lygia Clark," in *Lygia Clark,* exh. cat. (Barcelona: Fundació Antoni Tàpies, 1999), 42; Ferreira Gullar, "Lygia Clark's Trajectory," in *Lygia Clark,* exh. cat. (Barcelona: Fundació Antoni Tàpies, 1999), 65; and Jodi Kovach, "Lygia Clark, Bicho [Critter], 1961," in *The Geometry of Hope: Latin American Art from the Patricia Phelps de Cisneros Collection,* ed. Gabriel Pérez-Barreiro (Austin: Blanton Museum of Art, University of Texas at Austin, 2007), 184.
137. Lygia Clark, "*Bichos,*" in *Esculturas da Lygia Clark,* exh. cat. (Rio de Janeiro: Galeria Bonino, 1960), n.p. See also Mário Pedrosa, "Significação de Lygia Clark," *Suplemento Dominical do Jornal do Brasil,* October 22–23, 1960.
138. Ferreira Gullar, "Lygia Clark's Trajectory," 63.
139. Ferreira Gullar, "Arte Concreta, uma contribução brasilera," *Revista Critica de Arte* (Rio de Janeiro), no. 1 (1962), reprinted in *Projeto construtivo brasileiro na arte,* 127.
140. Mário Pedrosa, "Significação de Lygia Clark." In another text on the *Bichos,* written to accompany an all-Clark gallery at the 1963 São Paulo Bienal, Pedrosa wrote of their closeness to living organisms but remarked on operations that made them resemble insects or strange machines. Mário Pedrosa, "Sala Especial. Lygia Clark e os seus 'Bichos,'" in *VII Bienal de São Paulo,* exh. cat. (São Paulo: Fundação Bienal de São Paulo, 1963), 122. In 1963 Pedrosa also referred to these works as "animals," "monsters," and "objects"; see Mário Pedrosa, "A obra de Lygia Clark," in *Mário Pedrosa: Acadêmicos e modernos,* vol. 3, 351.
141. In addition to the Galeria Bonino exhibition of 1960, where Clark exhibited the first fifteen works in the series, the *Bichos* were seen in several other shows: the second

exhibition of neoconcrete art at the Ministry of Education and Culture (November 21–December 10, 1960); the exhibition of neoconcrete art at the Museu de Arte Moderna de São Paulo (April 27–May 14, 1961); the 1961 São Paulo Bienal, where Clark won the sculpture prize; her solo show at the Museu de Arte Moderna do Rio de Janeiro (May 30–July 7, 1963); and the 1963 São Paulo Bienal, where she was given the honor of a "Sala Especial" (Special Gallery). See for example Pedro Manuel, "A Linha e o 'Bicho,'" *Suplemento Literário* in *Diário de Noticias,* October 30, 1960; José Guilherme Merquior, "Galatéia ou a morte da pintura," *Suplemento Dominical do Jornal do Brasil,* November 26, 1960; *Antônio* Bento, "Os Bichos de Lygia Clark," *Diário Carioca* (Rio de Janeiro), October 1960; "Os 'Bichos' de Lygia Clark," *Módulo* (Rio de Janeiro) 4, no. 21 (December 1960): 16–21; and Walmir Ayala, "Os bichos: para a escultora Lygia Clark, a propósito dos seus bichos," *Jornal do Brasil* (Rio de Janeiro), December 9, 1961.

142. Lygia Clark, "1965: Do ato," Diário-2 folder, Archives of the Associação Cultural "O Mundo de Lygia Clark." The same ideas had been sketched in a diary entry from November 1, 1963, that was the basis of this text; see Diário-2 folder, Archives of the Associação Cultural "O Mundo de Lygia Clark." Clark initially referred to this piece as *Dentro e fora* (Inside and Outside).
143. Lygia Clark, "01–11–63," Diário-2 folder, Archives of the Associação Cultural "O Mundo de Lygia Clark."
144. Jack Reynolds, "Maurice Merleau-Ponty (1908–1961)," *Internet Encyclopedia of Philosophy,* accessed November 5, 2010, http://www.iep.utm.edu/merleau/.
145. Maurice Merleau-Ponty, *The Phenomenology of Perception,* 415.
146. Lygia Clark, "1965: Do ato," Diário-2 folder, Archives of the Associação Cultural "O Mundo de Lygia Clark." Clark is referring here to two works from 1963: *O dentro é o fora* (The Inside Is the Outside), which here she calls *Dentro e fora* (Inside and Outside); and *O antes é o depois* (The Before Is the After), which here she calls *Antes do depois* (Before What Comes After).
147. Mário Pedrosa, "A obra de Lygia Clark." The elusive exhibition history of this work has been recently addressed by Anna Dezeuze in "How to Live Precariously: Lygia Clark's *Caminhando* and Tropicalism in 1960s Brazil," *Women and Performance: A Journal of Feminist Theory* (London) (2013): 3–10.
148. Lygia Clark, "1963.2," Diário-2 folder, Archives of the Associação Cultural "O Mundo de Lygia Clark."
149. Maurice Merleau-Ponty, *The Phenomenology of Perception,* 415.
150. On immanence and transcendence in Merleau-Ponty's work, see the instructive essay by Jack Reynolds and Jon Roffe, "Deleuze and Merleau-Ponty: Immanence, Univocity and Phenomenology," *Journal of the British Society for Phenomenology* 37, no. 3 (October 2006): 228–51.
151. Lygia Clark, "1963.13, " Diário-2 folder, Archives of the Associação Cultural "O Mundo de Lygia Clark."
152. Lygia Clark, "1964: Caminhando (versão-1)," Textos de Lygia Clark publicados folder, Archives of the Associação Cultural "O Mundo de Lygia Clark." Several versions of this text exist. I am citing the so-called first version, which was written, like other texts published in *Livro obra,* on letterhead (in this case for "Editora artenova"). *Cami-*

*nhando* was clearly conceived in 1963, as most diary entries from that year are concerned with it.

153. Ibid.

154. Maurice Merleau-Ponty, *The Phenomenology of Perception,* 419–20.

155. Lygia Clark, "1964: Caminhando (versão-1)," Textos de Lygia Clark publicados folder, Archives of the Associação Cultural "O Mundo de Lygia Clark." This conception of total time was articulated in diary notes from 1963 and was conceived as a rejection of mechanical time: "*Caminhando* ~~for example~~ [strikethrough in original] only took on meaning for me when I took a trip and passed through the landscape over a period of time. It was not simply mechanical time but topology itself through the perceived moment." Lygia Clark, "1963.3," Diário-2 folder, Archives of the Associação Cultural "O Mundo de Lygia Clark."

156. "No separation between subject and object. It's a body-to-body embrace, a fusion." Lygia Clark, "1964: Caminhando (versão-1)," Textos de Lygia Clark publicados folder, Archives of the Associação Cultural "O Mundo de Lygia Clark." This *fusion* between subject and object—which is tempting to contrast with the constructivist-concrete *identification* between mind and work discussed in chapter 2—can be seen as confirming the critical dissolution of the concrete-constructivist Brazilian project and the loss of the object as an index of the artist's subjective projection or mind.

157. Maurice Merleau-Ponty, *The Phenomenology of Perception,* 424.

158. Ibid., 426.

159. Lygia Clark, "1963.10," Diário-2 folder, Archives of the Associação Cultural "O Mundo de Lygia Clark."

160. Lygia Clark, "1963.5," Diário-2 folder, Archives of the Associação Cultural "O Mundo de Lygia Clark."

161. Ibid.

162. Maurice Merleau-Ponty, *The Phenomenology of Perception,* 347.

163. Maurice Merleau-Ponty, *The Visible and the Invisible,* 8.

164. Lygia Clark, "1965: Do ato," Diário-2 folder, Archives of the Associação Cultural "O Mundo de Lygia Clark."

165. Ibid. In an article on Clark from December 1963, Pedrosa would refer to the paradox of "empty-plenitude" as an oscillation between two metaphysics, that of emptiness (meaning space) and that of time (meaning action). See Mário Pedrosa, "A obra de Lygia Clark." See also Lygia Clark, "O vazio-pleno," *Suplemento Dominical do Jornal do Brasil,* April 2, 1960, reprinted in English in *Lygia Clark,* exh. cat., 111–13.

166. While in 1963–64 Clark used the term *fusion*—"No separation between subject and object. It's a body-to-body embrace, a *fusion*" (emphasis added)—in 1965 she wrote of the same idea, "Subject-object essentially *identify* in the act" (emphasis added). While *fusion* suggests a relinquishing of boundaries, *identification* retains them. Clark seems to have used both terms to propose a feeling of totality and a shift away from the projective, spatially delimited positionality reliant on transference that representation implied. The fact that she used the term "empty-plenitude" (*vazio-pleno*), which described plenitude (a feeling of totality) in terms of a permanent incompleteness, complicates this notion of totality. See Lygia Clark, "1964: Caminhando (versão-1)," Textos de Lygia Clark

publicados folder, Archives of the Associação Cultural "O Mundo de Lygia Clark"; and Lygia Clark, "1965: Do ato," Diário-2 folder, Archives of the Associação Cultural "O Mundo de Lygia Clark."

167. Lygia Clark, "1965: Do ato," Diário-2 folder, Archives of the Associação Cultural "O Mundo de Lygia Clark."
168. Lygia Clark, "28–10–1963," Diário-2 folder, Archives of the Associação Cultural "O Mundo de Lygia Clark."
169. Lygia Clark, "Da supressão do objeto (anotações)," in *Navilouca*, ed. Lucio Urubatan de Abreu (Rio de Janeiro: Edições Gernasa e Artes Gráficas, 1974).
170. See for example Lygia Clark, "Breviário sobre o corpo," Diário-2 folder, Archives of the Associação Cultural "O Mundo de Lygia Clark."
171. Maurice Merleau-Ponty, *The Visible and the Invisible*, 131.
172. Ibid., 133–34.
173. Ibid., 137.
174. Ibid., 138. Again, regarding our relation to the phenomenal world: "[B]etween my body looked at and my body looking, my body touched and my body touching, there is overlapping and encroachment, so that we must say that the things pass into us as well as we into the things." Ibid., 123.
175. Ibid., 138.
176. Ibid., 142, 160.
177. Yve-Alain Bois, "Part Object," in *Formless: A User's Guide*, ed. Rosalind E. Krauss and Yve-Alain Bois (New York: Zone, 1997), 160.
178. Mark Yount, "Two Reversibilities: Merleau-Ponty and Derrida," in *Merleau-Ponty, Hermeneutics, and Postmodernism*, ed. Thomas W. Busch and Shaun Gallagher (Albany: State University of New York Press, 1992), 216–17, quoted in Jack Reynolds, "Maurice Merleau-Ponty (1908–1961)."
179. Maurice Merleau-Ponty, *The Visible and the Invisible*, 147.
180. Ibid., 148. Language, too, Merleau-Ponty argued, interrupts identity (perceptual and cognitive) by positing a screen between ourselves and the world. Yet this is not to be lamented: "[W]hat is lived is lived-spoken," he wrote. "[L]anguage is not a mask over Being, but . . . the most valuable witness to Being." Maurice Merleau-Ponty, *The Visible and the Invisible*, 126.

## 4. FORMS OF AFFECT: HÉLIO OITICICA'S *PARANGOLÉS*, 1964–65

1. Hélio Oiticica, "Anotações sobre o Parangolé" (November 1964), a mimeographed text that was first reprinted in Hélio Oiticica, *Aspiro ao grande labirinto*, ed. Luciano Figueiredo, Lygia Pape, and Waly Salomão (Rio de Janeiro: Rocco, 1986), 71.
2. Gregory J. Seigworth and Melissa Gregg, "An Inventory of Shimmers," in *The Affect Theory Reader* (Durham, NC, and London: Duke University Press, 2010), 3.
3. See Hélio Oiticica, "Bases fundamentais para uma definição do 'Parangolé,'" (November 1964), mimeographed text first reprinted in *Aspiro ao grande labirinto*,65–69, then reprinted in English in *Hélio Oiticica: The Body of Colour*, exh. cat., ed. Mari Carmen Ramírez, trans. Stephen A. Berg and Héctor Olea (London: Tate Publishing; Houston:

Museum of Fine Arts, 2007), 296. I am citing this English translation here. Also see "Anotações sobre o Parangolé"; "A dança na minha experiência" (November 12, 1965); and "Posição e programa" (July 1966) in *Aspiro ao grande labirinto,* 69–83. Lisette Lagnado Dwek undertook pioneering research on Oiticica's terminology in "Hélio Oiticica: O mapa do programa ambiental," vol. 1, and "Glossário do programa ambiental de Hélio Oiticica," vol. 2 (PhD diss., Universidade de São Paulo, 2003).

4. In a diary entry of May 25, 1967, Oiticica related this "processual" quality of the *Parangolés* to a "reformulation of established concepts." Oiticica, doc. no. 0111.67, Archives Hélio Oiticica / Projeto Hélio Oiticica, Rio de Janeiro. Or, as Oiticica put it in an explanatory text produced for Whitechapel Gallery in London in 1969 (where he exhibited the following year), the *Parangolé* cape "is not a finished object and its spatial sense is not definitive." Hélio Oiticica, doc. no. 0365.69, p. 6, Archives Hélio Oiticica / Projeto Hélio Oiticica. This unpublished text is part of the extensive Oiticica archive that includes the artist's copious writings and interviews from 1953 to 1980.
5. On continuities and breaks with neoconcretism in the *Parangolés,* see Michael Asbury, "Hélio Couldn't Dance," in *Fios soltos: A arte de Hélio Oiticica,* ed. Paula Braga (São Paulo: Perspectiva, 2008), 52–64.
6. See Waly Salomão, *Hélio Oiticica: Qual é o parangolé? e outros escritos* (Rio de Janeiro: Relume Dumará, 1996); and Cid Franco, *Dicionário de expressões populares brasileiras* (São Paulo: Unidas, 1970), 71.
7. Hélio Oiticica, "Feb. 17, 1965," doc. no. 0187.61, p. 122, Archives Hélio Oiticica / Projeto Hélio Oiticica. The Museu Nacional is a natural history museum where Oiticica worked from 1961 to 1964, assisting his father in cataloging insects.
8. Ibid. At the beginning of this handwritten text, Oiticica wrote (in parentheses) that this note should become part of his essay "Bases fundamentais para uma definição do 'Parangolé'" (see note 3 above).
9. Esther Emílio Carlos, "Atelier," *Diário de Noticias* (Rio de Janeiro), August 10, 1965.
10. While this line of thinking has been challenged in recent literature, my interest here is in a nuanced historical and theoretical analysis of this encounter as well as an exploration of the work's connection to Gullar's nonobject and the concerns of the neoconcrete period. See for example Michael Asbury, "Hélio Couldn't Dance"; and Sergio Bruno Martins, "Hélio Oiticica: Mapping the Constructive," *Third Text* 24, no. 4 (2010): 419. I agree that Oiticica's "discovery" of Mangueira should not be treated as a myth of origin, but the unique development of the artist's work is unthinkable without Mangueira. Ultimately, I am pursuing Asbury's argument that Oiticica's pre-Mangueira philosophical position and the political landscape of the early 1960s were fundamental to shaping his relationship with the favela and thus his work. This was, however, as we will see, an affective encounter fully informed by the unique material conditions and practices that Mangueira offered.
11. Hélio Oiticica (June 3, 1962), in *Aspiro ao grande labirinto,* 43.
12. See Hélio Oiticica, doc. no. 1863.sd, Archives Hélio Oiticica / Projeto Hélio Oiticica. In this undated text, probably prepared for an interview around 1964, Oiticica talks of his arrival in Mangueira, his encounter with samba, and his association of samba with the primordial and the archaic as well as with collective artistic work. The integrated work

of samba and carnival—the dance, the construction of costumes, the composition of music—is defined here as having unity and expressive force unlike anything found in "that other culture, which is ours, of European origin." The document's cover page reads: "This is the testimony of a young avant-garde Brazilian painter, Hélio Oiticica, who has just become one of the dancers of the famous Samba School of the First Station of Mangueira. He tells us of his experience with samba and its indubitable and 'sui generis' relationship to the ultra-avant-gardist art that he professes."

13. Ferreira Gullar had been the intellectual force behind the "Manifesto Neoconcreto" of 1959, which gave voice to a young generation of artists concerned with the limitations of concrete art, specifically its rational and objectivist dimension. Gullar's ideas—which emphasized perception and affect and were elaborated in his "Teoria do não-objeto" (1959) and "Diálogo sobre o não-objeto" (1960)—facilitated a rethinking of the conventional categories of painting and sculpture and the status of the spectator; see chapters 2 and 3.
14. An early assessment of Oiticica's relationship with the Left and Gullar's Marxist position was made by Carlos Zilio, "Da antropofagia à tropicália," in *Artes plásticas,* ed. Carlos Zilio, João Luiz Lafetá, and Lígia Chiappini Moraes Leite (São Paulo: Brasiliense, 1982), 13–56.
15. These included agrarian reform, the promotion of trade unions, civil liberties, anti-imperialism, and national initiatives that favored the working classes. Roberto Schwarz, "Culture and Politics in Brazil, 1964–1969," in *Misplaced Ideas: Essays on Brazilian Culture* (London and New York: Verso, 1992), 135.
16. Heloísa Buarque de Hollanda, *Impressões de viagem: CPC, vanguarda e desbunde, 1960–1970* (São Paulo: Editora Brasiliense, 1980), 16.
17. On the institute's role as a backdrop to notions of historical development implicit in the writings of Gullar at the end of the 1950s, see Irene Small, "Exit and Impasse: Ferreira Gullar and the 'New History' of the Last Avant-Garde," *Third Text* 26, no. 1 (2012): 91–101.
18. Carlos Estevam Martins, "Anteprojeto do Manifesto do CPC" (1962), reprinted in "Anos 60," a special issue of *Arte em Revista* (São Paulo), no. 1 (May 1981): 70. The manifesto probably circulated as a leaflet and was reprinted the year after it was written in Carlos Estevam Martins, *A questão da cultural popular* (Rio de Janeiro: Tempo Brasileiro, 1963), 79–109.
19. Ibid.
20. For an in-depth analysis of this document's reception, see Miliandre Garcia, "A questão da cultura popular: as políticas culturais do centro popular de cultura (CPC) da União Nacional dos Estudantes (UNE)," *Revista Brasileira de Historia* 24, no. 47 (2004): 127–62, accessed June 22, 2014, http://www.scielo.br/scielo.php?script=sci_arttext&pid=S0102-01882004000100006.
21. Heloísa Buarque de Hollanda, *Impressões de viagem,* 28. Miliandre Garcia also dwells on the failure of the CPC to reach the popular masses. She does, however, highlight several popular music events where a tentative integration among social classes (the students and artists associated with the CPC and popular artists and their audiences) was achieved. See Miliandre Garcia, "A questão da cultura popular," 148.

22. Carlos Estevam Martins, "Historia do CPC," *Arte em Revista,* no. 3 (March 1980): 81, cited in Carlos Zilio, "Da antropofagia à tropicália," 37.
23. Ferreira Gullar, depoimento à Funarte (Fundação Nacional de Artes), second semester, 1980, cited in Carlos Zilio, "Da antropofagia à tropicália," 37.
24. Carlos Estevam Martins, "Anteprojeto do Manifesto do CPC," 75.
25. Ferreira Gullar, *Cultura posta em questão* (Rio de Janeiro: Editora Civilização Brasileira, 1965). This book was written in 1963, initially published in 1964, and withdrawn from circulation before finally being republished in 1965.
26. Ibid., 4, 11, 22, 24, 38, 59. According to Carlos Zilio, "Oiticica established a dialogue with Gullar in which he reinterpreted, according to a point of view entirely consistent with his own work, Ferreira Gullar's position of 'engaged art.'" Carlos Zilio, "Da antropofagia à tropicália," 32. Likewise, Michael Asbury noted, "Although Oiticica's relation to popular culture was very different in nature, the influence which Gullar's critical position had on Oiticica should not be underestimated." Michael Asbury, "Hélio Oiticica and the Notion of the Popular in the 1960s," *Art and Architecture of the Americas,* no. 3, accessed September 3, 2004, http://www2.essex.ac.uk/arthistory/arara/issue_three/paper3.html.
27. Carlos Estevam Martins, "Anteprojeto do manifesto do CPC," 77.
28. See chapter 3, pages 123–24.
29. Ferreira Gullar, *Cultura posta em questão,* 95.
30. See Ferreira Gullar, "Depois do Neoconcretismo," in *Experiência Neoconcreta* (São Paulo: Cosacnaify, 2007), 68.
31. This argument is voiced by Miliandre Garcia, who said the manifesto was a point of reference more than a cultural project for the artists associated directly or indirectly with the CPC. See Miliandre Garcia, "A questão da cultura popular," 127–62.
32. Carlos Estevam Martins, "Anteprojeto do manifesto do CPC," 75.
33. Hélio Oiticica, "Bases fundamentais para uma definição do 'Parangolé,'" 65. This text, along with "Anotações sobre o Parangolé," was distributed to the public on the night of August 12, 1965, at the opening of *Opinião 65* at the Museu de Arte Moderna do Rio de Janeiro, where Oiticica presented the *Parangolés* in an institutional setting for the first time. I owe this information to Irene Small.
34. Ibid.
35. Ibid., 66. A similar concept, that of estrangement, would become increasingly important in Oiticica's work. See "Ivan Cardoso entrevista Hélio Oiticica," in R.F. Lucchetti and Ivan Cardoso, *Ivampirismo: O cinema em pânico* (Rio de Janeiro: Editora Brasil-America and Fundação do Cinema Brasileiro, 1979), 74.
36. Hélio Oiticica, "Bólides" (October 29, 1963), in *Aspiro ao grande labirinto,* 66. Ultimately, Oiticica's aesthetic agenda and distancing from CPC dictums might be indicative of his anarchist leanings. I want to thank Michael Asbury for calling my attention to this.
37. Hélio Oiticica, "Bólides," 63–65. In 1960 Lygia Clark recalled that Mário Pedrosa proposed the term *transobject* as an alternative to *nonobject.* To the critic, *nonobject* denied the form that conveyed the sensuousness of the object; *transobject,* according to Clark, suggested not a negation of form but a transcendence of it that departs from the object.

See Lygia Clark, Diário-2, Folder 1960–4, Archives of the Associação Cultural "O Mundo de Lygia Clark," Rio de Janeiro. Another text by Clark from 1960 questions the effectiveness of the nonobject in defining contemporary artistic production; see Lygia Clark, Diário-4, Folder 1960–8, Archives of the Associação Cultural "O Mundo de Lygia Clark."

38. Oiticica also rejected the straightforward appropriation of the readymade or found object, which remained associated with use and codified meaning.

39. Hélio Oiticica (September 19, 1963), doc. no. 0007.63, Archives Hélio Oiticica / Projeto Hélio Oiticica. A few years later, Oiticica described the *Bólides* as "focuses" of "visual-sensorial energy: they are like excercises [*sic*] for 'a perceptive transformation.'" See Hélio Oiticica, "Rhobo, Captions and Small Texts" (May 22–24, 1969), doc. no. 0363.69, Archives Hélio Oiticica / Projeto Hélio Oiticica; original text in English. Inspecting, manipulating, discovering were the next steps in a trajectory inaugurated with the nonobject and its rejection of representation.

40. Hélio Oiticica, "O objeto: Instâncias do problema do objeto," *GAM Galeria de Arte Moderna* (Rio de Janeiro), no. 15 (1968): 27.

41. Ibid.

42. Ibid. This object of immanence is close to what Gullar had attempted to define with the term *nonobject,* and was Clark's main preoccupation in *Caminhando.*

43. Hélio Oiticica, "Apocalipopotesis" (n.d.; ca. 1969), doc. no. 0534.69, p. 1, Archives Hélio Oiticica / Projeto Hélio Oiticica; original text in English.

44. Ibid.

45. Hélio Oiticica, "Depoimento 'Opinião 65' (para o Diário Carioca: Claudir Chaves)" (August 20, 1965), doc. no. 0119.65, Archives Hélio Oiticica / Projeto Hélio Oiticica.

46. Hélio Oiticica, "Côr, tempo e estrutura," *Suplemento Dominical do Jornal do Brasil,* November 26, 1960.

47. Hélio Oiticica, "Suporte" (1962), in *Aspiro ao grande labirinto,* 38.

48. Hélio Oiticica, "Côr, tempo e estrutura," 5.

49. In a handwritten text from March 17, 1964, pertinently entitled "O nascimento da estrutura" (The Birth of the Structure), Oiticica quoted the German phenomenologist Wilhelm Schapp at length to underline the interdependence of an order of color and the perception and representation of things. Color is not present in an objective space, but its various manifestations (i.e., colored shadows, lights, and reflections are modalities of these various manifestations) determine how the representation of objective reality is constructed. Wilhelm Schapp, *Beiträge zur Phänomenologie der Wahrnehmung* (Halle, Germany: Niemeyer, 1910). See also chapter 3, pages 115–16.

50. Hélio Oiticica, "Sôbre o 'núcleo médio no. 1 (NC3)'" (April 13, 1962), doc. 0182.59, p. 96, Archives Hélio Oiticica / Projeto Hélio Oiticica.

51. Hélio Oiticica (August 7, 1961), in *Aspiro ao grande labirinto,* 32–33.

52. "These are works of viewer participation." Hélio Oiticica (December 27, 1961), in *Aspiro ao grande labirinto,* 36–37.

53. Hélio Oiticica (December 28, 1961), doc. no. 0182.59, p. 72, Archives Hélio Oiticica / Projeto Hélio Oiticica. Early *Penetráveis* were conceived in 1961 as maquettes and referred to as "projects" or "maquette-projects." The first were labyrinthine, while later

ones involved rotating panels. Only *PN1*, an homage to Mário Pedrosa, was realized during the neoconcretist period; it consisted of a cabin with sliding doors painted yellow.

54. Vera Martins, "Oiticica: Transformação dialética da pintura," *Suplemento Dominical do Jornal do Brasil,* May 20–21, 1961.
55. Hélio Oiticica (August 28, 1961), in *Aspiro ao grande labirinto,* 35–36.
56. See Mário Pedrosa, "Os Projetos de Hélio Oiticica," in the flier for the exhibition *Projeto Cães de Caça de Hélio Oiticica* (Rio de Janeiro: Museu de Arte Moderna do Rio de Janeiro, 1961).
57. Hélio Oiticica, "Projeto Cães de Caça e pintura nuclear" (n.d.; ca. 1961 ), doc. no. 0024.61, p. 1, Archives Hélio Oiticica / Projeto Hélio Oiticica.
58. Reynaldo Jardim, "Teatro Integral," *Suplemento Dominical do Jornal do Brasil,* January 30, 1960.
59. Mário Pedrosa, "Os Projetos de Hélio Oiticica."
60. This defiance of established artistic categories was evident in a short article on the *Penetráveis* by Gullar, who also observed its collaborative and collective aspects. See Ferreira Gullar, "Os 'Penetráveis' de Oiticica," *Jornal do Brasil,* December 7, 1961.
61. Hélio Oiticica, "Cor tonal e desenvolvimento nuclear da cor" (March 17, 1962), in *Aspiro ao grande labirinto,* 40.
62. Ibid.
63. Hélio Oiticica, "Sôbre o 'núcleo médio no. 1' (NC3)" (April 13, 1962), doc. no. 0182.59, pp. 96–98, Archives Hélio Oiticica / Projeto Hélio Oiticica.
64. Hélio Oiticica, "A transição da cor do quadro para o espaço e o sentido de construtividade," *Habitat* (Rio de Janeiro), no. 70 (December 1962): 52. On the "structural" understanding of the "constructive"—as an operational term and not a stylistic category—see Sergio Bruno Martins, "Hélio Oiticica: Mapping the Constructive," 409–22.
65. Hélio Oiticica, "A transição da cor do quadro para o espaço e o sentido de construtividadc," 52.
66. Ibid.
67. Ibid., 54.
68. Ibid.
69. See Hélio Oiticica (December 28, 1961), doc. no. 0182.59, Archives Hélio Oiticica / Projeto Hélio Oiticica.
70. "The artist today has to create a structure to say something new. (Was it thus before?)" Lygia Clark, Diário-2 folder, 1960–1, Archives of the Associação Cultural "O Mundo de Lygia Clark."
71. Hélio Oiticica, "Bases fundamentais para uma definição do 'Parangolé,'" 297.
72. Hélio Oiticica, "Anotações sobre o Parangolé," 71.
73. Ibid., 67.
74. Hélio Oiticica (June 3, 1962), in *Aspiro ao grande labirinto,* 43.
75. "The *Parangolé* 'penetrable' assumes an important function: it is the 'shelter' of the spectator." Hélio Oiticica, "Anotações sobre o Parangolé," 71.
76. Hélio Oiticica, "Bases fundamentais para uma definição do 'Parangolé,'" 66.
77. Janice E. Perlman, *The Myth of Marginality: Urban Poverty and Politics in Rio de Janeiro* (Berkeley: University of California Press, 1976), 1.

78. Ibid., 129.
79. Hélio Oiticica, "A dança na minha experiência," 74.
80. Ibid.
81. Hélio Oiticica, "Cor tonal e desenvolvimento nuclear da cor," 41.
82. "Hélio Oiticica (March 4, 1968), in *Aspiro ao grande labirinto,* 108–9.
83. Ibid. Maria Laura Viveiros de Castro Cavalcanti has written that in the 1950s, samba schools enlarged their social base to include the middle class through the involvement of visual artists, among others, in the production of parades. She also observed that it was with the spectacularization of the carnival—epitomized by the 1984 construction of the Passarela do Samba, known as Sambódromo, through which the various samba schools and their floats parade—that the visual distinction between performer and spectator was reinforced. See Maria Laura Viveiros de Castro Cavalcanti, *Carnaval Carioca: Dos bastidores ao desfile* (Rio de Janeiro: Editora UFRJ and MinC/Funarte, 1994), 26, 52.
84. Marcelo Baumann Burgos, "Dos parques proletários ao favela-bairro—As políticas públicas nas favelas do Rio de Janeiro," in *Um século de favela,* ed. Alba Zaluar and Marcos Alvito (Rio de Janeiro: Editora Fundação Getúlio Vargas, 1998), 25–60; and Hermano Vianna, "Não quero que a vida me faça de otário! Hélio Oiticica como mediador cultural entre o asfalto e o morro," *Overmundo,* accessed January 15, 2008, http://www.overmundo.com.br/banco/helio-oiticica-como-mediador-entre-asfalto-e-morro.
85. Ibid.
86. Hermano Vianna, *The Mystery of Samba: Popular Music and National Identity in Brazil,* ed. and trans. John Charles Chasteen (Chapel Hill: University of North Carolina Press, 1999), 62–63.
87. Ibid., 74.
88. Ibid., 85.
89. Ibid., 88.
90. Other early parade designers included Marie Louise Nery, a Swiss museum exhibition designer who worked for the Musée d'Ethnographie in Neuchâtel, and her husband, Dirceu Nery, a stage designer. In 1960 they were joined at the school in Salgueiro by Pamplona, Nílton Sá, and Arlindo Rodrigues (who was also a stage designer for Theatro Municipal do Rio de Janeiro). See Maria Laura Viveiros de Castro Cavalcanti, *Carnaval Carioca,* 56.
91. Sérgio Cabral, *As escolas de Samba do Rio de Janeiro* (Rio de Janeiro: Lumiar Editora, 1996), 180.
92. Ibid., 186.
93. Ibid., 186–87. According to another witness, de Castro made metal sculptures that were heavy and expensive to transport from Mangueira to the center of Rio. According to this account, the commission benefited only the artist, who later exhibited the works in Europe. See Eduardo Giffoni Flórido, *Mangueira: estação primeira do samba* (Rio de Janeiro: Monte Castelo Idéias, 2005), 84.
94. Maria Julia Goldwasser, *O Palácio do Samba: estudo antropológico da Escola de Samba Estação Primeira de Mangueira* (Rio de Janeiro: Zahar Editores, 1975), 47.
95. Carlos Estevam Martins, "Anteprojeto do Manifesto do CPC," 76.

96. Hélio Oiticica in *H. O. Supra Sensorial: A obra de Hélio Oiticica,* directed by Kátia Maciel (Rio de Janeiro: UFRJ, 1997), CD-ROM, cited by Hermano Vianna in "Não quero que a vida me faça de otário."
97. A *componente* was clearly different from a *sócio* (associate), a word that described various people involved with the school. This terminology developed as a consequence of the penetration of the middle class into Mangueira, but it also addressed the differences between those for whom the samba school was a weekend entertainment and those for whom it was a "true experience of life and communitarian solidarity." Maria Julia Goldwasser, *O Palácio do Samba,* 66–69.
98. Goulart had been vice president in the Kubitschek government (1956–61). Elected vice president again in 1960, he assumed the presidency in 1961 after the resignation of President Jânio Quadros. During his presidency, Goulart developed ties with Communist countries and a program of radical reforms at home. Brazil's military leadership disliked these policies and deposed him in a coup in 1964.
99. For a concise analysis of the revolutionary demise of 1964, see Heloísa Buarque de Hollanda and Marcos Augusto Gonçalves, *Cultura e participação nos anos 60,* (São Paulo: Editora Brasiliense, 1982), 12–21. Despite the rise of the dictatorial Right, the cultural Left was allowed great freedom during the first five years of the regime. This public prominence, apparent in an array of cultural manifestations and spectacles (theater, concerts, film, exhibitions), implied the Left's break with the disenfranchised and the masses. Heloísa Buarque de Hollanda, *Impressões de viagem,* 30.
100. The exhibition was organized by the French critic Ceres Franco and the art dealer Jean Boghici at the Museu de Arte Moderna do Rio de Janeiro and featured French and Brazilian artists. It sprang from the musical event of the same name directed by Augusto Boal, director of Teatro de Arena, which was based in São Paulo, in December 1964. On this musical response from theater see Roberto Schwarz, "Culture and Politics in Brazil, 1964–1969," in *Misplaced Ideas: Essays on Brazilian Culture,* ed. Roberto Schwarz (London and New York: Verso, 1992), 146–49.
101. Heloísa Buarque de Hollanda and Marcos Augusto Gonçalves, *Cultura e participação nos anos 60,* 23.
102. Ibid.
103. Hélio Oiticica, "Bases fundamentais para uma definição do 'Parangolé'," 66.
104. Flora Süssekind addresses the theme of the political march in Oiticica's later work, which she sees prefigured in the *Parangolés*; see Flora Süssekind, "Chorus, Contraries, Masses: The Tropicalist Experience and Brazil in the Late Sixties," in *Tropicália,* ed. Carlos Basualdo (São Paulo: Cosac Naify, 2005), 50. Irene Small brilliantly elaborates on the semantic silence of the *Parangolés* in her dissertation on Oiticica's work, "Hélio Oiticica and the Morphology of Things" (PhD diss., Yale University, 2008), 214–16. By 1966, however, Oiticica was proposing the term *Parangolé poético e social* (Poetic and Social Parangolé) to refer to two capes made in collaboration with the artist Rubens Gerchman: *Capa da Liberdade* (Cape of Liberty) and *Cuidado com o Tigre* (Be Careful with the Tiger). These works, Oiticica pointed out, carried a clear polemical intention and introduced text as a key element of the *Parangolés* (the titles were legible in the works). Text had already appeared the year before in a cape entitled *Homenagem ao Mos-*

*quito* (Homage to Mosquito), dedicated to a young dancer of Mangueira who appears in several photographs of Oiticica's works. See Hélio Oiticica, "Para o globo: Parangolé poético e parangolé social" (August 14, 1966), doc. no. 0254.66, Archives Hélio Oiticica / Projeto Hélio Oiticica.

105. Claudir Chaves, "'Parangolé' impedido no MAM," *Diário Carioca* (Rio de Janeiro), August 14, 1965.

106. See Esther Emílio Carlos, "Atelier," *Diário de Notícias* (Rio de Janeiro), August 7, 1965; Esther Emílio Carlos, "Atelier-Parangolé," *Diário de Notícias* (Rio de Janeiro), August 10, 1965; Vera Pacheco Jordão, "Opinião 65," *O Globo* (Rio de Janeiro), August 11, 1965; "As criações—invenções de Hélio Oiticica," *Correio da Manhã* (Rio de Janeiro), August 13, 1965; "Ainda o 'Parangolé,'" *O Globo* (Rio de Janeiro), August 28, 1965; Esther Emílio Carlos, "Atelier," *Diário de Notícias* (Rio de Janeiro), September 1, 1965; and Claudir Chaves, "Opinião-65 dá Opinião," *Diário Carioca* (Rio de Janeiro), September 5, 1965.

107. See for example Ferreira Gullar, "Opinião 65," *Revista Civilização Brasileira* (Rio de Janeiro), no. 4 (September 1965); Mário Schenberg, "O ponto alto," *Artes* (São Paulo) 1 (January 1966): 5; and Sérgio Ferro, "Vale tudo," *Artes* 1 (January 1966): 6; all reprinted in *Arte em Revista,* no. 2 (May–August 1979). Curiously, none of these reviews mentioned Oiticica's *Parangolés,* possibly a consequence of their abbreviated inaugural presentation and marginalized display in the galleries as well as their semantic ambivalence, which was the opposite of an "opinion."

108. Heloísa Buarque de Hollanda, *Impressões de Viagem: CPC, vanguarda e desbunde: 1960/70* (Rio de Janeiro: Aeroplano, 2005), 32.

109. See for example Anna Dezeuze, "Tactile Dematerialization, Sensory Politics: Hélio Oiticica's Parangolés," *Art Journal* 63, no. 2 (Summer 2004): 58–71.

110. Carlos Zilio, "Da antropofagia à tropicália," 38.

111. Ibid., 39.

112. Hélio Oiticica to David Medalla, August 21, 1965, doc. no. 0586.65, Archives Hélio Oiticica / Projeto Hélio Oiticica. The letter was written in English.

113. Hélio Oiticica (March 4, 1968), in *Aspiro ao grande labirinto,* 108.

114. Hélio Oiticica, "A obra, seu caráter objetal, o comportamento" (December 1, 1968), doc. no. 0160.68, Archives Hélio Oiticica / Projeto Hélio Oiticica.

115. Hélio Oiticica, "Anotações sobre o Parangolé," 70.

116. Ibid., 71.

117. Ibid.

118. On provisional identities in Afro-Brazilian culture, and carnival and its impact on the body of the *Parangolés,* see Simone Osthoff, "Hélio Oiticica's Parangolés: Nomadic Experience in Endless Motion," in *Diaspora and Visual Culture: Representing Africans and Jews,* ed. Nicholas Mirzoeff (London: Routledge, 2000), 234–35.

119. Basualdo referred to the capes as prosthetic devices to describe the interdependence of work and body—that is, to indicate their supplemental relation to the body. See Carlos Basualdo, "Quelques annotations supplémentaires sur le Parangolé," in *L'art au corps: Le corps exposé de Man Ray à nos jours,* ed. Véronique Legrand and Philippe Vergne (Marseille: Mac, galeries contemporaines des Musées de Marseille, 1996), 256–73. More recently, Irene Small has picked up on this concept to discuss the unstable

body implied by the *Parangolés*; see Irene Small, "Hélio Oiticica and the Morphology of Things," 219.

120. Hélio Oiticica, "A dança na minha experiência," in *Aspiro ao grande labirinto,* 73. On the Dionysian aspect of dance and Nietzsche's influence on Oiticica, see Paula Braga, "Hélio Oiticica and the Parangolés: (Ad)dressing Nietzsche's Übermensch," *Third Text* 17, no. 1 (2003): 43–52. Anna Dezeuze has also observed that "the aerial dimension of samba could only have struck Oiticica as he learned dance steps such as the *parafuso,* or 'screw,' which, as Waly Salomão described it, consists in 'jumping from the floor and spinning in the air like a screw.' Significantly, as Salomão remarked, the Brazilian expression *entrar em parafuso* means to 'get into a state.' This 'state' of trancelike immersion or absorption, achieved through the body's movements, is what struck Oiticica most." See Anna Dezeuze, "Tactile Dematerialization," 67.

121. See Rachel T. Valença, *Carnaval: Para tudo se acabar na quarta-feira* (Rio de Janeiro: Relume Dumará and Rio Arte, 1996), 51–68. Oiticica celebrated the improvisation of samba dance but was well aware of its reliance on the highly structured organization of the parade and a hierarchy of roles. In 1967, in his famous prescription for contemporary Brazilian art entitled "Esquema geral da nova objetividade" (General Scheme of the New Objectivity), the artist discussed the organizational aspect of the carnival and other festive formations such as "samba schools, ranchos, *frevos,* holidays of every kind, soccer, fairs" (escolas de samba, ranchos, frevos, festas de toda ordem, futebol, feiras), noting that they were organized as popular manifestations and thus summoned the individual around the collective. Hélio Oiticica, "Esquema geral da nova objetividade," in *Aspiro ao grande labirinto,* 96. On the difference between the more choreographed roles of the *mestre-sala* (master of ceremonies) and the *porta estandarte* (flag bearer) versus the more spontaneous *passista* (lead dancer), see Hélio Oiticica, "Um pintor no samba," n.d., doc. no. 1863.sd, p. 3, Archives Hélio Oiticica / Projeto Hélio Oiticica.

122. Hélio Oiticica, "A dança na minha experiência," 74.

123. Hélio Oiticica, "Continuação" (April 10, 1966), in *Aspiro ao grande labirinto,* 75.

124. Irene Small, "Hélio Oiticica and the Morphology of Things," 188.

125. Lawrence Grossberg, "Another Boring Day in Paradise: Rock and Roll and the Empowerment of Everyday Life," *Popular Music* 4 (1984): 227.

126. Marguerite La Caze and Henry Martyn Lloyd, "Philosophy and the 'Affective Turn,'" ed. Marguerite La Caze and Henry Martyn Lloyd, special issue, *Parrhesia,* no. 13 (2011): 6–7. Ruth Leys analyzed and criticized the most important paradigm within affect theory in her article "The Turn to Affect: A Critique." This so-called "anti-intentionalist" position argues that affect operates outside signification and meaning because it is defined by unconscious bodily reactions. "The result," says Leys, "is that action and behavior are held to be determined by affective dispositions that are independent of consciousness and the mind's control." To oppose this (ultimate) reinsertion of the classical mind-body divide, she proposes a cognitive position that acknowledges the role of "affective dispositions" in our thinking process. Ruth Leys, "The Turn to Affect: A Critique," *Critical Inquiry* 37, no. 3 (Spring 2011): 434–72. I am not interested in mobilizing affect theory here, although it could certainly provide a productive framework for thinking about Clark and Oiticica's work. I do find, however, the figure of "movements in between,"

privileged in much of the literature on affect, helpful in understanding the looping between self and world, the affective and the social, in the *Parangolés*. Carlos Basualdo sheds light on this in-between movement between mind and body that so preoccupied Maurice Merleau-Ponty, arguing that the "Manifesto Neoconcreto," through the notion of the quasi-corpus, posited an unedited subjectivity with the potential to become tangible (unlike the traditional subject, which constitutes itself on the basis of an opposition between affect and reason, as in expressionism and constructivism). He observes that the utopian dimension of the quasi-corpus resides in its desire to alter our perception of ourselves, proposing an *unedited self* that tacitly implies the possibility of social change. Carlos Basualdo, "Quelques annotations supplémentaires sur le Parangolé," 256–73 (the original unpublished manuscript in Spanish is cited). For an account of Lygia Clark's work informed by affect theory, see Susan Best, *Visualizing Feeling: Affect and the Feminine Avant-Garde* (London and New York: I. B. Tauris, 2011), chapter 3.

127. Esther Emílio Carlos, "Parangolé," *Diário de Notícias* (Rio de Janeiro), August 10, 1965.
128. Hélio Oiticica, "Anotações sobre o Parangolé," 71.
129. Ibid., 72.
130. This is the title of a 1963 work by Clark; see chapter 3.
131. Gregory J. Seigworth and Melissa Gregg, "An Inventory of Shimmers," 3.
132. *H. O.*, directed by Ivan Cardoso (Rio de Janeiro, 1979). I am grateful to Cardoso for sharing the English version of his film script.
133. These words were written in the context of Oiticica's writings on his *Penetráveis* from the late 1960s. See Hélio Oiticica, doc. no. 0365.69-a, p. 1; "Rhobo. Captions and Small Texts," May 22, 1969, doc. no. 0363.69, p. 1; and "Whitechapel Gallery—experiência mostra" (January 27, 1970), doc. no. 0338.70, p. 1, Archives Hélio Oiticica / Projeto Hélio Oiticica.
134. Gregory J. Seigworth and Melissa Gregg, "An Inventory of Shimmers," 1–2.
135. Ferreira Gullar, "Manifesto Neoconcreto," in *Experiência Neoconcreta* (São Paulo: Cosacnaify, 2007), 42.
136. Gregory J. Seigworth and Melissa Gregg, "An Inventory of Shimmers," 3.

## 5. ANOTHER GEOMETRY: GEGO'S *RETICULÁREA*, 1969–77

1. Hanni Ossott, *Gego* (Caracas: Museo de Arte Contemporáneo de Caracas, 1977), 6.
2. On Venezuela's engagement with postwar geometric abstraction, see the enlightening texts by Luis Enrique Pérez-Oramas, "Caracas: A Constructive Stage," in *The Geometry of Hope: Latin American Art from the Patricia Phelps de Cisneros Collection*, exh. cat., ed. Gabriel Perez-Barreiro (Austin: Blanton Museum of Art, University of Texas at Austin, 2007), 74–85; and "Notes on the Venezuelan Constructive Scene, 1950–1973," in *Cold America: Geometric Abstraction in Latin America (1934–1973)*, ed. Osbel Suárez (Madrid: Fundación Juan March, 2011), 52–65.
3. While Bonatz is known to have opposed the Nazi regime's neoclassicism, which he regarded as pompous and ornamental, he is best remembered for the bridges that he designed for the National Socialist government.
4. Paul Bonatz, "Der Unterricht im Entwerfen an der Technische Hochschule Stuttgart,"

in *Paul Bonatz und seine Schüler,* ed. Graubner Gerhard (Stuttgart: Verlag Deutsche Bauten, 1931), 5–6.

5. A renowned urban planner, the Frenchman Maurice Emile Henri Rotival spent the late 1930s in Caracas, creating a plan for the city (1938), and was to remain an important presence in the field of city planning in Venezuela for years to come. See Lorenzo González, "Modernity and the City: Caracas, 1935–1958" (PhD diss., Cornell University, 1996), 150. See also Juan José Martín Frechilla, *Planes, planos y proyectos para Venezuela: 1908–1958 (Apuntes para una historial de la construcción en el país)* (Caracas: Universidad Central de Venezuela, 1994).
6. Fernando Coronil, *The Magical State: Nature, Money, and Modernity in Venezuela* (Chicago and London: University of Chicago Press, 1997), 76.
7. Lorenzo González, "Modernity and the City," 92.
8. Fernando Coronil, *The Magical State,* 146.
9. Laureano Vallenilla Lanz quoted in Andrés Stambouli, *Crisis política en Venezuela, 1945–1958* (Caracas: Ateneo, 1980), 94.
10. Fernando Coronil, *The Magical State,* 178.
11. May Lumsden, "Caracas—the Buildingest City in South America," *Architectural Forum* 101 (November 1954): 153.
12. "Highlights of Venezuela's Burgeoning New Architecture," *Architectural Record,* no. 3 (September 1957): 201–5.
13. *L'Architecture d'Aujourd'hui* (Paris) 27, nos. 67–68 (October 1956): 86–140.
14. Slum clearing had been part of the urbanization and modernization of the capital city since the 1940s but was intensified during the 1950s under the Marcos Pérez Jiménez dictatorship (1952–58), when the battle against the shanty became a motto of the regime. See Graziano Gasparini and Juan Pedro Posani, *Caracas a través de su architectura* (Caracas: Armitano Editores, 1998), 374.
15. For excellent recent work by historians on this point, see for example A. Almandoz, "Modernidad urbanística y Nuevo Ideal Nacional," in *La ciudad en el imaginario venezolano,* vol. 2, *De 1936 a los pequeños seres* (Caracas: Fundación para la Cultura Urbana, 2004), 119–62; and Manuel A. López Villa, "Gestión urbanística, revolución democrática y dictadura militar en Venezuela (1945–1958)," *Revista Urbana* (Caracas), nos. 14–15 (1994): 103–19.
16. Lourdes Blanco, *Gego: Reticulárea* (Caracas: Ediciones de la Galería Conkright, 1969), n.p. Original in English.
17. Michael John Gorman, *Buckminster Fuller: Designing for Mobility* (Milan: Skira, 2005), 177.
18. As Gorman indicates, tensegrity structures and geodesic domes are not the same. The main difference is that "while all of the metal struts in a geodesic dome are capable of bearing both compression and tension, some of the members in a tensegrity structure are only capable of bearing tension (Snelson's monofilament fishing line, for example)." Ibid., 180. Tensegrity elements could, however, be incorporated into geodesic domes. The Expo '67 dome in Montreal, the most famous of all, "made use of 'star tensegrity,' or tensegrity octahedral on each facet, providing additional strength through the creation of tensegrity octet truss elements." Ibid., 185. The artist Kenneth Snelson disagrees. He

observes that geodesic domes are not prestressed structures, as there is no play between tension and compression, and thus no tensegrity. Email to the author February 20, 2015. See also Kenneth Snelson, "The Art of Tensegrity," *International Journal of Space Structures* 27, nos. 2–3 (2012): 71–80; and "Letter from Kenneth Snelson to R. Motro, published in November 1990, International Journal of Space Structures," http://www.grunch.net/snelson/rmoto.html, accessed February 22, 2015.

19. Antoine Picon, ed., *L'art de l'ingénieur, constructeur, entrepreneur, inventeur* (Paris: Centre Georges Pompidou, 1997), 152.
20. Dana Miller writes: "Beginning in the mid-1950s Fuller was increasingly included in gallery and museum exhibitions, as well as art periodicals." Dana Miller, "Thought Patterns: Buckminster Fuller the Scientist-Artist," in *Buckminster Fuller: Starting with the Universe,* ed. K. Michael Hays and Dana Miller (New York: Whitney Museum of American Art; New Haven, CT: Yale University Press, 2008), 29.
21. Mark Wigley, *Constant's New Babylon: The Hyper-Architecture of Desire* (Rotterdam: Witte de With Center for Contemporary Art, 1998), 41.
22. Founded as the New Bauhaus by László Moholy-Nagy in 1937, the institution reopened in 1939 as the School of Design and changed its name to the Institute of Design in 1944, when it became an accredited college. In 1949 the institute was absorbed by the Illinois Institute of Technology. At that point Konrad Wachsmann became head of the department of building research. The previous year, Buckminster Fuller, as a visiting faculty member, had developed his pentahexaedron. Like the Ulm Hochschule für Gestaltung in Germany, the Institute of Design echoed but did not replicate the Bauhaus model. The Bauhaus, of course, had itself undergone various shifts between its founding in Weimar in 1918 and its closing in Berlin in 1933.
23. The architects working during the Venezuelan building boom of the 1950s were, as González has indicated, either foreigners or natives trained abroad and systematically exposed to or influenced by international architecture and the figure of Le Corbusier. Lorenzo González, "Modernity and the City," 181.
24. See Richard Pommer and Christian Otto, *Weissenhof 1927 and the Modern Movement in Architecture* (Chicago: University of Chicago Press, 1991).
25. Gego, "Reglamento para los cursos de composición," Personal Archives, Gego Foundation, Caracas. Gego seems to have been interested in the different levels of the basic design course. Handouts in her files, arranged chronologically, show that she was either involved in or attracted to progressively more complex architectural and urban problems and teaching activities as the years went by. But most records indicate that it was the introductory level for which she was responsible.
26. From 1964 to 1977 Gego was a professor at the Instituto de Diseño, Fundación Neumann, where she taught courses on "bi-dimensional and three-dimensional form" and "spatial solutions." She devoted great effort between 1971 and 1977 to developing a seminar on spatial relations, which culminated in the publication of two volumes of *Space, Volume, Organization,* the first issued by Fundación Neumann in 1976, and the second by Monte Ávila Editores in 1979.
27. Konrad Wachsmann, *The Turning Point of Building: Structure and Design* (New York: Reinhold, 1961), 172.

28. Larry Busbea, *Topologies: The Urban Utopia in France, 1960–1970* (Cambridge, MA: MIT Press, 2007), 147. It is important to note that Gego shared with this generation of experimental architects and engineers an interest in the organic. Busbea observes: "[T]he organic served as a more conceptual model—a source of principles rather than a source for forms. Increasingly, after the Second World War, architects and engineers seemed even more than before drawn to texts about crystals, plant structures, and microscopic organisms. D'Arcy Thompson's *On Growth and Form* (1917) [Gego owned a copy] was the most influential text in this regard." Ibid.

29. Lisa Blackmore has written intelligently about the monumental urban spaces, national discourses, and "technologies of display" deployed by Pérez Jiménez to boost the regime's reputation in a dissertation entitled "¡Venezuela Progresa! Dictatorship, Spectacle, and the Construction of Modernity" (PhD diss., Birkbeck College, University of London, 2011).

30. I have addressed the political inflections of Villanueva's project in two presentations: "The Topology of Exchange: Transnational Collaborations in Art and Architecture in Carlos Raúl Villanueva's City University," College Art Association Annual Conference, New York, February 20, 2003; and "Villanueva and Calder: The Poetics and Politics of a Dialogue," Newark Museum, New Jersey, April 10, 2010.

31. William Niño Araque, "Momentos de lo moderno," in *Carlos Raúl Villanueva, un moderno en sudamérica,* ed. William Niño Araque and Carmen Cecilia Araujo (Caracas: Galería de Arte Nacional, 2000), 38.

32. Sibyl Moholy-Nagy, *Carlos Raúl Villanueva y la arquitectura de Venezuela* (Caracas: Instituto del Patrimonio Cultural, 1999), 87.

33. Notable skyscrapers in the city at the time included Las Torres del Silencio (1948–57), with its twin towers of thirty-two floors each, which became a symbol of the modern Caracas; the Polar Tower (1951–54); the Banco Mercantil y Agrícola (1954); and Las Fundaciones (1954). On the range of architectural projects of the 1950s, most produced under the Pérez Jiménez dictatorship, see William Niño Araque, *1950: El espíritu moderno* (Caracas: Fundación Corp Group Centro Cultural, 1998).

34. Geometric abstraction in Venezuela was spearheaded by a group of artists who had been students at the Escuela de Artes Plásticas y Artes Aplicadas (School of Visual and Applied Arts) of Caracas in the early and mid-1940s, who were critical of the school's slow embrace of modernism and encountered European abstraction upon their arrival in Paris. It was in that city that Alejandro Otero, Narciso Debourg, Aimée Battistini, Belén Nuñez, Pascual Navarro, Mateo Manaure, Luis Guevara Moreno, Rubén Nuñez, Carlos González Bogen, Dora Hersen, and J. R. Guillent Pérez founded the group Los Disidentes and a magazine of the same name in 1950. From the pages of this publication, the young artists launched an attack on what they perceived as a profoundly conservative and anachronistic Venezuelan artistic milieu. Back home, artistic groups, galleries, and alternative spaces such as La Barraca de Guaicaipuro, La Barraca de Maripérez, El Taller Libre de Arte, and the Galería Cuatro Muros (owned by Bogen and Manaure) abetted the advance of abstraction.

35. Emblematic of this split between figuration and abstraction is the exchange between the artist Alejandro Otero and the writer Miguel Otero Silva in the pages of the Caracas

newspaper *El Nacional* in March and April of 1957. While Otero defended the universalist core of abstractionism—particularly a post-Mondrian variant that he associated with a project of collective social progress that would bring the Venezuelan arts into dialogue with the most advanced aesthetic practices—Silva refuted the solipsism of geometric abstraction and its absolute disregard for the realities of the Venezuelan people. For the full exchange between Otero and Silva, see Margarita Arias, ed., *Polémica sobre arte abstracto: Alejandro Otero Rodríguez / Miguel Otero Silva* (Caracas: Colección Delta Solar, Museo Alejandro Otero, 1999).

36. Edward E. Ashley, report of conference, June 30, 1952, Alexander Calder Archives, New York. Ashley was a consulting engineer on the project.

37. Larry Busbea, *Topologies*, 174–75.

38. Carlos Raúl Villanueva, "El Centro Comunal de la Ciudad Universitaria," *Ver y Estimar*, no. 2 (December 1954): 4–7.

39. Gego, n.d., Personal Archives, Gego Foundation. The handout itself was probably written by the coordinator of the workshop, Professor Eduardo Sanabria.

40. Lourdes Blanco, "Gego's Drawings Appeal to Visual," *Daily Journal* (Caracas), May 19, 1968. Original in English.

41. Lourdes Blanco, *Gego: Reticulárea*.

42. The seminal text here is that of Hanni Ossott, who, after careful discussions with the artist about her construction systems, wrote a catalogue/book for Gego's retrospective exhibition at the Museo de Arte Contemporáneo de Caracas in 1977. See Hanni Ossott, *Gego*.

43. Luis Enrique Pérez-Oramas has written lucidly on this topic: "At the beginning of the 1970s, the oil boom and the downfall of the guerrillas had brought bourgeois stability to Venezuela, and the country filled up with artworks—marvelous and monumental, abstract, kinetic, and parallactic." Luis Enrique Pérez-Oramas, "Caracas: A Constructive Stage," 82. Works by many abstract artists, including Gego, proliferated during this period, but the "three masters of abstraction"—as a catalogue dubbed the Venezuelan artists Alejandro Otero, Carlos Cruz-Diez, and Jesús Rafael Soto—had much more visibility than other artists. See *Otero, Cruz-Diez, Soto: Tres maestros del abstraccionismo en Venezuela y su proyección internacional*, exh. cat. (Caracas: Galería de Arte Nacional, 1994).

44. Cited in Hanni Ossott, *Gego*, 14. Barr became familiar with Gego's work when her piece *Sphere*, made in Iowa in 1959, entered the collection of the Museum of Modern Art in May or June 1960. The piece was included in MoMA's own take on kinetic art, the exhibition *The Responsive Eye* of 1965. The term "parallactical charm" appears precisely in Alfred H. Barr Jr., "Painting and Sculpture Acquisitions, 1960," in *The Museum of Modern Art: Painting and Sculpture Acquisitions*, exh. cat., January 1, 1960 through December 31, 1960, 5.

45. James Smith Pierce, "Contemplating Parallax," *Art International* (September 20, 1968): 20.

46. Luis Enrique Pérez-Oramas, "Gego: Laocoonte, las redes y la indecisión de las cosas," in *Gego: Obra completa, 1955–1990*, ed. Iris Peruga (Caracas: Fundación Cisneros, 2003), 396.

47. In an interview with José Antonio Pantin, Gego mentioned a disappointing encounter with Naum Gabo in New York: "He was only interested in selling me, Venezuela, a work . . . completely different than in the twenties." Interview with José Antonio Pantin, April 17, 1981, Personal Archives, Gego Foundation. Gego also met Josef and Anni Albers; see Clara Diament de Sujo, "Una mañana con Gego," *El Nacional* (Caracas), October 20, 1960. A close friend of Gego and Gerd Leufert's was the painter Leon Polk Smith, who may have introduced them to Betty Parsons. Other artists associated with Parsons whom they met or became aware of were Agnes Martin, Ellsworth Kelly, and Ad Reinhardt. Gego's gallerist in Caracas, Rachel Adler, confirmed these connections to me in an interview in October 1998.
48. Invitation to *New Names,* Betty Parsons Gallery, New York, December 20, 1960–January 7, 1961, Betty Parsons Papers, Archives of American Art, New York.
49. A press review indicates that Gego had worked on the *Reticulárea* for three months prior to the June opening. See "Reticulárea: Redes metálicas de Gego en un ambiente del museo," *El Nacional* (Caracas), June 6, 1969. On the other hand, a certificate dated 1974 marking the loan of the *Reticulárea* to the Museo de Bellas Artes dates the piece to 1968–69. This suggests that Gego might have started working on the individual pieces at the end of 1968. Personal Archives, Gego Foundation.
50. Lourdes Blanco, *Gego: Reticulárea.*
51. Miguel Arroyo, interview with the author, August 20, 2000.
52. Gego used the name *Reticulárea* for the individual nets that preceded and followed the large environmental work.
53. Hanni Ossott, *Gego,* 90.
54. Roberto Guevara, interview with the author, January 17, 1998.
55. Gego, sketches and checklists produced for the exhibition, Personal Archives, Gego Foundation.
56. Hanni Ossott, *Gego,* 98.
57. In December 1969 the *Reticulárea* was also shown in New York at the Center for Inter-American Relations as part of the exhibition *Latin America: New Paintings and Sculpture: Juan Downey, Agustín Fernández, Gego, Gabriel Morera.* In March 1975 the work was included in the exhibition *Relations and Contrasts in Venezuelan Painting* at the Museo de Bellas Artes de Caracas. Remaining in the same gallery, it was also featured in an exhibition that celebrated the official opening of the renovated Museo de Bellas Artes building on October 15, 1976. The exhibition, *Las Artes Plásticas en Venezuela* (Venezuelan Visual Arts), was organized as a salon that also featured works from the permanent collection. It was then that the *Reticulárea* was awarded first prize and acquired by the museum. At the end of 1976 the *Reticulárea,* along with the entire collection of Venezuelan art of the Museo de Bellas Artes, became part of the collection of the Galería de Arte Nacional, where at the beginning of 1977 it was installed in Gallery 1. Later that year it was included in another group show at the Galería de Arte Nacional titled *Arte Venezolano contemporáneo* (Venezuelan Contemporary Art). After three years of discussion, the permanent installation of *Reticulárea* took place in 1980. In 1982 Dietrich Mahlow, a German curator and critic and a friend of Gego, invited the artist to participate in a group exhibition at the Alte Oper in Frankfurt titled *Spielraum-Raumspiele*

(Playroom-Roomplay), which opened on August 28. In approximately four months, Gego created a new *Reticulárea,* which was shown along with *Roaratorio,* a sound piece by John Cage, in Frankfurt. More so than on previous occasions, the production of this iteration of the *Reticulárea* involved an intense amount of labor that required the participation of friends and colleagues.

58. Gego, Personal Archives, Gego Foundation.
59. Lourdes Blanco, *Gego: Reticulárea.*
60. "'Reticulárea': Redes metálicas de Gego en un ambiente del museo," *El Nacional* (Caracas), June 6, 1969; "Artes Plásticas," *La República* (Caracas), June 7, 1969; Roberto Guevara, "Reticulárea de Gego," *El Nacional* (Caracas), June 10, 1969; Roberto Montero Castro, "Una ambientación de Gego," *Imágen* (Caracas), no. 50 (June 1–15, 1969): 22; Ras-guños column, *El Nacional* (Caracas), June 19, 1969; Ras, "Ambientaciones de Gego y de Cruz-Diez, multiples de Soto," *Revista Nacional de Cultura* (Caracas) (June–September 1969).
61. Hanni Ossott, *Gego,* 9.
62. Marta Traba, *Gego* (Caracas: Museo de Arte Contemporáneo, 1977), n.p. On organic and constructivist metaphors in modern sculpture, see Rosalind Krauss, *Passages in Modern Sculpture* (Cambridge, MA: MIT Press, 1977), 57–67, 138–46.
63. Christian Thiel to Gego, November 12, 1983, Personal Archives, Gego Foundation.
64. Gilles Deleuze and Félix Guattari, *A Thousand Plateaus: Capitalism and Schizophrenia,* trans. Brian Massumi (Minneapolis: University of Minnesota Press, 1987), 5.
65. Ibid., 8.
66. According to Yves Christen, a nonevolutionary scheme might be required to substitute "reticular schemas . . . for the bush or tree schemas used to represent evolution." Cited in ibid., 10. Interestingly, on a floor plan for her 1977 retrospective at the Museo de Arte Contemporáneo de Caracas, Gego used the word *breñales* (terrain of weeds and undergrowth) to describe the installation of a group of *Spheres* (1970s) piled up on the floor. For an early "rhizomatic" description of the work (which does not use the term but invokes a less normative image of nature), see Salvador Garmendia, "Caracas por Gego," *Papel Literario, El Nacional* (Caracas), October 11, 1981.
67. Niklas Luhmann, "European Rationality," in *Rethinking Imagination: Culture and Creativity,* ed. Gillian Robinson and John Rundell (London: Routledge, 1994), 67.
68. Ibid., 73.
69. As Rosi Braidotti wrote in reference to a feminist imaginary keen on affecting the symbolic order: "I would like to stress that the point about being 'located' does not have to do with biological differences but with sociosymbolic positioning. . . . Speaking as a feminist I see this as confirming the importance of the 'politics of location' and of sexual difference as marking asymmetrical positions between the sexes." See Rosi Braidotti, "Of Bugs and Women: Irigaray and Deleuze on the Becoming-Woman," in *Engaging with Irigaray: Feminist Philosophy and Modern Thought,* ed. Carolyn Burke, Naomi Schor, and Margaret Whitford (New York: Columbia University Press, 1994), 133–34.
70. Peter Hönig to Gego, December 17, 1982, Personal Archives, Gego Foundation.
71. Roberto Guevara, "Reticulárea de Gego," *El Nacional* (Caracas), June 10, 1969.

72. Hanni Ossott, *Gego,* 6.
73. Gego, sketch, 1975, Personal Archives, Gego Foundation.
74. From Eva Hesse's description of *Right After* (1969) in her diary, cited by Lucy R. Lippard, *Eva Hesse* (New York: Da Capo Press, 1992), 161.
75. Roberto Guevara, "Revisión," *Papel Literario, El Nacional* (Caracas), June 21, 1970.
76. Greg Lynn, "Body Matters," in *Folds, Bodies & Blobs: Collected Essays* (Brussels: La Lettre Volée, 1998), 135.
77. Ibid., 137.
78. Ibid., 145.
79. Ibid., 146. On "becoming" and "connectedness," as well as on the differences between these important concepts in Deleuze and Irigaray's alternative philosophical proposals, see Rosi Braidotti, "Of Bugs and Women," 111–37.
80. Brian Massumi, *A User's Guide to Capitalism and Schizophrenia* (Cambridge, MA: MIT Press, 1992).
81. Rosi Braidotti, "Mothers, Monsters and Machines," in *Nomadic Subjects: Embodiment and Sexual Difference in Contemporary Feminist Theory* (New York: Columbia University Press, 1994). Braidotti's intention here is to delineate "a new figuration of feminist subjectivity" that takes into consideration recent developments in the field of biotechnology, "particularly artificial procreation." Ibid., 78.
82. Ibid., 80, 83. On the relevance of the Deleuzian text and the logics of the rhizome for feminism, see also Rosi Braidotti, "Toward a New Nomadism: Feminist Deleuzian Tracks; or Metaphysics and Metabolism," and Elizabeth Grosz, "A Thousand Tiny Sexes: Feminism and Rhizomatics," both in *Gilles Deleuze and the Theater of Philosophy,* ed. Constantin V. Boundas and Dorothea Olkowski (New York: Routledge, 1994).
83. Luis Enrique Pérez-Oramas has written extensively and intelligently about the relationship between Gego's work and Venezuelan kinetic art; see his essays "Gego and the Analytic Context of Cinetismo," in *Inverted Utopias: Avant-Garde Art in Latin America,* ed. Mari Carmen Ramírez and Hector Olea (New Haven, CT: Yale University Press, 2004); and "Gego: Laocoonte, las redes y la indecisión de las cosas," in *Gego: Obra completa, 1955–1990,* 298–311.
84. Elizabeth Grosz, "Architectures of Excess," in *Anymore,* ed. Cynthia C. Davidson (Cambridge, MA: MIT Press, 2000), 260–66.
85. Ibid., 264.
86. In 1969, the year that the *Reticulárea* was installed for the first time, Posani and Gasparini published *Caracas a través de su arquitectura* (Caracas Through Its Architecture). There, they assessed the current urban situation in the following terms: "Everything proceeds without cohesion. The incongruous repetition of studies, of research, is constitutive of all concerned institutions, working independently, of course, with Caracas. Confusion, lack of control, inappropriateness dominate. Decisions are not made, and when they are, they are either made late or do not become reality for lack of adequate organic, financial, judicial, and political means." They underlined the pervasive lack of permanence and the absence of spatial and temporal rigor in urban planning: "The city renovates itself continuously by superimposed remnants. . . . Next to empty lots, the product of collapsed houses that were never replaced, rise lot-line walls belonging to tall

office buildings and one-level commercial buildings. This produces a total absence of visual coherence, and does not achieve the quality of a congruent superimposition. But aside from that, for twenty years the people of the city have gotten used to living among buildings in demolition, being remodeled, or in construction, to circulating through streets in a permanent crisis of being open and closed between dust and noise." Graziano Gasparini and Juan Pedro Posani, *Caracas a través de su arquitectura* (Caracas: Armitano Editores, 1998), 514, 516–17.

87. A characteristic assessment was voiced by the architect Tomás José Sanabria in "Urbanization on an Ad Hoc Basis: A Case Study of Caracas," in *The Urban Explosion in Latin America: A Continent in Process of Modernization*, ed. Glenn H. Beyer (Ithaca, NY: Cornell University Press, 1967), 337–45.
88. An excellent assessment of state urban policy in Venezuela during the period of 1945–58 is made by Manuel A. López Villa in "Gestión urbanística," 103–19.
89. Ibid., 111.
90. Ibid., 114.
91. Not only was the aggressive deployment of the *superbloque* not based on any design research that would take into account the habits, traditions, and social and cultural texture of the expansive communities of rural migrants, but as López Villa emphasizes, the imperatives of massification and urgency required by the Nuevo Ideal Nacional had a crippling effect on the Le Corbusean model exemplified by the Swiss architect's Unité d'Habitation in Marseille. In Venezuela, the highly urbanized context in which Unité might make sense was nonexistent; what's more, in order to adapt this template to the "realities of the marginal population, the *pilotis*, the apartment *duplex* and its *loggias*, the collective services and the towers of vertical circulation disappeared." Ibid., 117.
92. Elizabeth Grosz, "Architectures of Excess," 265.
93. Hanni Ossott, "Gego: Dibujos para proyectos," Personal Archives, Gego Foundation. Interestingly, in his discussion of architecture as a framing activity, Bernard Cache indicates that while the "triangle [is] the minimal polygon, it is also the figure whose diagonals are identical to its sides, where thus legality and stability coincide. And it is perhaps the formal coincidence of these two principles of the frame that explains the fascination that this figure has exerted on many an architect." It is tempting to suggest that it was the anti-architect in Gego that led her to appropriate and warp the triangle in her nets. See Bernard Cache, *Earth Moves: The Furnishing of Territories* (Cambridge, MA: MIT Press, 1995), 60–61.
94. See for example Denis Hollier, *Against Architecture: The Writings of Georges Bataille* (Cambridge, MA: MIT Press, 1989); Greg Lynn, "Body Matters"; and Elizabeth Grosz, *Architecture from the Outside: Essays on Virtual and Real Space* (Cambridge, MA: MIT Press, 2001).
95. Gego, "Programación de unas charlas durante el 1er semester Febrero–Mayo 1965," Personal Archives, Gego Foundation. The highway was made possible by the construction of two tunnels and three viaducts through and across the mountain that separates Caracas from the port city of La Guaira. Via this engineering tour de force one can travel from Caracas to the coast in twenty minutes.
96. Ibid.

97. As Lorenzo González has indicated, the history of foreign urban planning in Latin America remains to be written. This narrative would include (to mention only the case of Venezuela): Maurice Rotival's *Plan Monumental* ("Plan Rotival") for Caracas (1938) and his *Plan of Caracas* (1949), Robert Moses in Caracas (1947–49), and Francis Violich's housing and zoning proposals for Caracas and other cities in Venezuela (1950–54). "This history," González writes, "would show the contributions of local professionals alongside foreign consultants; the reception of the plans by the public and authorities; the shortcomings and oversimplifications of foreign planners; and, of course, the reasons why many expectations created by those plans were not fulfilled. In any event, the rich history would illuminate issues of dependence, exploitation and unequal transfer of knowledge as well as affirmative cross-cultural relationships." Lorenzo González, "Modernity and the City," 61–63.

98. In 1972, the Everson Museum of Art in Syracuse, New York, planned to show Gego's *Reticulárea*. Gego, who had originally accepted the invitation, had to withdraw the project due to an accident that forced her to rest. In a letter, she wrote to James Harithas, then director of the museum, "I am sure you realized that to revive the sleeping beauty *Reticulárea* after three years will take a great deal of personal handicraft, but in my actual condition I am unable to handle this task. . . . A curious feature of my work is, as you know, the personal handling, staging, and displaying of the *Reticulárea* in a different architectural environment. I can only hope to develop a system by which it can be possible to arrange exhibitions without so much of my personal intervention." Gego to James Harithas, July 21, 1972, Personal Archives, Gego Foundation. In 1974, she was invited again to exhibit at the Everson Museum and at the Lowe Art Gallery of Syracuse University, then directed by Stanton L. Catlin. Her response was again negative; the nomadic potential of the piece was contradicted by its ephemeral quality, its delicate constitution. She wrote: "Your galleries at the Everson Museum of Art provoke to make a huge and environmental work—which again after two or three installations will be condemned to death, a fact I can't afford." Gego to Sandra Trop Blumberg, acting director of the Everson Museum of Art, July 18, 1974, Personal Archives, Gego Foundation. Despite Gego's struggles with the issues outlined above, the *Reticulárea* was reinstalled and reproduced a total of approximately seven times, always in a different form and with the help of assistants, friends, and colleagues.

# IMAGE CREDITS

FIGURES 0.1, 0.2, 3.1, 3.9: © Jornal do Brasil / CPDoc JB.

FIGURE 0.3: Photo: Moderna Museet, Stockholm. © Judd Foundation / Licensed by VAGA, New York.

FIGURE 0.4: Photo: Rudolph Burckhardt, courtesy Castelli Gallery, New York. © 2015 Robert Morris / Artists Rights Society (ARS), New York.

FIGURES 0.5, 2.1, 2.6: Marcel Gautherot / Acervo Instituto Moreira Salles.

FIGURE 0.6: Photo: Luis Becerra. Courtesy Atelier Soto.

FIGURE 1.1: Courtesy Colección Espinosa.

FIGURE 1.3: Photo: The Solomon R. Guggenheim Foundation / Art Resource, NY. © Artists Rights Society (ARS), New York.

FIGURE 1.4: Photo: The Museum of Modern Art / Licensed by SCALA / Art Resource, New York. © VAGA, New York.

FIGURE 1.5: Courtesy Gyula Kosice.

FIGURES 1.7, 1.8; PLATE 4: © Tomás Maldonado.

FIGURE 1.9: Courtesy Claudia Molenberg.

FIGURE 1.10: © Raúl Lozza.

FIGURE 2.2: © 2015 Artists Rights Society (ARS), New York / ProLitteris, Zurich. Collection of the Museu de Arte Contemporánea da Universidade de São Paulo, Brazil.

FIGURE 2.3: Private collection. © Família Geraldo de Barros.

FIGURE 2.4: Thomaz Farkas / Acervo Instituto Moreira Salles.

FIGURE 2.5: Arquivo Histórico Wanda Svevo / Fundação Bienal de São Paulo. Photographer unknown.

FIGURES 3.2, 3.4–3.8, 3.14–16; PLATES 11–13, 15: Courtesy "The World of Lygia Clark" Cultural Association.

FIGURE 3.3: Collection Tate Modern, London. Gift of the Josef and Anni Albers Foundation. © 2015 The Josef and Anni Albers Foundation, Artists Rights Society, New York.

FIGURES 3.10–3.12, 4.1–4.9; PLATES 9, 14, 16–18: Courtesy Projeto Hélio Oiticica, © César and Claudio Oiticica. Photos by the Museum of Fine Arts Collection, Houston (figs. 3.10, 3.12; plate 18), Desdemone Bardin (figs. 4.1, 4.4, 4.7. 4.8; plate 17), Claudio Oiticica (fig. 4.6; plates 9, 16), Hélio Oiticica (fig. 4.9). Figures 4.2 and 4.5 are from the Hélio Oiticica Archives.

FIGURES 5.1, 5.7, 5.9, 5.10, 5.13–5.24: © Fundación Gego. Photos by Paolo Gasparini (figs. 5.1, 5.10, 5.22, 5.23), Ana María Castillo (fig. 5.5), Juan Santana (fig. 5.7), Maxim (fig. 5.21).

FIGURE 5.2: Photo: Paolo Gasparini. © Fundación Archivo Fotográfico.

FIGURE 5.3: Courtesy *L'Architecture d'Aujourd'hui* (www.larchitecturedaujourdhui.fr).

FIGURE 5.4: Milwaukee Art Museum, gift of Friends of Art, 1970. © The Estate of Eva Hesse. Courtesy Hauser & Wirth. Image courtesy the Allen Memorial Art Museum, Oberlin College, Ohio. Gift of Helen Hesse Charash.

FIGURE 5.6: Courtesy Kenneth Snelson.

FIGURE 5.8: Courtesy the Josef and Anni Albers Foundation.

FIGURES 5.11, 5.12; PLATE 20: © Fundacion Villanueva. Photos by Paolo Gasparini (fig. 5.11; plate 20).

PLATE 1: © Fundacion Villanueva.

PLATE 2: Photo: Mark Morosse. Colección Patricia Phelps de Cisneros. © Raúl Lozza.

PLATE 3: Photo: José Cristelli. Private collection. Courtesy Colección Espinosa.

PLATE 5: Private collection.

PLATE 6: Institut Valencià d'Art Modern. Generalitat, Spain. Courtesy the Torres-García family.

PLATE 7: Colección MALBA / Museo de Arte Latinoamericano de Buenos Aires. Courtesy Gyula Kosice.

PLATE 8: © Angela Thomas Schmid, Artists Rights Society (ARS), New York / ProLitteris, Zurich.

PLATE 10: The Museum of Fine Arts Collection, Houston. The Adolpho Leirner Collection of Brazilian Constructive Art, museum purchase funded by the Caroline Wiess Law Foundation. © Família Geraldo de Barros.

PLATE 19: © Ivan Cardoso.

# INDEX

Titles of works are given in their original languages. *Italic* page references indicate illustrations. Plates are indicated by *pl.*

TEXT: 9.5/14 Scala Pro
DISPLAY: Scala Sans Pro
COMPOSITOR: BookMatters, Berkeley
INDEXER: Jim Fuhr
PREPRESS: Embassy Graphics
PRINTER/BINDER: Maple Press